Peterson Reference Guide to

SEAWATCHING

EASTERN WATERBIRDS
IN FLIGHT

THE PETERSON REFERENCE GUIDE SERIES

SEAWATCHING

EASTERN WATERBIRDS
IN FLIGHT

KEN BEHRENS

AND

CAMERON COX

HOUGHTON MIFFLIN HARCOURT
BOSTON   NEW YORK
2013

Sponsored by
the Roger Tory Peterson Institute
and the National Wildlife Federation

For information about permission to reproduce selections from this book, write to Permissions,
Houghton Mifflin Harcourt Publishing Company, 215 Park Avenue South, New York, New York 10003.

www.hmhbooks.com

PETERSON FIELD GUIDES and PETERSON FIELD GUIDE SERIES are registered trademarks
of Houghton Mifflin Harcourt Publishing Company.

Library of Congress Cataloging-in-Publication Data is available.
ISBN 978-0-547-23739-8

Printed in China
SCP 10 9 8 7 6 5 4 3 2 1

The legacy of America's greatest naturalist and creator of the field guide series, Roger Tory Peterson, is kept alive through the dedicated work of the Roger Tory Peterson Institute of Natural History (RTPI). Established in 1985, RTPI is located in Peterson's hometown of Jamestown, New York, near the Chautauqua Institution in the southwestern part of the state.

Today RTPI is a national center for nature education that maintains, shares, and interprets Peterson's extraordinary archive of writings, art, and photography. The institute, housed in a landmark building by world-class architect Robert A. M. Stern, continues to transmit Peterson's zest for teaching about the natural world through leadership programs in teacher development as well as outstanding exhibits of contemporary nature art, natural history, and the Peterson Collection.

Your participation as a steward of the Peterson Collection and supporter of the Peterson legacy is needed. Please consider joining RTPI at an introductory rate of 50 percent of the regular membership fee for the first year. Simply call RTPI's membership department at (800) 758-6841 ext. 226, or e-mail membership@rtpi.org to take advantage of this special membership offered to purchasers of this book. For more information, please visit the Peterson Institute in person or virtually at www.rtpi.org.

To Gail Dwyer and Shaun Bamford for the hot
coffee and good company that helped pass many
long hours at the Avalon Seawatch
—CDC

To my grandparents
—KDB

Peterson Reference Guide to
SEAWATCHING
EASTERN WATERBIRDS
IN FLIGHT

CONTENTS

PREFACE

This book started at New Jersey's Avalon Seawatch, where both authors worked as official counters in various years. As the long and salty but exhilarating days of counting the count wore on, and as we shared what we had learned and consulted with local seawatch veterans, we realized we were using very specific identification techniques, many of which had been discovered by other seawatchers but few of which had ever been published in any guide. We also noticed that while the hawk watch on Cape May received legions of visitors each fall, only a handful of them made their way north to visit the Avalon Seawatch. Although we both savor raptor watching and counting, we found the spectacles of waterbird migration at Avalon even more exciting and epic than the cape's raptor migration.

We decided to create this guide with the goal of sharing the waterbird flight identification techniques that we have learned, and also to inspire more birders to start seawatching, whether on the Atlantic Coast, Gulf Coast, Great Lakes, or elsewhere. Roughly 100 years ago, the identification of most birds in the field was thought impossible, and the focus of ornithology was the collection of birds for examination in the hand. Things changed with the invention of the modern field guide by Roger Tory Peterson. The field identification of birds became practical and enjoyable, and birding exploded in popularity. More recently, raptor flight identification was the esoteric purview of a handful of hardcore raptor watchers whose identification secrets were not widely known among other birders, most of whom viewed flying raptors as impossible to identify. A variety of good identification books, starting with *Hawks in Flight* by Pete Dunne, David Sibley, and Clay Sutton, changed that and turned hawk watching into a popular and mainstream form of birding. We hope this guide opens a doorway to seawatching in the way the Peterson Field Guide opened the doorway to bird watching for so many, and the way *Hawks in Flight* helped create legions of dedicated hawk watchers.

This book is not simply a technical manual of bird identification. We hope to capture some of the simple joy of being outside, being alive, and looking at birds. People do not go birding simply to put names on birds; they go birding for a variety of reasons, from marking the changing seasons, to aiding the conservation of wild creatures and environments, to challenging their skills and concentration. This book is indeed intended to aid identification, but also to inspire people to venture out and seek out these amazing sights for themselves, and even as a tribute to the beauty, nobility, and unreflective courage of the birds we are treating.

INTRODUCTION

WHAT IS SEAWATCHING?

In this book, we consider "seawatching" to be the observation of migrating waterbirds in flight. These observations can take place anywhere: a lake, river, bay, mountain ridge, or even a Midwestern corn field, not to mention the sea. Sometimes birders refer to a river observation as a "riverwatch" and to a lake observation as a "lakewatch." The important point is that this book encompasses all such observations.

Bird migration is complex and poorly understood, and it is not always easy to know which birds are migrating. This is part of the challenge and the appeal of seawatching, and one of the areas in which seawatching can make significant contributions to our knowledge of birds. There are many reasons for waterbirds to fly, ranging from long-range migration, to local commuting between roost and feeding sites, to fleeing from a hungry Bald Eagle. Although we are particularly interested in their long-range migration, this book will equip you to identify waterbirds in many different contexts. Hawk watching started with migration watches, but it inspired guides that are applicable to any raptor in flight. Likewise, our book was inspired by the conspicuous and fascinating migration of waterbirds, but it will help you identify waterbirds anytime you see them in flight.

Tropical storms and hurricanes can blow tubenoses, "tropical" terns, and other rarities close to shore or even inland, and in the wake of these events birders are drawn to promontories and other likely locations for the chance of spotting a rarity. Such events are exciting but infrequent. Our book will help you identify these storm-blown waifs, but they are not its primary focus. Far fewer birders spend extended periods watching and documenting the normal, biannual waves of migrating waterbirds that sweep across North America's coasts, lakes, and rivers. This book is concerned more with the usual than the unusual. Even the usual ebb and flow of our continent's waterbird migration is barely known, and much remains to be discovered, even in the shadow of some of the largest cities.

Part of the reason we are particularly interested in waterbird migration is that these birds become more distinctive on migration. Species associations become stricter, flight paths become well defined, and flocks take on distinctive shapes. Identification based on this kind of information is one of the things that put seawatching at the cutting edge of birding. Unfortunately, many of these tendencies become weaker when birds are not migrating. The task of long-distance migration seems to bring a single-mindedness that creates distinctive behav-

"Seawatching" is not restricted to the coast. The Great Lakes, rivers, and interior lakes offer excellent opportunities to "seawatch" (or "lakewatch" or "riverwatch" if you favor accuracy over a catchall label). Any location that offers the opportunity to observe migrating waterbirds can be a seawatching site. The potential to find an occasional rarity while seawatching, like this Black-legged Kittiwake on a reservoir in Colorado, keeps things exciting. Colorado, Nov. Bill Schmoker.

Seawatchers at New Jersey's Avalon Seawatch. Michael O'Brien.

iors. These behaviors never disappear, but they are relaxed when other tasks such as feeding and breeding are at hand.

We hope this book will challenge birders to expand their interest in migration watching. Raptor watching has grown into a huge activity in recent decades, resulting in an explosion of knowledge about raptors. New sites where concentrations of migrating raptors can be observed have been found in almost every corner of the continent. We believe the potential for discovering points of concentration for waterbirds is just as great; all kinds of geography can produce concentrations of waterbirds.

Franklin's Gull with Willets, Short-billed Dowitchers, a Ruddy Turnstone, and a Sanderling. The term "waterbirds" could include shorebirds, rails, and others. The definition we use in this guide is narrower, limited to groups of birds that are often observed in diurnal migration. Texas, April. Ken Behrens.

And the amount that can be learned from an increased number of people seawatching is tremendous. Raptor watching is popular because it is fun and challenging, and it connects the observer with the great flow of the natural world in which we live. Seawatching has all these elements and more. It certainly offers a challenge. There are more than 100 species of waterbirds in the region covered by this book, compared with only 30-some raptors. Many of these waterbirds rocket by at astounding speed, never stopping to wheel over the observer's head in hawk fashion. And seawatching specializes in providing astounding natural spectacles. Both of us have seen incredible days at some of the best hawk watches and seawatches on the continent. We both agree that our most remarkable and memorable experiences have been at seawatches: days of wind and scoters, rain and loons, captivated by the tenacity of migrating birds, and governed by the ceaseless beat of waves against the shore.

THE SPECIES COVERED IN THIS BOOK

Early in the creation of this guide, we faced a challenge: we had to decide on the group of birds we would cover. Whereas most guides cover groups defined by clear geographical or taxonomic lines, "waterbird" is an imprecise term. In its widest sense, it could encompass species such as Osprey or waterthrushes that spend most of their time in and around water. We quickly realized we would be unable to do justice to the full range of "waterbirds" and would have to exclude some groups.

By most accounts, shorebirds are waterbirds, but we have not included them in this guide. The main reason for this is that shorebirds are largely nocturnal migrants, and it is rare to see large diurnal movements. We acknowledge that shorebirds are sometimes a part of seawatching and do stage diurnal migrations. For example, phalaropes are a feature of seawatches in the Atlantic Provinces, and watch sites such as Miller Beach in Indiana and Whitefish Point in Michigan see a range of shorebirds. A secondary reason for excluding shorebirds is *The Shorebird Guide* by Michael O'Brien, Richard Crossley, and Kevin Karlson. This excellent identification guide already covers shorebirds in flight.

Wading birds (herons, egrets, ibis, and so on) are certainly aquatic, but we have excluded them as well. Once again, most of them migrate at night. Diurnal migrations do occur, as on the Gulf Coast in spring and in Atlantic salt marshes in fall. Including these species would have significantly increased the number of species in the book, however, and would have detracted from our ability to cover the core seawatch species well.

We have excluded all of the rallids, as they are virtually never seen in flight as migrants. We cover Horned and Red-necked Grebes, as these are exceptional among grebes in that they are frequently seen as diurnal migrants. We excluded Pied-billed, Eared, Least, Clark's, and Western Grebes, as they're rarely seen in flight in any context, and most are rare in most of the area we cover.

Like many guides, this one does not cover extreme rarities, such as Yellow-nosed Albatross, Red-footed Booby, and Ancient Murrelet. If you focus on intimately knowing the species covered in this guide, you'll be well prepared to pick out an exceptional vagrant.

Although we have excluded certain species from this guide, we by no means recommend a narrow focus when seawatching. All migrating birds are fascinating and anyone spending time at a seawatch is bound to see a variety of things fly by. Observe, marvel, record, and learn!

TAXONOMY

We have chosen to follow the family sequence proposed by Howell et al. in the November 2009 *Birding* magazine article "The purpose of field guides: taxonomy vs. utility?" This sequence places more emphasis on superficial similarity than on underlying genetics, a more helpful approach for an identification guide. In an era when the once-familiar order of species in a field guide is no longer familiar as taxonomists have reshuffled the deck so frequently and significantly, the proposal by Howell et al. that the sequence of families remain constant is particularly appealing. We echo their plea that more authors of guides and checklists that target birders rather than professional ornithologists adopt the order proposed by Howell et al. A stable sequence of bird families that emphasizes utility and stability over precise taxonomic relationships is in the best interest of the casual birder and does not hamper more advanced birders from exploring taxonomic relationships if they choose to do so. Within each family we have also diverged from more established taxonomy and shuffled species into the sequence we consider most helpful and intuitive for identification purposes. Neither the order of families nor the order of species within families is perfect, but the goal of this guide is to be an aid in field identification and we believe that a species order that emphasizes utility is the best way to aid that goal.

NORTH AMERICAN WATERBIRD FAMILIES

The numbers of species covered in each of the 15 families represented in this guide are as follows:

Waterfowl (swans, geese, ducks): Anatidae—44 species
Cormorants: Phalacrocoracidae—3 species
Anhinga: Anhingidae—1 species
Loons: Gaviidae—3 species
Grebes: Podicipedidae—2 species
Alcids: Alcidae—6 species
Shearwaters and petrels: Procellariidae—7 species
Storm-petrels: Hydrobatidae—3 species
Frigatebirds: Fregatidae—1 species
Gannets and boobies: Sulidae—3 species
Pelicans: Pelecanidae—2 species
Skuas and jaegers: Stercorariidae—5 species
Gulls: Laridae—18 species
Black Skimmer: Rynchoptidae—1 species
Terns: Sternidae—13 species

Carefully scan through billowing flocks of migrating scoters to pick out other species. This flock includes both Surf and Black Scoters as well as three Long-tailed Ducks, a Bufflehead, and a Hooded Merganser. New Jersey, Nov. Ken Behrens.

MIGRATION

North American waterbird migration is a huge topic that we can only touch on here. The basic reason that birds migrate is that it allows them to take advantage of different resources in different parts of the globe at different times of the year. The fact that birds can undertake such journeys is one of the most remarkable things about them, and it has captured the human imagination throughout history.

The most important point in the context of this guide is that waterbird migration is complicated and imperfectly understood, and should not be oversimplified. A variety of strategies are exhibited by North American waterbird species, which range from the sometimes entirely sedentary Canada Goose, resident on many golf courses, to the remarkable Arctic Tern, which breeds in the high Arctic, winters in the Antarctic Ocean, and spends the rest of the year traveling between these areas. Most of the continent's waterbirds have a strategy somewhere between these two extremes. Many species are present in part of their range year-round but withdraw from the remainder of the breeding range during the winter and move south into areas that are unoccupied during the summer. Some species undertake a "leapfrog" migration in which the birds that breed the farthest north also winter the farthest south, leapfrogging birds in the middle that are resident or that undertake shorter migrations.

The majority of species covered in this guide undertake classic northbound spring and southbound fall movements, but this stereotype is usually an oversimplification. Some species, including some gulls and many waterfowl, stay as far north as the availability of open water will allow, withdrawing to the south as bodies of water freeze over and moving back north the moment open water begins to appear. So

American Coots are waterbirds, but because they migrate nocturnally and are rarely seen in flight, we exclude them from this guide. Their inclusion in the introduction ensures that readers are not totally deprived of their unsurpassed elegance in flight. Utah, Jan. Ken Behrens.

in a given year, these species' "fall" migration might not take place until far into winter, and their spring migration may also begin in winter. There are even species such as Great Shearwater that breed in the Southern Hemisphere and migrate north to spend the austral winter (which is the boreal summer) in the North Atlantic.

Referring to migrations as being south-to-north and north-to-south is also overly simplistic. The bulk of the North American Arctic lies west of Hudson Bay, meaning that many Arctic-breeding species that winter in the Atlantic off the East Coast have to angle all the way across the continent on migration, perhaps following the Great Lakes for part of the journey. The direction of their fall migration is as much west-to-east as it is north-to-south. Some species fly almost nonstop to complete their migration in a few days or a week, whereas others migrate in a much more leisurely manner, with frequent detours and backtracks.

A significant example of breaking with stereotypical migration is found in ducks. Leaving their mate soon after the young hatch, the males of many species undertake a molt migration that may take them hundreds or even thousands of miles in any direction. They do this to find good cover and food sources to sustain them during the period when they are flightless due to the molt. This additional migration may even carry them north, mere weeks before they begin their southbound fall migration.

Some birds migrate exclusively nocturnally, some exclusively diurnally, and some migrate both day and night when conditions allow. The daily schedule during migration of many waterbirds is poorly known. Most swans, geese, and ducks seem to be mainly nocturnal migrants that will continue their movements into daylight hours when conditions are favorable. This may also be true of many gull species, though this is less certain. Some individuals of Arctic-breeding species that are pelagic on their wintering grounds, such as jaegers, Sabine's Gull, and Black-legged Kittiwake, cut across the interior of the continent to reach the ocean, but they do so either at night or at great altitude and are rarely witnessed on this migration except when bad weather forces them down.

The "routes" taken by migrating birds are incredibly diverse. A widely known but vast oversimplification of these routes is the concept of "North American flyways." Some species do follow well-established routes during migration, but others move across a broad front and can show up almost anywhere. Certainly there are more waterbirds migrating through the Mississippi Valley than the Appalachians, so there is some merit to the "flyway" concept. The same is true of migratory routes on a smaller scale. Some species have strong preferences in the flight line they take—for example, their altitude and position along a coastline—whereas others may be seen in flight almost anywhere. Red-throated Loons and Northern Gannets have a strong tendency to follow the Atlantic Coast on migration and avoid flying over land, at least diurnally and at low altitude. Snow Geese can show up anywhere, though concentrations sometimes occur along coastlines or rivers. Many species have a strong tendency to follow "leading lines" on migration, especially when these lines are formed by shorelines. Rivers, lakeshores, bays, and peninsulas are all features that attract and concentrate migrating waterbirds. Following waterways keeps the birds close to suitable feeding and roosting habitat, and they may also use such features to navigate. Many waterbirds, such as scoters, loons, and jaegers, seem willing to migrate at low altitudes over the ocean and Great Lakes but are hesitant to do so over land or smaller bodies of water. A large portion of waterbird migration may take place nocturnally at high altitudes. This is one respect in which waterbird migration definitely varies from raptor migration, which seems to take place mainly diurnally and at low to middle altitudes.

This brief section should make it obvious what a complex set of phenomena is subsumed under the label "waterbird migration." Although some of the species accounts contain information on migration strategies, it is beyond the scope of this guide to cover this in detail for every species. Even if we aimed to treat this subject in detail, the migratory behavior of many species is poorly known. What is important is that seawatchers "tune in" to the great continental dynamic of waterbird migration, which comprises an incredible range of varied and fascinating strategies. There is still a great deal to learn about waterbird migration, and careful observers stationed anywhere on the continent can make significant contributions to the field.

CONSERVATION

There are dozens of regularly operated hawkwatches throughout North America, with a concentration in the northeastern United States. Several of these watches have annual data going back to the 1970s or earlier. These watches form a powerful network whose data are analyzed together, with the aim of tracking population trends in North American raptors. They have succeeded admirably in this goal, documenting the recovery of the Bald Eagle and Peregrine Falcon, the rise of Cooper's Hawk, and the decline of American Kestrel and Sharp-shinned Hawk. The data from any one watch could easily be dismissed, but data from dozens of watches over a broad area that reflect similar trends are hard to ignore. Unfortunately, no such network exists for waterbirds, despite the conspicuous diurnal migrations most species undertake and an abundance of sites with significant concentrations of migrants. The fall seawatch in Avalon, New Jersey, administered by Cape May Bird Observatory and New Jersey Audubon Society, and the waterbird count at Whitefish Point, Michigan, administered by Whitefish Point Bird Observatory, are the only official long-term watches collecting data on the trends in waterbird migration. Certainly there are other means of monitoring waterbirds, and the population trends in game species such as geese and ducks are carefully tracked by government agencies. Even among ducks, though, a cohesive strategy for monitoring the sea ducks that nest in the far north, such as scoters and eiders, does not exist. Admittedly, some of the least-known species in the direst need of population monitoring, such as Black-capped Petrel and Ivory Gull, are not well suited to monitoring by seawatching. Even so, what additional knowledge might be gained about waterbird populations, trends, and movements if there were a network of regularly operated waterbird counts similar to the network of hawk-watches? The steady decline in the numbers of Common Loons at the Avalon Seawatch, and the timing of their movements, are not paralleled by the data gathered at less formal watches on the eastern Great Lakes. Are the birds recorded in the Mid-Atlantic coming from a different breeding population than those passing through the Great Lakes? What is the meaning of the occasional huge incursions of Razorbills to the Carolinas south of the normal range of this species? So far there has been little effort to systematically gather and compare numbers of Razorbills seen in the Southeast over time and correlate them to larger population trends in this species or with the status of the fish on which Razorbills depend. Such examples only touch on what could be discovered if there were more birders seawatching and recording numbers in a systematic manner.

IDENTIFICATION

In addition to the feeling of being plugged into the incredible spectacle of migration, feeling the flow of the seasons wash over you, one of the main attractions of seawatching is the challenge it presents. Birds are generally distant and flying fast, and the best days often coincide with difficult observation conditions such as wind or rain. An additional challenge is the large range of possible species at most observation points, even those located inland. Simply put, seawatching is one of the most demanding types of birding in North America, and this is just what makes it exciting! There is always more to learn, new ground to break, and the opportunity to expand your birding skills.

The identification methods that most field guides stress bear little resemblance to those that expert seawatchers use. At normal seawatch distances, traditional field marks are simply not visible. Most of the techniques used at a seawatch will be familiar to any hawk watcher or skilled birder, some of whom may use the techniques outlined below instinctively, without even realizing it. Seawatching differs, even from hawk watching, in the amount of emphasis placed on the shape and behavior of flocks. Although the idea of flock analysis and identification may seem difficult to birders accustomed to looking at birds one by one, this technique is a key element in identifying distant, flying waterbirds. Another important difference between seawatching and more traditional methods of identification is the attempt to carry information gained from one identified bird over to adjacent birds. Once they've identified one member of a flock, seawatchers use it as a reference to compare its size, structure, behavior, and any vis-

More seawatch data gathered by observers in different places could become a powerful tool for monitoring and conserving North American waterbird populations. Derek Lovitch.

ible plumage traits with those of unknown birds in the flock. This is an incredibly powerful method, which at long distances is always superior to the traditional tendency to treat each bird as an individual and look for its specific field marks.

Because most seawatching is done through spotting scopes at powers of at least 20x magnification, birds often initially appear as little more than specks at extreme distances. The first step is to place the speck or flock of specks into the correct category, such as duck, loon, pelican, or tern. Only then can the specific identification begin. The process used to determine what group a distant waterbird belongs to is basically the same as that used to identify a bird to species. For this reason it may be necessary to go through the process outlined below more than once in order to reach a specific identification. Here we discuss the main identification criteria, from most to least important. Of course this list is only a guide; in the field everything is evaluated simultaneously, and each piece of information that you can mine is important, even though you may not acquire it in this precise order. As stated above, it may first be necessary to go through this list once just to narrow down a distant bird to a category, then go through it again to pin the bird down to species. With the most difficult identifications, you may need to consider each point below several times, whittling down the list of possible species until you can reach a conclusion or the birds disappear for the last time behind a wave, eliciting a round of wry looks and shoulder shrugging from the observers.

RELATIVE SIZE

Size is always the most important trait, and it is generally easy to determine size on a broad scale. For example, is the bird closer in size to a gannet,

Many large flocks of birds form characteristic shapes, and some species also have distinctive flocking behaviors that can be used to identify the species at distances where the specific traits of individuals cannot be seen. A Double-crested Cormorant flock, like this one, constantly and slowly shifts its shape, like a huge macroorganism crawling across the sky. New Jersey, Oct. Cameron Cox.

a duck, or a storm-petrel? Establishing this is a key first step, but given that viewing birds in vast, open spaces such as a large body of water may skew size perception, how do we accomplish this? The very fact that the birds we are discussing are in flight provides one of the best bases for making rough judgments of size: the speed of the wingbeats. The speed of the wingbeats is linked to a bird's size and weight, and wingbeats tend to be obvious at great distances, flashing information to the observer almost like a semaphore. Once you've established size on a macro scale, you may need to evaluate other features in order to place a distant speck in the correct bird family. Once you've established which family the bird belongs to, size again becomes the first factor to consider in narrowing the list of possible species.

STRUCTURE

Initially, basic considerations such as whether a bird is long-winged or short-winged, long-tailed or short-tailed (or has no visible tail), help you narrow a bird down to a group. As a bird or flock moves closer, constantly refine and reassess your perception of its shape. Many species covered in this guide can be identified by silhouette alone once they are close enough for structure to be accurately judged. As soon as they can be seen, carefully evaluate the precise structure of the head and wing and the shape of the body, as these characteristics play a role in virtually every identification made at a seawatch.

FLIGHT STYLE AND FLOCK STRUCTURE

Most of the identification criteria we discuss here are interconnected, and flight style is a good example. The speed and strength of the wingbeats are one of the best ways to determine a bird's size, but

additional information can be gathered from the precise way a bird moves through the air. How far below the body are the wings at the bottom of the downstroke? Does the bird hold its wings straight or swept back? Does a bird speed up and slow down, or does it maintain a steady course? Does the bird beat its wings constantly, or does it periodically glide?

Flocks behave almost like macroorganisms and often have distinctive flight styles and behaviors all their own. Some of the important traits to consider include the size of a flock, the shape of the flock and how it changes over time, the height at which the flock flies, and if the flock dips up and down or maintains a level course. Careful observation of flock behavior can sometimes allow identification at tremendous distances, or at least probable identification of the majority of members of a distant flock.

OVERALL COLORATION

Does a distant bird look largely dark or pale? This sounds simple, but it can greatly help in narrowing down the possibilities on a distant bird. Even more important is the presence or absence of contrasting areas of white on the wings or body. Such patches tend to be visible at great distances, and their position on a distant bird can quickly narrow the list of possible species.

PROBABILITY

Probability comes into play with every identification, not just when seawatching. It is one of the things experienced birders constantly use to their advantage, a quick shortcut to many correct identifications. Given the difficulty of identifying passing waterbirds, knowing what to expect is a huge advantage, as it allows you to concentrate first on a short list of the most probable species, then consider other possibilities only once you've eliminated the more likely ones. The best way to learn about the timing of migration locally is to spend time in the field, to interact with other local birders, and to make use of resources such as checklists, e-mail listservs, and local periodicals. Knowing what species are likely at a given time of year, or even time of day, is one of the things experienced observers use to make impressively quick and accurate identifications. Finding unusual species is certainly part of the thrill of seawatching, so it's best to strike a balance. It is unwise to blindly base all your identifications on what is expected, but attempting to identify birds without a framework of probability is reckless and leads to numerous errors. Two aspects of probability come into play when identifying waterbirds:

YEARLY TIMING Most waterbirds have protracted migration periods. At any given month in any given location, some of the species covered in this guide are on the move. It is essential to know what species are likely to occur at a given location on a given date. If you know what species are at their peak, what species are early or late but still might be observed, and what species are unlikely to be found on a given date, you'll greatly improve your chances of making quick and accurate identifications.

DAILY TIMING Early morning is the most diverse time at most migration watches, as many waterbirds are primarily nocturnal migrants but may extend their migration into the first few hours of the morning. Likewise, just before dusk is often productive as species may begin their evening flight several hours before it is actually dark. Knowing this, be prepared to consider a greater variety of species during these more diverse periods. Hooded Mergansers and Ruddy Ducks are examples of species you are far more likely to see early and late rather than in the middle of the day. At the Avalon Seawatch in southern New Jersey, where alcids are rare, most Razorbill sightings occur during the first 2 hours after dawn. Loons offer a slightly different illustration of daily timing at Avalon. Common Loons move primarily in the morning, drop off in the late morning, and are almost nonexistent in the afternoon. By contrast, Red-throated Loons move throughout the day, though often with an afternoon spike in numbers.

FLIGHT LINES

At each watch site, certain species will consistently fly along invisible corridors, referred to as "flight lines." For some species, flight lines may be consistent over time, whereas other species establish new flight lines daily, as conditions change. When seawatching, you can gain a "feel" for flight lines at a given location over the course of a day, as well as over the course of weeks, months, and even years of observations. Gulls, terns, some tubenoses, and some waterfowl are the birds most likely to use predictable flight lines. Northern Gannets may use certain flight lines in some conditions, only to spread out widely as conditions change. Although it may not be possible to identify a bird or flock solely by the flight line it is following, immediately knowing what characteristics to look for to confirm a hunch based on the flight line can be quite useful. Knowledge of flight lines may also allow you to locate less common species with greater frequency by repeatedly checking along known flight lines.

ASSOCIATIONS

Knowing which species frequently flock together is another helpful identification shortcut. Waterfowl in particular tend to form mixed-species flocks. Once you've identified one species in a flock,

Knowledge of frequent species associations can be helpful when trying to identify all the members of large flocks of birds, particularly waterfowl. In northeastern North America, a large flock of Mallard, like this one, will almost always include at least a few American Black Ducks. An observer who is aware of this is much more likely to pick out the Black Ducks than one who isn't aware of it. New Jersey, Dec. Ken Behrens.

knowledge of which other species often associate with that species can help you piece together the identity of the rest of the flock. For example, along the East Coast large flocks of Mallard almost always include America Black Ducks and vice versa. Most other dabblers do not join Mallard/Black Duck flocks, though Gadwall occasionally will. So when the green head of a male Mallard is visible in a distant flock, it is likely that the similar-sized brown ducks with it are female Mallard and that the darker ducks of similar size are American Black Ducks. If there is a bird in the flock that looks extremely skinny, check it first for Gadwall characteristics. As another example, Blue-winged Teal flocks on the Gulf Coast often include Northern Shoveler and Green-winged Teal. In contrast, large flocks of Northern Pintail are usually monospecific in migration, though small flocks will join other ducks.

BEHAVIOR

Several behaviors can serve as clues to the identity of migrating birds. Red-throated Loons often droop their neck well below their body and bob their head up and down. Common Loons often fly with their bill open. Horned Grebes have a strong tendency to fly short distances and plop back down in the water. These behaviors can clinch the identification of a distant bird when you can't see plumage traits, as in poor light.

PLUMAGE DETAILS

Specific plumage details are typically the last identification traits to consider at a seawatch, as they are usually the last traits to be visible. With most species, you can nail down the identification long before you can clearly see plumage details. There are identifications for which plumage traits are essential, such as the separation of Thayer's Gull from Herring Gull, or at least very useful, such as the wing stripe differences on scaup. Plumage is also essential to aging and sexing most species. As a bird flies closer to you, you can also use plumage traits to double-check conclusions you reached at a distance based on other characteristics. Misinterpreting any piece of information preceding the evaluation of plumage can throw the identification process off track. Making sure the plumage of a bird meshes with the identity assigned at a distance provides the last line of defense against misidentification. Watching as a bird confidently called a Lesser Scaup at a distance approaches and morphs into a Green-winged Teal is a humbling experience, but it provides a learning opportunity!

VOICE

Most of the species we cover here are not particularly vocal in flight or are too far away for vocalizations to be useful, but there are exceptions. Tundra and Trumpeter Swans have far-carrying calls that are the most reliable way of separating these species. Swans and geese often fly high enough that their vocalizations may be heard even when the birds themselves are hidden in cloud cover. Terns are also vocal, and unusual species may be picked out by their vocalizations. And although the gurgles of Long-tailed Ducks and the cackles of Brant may not be needed for identification purposes, their contribution to the quality of a day of seawatching cannot be overestimated.

IDENTIFICATION PITFALLS

As with any challenging kind of bird identification, there is always potential for errors when seawatching. Because the birds are often distant and tend to move by without stopping, there is less "accountability" than in most types of birding, and therefore the potential to let errors slip by unchecked. Knowledge of what can cause errors is one way to ward against them.

When the sun is directly behind the observer, birds are lit up and plumage traits can be seen at much greater distances. Conversely, strong backlighting or glare can make plumage traits invisible and can even burn out the edges of silhouettes, compromising the usefulness of structure. Strong midday light washes out colors, making it difficult to assess the mantle shades in gulls and to discern

The stark black-and-white plumage of American White Pelican serves as an example of how dark and light colors are perceived differently at a distance. Against a pale background such as clouds, the pelican's black wings would stand out sharply, whereas its white body would blend into the background; the reverse is true against a dark background as in this photo. The way the color of a bird interacts with its background affects our perception of its size and structure. Texas, Jan. Ken Behrens.

Light conditions have a huge impact on how we perceive and identify birds. Focusing on size, structure, and behavior is the best approach when confronted with backlit birds, but be aware that these conditions change our perception of birds' shapes and wingbeats. These nuances can be learned only by spending time studying birds in a variety of light conditions. These birds are Black-bellied Whistling Ducks, a species with a distinctive structure and flight style that can be identified under almost any circumstances. Louisiana, Jan. Ken Behrens.

other subtle differences in color. Heat haze is also a major problem; strong heat haze can make sea-watching all but impossible, turning the distant flicker of a small bird's wing into something that seems to explode on the horizon. Fog and mist are also problematic, although birds may venture much closer to shore during these conditions. Low light causes wingbeats to appear faster than during sunny conditions and thus throws off size evaluations. At the same time, low light also makes birds look bulkier. Every jaeger looks like a Pomarine in the period between sunset and complete darkness! Also be aware that dark birds will appear smaller against a dark background than against a pale background, whereas the reverse is true of pale birds.

Flight style is frequently relied on to identify distant waterbirds, but be aware that when joining a flock of another species, many birds alter their flight style so that it becomes less distinctive. For example, Canada Geese tend to form orderly flocks arranged in neat lines and have slow, methodical wingbeats, whereas Cackling Geese tend to bunch up more, forming messy skeins or balls and have faster, looser wingbeats. However, when small numbers of Cackling Geese join a flock of Canada Geese, they will adopt a wingbeat more like that of their larger flock-mates, and stay

within the confines of the more structured flock. A similar phenomenon takes place in the wingbeat of White-winged Scoters when they join a flock of dark-winged scoters. They alter their deeper, slower wingbeats to synchronize better with the rest of the flock, though they still tend to maintain greater spacing between individuals than do the smaller scoters. Birds that are not able to modify their flight tend to be found on the margins of a flock. Large alcids in flocks of scoters are usually found near the rear, trailing slightly behind the main flock.

There are many things other than differences in species that create variation within birds, and when variation falls outside the experience or expectations of an observer, it can create confusion. Below we discuss some of the causes for potentially confusing variation that you may encounter at a seawatch.

SEX- AND AGE-RELATED SIZE VARIATION

Size is a primary identification characteristic, so when it is misjudged it can lead to drastic errors. For example, when you are trying to determine how many species are present in a distant flock, size is the main characteristic to consider, so intraspecific variation can create significant confusion. In general, larger birds show more obvious variation in

Age-related variation is another consideration when identifying distant birds in flight. The plumage of immature birds often differs from that of adults, and many large waterbirds in the first cycle, like these Double-crested Cormorants, migrate south before their bills are fully grown or their bodies have fully filled out. Some individuals can be strikingly smaller than the norm, such as the bird in the lower left of this photo. Some observers would be tempted to call this slender, short-billed cormorant a Neotropic, but it is actually just a runt Double-crested Cormorant. New Jersey, Dec. Ken Behrens.

size, but even the smaller waterfowl can show size variation. Size variation between sexes is one of the main causes for size differences. In most birds covered in this book, males are at least somewhat larger than females, the exception being the skuas and jaegers, in which females are significantly larger. In many cases in which size varies by sex, the larger sex will have a larger head, heavier bill, or broader wings, which further increases the likelihood of confusion. Age-related differences in size also come into play with some species. Cormorants, Common Loon, and some of the larger waterfowl all show this type of size variation; during fall migration many young birds are more slender than adults and therefore appear smaller. In contrast, some well-fed juvenile gulls, terns, and jaegers may be plumper than the average adult and appear larger. Variation within a species tends to be subtler than that among species, but this is not always true. Experience is the best guard against mistaking size variation within a species for variation among species.

HYBRIDS

In eastern North America, hybrid waterbirds are generally rare. Mallard x American Black Duck is by far the most likely hybrid to be encountered at a seawatch in the Northeast. Aside from this regular hybrid combination, most waterbird counts are unlikely to record more than one or two hybrids in a season. Although none of them are very frequent, there are several interesting hybrids among gulls and waterfowl that can potentially occur at a migration watch. Herring Gull x Glaucous Gull and Blue-winged Teal x Cinnamon Teal are two of the most likely. Although hybrids do occur in other groups of waterbirds, they are far less frequent than in waterfowl and gulls. Except for a few of the most frequent and distinctive hybrids, most will be very difficult or impossible to identify with only a flyby view.

PIGMENT ABERRATIONS

Variation caused by birds with aberrant pigment is also rare, but given the large numbers of birds that may be seen at a good migration watch point, a few birds with aberrant pigment can be expected per season. Leucism, reduced amounts of pigment resulting in abnormal paleness, is the most frequent pigment aberration. Leucistic birds may range from having just a few pale feathers to being almost completely white. True albinism, the complete lack of pigment, is far rarer. Melanism, increased amounts of dark pigment, is also rare, as are several other pigment abnormalities that may cause a particular color to be more prevalent than normal. When viewing a bird with a pigment abnormality, concentrate on the bird's structure and behavior rather than the affected plumage. Often such birds are part of a flock and can be compared with normal members of the same species and identified by that means.

In addition to the normal identification challenges that come with seawatching, occasional curveballs come in the form of aberrant birds such as this leucistic Laughing Gull. Although the plumage is odd, the bird's size and structure remain typical for the species. Georgia, Sept. Lauren Deaner.

The molt is less obvious on this Lesser Black-backed Gull than it is on the Bonaparte's Gull in the next photo, but careful examination shows that the outermost primary (P10) is still growing. Lesser Black-backed Gull typically has very pointed wings, at least for a large gull, but molt in the outer primaries can alter the shape of the wingtip. New Jersey, Sept. Cameron Cox.

MOLT AND PLUMAGES

MOLT Feathers are incredible structures that provide insulation, allow birds to fly, and perform a variety of other functions. Biologically, feathers are central to what makes a bird a bird. But feathers are fragile. They are made of keratin, the same protein that makes up human hair and nails, and exposure to the sun and elements wears them out so that they need to be replaced. Unlike human hair and nails, feathers do not grow continuously; they grow in orderly and regular waves known as "molts." Defined simply, molt is normal feather growth. Although it may be the most noticeable indication of molt, feather loss is only a side effect of feather growth, not a part of the process of molt; old feathers are pushed out by newly emerging feathers.

The broad range of species covered in this guide displays a wide variety of molt strategies. Waterfowl and alcids become completely flightless for several weeks and regrow all their flight feathers at the same time. In contrast, large gulls replace their flight feathers individually in an orderly sequence and may take 6 months or more to complete a molt. These differences reflect different life history strategies beyond the scope of this guide. For those interested in this subject, we recommend the Peterson Reference Guide *Molt in North American Birds* by Steve N. G. Howell.

A seawatcher needs a working knowledge of molt, as molt can have a significant effect on the silhouettes and flight styles that play key roles in the identification of distant waterbirds. Molt in the outer primaries can give the wing a more rounded appearance. Molt in the inner primaries and secondaries can break up the silhouette of the wing, making it more difficult to get a feel for the true structure of a bird. Molt in the tail feathers can make the tail appear shorter than normal, forked, notched, or graduated. Gaps in the wing cause the wingbeats to be faster than normal, creating an unfamiliar cadence to the wingbeats and potentially throwing off an evaluation of size.

Molt can also be an aid to identification. For example, it appears that molt timing may be vital to sorting out the Band-rumped Storm-Petrel complex in the field (see pp. 325 and 591). As another example, active flight-feather molt on a puzzling jaeger is enough to eliminate Long-tailed from contention, as Long-tailed Jaegers molt flight feathers only after arriving on their wintering ground in the Southern Hemisphere.

PLUMAGES We have chosen to use the Humphrey-Parkes (H-P) system (Humphrey and Parkes 1959), as modified by Howell et. al. 2003, for naming molts and plumages in this guide. There are detractors of this system, as aspects of it are difficult to understand, but it lacks the inconsistences that plague other systems of naming plumages. The H-P system is based on the terminology of "basic," "alternate," and "formative" plumages.

All birds have a base plumage referred to by the H-P system as "basic plumage," brought about by a prebasic molt. In most cases the prebasic molt is a complete molt replacing all feathers, and it occurs on a roughly annual basis. Some birds add an additional plumage to their annual molt cycle, and this is referred to as "alternate plumage," brought about by a prealternate molt. The prealternate molt is usually only partial, including few if any flight feathers. One of the few exceptions is a species covered in this guide; Franklin's Gull has a complete prealternate molt in addition to a complete prebasic molt. In other words, it replaces every feather on its body two times each year. Some birds have an extra plumage in the first cycle that is not repeated in the following cycles; this is known as "formative plumage," brought about by a preformative molt. Formative plumage is referred to as "first-winter" plumage in most other naming systems. As formative plumage is not as widely understood as the other terms we use for molts and plumages, we have used it sparingly. In many species that forage primarily on the wing, such as Wilson's Storm-Petrel and most species of terns and

Fresh inner primaries contrast with worn and faded outer primaries and secondaries on this Bonaparte's Gull. During this stage of molt, the wingbeat is noticeably affected, potentially altering the impression the bird gives at a distance. The brown areas on the worn feathers were once black, like the tips of the fresh primaries. Such heavy fading dulls strong patterns, reducing the distance at which they can be discerned. Massachusetts, July. Cameron Cox.

jaegers, the preformative molt is complete, including all flight feathers, though it may drag out over 9 months or more and overlap with other molts. In most other species, such as small gulls and ducks, the preformative molt does not include flight feathers.

Bird molt is clearly cyclical in nature, repeated over and over again, so the idea of plumage cycles is one of the underpinnings of the H-P system. A plumage cycle begins with the onset of one molt and ends the next time the same molt is repeated. For example, a bird acquires its first true set of (juvenile) feathers via its complete (first) prebasic molt, initiating the first cycle. The first cycle ends with the onset of the second prebasic molt roughly a year later. The second cycle ends with the onset of the third prebasic molt, and so on. Cycles may be initiated by any repeated molt, so there can be both alternate cycles and basic cycles. Alternate cycles begin with a prealternate molt and end with the next prealternate molt. In this guide, however, "cycle" always refers to the basic cycle, beginning with a prebasic molt and ending at the beginning of the next prebasic molt.

Why refer to cycles rather than exact plumages? Although it is preferable to precisely identify plumage, such as first alternate or second basic, we often cannot do so in the field or in a photograph with absolute confidence. It is easier to determine a bird's cycle, and if the cycle can be discerned, it can be used to give a rough framework of age. It is a case of being less precise but more correct. Since cycles are roughly a year in length, calling a Roseate Tern a "first-cycle" bird is similar to calling it a "first-year" bird. The advantage of referring to cycles is that they are based on the molt sequence of each individual bird rather than an arbitrary date, so whereas all first-year Roseate Terns become second-year Roseate Terns on a date sometime in midsummer regardless of their appearance or molt, first-cycle Roseate Terns do not become second-cycle Roseate Terns until the second prebasic molt begins, and the timing of this may differ significantly between Roseate Terns breeding in Florida and Roseate Terns breeding in New England.

HOW TO USE THIS GUIDE

This book consists of two major sections. The first and largest section comprises species accounts for all of the eastern North American waterbirds that we have chosen to cover. The accounts contain text, maps, and photos. More information about the format and content of the species accounts is included below. The second section, called "Where to Watch," is a guide to some of the seawatch sites in eastern North America.

SPECIES ACCOUNTS

Each account starts with a photo, followed by the species' name and dimensions, spring and fall arrival dates (not included for all species, and sometimes given for only one season), and then a range map. Next comes the text, which consists of an introduction followed by five or six subcategories, and finally the main section of photographs. The text and photos are complementary, so if something in the text isn't clear, refer to the photos and accompanying captions. Likewise, if a caption isn't clear, refer to the text, which likely treats the same subject in more detail.

DIMENSIONS: These are given as average length (L), wingspan (WS), and weight (WT).

SPRING ARRIVAL AND FALL ARRIVAL: We include (for most species) average arrival dates on spring and fall migration in different locations. There is a focus on rather "clean" migrations, in which a species passes during a specific period, or completely evacuates part of its range for part of the year. Bird migration can be more complex than this. For example, Herring Gulls occupy much of their North American range throughout the year, although there is a great deal of movement within that range, and winter and summer see very different distributions of the continent's Herring Gulls, even though much of the "range" remains occupied year-round. We use standard state and provincial abbreviations.

RANGE MAP: These maps are annotated to focus more on migration than do traditional range maps, which prioritize breeding and wintering ranges.

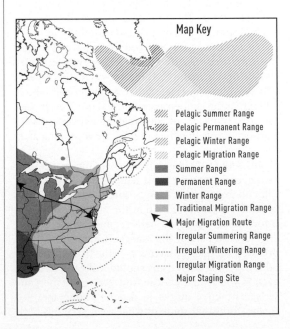

Map Key

	Pelagic Summer Range
	Pelagic Permanent Range
	Pelagic Winter Range
	Pelagic Migration Range
	Summer Range
	Permanent Range
	Winter Range
	Traditional Migration Range
	Major Migration Route
	Irregular Summering Range
	Irregular Wintering Range
	Irregular Migration Range
•	Major Staging Site

TEXT SUBCATEGORIES

INTRODUCTION This is a variable paragraph that contains a few different categories of information, often things that don't fit in other sections of the account, and that aren't consistently important enough to merit their own section but still bear mention for some species. The length of the introduction thus varies considerably depending on the species. It often starts with a sentence or two that place the bird within our lives. Some species are common and iconic, whereas others are rare vagrants from elsewhere in the world. There is usually a quick summary of the bird's distribution, to augment the range map. We mention subspecies when these are distinctive and relevant to identification but cover this topic in more depth further into the account. Finally, we describe the call for those species that are distinctive and vocal in flight.

SIZE Although size can't be divorced from the next category, structure, it is so important to flight identification that it merits its own category. Here we note the bird's size in the context of other species. We've chosen these index species because they are either common and well known or are closely related to the species in question. It is useful to know that a Lesser Scaup is larger than a Blue-winged Teal since Blue-winged Teal is a familiar species, but Lesser Scaup is more likely to be in the company of Greater Scaup, so we mention both.

STRUCTURE This is the second fundamental of identification, and closely related to size. Here we describe the way the bird is put together: the length and thickness of its neck, the prominence of its belly, shape and length of its tail, how its wings are shaped and how the bird holds them, and so on. Although some of this may sound incredibly subtle to inexperienced observers, you don't have to watch birds for long before you start to observe the subtleties of bird structure. These are often the aspects of each bird's character that we don't talk about when making an identification, and don't even consciously think about, but that nonetheless play a significant role in telling us what we're looking at.

FLIGHT AND FLOCKING Here we cover the most interesting, and often the most telling but also the most difficult to communicate, aspects of how waterbirds fly. Even more than in the other sections, the information conveyed here requires some experience on the part of the reader. If the idea of Red-breasted Merganser having a "wing twitch" sounds odd, watching a few fly by should make things clear, even if you would choose to describe the merganser's distinctive quirks in different language. We freely admit that some of what we describe is both subjective and difficult to capture in words. Although birders have developed an unofficial lexicon of words to describe flight, we have had to standardize and in some cases improvise our descriptive language.

Flocks of birds take on a character all their own, which can tell you a great deal about the constituent species. This is an aspect of bird identification that has often been ignored in the past. Are the birds in a flock packed tightly together or well spaced? Do they form a line, a ball, a V, or some other shape? Are the spatial relations within a flock constant, or do the birds shift, or jockey, for position? Is the overall structure of the flock shifting or constant? How high above the ground or water are the birds flying? As a slightly far-fetched example, you might agonize over whether you'd just seen a line of mergansers or loons on the distant horizon if you didn't know that loons never fly in an ordered line, whereas it's the rule of merganser flight. Much like seasonality, this is another kind of "macro" information that experienced observers use when making an identification. By the time a serious birder gets down to examining the details of one bird's structure and plumage, he or she has usually discarded a large range of possible species based on things that might be neglected by the novice.

In discussing flock structure, we give priority to the angles that are most common and most instructive. For waterfowl that frequently migrate low over large bodies of water, we mostly discuss side-on flock structure, whereas for gulls and terns that form high-flying migrant flocks, we are more interested in the structure as seen from underneath.

We often refer to the height of a species' flight, particularly for waterfowl. As a rough index, low flight is 1 to 10 yards above the water or ground, moderate height is 10 to 100 yards, and high is 100 yards or above.

Everything we say regarding flight and flocking applies most strongly to migrating birds and is blunted in nonmigrating birds. For example, migrating ducks have strong tendencies regarding which species they will associate with, but on the wintering grounds these rules seem to go lax, and almost any species will fly together when commuting between two adjacent pools at a wildlife refuge. When waterbirds are not migrating, their flocking tendencies become less distinctive. We have decided that the best strategy is to describe flight and flocking characteristics at their most distinctive, during migration, with the caveat that what we say softens when applied to nonmigrants. Bear in mind that many of the photos in this guide were taken of nonmigrants and show species associations that would be highly unusual for migrating birds. Although such photos might show only a

Wilson's Storm-Petrel breeds in the Southern Hemisphere and migrates north to spend the austral winter—the boreal summer—in the North Atlantic. Adults are molting at this time, so most of the adults seen in North American waters look like this individual. This affects the flight style and silhouette and can alter plumage traits, such as the pale ulnar bar on this bird. Massachusetts, July. Ken Behrens.

rare or incidental association, they are still of great value for comparing species. But just because we show a photo with multiple species in it doesn't mean they frequently fly together. Getting some of our comparison photos, such as American White Pelican with Brown Pelican, became major projects, as these species simply don't like to fly in close proximity!

APPEARANCE Here we cover the colors and patterns of a given species, particularly the different plumages held by different ages and sexes. A few species also have different color morphs. Where these are distinct they receive separate treatment. We have

intentionally placed appearance after size, structure, and flight and flocking. Although this aspect of identification has traditionally been discussed more than the other aspects combined, we view it as less important, particularly in a book concerned with flight identification. The size, structure, and flight style of a bird are still apparent at distances where all or most of its colors become indistinct. The appearance section starts with a summary of the patterns and colors of the species that are common across age and sex. What follows is a more detailed description of the different plumages. This section is not intended to be a complete catalog of the different plumages that can theoretically be differentiated. It is intended to allow separation of distinctive plumages in flight at moderate range. Although certain fourth-cycle gulls might be easy to differentiate with a good photo of a perched bird, information on this plumage is not relevant to a book whose focus is identification of distant flying birds. The appearance section ends with a "Distant" subsection that describes the traits that are obvious at long range.

SIMILAR SPECIES Here we treat species that could cause confusion. We typically start with the most similar species and proceed to ones that are also similar but less confusing, or perhaps only confusing at great distances or in bad viewing conditions. Although sections like this have been a feature of field guides for a long time, in this book we consider some novel identification challenges that crop up as you attempt to identify birds at long range. Northern Gannet and Brown Pelican really don't cause confusion until you're trying to differentiate shimmering dots on the horizon!

DISTANCES

Throughout this book we use arbitrary-sounding phrases to describe the distances of birds and to address the way their plumage and structure are perceived at different distances. Although the vagueness of the language is unfortunate, relying on such phrases is a necessary evil in taking on the subject of flight identification, particularly distant flight identification. Below we attempt to provide a framework for understanding these terms, in hopes of making them seem less arbitrary than they might appear.

One thing that affects perception of a bird's size and distance is the kind of optics you use. Birds will "feel" closer when viewed through a high-powered spotting scope than through normal binoculars. Perception of distance is also altered by the size of an object. If a Dovekie and a Northern Gannet are both 500 yards away, an observer would likely describe the Dovekie as far away and the gannet as at a moderate distance. Since such biases are an inevitable part of seawatching, we use "perceptional" terms for distance rather than absolute ones. Therefore, when describing what a Dovekie looks like at "long distance," we might be describing what a Dovekie looks like at 500 yards, but when describing what a Northern Gannet looks like at "long distance," we might be describing what a gannet looks like at a mile or more. We hope the following definitions of terms used in the book will be helpful.

• **CLOSE/CLOSE RANGE:** Most if not all typical field marks are readily visible. Most observers focus mainly on colors and patterns and less on structure and behavior. Very little knowledge of seawatching techniques is required to make identifications at this distance.

• **MEDIUM/MODERATE DISTANCE:** Colors and patterns are still visible, but fine details disappear. Structure and behavior play a larger role in the identification process. Learning birds at this distance lays the framework for developing better seawatching skills.

• **LONG DISTANCE:** Bold patterns are usually still visible, particularly bright white patterns, but even these may be visible only in brief flashes or not at all in poor light. Overall color is often the only color that is visible; for example, an observer can tell that a bird is fairly light or fairly dark but cannot see any pattern. Structure and behavior are the primary identification criteria. Unless the light is very poor, most structural aspects can be judged with accuracy, though some fine differences in structure become so muted they can no longer be used.

• **EXTREME DISTANCE:** The only color visible is large patches of white. Most birds look black irrespective of their actual color. Silhouettes may be visible in good light, though species with a compact or otherwise indistinct structure will start to look like dots. Differences in wingbeat speed and cadence are apparent on most birds, but the distinctiveness of these traits begins to fade, particularly in small and medium-sized birds. Depending on the size of the birds and the size of the group, flocks are usually visible but may fade in and out as the flock shifts. How these flocks shift and move may allow the experienced seawatcher to identify them to a broad group, such as scoters, cormorants, or loons.

PHOTOGRAPHS

As soon as you start flipping through this book, you will notice that we are using some different kinds of photographs than normally appear in a bird guide. We chose the photos to convey several aspects of what is distinctive about each species. Most basically, the characteristic shapes and colors of each species are shown. Beyond that, we attempt to capture the less tangible aspects of the way a bird flies. Identifications are rarely based on simple realizations that "this bird has these colors" or "it is shaped like so," but rather on an entire suite of traits that are perceived instantaneously and simultaneously. We attempt to impart the "feel" of each species in flight and to place them in their environment. Oftentimes, distant photos tell you more about how to identify a bird than do close-ups, so our photos run the gamut from well-lit, frame-filling portraits to backlit specks on the horizon. This is the same range of possibilities that occurs in the field, especially at a migration watch, where birds are often distant and poorly lit.

Beyond shape and color, we also attempt to capture what is distinctive about the *way* a bird flies. How does it move its wings and body? Does it look lanky and languid or compact and frantic? Photos often mislead, particularly when it comes to birds in flight, but our aim has been to select photos that accurately portray each species. Experienced observers will agree that certain photos have the "feel" of a species much more than others. Few bird books in the past have included illustrations of flocks of birds, yet that is another important clue to the identity of a flying bird. How is it flying in relation to other members of its species, and even other species? Bird flocks take on a huge range of distinctive structures, and these can be readily seen at distances where the details of the individual birds in the flock are impossible to discern.

We also aim to place birds in their environment. In its way, a deep yellow autumn salt marsh tells you as much about what makes a Brant a Brant as does any other piece of information about the species. Whenever possible, we have chosen photos that include the bird's favored environment.

Our approach has led to unconventional choices of photographs. Many of them would be considered too distant or poorly lit to be included in most guides. Until we find a migration watch with perpetual, directionless light, and birds that fly by 30 feet away, we will defend our choice of photos!

In general, we have tried to select photos that communicate what a birder actually sees in the field. The vast majority of photos in this book were only slightly edited in Photoshop to optimize them for printing. In limited cases we use composite images. Three different kinds of composites are used in the book: (1) Cutting a bird from one image and placing it onto another image, beside a bird with which we want to compare it. We have done this only a handful of times and have labeled these "Composite" in the captions. (2) Composites of two or more frames with different backgrounds, usually to compare different species. These are slightly more common, and the variety of different backgrounds will make them obvious to the reader. (3) Slight shifts of birds within an image, usually to create more effective comparisons. We have carefully prepared these composites to represent things that might actually be seen in the field. In other words, with some more time and luck these photos could actually be taken; we are just using Photoshop as a shortcut in their creation. The composites of this third type are Brant page 63 (middle); Mallard page 85 (top); American Black Duck page 86, page 88 (top), page 89 (bottom); Mottled Duck page 91 (top); Gadwall page 94; Ring-necked Duck page 148; Hooded Merganser page 222 (top); Common Loon page 255 (bottom); Common Murre page 276 (bottom right); Atlantic Puffin page 280 (bottom); Great Shearwater page 295 (bottom); American White Pelican page 350 (bottom left); Parasitic Jaeger page 375 (bottom); Long-tailed Jaeger page 381 (top right); Great Black-backed Gull page 427 (bottom); Little Gull page 448 (top); and Gull-billed Tern page 489 (top).

In a few cases we include photos of a subspecies that is either extremely rare or unrecorded in eastern North America, and we usually don't mention this fact in the captions. For example, in the Brant account we include a series of photos that were taken in Wales of the *bernicla* subspecies, which is extremely rare in eastern North America. Although some details of these birds may be different than the normal subspecies in our area, we use such photos cautiously, and only to illustrate features that are the same across subspecies, such as overall structure or flock structure and behavior.

Some photo captions include questions about the birds shown in the photo. These are always italicized, and the answers are found in Appendix 1 (page 582). Quizzes like this can be a powerful tool in learning a challenging subject like flight identification. Even if some of these questions seem intimidating, we challenge our readers to give them a try. Even a drastic misidentification can be a learning experience!

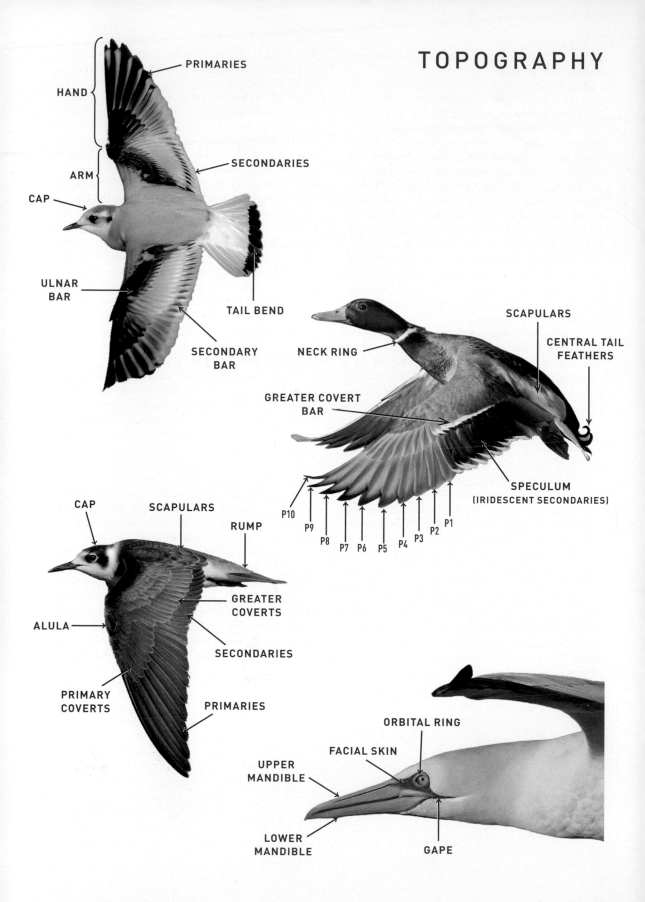

TOPOGRAPHY

PRIMARIES

HAND

ARM

SECONDARIES

CAP

ULNAR BAR

TAIL BEND

SECONDARY BAR

SCAPULARS

CENTRAL TAIL FEATHERS

NECK RING

GREATER COVERT BAR

SPECULUM (IRIDESCENT SECONDARIES)

P10
P9
P8
P7
P6
P5
P4
P3
P2
P1

CAP

SCAPULARS

RUMP

GREATER COVERTS

ALULA

SECONDARIES

PRIMARY COVERTS

PRIMARIES

ORBITAL RING

FACIAL SKIN

UPPER MANDIBLE

LOWER MANDIBLE

GAPE

MIRRORS

UNDERWING
COVERTS

SUBTERMINAL
RING

AXILLARIES

WING
TIP

TAIL
EATHERS

NARICORNS

ARM

HAND

NAIL

GULAR POUCH

WING
BEND

SECONDARIES

PRIMARY
"FINGERS"

SECONDARY BAR

GREATER COVERT
BAR

INNER PRIMARY
WINDOW

SPECIES
ACCOUNTS

SWANS

Swans are massive, beautiful waterbirds that have a prominent place in folklore. They comprise one of the most distinctive groups of birds covered in this guide. Along with geese, swans form the sub-family Anserinae within the family Anatidae, which also includes whistling-ducks and typical ducks. We cover three species of swans in this guide: two native species and the introduced Mute Swan. All three are white as adults and are washed with pale gray or brown in the first cycle, gradually turning white over the course of the first winter.

Over most of eastern North America, Tundra Swan is the default swan, and the most migratory swan by far. Trumpeter Swan has been widely re-introduced into the region but is still fairly local, and many introduced populations are sedentary or nearly so. Mute Swan is an Old World species that was introduced to many parts of eastern North America. It tends to be sedentary but does make short-distance flights.

All three swans are typically found in shallow wetlands and small lakes, and the native species often forage in damp fields. Unlike ducks, swans tend to stay in tight family groups throughout the winter. Migrating flocks often fly at great heights, sometimes so high that they can be heard but not seen.

Although just about anybody can recognize a swan as a swan, separating species in flight can be incredibly difficult, especially when they are distant. Separating distant Trumpeter and Tundra Swans when their vocalizations cannot be heard can be nearly impossible. Fortunately, both species are very vocal in flight, and this is the best means of separating them. Given how difficult swan identification is at long range, knowledge of each species' probability at a given location can be an excellent clue. The sexes are similar in all three species covered here and the appearance of adults remains unchanged throughout the year. They also show differences between first-cycle birds and adults. They acquire adult appearance in the second cycle.

Swans are a distinctive group, but separating distant Tundra and Trumpeter Swans visually is extremely difficult. Separation becomes much easier when the two species fly together, like the two wing-tagged Trumpeter Swans (top and bottom) and one Tundra Swan shown here. Ontario, May. Raymond Barlow.

TUNDRA SWAN
Cygnus columbianus
DIMENSIONS
L: 52 in.; WS: 66 in.; WT: 14.4 lb.

SPRING ARRIVAL

se. PA: mid-Mar.; Lake Erie: late Mar.;
s. MB: late Apr.

FALL ARRIVAL

ND/MN: early Oct.; s. ON: early Nov.;
Chesapeake Bay: mid-Nov.

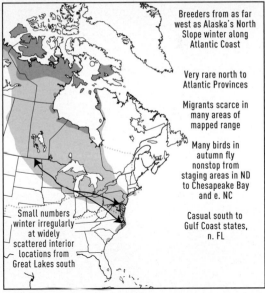

Breeders from as far west as Alaska's North Slope winter along Atlantic Coast

Very rare north to Atlantic Provinces

Migrants scarce in many areas of mapped range

Many birds in autumn fly nonstop from staging areas in ND to Chesapeake Bay and e. NC

Casual south to Gulf Coast states, n. FL

Small numbers winter irregularly at widely scattered interior locations from Great Lakes south

Tundra Swan is a long-distance migrant; the birds wintering in eastern North America breed on the tundra between the north slope of Alaska and Hudson Bay and winter primarily in freshwater wetlands of the Mid-Atlantic region. This is the swan most likely to be observed in long flights in eastern North America, often at great altitudes. Flying Tundra Swans often reveal their presence with their call, a high-pitched, gurgling yodel drifting down from high overhead. Although this is not the most enticing description, it is one of the continent's most beautiful and intensely wild sounds.

SIZE: Substantially larger than even the largest Canada Goose. Significantly smaller than Trumpeter

and Mute Swans. Despite the great disparity in size between Tundra and the two larger swans, the difference can be very difficult to detect at a distance, as all swans appear massive at long range.

STRUCTURE: Classic swan shape, with a long, slender neck; heavy body; and very long, broad wings. The bill is wedge-shaped and slightly shorter than that of Trumpeter Swan, with a slightly concave culmen that is difficult to see in flight but can be seen at moderate distances under good conditions. The belly tends to be fairly flat or bulges only slightly at the "hips," whereas the larger swans expand noticeably in this region. The tail is short and rounded, unlike Mute Swan's. The feet are significantly smaller than those of Trumpeter Swan, but this is difficult to judge without comparative experience or direct comparison.

FLIGHT AND FLOCKING: The smaller size compared with that of other swans translates into slightly faster, less labored wingbeats. Typically migrates in small groups of 6–30, though flocks can swell to several hundred individuals. Small flocks form lines or Vs; large flocks form less orderly Us. Birds in a flock are precisely and neatly spaced, and there is little shifting or jockeying for position. Migrants usually fly quite high, though smaller flocks occasionally fly low over large bodies of water.

APPEARANCE: Adult: All white with black bill and feet. The variably sized yellow patch at the base of the bill is difficult to see in flight, and some birds lack it entirely. **First Cycle:** Pale dusky gray overall with white patches becoming evident later in fall. Molts earlier than Trumpeter Swan; many Tundras are virtually all white by late December. **Distant:** All white. Adults tend to gleam slightly, whereas dusky first-cycle birds do not. Like other swans, easily fades into pale backgrounds and can be maddeningly difficult to spot, even when the call can be plainly heard.

SIMILAR SPECIES: Trumpeter Swan: Larger and longer-necked, sporting a longer bill with a straight culmen. Tends to show a more bulging undercarriage and broader wings than Tundra. Wingbeats are slightly slower than Tundra's. Extremely difficult to separate visually at a distance but frequently gives its diagnostic call in flight. **Mute Swan:** Larger than Tundra, with a longer, pointed tail. The knob on the bill gives the head a more rounded look at a distance. Usually silent in flight but occasionally gives odd screeching calls that do not carry well.

UTAH, JAN. KEN BEHRENS.
- Swans are beautiful and elegant in flight. A wedge-shaped head and short tail are characteristic of both native species.
- The bill of Tundra is fairly short, with a concave profile that can be resolved at medium distance under perfect conditions but is often difficult to see.

ADULT WITH ADULT TRUMPETER SWAN (L). ONTARIO, MAY. RAYMOND BARLOW.
- Size difference is immediately apparent in comparison but difficult at long range because proportions are similar.
- Note longer bill, broader wings, and larger feet of Trumpeter.
- At close range, Trumpeter's pink tomial stripe on the gape and more muscular neck are evident.

WITH ONE CANADA GOOSE. NEW YORK, MAR. DON ARMSTRONG.
• Typical flock of Tundra Swans; such flocks emit a haunting, far-carrying yodel.
• Their brilliant white color causes them to gleam when they catch the sun.

ADULTS AND ONE FIRST CYCLE (MIDDLE R). UTAH, JAN. KEN BEHRENS.
• First-cycle Tundras lose their gray plumage earlier in the year than first-cycle Trumpeters; this one is already showing white patches on the back and wing coverts.
• Significant individual variation occurs among first cycles in late fall and early winter; in the same flock, some birds may be entirely gray and others almost fully white.

**NEW JERSEY, DEC.
KEN BEHRENS.**

- In silhouette, note the relatively slim, pointed wings. The bills look short compared with the large heads.
- On the birds with the wings up (third from R and fourth from L), notice how the belly is almost flat.

**ADULTS. UTAH, JAN.
KEN BEHRENS.**

- Note the slim wings and modest-sized feet.
- The longer-necked bird (L) is likely a male.

ADULTS. UTAH, JAN. KEN BEHRENS.

- Their coloration causes swans to melt into pale backgrounds, such as cloudy skies, and to be difficult to locate even when their vocalizations can be heard.

TRUMPETER SWAN
Cygnus buccinator
DIMENSIONS
L: 60 in.; WS: 80 in.; WT: 23 lb.

Trumpeter Swan is one of the largest flying birds in the world but maintains an elegant appearance despite its massive bulk. This species was formerly more widespread in eastern North America but in many areas was extirpated before its range could be documented, so the true extent of its historical distribution is unknown. Trumpeter Swan's current presence in eastern North America is thanks almost exclusively to reintroduction programs that started in the late 1970s and early 1980s, and that are underway in Ohio, Michigan, Minnesota, Wisconsin, Iowa, Arkansas, and southern Ontario. These reintroductions have been highly successful, and in many areas the new populations are booming. Many of the vagrant records of Trumpeter in eastern North America likely originate from one of these introduced populations, though most of the birds in these introduced populations are fairly sedentary. Trumpeter's low-pitched honking call separates it from Tundra Swan and is often the best way to locate and identify this species in flight.

SIZE: The largest species of North American waterfowl. Significantly larger than Tundra Swan, slightly larger than Mute Swan.

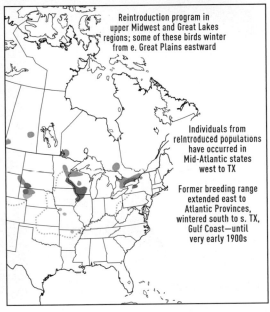

Reintroduction program in upper Midwest and Great Lakes regions; some of these birds winter from e. Great Plains eastward

Individuals from reintroduced populations have occurred in Mid-Atlantic states west to TX

Former breeding range extended east to Atlantic Provinces, wintered south to s. TX, Gulf Coast—until very early 1900s

STRUCTURE: Enormous and long-necked, with a long, wedge-shaped bill and long, broad wings, with obvious primary "fingers." The bill is shaped like a doorstop, with a perfectly straight culmen. The huge feet, almost the size of a small dinner plate, extend almost to the tip of the short, squared-off tail. The back slopes down sharply to the base of the neck, creating a more humpbacked appearance than in Tundra.

FLIGHT AND FLOCKING: Wingbeats are slow and heavy. Although true migrants fly high, birds commuting around the Great Lakes and other parts of the reintroduced range typically fly much lower. Flocks found in eastern North America are small—family groups or pairs—and fly in short lines. In the West, larger flocks form Vs.

APPEARANCE: Adult: All white with a jet-black bill and feet. **First Cycle:** Mottled white and pale gray-brown. Molts later than Tundra Swan; most Trumpeters maintain a large amount of gray-brown plumage until late winter. **Distant:** All white. Adults tend to gleam slightly, whereas first-cycle birds do not.

SIMILAR SPECIES: Tundra Swan: Very difficult to separate. Best distinguished by voice; a higher-pitched yodeling compared with the lower honking of Trumpeter. Tundra Swan is smaller, with shorter neck and bill, flatter belly, and less hump-backed appearance. At the distances at which swans are often observed, however, these traits are of little help. **Mute Swan:** Also difficult to separate at great distances. The tail is longer and wedge-shaped. The knob above the bill creates a more rounded head profile at a distance. The wings create a low-pitched creak that is audible at close range, but vocalizations do not carry far enough to be heard in flight.

ADULT WITH ADULT TUNDRA SWAN. NEW YORK, NOV. TOM JOHNSON.
- Massive size dwarfs Tundra swan.
- Note Trumpeter's substantially larger, wider body and huge feet.

ADULT WITH ADULT TUNDRA SWAN. OKLAHOMA, JAN. JIM ARTERBURN.
- Trumpeter has a longer neck, hunched back, broader and blunter wings with obvious primary "fingers," and bulging belly compared with the smaller Tundra.
- Trumpeter's head and bill look proportionate: both are large. Tundra has a large head, but its bill seems disproportionally small.
- Trumpeters often root in the mud, resulting in a dirty bill, as shown on this bird.

MUTE SWAN
Cygnus olor
DIMENSIONS
L: 60 in.; WS: 75 in.; WT: 22 lb.

FALL ARRIVAL

IA: mid-Sept.; NC: mid-Oct.

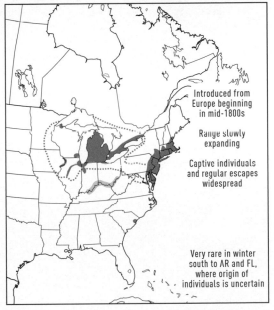

Introduced from Europe beginning in mid-1800s

Range slowly expanding

Captive individuals and regular escapes widespread

Very rare in winter south to AR and FL, where origin of individuals is uncertain

This graceful and impressive Old World species is widely kept in captivity in North America to add ornamental flair to lakes and ponds. Some individuals long ago escaped and established feral populations in the Mid-Atlantic region, southern New England, and around the Great Lakes, and these populations continue to expand despite efforts to curb their growth. Mute Swans do show up elsewhere, but most of these are probably recent escapees, as the feral populations are largely sedentary. As the name suggests, Mute Swan is largely silent in flight, though the wings produce an odd creaking noise that can be heard at close range.

SIZE: Massive. Slightly smaller than Trumpeter Swan. Clearly larger than Tundra Swan.

STRUCTURE: Typical swan silhouette in flight. The weight distribution of the body averages slightly different than in other swans, particularly Tundra.

There is more weight farther back, near the feet. As a result, the body tilts up slightly, while the neck remains straight, producing a slight kink at its base. Although this characteristic is very subtle, and can be approximated by the other swans (especially Trumpeter), it can be useful with practice. Unlike native swans, Mute has a knobby growth at the base of the bill that gives the head a more rounded appearance. The wings are slightly shorter and more rounded than in other swans. The tail is wedge-shaped and longer than in other swans, extending well beyond the feet.

FLIGHT AND FLOCKING: Slow, heavy wingbeats create a loud creaking sound. Wingbeats are slightly looser and less determined than those of the native swans. Usually flies at low to medium height, lower than other swans. Swans seen flying just over the water along coastlines are apt to be this species. Usually in small flocks or family groups, rarely more than 10 individuals. Flocks typically form lines or small Vs.

APPEARANCE: Adult: White plumage with an orange-red bill, distinct black knob above the bill, and black feet. **First Cycle:** Bill is pinkish, and the black knob is much reduced. Most birds are pale gray-brown mottled with white. White-morph juveniles, sometimes referred to as "Polish morphs," occur occasionally. **Distant:** All white. Adults tend to gleam slightly. First-cycle birds appear dull gray at great distances, the mottled appearance of their plumage visible only at moderate range.

SIMILAR SPECIES: Trumpeter and Tundra Swans: Compared with native swans, Mute Swan has slightly looser wingbeats and a more pronounced humpbacked appearance, with the body and neck held at slightly different angles. Overall, it lacks the feel of a long-distance migrant such as Tundra Swan. The other swans also have a shorter, squared-off tail, black, wedge-shaped bill, and more wedge-shaped head. They are quite vocal, whereas Mute Swan is typically silent.

ONE ADULT AND THREE FIRST CYCLES: ONE WHITE MORPH (TOP R) AND TWO TYPICAL GRAY BIRDS. NEW JERSEY, SEPT. CAMERON COX.
- Note the considerable plumage variation in the first cycle.
- The tilted body vs. straight neck is apparent on the bottom right bird.

TWO ADULTS. SWEDEN, APR. KEN BEHRENS.
- Note how the feet fall well short of the tip of the tail, which is longer and more wedge-shaped than those of native swans.

TWO ADULTS AND THREE FIRST-CYCLE WHITE-MORPH BIRDS WITH RING-NECKED DUCK, RUDDY DUCK, AMERICAN WIGEON, AND GADWALL.
NEW JERSEY, SEPT. CAMERON COX.

- Small groups of Mute Swans often make short flights between shallow wetlands. These movements account for most in-flight sightings.

ADULTS. SWEDEN, MAY. LASSE OLSSON.

- The head and neck are virtually straight whereas the body tilts slightly downward, a posture unique to Mute among swans.
- Head is slightly more rounded than that of native swans, and the forehead profile is distinctly concave.
- The only swan likely to be seen flying low over the ocean, usually in small, tight flocks.

All geese share a characteristic overall shape: long-necked and heavy-bodied, with long and broad-based wings. Plumage differences easily separate most species, but each species also shows subtle differences in structure that can be used to separate distant or backlit birds. This photo illustrates two of the distinct groups within geese: the Cackling Goose (L) is a "white-cheeked" goose, and the Snow Goose (R) is a "white," or "*Chen*," goose. Maryland, Dec. Michael O'Brien.

GEESE

Geese are medium-sized waterfowl with stocky and somewhat awkward bodies, long necks, and long, pointed wings. Along with swans, they are members of the subfamily Anserinae, and both groups are part of the family Anatidae. Some species of geese have been domesticated for centuries, contributing to widespread awareness of geese and their features by the general population. The highly visible passage of wedges of geese, heralded by their loud honking calls, has long been regarded by many cultures as a sign of the change of seasons and the passage of time, ingraining geese even further into human consciousness.

Geese are highly social and, more than any other group of birds in this guide, are known for their flocking behavior. This is for good reason, as there is little one can do in the face of the spectacle and the cacophony of sound created by a flock of tens of thousands of geese besides stand in awe! Although geese do not regularly mix with other birds, flocks of multiple species of geese are a regular occurrence, particularly in middle and western North America where geese are at their most diverse. Canada Goose is the only species that seems reluctant to mix with other geese, though stray singles or small groups of other species of geese will join flocks of Canada Geese. This tendency to form mixed flocks makes it advisable to check every flock of geese for less common species. Whereas a Barnacle Goose should be easy to pick out, distinguishing a Cackling Goose in a flock of Canada Geese or a Ross's Goose in a flock of Snow Geese requires experience, luck, and a careful eye.

Like swans, but unlike ducks, geese stay together in family groups for the fall and winter, and individual family groups can sometimes be identified within a larger flock of geese, particularly when one or two family groups of one species join a flock composed primarily of another species. When a family group can be recognized, it is useful to evalu-

Geese are well known for their tendency to fly in V formations, like the one formed by these Greater White-fronted Geese. Texas, Nov. Cameron Cox.

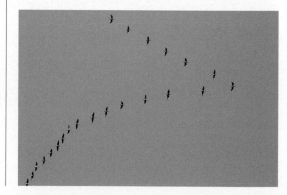

Large flocks of geese possess a unique beauty and vitality. They also often present a fun challenge, and this flock is a good example; amid the Greater White-fronted and Snow Geese are a few Ross's Geese. Louisiana, Jan. Ken Behrens.

ate the subtle differences in structure between adult males, adult females, and first-cycle birds, as well as any visible plumage differences between adults and first-cycle birds. Many of these differences are only discernible within the context of a family group, but paying attention to these small details allows you to understand variability within a species.

We cover seven species of geese in this guide. Six breed in continental North America and one, Barnacle Goose, is a vagrant from Europe and Greenland. There is some controversy about the records of Barnacle Goose, but it is clear that many of the Barnacle Geese observed in eastern North America are wild vagrants. The geese in this guide fall into three main groups: the "black" or *Branta*, geese, Brant, Barnacle, Canada, and Cackling Geese (the latter two are often known collectively as "white-cheeked" geese); the "white," or *Chen*, geese, Snow and Ross's Geese; and the "gray" geese, represented in North America by Greater White-fronted Goose. (The Old World has several other species of "gray" geese, one of which, Pink-footed Goose, is a rare vagrant to eastern North America, though it appears to be increasing. Another of the European "gray" geese, Graylag Goose, is a common domestic species in North America and there are a few reports that may represent wild birds.)

The ranges and populations of most North American goose species are expanding, in part because these birds seem to benefit from human modifications to the landscape. The expansion of farmland and creation of wildlife refuges have allowed Snow and Ross's Geese to spend the winter much farther north than ever before, decreasing their annual mortality and resulting in massive increases

in their populations. In many areas of their Arctic breeding grounds, white geese have become so numerous that they consume most of the vegetation, degrading the habitat for other species. Likewise, Canada Geese have altered their habits in response to the changes humans have made to the continent. Some Canada Geese have ceased to migrate, becoming resident on golf courses and parks in such numbers that they are now a nuisance. The breeding range of Canada Goose continues to expand, and there seems to be little to halt the progress of this avian lawnmower.

With the exception of Brant, a bird tied primarily to coastal salt marshes, geese migrate in greater numbers in the interior of eastern North America than they do coastally. Although coastal locations can see significant movements of Canada and Snow Geese following strong fall cold fronts, these events are the exception. More often geese pass in a broad front over much of the continent, with some concentration of their movements along major river valleys. Although geese are primarily nocturnal migrants, they often begin their movements well before sunset and continue them long after dawn, creating the iconic sight of migrating geese cutting across the sky. Flocks of geese usually fly high and are often heard before they are seen. They may even fly at heights where their calls can be heard faintly but the human eye cannot see them.

The sexes are similar in all seven species covered here and the appearance of adults remains unchanged throughout the year. They show differences between first-cycle birds and adults. They acquire adult appearance in the second cycle.

CANADA GOOSE
Branta canadensis
DIMENSIONS
L: 45 in.; WS: 60 in.; WT: 9.5 lb.

SPRING ARRIVAL

(migratory populations):
WI: mid-Mar.; n. ON: late Mar.; n. MB: late Apr.

FALL ARRIVAL

(migratory populations):
ND: late Sept.; WI: late Sept.

Between the iconic V-shaped flocks of chilly fall afternoons and antagonistic geese at local parks, everyone recognizes Canada Geese. Recently, many Canada Geese have developed a liking for golf courses, parks, and other human-made habitats and have become sedentary. However, Arctic-nesting Canada Geese still traverse their traditional migratory routes, and these birds receive the focus of this account. Migrants often fly quite high, and their characteristic deep, resonant honking is often the best clue to the passage of a flock overhead.

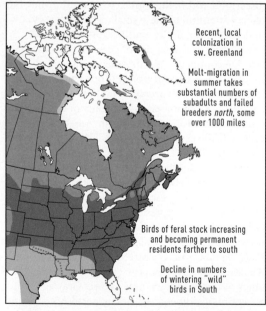

Recent, local colonization in sw. Greenland

Molt-migration in summer takes substantial numbers of subadults and failed breeders *north*, some over 1000 miles

Birds of feral stock increasing and becoming permanent residents farther to south

Decline in numbers of wintering "wild" birds in South

SIZE: Variable, though most are large, and this is clearly the largest goose. Some approach the size of a small Tundra Swan. Others are only about the size of Snow Goose. Adult males are larger than adult females, which in turn are usually slightly larger than first-cycle individuals.

STRUCTURE: Extremely bulky body with a long, slender neck. Wings are long and exceptionally broad-based, with blunter tips than in other geese, and show individual fingerlike primaries at their tips, rather like a raptor does. The overall flight silhouette is more similar to that of a small swan than to other geese.

FLIGHT AND FLOCKING: Wingbeats are slow, heavy, even, and powerful. Small flocks form lines with even spacing among members; larger flocks take the shape of a V, U, or W. Flocks are well organized, and individuals hold their place in line with little movement within the flock. A flock spotted from a distance will appear to move at a glacial pace. Often a flock will be spotted at a great distance and initially be identified as cormorants, only to be correctly identified as Canada Geese minutes later when the observer notices that the flock has made little forward progress. Usually seen in single-species flocks but can be joined by other geese, particularly Cackling Geese. Migrants inland tend to fly at high altitudes, but migrants over large lakes or the ocean occasionally stay very low. Birds making short movements often fly at low to moderate altitudes.

APPEARANCE: Adult: Dark overall. The head and neck are black except for a white cheek patch that wraps around the bottom of the throat. The body and wings are gray-brown to brown with a paler breast and white vent. The uppertail coverts form a white band. The highly migratory subspecies that winters along the Atlantic Coast, *canadensis*, tends to be paler with a frosty appearance, but there is much variation. **First Cycle:** Virtually identical to adult but may show a reduced or dusky cheek patch. **Distant:** Dark brown. The paler belly is difficult to detect except in very good light.

SIMILAR SPECIES: Cormorants: Flocks of cormorants can be mistaken for Canada Geese at long range. However, cormorants glide frequently, have billowing disorganized flocks, and move more rapidly. **Brant:** Smaller, with slimmer and more pointed wings. Tends to move in disorganized, shifting flocks that move more rapidly than flocks of Canada Geese. **Greater White-fronted Goose:** Smaller, with a shorter, thicker neck that creates the more compact silhouette of a "typical" goose, in contrast to the rather swanlike silhouette of Canada Goose. Flocks are less rigidly organized than those of Canada Goose and move more rapidly.

ILLINOIS, DEC. KEN BEHRENS.
• Stocky and long-winged like other geese, but with a longer, narrower neck that is almost swanlike.

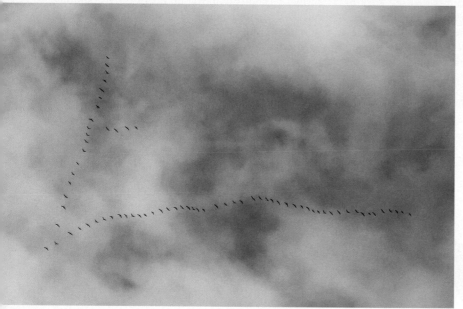

ILLINOIS, DEC. KEN BEHRENS.
- Note the distinctive plumage, which at close range is similar only to that of Cackling Goose.

ENGLAND, OCT. PAUL SCHROEDER.
- High-flying Vs are orderly, with wide and even spacing.
- Flocks crawl across the sky at a slower rate than those of other dark flocking birds, such as cormorants and Brant.

WITH CACKLING GOOSE (TOP C). MARYLAND, FEB. BILL HUBICK.
- It is always worth checking a flock of Canadas for their smaller look-alikes; most Cackling Geese occurring on the East Coast are with Canadas.
- Cackling is clearly smaller, with a shorter neck and more pointed wings.

(RIGHT) ILLINOIS, DEC. KEN BEHRENS.

ILLINOIS, DEC. KEN BEHRENS.
- The elegance of the slim neck contrasts with the heavy body and broad wings.
- Many species of geese have a white U at the base of the tail, but it is often invisible in flight.

NEW JERSEY, DEC. KEN BEHRENS.
- The largest flocks form huge Vs, Us, and Ws. Although the organization of these flocks tends to break down, the birds still maintain greater spacing than do smaller geese.
- Throngs of migrating Canada Geese mark the changing seasons and make such a tremendous din that they may cause people who ignore most birds to pause and look up.

WITH TWO MALLARD (TOP). UTAH, JAN. KEN BEHRENS.
- Note the size difference between one of the largest duck species and the largest goose.

WITH BONAPARTE'S GULLS, BUFFLEHEAD, AND NORTHERN SHOVELER (LATTER TWO ON WATER). ONTARIO, APR. KEN BEHRENS.
- Many ponds and golf courses have geese that birders largely ignore; however, studying these birds as they fly around their home territories helps build confidence in identifying flocks seen at tremendous distances.
- Birds making short flights lack the structure and spacing of migrating flocks.

UTAH, JAN. KEN BEHRENS.
- At close range the black, white, and brown markings are striking, but at a distance Canada Goose appears uniformly dark brown.

MASSACHUSETTS, JAN. KEN BEHRENS.
- Note the swanlike silhouette. Uniformly dark at a distance, though a hint of the paler breast may be apparent in good light.

CACKLING GOOSE
Branta hutchinsii
DIMENSIONS
L: 25 in.; WS: 43 in.; WT: 3.5 lb.

SPRING ARRIVAL

NE: late Feb.; SD: mid-Mar.

FALL ARRIVAL

s. SK: early/mid-Sept.; NE: late Sept.;
n. TX: mid-Nov.

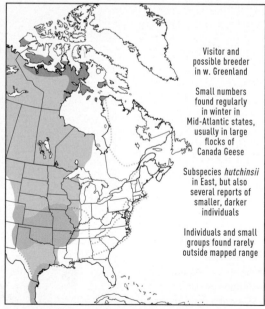

Visitor and
possible breeder
in w. Greenland

Small numbers
found regularly
in winter in
Mid-Atlantic states,
usually in large
flocks of
Canada Geese

Subspecies *hutchinsii*
in East, but also
several reports of
smaller, darker
individuals

Individuals and small
groups found rarely
outside mapped range

Cackling is a small Canada Goose look-alike that was recognized as a distinct species in 2004. It has four fairly distinctive subspecies, though only the nominate subspecies, known as "Richardson's" Goose, is regularly seen in eastern North America. In this book the name "Richardson's" Goose is used to refer to the nominate race, whereas Cackling Goose refers to the species as a whole. "Richardson's" occurs commonly in the Midwest and is a rare but regular stray to the Atlantic Coast. In eastern North America, "Richardson's" Goose is usu-ally seen in the company of Canada Geese but will also join flocks of Snow Geese. The call is a squeaky honk that is higher pitched than the throaty bass of Canada Goose.

SIZE: Generally small for a goose, though variable.

Averages slightly larger than Ross's Goose, though some large males approach the size of a small Canada Goose.

STRUCTURE: Silhouette is similar to that of Canada Goose but more compact. The neck is short and thinner at the base than on a Snow or Greater White-fronted Goose. The small, rounded head bulges slightly out of the neck and is often held above the body—more noticeably so than in Canada Goose. At close range the stubby bill can be evident. The body looks strongly potbellied compared with the longer body and more subtle curves that somewhat mask the bulk of Canada Goose. The wings are slimmer and more pointed than Canada's.

FLIGHT AND FLOCKING: Wingbeats are quicker, deeper, and looser than the heavy, even, controlled wingbeats of Canada Goose. Cackling Goose tends to rock from side to side and to form denser, less organized flocks than Canada Goose. When small groups join flocks of Canada Geese, however, they tend to adopt a more stable flight style similar to that of their larger cousins.

APPEARANCE: Adult: Very similar to Canada Goose, with black head and neck and white cheek patch. Unlike in most Canada Geese, the cheek patch is often broken on the throat. Also much more likely than Canada to show a strong white collar around the base of the neck; 20–30 percent of "Richardson's" Geese show a neck collar. The chest and belly of "Richardson's" are silvery gray, whereas birds of the western subspecies tend to be much darker-breasted than Canada Goose. First Cycle: Like adult, but white cheek patch is often reduced

and washed with pale brown. The breast of "Richardson's" tends to be creamy white, much like in most subspecies of Canada Goose, whereas the breast of the western subspecies of Cackling Goose tends to be dull brown. Distant: Solidly dark like Canada; the pale belly is evident only in good light.

SIMILAR SPECIES: Canada Goose: The basic pattern of Cackling Goose is virtually identical to that of Canada Goose, so structure and vocalizations are key to identification. Although Cackling Goose is small enough to stand out in flocks of Canada Geese, size alone is not enough to clinch its identification because of two factors. First, some of the interior races of Canada Goose are small enough to also stand out in a flock of large Canada Geese. Second, runt Canada Geese exist, and are an even more difficult problem. If a bird is seen at close range, supporting traits include the short, steeply sloping bill and silvery breast color of "Richardson's." In addition, many Cackling Geese have a broad white neck ring separating the neck from the breast, a feature that Canada Goose shows only weakly. Cackling Goose also tends to have a longer hand and more pointed wings. The higher-pitched vocalizations of Cackling are useful for identification if not swept away in the din of Canadas.

SUBSPECIES: Cackling Goose was split from Canada Goose in 2004 and comprises four subspecies: *hutchinsii*, *minima*, *taverneri*, and *leucopareia*. The nominate *B. h. hutchinsii*, known as "Richardson's" Goose, is the only expected subspecies in eastern North America, though there are a few records of other subspecies. See Taxonomic Notes (p. 590) for more information.

WITH SNOW AND ROSS'S GEESE. TEXAS, JAN. CAMERON COX.

- Stocky body, very short neck, and long, pointed wings are typical of Cackling Goose.
- Similar in size to the two Ross's (first and third white geese from L) but not as large or heavy as the two Snow Geese.

WITH CANADA GEESE. PENNSYLVANIA, DEC. TOM JOHNSON.
- Although small Canadas can approach the size of this Cackling (second from L), compare these species' body shapes. The short, compact shape is characteristic of Cackling Goose.

TEXAS, JAN. KEN BEHRENS.
- Chaotic, wedge-shaped flocks are typical of Cackling Geese, and unlike the more regimented flocks of Canada Geese that show greater spacing between individuals.
- Even at a distance, the stocky shape, short neck, and long wings are noticeable.

CACKLING GEESE (TOP R, BOTTOM L, AND TOP C) WITH CANADA GEESE (BOTTOM C AND C) AMBIGUOUS BIRD (TOP L). MANITOBA, MAY. TOM JOHNSON.
- Cackling Goose has a shorter neck, shorter bill, and more rounded head than Canada Goose.
- Size sometimes provides an immediate way to separate these two species, but some Canadas, such as those breeding around Hudson Bay, can be quite small, so subtle aspects of structure must be employed to separate them from Cackling. There is enough variation that some birds cannot be identified in flight.

GREATER WHITE-FRONTED GOOSE
Anser albifrons
DIMENSIONS
L: 28 in.; WS: 43 in.; WT: 4.8 lb.

SPRING ARRIVAL

s. NE: late Feb.; SD. early Mar.;
Hudson Bay: mid-May

FALL ARRIVAL

n. Great Plains: mid-Sept.; MO: late Sept.;
TX: early Oct.

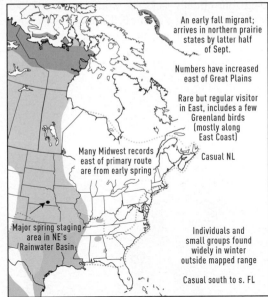

An early fall migrant; arrives in northern prairie states by latter half of Sept.

Numbers have increased east of Great Plains

Rare but regular visitor in East, includes a few Greenland birds (mostly along East Coast)

Many Midwest records east of primary route are from early spring

Casual NL

Major spring staging area in NE's Rainwater Basin

Individuals and small groups found widely in winter outside mapped range

Casual south to s. FL

This is the sole native representative of the "gray" geese, though several other Old World "gray" geese occur rarely in North America. Greater White-fronted is primarily a species of western and middle North America, though strays are found regularly throughout the East. In addition to its unique appearance, it has a distinctive piercing two- or three-part yelping call unlike that of any other regularly occurring goose, further simplifying identification.

SIZE: Virtually identical to Snow Goose and therefore a quintessentially midsized goose. Clearly larger than Cackling Goose. Much smaller than Canada Goose.

STRUCTURE: Silhouette is similar to that of Snow Goose but with a slightly longer, slimmer neck and more obviously rounded head. The neck is held straight out from the body rather than raised in the manner of Snow and Ross's Goose. The wings are long, but broad at the base, which disguises their length.

FLIGHT AND FLOCKING: Wingbeats are quick, deep, and steady. Flock structures are far more organized than those of Brant and Cackling Goose, and are generally more organized than those of Snow Goose, without quite reaching the military precision usually shown by Canada Goose. Small flocks form short lines, but most flocks of moderate to large size fly in well-defined Vs, though the V is often distorted by solitary individuals or short, isolated lines in the interior of the V, and by birds jockeying for position along the edges of the flock. Huge masses, particularly those mixed with Snow Geese, are far less organized and tend to create a thick, drawn-out, snaking structure. Most often mixes with Snow Geese but may be found in any flock of geese, though associations with Brant are extremely rare.

APPEARANCE: Adult: Gray-brown overall with darker brown wings, white vent, and bold white U around the uppertail coverts. A small white ring around the base of the bill accounts for the species' common name; its colloquial name, "specklebelly," comes from the variable pattern of black splotches on the underparts. The bill is usually pinkish orange and the feet bright orange, but there is some subspecific variation in bare part color. **First Cycle:** Like adult but initially lacks the white ring on the face and black speckling on the belly. Acquires the white "front" in late winter, and by spring migration may show traces of black speckling on the underparts. **Distant:** Dark and uniform. Lighter portions of plumage tend to disappear.

SIMILAR SPECIES: "Blue" Snow Goose: Adult has a white head, strongly two-toned upperwings, and extensive white underwing. First-cycle birds are more similar to White-fronted but still show strongly contrasting white axillaries. Structurally, Snow Goose has a stouter neck that is raised slightly, whereas Greater White-fronted keeps its neck straighter. **Pink-footed Goose** (not included in this guide): A Eurasian member of the "gray" goose clan, formerly extremely rare in eastern North America but the number of records has been increasing in recent years. Quite similar to Greater White-fronted but slightly smaller with a much smaller, mostly black bill. It also has a darker head, lacks the black-speckled belly, and has a strongly two-toned upperwing.

SUBSPECIES: Complex and poorly understood. Inseparable for flight identification purposes. Both *A. a. frontalis* and *A. a. gambeli* winter along the western Gulf Coast and stray farther east. *A. a. flavirostris*, which breeds in Greenland and winters in Europe, is a vagrant in the Northeast.

ADULTS. LOUISIANA, JAN. CAMERON COX.
- All geese have an odd and distinctive combination of long wings and stocky body.
- Greater White-fronted's shape is very similar to that of Snow Goose, but the neck is pinched near the top, emphasizing the rounded head. Greater White-fronted also tends to hold its neck straighter than Snow Goose.
- With a striking face pattern, speckled belly, and subtle gradations of brown, Greater White-fronted's appearance at close range is intricate; at a distance, these details melt away and they appear uniformly dull brown.

ADULTS. LOUISIANA, JAN. KEN BEHRENS.
- Even at medium distance much detail is lost, and the geese start to appear uniformly brown.
- *What are the two species of ducks in the photo?*

FIRST CYCLE (R) WITH ADULT. BRITISH COLUMBIA, NOV. GLENN BARTLEY.
- Note how first cycle's clean underparts contrast with its dark underwings.
- The black speckling of the adult breaks up the contrast and contributes to a uniform appearance at a distance.

TEXAS, JAN. CAMERON COX.
- Typical flock formation.
- They tend to form more organized V-shaped flocks than Snow Geese, though additional birds within the V are typical.

ADULTS WITH CANADA GEESE (FAR L AND R). SWEDEN, JAN. THOMAS SVANBERG.
- Although both species look brown at a distance, White-fronted is smaller and more compact than Canada, with slimmer, more pointed wings and a shorter, thicker neck.

ADULTS AND FIRST CYCLES WITH SNOW GEESE. TEXAS, JAN. KEN BEHRENS.
- The two species are similar in size and shape, and often flock together.
- Overhead, the slightly longer, more pointed hand of Greater White-fronted is apparent.
- The four first-cycle Greater White-fronteds in this flock are easily recognizable by their pale bellies.

SNOW GOOSE
Chen caerulescens
DIMENSIONS
(Greater) L: 31 in.; WS: 56 in.; WT: 7.4 lb.
(Lesser) L: 28 in.; WS: 53 in.; WT: 5.3 lb.

SPRING ARRIVAL

SD: mid-/late Mar.; s. MB: early Apr.;
Hudson Bay: mid-May

FALL ARRIVAL

SD: late Oct.; Lake Erie: mid-/late Oct.,
NJ: mid-Oct.; w. Gulf Coast: mid-Nov.

Snow Goose is the most common white goose in most of North America. It is often observed in flocks high overhead, where the predominately white color allows the birds to disappear against a pale blue sky or white clouds. Even large flocks can vanish with incredible ease, and are visible only when the flock catches the sun and the white plumage flashes brightly. A flock seen this way hardly seems to pertain to a terrestrial being! In the interior of the continent, the dark morph known as

Weakly differentiated "Greater" Snow Goose nests in e. Canadian arctic and Greenland, winters along Atlantic Coast

Fall and spring migrants overfly boreal forest to and from Upper St. Lawrence Estuary

Northeast fall staging sites

Numbers have increased in recent years

Individuals and small groups found widely outside mapped range

"Blue" Goose can make up one-third of the population or more, whereas along the Atlantic Coast fewer than 10 percent are "Blue" Geese. In recent years the percentage of "Blue" Geese in the Snow Goose population has steadily increased. Snow Geese constantly give a raucous, harsh, yelping call in flight.

SIZE: Larger than Brant. Clearly smaller than Canada Goose. Similar in size to Greater White-fronted Goose or even Double-crested Cormorant.

STRUCTURE: A compact goose with a stout neck and heavy body. The wings are long and slender, noticeably more pointed than those of Greater White-fronted Goose but broader and blunter than Brant's.

FLIGHT AND FLOCKING: Wingbeats are strong and steady, pausing only when a bird is landing or evaluating a potential location for landing. Extremely gregarious; singles and even pairs are rarely seen. Small groups move in tight, clean lines that often slant slightly. Moderately sized flocks often take a V shape but tend to hold this formation less rigidly than Canada Geese do. Larger groups form messy Us or wedges with much jockeying for position among the members. The largest flocks are huge conglomerations that may be vaguely wedge- or W-shaped, with one or more long trailing tails. Virtually always flies high, often extremely high. Flocks are often joined by other species of geese, particularly Greater White-fronted and Ross's, sometimes Cackling, and most rarely Canada.

APPEARANCE: The edges of the upper and lower mandibles curve away from each other creating an opening called a "grinning patch" on the sides of the bill, which can be seen up to moderate range. **Adult White:** All white with a coral bill and legs, black primaries, and dusky greater primary coverts. **First-cycle White:** White plumage is extensively washed with gray, particularly on the crown and back. Late in winter the back becomes blotched with pure white as new scapulars are acquired. The primaries are blackish; the secondaries vary among individuals, ranging from whitish to slate gray. The bill is pinkish gray, and the legs are dark. **Adult Blue:** The head, vent, and underwing are bright white, and the breast, back, and nape are dusky navy. The upperwing coverts are paler blue, and the flight feathers are black. "Blue" Geese show much variability; many have a pure white belly or show other characteristics that fall between the classic white and blue morphs. **First-cycle Blue:** Virtually all dull blue-gray with white flecking around the face and vent and bright white underwing coverts. **Distant:** White-morph adults are bright white and appear to flash and gleam in sunlight, their black wingtips often invisible. They blend easily into both cloudy and clear skies. White morphs in their first cycle appear pale but do not gleam white as readily as adults. Both adult and first-cycle blue morphs appear blackish, as their white underwings and lower bellies are difficult to detect at long range. The presence of small numbers of blue birds does not affect the ability of a flock to disappear into the sky, but large blocks of "Blue" Geese are more evident against pale skies and give flocks a patchy appearance.

SIMILAR SPECIES: Ross's Goose: Like a Snow Goose in miniature, being approximately one-third smaller. It has a shorter, thicker neck and smaller, wedge-shaped bill. In direct comparison it is obviously smaller, with quicker wingbeats and a higher-pitched call. See Ross's Goose account for more information.

SUBSPECIES: Two subspecies, *C. c. caerulescens* and *C. c. atlantica*. The nominate *caerulescens*, known as "Lesser" Snow Goose, breeds along Hudson Bay and in the lower reaches of the Canadian Arctic as well as on Wrangel Island in the Siberian Sea and in small numbers in Alaska. It winters in the interior of the continent, on the Gulf Coast, and along the Atlantic Coast in small numbers. "Greater" Snow Goose, *atlantica*, breeds in the high Canadian Arctic and northern Greenland and winters on the Atlantic Coast, primarily in the Mid-Atlantic. "Greater" Snow Goose is marginally larger and thicker-necked than "Lesser," but this difference is not consistent enough to allow subspecific identification in flight. "Greater" Snow Goose rarely produces "Blue" Geese, so "Blue" Geese on the Atlantic Coast are likely the nominate race, *caerulescens*.

**ADULTS. TEXAS, JAN.
CAMERON COX.**

- Medium-sized, with a "classic" goose shape: the long, slender wings seem almost at odds with the stocky body.
- The white plumage gleams in bright light.

LOUISIANA, JAN. CAMERON COX.
- A sample (from L to R) of the variation that can be present in a flock: adult white, first-cycle blue, adult blue, and adult intermediate morph.
- First-cycle blue morphs are very uniform at a distance, like Greater White-fronted but with bright white underwing coverts.

NEW JERSEY, DEC. KEN BEHRENS.
- Similar to Greater White-fronted in shape, but thicker-necked and usually hold the head slightly above the body.

WITH ROSS'S AND GREATER WHITE-FRONTED GEESE. TEXAS, JAN. CAMERON COX.
- Large flocks are usually messier than those of Greater White-fronted and are often joined by other geese.
- *There are 10 Ross's Geese in this flock; how many Greater White-fronteds?*

(LEFT) SNOW GEESE. NEW MEXICO, NOV. OSWALD PFENNINGER.

WITH TWO GREATER WHITE-FRONTED GEESE. TEXAS, JAN. KEN BEHRENS.
- Small flocks are more organized than large ones, frequently in Vs that maintain a fairly steady shape.
- Greater White-fronted is similar in structure but has a subtly more elegant shape.

SNOW GOOSE WITH ROSS'S GOOSE (BELOW). TEXAS, JAN. KEN BEHRENS.
- The neck of Snow Goose is much longer and appears thinner; Snow Goose looks lankier overall.
- Ross's is much smaller, and its stubby bill lacks the noticeable "grinning patch" of Snow's.

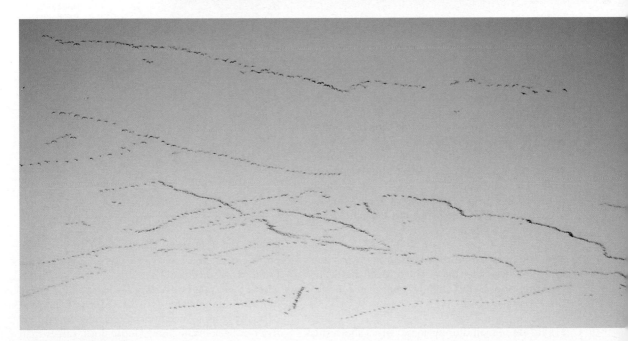

TEXAS, JAN. CAMERON COX.
- Massive flocks fill the sky with twisting ribbons of birds and a cacophony of honking; a breathtaking experience!

ROSS'S GOOSE
Chen rossii
DIMENSIONS
L: 23 in.; WS: 45 in.; WT: 2.7 lb.

SPRING ARRIVAL

Hudson Bay: early June

Ross's Goose is a smaller, thicker-necked version of Snow Goose that is not nearly as common in eastern North America. Identification can be tricky but is aided by the species' tendency to flock with Snow Geese, making its smaller size obvious. Like Snow Goose, Ross's is a polymorphic species, with both white and blue morphs, but blue-morph Ross's are extremely rare. Ross's call is higher pitched and squeakier than that of Snow Goose but is difficult to pick out in the din created by large flocks of Snow Geese.

SIZE: The smallest North American goose on average. Slightly smaller than Brant and "Richardson's" Cackling Goose. Only slightly larger than American Black Duck.

STRUCTURE: Small dumpy goose with a short, thick neck; tiny, triangular bill; and long wings that are slightly more slender and pointed than those of Snow Goose.

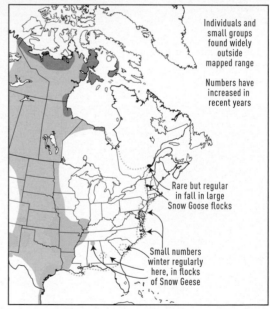

Individuals and small groups found widely outside mapped range

Numbers have increased in recent years

Rare but regular in fall in large Snow Goose flocks

Small numbers winter regularly here, in flocks of Snow Geese

FLIGHT AND FLOCKING: Usually seen in flocks of Snow Geese, where Ross's smaller size and slightly faster wingbeats can be quite obvious. In areas where their ranges overlap, flocks of Snow Geese often include small knots of Ross's Geese composed of family groups. Such bunches are often toward the front or back of the Snow Goose flock, rather than at its center. Aside from Snow Geese, Ross's Geese are most likely to be seen with Cackling Geese, and more rarely with Greater White-fronted and Canada Geese. Monospecific flocks of Ross's Geese or even flocks made up primarily of Ross's are rare in eastern North America.

APPEARANCE: Some, particularly males, can show a slight "grinning patch," less obvious than that of Snow Goose. **Adult White:** All white with coral bill and legs, black primaries, and dusky greater primary coverts. The base of the bill has dusky, wart-like growths never shown by Snow Goose, but this is difficult to see from a distance. **First-cycle White:** Nearly all white with faint dusky patches on the head and back. Far whiter than first-cycle Snow Goose, and similar enough to adult Ross's that a careful look is required to separate adults from first-cycle birds. The primaries, but not the secondaries, are blackish. The bill and legs are dull pink, and the warty growths at the base of the bill are much reduced or absent. **Adult Blue:** Extremely rare. Dark blackish blue on the crown, neck, upper back, breast, and flanks, setting off an isolated white face. The belly, vent, rump, underwing coverts, and much of the upperwing coverts are white. **First-cycle Blue:** Like adult Blue but with a dark face and the white portions of the body masked with faint duskiness. **Distant:** Shimmering white.

SIMILAR SPECIES: Snow Goose: In direct comparison, Snow's larger size is obvious. Some Snow Geese, however, can be noticeably smaller than others. For this reason, note Ross's proportionally chunkier build, with shorter, thicker neck; tiny bill; and slimmer, more pointed wings. **Snow x Ross's Hybrid:** Flight identification of the Snow/Ross's complex is further complicated by the fact that these two species hybridize. In recent years, reporting of hybrid white geese has been overzealous, and some observers have underestimated the variability of pure Ross's and Snow Geese. Nonetheless, hybrids do occur and this possibility should be considered for odd-looking individuals. Hybrids can be nearly as small as Ross's, blunting the effectiveness of using size, which is the only characteristic that is effective at long distances. Given this difficulty, identify flying Ross's Geese with care. At close range look for a distinct "grinning patch," reduced or absent warty facial skin, and a slightly longer bill to identify a hybrid.

MALE AND FEMALE. UTAH, MAR. PAUL HIGGINS.
- The male (R) is clearly larger-headed and larger-billed than the female (L).
- Both have a short, thick neck and a shorter bill than Snow Goose, making the face appear squared-off.
- Adults acquire warty blue-gray growths at the base of the bill, and males show a slight "grinning patch," though it's far smaller and less noticeable than that of Snow Goose or hybrids.

WITH TWO SNOW GEESE. TEXAS, JAN. KEN BEHRENS.

- Ross's (C) is distinctly smaller than Snow, which is especially obvious in flocks directly overhead.
- Note the slight differences in wing shape and Ross's shorter neck and bill.

WITH THREE SNOW GEESE (TOP R). TEXAS, JAN. KEN BEHRENS.

- The much smaller Ross's often fly in tight knots near the front or back of a flock of Snow Geese. These knots often comprise family groups.
- The tiny bills of Ross's almost disappear at a distance, giving their faces a squared-off appearance.

ADULTS WITH SNOW GOOSE. UTAH, MAR. PAUL HIGGINS.

- Compare the Snow Goose (out of focus top C) to Ross's; Ross's heads are barely differentiated from their necks, and their bills are very short.
- The staining on the face of the Snow Goose is characteristic of this species because it roots in the mud for food. Ross's graze rather than dig for food, which keeps their heads immaculately white.

WITH SNOW GOOSE (BEHIND). COMPOSITE. UTAH, MAR. PAUL HIGGINS.

- Ross's wings are proportionally slimmer.
- Snow Goose sports a large "grinning patch," whereas the base of Ross's bill is covered with warty growths.
- Compare the subtle difference between where the eye is located on each bird.

BARNACLE GOOSE
Branta leucopsis
DIMENSIONS
L: 27 in.; WS: 50 in.; WT: 3.7 lb.

FALL ARRIVAL

(vagrants):

Atlantic Coast: early Oct.

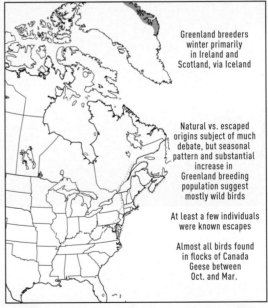

Greenland breeders winter primarily in Ireland and Scotland, via Iceland

Natural vs. escaped origins subject of much debate, but seasonal pattern and substantial increase in Greenland breeding population suggest mostly wild birds

At least a few individuals were known escapes

Almost all birds found in flocks of Canada Geese between Oct. and Mar.

In ancient times, the Arctic breeding grounds of this European species were unknown, and popular belief held that the birds sprang from barnacles! Barnacle Goose is an increasingly common vagrant to eastern North America from Europe and Greenland. There is some controversy about the North American records, because of some well-documented cases of Barnacle Geese that were found in the wild only to be traced back to a waterfowl collection. There are even records of escaped Barnacle Geese breeding in the wild. However, the recent increase in Barnacle Goose records from northeastern Canada and the U.S. has paralleled a massive increase in the populations that breed in Greenland and winter in Scotland and Ireland. The body of evidence has built to the point that it is clear that many of the Barnacle Geese observed in eastern North America are wild vagrants. The call is a distinctive, almost canine yelp, though it may be difficult to hear among the louder Canada Geese with which vagrant Barnacles frequently associate.

SIZE: Clearly smaller than Snow Goose. Slightly larger than Ross's Goose. Similar to Brant and Cackling Goose.

STRUCTURE: Similar to Brant, and like that species, has a smooth body, without the potbelly of most geese. Compared with Brant, the neck is slightly longer and the head more pronounced. The wings are both broader and longer than the unusually short and slim ones of Brant, giving Barnacle a more typical goose wing shape.

FLIGHT AND FLOCKING: Probably because of the larger wings, the wingbeats are more like those of a larger goose than of Brant. They are fairly heavy and steady, and the flight is significantly slower. In North America, Barnacle Goose is almost always found with Canada Goose. Although Cackling Goose is rare on the northeastern seaboard, where Barnacle is most frequent, when the two species do come into contact, they quickly begin associating. Despite their similarity, and frequent association in the Old World, Barnacle Goose and Brant are rarely found together in our area.

APPEARANCE: Adult: Distinctive, with lots of contrast. Black breast, neck, and crown, with a contrastingly white face and pale underparts. The white face patch accentuates the mildly bulbous head. The back is gray, with black bars across the upperwing coverts. The tail is black with white uppertail coverts. **First Cycle:** Very similar to adult, though the pattern of the back and the barring on the flanks are slightly more diffuse. **Distant:** Although the white patch on the head may disappear, the strong contrast between pale and dark areas remains more conspicuous in this species than in any other goose species we cover.

SIMILAR SPECIES: Brant: Slimmer and shorter wings result in quicker wingbeats that are atypical for a goose; Barnacle flies more like a larger goose. Although the white head of Barnacle is distinctive, it can disappear at long ranges, where the sharp contrast between the black breast and pale gray underparts will still serve to separate it from Brant. A single Brant with a flock of Canada Geese would be an unusual sight, whereas it is the expected context for a Barnacle Goose in the region. **Cackling Goose:** Similar in size but has much more uniform dark brown coloration, lacking the contrasts of Barnacle.

WITH CANADA GEESE. NEW JERSEY, NOV. TOM JOHNSON.
• Vagrants often join flocks of Canada Geese, where their small size, frosty pale upperwings, and black-and-white body immediately set them apart.

SWEDEN, MAR. KEN BEHRENS.
• Neck and body are similar to Brant's, but Barnacle Goose has longer and broader wings, more like those of a "typical" goose. Its flocks are also more orderly and widely spaced.

BRANT
Branta bernicla
DIMENSIONS
L: 25 in.; WS: 42 in.; WT: 3.1 lb.

SPRING ARRIVAL

James Bay: early June

FALL ARRIVAL

James Bay: early Sept.;
s. ON: early Oct.; Long Island: mid-Oct.

Several populations of this dapper goose breed in different areas of northern Canada and winter in different regions. This account refers to the eastern subspecies, *B. b. hrota*, or "Atlantic" Brant, which winters in coastal bays and salt marshes of the Mid-Atlantic and southern New England. Brant is generally a later migrant in spring and earlier migrant in fall than other geese. Although some diurnal migration can be seen along large bodies of water, the species probably migrates mostly at night, explaining the rarity of sightings in the interior between its Arctic breeding grounds and the Atlantic Coast. Brant's pleasant, gurgling call is quite different from the boisterous calls of most other geese.

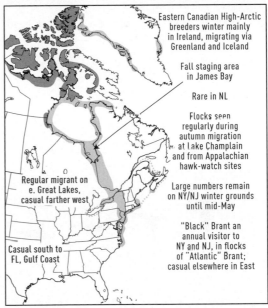

Eastern Canadian High-Arctic breeders winter mainly in Ireland, migrating via Greenland and Iceland

Fall staging area in James Bay

Rare in NL

Flocks seen regularly during autumn migration at Lake Champlain and from Appalachian hawk-watch sites

Large numbers remain on NY/NJ winter grounds until mid-May

"Black" Brant an annual visitor to NY and NJ, in flocks of "Atlantic" Brant; casual elsewhere in East

Regular migrant on e. Great Lakes, casual farther west

Casual south to FL, Gulf Coast

SIZE: Marginally larger than Ross's Goose. Significantly smaller than Snow Goose. About the size of Cackling Goose.

STRUCTURE: Trim, elegant appearance with a short, stout neck that merges smoothly into a streamlined body. Brant lacks the potbellied look of most other geese. The wings are quite short, narrow, and pointed for a goose, and are arched downward and slightly swept back. These features result in a structure unlike that of any other native goose.

FLIGHT AND FLOCKING: Brant has smooth, quick wingbeats and faster flight than other geese. Its arched wings and smooth flight action create the impression that it is constantly cupping the air rather than batting at it or rowing through it like other geese. Smaller flocks can form short, tight lines similar to those of other geese. Large flocks form distinctive, tightly packed, disorganized clumps that occasionally give glimmers of more ordered, wingtip-to-wingtip flight before dissolving back into seeming chaos. Some large flocks take on a boxy look, created by parallel lines with birds packed in between, particularly toward the front. Birds frequently switch places within a flock, which adds to the disorganized look. Brant is the only goose that frequently flies low over the ocean for extended periods of time, and it rarely makes the high-altitude flights of other geese, at least diurnally. Small groups of 5–30 are typical, though flocks of hundreds do occur. Rarely mixes with other geese and is usually seen in monospecific flocks, though it occasionally joins Double-crested Cormorants or scoters.

APPEARANCE: Adult: Very dark overall. Black head, neck, and upper breast with a broken white necklace on the throat. The back and upperwings are dark gray, and the flight feathers are slightly darker slate gray. The lower breast and belly are pale gray but variable; some birds are noticeably darker than others. The bright white uppertail coverts form a U shape, and the vent is also white. **First Cycle:** Like adult but the head is slightly duller with a reduced or sometimes absent white necklace. The secondaries and greater coverts are fringed in white, though this is evident only at close or moderate range. **Distant:** Uniformly blackish.

SIMILAR SPECIES: Double-crested Cormorant: Often confused with Brant at great distances but has a thinner, crooked neck and long tail, glides often, and tends to fly in undulating, evenly spaced flocks. **Scoters:** Can be briefly confused with Brant, but a few seconds of observing scoters' smaller size, shorter wings, and much faster wingbeats should clear things up. Flocks also undulate and shift much more quickly than those of Brant and appear to move more quickly. **American Black Duck and Mallard:** Also appear dark at a distance, but these ducks are smaller, with quicker wingbeats, pale underwings, and fundamentally different structure.

SUBSPECIES: See Taxonomic Notes (p. 590)

NEW JERSEY, DEC. KEN BEHRENS.
• Flies in messy lines or wedges that are very similar in shape to scoter flocks.
• Wings are more angular and pointed than those of any other species of goose.

NEW JERSEY, DEC. KEN BEHRENS.
- A typical, roughly rectangular flock.
- Large flocks lack precise structure and shift constantly like flocks of scoters.
- Flocks of cormorants are similar, but they glide frequently, whereas Brant flap continuously.
- Migrants coming off the ocean gain height to cross land.

ADULTS AND FIRST CYCLE (R). NEW JERSEY, OCT. CAMERON COX.
- Black neck contrasts with pale belly, and the U-shaped uppertail coverts are clearly visible from some angles.
- Salt marshes are prime wintering habitat for Brant. American Black Duck is the only other large dark species of waterfowl regularly found in this habitat.

THREE FIRST CYCLES WITH TWO ADULTS (LOWER R). NEW JERSEY, DEC. KEN BEHRENS.
- First cycles have pale-edged wing coverts.
- Although the black neck contrasts with the pale belly, it blends into the gray back, contributing to a uniform appearance at a distance.

CONNECTICUT, JAN. KEN BEHRENS.
- Slim-winged geese with a sharply pointed hand.
- Notice how shadow obscures the contrast between the pale belly and black neck.

ADULT. NEW JERSEY, JAN. KEVIN KARLSON.
- A small broken neck collar and a pale belly that contrasts sharply with the black neck are characteristics of the "Atlantic" Brant that winter along the East Coast.

ONE ADULT (SECOND FROM L) AND THREE FIRST-CYCLE BIRDS. NEW JERSEY, NOV. KEN BEHRENS.

- Brant often migrate and commute between foraging areas by flying low over the ocean. This is unlike other geese, which typically do not fly over the ocean, or fly quite high when they do.
- Although they form huge flocks on the ground, Brant seem to prefer to fly in small groups, unlike other geese.
- Uniformly dark at a distance.

WITH FIVE MALLARD. NEW JERSEY, DEC. KEN BEHRENS.

- Brant are longer-winged, but not substantially larger-bodied than large ducks like these Mallard.
- Although the sizes are close, Brant have significantly slower wingbeats than large ducks like Mallard or American Black Duck.

THREE FIRST CYCLES AND NINE ADULTS. NEW JERSEY, NOV. CAMERON COX.

- Necks are stocky, particularly at the base, and the head is barely differentiated from the neck.
- At close range, their low, pleasant, gurgling call is frequently heard.

DABBLING DUCKS

Dabbling ducks are part of the family Anatidae, often referred to as the tribe Anatini. They are small to medium-sized waterfowl with stocky bodies, short to medium-length necks, and the ability to take flight almost vertically, without first running across the water. They are often considered the "typical" ducks. Most members of this group are in the genus *Anas* and are quite similar in most aspects of their life history. Wood Duck is an exception and belongs to the genus *Aix*, nests in cavities, and frequently perches in trees. We also include whistling-ducks in this section, although they are in their own subfamily, Dendrocygninae. Although whistling-ducks are quite different from dabbling ducks, having some gooselike traits, some ducklike traits, and sharing Wood Duck's arboreal habits, they are most likely to be confused with dabbling ducks, hence their inclusion in this section.

Male dabbling ducks tend to be quite colorful for most of the year, whereas the females always wear a camouflage of brown and gray mottling. One difference whistling-ducks show from dabbling ducks is the sexes are similar and their appearance does not change during the year. Most male ducks leave their mate after the young have hatched and undertake a molt migration, joining other males at a location with abundant cover and food. Here they undergo a prealternate molt, acquiring a dull femalelike plumage often referred to as "eclipse" plumage. Soon afterward, they drop all their flight feathers and become flightless for several weeks while these feathers regrow simultaneously. It was once thought that the molt of the body feathers to eclipse plumage and the molt of the flight feathers were two parts of the same molt. It is now known that the flight feather molt is the beginning of the prebasic molt; therefore two distinct molts occur in quick succession. It was also previously thought that the molt to the dull plumage was a molt unique to ducks. It is now known that while the timing of this molt is different than in most birds, it is not unique and therefore the term "eclipse" is unnecessary. Following Pyle 2005, we consider the dull plumage held by male ducks in late summer to be alternate plumage and the bright plumage held for most of the year to be basic plumage. Female dabbling ducks have their prealternate molt in the spring, though their appearance is unchanged, during the time frame that is considered normal for this molt and begin their prebasic molt by dropping their flight feathers while their young are growing their first set of true feathers, and may even undertake a molt migration if a brood is lost.

Dabbling ducks have a tendency to form diverse flocks. This flock includes Northern Pintail, American Wigeon, a few Blue-winged Teal, and two skulking Gadwall, as well as two White Ibis. *Applying the process for breaking down mixed flocks of ducks outlined in this section, can you pick out all four species of ducks?* Florida, Jan. Cameron Cox.

Whistling-ducks, like this Black-bellied Whistling-Duck (L), are not closely related to dabbling ducks, but we place them with the dabbling ducks in this guide because of many basic similarities. Although Wood Ducks, like this female (R), truly are part of the dabbling duck clan, they also differ from most dabblers. Their large eyes, long and rudderlike tail, and short wings are adaptations that allow them to navigate and maneuver through dim, densely forested swamps. Texas, May (L); South Carolina, Nov. (R). Ken Behrens.

Dabbling ducks are one of the great joys of the seawatcher because of their tendency to form diverse mixed flocks, creating significant identification challenges and boosting a watch's daily species total. Flocks are often spotted at extreme distances, allowing the observer to watch a tiny group of dots gradually change into indistinct ducklike shapes; then watch those shapes solidify into clear silhouettes; then, with any luck, into flashes of color that can be identified with no ambiguity. It can take a while to thoroughly evaluate the identity of a mixed flock of dabblers, and it is easy to miss some of its members, so we recommend starting the identification process outlined below as soon as you spot a flock. This process is similar to the one described in the identification portion of the introduction, but is specifically tailored to mixed flocks of ducks.

MIXED DUCK FLOCK IDENTIFICATION PROCESS:

1. As soon as you spot the flock, even and especially if you cannot distinguish color or silhouette, evaluate size. Are the flock members uniform in size or can you discern differences? If you can pick up size differences at a distance, the flock probably contains multiple species. Note how many different sizes you can see and use this as a guide for how many species to look for as the flock comes closer.

2. Assess behavioral traits. How high above the water is the flock? Does it maintain a straight flight line or dip and rise? How much spacing is there between individuals? Does the spacing remain static or is there constant shifting of individuals within the flock? Is the overall flock shape constantly changing or relatively stable?

3. As the flock comes closer, look for distinctive structural characteristics. Many species, such as Northern Pintail and Northern Shoveler, have highly visible structural traits that allow them to be identified at great distances. Once you've identified one species in the flock, use it as a reference point to evaluate the size and structure of other members of the flock.

4. Long before you can discern specific color patterns, an overall impression of color is usually apparent. Does the entire flock have a dark appearance, a pale appearance, or a mix of dark and light individuals that creates a mottled appearance? At the same time that overall color becomes noticeable, some more subtle aspects of structure will also be more apparent, allowing you to better evaluate the birds' shapes.

5. Look for striking color patterns, such as the bold white ovals on the upperwings of adult male wigeons. White is visible at greater distances than other colors and becomes even more obvious when surrounded by dark plumage or set off by a dark background such as a dark lake or ocean. Since many of the most striking plumage traits are present only on adult males, once you have identified a species using obvious plumage traits, look for other members of the flock with the same size and structure that could be members of the same species that lack obvious plumage traits.

Dabbling ducks are not usually associated with the ocean, but many species migrate along coastlines. This mixed flock of Cinnamon, Blue-winged, and Green-winged Teal is part of an incredible and largely overlooked spring movement of ducks that occurs along the Gulf Coast, particularly in the western gulf. Texas, Feb. Tom Johnson.

6. If striking aspects of structure or obvious plumage traits are not visible as the flock approaches, you can use their absence to eliminate species that show distinctive characteristics, such as Northern Pintail, Wood Duck, American Black Duck, and several others. The lack of obvious characteristics basically eliminates all possibilities except Blue-winged Teal, Gadwall, and possibly a flock of all-female American Wigeon. This is a very workable list, and the combination of overall color and any size data you may have already gleaned should help you complete the identification process.

7. If possible, check your conclusions when the flock is closest to the observation point. Trying to evaluate all of the things listed above while the flock is at its closest is difficult, but if most of the work of identification is already done, you can quickly verify identifications at this point. Doing so forces you to confront any errors you may have made, consider the reason for the errors, and use this information to improve your skills.

The method above works well for sorting through flocks of dabbling ducks, and also for diving ducks or any group that regularly forms mixed flocks. It sounds complicated, but most of the analyses happen instantaneously and simultaneously in the minds of skilled observers. For less seasoned watchers, having a system gives you a starting point when you're confronted with the challenge of a distant and fast-moving mixed flock. The first few hours of the morning often have significantly higher duck diversity than the rest of the day does, so it is helpful to pay special attention to dabbler flocks during this time.

Dabbling ducks do not mix only with other dabbling ducks; they form mixed flocks with diving ducks as well, particularly *Aythya* ducks, scoters, Bufflehead, and Hooded Merganser. Virtually all species of ducks are drawn to flocks of scoters, and dabbling ducks are no exception. Wood Duck, Green-winged Teal, and American Wigeon are particularly prone to join scoters. Since the scoters provide a definitive way to judge size, the identification process for dabbling ducks with scoters becomes easier. For example, a tight knot of uniformly dark ducks that are half the size of the scoters will be Green-winged Teal. There is no need to see any other characteristics.

Although many species of dabbling ducks breed over large areas, the "prairie potholes region" of the Canadian Prairie Provinces and the northern Great Plains of the U.S. has a density and diversity of breeding ducks that are unmatched elsewhere in North America. The region is often referred to as a "duck factory" and is vitally important for the health of continental waterfowl populations. Fortunately this fact is well recognized, and partnerships between government agencies and landowners have allowed waterfowl and other wildlife to thrive in this region.

The sexes differ in all species covered here except whistling-ducks. Males show a distinct alternate plumage, sometimes referred to as "eclipse" plumage. Females also have an alternate plumage but it does not change their appearance. Differences between first-cycle birds and adults are apparent initially but are often difficult to detect by the end of the first cycle. By the second cycle they have acquired full adult plumage.

FULVOUS WHISTLING-DUCK
Dendrocygna bicolor
DIMENSIONS
L: 19 in.; WS: 26 in.; WT: 1.5 lb.

SPRING ARRIVAL

TX: early/mid-Mar.

It is always a pleasure to watch tawny brown Fulvous Whistling-Ducks as they explode from the brilliant green of a newly sprouted rice field, one of their favored habitats. Many birders don't realize that this species follows the Gulf Coast on migration, creating the odd sight of flocks of gangly whistling-ducks flying just above the waves. There is a small resident population of Fulvous Whistling-Duck in central Florida and a much larger western Gulf Coast population that is migratory. In flight, Fulvous frequently gives a loud, shrill, two-part whistle.

SIZE: Only about the size of Northern Shoveler, though it gives the impression of being much larger. Clearly smaller than Black-bellied Whistling-Duck.

STRUCTURE: Gives a bulky impression, with a heavy body and very broad, blunt wings. The head is rounded, with a long, sloping bill and a long neck that tapers down to almost nothing before expand-

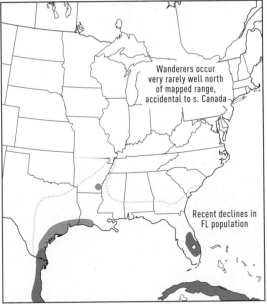

Wanderers occur very rarely well north of mapped range, accidental to s. Canada

Recent declines in FL population

ing rapidly into the stout body. This combination makes for a rather bottle-shaped bird, and the large trailing feet only add to its strange appearance.

FLIGHT AND FLOCKING: Distinctive. Wingbeats are stiff and heavy, creating the appearance of a slow flight, though in reality this species moves fairly rapidly. Like geese, but unlike typical ducks, both whistling-ducks keep their wings distinctly cupped throughout the wingbeat. Quite gregarious; often seen in dense flocks of 10–100 birds. Large flocks may have several messy lines trailing behind the main clump. During migration, especially in spring, migrating flocks may be seen over the western Gulf of Mexico flying parallel to the coast. Does not usually flock with other species except Black-bellied Whistling-Duck, and even this is rare and largely incidental.

APPEARANCE: Adult: Distinctive. The body and neck are a warm tawny brown, the back and wings much darker. Blackish underwings contrast sharply with the tawny flanks, creating a highly conspicuous and unique pattern. The vent is white, and a crisp white band wraps around the uppertail coverts, which makes identification of birds flying directly away quite simple. **First Cycle:** Like a washed-out version of adult; not significantly different. **Distant:** Often gives a very blackish impression, giving only glimpses of the tawny breast, but eventually the

bird or flock will turn and the sharply contrasting brown-and-black pattern will become apparent.

SIMILAR SPECIES: Black-bellied Whistling-Duck: Very similar in overall shape but huskier and broader-winged. For the first 5–8 months of life, first-cycle birds lack the black and chestnut underparts of adults and instead have a dull grayish brown belly and gray bill, similar to Fulvous. They do, however, still sport the bold white wing band, so identification is simple, and they confuse only those unaware of this plumage. Most first-cycle birds acquire distinct black mottling on the belly by December, though a few retain an almost entirely brown belly through the following spring. The two whistling-duck species can also be confused in silhouette at great distances, but Black-bellied's far-carrying vocalization, broader wings, slower wingbeats, and greater spacing between individuals in flocks are usually enough to allow identification.

WITH FOUR BLUE-WINGED TEAL. TEXAS, MAY. KEN BEHRENS.
- The unique tawny brown of the body and black wings create an unmistakable pattern.
- The odd structure of whistling-ducks is striking when they are seen next to typical ducks.
- These two species are often found together, both in freshwater wetlands in the southern U.S. and as migrants along the western Gulf Coast.

WITH BLACK-BELLIED WHISTLING-DUCKS. TEXAS, MAY. KEN BEHRENS.
- Even at this distance, the white wing panel and larger size of Black-bellied are evident. Fulvous look uniformly dark but show a hint of the tawny underparts.
- Fulvous can form huge flocks, sometimes joined by Black-bellieds, which tend to stick to the fringes.

TEXAS, MAY. KEN BEHRENS.
- Broad wings and trailing legs reveal these birds as whistling-ducks.
- Fulvous can be separated from Black-bellied by their longer, thinner necks; smaller heads; and slimmer bodies.
- Small flocks like this one may be quite organized, but large flocks always form messy clumps.

TEXAS, MAY. KEN BEHRENS.
- Wings are broad and blunt-tipped, almost rectangular. Body is oddly bottle-shaped, and the feet trail behind.
- The contrast between the body and wings is visible at great distances.
- Wings are black both above and below, unlike Black-bellied Whistling-Duck's.

BLACK-BELLIED WHISTLING-DUCK
Dendrocygna autumnalis
DIMENSIONS
L: 21 in.; WS: 30 in.; WT: 1.8 lb.

SPRING ARRIVAL

OK: mid-Apr.

This showy species sports gaudy colors and a loud, attention-grabbing call. Unlike Fulvous Whistling-Duck, is seems fairly open-minded about habitat selection; almost any shallow wetland will do. Formerly restricted in the U.S. to south Texas, it has expanded its range dramatically in recent years, even gaining a central Florida population thought to have emigrated from the Yucatán. In recent years, individuals and small flocks have occurred at far-flung locations, showing that this species has the potential to show up almost anywhere. In flight, it constantly gives a loud three-part whistle, simplifying an already simple identification.

SIZE: Similar to Mottled Duck and Gadwall. Slightly smaller than Mallard. It gives the appearance of being larger than it actually is.

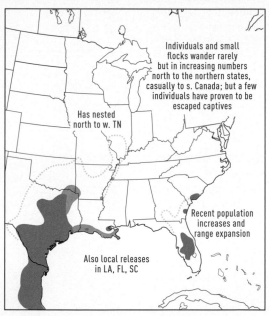

Individuals and small flocks wander rarely but in increasing numbers north to the northern states, casually to s. Canada; but a few individuals have proven to be escaped captives

Has nested north to w. TN

Recent population increases and range expansion

Also local releases in LA, FL, SC

STRUCTURE: Like Fulvous but larger and heavier. Appears more hunchbacked, potbellied, and larger-headed than Fulvous. The wings are extremely broad with rounded wingtips. The bill is larger than that of Fulvous. Both species have exceptionally large feet that trail behind the body.

FLIGHT AND FLOCKING: Extremely heavy, shallow wingbeats on stiff wings. Like Fulvous, holds the wings rigidly cupped. Flight speed is slower than that of Fulvous but can be deceptive, appearing slower than it actually is. Typically seen in smaller flocks than Fulvous, generally 4–30 though flocks of up to 200 occur more rarely. Lines often stack up vertically, with several layers of birds on top of one another so that flocks may be taller than they are long, unlike the long lines preferred by most waterfowl species. Sometimes joins Fulvous Whistling-Duck, though it prefers to stay in monotypic flocks.

APPEARANCE: Adult: The stone gray face contrasts with a brilliant carmine bill and chestnut chest and neck, which end abruptly at the trademark black belly. The wings are black below but have a broad white band running the entire length of the upperwing, which is the most obvious plumage feature of the species in flight. **First Cycle:** Unlike the striking adult, has a gray rather than pink bill and a dull gray-brown belly. Patches of black appear on the belly by midwinter, and most birds have a completely black belly by the following spring. The wing pattern is identical to adult's. **Distant:** Bicolored, and in good light tricolored. The black-and-white aspects of the plumage are always evident, and the chestnut brown of the chest is visible in some conditions.

SIMILAR SPECIES: Fulvous Whistling-Duck: Slimmer overall. The tawny body contrasts sharply with the black underwing. Lacks the black-and-white flashing wings and more raucous call of Black-bellied. See Fulvous account for more information.

WITH FULVOUS WHISTLING-DUCKS. COMPOSITE. TEXAS, MAY. KEN BEHRENS.

- Broad wings, a bottle-shaped body, hunched back, and big, trailing feet characterize both whistling-ducks.
- At virtually any angle, the white wing panel of Black-bellied is distinctive.
- Black-bellied has a larger head, slightly shorter neck, heavier chest, bulkier body, and even broader wings than Fulvous.
- Notice how both species change their neck posture and how this alters the overall appearance of the bird.

FIRST CYCLE (TOP) AND ADULT. LOUISIANA, JAN. CAMERON COX.
- First cycle lacks the black belly and pink bill and is more like Fulvous in color, but it has the heavy build of Black-bellied.
- Although not evident in this photo, the white wing panel of first cycle also separates it from Fulvous.

TEXAS, NOV. CAMERON COX.
- They tend to form smaller flocks than Fulvous; groups like this are on the large side for the species.
- Broad, U-shaped flocks are typical.

ADULT. MEXICO, MAR. STEVE MLODINOW.
- Striking! At a distance, the chestnut breast blends into the black belly, and the bird looks dark except for the flashing white wing panels.

TEXAS, NOV. CAMERON COX.
- Noisy flocks are often on the move at dawn and dusk.

WOOD DUCK
Aix sponsa
DIMENSIONS
L: 18.5 in.; WS: 30 in.; WT: 1.3 lb.

SPRING ARRIVAL

MA: early Mar.; MI: late Mar.;
MB: late Mar./early Apr.

FALL ARRIVAL

s. NJ: late July; VA: late July;
TX coast: early Nov.

Although usually thought of as a bird of flooded woodlands and marshes, Wood Duck can be seen in several different situations during migration, including over the ocean. If watching Wood Ducks fly just above breaking waves is not enough of a mindbender, the species is regularly seen winging along amid flocks of scoters! Whether mixed with hundreds of scoters over the Atlantic or dabbling in cypress swamps along the lower Mississippi, Wood Duck is a spectacular creature, distinctive on the water and in flight.

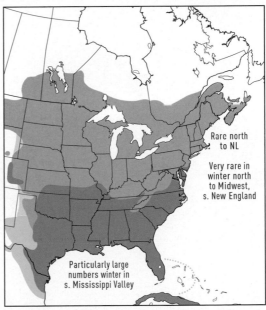

Rare north to NL

Very rare in winter north to Midwest, s. New England

Particularly large numbers winter in s. Mississippi Valley

SIZE: About the same size as Northern Shoveler. Slightly smaller than American Wigeon.

STRUCTURE: Distinctive. The head is held well above the body on a spindly neck, and the bushy crest causes the head to appear oversized and smoothly rounded, as if the bird were wearing a helmet. It is distinctly potbellied and has a long, squared-off tail. The wings are located at the center of the body and are very broad-based, with rounded tips. First-cycle birds are slimmer and have a significantly reduced crest, which causes them to appear smaller-headed.

FLIGHT AND FLOCKING: Wingbeats are fairly rapid and distinctively "soft," with a tremendous amount of flex at the tips of the primaries. Flocks usually form small oval-shaped clumps that maintain a fairly consistent shape. Migrating flocks are usually found at medium height, similar to scaup but lower than Mallard. Along the coast, migrants often join scoters, usually only in singles or pairs.

APPEARANCE: Uniformly grayish underwings and sharply defined pale belly in all plumages. **Basic Adult Male:** Spectacular at close range but in flight appears mainly dark. At medium range a pale throat and two spurs that extend onto the face are evident. Appears more uniformly dark than other age/sex classes, and the white trailing edge to the wing is narrower and usually not evident. **Adult Female:** Grayer than male with a less extensive white throat patch and smaller crest. Large white patch around the eye that looks like a mask when seen well. Shows the broadest, most evident white trailing edge to the wing of any plumage. **First Cycle:** Like female but smaller and duller with a narrower white trailing edge to the wing. **Distant:** Uniformly blackish but with a sharply defined white belly. The white throat markings are generally not visible except at moderate to close range, but the white trailing edge to the wing can be surprisingly evident at long distances.

SIMILAR SPECIES: American Wigeon: Similar in shape but more compact, with more slender, angular, and pointed wings, and without the puffy crest of adult Wood Duck. At long distances tends to look pale, whereas Wood Duck looks dark. **Scoters:** Although significantly heavier, Black and Surf Scoters have similar length and wingspan as Wood Duck, and a Wood Duck can easily be overlooked amid a flock of scoters. However, scoters are quite different in structure, being heavier and more compact than Wood Duck. With a good look, the rangy structure, long and squared-off tail, and oddly shaped head will allow an observer to home in on a Wood Duck hiding in a flock of scoters.

ONE FEMALE (BOTTOM) AND FOUR MALES. TEXAS, NOV. GREG LAVATY.
- Potbelly, broad wings, long tail, spindly neck, and oddly shaped head usually held well above the body create a distinctive silhouette.
- Spectacular up close, but mainly dark with a pale belly at a distance. The double spur of the male's throat and the eye patch and pale throat of the female are sometimes visible.
- The all-gray underwing and bold white trailing edge to the female's wing are also relevant plumage features.

FIVE MALES AND ONE FEMALE (THIRD FROM L). NEW JERSEY, NOV. CAMERON COX.

- Plumage details largely disappear at a distance, but structure is plainly visible.
- The pale belly is the most obvious plumage trait at a distance.

FEMALE. UTAH, JUNE. KEN BEHRENS.
- Wood Duck has broader, blunter wings and a longer tail than other ducks.

MALES. TEXAS, DEC. JUSTIN INMAN.
- One of the most spectacular ducks up close, but most of this finery disappears at a distance.

NEW JERSEY, NOV. KEN BEHRENS.
- Typical migrating flock, small and vaguely oval-shaped.
- Flocks may also form a messy line for short periods, but soon return to a more bunched-up shape.

THREE MALES AND ONE FEMALE. NEW JERSEY, NOV. KEN BEHRENS.
- Distinctive even overhead; the long tail looks squared-off, and the neck appears spindly.
- Sharply defined pale belly creates contrast that is clearly visible at a distance.
- Females (such as top bird) have a smaller head than males, resulting in a slightly different silhouette.

TWO MALES WITH FIFTEEN BLACK AND FOUR SURF SCOTERS. NEW JERSEY, NOV. KEN BEHRENS.
- The male Wood Duck (sixth from L on bottom) blends easily into this flock, but its slender shape, slim neck, and distinctly raised head are apparent.
- *Can you spot the second Wood Duck?*

MALE (BOTTOM C) WITH MALLARD. ONTARIO, FEB. RAYMOND BARLOW.
- The two best-known species of duck, both widespread and numerous.
- Compared with a typical duck such as Mallard, Wood Duck has a shorter, more rounded hand and longer tail that aids it in navigating its wet woodland habitat at high speed.

NORTHERN PINTAIL
Anas acuta
DIMENSIONS
L: 21 in.; WS: 34 in.; WT: 1.8 lb.

SPRING ARRIVAL

ME: early Mar.; IA: early Mar.; ON: mid-Mar.;
Hudson Bay: early/mid-May

FALL ARRIVAL

MO: late Aug.; NJ: late Aug.; n. FL: mid-Sept.

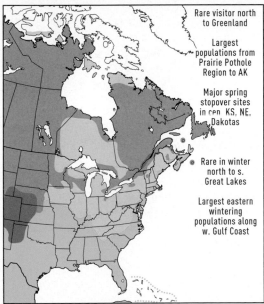

Rare visitor north
to Greenland

Largest
populations from
Prairie Pothole
Region to AK

Major spring
stopover sites
in cen. KS, NE,
Dakotas

Rare in winter
north to s.
Great Lakes

Largest eastern
wintering
populations along
w. Gulf Coast

Lithe and agile, Northern Pintail can be recognized at great distances by silhouette only. Its long, lean build often draws comparisons to a greyhound. The species is most numerous in western North America but is common along the Atlantic and Gulf Coasts and locally common in the interior.

SIZE: One of the largest dabblers; excluding the long "pintail" of the male, it falls between Mallard and Gadwall.

STRUCTURE: Slender, even proportions and long, clean lines create an elegant impression. The long, slim neck merges smoothly with the head, which is held slightly lifted. The long, narrow wings are centered on the body, creating a balanced appearance. The long "pintail" of the male disappears at a distance, particularly against a blue sky.

FLIGHT AND FLOCKING: Flight is fast, direct, and steady with fairly rapid wingbeats. Flocks typically fly high, higher on average than any other duck. Although small groups of 10 or fewer may join other species, large flocks are usually monospecific. The largest flocks form a wedge or U shape, with each member holding its order and spacing with military precision. Smaller flocks fly in straight, clean lines.

APPEARANCE: In all plumages has dusky underwings that do not contrast with the body. **Basic Adult Male:** Attractive in an understated way. The head is chocolate brown, and the neck, breast, and belly are white. The back and upperwings are gray with a broad white trailing edge to the secondaries. **Female and Alternate Male:** Very uniform pale brown overall. The white trailing edge of the wing is visible at surprising distances. **Distant:** As both sexes are quite pale, flocks have a uniform appearance that is unlike that of most species of dabblers. The dark heads of males may be evident, but flocks often take on the overall pale brown color of the females.

SIMILAR SPECIES: Northern Shoveler: At great distances can appear surprisingly similar. As in Northern Pintail, male has a dark head and white breast and female is a warm tan. Both species are slim, and the shoveler's long bill can easily be misconstrued as a long neck. Usually, though, with more than a few moments of observation the long downward-angled bill of the shoveler will become apparent. Also, the shoveler appears front-heavy, with the wings pushed back toward the rear of the bird, not balanced as in the pintail. Flocks of shoveler lack the military precision of pintail and tend to bunch up. **American Black Duck and Mallard:** Both species are long-necked and sometimes flock similarly, but they are larger-headed and broader-winged than Northern Pintail, and lack its attenuated elegance in flight. They also show bright white underwings, visible at great distances.

NEW JERSEY, DEC. KEN BEHRENS.
- The head-and-breast contrast on males is striking, but pintail flocks appear uniform at a distance, typically pale grayish or faintly rusty brown.
- Subtle shape differences between the sexes: males are slightly broader-winged and longer-necked.
- The first-cycle male (second bird from R) has female-like plumage (though with a whitish chest) but the structure of a male.

ADULT MALES. UTAH, JAN. KEN BEHRENS.
- Structure is unlike that of any other duck, slender and long-necked with a sharply pointed hand.
- The "pintails" of males disappear even at moderate range, but the silhouette remains long and slender.

INDIA, DEC. KEN BEHRENS.
- Wings are slender and falconlike, centered perfectly on the body.
- Flocks making short-distance flights in winter are less organized than migrating flocks.

ADULT MALES AND FEMALES. CALIFORNIA, DEC. JERRY TING.
- Unmistakable at close range!
- Note the plain gray wings with a bold white trailing edge to the secondaries.

UTAH, JAN. KEN BEHRENS.
- Unmistakable at long range!
- Long neck, lean body, and falconlike wings create a unique silhouette.

ADULT MALE. NORTH DAKOTA, MAY. KEN BEHRENS.
• Underwing is almost entirely gray, a trait shared only with Wood Duck and Eurasian Wigeon.

NEW JERSEY, DEC. KEN BEHRENS.
• Even when jumping from one pond to another, they tend to spread out rather than form tight clumps as most other dabbling ducks do.

SWEDEN, APR. KEN BEHRENS.
• Clean, even lines are typical of migrating flocks, particularly smaller flocks.
• Northern Pintail can be provisionally identified at great distance on flock structure alone.

THREE ADULT MALES AND ONE FIRST-CYCLE MALE (R). LOUISIANA, JAN. KEN BEHRENS.
- Even at medium distance, the color difference between the sexes is blunted, and flocks look quite uniform.
- As migrants, they tend to fly higher than any other duck species.

ONTARIO, APR. KEN BEHRENS.
- Typical formation for a medium-sized to large migrating flock.
- This type of flock holds its shape with only minor adjustments. Large flocks of most other ducks change shape constantly.

FEMALE. BRITISH COLUMBIA, JAN. GLENN BARTLEY.
- Drab but attractive. The only plumage traits visible at a distance are the warm, rusty head and thin, but distinct, white trailing edge to the secondaries.

MALLARD
Anas platyrhynchos
DIMENSIONS
L: 23 in.; WS: 35 in.; WT: 2.4 lb.

SPRING ARRIVAL

(migratory populations):
s. MB: late Mar.; s. QC: late Mar.;
Hudson Bay: early May

FALL ARRIVAL

(migratory populations):
Lake Erie: late Aug.; s. NJ: late Sept.;
w. Gulf Coast: early Oct.

Mallard is the most abundant duck in North America, widely recognized by birders and non-birders alike. Despite its well-known appearance, it can be surprisingly difficult to identify at the distances typical of a migration watch site. It is generally common, and is particularly abundant along the Mississippi flyway, where it is by far the most numerous duck.

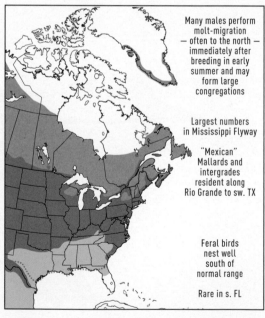

Many males perform molt-migration — often to the north — immediately after breeding in early summer and may form large congregations

Largest numbers in Mississippi Flyway

"Mexican" Mallards and intergrades resident along Rio Grande to sw. TX

Feral birds nest well south of normal range

Rare in s. FL

SIZE: Slightly smaller than American Black Duck. Larger than Northern Pintail and Gadwall. Body size approaches that of a small Ross's Goose or a small Cackling Goose, but Mallard is shorter-winged.

STRUCTURE: A bulky, heavy-bodied, broad-winged dabbler. The bill is long and prominent but merges smoothly into the forehead. The large head is held just above the bulky body and usually appears rounded, though at times the crown appears flat. This combination of features—raised head, pot-belly, short tail, and broad-based wings set well back on the body—creates a rear-heavy, slightly up-ward-tilted impression. Males have curled central uppertail coverts than can be detected at surprising distances.

FLIGHT AND FLOCKING: Wingbeats are fairly even and moderate in depth. They are quite slow, such that even at a distance individual wingbeats can be counted—a trait shared only with American Black Duck and a few of the largest diving ducks. Small flocks may fly in even lines but more frequently form irregularly shaped clumps or staggered lines in which each individual is on a slightly different plane. Large flocks (20 or more) fly in messy wedges. Mallard shows a tendency to form subflocks within a flock: groups of two to four birds packed tightly within the looser overall flock formation. Readily joins American Black Duck; most large flocks of Mallard in the Northeast will include Black Ducks and vice versa. Gadwall and, to a lesser degree, wigeons also join flocks of Mallard. Mallard are far less likely than smaller dabblers to join flocks of scoters.

APPEARANCE: Basic Adult Male: The iridescent green head is set off by a bright yellow bill, and the chocolate breast is separated from the head by a narrow white neck ring. The body is mostly pale gray with a black rump and vent that contrast with the bright white tail. The brilliant orange feet can be seen tucked underneath the tail at moderate distances. The underwing is bright white but contrasts little with the body; the upperwing is gray with a dark speculum bordered by obvious white lines. **Adult**

Female: A cold gray face contrasts slightly with a richer brown breast. The belly can be identical to the breast but is typically paler and less mottled, sometimes obviously so, but never pure white. The wing pattern is like the male's but browner with slightly narrower borders to the speculum. **Alternate Adult Male:** Much like female but retains a variable amount of basic plumage, creating a mottled, patchy appearance. The basic wing pattern is also retained, and the yellow bill becomes quite dull. **First Cycle:** Same as female, though very young birds have an all-dark bill. **Distant:** Medium brown or gray. Males are conspicuously dark-headed. The underwings are white but lack the same degree of contrast shown by American Black Duck, and are therefore far less obvious at a distance.

SIMILAR SPECIES: American Black Duck: Almost identical in structure but slightly bulkier than Mallard with marginally more rounded wingtips and a noticeable peak above the eye rather than a rounded crown. Overall much darker than female Mallard, lacking the white borders to the speculum. The contrast between white underwing and dark body is much more striking than in Mallard. **Mottled Duck:** Slightly smaller, with significantly quicker wingbeats and a smaller head that is barely differentiated from the neck. Darker overall than female Mallard, with a clean buffy throat that contrasts sharply with the body. Lacks the white outer tail feathers and bold white borders to the speculum of Mallard. **Gadwall:** Smaller and slimmer with a balanced appearance, rather than the rear-heavy, upward-tilted appearance of Mallard. Gadwall's wings are narrower and more pointed, and its wingbeats are faster. The white belly contrasts clearly with the dark chest and flanks. The white inner secondaries are often difficult to see but are diagnostic when visible, and Gadwall also lacks the bold speculum borders of Mallard.

ONE MALE AND THREE FEMALES. NEW MEXICO, NOV. CAMERON COX.

- Quite large, and the silhouette is somewhat gooselike: bulky body, broad-based and some-what blunt-tipped wings, and small head in relation to the body.
- Underwings are white but contrast little with the body, far less so than those of American Black Duck. The dark female here (L) is an exceptional.

MALE AND FEMALE. UTAH, JAN. KEN BEHRENS.
- Although the male's green head is the species' hallmark, the broad white lines that border the speculum are more important, as they are prominently displayed by both sexes.
- The male's curled uppertail coverts can be visible at surprising distances; birds that look like American Black Duck but show this trait carry Mallard genes.

NEW YORK, MAR. COLIN CLEMENT.
- Frequently forms wedges or disorderly clumps. American Black Duck may form similar flocks, particularly in large groups, but more often flies in loose lines.
- Underwings are bright white but contrast little with the body.
- The bottom bird is a male American Black Duck x Mallard hybrid.

WITH AMERICAN BLACK DUCKS. NEW JERSEY, DEC. KEN BEHRENS.
- Large flocks of Mallard and American Black Ducks form distinctive messy wedges.
- At this distance, the shape and height of the flock, bulky bodies, and triangular, broad-based wings identify these birds as Mallard/American Black Ducks. In poor light it may be impossible to differentiate the species. This flock is primarily Mallard.

WITH TWO AMERICAN BLACK DUCKS (L). NEW JERSEY, DEC. KEN BEHRENS.

- The darker color of American Black Duck causes its silhouette to stand out distinctly. Mallard is paler and consequently looks smaller.

MALES WITH NORTHERN SHOVELER. UTAH, JAN. KEN BEHRENS.

- Males of both species have a bold green head that appears dark at a distance, but the similarities largely end there.
- This is a fleeting association; these two species rarely migrate together.

MALES WITH TWO MALE NORTHERN PINTAIL. NORTH DAKOTA, MAY. KEN BEHRENS.

- These species are similar in size but built completely differently. Mallard is bulky and broad-winged, whereas Northern Pintail has slim wings and body and a long neck.
- The dark head of male Mallard is visible at much greater distances than that of male Northern Pintail.

AMERICAN BLACK DUCK
Anas rubripes
DIMENSIONS
L: 23 in.; WS: 35 in.; WT: 2.6 lb.

SPRING ARRIVAL

MN: mid-Mar.; cen. ON: late Mar.; NL: late Apr.

FALL ARRIVAL

GA: late Sept.; IA: late Oct.; AR: early Nov.

This large, dark dabbler nests in small freshwater wetlands in the boreal forests of eastern Canada and in coastal salt marshes along the northeast Atlantic Coast. It was once much more common but has declined because of logging and other human activities, which have allowed Mallard, which is more tolerant of disturbed habitats, to expand north and east into the Black Duck's breeding range. The two species now hybridize frequently, threatening the viability of pure Black Duck populations. Black Duck is only truly common along the Atlantic Coast, particularly in its winter stronghold, the marshes of Chesapeake and Delaware Bays.

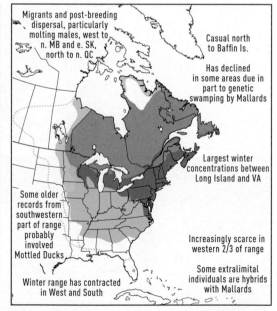

Migrants and post-breeding dispersal, particularly molting males, west to n. MB and e. SK, north to n. QC

Casual north to Baffin Is.

Has declined in some areas due in part to genetic swamping by Mallards

Largest winter concentrations between Long Island and VA

Some older records from southwestern part of range probably involved Mottled Ducks

Increasingly scarce in western 2/3 of range

Some extralimital individuals are hybrids with Mallards

Winter range has contracted in West and South

SIZE: The largest dabbling duck, averaging slightly larger than Mallard, though small females overlap with Mallard. Slightly smaller than Common Eider, though both species approach the size of a small goose.

STRUCTURE: Like Mallard but subtly bulkier, especially in the neck. Compared with Mallard, Black Duck has slightly broader wings with blunter wingtips and a slightly peaked crown rather than a rounded head. Experienced observers can pick out Mallard candidates from a flock of American Black Duck on size and structure alone, but the existence of hybrids and small female Black Ducks makes it unwise to separate these species without also using plumage characteristics.

FLIGHT AND FLOCKING: As in Mallard, though flocks are often more organized with slightly greater spacing between individuals. Along the Atlantic Coast, both Black Duck and Mallard tend to fly quite high as migrants, higher than any other duck except Northern Pintail. They have strong flight line tendencies. American Black Ducks occasionally join flocks of migrating scoters or Brant.

APPEARANCE: In all plumages, the snowy white underwing contrasts sharply with the dark body, a trait visible at considerable distance. **Adult Male:** Cold gray face and bright yellow bill contrast sharply with blackish body. **Adult Female:** Like male but slightly paler overall with a duller greenish yellow bill. **First Cycle:** Essentially identical to adult female for flight identification, but marginally paler. **Distant:** Uniformly blackish with sharply contrasting white underwing coverts. At moderate distance the wing coverts create an extensive white flash every time the wing is raised. At extreme distances the white underwing appears much reduced and is visible only as a small white triangle at the base of the wing.

SIMILAR SPECIES: Mallard: Slightly slimmer overall with a smaller head. Male is very different in appearance. Female is paler than American Black Duck, and the white underwing does not contrast as sharply as it does in Black Duck. **Mallard Hybrids:** The number of hybrids makes flight identification of American Black Duck tricky. As a general rule, hybrids have the structure of Mallard and more of the appearance of Black Duck, though there is much variation. In the Mid-Atlantic, most large flocks of either species will include some hybrids. At a distance, hybrids often look like skinny Black Ducks with a slightly paler belly. Other indications of a hybrid include faint white speculum borders, white tail feathers, and green patches on the head. Some hybrids may look like Black Duck but show one or two curled uppertail coverts, which are visible even at long distances. Some hybrids are just too similar to one of the parent species to be identifiable in flight. **White-winged Scoter:** In silhouette can be surprisingly similar to Black Duck but is more compact, heavier, and thicker-necked. Its bill angles downward slightly, whereas Black Duck holds its bill straight. White-winged Scoter has wings that are longer and more swept back at the wrist. It also has deeper wingbeats and tends to fly lower, in crisp lines with precise spacing between individuals.

MASSACHUSETTS, JAN. KEN BEHRENS.
- American Black Duck and Mallard are very similar in structure: both have broad-based, triangular wings; a long but bulky body; and a fairly large, long bill.
- A slight but noticeable peak above the eye gives American Black Duck's head a boxier appearance than Mallard's.

WITH TWO MALLARD (L AND C). NEW JERSEY, NOV. KEN BEHRENS.
- Note American Black Duck's more peaked forehead and slightly thicker neck.
- The contrast with the dark flanks causes the American Black Duck's white underwing to pop; Mallard shows far less contrast.

NEW JERSEY, MAR. TOM SMITH.
- The cold gray face contrasts with the dark body and dull yellow-green bill.
- A purple speculum bordered with solid black is indicative of an American Black Duck untainted by Mallard genes.

WITH TWELVE MALLARD AND TWO NORTHERN PINTAIL (FAR R). NEW JERSEY, NOV. KEN BEHRENS.
- Compare the wing shape of the American Black Ducks and Mallard to that of the pintail.
- American Black Duck has slightly blunter wingtips than Mallard.
- Along much of the Atlantic Coast, flocks of American Black Ducks usually include Mallard or Mallard hybrids.

MIXED FLOCK: PRIMARILY AMERICAN BLACK DUCKS WITH MALLARD, NORTHERN PINTAIL, AND UNIDENTIFIED SMALLER DABBLERS, LIKELY GADWALL. NEW JERSEY, NOV. KEN BEHRENS.

- Although it includes several species, this flock is typical of American Black Duck: quite high and not as bunched as a Mallard flock, with birds on several different planes.
- Distant mixed dabbler flocks are challenging. The best strategy is to identify the most distinctive bird(s) and then compare the size, structure, and any visible plumage traits of the unknown birds with those of the known ones.

WITH TWELVE MALLARD AND ONE MALLARD X AMERICAN BLACK DUCK HYBRID. NEW JERSEY, NOV. KEN BEHRENS.

- The contrast between the underwings and flanks of the American Black Duck is striking; although Mallard also have white underwings, they lack the strong contrast, so their underwings are not visible at the same distances.
- The hybrid (top C, wings down) is a classic example of a hybrid male.

WITH SURF SCOTERS. NEW JERSEY, NOV. KEN BEHRENS.

- American Black Ducks (R) infrequently join scoter flocks. The American Black Duck is slightly larger than the Surf Scoters, approaching the size of a White-winged Scoter.
- Underwing coverts flash bright white even at this distance and angle.

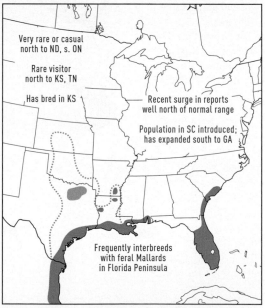

MOTTLED DUCK
Anas fulvigula
DIMENSIONS
L: 22 in.; WS: 30 in.; WT: 2.2 lb.

SPRING ARRIVAL

OK: mid-Feb.

This southern counterpart to American Black Duck is found along the Gulf Coast and in peninsular Florida, and an introduced population exists in South Carolina. The Florida population is slightly paler and prefers freshwater wetlands; the darker birds of the western Gulf Coast are found in brackish marshes near the coast. The Florida population is threatened by interbreeding with feral Mallard.

SIZE: Slightly, but distinctly, smaller than Mallard. Very similar to Gadwall, though slightly heavier.

STRUCTURE: Very similar to Mallard but with a thinner neck and smaller head that barely expands out of the neck. Wings are slightly slimmer-based and more pointed.

Very rare or casual north to ND, s. ON

Rare visitor north to KS, TN

Has bred in KS

Recent surge in reports well north of normal range

Population in SC introduced; has expanded south to GA

Frequently interbreeds with feral Mallards in Florida Peninsula

FLIGHT AND FLOCKING: As in Mallard, but wingbeats are clearly faster and flight is not quite so strong and steady. Flocks typically include 2–25 birds. Large flocks are generally rare, though large numbers gather at concentrations of food and can be seen commuting in and out in sizable flocks. Readily mixes with both wintering and feral Mallard around the Gulf Coast.

APPEARANCE: In all plumages the underwing coverts are bright white and easily visible. **Adult Male:** Dark to medium brown overall with a contrasting paler neck and face and a bright yellow bill. The neck and throat are free of streaking and stippling, and the entire face is a warm buff. Comparatively, the faces of American Black Duck and female Mallard look cold and dirty with finely streaked throats. **Adult Female:** Like male but slightly paler with a duller bill. **Distant:** Uniformly blackish with sharply contrasting pale underwing coverts. As in Black Duck, the underwing coverts create an extensive white flash at moderate distance; it is still visible at extreme distances but only as a small white triangle at the base of the wing.

SIMILAR SPECIES: American Black Duck: Darker and larger with a blockier head and colder, dark-streaked throat. Rare anywhere in Mottled Duck's range. **Mallard:** Female is slightly larger, with a thicker neck, larger head, and slower wingbeats. The strong white borders to the speculum are obvious, along with a colder gray throat and paler belly. Mallard x Mottled Duck hybrids present an additional challenge that is most frequently encountered in Florida where such hybrids are regular. The most difficult hybrids look slightly paler than the average Mottled Duck, with a faintly paler belly than chest and thin but distinct white borders to the speculum. **Gadwall:** Similar in structure but with a more balanced appearance. The peaked forehead and sharply defined white belly separate it from Mottled Duck.

MAY, TEXAS. KEN BEHRENS.
- Silhouette is like that of Mallard but with notable differences: shape is slimmer overall, with thinner, more pointed wings and a much thinner neck.
- Found in pairs throughout the year more consistently than any other duck.
- Like Mallard and American Black Duck, often elevates the head slightly above the body.

TEXAS, APRIL. WITH EIGHT NORTHERN SHOVELER AND THREE GREEN-WINGED TEAL. KEN BEHRENS.
- The speculums of the two lead birds are catching the light and look purple, like those of American Black Duck, but the slender necks, small heads, and size, only slightly larger than Northern Shoveler, indicate that they are Mottled Ducks.

MALE AND FEMALE. FLORIDA, JAN. CAMERON COX.
- White underwing contrasts sharply with the dark body, as on American Black Duck, but Mottled Duck is warmer-toned, with a buffy throat and golden-fringed body feathers.
- Male (foreground) has a brighter yellow bill and is slightly darker than female.
- Often unnoticed in the field, the narrow white trailing edge of the wing is typical of pure Mottled Duck.

WITH MALLARD x MOTTLED DUCK HYBRID (L). FLORIDA, DEC. CAMERON COX.
- Particularly in Florida, hybrids with Mallard are becoming alarmingly common.
- This particular hybrid is much like a Mallard in plumage but has the structure of Mottled Duck.
- Both birds show the buff throat typical of Mottled Duck.

WITH MALLARD x MOTTLED DUCK HYBRID (THIRD FROM L). LOUISIANA, JAN. KEN BEHRENS.
- With slimmer body and wings, Mottled Duck gives a more balanced impression than Mallard.
- Note how the pale underwings flash in the sun, contrasting sharply with the body.
- The female of the center pair is pale, with an orange bill and distinct speculum borders, indicating a hybrid.

GADWALL
Anas strepera
DIMENSIONS
L: 20 in.; WS: 33 in.; WT: 2 lb.

SPRING ARRIVAL

OH: late Feb.; ON: late Mar.;
ND: late Mar.; MB: mid-Apr.

FALL ARRIVAL

VA: early Sept.; MO: mid-Sept.;
Gulf Coast: mid-Oct.

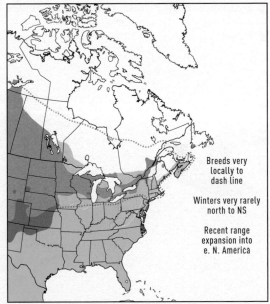

Breeds very
locally to
dash line

Winters very rarely
north to NS

Recent range
expansion into
e. N. America

This unassuming species lacks the gaudy colors of many dabbling ducks but possesses a subtle beauty when viewed closely. Historically, Gadwall bred primarily in western North America, but it has expanded to the Great Lakes and southeast Canada. It is intermediate in size between Mallard and the smaller dabbling ducks and often associates with both Mallard and American Wigeon.

SIZE: Clearly smaller than Mallard. Similar to American Wigeon but appears larger because of its stocky shape and darker color.

STRUCTURE: Boasts perhaps the most "generic" of all duck silhouettes. The head, which looks oversized and blocky when resting on the water, looks average in flight except for a slight peak to the crown shown by males. The neck is slightly longer and slimmer than one might expect having seen Gadwall on the water, but is still unremarkable. The body is medium-sized; the wings are broad-based and set directly in the middle of the body, giving the bird a balanced appearance.

FLIGHT AND FLOCKING: Wingbeats are faster and deeper than those of Mallard, and counting the wingbeats at a distance is impossible, though the wings do not completely blur as is the case with teal. Typically flies high, usually in pairs or small groups of fewer than 10. The small, messy flocks often feature a central bunch of birds with one or two more isolated birds leading or trailing the main group. Readily joins flocks of Mallard or American Black Duck and can easily disappear into them. Also joins and vanishes just as easily into flocks of wigeons and occasionally scoters.

APPEARANCE: Adult Male: Dull overall with a black bill, gray face, and slightly darker crown. The chest and flanks are a darker gray and coarsely marked with black barring. The belly is white and contrasts clearly with the chest and black rump. The underwing coverts are white; the upperwing is mostly gray-brown, though there is an inconspicuous pattern of maroon and black secondary coverts. A few inner secondaries are white, but owing to their close proximity to the body, they are often difficult to see at a distance. **Adult Female:** Plain mottled brown with a slightly paler throat and sharply defined white belly. The wings are brown above with a tiny patch of white inner secondaries that become invisible at even moderate distances. The underwing coverts are bright white. **Distant:** Uniformly dull gray or dull brown with a sharply defined pale belly and white underwing coverts. The pale underwings are far less evident at a distance than those of American Black Duck or Mottled Duck, and the white inner secondaries are often not visible.

SIMILAR SPECIES: Mallard and American Black Duck: Both species are larger and heavier-bodied with a larger head, thicker neck, and broader wings. Both have noticeably slower wingbeats than Gadwall. **American Wigeon:** Similar in size but appears more compact with a plumper body, shorter neck, and rounded head that is usually slightly elevated. Its tiny bill disappears at a distance, emphasizing the rounded head. The wings are slimmer, more angular and pointed, and appear to be placed farther up the body because of the longer, pointed tail. **Blue-winged Teal:** Similar shape but much smaller head and smaller overall. Has much faster wingbeats, a darker belly, and a pale blue upperwing patch. Forms tightly packed flocks that move with greater speed and agility than those of Gadwall.

TWO MALES, TWO FEMALES. TEXAS, JAN. KEN BEHRENS.
• Males have an intricate wing pattern and a black rump, but these disappear at a distance, leaving birders without their two favorite field marks. All that is left is a plain gray-brown bird, which is exactly how Gadwall appear at a distance. Very few ducks can match it in plainness, and the lack of field marks becomes the key trait.

MALE AND FEMALE WITH FEMALE GREEN-WINGED TEAL (C). TEXAS, JAN. KEN BEHRENS.

- Wings are almost perfectly centered on the body, and the hand is pointed.
- Clearly larger, with slower wingbeats than small dabblers such as this teal.
- Quite lean in comparison with Green-winged Teal, which is very small but appears stocky.

MALE (R) WITH FEMALE LESSER SCAUP. UTAH, JAN. KEN BEHRENS.

- Both species of scaup are smaller than Gadwall, with more angular wings and faster wingbeats.
- Medium-sized diving ducks form tighter flocks than Gadwall.
- The slight peak above the eye on Gadwall is the only trait that stands out in the bland silhouette.

WITH SNOW GEESE (BACKGROUND). LOUISIANA, JAN. KEN BEHRENS.

- The silhouette is remarkably unremarkable: like Mallard's but leaner and more balanced, with thinner, more pointed wings.
- Flock shape is much more similar to that of Mallard than that of wigeon: loose bunches with individuals at several different heights, often with outlying birds at the front or back.
- Often looks like a skinny, unmarked Mallard, which is enough to identify Gadwall in most locations, though if birding in the south remember that Mottled Duck can give the same impression.

WITH ADULT FEMALE AMERICAN WIGEON (SECOND FROM R). NEW JERSEY, OCT. CAMERON COX.
- Gadwall are often joined by the similar American Wigeon.
- Gadwall is lankier, with a larger, boxy head and slightly darker overall color.

PAIR WITH AN ADULT MALE NORTHERN PINTAIL (L). NORTH DAKOTA, MAY. KEN BEHRENS.
- Gadwall's generic silhouette is utterly unlike that of Northern Pintail, which has the most distinctive silhouette among ducks.

MALE. UTAH, JUNE. KEN BEHRENS.
- Dull at a distance but spectacular at close range!

FEMALE (TOP) WITH FIRST-CYCLE MALE. UTAH, JUNE. KEN BEHRENS.
- The belly is white but rather dull so does not show up clearly at a distance, unlike the bright belly of wigeon.
- Female and first-cycle male look very similar, but note the black coming into the male's undertail coverts and chest.

WITH MALE NORTHERN SHOVELER (BELOW). UTAH, JAN. KEN BEHRENS.
- Gadwall's generic silhouette is very different from that of shoveler, with its distinctive bill, thick neck, and indistinct head.
- Gadwall has a bright white underwing, like Mallard and American Black Duck. Like Mallard, its underwing appears muted at a distance, whereas American Black Duck's is strongly contrasting.

AMERICAN WIGEON
Anas americana
DIMENSIONS
L: 20 in.; WS: 32 in.; WT: 1.6 lb.

SPRING ARRIVAL

s. Great Lakes: early Mar.; IA: mid-Mar.;
NS: mid-Mar.; Hudson Bay: mid-/late May

FALL ARRIVAL

IA: early Sept.; Lake Erie: mid-Sept.;
MA: mid-Sept.; FL: late Sept.

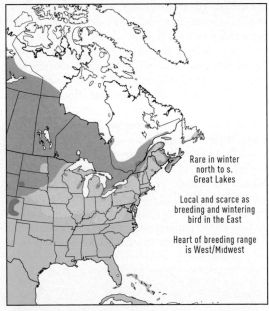

Rare in winter
north to s.
Great Lakes

Local and scarce as
breeding and wintering
bird in the East

Heart of breeding range
is West/Midwest

This medium-sized dabbler has a dashing flight style and flashy plumage. It is most numerous along the Pacific Coast but still relatively common, though local, in eastern North America. In the winter it is often found around concentrations of American Coot, from which it steals food. Males are very vocal and frequently give a two- or three-part ringing wolf whistle in flight.

SIZE: Perhaps the most medium-sized of the medium-sized dabblers. Slightly smaller than Gadwall. Slightly larger than Northern Shoveler.

STRUCTURE: Body is rather plump, whereas the wings are slender, cut back at the wrist, and pointed—jet-fighter wings on a blimp. The bill is small and disappears at moderate distance, emphasizing the very round head, which is held slightly above the body. The rounded belly tapers into a long, sharply pointed tail. This combination is unique, though distance can blunt its distinctiveness.

FLIGHT AND FLOCKING: Wingbeats are deep and rapid without quite reaching the blurred appearance of smaller ducks. Flight is agile and gives the impression of great swiftness, though this species is no faster than any other medium-sized dabbler. Pairs fly in a steady manner, but small flocks form tight clumps that can behave quite erratically. Large flocks fly in messy wedges that are more tightly packed and have more individuals shifting within the flock than do flocks of larger dabblers such as Gadwall or Mallard, without reaching the level of chaos that typifies flocks of teal. Larger clumps often have trailing lines. Migrating flocks typically number 4–20, occasionally larger in the interior. Frequently seen flying with other ducks: Gadwall and Northern Pintail most frequently, but also Mallard, scoters, and even scaup.

APPEARANCE: In all plumages, axillaries and underwing coverts are white or very pale gray and contrast with the gray flight feathers. **Basic Adult Male:** Striking. The face is tricolored: white crown, broad green eye stripe, and cold gray throat and neck. The bill is pale blue, which allows it to blend into almost any background. The chest and flanks are peachy orange to pinkish and contrast sharply with the throat. The white belly expands to wrap around the "hips" just in front of the black rump. The upper surface of the wing has a large oval white patch that gleams and flashes in flight. **Adult Female:** Cold gray head and throat contrast sharply with the more warmly colored breast and flanks, which range from orange-brown to a rich rust. The belly is white, and the wings are plain brown with a narrow but obvious white greater covert bar. **Alternate Adult Male:** Like female, but chest and flanks are typically a richer, mottled rust color. The bold white wing patch of basic plumage is retained. **First-cycle Male:** Like female or alternate adult male. Has a wing patch like adult male, but the white is clouded with gray so it does not stand out as on the adult. A few adult females also show this pattern. By spring, much like basic adult male but maintains the clouded upperwing patch. **First-cycle Female:** Like adult female but drabber overall with a completely plain upperwing. **Distant:** Fairly nondescript pale brown overall but with a bright white, crisply defined belly. The white ovals on the upperwings of male are obvious but may appear only in flashes because of the slightly rocking flight style. The greater covert bar of adult female is clearly visible at moderate distances. At great distances the impression of white on the female's wing remains clear, though the exact pattern is hard to discern.

SIMILAR SPECIES: Eurasian Wigeon: All plumages except adult males should be separated with great caution. See Eurasian Wigeon account for more information. **Gadwall:** Similar in size but is deepest at the chest whereas the belly is flat, creating a leaner, more athletic appearance. Also has a longer, thinner neck and broader wings, and its flight is steadier and more Mallard-like. Both Gadwall and American Wigeon have a pale belly and axillaries, but these regions appear dull and subdued in Gadwall whereas they shine brightly in American Wigeon. **Wood Duck:** Like American Wigeon, has a long tail, deep wingbeats, and a large rounded head. Wood Duck's soft quality to the wingbeats caused by flexible wingtips, broader and more rounded wings, and darker overall color serve to separate it from American Wigeon. Wood Duck also tends to look long and rangy, whereas American Wigeon is plump and compact. Both species form oval-shaped clumps, but Wood Duck flocks hold their shape and show minimal movement of individuals within the flock. Small flocks of wigeons tend to be more tightly packed and often change shape. **Greater Scaup:** Similar in size and head shape but more compact, deepest at the chest rather than the belly, and has shorter, slimmer wings and faster wingbeats. The darker head and chest and long white stripe along the trailing edge of the wing, if visible, eliminate wigeon. **Lesser Scaup:** Same differences as Greater Scaup but even smaller, with a smaller head, faster wingbeats, and shorter, less distinct wing stripe.

ADULT MALES. NORTH DAKOTA, MAY. CAMERON COX.

- Head is large, appearing slightly puffy, and has either a rounded or slightly squared-off shape, depending on posture.
- Body tends to look rounded and tapers into a long, sharply pointed tail.
- Male on the left is an uncommon variant known as "white-faced" or "storm" wigeon.

NEW JERSEY, NOV. KEVIN KARLSON.

- Flocks tend to bunch up like those of small ducks and, at a distance, look paler brown than the species most similar in size and silhouette: Gadwall and Wood Duck.
- Wings are set forward on the body and are slim, with a sharply pointed hand.
- From a distance, the head tends to look boxy, whereas at close range it often looks rounded.

WITH BLUE-WINGED TEAL. FLORIDA, JAN. CAMERON COX.

- The males' wing patches flash bright white even at tremendous distances; often the white greater covert bar running down the wing of adult females is also conspicuous, as darker areas border it on both sides.
- The teal are smaller and have a noticeably slimmer build.

PAIR WITH TWO NORTHERN SHOVELER (TOP). LOUISIANA, JAN. KEN BEHRENS.

- Although dissimilar up close, these species are similar enough in size to cause momentary confusion at a distance.
- Note the different distribution of pale and dark areas, as these are the only aspects of the plumage visible at great distances.
- Along with Snow Geese, there are also Northern Pintail and more Northern Shoveler in the background.

WITH TWO BLUE-WINGED TEAL. FLORIDA, JAN. CAMERON COX.

- The black bills of the teal are clearly apparent and seem like part of the head shape, whereas the wigeons' pale bills are barely apparent.

ADULT MALE. TEXAS, JAN. KEN BEHRENS.

- American Wigeon has bright white underwing coverts, whereas those of Eurasian Wigeon are dull gray.
- The pale bill, particularly on males, disappears at a distance, emphasizing the rounded head shape.

WITH ONE FEMALE NORTHERN PINTAIL (R). UTAH, JAN. KEN BEHRENS.

- American Wigeon are less colorful at a distance, but they never look completely uniform because of their white belly, which always creates some degree of contrast.
- Northern Pintail, especially females, often appear uniform at a distance, but they have a unique structure.

WITH TWO GADWALL (UPPER R). NEW JERSEY, DEC. KEN BEHRENS.

- Pudgy body and slender, pointed wings of wigeon create a subtly unique silhouette.
- Gadwall are similar, but the wings are broader, the tail is squared off, and the neck is longer and slimmer, though at this angle the head shapes are misleading.

WITH THREE MALLARD (ONE FAR L AND TWO AT C). UTAH, JAN. KEN BEHRENS.
- Mallard is larger overall but with a similarly sized head, hence the large-headed look of American Wigeon.
- Compare wing shapes; Mallard has broader wings that are not as swept back.

NEW JERSEY, NOV.
CAMERON COX.
- Flocks are remarkably agile in flight.
- Males are very vocal, giving a loud, distinctive wolf whistle.
- *Four of these birds are males in basic plumage. What are the age and sex of the second bird from the right?*

EURASIAN WIGEON
Anas penelope
DIMENSIONS
L: 20 in.; WS: 32 in.; WT: 1.6 lb.

SPRING ARRIVAL

(vagrants): NE: mid-Mar.;
s. ON: late Mar.; ME: late Mar.

FALL ARRIVAL

NJ (vagrants): late Sept.;
s. ON: late Sept.; NC: early Oct.

This regular vagrant from the Old World can occur anywhere in North America but is most frequently seen in the Northeast and particularly the Pacific Northwest. It usually occurs in the company of American Wigeon. Adult males are distinctive, but birds in other plumages are difficult to separate from American Wigeon, especially in flight. Males are quite vocal in flight, giving a loud, piercing, single-note whistle.

SIZE: Slightly smaller than American Wigeon.

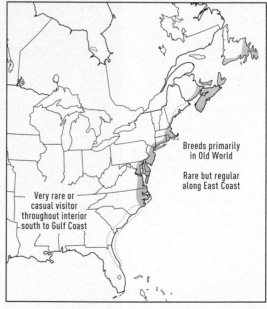

Breeds primarily in Old World

Rare but regular along East Coast

Very rare or casual visitor throughout interior south to Gulf Coast

STRUCTURE: Virtually identical to American Wigeon but averages smaller-headed and slightly shorter-tailed.

FLIGHT AND FLOCKING: Same as in American Wigeon. Almost always seen with American Wigeon in North America.

APPEARANCE: In all plumages the axillaries and underwing coverts are uniformly gray, though in bright light the axillaries can appear pale. **Basic Adult Male:** Similar to American Wigeon in pattern but with a different color scheme: a bright rufous head with a yellowish crown and pale gray back and flanks. **Adult Female:** Averages browner and warmer overall than American Wigeon, particularly on the head. The head, breast, and flanks are more uniform in color than on American Wigeon. The upperwing lacks distinct markings. **Alternate Adult Male:** Full alternate individuals are uniformly rusty brown with white secondary coverts, but often show some scattered gray patches on the body. **First-cycle Male:** Typically significantly duller than alternate male but slightly brighter than adult female. Unlike first-cycle male American Wigeon, has mostly grayish secondary coverts with ragged white tips that form a white bar in the center of the wing, like that of adult female American Wigeon but less distinct. By the first spring, has acquired a brighter plumage, much like that of basic male but duller, with grayish secondary coverts. **First-cycle Female:** Like adult female but drabber overall. The brown head and body are often paler and grayer, more like that of American Wigeon. The greater secondary coverts have small white tips that create a thin pale bar running up the center of the wing, though this is often difficult to detect in flight. **Distant:** Colorful males can be picked out in good light, but other plumages similar to those of American Wigeon.

SIMILAR SPECIES: American Wigeon: Virtually identical structurally, though with a larger, more rounded head. This is not enough to clinch identification, but observers should look carefully at any oddly small-headed wigeon. Adult males are easily separated by plumage characteristics; however, separating females, particularly first-cycle female Eurasian Wigeon from non-adult male American Wigeon, is a challenge. If possible, note the color of the axillaries, which are evenly gray in all plumages of Eurasian Wigeon and bright white in American Wigeon. First-cycle male Eurasian Wigeon will always be largely rusty brown, whereas female American Wigeon has pinkish or orangish flanks with a dull gray head. Dull female Eurasian Wigeon are separated from American Wigeon by their uniform head and breast with no contrast between head and breast or breast and flanks. The existence of hybrids adds more uncertainty to the issue, and possible flyby female-type Eurasian Wigeon are probably best left unidentified in the absence of photos that show the details of the head and underwing.

TWO ADULT MALES AND TWO FEMALES. WALES, MAR. KEN BEHRENS.
- The female leading the flock clearly displays the solid gray underwing that separates it from American Wigeon.
- Both females have dull brown heads that blend seamlessly into the brown chest.

WITH MALE AMERICAN WIGEON (C) AND GADWALL. SWEDEN, APR. TOMMY HOLMGREN.
- Differences in head color between males of the two wigeon species are striking even at a distance.
- American Wigeon has a larger, more rounded head.
- *How many Gadwall are there?*

MARYLAND, JAN. FIRST-CYCLE
MALE (LEFT) WITH ADULT MALE
AMERICAN WIGEON.
DAVID A. PALMER.
• After mid-winter, most
first-cycle wigeon of
both species look
almost like adult males
but retain a smaller and
duller wing patch,
unlike the large,
brilliant white wing
patch of adult males.

SWEDEN, APRIL. KEN BEHRENS
• Eurasian Wigeon share
the plump, rounded
bodies and slim,
angular wings of
American Wigeon but
have slightly smaller
heads.

NORTHERN SHOVELER
Anas clypeata
DIMENSION
L: 19 in.; WS: 30 in.; WT: 1.3 lb.

SPRING ARRIVAL

MO: early Mar.; WI: mid-Mar.;
s. ON: mid-Mar.; MB: mid-Apr.

FALL ARRIVAL

NJ: late Aug.; AR: late Aug.;
w. Gulf Coast: late Aug.

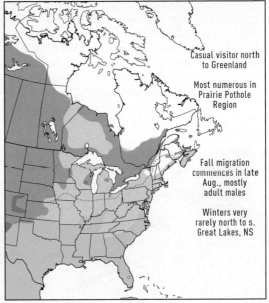

Casual visitor north
to Greenland

Most numerous in
Prairie Pothole
Region

Fall migration
commences in late
Aug., mostly
adult males

Winters very
rarely north to s.
Great Lakes, NS

This colorful dabbler takes its name from its highly modified bill which allows it to strain small organisms out of the water. This distinctive bill makes identification of the species straightforward. Like its close relative Blue-winged Teal, Northern Shoveler moves north late in spring and south very early in fall, and the two are often seen together on migration.

SIZE: Smallest of the medium-sized dabblers. Slightly smaller than American Wigeon. Distinctly larger than Blue-winged Teal.

STRUCTURE: Structure is dominated by the large scooplike bill that is held angled downward, whereas the head is slightly raised. The neck is long and fairly stout, and the head is virtually indistinguishable from the neck, causing the species to look even more long-necked and emphasizing the distinctive bill. The body is long and slim but bulges slightly in line with the leading edge of the wings and then tapers back to the tail, giving an athletic impression. The wings are long and angular, cut back at the wrist, and sharply pointed.

FLIGHT AND FLOCKING: Rapid wingbeats create the impression of swift, powerful flight. Generally steadier in flight than teal or wigeon. Small groups of 4–12 are typical, though flocks may grow to more than 100. Typical flock structure is tight, usually with a small knot of birds leading the flock. Large flocks may form neat lines but more typically form messy clumps, though some short, straight lines may occur within the clumps. Individuals often change location within the flock, like Blue-winged Teal do, but they do so more slowly and with greater control. Unlike teal, they occasionally hold a rigid line for a long period. Readily flocks with Blue-winged Teal and infrequently with other dabblers. Large flocks are often monospecific in the fall but usually include Blue-winged Teal in the spring, when the migration timing of these two species overlaps to a greater degree. Occasionally joins other ducks, including scoters.

APPEARANCE: Basic Adult Male: Striking. The bright white chest contrasts with the bold green head, black bill, and reddish belly. Bright, golden eye visible at close range in both basic and alternate adult males. An extensive powder blue patch on the upperwing is separated from the dull green speculum by a strong white greater covert bar. Among dabblers, the white chest is shared only with Northern Pintail. **Adult Female:** Light grayish tan overall with a paler chest and belly that show warmer tones. The bill is largely black with narrow, bright orange edges. The underwing is bright white; the upperwing is mostly gray with a narrow white bar running up the middle of the inner wing, similar to that of adult female American Wigeon. **Alternate Adult Male:** Like female but more richly colored, with more reddish tones on the body and a stronger wing pattern. This is the plumage worn by most males during fall migration. **First-cycle Male:** Early in the first fall appears similar to adult female, but with a wing pattern more like an adult male's. Over the winter, plumage begins to resemble that of adult male, but with patches of brown barring, particularly on the breast. **First-cycle Female:** Like adult female but duller and paler with a narrower white bar on the upperwing. **Distant:** Basic males appear almost black and white. However, most fall migration occurs when males are in alternate plumage and, like females, are warm tan overall with bright white underwings. Flocks in the fall have this pale brown aspect, whereas spring flocks are a mixture of pale brown and the dark and white of basic males.

SIMILAR SPECIES: The oversized bill makes identification straightforward at all but the longest distances. **Northern Pintail:** Similar overall color scheme and long neck can create confusion at great distances. Tends to fly higher and in more precise lines. Also appears slimmer and more balanced, with wings that are centered on the body. Has dull gray underwings, whereas Northern Shoveler shows pale flashes as the wing is raised.

THREE ADULT MALES, FIRST-CYCLE MALE (LEAD), ADULT FEMALE (C), AND FIRST-CYCLE FEMALE (LAST). UTAH, JAN. KEN BEHRENS.
• Midsized duck of moderate length with an exceptionally large bill and slim wings.
• Winter and late-fall flocks are quite varied in appearance; the three adult males shown here are still undergoing their prebasic molt that began in fall.

WITH BLUE-WINGED TEAL. TEXAS, APR. CAMERON COX.

- Typical flock of migrants along the Gulf Coast in spring. Pure flocks of Northern Shoveler are slightly more organized, and those of teal are more tightly packed and ball-shaped. This mixed flock is predictably intermediate.
- Shoveler's blue wing patches are duller than those of teal and do not reflect light as brightly.

ADULT MALE AND FIRST-CYCLE FEMALE (L). UTAH, JAN. KEN BEHRENS.

- Head is slightly raised, and the huge bill is angled downward.
- In early fall, males are mostly brown like this female, but they retain the bright golden eye and brighter wing pattern year-round.

UTAH, JAN. KEN BEHRENS.

- At great distances the bill and head merge into the long neck, creating a pintail-like impression.
- Flocks are less organized than those of Northern Pintail, though more orderly and spread out than those of small ducks.
- Wings are more angular, pointed, and shorter than those of Northern Pintail.

TWO ADULT MALES AND A FEMALE. UTAH, JAN. KEN BEHRENS.
- Distinctive scooplike bill dominates the silhouette.
- The head barely expands out of the neck and at a distance often looks like part of the neck.

FOUR ADULT MALES AND ONE FEMALE. UTAH, JAN. KEN BEHRENS.
- At a distance, males appear to have a dark head and body separated by a broad white band.
- Among dabblers, only male Northern Pintail share the shoveler's dark head and white breast, but they lack the dark belly.

FIRST-CYCLE FEMALE. UTAH, JAN. KEN BEHRENS.
- Overall coloration of females is similar to that of female Northern Pintail, thus early-fall flocks of these two species can look similar in overall color.

WITH THREE COMMON GOLDENEYE AND THREE BARROW'S GOLDENEYE. UTAH, JAN. KEN BEHRENS.
- In general, diving ducks look bulkier than dabblers, which can drastically affect how size is perceived; the goldeneyes appear heavier, but the shoveler seems longer in the wings and body.

BLUE-WINGED TEAL
Anas discors
DIMENSIONS
L: 15.5 in.; WS: 23 in.; WT: 13 oz.

SPRING ARRIVAL

w. Gulf Coast: late Feb.; Dakotas: late Mar.;
s. Great Lakes: late Mar.; ME: late Mar.

FALL ARRIVAL

KY: mid-Aug.; n. TX: mid-Aug.;
Gulf Coast: mid-Aug.

This sharp-looking species is the longest-distance migrant among North American waterfowl. The bulk of the population travels to northern South America, though many winter along the Gulf Coast. Blue-winged Teal are among the latest dabblers to move north in spring and the earliest waterfowl to head south in fall. Although most birders associate the Gulf Coast with warbler migration, the spring hordes of migrating Blue-winged Teal along the coasts of Texas and Louisiana can be almost as impressive.

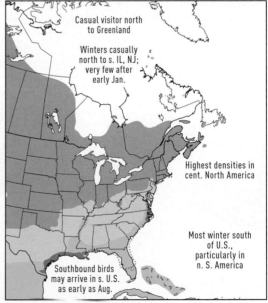

Casual visitor north to Greenland

Winters casually north to s. IL, NJ; very few after early Jan.

Highest densities in cent. North America

Most winter south of U.S., particularly in n. S. America

Southbound birds may arrive in s. U.S. as early as Aug.

SIZE: Small. Clearly smaller than Northern Shoveler. Only slightly larger than Green-winged Teal. Similar to Lesser Scaup.

STRUCTURE: Despite the small size, a long, lean shape causes this species to appear modestly large in flight. The head is small, barely expanding out of the neck, and is generally held slightly above the body. The wings are slim and set just ahead of center, though the long neck and bill balance the impression. Overall the silhouette is generic, like Gadwall's but slimmer.

FLIGHT AND FLOCKING: Very fast wingbeats and swift, agile flight. Typically flies at low to medium heights. Over the ocean, sometimes skims the waves, though it flies higher than Green-winged Teal on average. Usually moves in tightly packed flocks of 4–80 that shift direction frequently. Flocks can swell to several hundred birds, and these large flocks tend to maintain a fairly consistent shape despite the constant shifting of individuals within them. Often associates with Northern Shoveler when migrating along the Gulf of Mexico. Also frequently joins Green-winged Teal, and rarely scoters.

APPEARANCE: Basic Adult Male: Steel blue head marked with a bold white crescent. When seen well, the body is a dingy gold color and covered with black dots and bars, but in flight it usually just looks dull brown. The underwing coverts are bright white and contrast strongly with the flanks. The extensive powder blue patch on the upperwing that gives the species its name is set off by a strong white greater covert bar. **Adult Female:** Medium brown overall, with cold tones to the plumage and a pale area around the base of the bill. The upperwing is pale

blue, slightly duller than in the adult male, and the greater covert bar is much thinner. **Alternate Adult Male:** Same as female but retains stronger wing pattern. The vast majority of southbound males are in this plumage. **First-cycle Male:** Same as female during the fall but with a slightly stronger wing pattern. By midwinter virtually identical to basic adult male but slightly duller overall. **First-cycle Female:** Same as adult female, but duller blue upperwing lacks a white border. **Distant:** Generally appears dull gray-brown. In dull light the blue upperwings are not very obvious, but in sunny conditions they reflect light and shine brightly.

SIMILAR SPECIES: Green-winged Teal: Even more "teal-like" than Blue-winged Teal. Smaller and more compact, with shorter, more swept-back wings, faster wingbeats, and tighter flocks that behave more erratically. Lacks the blue upperwing patch of Blue-winged Teal, and the male's head looks blackish. **Gadwall:** Similar in overall structure but larger-headed and with broader, straighter wings and shallower wingbeats. Lacks the blue upperwing patch and has a pale belly that contrasts with the dark flanks. **Mottled Duck:** Flight is ponderous compared with that of frenetic Blue-winged Teal. Mottled is much larger, with broader wings, and is usually seen in pairs that fly more widely spaced than Blue-winged Teal.

NEW JERSEY, SEPT. CAMERON COX.

- Small and slender, with a balanced, unremarkable silhouette.
- Males migrate south in fall in their dull alternate plumage, so fall flocks are uniformly brown, though the powder blue wing patches reflect light and flash paler than the body in bright light.
- *This photo includes three age/sex classes. What are they?*

ADULT MALE AND FIRST-CYCLE FEMALE WITH ONE GREEN-WINGED TEAL (R). FLORIDA, FEB. TOM DUNKERTON.

- Both species are among the smallest ducks, though Green-winged is smaller.
- Blue-winged is larger than Green-winged but appears leaner, with a longer neck and wings.

TEXAS, APR. CAMERON COX.

- Huge flocks migrate along the Gulf Coast.

WITH SIX GREEN-WINGED TEAL. TEXAS, APR. KEN BEHRENS.

- Larger size and clean white underwings make Blue-winged easy to pick out.
- Blue-winged are long and slender, whereas Green-winged look stocky and compact, exaggerating the actual small difference in size.

- Forms small, tight flocks but not as tightly packed or as ball-shaped as flocks of Green-winged Teal. Blue-winged flocks are often very linear.

ADULT MALE, FIRST-CYCLE MALE (L), AND FIRST-CYCLE FEMALE (R). NORTH DAKOTA, MAY. KEN BEHRENS.

- The male's diagnostic white facial crescent is present from early winter through early summer and is visible at great enough distances to be a useful seawatching characteristic in spring.
- Females have a cold gray appearance.

WITH TWO AMERICAN WIGEON (L AND C) AND A TRICOLORED HERON. FLORIDA, JAN. CAMERON COX.

- The wigeon's white underwings are not as bright as the teal's; though subtle, these differences affect how distantly such a trait can be detected.
- When other duck species are not present, even a very different species like this heron can serve to place a distant duck into a size context and greatly aid in identification.

CINNAMON TEAL
Anas cyanoptera
DIMENSIONS
L: 16 in.; WS: 22 in.; WT: 14 oz.

This eye-catching western sibling of Blue-winged Teal is so closely related to it that they hybridize with some regularity. Cinnamon Teal occurs regularly along the Texas coast but is scarce elsewhere in eastern North America. Vagrants in the East occur most frequently along the Gulf Coast to Florida and along the Mississippi corridor, but they have occurred throughout the East, particularly in spring.

SIZE: Slightly larger than Blue-winged Teal. Noticeably smaller than Northern Shoveler.

STRUCTURE: Same as Blue-winged but slightly larger-billed, thicker-necked, and larger-headed.

FLIGHT AND FLOCKING: Same as in Blue-winged Teal. Vagrants are usually in the company of Blue-winged Teal.

APPEARANCE: Basic Adult Male: An absolute showstopper! Deep maroon overall with a glowing red eye, dark rump, and gold highlights on the scapulars and upper back. The wing pattern is identical to

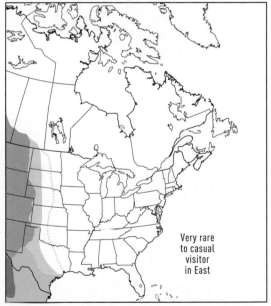

Very rare to casual visitor in East

that of Blue-winged, with powder blue coverts and a bold white greater covert bar. **Adult Female:** Like female Blue-winged but with faint to fairly intense rusty wash and less distinct pale area at the base of the bill. **Alternate Adult Male:** Warm dull brown overall with a plain brown face. Wing pattern is same as in basic. This is the plumage seen during fall migration. **First Cycle:** Like female but slightly duller and colder-toned, consequently more like Blue-winged. **Distant:** Maroon males are unmistakable, but other plumages are like those of Blue-winged.

SIMILAR SPECIES: **Blue-winged Teal:** Adult male is utterly distinctive, but nonadult males are very difficult. In flight and out of range, they are best left unidentified without good photos. Blue-winged has a smaller bill, whereas the bill of some Cinnamon can look almost shoveler-like. Blue-winged also has a slightly smaller head and thinner neck. The overall color of Blue-winged is much colder than that of adult female Cinnamon Teal, but first-cycle Cinnamon can be similar. The face pattern of female Blue-winged is pronounced, almost mirroring the crescent of male Blue-winged Teal, whereas Cinnamon shows a very low-contrast face. Overall these traits do not hold up at a distance and are hard to judge on a fast-moving bird. Hybrids create an additional problem—only basic male hybrids can possibly be identified in flight. Most hybrid males are largely maroon like Cinnamon Teal but have a hint of the white facial crescent of Blue-winged Teal and a blue-gray stripe running behind the eye to the nape.

MALE AND FEMALE. CALIFORNIA, OCT. PETER LATOURRETTE.
- The gorgeous male (L), distinctive at almost any distance, is among the most beautiful of ducks.
- Female has a plainer face than female Blue-winged Teal, along with a larger head, slightly longer bill, and thicker neck.

WITH TWO BLUE-WINGED TEAL, ONE GREEN-WINGED TEAL, AND FIVE NORTHERN SHOVELER. MEXICO, MAR. STEVE MLODINOW.

- Compare the bill shape of Cinnamon Teal to that of Blue-winged and Northern Shoveler. Also compare the silhouettes of male Cinnamon and Blue-winged.
- If such a flock were seen at a distance, the distinct differences in size would immediately suggest at least three species. The unique silhouette of Northern Shoveler and the tiny, compact shape of Green-winged would identify those two species. What ducks fall between these two species in size and have a generic silhouette? Only Blue-winged and Cinnamon Teal! Depending on conditions, separation of the teal might not be possible, but with relatively little information the makeup of the flock can be deduced.
- *In addition to the obvious male, there are two other Cinnamon Teal and one more Blue-winged. Can you find them?*

GREEN-WINGED TEAL
Anas crecca
DIMENSIONS
L: 14 in.; WS: 23 in.; WT: 12 oz.

SPRING ARRIVAL

IA: early Mar.; s. ON: mid-Mar.; MB: early Apr.;
Hudson Bay: late May

FALL ARRIVAL

MO: mid-Aug.; NC: late Aug.;
w. Gulf Coast: late Aug.

This tiny, dapper dabbler is abundant and widespread. Although it prefers freshwater ponds and wetlands for feeding and breeding, it is one of the most common dabbling ducks over the ocean during migration. Green-wingeds move in small, agile, tightly packed flocks that, more than those of any other species of waterfowl, closely resemble flocks of small sandpipers.

SIZE: Very small. Slightly smaller than Blue-winged Teal. Very similar to Bufflehead; the two species compete for the title of smallest duck.

"Eurasian" subspecies rare but regular in migration and winter along Atlantic Coast, casual well inland

•A few may winter north to s. Great Lakes

May appear south of breeding range as early as July

Casual breeder south to KS, NJ

STRUCTURE: Tiny and compact, with an oversized head that is virtually always lifted noticeably in flight. The bill is small and disappears at a distance, causing the head to appear quite square. The body seems too short for the rest of the bird but is otherwise unremarkable and barely factors into the impression of the bird. The wings are narrow and cut back at the wrist, with fairly pointed tips.

FLIGHT AND FLOCKING: Very rapid, almost whirring, wingbeats. Usually seen in small, tightly packed flocks that give the impression of great speed and agility, changing direction with almost whimsical suddenness. They can give an impression similar to that of a flock of sandpipers, but teal cannot quite pull off the synchronized twists and turns of small shorebirds, and the birds in the back of a flock look like they are a half-step off the beat as they gamely try to mimic the actions of their neighbors. Over the ocean, flocks of teal usually skim the water but occasionally rise up to a modest height before plunging back to the surface. Rarely seen singly in flight; most flocks are small, with 3–20 typical and rarely up to 50. Often joins other ducks as singles, pairs, or small flocks. Frequently joins scoters along the Atlantic Coast, though teal are half the size of a scoter. The only ducks that are as small are Bufflehead and Ruddy Duck, but Ruddy Duck is rarely seen in flight and Bufflehead rarely joins scoters, so tiny ducks in flocks of scoter are likely to be Green-winged Teal.

APPEARANCE: Basic Adult Male: Sports a rich chestnut head with an iridescent green slash through the eye, though at a distance this pattern is lost and the bird appears uniformly dark-headed. The uniform gray of the body is broken by a white vertical slash just before the wings and a creamy yellow patch on the side of the rump. The chest is buffy, and the pale belly contrasts sharply with the body. **Adult Female:** Uniformly medium brown with a sharply defined pale belly. **Alternate Adult Male and First Cycle:** Essentially identical to female for flight identification purposes. **Distant:** Flocks appear evenly dark brown but flash pale bellies. Even the gray plumage of basic males takes on a brown appearance within the context of the flock, though they appear slightly darker and their heads are distinctly blackish.

SIMILAR SPECIES: Ring-necked Duck: Can create confusion, as it is somewhat similar in shape and has similar flock structures. Unlike Green-winged Teal, Ring-necked rarely flies low over the water for extended periods. It usually maintains a constant altitude at a moderate height, not rising and falling like Green-winged Teal. Ring-necked is larger, with a heavier body and broader wings that are held quite straight, unlike the swept-back wings of Green-winged Teal. At a distance looks blackish, whereas Green-winged Teal typically looks brown. **Blue-winged Teal:** Slightly larger and appears significantly lankier and longer-necked. Flock structure is looser than in the jam-packed oval-shaped flocks of Green-winged, and Blue-winged flies more constantly at medium height. Blue-winged has blue upperwing coverts and a pale brown belly instead of the whitish belly of Green-winged. **Ruddy Duck:** Much stockier, with shorter, straighter wings and a long tail. Flight is grebelike: heavy and awkward with ultrafast, frantic wingbeats, unlike the sweeping, agile flight of Green-winged Teal.

SUBSPECIES: The nominate race of Green-winged Teal, known as "Common" Teal, is rare but regular in North America, but accurate identification in flight is extremely unlikely except at very close range. This account refers to *A.c. carolinensis*, the only subspecies to normally occur in eastern North America.

WITH SIX BUFFLEHEAD AND TEN BLACK SCOTERS. NEW JERSEY, DEC. KEN BEHRENS.
- Green-winged Teal migrating along the Atlantic are typically seen as a dark flock of tightly packed birds low over the water.
- Occasionally mixes with Bufflehead, which forms similar though slightly less dense flocks; more frequently, both of these species migrate in single-species flocks.
- Groups this size fly alone. Smaller flocks often join scoters but retain their tightly packed structure within the looser scoter flock.

TWO ADULT MALES AND ONE ADULT FEMALE. UTAH, DEC. PAUL HIGGINS.
- The beautiful heads of males look large, blocky, and uniformly blackish at a distance.
- Underwing is mostly dingy gray, unlike the bright white underwing of Blue-winged Teal.

WITH FOUR BLUE-WINGED TEAL, THREE NORTHERN SHOVELER, AND ONE GADWALL. TEXAS, JAN. KEN BEHRENS.
- Tiny and uniformly dark brown, with a flock formation reminiscent of sandpipers, these can only be Green-winged Teal.
- Head is often held noticeably above the body.
- In tightly packed flocks of small ducks, other species are found primarily along the fringes.

WITH SURF AND BLACK SCOTERS. NEW JERSEY, NOV. FRANÇOIS DEWAGHE.

- In fall, Green-winged Teal is the most frequent additional species found in scoter flocks.
- The teal are easily recognized as the only uniformly brown ducks that look half the size of the scoters, though at times their compact subflocks may be hidden by the scoters' massed bulk.

WITH ONE BLUE-WINGED TEAL (BOTTOM C). TEXAS, APR. KEN BEHRENS.

- Underwings of Blue-winged are clean and bright. Those of Green-winged look dirty.

UTAH, JAN. KEN BEHRENS.

- Small but stocky and short-necked, with a slightly oversized head.

WITH ONE BUFFLEHEAD (C). NEW JERSEY, NOV. FRANÇOIS DEWAGHE.

- Most birds in this flock are banking, but not all have gotten the message yet. Small groups resemble sandpiper flocks but cannot quite match their perfectly synchronized maneuvering.
- Even in bright light, the underwings appear dirty and the dark heads of the males stand out.
- The Bufflehead is a first-cycle male with a whiter chest and larger cheek spot than female Bufflehead.

MIXED DUCKS SPECIAL SECTION

FIRST-CYCLE FEMALE (L), ALTERNATE ADULT MALE (C), AND FIRST-CYCLE MALE NORTHERN SHOVELER; AND A FEMALE GREEN-WINGED TEAL. NEW JERSEY, SEPT. CAMERON COX.

- Green-winged Teal (second from R) is tiny, compact, and uniformly dark.
- Northern Shoveler are medium-sized, with narrower, more pointed wings than the similarly sized Gadwall and American Wigeon.

FIVE AMERICAN WIGEON AND A FEMALE GREEN-WINGED TEAL (TOP R). NEW JERSEY, OCT. CAMERON COX.

- American Wigeon have a rounded, slightly pudgy body shape, and their bright white bellies catch the eye at a distance. The teal looks small, compact, and uniform.

TWO RUDDY DUCKS AND A NORTHERN SHOVELER. UTAH, JAN. KEN BEHRENS.

- Although Ruddy Duck is extremely stocky even by diving duck standards, dabbling ducks are typically more slender and appear lighter and more agile than diving ducks, which typically appear stockier and less elegant.

SEVEN NORTHERN SHOVELER AND SIX CANVASBACK. NORTH DAKOTA, MAY. CAMERON COX.

- Canvasback have a distinctive, loonlike silhouette.
- Notice how the scoop-shaped bills of Northern Shoveler are less obvious at this distance and begin to give the birds a long-necked, Northern Pintail–like impression. Look for the slight downward tilt to the bill and the elevated head on the shoveler, emphasizing the smoothly rounded belly, to separate it from Northern Pintail at a distance.

TWO ADULT MALE AMERICAN WIGEON, TWO NORTHERN PINTAIL, AND ONE MALE GADWALL. UTAH, JAN. KEN BEHRENS.
- The slender, elegant shape of the Northern Pintail (C) is obvious, whereas the flashing, oval-shaped white wing patch easily identifies the two adult male American Wigeon (L and R).
- The lowest bird is more difficult. It has a Mallard-like shape but is clearly smaller than the pintail though similar in size to the wigeon. Lack of obvious identifying characteristics is a strong indication of a Gadwall, and the Mallard-like shape and similarity in size to American Wigeon clinch the identification.

SIXTEEN GADWALL, FIVE NORTHERN SHOVELER, AND TWO NORTHERN PINTAIL. TEXAS, NOV. CAMERON COX.
- The silhouettes of the pintail and shoveler should be obvious. The Gadwall are again identified by a combination of their size and Mallard-like structure.

TWELVE NORTHERN PINTAIL AND SIX MALLARD. UTAH, JAN. KEN BEHRENS.
- Only a few ducks are obviously larger than Northern Pintail, and the stocky build, short tail, broad wings, and extensive white underwing clearly point to Mallard. The hint of the white borders to the secondaries serves as a supporting characteristic.

EIGHT NORTHERN SHOVELER, THREE GREEN-WINGED TEAL, TWO NORTHERN PINTAIL, ONE MOTTLED DUCK, AND ONE UNIDENTIFIED (POSSIBLY MOTTLED DUCK X MALLARD HYBRID). TEXAS, APR. KEN BEHRENS.
- Location, size, and dark color identify the Mottled Duck (third from L). The bird three ducks behind the Mottled Duck has Mallard-like characteristics but seems too slender and dark and may be a hybrid. Ducks hybridize somewhat regularly, but it's rarely possible to see the level of detail required to identify a hybrid in flight.

EIGHT NORTHERN SHOVELER AND THREE ADULT MALE NORTHERN PINTAIL. ETHIOPIA, FEB. KEN BEHRENS.
- These two species appear similar at long distances, but Northern Shoveler has a deeper, more rounded belly and white underwings in addition to the differences in head structure.

SEVEN GREEN-WINGED TEAL AND ONE FEMALE LESSER SCAUP (TOP R). NEW JERSEY, NOV. FRANÇOIS DEWAGHE.
- These species are surprisingly easy to confuse at a distance. Lesser Scaup tends to form slightly more spread-out flocks, is slightly larger and rangier, and tends to flash black and white, whereas Green-winged Teal appears uniformly dark.

NINE MALLARD AND ONE AMERICAN WIGEON. NORTH DAKOTA, MAY. KEN BEHRENS.
- *Can you find the American Wigeon? What makes it stand out from the Mallard?*

FOUR LESSER SCAUP AND FOUR COMMON GOLDENEYE. UTAH, JAN. CAMERON COX.
- Note the blocky shape, blunt wings, and oversized head of the Common Goldeneye. Both species show the compact look typical of diving ducks.

ONE MALE NORTHERN SHOVELER, ONE FIRST-CYCLE MALE COMMON GOLDENEYE, AND ONE ADULT MALE LESSER SCAUP. UTAH, JAN. KEN BEHRENS.
- Compare the long wings and slender shape of Northern Shoveler with the shorter, blunter wings and more compact shape of the diving ducks.

SIX GREEN-WINGED TEAL AND THREE CANVASBACK. NEW YORK, MAR. COLIN CLEMENT.

• Canvasback display a degree of sexual dimorphism that is typical of ducks. This can give distant flocks a patchwork appearance. Not all ducks show this variation, however; sexual dimorphism in Green-winged Teal is not noticeable at a distance, resulting in uniformly dark-looking flocks.

TWO GADWALL, ONE AMERICAN WIGEON (SECOND FROM R), AND ONE COMMON GOLDENEYE (L). UTAH, JAN. KEN BEHRENS.

• The head of the female Common Goldeneye seems oversized, which is apparent even at long distances.
• The two Gadwall lack any traits that draw the eye. Few ducks are this plain, and this becomes the primary identification characteristic. The shape is similar to that of Mallard, though the head is smaller and the neck thinner.
• The American Wigeon is in the midst of bobbing its head, something most ducks do in flight, some species more noticeably than others.

SEVEN AMERICAN WIGEON, SIX GADWALL, THREE MALLARD, AND ONE NORTHERN SHOVELER. UTAH, JAN. KEN BEHRENS.
- How to approach a challenging flock like this? First, pick off the easy birds: the huge Mallard and adult male American Wigeon with the obvious white wing patches. Then use the size and shape of the obvious American Wigeon to find the non-adult male American Wigeon. The plain, wigeon-sized, Mallard-like birds must be Gadwall.
- *The Northern Shoveler is a female and is less obvious than a male would be. Can you find her?*

SIX GREEN-WINGED TEAL, THREE RED-BREASTED MERGANSERS, TWO LESSER SCAUP (TOP R), ONE COMMON GOLDENEYE (CENTER L), AND ONE BLACK SCOTER (TOP L). MICHIGAN, OCT. CHRIS NERI.
- With their ultra-skinny shape and twitchy cadence to the wingbeats, Red-breasted Mergansers always stick out in a flock. The tiny, uniform Green-winged Teal provide a clear size reference. The main challenge here is not lumping the Lesser Scaup in with the teal, although their slightly larger size and more contrasting plumage should be apparent. The large size, dark color, and contrasting pale cheek patch identify the Black Scoter, and at this distance the Common Goldeneye is easy.

TWELVE GREEN-WINGED TEAL AND THREE AMERICAN WIGEON. TEXAS, JAN. KEN BEHRENS.
- Green-winged Teal are tiny, with a compact structure. The males have oversized, obviously dark heads.
- Adult male American Wigeon have an obvious bright white oval wing patch. First-cycle males and some adult females have a cloudy, grayish wing patch like the American Wigeon at the center of the photo.
- *There is a single individual of a third duck species in this photo. What is it?*

SEVEN NORTHERN SHOVELER, ELEVEN GADWALL, THREE GREEN-WINGED TEAL, FIVE AMERICAN WIGEON, AND THREE NORTHERN PINTAIL. UTAH, JAN. KEN BEHRENS.

- The uniquely shaped Northern Pintail are the largest birds in this flock. The tiny Green-winged Teal are obviously smaller than all the other birds, so the majority of this flock must be medium-sized ducks.
- The Gadwall appear short-tailed, like Mallard, whereas the American Wigeon have a rounded, pudgy body that tapers into a long, pointed tail.
- At a distance, differences in size become apparent first, then differences in shape, then glimpses of color, with white being the color most easily seen from a distance.

DIVING DUCKS

Several different branches of the waterfowl family Anatidae are loosely grouped together under the name "diving ducks." All members of this large and diverse group share the tendency to catch their prey by diving. They also tend to have proportionally heavier bodies than dabbling ducks and require a running start across the water to take flight. We cover 20 species of diving ducks representing several distinct groups: the *Aythya* or bay ducks, eiders, scoters, the distinctive Harlequin Duck, Long-tailed Duck, the *Bucephala* ducks or goldeneyes, the mergansers, and a single "stiff-tail," Ruddy Duck. One subset of diving ducks is often called the "sea ducks." Sea ducks comprise eiders, scoters, Harlequin Duck, and Long-tailed Duck. Goldeneyes are also sometimes considered sea ducks. Sea ducks tend to be more powerfully built than other diving ducks and winter primarily along the immediate coast, though many are also common in the Great Lakes.

The genus *Aythya*, also known as "bay ducks" or pochards, consists of Greater and Lesser Scaup, which present a well-known identification challenge; Ring-necked Duck; Redhead; and Canvasback. These ducks do often inhabit calm coastal bays, as the group name suggests, but they also frequent fresh water, particularly the Great Lakes, where enormous flocks can sometimes be found. *Aythya* ducks mix readily among themselves but less frequently with other ducks, including scoters and dabbling ducks. They are prone to hybridize with other members of the genus, and the hybrid offspring have a disconcerting tendency to resemble other species of *Aythya;* for example a Ring-necked Duck x Greater Scaup hybrid could superficially resemble a Tufted Duck. For this reason, claims of flyby Common Pochard or Tufted Duck at a seawatch need to be accompanied by excellent photos. Migrating flocks of *Aythya* most frequently fly at medium heights.

Eiders are large, hardy sea ducks found primarily in northern regions. Males are boldly and beautifully patterned, whereas females are garbed in rusty browns and grays. It takes male eiders at least 2 years to reach adult plumage, and during the first cycle in particular, the speed at which individuals acquire the adult appearance varies significantly. Because of this, birds of the same age can be distinctly different in appearance. The variability of immature males, the bold pattern of adult males, and the subtle coloration of females combine to give distant eider flocks a unique, boldly checkered appearance. Migrating eiders usually fly low over

This photo shows two Lesser Scaup, which are diving ducks, and in the center a Blue-winged Teal, a typical dabbling duck. The names of these groups reflect their different manners of foraging, but diving ducks also differ in being more heavily built than dabbling ducks and having proportionally shorter, broader-based wings. North Dakota, May. Ken Behrens.

These striking Harlequin Ducks are a good example of the stocky, compact shape that all sea ducks share. They are built to stand up to constant battering by the ocean. Massachusetts, Jan. Ken Behrens.

the ocean, though in the northern parts of their range they may also fly high in huge flocks.

Along much of the Atlantic Coast, massive flocks of scoters form the heart of the seawatch spectacle. Scoters are large, dark sea ducks. Like eiders, they breed in northern regions, but they winter much farther south than most eiders. Males are black with distinctive markings on the head; females are dark brown; first-cycle birds have a pale belly. There are three species, and they mix readily on migration, forming large, billowing flocks. They are often joined by other species of ducks, and less frequently by other migrating waterbirds such as Brant, cormorants, large alcids, and grebes. Scoters are primarily coastal, but large flocks can be found in parts of the Great Lakes, and small numbers often occur on inland bodies of water, particularly following late fall storms. Migrating scoters usually fly fairly low over the water.

The genus *Bucephala* includes goldeneyes and Bufflehead, all of which are very compact, large-headed, short-winged diving ducks. Males are mostly gleaming white, set off by sharp black markings and a dark iridescent head; females are gray with a dark head. There are two species of goldeneyes—Common and Barrow's—though the eastern population of Barrow's Goldeneye numbers only a few thousand and most birds stay in Quebec year-round. Although the two goldeneyes readily mix, they tend not to join other ducks, though they are occasionally found in scoter flocks. Bufflehead also tend not to join other ducks, though they are less reluctant to do so than goldeneyes. Goldeneyes typically fly at medium height, whereas Bufflehead are usually low.

Mergansers are the lean speedsters of the diving duck group. They are unique in that fish make up a large part of their diet and their slender bills are serrated, which aids in grasping their slippery prey. There are two large mergansers: Red-breasted, which winters mainly along the coast, and Common Merganser, which favors large freshwater lakes and rivers. Hooded Merganser is the outlier in appearance and behavior, being a cavity nester and often using tiny, shallow bodies of water. Mergansers tend to be found in single-species flocks, though Red-breasted and Common Mergansers will mix in locations where both are found. Singles or small flocks of Red-breasted and Hooded Mergansers also sometimes join scoter flocks. Mergansers usually fly at medium height and often show strong fidelity to specific flight lines.

Harlequin Duck is a medium-sized and oddly shaped but beautifully plumaged sea duck in the monotypic genus *Histrionicus*. It winters along rocky coastlines, and the construction of jetties and breakwaters has enabled it to spread south along the Atlantic Coast into areas predominated by sandy shoreline. In the heart of their range, Harlequins fly in short, monospecific lines; farther south they often are seen singly or in scoter flocks. When they join scoters, Harlequins can be very difficult to pick out, as they look like skinny scoters at a distance. Migrating Harlequins fly just above the ocean.

Long-tailed Duck is a medium-sized, distinctively plumaged sea duck in the monotypic genus *Clangula*. Its common name comes from the long spikelike "tail" of adult males. Long-tailed Ducks have several subtly distinctive flight mannerisms

Many male diving ducks have a strong black-and-white pattern that stands out at great distances. Utah, Jan. Ken Behrens.

that allow flocks to be identified when they appear as nothing but tiny dots dancing on the horizon. Singles and small flocks join scoters, but Long-tailed Ducks usually fly in monospecific flocks. Migrating birds tend to skim just above the water.

Ruddy Duck is a small, squat, oddly proportioned duck that seems to be flying on a learner's permit; its ineptitude in flight borders on the comical, and its migrations are almost exclusively nocturnal. It is the only representative of the tribe Oxyurini, known as "stiff-tails." Diurnally, it flies just barely above the water.

Like dabbling ducks, diving ducks form mixed flocks, but they tend to do so on a more limited basis (see the dabbling duck introduction for techniques to sort out mixed flocks). Certain pairs or groups of species often fly together but rarely join other ducks. Mixed flocks of five or six species are rare, whereas dabbling ducks form such flocks regularly. Many species of diving ducks form flocks chiefly or exclusively with fellow members of one of the groups described above. The major exception is scoter flocks, in which virtually any species of waterfowl can be found at times. It seems that single birds or very small flocks would rather join flocks of scoters than fly without the protection and aerodynamic assistance of a large flock. This holds true even for those species that do not typically form mixed flocks.

There is a general tendency among all ducks for larger species to fly in cleaner and more widely spaced flocks, and smaller species in more messy and clumped flocks. When looking for different species in a larger flock, it is helpful to look for "subflocks," as these may consist of ducks of a different species. A subflock is a small clump of birds that consistently maintain a little space between themselves and the rest of the flock while still remaining part of the greater flock. Subflocks can form in any flock of birds but are particularly prevalent in waterfowl and alcids.

The majority of diving duck migration probably occurs nocturnally and at high altitudes. However, the first few hours of the morning during migration often see strong waterfowl movements. It is

The diving ducks comprise several distinct groups. These groups are usually are not difficult to separate; the five scaup in this photo are part of the *Aythya* group and are quite different from the four scoters. At a distance, though, separating Surf from Black Scoter or sorting out members of the *Aythya* clan can be very challenging. This flock contains four Greater Scaup, one Lesser Scaup, two Surf Scoters, and two Black Scoters. New Jersey, Dec. Ken Behrens.

theorized that these morning movements are the continuations of ducks' nocturnal migrations. There are some species, such as scoters, that seem to migrate mainly diurnally, frequently staging strong afternoon movements. The sexes differ in all species covered here. Males show a distinct alternate plumage, sometimes referred to as "eclipse" plumage. Females also have an alternate plumage but it does not change their appearance. Differences between first-cycle birds and adults are apparent initially but are often difficult to detect by the end of the first cycle in most species. By the second cycle most have acquired full adult plumage. The exception is the eiders and Surf and White-winged Scoters, which aquire adult plumage with the third cycle.

Diving ducks generally have shorter wings and stockier bodies than similarly sized dabbling ducks. These Black Scoters show the chunky and even awkward silhouette typical of divers, compared with the more elegant dabbling ducks. New Jersey, Jan. Cameron Cox.

CANVASBACK
Aythya valisineria
DIMENSIONS
L: 21 in.; WS: 29 in.; WT: 2.7 lb.

SPRING ARRIVAL

Lake Erie: late Feb.; WI: early/mid-Mar.;
s. MB: mid-Apr.

FALL ARRIVAL

Upper Mississippi Valley: early/mid-Oct.;
Lake Erie: late Oct.; Chesapeake Bay: late Oct.;
LA: late Oct./early Nov.

This large bay duck possesses an understated elegance and is easily identified by its distinctive structure. One of the least abundant of North American waterfowl, it is highly sought after by birders for its beauty and by hunters for its flavor. Despite the fact that Chesapeake Bay hosts a huge concentration of wintering Canvasback and that half the population winters in the Mid-Atlantic region, this is a surprisingly scarce migrant along the Atlantic Coast.

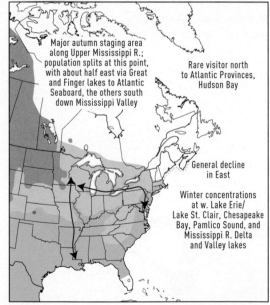

Major autumn staging area along Upper Mississippi R.; population splits at this point, with about half east via Great and Finger lakes to Atlantic Seaboard, the others south down Mississippi Valley

Rare visitor north to Atlantic Provinces, Hudson Bay

General decline in East

Winter concentrations at w. Lake Erie/Lake St. Clair, Chesapeake Bay, Pamlico Sound, and Mississippi R. Delta and Valley lakes

SIZE: Slightly larger than Redhead. Smaller than Mallard. About the same size as Surf Scoter but gives a leaner impression.

STRUCTURE: Bulky but elegant bay duck with a long and sloping bill, long neck, and long, slender wings. The neck always appears to be stretched out to its greatest length, and is surprisingly slender compared with how stout it looks when the bird is swimming. The stretched neck is very loonlike, and like loons, Canvasback can droop its head slightly below the body or elevate it slightly above the body, changing its silhouette. The wings are set forward on the body and have a particularly long, pointed hand. Canvasback holds its wings almost completely straight, giving a very different silhouette from that of most ducks, which display more angular wing shapes.

FLIGHT AND FLOCKING: Among the swiftest of all waterfowl. Wingbeats are fast and deep, with every movement appearing precise and powerful. In flocks, individuals are widely spaced, far more so than in any other bay duck. Even when flying in pairs, individuals keep a fairly large "personal space" buffer. Flocks typically form fairly straight lines in small numbers (fewer than 20), but as flocks grow they become more irregular. Larger flocks often form a messy U or V shape.

APPEARANCE: All have a blackish bill, extensive white underwings, and pale gray upperwings with low-contrast wing stripe. **Basic Male:** The head and neck are deep maroon, with a narrow black breast, creamy white belly and back, and a small black rump. **Female:** The head and neck are pale sandy brown; the breast and body are a slightly darker and colder gray. The belly and underwing are pale gray in dim light but shine silvery white in direct sunlight. **Alternate Male:** Like basic male but slightly duller with a mottled gray back and patchy black and gray breast. **Distant:** Females appear pale gray. Males generally also appear pale gray, with a blackish head, though in good light their bellies and underwings can shine bright white.

SIMILAR SPECIES: Redhead: Easily separated from Canvasback by its large, square head, surprisingly skinny neck, darker coloration, and shorter and stockier overall shape. Redhead flocks tend to bunch up more than Canvasback flocks do, forming clumps with trailing tails or disorganized wedges. **Common Merganser:** Similar structure but has a flatter head, lacking the peaked crown of Canvasback, a shorter neck, and the body is deepest at the "thighs," whereas Canvasback is deepest at the chest. Has faster, shallower wingbeats, and the wings are more swept back. Male shows a strongly contrasting black-and-white pattern; female is darker with white wing patches. As a result, flocks show more contrast overall than fairly uniform Canvasback flocks.

UTAH, JAN. KEN BEHRENS.
• Largest of the *Aythya* ducks, Canvasback is long and lean, with slender wings that are held very straight.
• Unlike other *Aythya*, they usually spread out widely, bunching up only to land and take off.
• Flocks form clean lines that are often slanted but may also be perfectly level.

FOUR MALE CANVASBACK WITH ONE MALE REDHEAD (R). NORTH DAKOTA, MAY. KEN BEHRENS.
- Canvasback is noticeably larger and paler than Redhead. The upperwing of Canvasback is evenly pale gray, lacking the contrast shown by Redhead. The belly and underwing of Canvasback are also evenly pale.

TWO MALES AND TWO FEMALES. UTAH, DEC. PAUL HIGGINS.
- The long, wedge-shaped head is as distinctive at a distance as it is up close.
- The black chest band is narrower than on scaup and Redhead.
- Males appear black-headed at a distance, but flocks are paler overall than those of other *Aythya*.

WITH SIX COMMON GOLDENEYE AND ONE CANADA GOOSE. UTAH, JAN. KEN BEHRENS.
- Whereas dabbling ducks spring up lightly, diving ducks are heavier and must run across the water with wings churning in order to take flight.
- Note the head shapes of the Canvasback and goldeneye, two of the most structurally distinctive ducks.

PAIR. NORTH DAKOTA, MAY. CAMERON COX.

- The immediate impression is almost loonlike. The neck always appears to be stretched to its limit.
- Even pairs maintain large "personal space" buffers.

TWELVE MALES AND ONE FEMALE. NORTH DAKOTA, MAY. KEN BEHRENS.

- Pale, frosty males are distinctive and beautiful.

MALE WITH SIX LESSER SCAUP. FLORIDA, JAN. KEN BEHRENS.

- Scaup are clearly smaller and appear pudgy in comparison.
- Scan back through the photos and observe how many times Canvasback wings are captured straight or nearly straight, and then compare the species to any other duck covered in this guide.

REDHEAD
Aythya americana
DIMENSIONS
L: 19 in.; WS: 29 in.; WT: 2.3 lb.

SPRING ARRIVAL

MI: late Feb.; NE: late Feb.; s. ON: early Mar.;
MB: late Mar.

FALL ARRIVAL

NE: mid-Sept.; MO: mid-Sept.; w. Gulf Coast:
early Oct.; NC: late Oct.

This large, chunky bay duck is intermediate between Canvasback and Greater Scaup in many respects. It uses a wider array of habitats than most bay ducks, reflecting a rather catholic approach to dining. Among ducks, Redhead shows a unique winter distribution. Although it occurs over a large area, the vast majority of birds winter in a small area along the coast of south Texas and northern Mexico in the long, shallow bay known as the Laguna Madre.

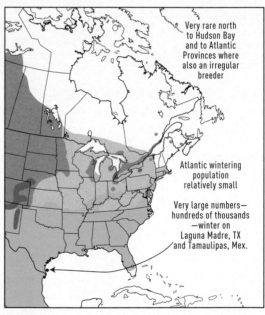

Very rare north to Hudson Bay and to Atlantic Provinces where also an irregular breeder

Atlantic wintering population relatively small

Very large numbers—hundreds of thousands—winter on Laguna Madre, TX and Tamaulipas, Mex.

SIZE: Falls directly between Canvasback and Greater Scaup. Significantly smaller than Mallard.

STRUCTURE: Compact and stocky build makes Redhead appear larger than it really is. The large, boxy head pinches down to a surprisingly skinny neck, and this combination is the key feature for flight identification. The wings are broad for an *Aythya*, with a fairly short, blunt-tipped hand. The body swells markedly right at the belly, and consequently, Redhead appears stockier than any other bay duck.

FLIGHT AND FLOCKING: Shallow, relatively slow wing-beats give the impression of slower flight speed than in any other *Aythya*. Flock structure falls between that of Canvasback and Greater Scaup, with moderate spacing between individuals. Small flocks typically form muddled lines, more tightly spaced than in Canvasback. Large flocks fly in tight wedges or large clumps with long lines extending behind.

APPEARANCE: All show a medium-gray upperwing with a weakly contrasting silvery wing stripe and pale gray underwings. **Basic Male:** Rufous head, brighter than Canvasback, with a pale bill tipped in black. The white belly contrasts strongly with the black breast and rump but blends into the gray flanks. **Female:** Medium brown overall with a dingy white belly. Some show a paler area at the base of the bill and along the throat that is visible in flight. **Alternate Male:** Similar to basic but duller, browner, and darker-billed. **Distant:** Uniformly dull gray-ish at great distances. Slightly closer, the pale belly and underwings are visible, but not striking, and some unevenness of color is visible. Males appear duller gray and slightly paler; females are marginally darker and browner than males.

SIMILAR SPECIES: Canvasback: Similar in color but paler overall, particularly the male with its whitish body. Appears longer and leaner with a longer, thicker neck and longer, tapered head. Also has faster wingbeats and spaces itself out more widely in flocks. **Greater Scaup:** Slimmer overall with narrower, more angular wings, disproportionally thicker neck and smaller head, and faster wingbeats. Flocks are slightly tighter and more clumped. Tends to look distinctly black and white at a distance, whereas Redhead appears uniformly dull gray. At moderate to close range, scaup display a strong white wing stripe, unlike the silvery gray one of Redhead. **Mallard and American Black Duck:** Larger and lankier, with longer, broader-based wings and a longer neck. Wingbeats are slow enough to count. Lacks a contrasting white belly, but the white underwing is visible from great distances, and crisp white borders the speculum.

TEXAS, JAN. CAMERON COX.
• The large, boxy head and surprisingly slender neck are the key characteristics in flight.
• Appears stockier than any other *Aythya* and has broader wings than scaup.

FEMALE (BOTTOM L) WITH TEN LESSER SCAUP. FLORIDA, JAN. KEN BEHRENS.
• Neck of Redhead is slightly longer and thinner than on Lesser Scaup, but head is larger.
• Scaup have much black-and-white contrast, whereas Redhead have little.

TWO MALES AND ONE FEMALE. UTAH, JUNE. KEN BEHRENS.
• The neck almost disappears at a distance, recalling that of Northern Pintail in its slimness, but the head remains large and obvious.

PAIR WITH PAIR OF LESSER SCAUP (UPPER L). NORTH DAKOTA, MAY. CAMERON COX.
• Redhead are larger, with a larger head and longer neck, than scaup.
• Note the sheen on the male Redhead's underwing, which is usually dull; when lit strongly from underneath, as over snow or water on a sunny day, it can glow far more brightly than that of scaup, an unexpected effect that can cause Redhead to be mistaken for Canvasback.

MALE AND FEMALE. NORTH DAKOTA, MAY. CAMERON COX.
• Stocky and broad-winged with blunter wingtips than other *Aythya*.
• Usually shows a bulging belly, but the bulge may be up near the chest, almost behind the wings (as in this female) or in between; regardless of location, it contributes to the bulky impression.

WITH LESSER SCAUP. FLORIDA, JAN. CAMERON COX.
• Even at a moderate distance, the plumage aspects that separate the sexes start fading and uniformity begins to emerge.
• All Redhead have a belly that is pale but dingy and not as obvious as that of scaup.
• Compare the silhouettes of the male scaup at the center to those of the Redhead.
• *How many additional scaup are in this photo? Hint: Some are partially out of the frame.*

GREATER SCAUP
Aythya marila
DIMENSIONS
L: 18 in.; WS: 28 in.; WT: 2.3 lb.

SPRING ARRIVAL

s. Great Lakes: mid-Mar.;
Hudson Bay: late May

FALL ARRIVAL

WI: early Oct.; Long Island: late Oct.;
MO: late Oct.; Gulf Coast: early Nov.

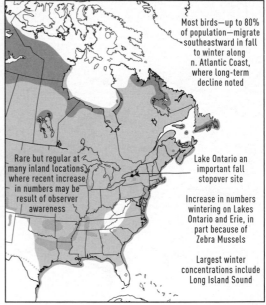

Most birds—up to 80% of population—migrate southeastward in fall to winter along n. Atlantic Coast, where long-term decline noted

Rare but regular at many inland locations, where recent increase in numbers may be result of observer awareness

Lake Ontario an important fall stopover site

Increase in numbers wintering on Lakes Ontario and Erie, in part because of Zebra Mussels

Largest winter concentrations include Long Island Sound

Greater Scaup is the classic bay duck. Although widespread and common, it is most at home in calm coastal estuaries. Greater was formerly considered inseparable from Lesser Scaup in the field. This attitude has changed, though these two species are among the most difficult to separate in flight of any covered in this guide. In fact, their similarity causes them to be lumped when aerial population surveys are conducted, clouding their true abundance, and hunters still lump them under the name "Bluebill." The majority of the North American Greater Scaup population winters on the Atlantic Coast, concentrating in Long Island Sound. Greater typically migrates somewhat earlier in spring and later in fall than Lesser, though there is wide overlap in migration timing.

SIZE: Slightly but discernibly larger than Lesser Scaup. Slightly smaller than Redhead. About the same size as Black Scoter but appears smaller because it is paler.

STRUCTURE: Fairly balanced overall impression with

no outstanding structural features. The head is large with a boxy shape, but the thick neck disguises this fact in flight, resulting in a rather evenly thick head and neck. The body is stout, but Greater lacks the potbelly of Redhead and Lesser Scaup. The wings are slimmer and more angular than those of Redhead and Canvasback, and are slightly more centered on the body.

FLIGHT AND FLOCKING: Wingbeats are rapid but otherwise unexceptional. Flight speed is faster than Redhead's. Migrants are virtually always in flocks, and groups smaller than five will join other species in order to fly with a larger crowd. Larger flocks typically fly at midheight, whereas singles and small flocks stay low. Readily mixes with Lesser Scaup, less frequently with Ring-necked Duck and the larger *Aythya*. Small to medium-size flocks frequently join migrating scoters, though on days of strong movement, large flocks tend to desert the ocean-hugging scoters and fly at a higher altitude. Flock structure is typical of bay ducks: small flocks in oval-shaped clumps or messy lines; larger flocks in wedge-shaped clumps with trailing lines that sometimes resolve into broad Us.

APPEARANCE: In all plumages the wing stripe extends seamlessly from the secondaries onto the inner primaries and may reach almost to the tip of the wing. The wing stripe is more variable than depicted in many guides, and there is overlap in length with some Lesser Scaup. The stripe is also slightly thicker than that of Lesser Scaup, often curving slightly along the upper border, whereas the wing stripe of Lesser Scaup is thin and straight. The thickness of the wing stripe is often more useful than the length,

as it is less variable and causes the wing stripe to be more obvious at a distance. **Adult Male:** A close look shows the head to be iridescent green, but in flight both the head and chest look black, contrasting with the white belly and flanks. The back and upperwing coverts are pale gray. **Adult Female:** Medium brown overall with contrasting pale belly. There is a white ring around the base of the bill that is typically quite broad, though significant individual variation occurs. Many females show a light cheek patch. **First Cycle:** Generally very similar to adult female, but some show a shorter white wing stripe and reduced white around the bill, making structural differences essential in separation from Lesser Scaup. **Distant:** In all but the poorest light conditions, scaup appear largely dark but with white highlights that are clearly discernible. The difference in wing stripe cannot be distinguished with accuracy until moderate range or closer.

SIMILAR SPECIES: Lesser Scaup: Slightly smaller, and the size difference is usually apparent in direct comparison. Thinner neck and slightly more elevated head. Has slightly faster wingbeats and forms tighter flocks that show more movement of individuals within the flock. The wing stripe is usually shorter, thinner, and less apparent at a distance. See *Aythya* special section, page 154, for more information. **Mallard and American Black Duck:** Basic silhouette is similar, but these dabbling ducks are much larger with slower wingbeats and broader wings. **Gadwall:** Silhouette is surprisingly similar, but Gadwall is larger with a longer body and broader wings that are held straight out from the body. It is browner overall, lacking the contrasting black-and-white appearance of scaup.

PAIR. NEW YORK, APR.
KEN BEHRENS.

- In silhouette, the thick neck is one of the only differences from Lesser Scaup.
- The slight peak above the eye and the flat crown shown by this male are also differences from Lesser Scaup. These differences tend to be more striking on males and are not always this obvious.
- Head shape in flight is almost opposite that on the water. In flight, head is flat and boxy in Greater, rounded in Lesser.

WITH FOUR LESSER SCAUP AND ONE RED-BREASTED MERGANSER. NEW JERSEY, DEC. KEN BEHRENS.
- Typical flock formation for Greater Scaup or flocks dominated by Greater: tightly packed but linear. Flocks of Lesser Scaup form bunches.
- The first bird behind the merganser is a Greater and the second is a Lesser, with head and neck shapes clearly differing and wing stripes being more similar than indicated in field guides; they are more different in width than in length. Note size difference.
- *Can you find the other three Lesser Scaup?*

MALES AND ONE FEMALE (BACK C) WITH ONE CANVASBACK (NEAR L). NEW YORK, FEB. COLIN CLEMENT.
- Typically holds neck straighter than Lesser Scaup or lifts it less obviously. Lesser tends to lift its head conspicuously, like Green-winged Teal.

WITH LESSER SCAUP AND RED-BREASTED MERGANSERS. MICHIGAN, OCT. CHRIS NERI.
- Large flocks of both Greater Scaup and Red-breasted Mergansers tend to form wedges. Lesser Scaup does this infrequently on its own but readily adjusts flight style to fly with more regimented species.

(RIGHT) MALES. BRITISH COLUMBIA, MAR. MIKE YIP.

- Scaup tend to fly slightly higher than scoters in most conditions.
- Flocks smaller than this typically fly with scoters, whereas larger flocks tend to fly separately; flocks this size often join scoter flocks, split off, then rejoin the scoters, and so on.

PAIR. NEW YORK, MAR. COLIN CLEMENT.

- Classic head shape and neck thickness on this male easily eliminate Lesser Scaup; the female shows the same distinctive traits almost as strongly.
- The extensive bright white ring at the base of the bill and faint, pale cheek patch are good supporting characteristics for the female, but only the ring around the bill shows up clearly beyond moderate distances.

WITH EIGHT LONG-TAILED DUCKS. ONTARIO, NOV. BRANDON HOLDEN.

- Among *Aythya*, only scaup show strong black-and-white contrast, and it is visible at longer distances on Greater Scaup than on Lesser Scaup.

LESSER SCAUP
Aythya affinis
DIMENSIONS
L: 16.5 in.; WS: 25 in.; WT: 1.8 lb.

SPRING ARRIVAL

IA: early Mar.; ME: mid-Mar.;
Hudson Bay: late May

FALL ARRIVAL

IA: late Sept.; w. Gulf Coast: late Sept./early Oct.;
NJ: mid-Oct.; FL: mid-Oct.

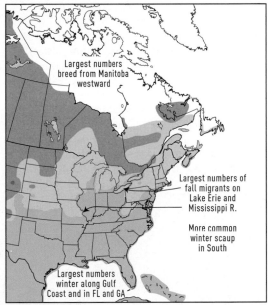

Largest numbers breed from Manitoba westward

Largest numbers of fall migrants on Lake Erie and Mississippi R.

More common winter scaup in South

Largest numbers winter along Gulf Coast and in FL and GA

This smaller cousin to Greater Scaup is equally widespread and abundant though it is more southerly in its distribution. A prevalent assumption about scaup is that Lesser Scaup are found on fresh water and Greater Scaup on salt water. It's true that Greater Scaup prefer salt water, but they use both, particularly during migration, and Lesser Scaup use both extensively. Wherever they are found, it is a good practice to check the identity of scaup rather than assume, because they frequently mix in both habitats. In the fall, Lesser Scaup move south slightly earlier than Greater Scaup, though there is much overlap. In spring the overlap in migration is nearly complete.

SIZE: Slightly smaller than Greater Scaup. Larger than Blue-winged Teal. Almost identical to Ring-necked Duck.

STRUCTURE: Like Greater Scaup, Lesser Scaup has an unremarkable silhouette and appears quite balanced. It gives the impression of being even smaller than Greater Scaup than it actually is. In mixed flocks, Lesser Scaup appears thinner-necked than Greater, though there is some overlap. Although both scaup can elevate their heads above their bodies, this is barely noticeable in Greater but is pronounced in Lesser, recalling Green-winged Teal. Whereas Greater Scaup often shows a slight peak to the crown and a boxy head shape, Lesser virtually always shows a rounded crown, the opposite of how it appears when sitting on the water, and tends to look small-headed.

FLIGHT AND FLOCKING: Flight is agile and swift, quite similar to that of Greater Scaup though Lesser's wingbeats are slightly faster. Larger groups are typically at medium height; singles and small groups fly low, often with scoters or other waterfowl. Flocks are more tightly bunched than those of Greater Scaup, and individuals constantly shift position. Overall flock structure is surprisingly similar to that of Green-winged Teal. Often mixes with Greater Scaup, simplifying identification, but can also occur in flocks with Ring-necked Duck, scoters, Green-winged Teal, and almost any other species of duck.

APPEARANCE: In all plumages has a narrow white stripe that incorporates only the secondaries, though on a minority (mostly adult males), the wing stripe extends into the inner primaries, overlapping in extent with that of some Greater Scaup (mostly females). In bright light, the stripe can appear longer as the strong light intensifies the paleness of the gray stripe on the primaries. The wing stripe is also thinner and straighter on Lesser, a trait that is subtle but is less variable than the length. Adult Male: The true color of the head, an irides-

cent purple, is rarely visible in flight. The head and chest appear blackish, contrasting with the white belly and flanks. The back and upperwing coverts are gray, and the rump is black. Female: Medium brown overall with contrasting pale belly and white ring around the base of the bill. Tends to be darker-headed than female Greater Scaup, with a smaller area of white at the base of the bill. Usually lacks the pale cheek patch shown by many female Greaters. Distant: In all but the poorest light conditions, scaup appear largely dark but with white highlights that are clearly discernible. The differences in wing stripe cannot be distinguished with accuracy until moderate range or closer.

SIMILAR SPECIES: Greater Scaup: Larger, thicker-necked, and usually holds the head straight out from the body. Tends to form more linear flocks than Lesser, with more space between birds and less movement of individuals within the flock. Greater Scaup usually has a longer, bolder wing stripe that is visible at greater distances, and female has a slightly paler, warmer-toned head. See *Aythya* special section, page 154, for more information. Ring-necked Duck: Flocks are uniformly dark, unlike the black-and-white flocks of scaup. Ring-necked Duck has slightly faster wingbeats that appear to be straight up and down. See *Aythya* special section, page 154, for more information. Green-winged Teal: The two species share similar individual and flock structure, but the teal's smaller size and utterly dissimilar plumage are useful identification tools. Flocks of teal look uniformly dark at a distance and solidly brown at closer range, whereas scaup have a contrasting black-and-white appearance even at a distance. The flight style of teal is more erratic than that of scaup, with flocks often twisting back on themselves, like a flock of sandpipers, rising to a moderate height, then diving back toward the surface.

FOUR MALES AND ONE FEMALE (C). NORTH DAKOTA, MAY. KEN BEHRENS.
• Unlike on the water, in flight has a fairly rounded head, which looks small at a distance. The larger, boxy head of Greater Scaup is more visible at a distance.
• Smaller than Greater, with a thinner neck and the head often noticeably lifted above the body.
• Slightly slimmer wings and faster wingbeats than Greater; also less "chesty" than Greater.

TWO MALES AND FOUR FEMALES. UTAH, JAN. KEN BEHRENS.

- Wing stripe is generally bright white along the secondaries but becomes dull gray in the primaries.
- Wing stripe sometimes extends onto the primaries, as on the lead bird. Length and intensity of the wing stripe vary among individuals, and bright light can heighten the appearance of white on the inner primaries.
- *What other species is shown?*

MALE. NORTH DAKOTA, MAY. CAMERON COX.
- Neck is narrow and looks pinched at the base.

FEMALE. OKLAHOMA, DEC. JIM ARTERBURN.
- The wing stripe shining through the wing below is usually visible on Lesser only in photos but can be noticeable in the field on Greater.

WITH TWO BROWN PELICANS. FLORIDA, JAN. KEN BEHRENS.
- Despite a reputation for preferring fresh water, Lessers winter in hordes along the Gulf and Atlantic Coasts of Florida, often seen in flight as they commute or flee from boats. Small numbers of Greater Scaup, scoters, and even Long-tailed Ducks are occasionally found among them.

WITH ONE FEMALE GREATER SCAUP (UPPER R). FLORIDA, JAN. CAMERON COX.
- Greater gives a powerful impression and is clearly larger and bulkier.
- Greater's head is larger, and the white ring at the base of the bill is more apparent. The thick neck enhances the large, boxy appearance of the head.

MICHIGAN, MAY. KEN BEHRENS.
- Even in poor light, has the strongly contrasting overall black-and-white appearance typical of both species of scaup— Greater Scaup slightly more so than Lesser.

FLORIDA, JAN. CAMERON COX.
- Large flocks of *Aythya* ducks (except Ring-necked) fly in wedge-shaped formations during migration.
- Flocks of Lessers tend to contract into chaos and then expand back into a wedge, whereas larger *Aythya* show greater spacing and flock stability.

(LEFT) FLORIDA, JAN. CAMERON COX.

RING-NECKED DUCK
Aythya collaris
DIMENSIONS
L: 17 in.; WS: 25 in.; WT: 1.5 lb.

SPRING ARRIVAL

s. ON: early Mar.; IA: early Mar.; ME: mid-Mar.

FALL ARRIVAL

MO: late Sept.; MD: mid-Oct.;
Gulf Coast: mid-Oct.

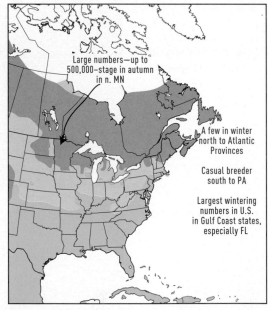

Large numbers—up to 500,000—stage in autumn in n. MN

A few in winter north to Atlantic Provinces

Casual breeder south to PA

Largest wintering numbers in U.S. in Gulf Coast states, especially FL

This small and versatile diver is far less likely than other bay ducks to be found in saltwater bays. It prefers ponds, marshes, and other shallow wetlands, though it also makes use of more open, deeper bodies of water used by other bay ducks. During migration this is the stealth *Aythya*, infrequently seen and often overlooked. It often mixes with flocks of scaup, creating a significant challenge. Skillful seawatchers double- and triple-check flocks of scaup, as singles and small groups of Ringneck in a scaup flock can be easily overlooked.

SIZE: A small diver, slightly larger than Hooded Merganser and Blue-winged Teal. Almost the same size as Lesser Scaup, averaging slightly smaller; when the two species are compared at close range, however, Ring-necked often gives the impression of being slightly larger than Lesser Scaup.

STRUCTURE: Compared with Lesser Scaup, has a slightly larger head, shorter neck that is held straighter, and a body that is shorter but broader with a more prominent bulging belly. The wings are noticeably shorter, slightly broader-based, and held almost straight, unlike the wings of Lesser Scaup, which angle back distinctly at the wrist.

FLIGHT AND FLOCKING: Wingbeats are rapid and slightly stiff, differing from those of Lesser Scaup in several subtle ways. They are slightly quicker and deeper and have a more even up-and-down action. The more angular wings of scaup make their wingbeats appear swept back. Flies quickly, usually at midheight, and tends to look more stable than Lesser Scaup. Migrating flocks are usually small, commonly 5–12 birds in a tightly packed line or oval. Regularly joins flocks of scaup, where it is extremely difficult to pick out, or sometimes other waterfowl, though large flocks tend to be monospecific.

APPEARANCE: In all plumages has dull gray, low-contrast wing stripes and dull gray underwings. **Adult Male:** The chest, back, and upperwings are black, and the head is blackish. The gray bill has a black tip and a subterminal white ring that is difficult to see in flight. The light gray flanks are separated from the breast by a vertical white bar, though at a distance the sides, belly, and underwing all appear off-white. **Female:** Uniformly brown with a darker crown, back, and chest and paler gray face and small pale belly. **Distant:** Despite the pale belly and gray flanks, at a distance both males and females look quite dark. This is unlike flocks of scaup, which flash black and white even at great distances.

SIMILAR SPECIES: Greater and Lesser Scaup: Tend to appear black and white at a distance, whereas Ring-necked appears all dark. Scaup have more angular wings and slightly slower wingbeats. At moderate to close range the well-defined white wing stripe is a diagnostic difference from Ring-necked. See *Aythya* special section, page 154, for more information. **Green-winged Teal:** Similar overall structure and flock structure, but Green-winged Teal is smaller, has a more careening flight style, raised (and often bobbed) head, slimmer and more swept-back wings, and looks brown rather than black overall.

MALES AND FEMALES. FLORIDA, DEC. KEN BEHRENS.
- Flocks look uniformly dark at a distance, whereas scaup show black-and-white contrast.
- Flocks are often more tightly packed than even those of Lesser Scaup.

FLORIDA, DEC. KEN BEHRENS.
- Tight, oval-shaped flocks are typical.
- Unlike other *Aythya*, does not form large wedge-shaped flocks; groups larger than 30 are rare.

FLORIDA, DEC. KEN BEHRENS.
- Wings are slightly shorter and blunter than Lesser Scaup's.
- Wingbeats are almost straight up and down and are slightly faster and deeper than those of scaup.

FEMALE. FLORIDA, DEC. KEN BEHRENS.
- As in Redhead, belly is pale but dingy, contrasting little at a distance and contributing to a uniform appearance.

MALE WITH SEVEN LESSER SCAUP. FLORIDA, JAN. KEN BEHRENS.
- The male Ring-necked (bottom, second from R) is slightly duller looking than the Lesser Scaup, with slightly broader, blunter wings and larger head.
- When backlit, the wing stripe of Lesser Scaup bleeds through, but it never does on Ring-necked; this is usually difficult to observe in the field on Lesser (more evident in photos) but is often obvious on Greater Scaup.

FOUR MALES AND THREE FEMALES. FLORIDA, FEB. KEVIN KARLSON.
- Typical flock: small and tightly packed.
- Nearly identical in size to Lesser Scaup, but Ring-necked's head is larger and its body appears shorter and chunkier, conveying a compact, stocky look.
- Ring-necked has almost as much whitish plumage as scaup, but even at moderate distances it looks dark, whereas scaup are clearly black and white.

FLORIDA, DEC. KEN BEHRENS.
- Silhouettes can be identified without even a glimpse of color. Compare this photo with the photos in the Lesser Scaup and Redhead accounts. In silhouette it is possible to confuse totally dissimilar birds, so it would also be useful to compare Ring-necked to some of the dabbling ducks such as wigeon and Gadwall.
- *What traits definitively separate Ring-necked Duck from the most likely confusion species, Lesser Scaup?*

TUFTED DUCK
Aythya fuligula
DIMENSIONS
L: 17 in.; WS: 26 in.; WT: 1.6 lb.

This widespread Old World species is very similar to both Lesser and Greater Scaup but sports a funky crest. It is a frequent vagrant to North America, most common in the Pacific Northwest but regular in the Northeast and possible anywhere.

SIZE: Slightly smaller than Greater Scaup. Very similar to Lesser Scaup and Ring-necked Duck. Significantly larger than Green-winged Teal.

STRUCTURE: Quite similar to Greater Scaup. As in Greater Scaup, the head looks large and boxy, though the neck of Tufted is slightly thinner and shorter. Like Greater Scaup, Tufted looks almost blunt-fronted, especially at distances where the bill disappears, whereas Lesser Scaup looks round-fronted. Both sexes have a tuft at the back of the head, males a large one and females one that is much reduced. Although this tuft is usually depressed in flight, it still contributes to the bird's big-headed look, and when it is lifted off the back

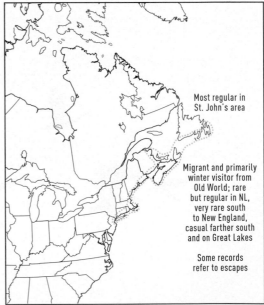

Most regular in St. John's area

Migrant and primarily winter visitor from Old World; rare but regular in NL, very rare south to New England, casual farther south and on Great Lakes

Some records refer to escapes

of the neck, it renders the silhouette unmistakable. The wings are slightly narrower and the hand more sharply pointed than those of scaup.

FLIGHT AND FLOCKING: Very similar to that of both scaup. Like Lesser Scaup, Tufted Duck often raises its head, and sometimes even bobs it, something that Greater Scaup rarely does. Usually seen with scaup in North America.

APPEARANCE: Generally similar to scaup. In all plumages shows a bright white stripe through the primaries and secondaries that runs almost to the leading edge of the wing. **Male:** The head and chest are very dark, contrasting with the pure white belly and flanks. The iridescent purple of the head is rarely visible in flight. The back and upperwing coverts are uniformly black. **Female:** More uniformly dark brown than female scaup, with a bright white belly. Most show very little white at the base of the bill, though an occasional bird will display a female scaup–like pattern. **Distant:** Even more sharply black and white than scaup.

SIMILAR SPECIES: Greater Scaup: Shares the general structure of Tufted Duck and the extensive white wing stripe. Although its head is large and boxy, it lacks the tuft, which is diagnostic for Tufted when seen. Greater Scaup also has a slightly longer, thicker neck, which makes its big head less obvious. It is slightly paler overall, with a barred gray back as opposed to the solid black or dark brown back of Tufted. Separation of these species in flight should be undertaken with caution, especially at distances where it is difficult or impossible to distinguish the crest of Tufted. **Lesser Scaup:** Quite similar to Tufted in structure, though the head is smaller and rounded instead of boxy, and lacks the tuft. The wing stripe of Lesser Scaup is variable but typically consists of a bright patch on the secondaries followed by a dull gray stripe on the primaries, with some contrast between the two. Tufted has a stripe that is bright throughout, with no internal contrast. **Ring-necked Duck:** Structurally similar but generally appears smaller and more compact. Has a thinner neck and smaller head that lacks a tuft. At most distances and in most lights, the dull gray wing stripe of Ring-necked will separate it from Tufted.

PAIR. WALES, APR.
KEN BEHRENS.

- Much like scaup in appearance but like a small-headed Ring-necked Duck in structure: stocky and short-winged.
- The tuft is held close to the head in flight and is unfortunately difficult to observe, as it is an important trait for identifying this species out of range.

MALE WITH TWO MALE GREATER SCAUP (L). NEWFOUNDLAND, DEC. CORY GREGORY.
- Hand is a little more pointed, underwing cleaner, head smaller, and wing stripe slightly stronger than in Greater Scaup, but the likelihood of identifying a flyby Tufted is pretty low.

AYTHYA SPECIAL SECTION

FOUR GREATER SCAUP AND ONE LESSER SCAUP (SECOND FROM R) WITH TWO SURF SCOTERS AND TWO BLACK SCOTERS. NEW JERSEY, DEC. KEN BEHRENS.

- Greater Scaup is similar to Black Scoter in size but appears slightly slimmer. Lesser Scaup is noticeably smaller than Black Scoter.
- Scaup can blend into large flocks of scoters surprisingly well but can be picked out by their slimmer shape. They also tend to show flashes of white in places where scoters do not.
- Small flocks of scaup often split away from a scoter flock and fly on their own slightly above the scoters before eventually rejoining the scoters.

TWELVE LESSER SCAUP AND ONE FEMALE GREATER SCAUP (C). FLORIDA, JAN. KEN BEHRENS.

- A flock that contains a female scaup that is obviously larger than nearby male scaup will consist of a female Greater in a flock of Lessers.
- The slightly thicker neck of Greater Scaup can be detected in flight but is a subtle distinction.
- Greater has a wing stripe that is broader, not just longer, than that of Lesser.
- The male Lesser directly above the female Greater is a lesson in why it is best to rely on multiple characteristics, not just the wing stripe.

TEN GREATER SCAUP AND TWO LESSER SCAUP (LOWEST BIRDS). NEW JERSEY, DEC. KEN BEHRENS.

- Bolder wing stripe and slightly more contrasting plumage allow Greater Scaup to be identified in poor light at distances where it would be difficult to identify Lesser Scaup.

FEMALE LESSER SCAUP (L) WITH FEMALE GREATER SCAUP. FLORIDA, JAN. CAMERON COX.

- In direct comparison, the differences in structure are obvious.
- The larger white ring at the base of the bill is a useful trait for adult female Greater Scaup.
- The higher peaked forehead of Greater creates a boxy appearance to the head, whereas Lesser appears more round-headed.

FEMALE LESSER SCAUP (L) AND RING-NECKED DUCK. NEW JERSEY, NOV. FRANÇOIS DEWAGHE.
- Lack of a noticeable wing stripe is one reason why Ring-necked Duck appears dark at a distance, whereas both scaup typically show flashes of white.
- Note how Ring-necked holds its wings straighter.

GREATER SCAUP WITH FOUR REDHEAD. NEW YORK, FEB. COLIN CLEMENT.
- Redhead is slightly larger and huskier than Greater Scaup.
- Neck of Redhead is pinched in, emphasizing the large head that has an even more pronounced boxy shape than Greater Scaup's.

FIVE GREATER SCAUP AND ONE FEMALE LESSER SCAUP. OKLAHOMA, NOV. JIM ARTERBURN.
- Seen from below, the wing stripe bleeds through the secondaries of Greater Scaup much more strongly. A scaup that shows such obvious wing stripe "bleed" in the field it is almost certainly a Greater.
- On the upperwing of Greater, the wing stripe tends to curve slightly along the upper border, whereas the wing stripe of Lesser is narrow and more straight.

EIGHT LESSER SCAUP AND ONE GREATER SCAUP (UPPER R). FLORIDA, JAN. CAMERON COX.
- At times, the larger size, heavier build, and more contrasting pattern of Greater Scaup allow it to stand out clearly from Lesser, but the distinction can also be very subtle, and impossible to discern at long distances.

FOUR CANVASBACK AND TWO REDHEAD (L). UTAH, JAN. KEN BEHRENS.
• Canvasback is clearly larger than Redhead and has an elegant shape unlike that of any of the other North American *Aythya* ducks.

THREE CANVASBACK AND TWO REDHEAD. NORTH DAKOTA, MAY. KEN BEHRENS.
• Redhead is short-tailed and stocky, with broad-based wings; it has a Mallard-like, typical duck structure.
• Long neck; sloping, lean shape; and wings set forward on the body give Canvasback a unique loonlike shape.

FIVE LESSER SCAUP AND ONE FEMALE GREATER SCAUP. FLORIDA, JAN. CAMERON COX.
• Lesser Scaup often raises its neck noticeably so the head is held slightly above the body. Greater Scaup does this as well, but the thicker neck masks the elevated head and makes it far less obvious.

ELEVEN GREATER SCAUP AND ONE LESSER SCAUP WITH ONE HOODED MERGANSER. OKLAHOMA, NOV. JIM ARTERBURN.
• After identifying the majority of this flock as Greater Scaup, it would be easy to shift attention to the Hooded Merganser at the back and completely miss the female Lesser Scaup near the front.
• Once you've identified the majority of a flock of scaup, it is good practice to go back through the flock looking for "stealth" members of the other scaup species and for Ring-necked Duck, which can sometimes be found even after several rounds of scrutiny.

COMMON EIDER
Somateria mollissima
DIMENSIONS
L: 24 in.; WS: 38 in.; WT: 4.7 lb.

SPRING ARRIVAL

NL: late Mar.; w. Hudson Bay: early Apr.

FALL ARRIVAL

MA: early Oct.; NJ: late Sept./early Nov.
(two pulses); VA: early Nov.

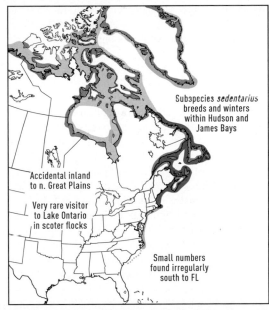

Subspecies *sedentarius* breeds and winters within Hudson and James Bays

Accidental inland to n. Great Plains

Very rare visitor to Lake Ontario in scoter flocks

Small numbers found irregularly south to FL

This hardy resident of the far north is the largest duck in North America. It is a strictly coastal species, with few modern records in the interior. It was formerly regular on the Great Lakes but has become extremely rare there. Common Eider is so abundant as to seem an inseparable part of the coasts of New England and eastern Canada. It is far less common as a wintering species south of Long Island, and quickly becomes rare south of Delaware Bay. Tremendous migrations of this species occur in northern Europe, where it the dominant species of migrating waterfowl, similar to scoters on North American coasts, with many species joining its im-

mense flocks. The same phenomenon seems to occur in the Atlantic Provinces and Arctic Canada but is less well documented.

SIZE: Massive. The largest duck, exceeding small geese such as Ross's and Brant in overall size, though it is not as long-winged as geese. Clearly larger than other large ducks, such as King Eider, White-winged Scoter, and American Black Duck.

STRUCTURE: Manages to impart a sense of great size and weight while still appearing fairly sleek. Like Surf Scoter, it distributes its weigh over a long, oval-shaped body, though some appear to have a Common Loon–like hanging paunch. The thick neck supports the huge anvil-shaped head with a long sloping forehead that is discernible at incredible distances. Females are slightly slimmer; most have the same sloping forehead as the males, but some appear decidedly smaller-headed, with a more concave forehead profile, and can be confused with King Eider. The wings are very broad, slightly angled back at the wrist, and fairly pointed considering their breadth.

FLIGHT AND FLOCKING: The slow, heavy wingbeats communicate from any distance the size and bulk of this enormous diving duck. Small flocks typically form organized, horizontal lines with roughly a full bird's length separating each member of the flock. Larger flocks may form Vs or bunches with long lines trailing behind and tend to be less widely spaced. In the northern parts of the range, flocks of multiple hundreds may be seen, but 5–50 are normal farther south. Usually seen close to the water in winter and in fall migration. At northern latitudes may fly quite high, even crossing land, particularly in spring.

APPEARANCE: Basic Adult Male: Creamy white face, breast, and back, with a small black crown and a pale horn-colored bill fading into dull green or yellow frontal lobes. The upperwing coverts form a white wedge halfway out the wing, contrasting with the black primaries and primary coverts. The belly is jet-black, contrasting with a small pale triangle on the underwing and separated from the breast by a sharp line. **Adult Female:** Evenly brown overall, but the color varies from bright reddish brown to a dull pale brown on older females. The bill is dark with a pale tip. The only noticeable bit of color is the pale axillaries, which are easily seen from a distance when the wings are raised. **Alternate Adult Male:** Like ba-

sic except the white chest is marred with extensive brown mottling and can appear almost wholly dark on some individuals, and the white areas of the face become mostly gray or brownish. **First-cycle Male:** Incredibly variable in fall. Mostly blackish with a yellow bill and patchy white chest. As winter progresses and molt progresses, white extends onto the back and then out onto the upperwings. The white on the wings is always contiguous with the white on the back. Throughout fall and winter, birds in the same flock may show significantly different plumage progression and may appear quite different. **Distant:** The combination of the strikingly black-and-white adult males, uniformly dark females, and patchy first-cycle males makes for a distinctly mottled appearance. Flocks show more contrast and a greater variety of appearances than any other monospecific flock of ducks. In the southern parts of the range, adult males are far less common, and flocks of females may resemble flocks of American Black Ducks, as both are dark with pale underwings, though only the axillaries are pale in female eider.

SIMILAR SPECIES: King Eider: Smaller and more compact, with a smaller head, concave forehead, and slimmer wings. First-cycle male is similar in plumage to first-cycle Common Eider—dark with a white chest—but King has a shorter, orange bill and acquires less white on the back and wings during the first winter, and some retain a fully brown back throughout the first-cycle. Females are similar in plumage, but King is noticeably smaller, with a short dark bill and concave forehead. Differences in flight style are subtle, but King has faster wingbeats and is slightly less stable, enhancing the impression that it is a smaller species. **White-winged Scoter:** Very similar silhouette, but darker with bold white secondaries. Additionally, the wings are narrower and more pointed, and the sloping forehead is shorter and slightly concave. **American Black Duck:** Large and broad-winged like Common Eider but has a smaller head and longer, slimmer neck; a paler face that contrasts sharply with the body; and more extensively white underwing.

SUBSPECIES: See Taxonomic Notes (p. 590).

- Flocks of this size and height are most typical of spring birds approaching the Arctic breeding grounds, but they occasionally occur farther south.
- Note the mottled appearance of the flock.

FEMALE. NEW JERSEY, FEB. MIKE DANZENBAKER.

- Always appears large and heavy.
- Imposing, anvil-shaped head is the key trait at a distance.
- Females usually appear all dark at a distance, though a small pale triangle may be visible on the axillaries.
- Females of the southern race, *dresseri*, typically have a rusty coloration, but there is much variation.

ADULT MALE. NORWAY, MAR. HUGH HARROP.

- Black-and-white plumage, angular head, and thick neck make males unmistakable.
- Almost strictly coastal; even less likely than King Eider to stray to fresh water.

TWO FEMALES AND ONE FIRST-CYCLE MALE (R). MASSACHUSETTS, JAN. KEN BEHRENS.
- Recalls American Black Duck, but the pale underwing is smaller and different in shape.
- Typical first-cycle male in fall or early winter. Most show extensive white patches on the back and upperwings by late winter.

ADULT MALE *SEDENTARIA*. MANITOBA, JUNE. GLENN BARTLEY.
- At close range, males can be identified to subspecies by the shape and pattern of the frontal lobes. This individual represents the subspecies *sedentaria*, which is restricted to Hudson and James Bays.
- Regardless of subspecies, the anvil-shaped head is a key identification trait.

WITH TWO ADULT MALE KING EIDER. NEWFOUNDLAND, MAY. BRUCE MACTAVISH.
- Check every flock of Common Eider for Kings!
- King Eider is the second-largest duck, but it does not project size and bulk like Common Eider does.
- The huge difference in appearance between males and females gives eider flocks a distinctively mottled appearance.

(RIGHT) SWEDEN, APR. KEN BEHRENS.

- The huge eider dwarf the midsized shoveler.
- The very blunt wingtip obvious in some of these birds' postures is unique to Common Eider.

ADULT MALES WITH ONE FIRST-CYCLE MALE KING EIDER (MIDDLE BOTTOM). SWEDEN, MAY. LASSE OLSSON.
- Check every flock of Common Eider for King Eider! Note King's smaller size, more compact shape, and blunter, less anvil-shaped front.
- Such a tightly packed flock is unusual. Eider typically look like flocks of scoters but with wider spacing between individuals.

ALTERNATE MALES. MAINE, JULY. KEN BEHRENS.
- The appearance of males in summer is variable— often blotchy—but their distinctive wing pattern remains largely intact.

FEMALES. MAINE, JULY. KEN BEHRENS.
- The deep, rounded, gooselike belly and exceptionally broad wings are almost as distinctive as the anvil-shaped head.

KING EIDER
Somateria spectabilis
DIMENSIONS
L: 22 in.; WS: 35 in.; WT: 3.7 lb.

SPRING ARRIVAL

e. Beaufort Sea: late May; Hudson Bay: early
June; Bathurst Is.: mid-June

FALL ARRIVAL

ME: late Oct./early Nov.;
s. Great Lakes: mid-Nov.

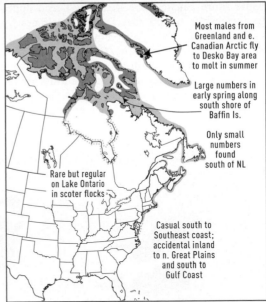

Most males from Greenland and e. Canadian Arctic fly to Desko Bay area to molt in summer

Large numbers in early spring along south shore of Baffin Is.

Only small numbers found south of NL

Rare but regular on Lake Ontario in scoter flocks

Casual south to Southeast coast; accidental inland to n. Great Plains and south to Gulf Coast

This stunningly beautiful duck resides along the coasts of the far north. A few trickle down the Atlantic Coast in winter, and vagrants are regular on the Great Lakes, but this handful is not nearly enough to satisfy the dedicated seawatcher! In the spring most King Eider leave the wintering areas late, as they have to wait for the ice to thaw in the Arctic waters of their breeding grounds. In some years they miscalculate and arrive before the ice has melted, resulting in mass die-offs.

SIZE: Clearly smaller than Common Eider. Slightly larger than White-winged Scoter. Whereas Common Eider always looks huge, King Eider, though large, is not as obviously massive as Common Eider, and can blend into flocks of scoters.

STRUCTURE: Stocky, not as long and sleek as Common Eider, with a short wedge-shaped head, concave forehead, and small bill. Adult male has a prominent bulge above the bill that creates an oversized and squared-off rather than wedge-shaped head. The wings are clearly thinner than Common Eider's, and have a rather short hand that may appear to end in a slightly blunter tip than that of Common.

FLIGHT AND FLOCKING: Wingbeats are quicker and less ponderous than in Common Eider, though King still imparts the impression of a large bird. Along the Atlantic Coast, King Eider are usually seen as a bird or two mixed with flocks of Common Eider or scoters. All but the brightly colored adult males seem to be able to blend equally well with flocks of Common Eider or scoters, matching the flight speed and wingbeats of their fellow travelers, and it may not be until the second or third scan through a flock that an observer notices a King Eider. During migration in the Arctic, they can form flocks thousands strong.

APPEARANCE: Basic Adult Male: At close range, the multicolored head is striking. It sports a glowing coral bill, a large orange knob projecting above the bill, a face washed with lime green, and a sky blue crown and nape. The upperwing is black but marked with wigeonlike white patches that are separated from the pale upper back by black scapulars. The belly and lower back are black, broken only by white rump patches. The neck, chest, and upper back are white, but the chest is washed with peachy orange. **Female:** Plain warm brown, with a slightly paler face and white axillaries. **First-cycle Male:** Dull brown head and blackish belly are separated by a white chest. The speed with which the white upperwing coverts are acquired varies greatly. Some birds begin to show white patches in the upperwing early in winter; others retain almost completely brown

upperwings for most of the first cycle. The bill is bright yellow-orange. **Second-cycle Male:** Much like first cycle, but the upperwing coverts are largely white, the back is extensively white, and the adult head pattern begins to develop, including a small orange knob on the forehead. **Distant:** Like Common Eider, but males show less white and females are more buffy.

SIMILAR SPECIES: Common Eider: Larger, with a long sloping forehead and broader wings. A sprawling hulk of an eider, whereas King is much more compact. First-cycle male is similar in plumage to first-cycle King—dark with a white chest—but Common has a much longer, dull gray bill and acquires more white on the back and wings during the first winter. Females of both species are similar in plumage, though Common Eider has a gray bill and is typically dull gray or reddish brown overall, whereas female King has a black bill and is medium brown, often with a buffy face. Structural differences are also crucial to separating them, particularly Common's larger, anvil-shaped head and straighter angle to the forehead. **Gadwall:** Overeager observers can mistake a Gadwall for a female King Eider, especially if a Gadwall joins a flock of Common Eider. Gadwall is much smaller, with a thinner body and neck, pale belly, and more extensive white underwings. **White-winged Scoter:** Very similar in size but has a leaner build and is darker overall with conspicuous white secondaries. **Black and Surf Scoters:** Smaller and darker, lacking white on the chest and underwing. Scoters have narrower wings and a slimmer, less "chesty" body shape.

ADULT MALE WITH TWO ADULT MALE COMMON EIDER. SWEDEN, APR. LASSE OLSSON.
• At a distance the protuberance above the bill of King Eider causes the head to appear square, whereas Common Eider has a wedge-shaped head profile.
• The white wing patch is separated from the white on the back by a narrow black band. The white on Common Eider's wings is always connected to the white on the back.

SECOND-CYCLE MALE KING EIDER WITH EIGHT BLACK SCOTERS. NEW JERSEY, OCT. CAMERON COX.

- King Eider is larger, with a heavier body and broader, more blunt-tipped wings, but does not stand out amid the scoters, whereas Common Eider are obvious in a scoter flock.

FIRST-CYCLE MALE WITH FIRST-CYCLE MALE COMMON EIDER (L). NEW JERSEY, JAN. MIKE DANZENBAKER.

- The shape of King Eider is relatively bland, whereas the silhouette of Common is dominated by the wedge-shaped head.
- Both individuals are typical of first-cycle males in early fall. More white will appear on the backs of both birds later in winter.

WITH SPECTACLED EIDER (BOTTOM R). NORWAY, MAR. HUGH HARROP.

- Large flocks of adult males are usually seen only at very high latitudes. At most lake- and seawatches, even one adult male King Eider is exceptional. Spectacled Eider has not been recorded in eastern North America.

- Unlike female Common Eider, female King has an all-dark bill.
- The gape curves slightly on females, giving them a "smiling" appearance.
- Overall, female King Eider is smaller and more compact, with a much smaller head than female Common Eider.
- In most areas, female Common Eider are very drab gray whereas female King Eider look noticeably warmer and more reddish, but the southernmost subspecies of Common, *dresseri*, is also quite reddish.

ALASKA, MAY. TED SWEM.

- At a distance the head shape of the female and first-cycle male (C, with dark head and white breast) is wedge-shaped, like Common Eider's, but is shorter and less obvious, not as exaggerated or drawn-out as in Common.
- Wings are slimmer and not as broad-based as Common Eider's.

(BELOW) NORWAY, MAR. HUGH HARROP.

WHITE-WINGED SCOTER
Melanitta fusca
DIMENSIONS
L: 21 in.; WS: 34 in.; WT: 3.7 lb.

SPRING ARRIVAL

n. MI: early May; s. ON: mid-May;
s. MB: mid-May

FALL ARRIVAL

ME: late Sept.; s. Great Lakes: early Oct.;
MD: early Oct.

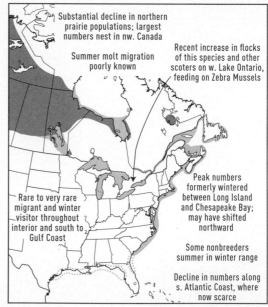

Substantial decline in northern prairie populations; largest numbers nest in nw. Canada

Summer molt migration poorly known

Recent increase in flocks of this species and other scoters on w. Lake Ontario, feeding on Zebra Mussels

Rare to very rare migrant and winter visitor throughout interior and south to Gulf Coast

Peak numbers formerly wintered between Long Island and Chesapeake Bay; may have shifted northward

Some nonbreeders summer in winter range

Decline in numbers along s. Atlantic Coast, where now scarce

This is the largest scoter, and its movements and bearing are almost eiderlike, though its plumage is similar to that of the other scoters. White-winged is far less gregarious than the other scoters; even where it is common, it rarely forms flocks larger than 100, and flocks of 5–20 are more typical. Unlike the other two scoters, which winter primarily in the Mid-Atlantic, most eastern White-winged Scoters overwinter in New England and the Great Lakes. While all three scoters have increased on the Great Lakes since the accidental introduction of the Zebra Mussel (*Dreissena polymorpha*), White-winged has particularly benefited from this new source of food. Like Surf Scoter, White-winged is rare but regular on inland bodies of water, particularly after late fall storms.

SIZE: The largest North American scoter. Only slightly smaller than King Eider but clearly smaller than Common Eider. Similar to American Black Duck but has a heavier structure.

STRUCTURE: Large and heavy, with a silhouette similar to that of Common Eider, though slightly more trim. The head is large, with a long sloping forehead that is shorter and slightly more concave than the long straight forehead of Common Eider. As in Common Eider, but unlike in the smaller scoters, the slanted forehead causes the entire head to appear to be angled downward. Although the head shape is similar to that of Common Eider, this is not the most dominant structural feature of White-winged Scoter. Instead, the eyes of an observer are drawn to the broad-based wings that are cut back more distinctly at the wrist than in the other scoters and that are pointed despite their width. At a distance the white secondaries can disappear, creating the illusion of a large bird with abnormally narrow wings and causing the wings to appear even more angular than they actually are.

FLIGHT AND FLOCKING: Wingbeats are decidedly slower than those of Black and Surf Scoters, as well as a bit deeper. Flight is more stable than that of other scoters, and lacks their subtle rocking motion. Flocks form nearly perfect lines, with each bird spaced almost a full bird's length apart. Usually stays close to the water but has a greater tendency than smaller scoters to fly at medium height or even fairly high. Regularly joins flocks of other scoters, though it does not mix as readily as the smaller species. Occurs in monospecific flocks wherever there are sufficient numbers, usually flocks larger than five or six. Despite their similarities, rarely flocks with Common Eider.

APPEARANCE: In all plumages the secondaries are completely white. **Adult Male:** Blackish overall with an orange-tipped bill and a small white "comma" that surrounds the eye. **Adult Female:** Dark brown with two pale, dusky spots on the face. **First-cycle Male:** Similar to adult female but with a pale belly, and the rest of the body plumage can be darker, particularly the head, with less distinct pale spots. In late fall or winter the bill turns dull orange. **First-cycle Female:** Like adult female but duller brown with a pale belly. The pale spots on the face are larger, and the dark crown contrasts more distinctly than on adult females. **Second-cycle Male:** Similar to adult male but dark brown rather than black, with no white eye comma. **Distant:** Blackish, with bright flashing white secondaries. The white patches on the wings are visible at tremendous distances; they can almost be inferred by the experienced observer before they are clearly seen, based on the appearance of a dark bird missing a large section of its wings.

SIMILAR SPECIES: **Black and Surf Scoters:** Smaller, with faster and shallower wingbeats. They form less organized flocks with less space between birds. Neither has the highly distinctive white secondaries of White-winged Scoter, nor does either angle its head downward in flight. See the scoters special section, page 184, for more information. **Common Eider:** Larger, with a longer and straighter forehead. Much more variable in appearance, from dingy brown females, to white-breasted and blackish young males, to strikingly black-and-white adult males. Flocks look like a motley mess at a distance. Common Eider also lacks the large white secondaries of White-winged Scoter.

WITH TWO SURF SCOTERS (REAR). NEW JERSEY, NOV. FRANÇOIS DEWAGHE.

• Broad and uniform spacing is characteristic of lines of White-winged Scoters.
• Surf Scoters can occasionally approximate the precise flock structure of White-winged, but there is less space between individuals, as shown by the two rear birds in this line.
• Black Scoters rarely maintain clean lines and always show tight spacing.

WITH BLACK AND SURF SCOTERS. NEW JERSEY, NOV. KEN BEHRENS.

• White-wingeds are sometimes obvious in flocks of dark-winged scoters but can be hard to pick out at other times, particularly in densely packed flocks.

• Note how the white secondaries disappear, creating the illusion of narrow-based wings.

FOUR FEMALES, FOUR SURF, AND SIX BLACK SCOTERS. NEW JERSEY, DEC. KEN BEHRENS.

• At close range the white secondaries and larger size instantly identify White-wingeds.

• Notice that White-winged and Surf Scoters are fairly similar in shape, whereas Black Scoter is structurally quite different.

ONTARIO, JAN. BRANDON HOLDEN.

• Structure is very similar to that of an eider, but the plumage is distinctive.

• Flocks often form parallel lines with broad spacing between individuals. Parallel lines are rarely seen among the smaller scoters; they usually form more irregular and often vaguely V-shaped flocks instead.

ONTARIO, JAN.
BRANDON HOLDEN.
• Wingbeats slower, so wing shape is visible at greater distances. The two upper-left birds are captured at the apex of their upstroke, when the swept-back hand is most apparent.

DELAWARE, FEB.
CAMERON COX.
• Large, bulky, and broad-winged.

ADULT FEMALE. UTAH, NOV.
PAUL HIGGINS.
• The hand angles back at the wrist even more distinctly than in Surf Scoter.
• Heavy build, broad wings, and wedge-shaped head are reminiscent of Common Eider.
• On female White-winged Scoter the white spot in front of the eye is large and extends onto the bill. In female Surf Scoter this spot is smaller and abuts the base of the bill but does not extend onto it.

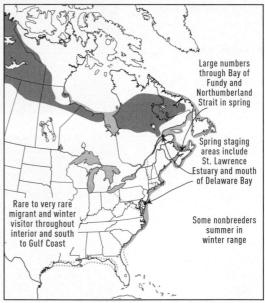

SURF SCOTER
Melanitta perspicillata
DIMENSIONS
L: 20 in.; WS: 30 in.; WT: 2.1 lb.

Large numbers through Bay of Fundy and Northumberland Strait in spring

Spring staging areas include St. Lawrence Estuary and mouth of Delaware Bay

Rare to very rare migrant and winter visitor throughout interior and south to Gulf Coast

Some nonbreeders summer in winter range

SPRING ARRIVAL

WI: mid-Apr.; St. Lawrence estuary: late Apr.; n. QC: late May

FALL ARRIVAL

n. MI: late Sept.; NJ: late Sept.; VA: mid-Oct.

This striking sea duck is one of the most obvious coastal waterfowl migrants in the fall because of its habit of migrating diurnally in huge flocks. On a peak day, mixed flocks of Black and Surf Scoters may pour past a watch site with flocks numbering in the thousands. The sight of thousands of silent black wings in billowing lines is indescribably powerful. Owing to its abundance and widespread distribution, Surf Scoter is a useful species to learn as a basis for comparison with other sea ducks. Considering the species' conspicuous fall migration, one might assume that an equally impressive event would occur in spring. This is not the case, though, and if fall migration is a shout, spring migration is a whisper, with most movements thought to occur nocturnally. Huge aggregations at a few key staging areas are the only hint of the numbers of birds returning north.

SIZE: Slightly larger than Black Scoter. Clearly smaller than White-winged Scoter. About the same size as Redhead.

STRUCTURE: Bulky and powerful but with a long body and sleek, aerodynamic silhouette. The distinctive wedge-shaped head is a major key to identification. In adult males the head looks slightly swollen, and the crown-to-bill profile may be slightly convex. Females and immatures have a smaller head with a straight to slightly concave profile. The wings are cut back at the wrist with a longer, more pointed hand than on Black Scoter. The long, evenly heavy undercarriage stands in contrast to the round potbelly of Black Scoter.

FLIGHT AND FLOCKING: Wingbeats are very fast and powerful, driving a swift flight. Surf Scoter typically stays just above the water except when flying into a headwind or on a very calm day when flocks sometimes rise to medium height. May also fly higher when crossing land. Flock size usually varies from 2 to 500 but may grow much larger during migration peaks. Scoter flocks are utterly distinctive, comprising disorganized knots of birds connected by constantly shifting and snaking lines. Surf Scoter mixes freely with Black and to a lesser extent White-winged Scoters. Virtually any species of waterfowl may join scoter flocks, with Green-winged Teal, Wood Duck, and scaup being among the most regular, but even large alcids, cormorants, and grebes join flocks of scoters at times.

APPEARANCE: In all plumages the underside of the flight feathers can show a dull silver sheen, but this is noticeable only in excellent light. **Basic Adult Male:** Striking. All black with white patches on the nape, crown, and at the base of the bright orange bill. The feet are bright red-orange and, when well lit, stand out against the black body at tremendous distances. **Adult Female:** Very dark brown to blackish with two pale spots on the face. Older females are darker and can show a white patch on the nape. **First-cycle Male:** During fall migration, typically shows a blackish head with a hint of orange on the bill and white at its base, a browner body and wings, and a pale tan belly. During late winter and spring, the body becomes largely black, but the white patches on the face are less extensive than those of adults and the pale belly is retained. **First-cycle Female:** Like adult female but paler brown overall with a pale tan to whitish belly. Some can be very pale. **Second-cycle Male:** Like adult male, but the white patches on the nape and crown are smaller or absent. **Distant:** Uniformly blackish, though large flocks often show a scattering of pale brown first-cycle females. The orange and white on the head and bill, and the red-orange feet of adult males, can be visible at incredible distances in good light. Female Surf Scoters are darker than female Black Scoters, causing distant lines of Surf Scoters to appear more uniformly dark than flocks of Black Scoters.

SIMILAR SPECIES: **Black Scoter:** Smaller, with a small bill; smaller, rounded head; and shorter and stockier, with a unique potbellied appearance. See the scoters special section, page 184, for more information. **White-winged Scoter:** Larger, with large white wing patches. See the scoters special section, page 184, for more information. **Common Eider:** Shows some similarities in silhouette but is much larger, with broader wings, and has slower wingbeats. Females are brown, not black or blackish brown, and while they may appear dark at a distance, their white axillaries are usually visible.

FOUR MALES AND ONE FEMALE. NEW JERSEY, FEB. KEVIN KARLSON.
• Large and dark with a sleek silhouette, wedge-shaped head, and angular wings.
• Structure can be judged accurately against the sky. With a dark background such as the ocean, judging structure is more difficult, though colors can be seen more clearly.

WITH ADULT MALE BLACK SCOTER (L), NEW JERSEY, MAR. GERRY DEWAGHE.

- Against a dark background, the white areas on Surf Scoter stand out, allowing it to be identified by plumage at greater distances than Black Scoter.
- Flight feathers are dull silver on the Surf Scoters but bright silver on the Black Scoter.
- The middle bird is a first-cycle male Surf Scoter.

WITH BLACK SCOTERS. NEW JERSEY, NOV. KEN BEHRENS.

- Typical flock formation for a large group of dark-winged scoters. The fairly linear structure with modest spacing between most individuals suggests that Surf Scoter is the predominant species in this flock, though Black Scoters are also present.
- Flocks of this size often include other species of waterfowl, but several careful scans may be necessary to locate all the non-scoters.

THREE MALES AND ONE ADULT FEMALE WITH THREE BLACK SCOTERS (REAR). NEW JERSEY, OCT. TONY LEUKERING.

- Surf Scoters appear slightly longer compared with the stocky and compact Black Scoters.
- Black Scoters have a small blocky head. Surf Scoters have a smoothly sloping forehead.
- Although the heads of the two male Black Scoters at the rear of the flock cannot be seen, the birds can be identified by their potbellied shape and by the wing shape on the rear bird.

(RIGHT) ADULT MALES. NEW JERSEY, FEB. KEVIN KARLSON.

WITH ONE FEMALE BLACK SCOTER (THIRD FROM REAR). NEW JERSEY, NOV. FRANÇOIS DEWAGHE.
- If they catch the light perfectly, the flight feathers of Surf Scoter can shine as brightly as those of Black Scoter.
- The birds with pale bellies are first-cycle birds. The female with a slightly paler brown belly (C) is likely a second-cycle individual.

ADULT MALE WITH GREATER SCAUP. BRITISH COLUMBIA, MAR. MIKE YIP.
- The bright red-orange feet of male Surf Scoter can be apparent from surprising distances.

WITH BLACK SCOTERS. NEW JERSEY, OCT. CAMERON COX.
- A tightly bunched flock like this could indicate that Black Scoters dominate the front of the flock, which is the case here, or that the birds are flying into a headwind.

**ADULT MALES AND FEMALES.
NEW JERSEY, FEB.
KEVIN KARLSON.**

• Late-afternoon sun lighting up the spectacular clownlike facial pattern and red-orange feet of male Surf Scoters is one of the pleasures dedicated seawatchers savor.

TWO ADULT MALES AND ONE ADULT FEMALE (R). NEW YORK, OCT. JERRY TING.

• Although Surf Scoters are large and bulky, their clean lines give them an aerodynamic appearance.
• Some adult females are very dark, lacking white areas on the face.

**WITH EIGHT BLACK SCOTERS AND NINE GREATER SCAUP.
NEW JERSEY, NOV. KEN BEHRENS.**

• Scaup that appear scoter-sized or slightly smaller are Greaters; those that appear much smaller than scoters are Lessers.

**ADULT FEMALE WITH FEMALE BLACK SCOTER (ABOVE).
NEW JERSEY, OCT. FRANÇOIS DEWAGHE.**

• Differences in shape are subtle, but at a distance Black Scoter appears to have a potbelly whereas Surf appears leaner and more attenuated.

BLACK SCOTER
Melanitta americana
DIMENSIONS
L: 19 in.; WS: 28 in.; WT: 2.1 lb.

SPRING ARRIVAL

St. Lawrence Estuary: late Apr.;
n. MI: early May; n. QC: late May

FALL ARRIVAL

ME: late Sept.; s. ON: late Sept.;
NJ: late Sept.; Gulf Coast: early Nov.

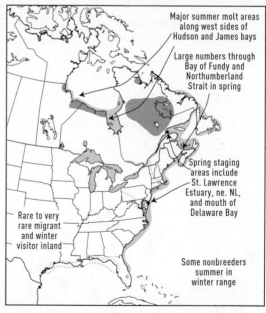

Major summer molt areas along west sides of Hudson and James bays

Large numbers through Bay of Fundy and Northumberland Strait in spring

Spring staging areas include St. Lawrence Estuary, ne. NL, and mouth of Delaware Bay

Rare to very rare migrant and winter visitor inland

Some nonbreeders summer in winter range

This gregarious species is the smallest of the three scoters. It can be surprisingly vocal, as males utter a low melancholy whistle when pursuing females, and this distinctive call emanates from any large flock of Black Scoters in late winter or spring. Migration timing and behavior are very similar to that of Surf Scoter, and the two species are frequently seen together. Black Scoter is fairly common on most of the Great Lakes but tends to be far less common than Surf Scoter on interior lakes and rivers during migration and winter.

SIZE: Slightly smaller than Surf Scoter. About the same size as Greater Scaup, though bulkier.

STRUCTURE: Medium-sized diving duck with a chunky, potbellied appearance. The bill is small, easily disappearing at a distance, and the forehead rises sharply. Together, these traits give Black Scoter a very distinctive blunt-fronted look that is obvious and diagnostic with some practice. The body appears short and rounded, with the deepest point about even with the trailing edge of the wing. Overall looks shorter-bodied and dumpier than Surf Scoter. Whereas the rear end of a Surf Scoter tapers smoothly up to the tail, on Black Scoter the rear curves upward more abruptly, a trait emphasized by the toes that often project beyond the tail and curl up slightly. The wings also look short, particularly the hand, and they angle back only slightly at the wrist, ending in blunter tips than on Surf Scoter.

FLIGHT AND FLOCKING: Wingbeats are fast but appear subtly less powerful than those of Surf Scoter. Despite this, the two species often fly together at identical rates of speed. Both of these scoters possess a certain distinctive quality in flight. Although they hold course well, they do so while subtly rocking back and forth, simultaneously communicating stability and instability. This is true on the individual as well as the flock level; the birds are swift and powerful on the one hand, but on the other hand they shift and jockey enough that at any moment it seems the entire flock may plummet headfirst into the water! Flock structure is very similar to that of Surf Scoter, though Black Scoters do more shifting within a flock, and small flocks are more likely to form bunches than organized lines. Blacks are even more likely than Surfs to stay close to the water in flight, though they sometimes rise when flying into a headwind or when flying over land.

APPEARANCE: In all plumages the undersides of the flight feathers are silvery and contrast with the black coverts. This can be quite apparent in excellent light and can be a good characteristic for separating Black from Surf, as Surf Scoter shows only modest contrast. In dull light, however, this contrast is far less apparent. For unknown reasons, Black Scoter shows much more silvery contrast in the flight feathers in spring, whereas the level of contrast in the wing of Surf remains the same year-round. **Basic Adult Male:** Solid black with a bright orange knob above the bill. **Adult Female:** Medium brown to blackish brown, averaging paler than female Surf Scoter. The sharply defined pale face contrasts sharply with the dark cap. Older females may show a hint of orange at the base of the bill. **First-cycle Male:** In fall similar to adult female but may show the beginnings of the orange knob above the bill and have a pale belly. During the winter the head turns black, and more orange appears above the bill. **First-cycle Female:** Like adult female but paler brown with a pale belly. **Distant:** Uniformly blackish, though large flocks often show a scattering of pale brown first-cycle females. The orange knob on the bill of adult males can be visible at a significant distance, particularly in good light and against the water. However, it tends not to be visible from as great a distance as the orange and white on a male Surf Scoter. Despite the species' name, females average paler than female Surf Scoters, and a distant flock that appears uniformly brown rather than blackish is probably mostly female Blacks.

SIMILAR SPECIES: Surf Scoter: Longer and leaner with a long sloping forehead and smooth undercarriage. See the scoters special section, page 184, for more information. **Harlequin Duck:** Fairly similar in structure, but smaller, with a smaller head, thinner and more pointed wings, and a longer tail. Tends to pop the head up and down or hold it elevated, giving the impression of an anxious turtle. Lacks the large pale cheek patch of Black Scoter, instead sporting small, sharply defined white markings on the face that are visible at medium distance but that fade away at greater distances.

NEW JERSEY, NOV. KEN BEHRENS.
- Very dark and stocky with a small head that is boxy but rounded at the corners.
- At a distance the bill disappears, creating the appearance of a flat forehead.
- The belly curves upward dramatically toward the tail. In Surf Scoter this angle is gradual.
- The toes stick out beyond the tail and often curl upward, emphasizing the strongly curved belly.

- Compared with flocks of other scoters, those dominated by Black Scoters are slightly more bunched with more movement of individuals within the flock.

FOUR ADULT FEMALES AND SEVEN ADULT MALES. NEW JERSEY, DEC. CAMERON COX.

- The orange knob of male Black Scoter disappears at long range more quickly than do the white head markings of male Surf Scoter.
- The wings of Black Scoter appear slightly shorter than those of Surf, and the wingtips are blunter.

WITH SURF SCOTERS. NEW JERSEY, NOV. KEN BEHRENS.

- This flock structure is more typical of Surf Scoters, but during certain wind conditions Black Scoters also form clean lines. It is helpful to calibrate your eye to the way scoters are behaving on a given day. Also watch for shifts in behavior as weather conditions change.

(RIGHT) BLACK SCOTERS. NEW JERSEY, FEB. KEVIN KARLSON.

- The sharply defined pale cheek of the female is evident at great distances, sometimes even when the orange knob of males cannot be detected.

ADULT MALES. NEW JERSEY, FEB. KEVIN KARLSON.

- The contrast between the silver flight feathers and black coverts is greater than that shown by Surf Scoter in all situations but is particularly obvious in dull light.
- For unknown reasons, Black Scoters show even greater contrast between the flight feathers and coverts in spring. This contrast remains the same on Surf Scoters year-round.
- Males lack the bright red-orange feet of male Surf, and this can be a useful identification trait on birds flying directly away.

NEW JERSEY, NOV. KEN BEHRENS.
- At this range the bill is practically invisible and the forehead appears almost flat.
- Notice how the belly shows an abrupt upward curve near the rear on the birds with the wings up.
- On the birds with the wings down, notice how blunt the wingtips appear.

ONE MALE (BOTTOM C) WITH FIVE MALE SURF SCOTERS. NEW JERSEY, OCT. CAMERON COX.
- In poor light plumage differences disappear and structure becomes essential.
- The difference in head shape is by far the most obvious difference.
- Body and wing shape differences are subtle but key supporting identification traits.

SEVEN SURF SCOTERS, THREE BLACK SCOTERS, AND TWO GREATER SCAUP (ABOVE). NEW JERSEY, NOV. FRANÇOIS DEWAGHE.
- Silhouetted against a pale sky, shape—particularly differences in wing shape—becomes especially apparent. When dark birds such as scoters are seen against a dark background such as water, it is more difficult to perceive subtle aspects of structure.
- Flocks entirely or mainly of Surf Scoters tend to form cleaner lines; Black Scoters are more apt to form tight clumps. These are only tendencies, however, and flock structure varies greatly with weather. On some days flocking tendencies are highly useful, and on others they are completely useless.

THREE BLACK SCOTERS AND TWO SURF SCOTERS (C). NEW JERSEY, OCT. CAMERON COX.
- Against a background of water, the pale areas of plumage, such as the white on the head of a male Surf Scoter or the pale cheeks of a female Black Scoter, are more obvious than when they are silhouetted against the sky.
- Head shape is always the most important trait in scoter identification; but on flocks flying right along the horizon, silhouette is the key secondary trait as birds rise above the horizon, whereas plumage and color become secondary traits to focus on when birds sink below the horizon. The ability of an observer to seamlessly switch between these two techniques is an essential "trick of the trade."

TWO SURF SCOTERS, TWO BLACK SCOTERS, FOUR GREATER SCAUP, AND ONE LESSER SCAUP (SECOND FROM R). NEW JERSEY, DEC. KEN BEHRENS.
- Scaup and other ducks frequently join scoter flocks. Most ducks appear slimmer than scoters, so it is useful to look carefully at birds that seem small or slender.

EIGHT BLACK SCOTERS AND ELEVEN SURF SCOTERS. NEW JERSEY, NOV. KEN BEHRENS.

- Dim light makes it more difficult to judge both color and structure, reducing the distance at which scoters can confidently be separated. It is often possible to identify birds as scoters without being able to identify the species, making the designations "scoter sp." or "dark-winged scoter" useful.
- Black Scoters appear compact and pudgy. Surf Scoters are comparatively lean and rangy.
- *What are the two non-scoters?*

SIX BLACK SCOTERS (FIVE ADULT MALES AND ONE FIRST-CYCLE MALE) AND THREE WHITE-WINGED SCOTERS (TWO ADULT MALES AND ONE ADULT FEMALE). BRITISH COLUMBIA, APR. MIKE YIP.

- White-winged Scoters are huge—almost eider-sized—and have significantly slower, deeper wingbeats than other scoters.
- The white secondaries of White-winged Scoter can be seen at tremendous distances, but with practice White-winged Scoter can be identified at distances even beyond where the white wings can be discerned, based on wing shape, speed of the wingbeats, and flocking tendencies.

FIVE SURF SCOTERS AND TWO WHITE-WINGED SCOTERS (FRONT). NEW JERSEY, NOV. KEN BEHRENS.

• Silhouette of White-winged Scoter is intermediate between that of Surf Scoter and Common Eider but distinctly different from that of Black Scoter.

• White-winged Scoters show an even stronger tendency than Surf Scoters to form clean, organized lines with precise spacing between individuals.

SURF SCOTERS, BLACK SCOTERS, AND FIVE GREEN-WINGED TEAL (FRONT). NEW JERSEY, NOV. FRANÇOIS DEWAGHE.

• When counting large flocks of scoters, first count the entire flock by fives, tens, or hundreds, depending on the flock size, then go back and work on the species breakdown. Small flocks may allow for each bird to be identified, but more often, given their flight speed, estimating the percentage of the whole is the best that can be done. For example, this flock breaks down to 60 percent Surf, 35 percent Black, and 5 percent dark-winged scoters, plus five Green-winged Teal.

NINE BLACK SCOTERS AND THREE SURF SCOTERS. NEW JERSEY, FEB. KEVIN KARLSON.

• Both Surf and Black Scoters can show a silver sheen on the primaries, but the sheen is much brighter and more obvious on Black Scoter and seems to become more apparent as the primaries wear, so that it is particularly obvious in spring.

FOURTEEN SURF SCOTERS AND FIVE BLACK SCOTERS. NEW JERSEY, OCT. CAMERON COX.

- The convex forehead profile of adult male Surf Scoter is absolutely distinctive. Most adult females and immature males have a fairly straight to slightly concave forehead profile. Some first-cycle females, however, have a distinctly concave forehead and at a distance appear more similar to Black Scoter.
- The small-headed appearance is distinctive on the out-of-focus Black Scoters in the background.

FORTY-ONE BLACK SCOTERS AND SEVEN SURF SCOTERS. NEW JERSEY, NOV. CAMERON COX.

- Separating distant flocks of scoters from distant cormorants can be more difficult than might be expected. Scoter flocks move faster than cormorant flocks, undulate and alter their shape more rapidly, and show tighter individual spacing than cormorants. But on extremely distant flocks it may take some time to fully evaluate these characteristics.

FOUR SURF SCOTERS AND TWO BLACK SCOTERS (R AND C). NEW JERSEY, OCT. FRANÇOIS DEWAGHE.
• At first glance these two species are extremely similar, but with practice, discerning the differences in head shape and overall silhouette becomes second nature. Learning scoter identification is aided by the fact that the species often fly side by side, allowing easy comparison. Over the course of a day when thousands or even tens of thousands are seen, as is often the case at prime seawatching locations, the differences become more and more apparent.

ADULT MALE AND ADULT MALE SURF SCOTER (R). NEW JERSEY, FEB. KEVIN KARLSON.
• Obvious males present a good opportunity to carefully study shape.
• Note how the primaries of Black Scoter are bright silver, whereas Surf Scoter has dull silver primaries. Also note slight differences in wing shape.

THREE BLACK SCOTERS AND TWO SURF SCOTERS (ADULT MALE L AND FIRST CYCLE C). NEW JERSEY, NOV. KEN BEHRENS.
• First-cycle scoters are often slightly smaller than adults and can be mistaken for other species of ducks. Their pale bellies and paler overall coloration add to the perception that they are smaller than adults. After a momentary struggle to find an alternative identification for such a bird, the realization dawns that nothing else fits and it must be an undersized scoter.

TWELVE SURF SCOTERS AND THREE WHITE-WINGED SCOTERS. NEW JERSEY, NOV. KEN BEHRENS.
• White-winged Scoters are most often seen at the back or front of a flock of dark-winged scoters. Less often they are in the middle, but in this position a large gap often forms in front of them so they appear to be holding up the flock.

SPRING ARRIVAL

s. QC: early Apr.; w. Hudson Bay: early June

FALL ARRIVAL

e. NL: late Sept.; ME: early Oct.; NJ: early Nov.

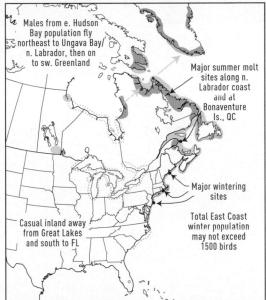

Males from e. Hudson Bay population fly northeast to Ungava Bay/ n. Labrador, then on to sw. Greenland

Major summer molt sites along n. Labrador coast and at Bonaventure Is., QC

Major wintering sites

Casual inland away from Great Lakes and south to FL

Total East Coast winter population may not exceed 1500 birds

This crown jewel among diving ducks is a regrettably scarce wintering species on the Atlantic Coast. Males are stunning, and though females are subtler, both possess a unique structure and behavior that make them a joy to watch. Harlequin Duck was formerly rare south of New England, but its ability to use human-made jetties and breakwaters as a substitute for natural habitat has allowed it to spread farther south in the winter and become locally common in many parts of the Mid-Atlantic. Large-scale migratory movements are rarely detected in eastern North America, and they may occur nocturnally, though Harlequins are occasionally seen with migrating scoters.

SIZE: Small to medium-sized, about the same size as Lesser Scaup. Clearly larger than Green-winged Teal and Bufflehead. Smaller than Black Scoter.

STRUCTURE: Pudgy and unathletic, with a tiny bill, large head with steep forehead, and thick neck. The body is oval-shaped and strongly potbellied, traits that are made even more obvious by the species' habit of holding the head above the body. The slim wings are centered on the body, with a long, sharply pointed hand. The tail is long and wedge-shaped. Females have the same basic structure as males but are noticeably slimmer-necked and smaller-headed, which can strongly influence the impression they give. In flight, Harlequins bob their head up and down more noticeably than any other sea duck.

FLIGHT AND FLOCKING: Wingbeats are swift but lack power, and the flight speed appears fairly slow for a diving duck. Flocks are typically small, fewer than 15, and form wedges or short, loose lines. Usually flies close to the shoreline and just above the water in monospecific flocks, though migrants will join scoter flocks and may be easily overlooked as runty Black Scoters.

APPEARANCE: Basic Adult Male: Steel blue with bold white slashes down the chest, white spots at the base of the bill and on the face, and flanks that are washed with rusty red. **Adult Female:** Dark brown with two white spots on the face. **First-cycle Male:** Plumage becomes similar to basic adult male early in fall but is duller, with reduced white markings and a mottled brown belly. **First-cycle Female:** Like adult female but slightly paler brown, with duller pale markings and a tan mottled belly. **Distant:** Blackish from any distance. Flocks of Harlequins actually look more evenly dark than most flocks of scoters, as the immature females are not as pale. The white markings on the face and chest of the males are sharply defined and contrast sharply, so they are visible at surprising distances, but these markings are also small and often difficult to discern. Although all but the adult males have paler bellies, the pale bellies are dull and fairly small so they are indistinct at any distance.

SIMILAR SPECIES: Black Scoter: Similar head shape but is heavier, shorter-tailed, and has shorter wings with more rounded wingtips. Adult males are darker and all lack pale spots on the face.

FOUR MALES AND ONE FEMALE. NEW JERSEY, FEB. KEVIN KARLSON.
- Overall structure is like a skinny Black Scoter with thin, pointed wings and a wedge-shaped, pointed tail.
- Males are stunning and unmistakable in good light!
- Adult females like the lead bird have an indistinct pale belly. First-cycle birds of both sexes have a much more prominent pale belly.

ADULT MALE. MONTANA, MAY. PAUL HIGGINS.

- Much like Black Scoter in head and body structure but appears more attenuated because of the slender wings and long tail.
- Harlequins are unafraid of turbulent water and fly very close to shore, often just out of reach of the waves crashing on a rocky shoreline or jetty.

ADULT MALES WITH A THICK-BILLED MURRE (L). ALASKA, JUNE. CAMERON COX.

- Nondescript in dull light except for the white markings on the face and shoulder.
- Small; similar in size to a large alcid.

WITH A FEMALE BLACK SCOTER (SECOND FROM REAR). ALASKA, JUNE. CAMERON COX.

- Harlequins are easily overlooked in a flock of scoters as they can look like small, skinny scoters. The slimmer, more pointed wing is the characteristic that usually tips off the presence of a Harlequin.

LONG-TAILED DUCK
Clangula hyemalis
DIMENSIONS
L: 16.5 in.; WS: 28 in.; WT: 1.6 lb.

SPRING ARRIVAL

w. Hudson Bay: early June;
Baffin Is.: mid-June

FALL ARRIVAL

ME: early Oct.; s. Great Lakes: mid-Oct.;
MD: late Oct.

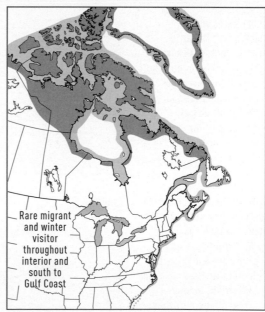

Rare migrant and winter visitor throughout interior and south to Gulf Coast

This trim sea duck, formerly known as Old-squaw, is common and distinctive. Although its striking and almost comical appearance would befit a tropical bird, this is among the hardiest of ducks, with many enduring the icy North Atlantic through the winter. For the seawatcher, small pods of Long-tailed Ducks dodging among waves signify the coming of cold weather and the fall season's drawing to a close. Long-tailed Duck was once thought to be unique among waterfowl in having three distinct plumages, but it is now known that variation in plumage and molt timing created this misconception and that there are just two plumages in the adult cycle, as in other ducks. Although found primarily along the Atlantic Coast and on the Great Lakes, this species also occurs on bodies of fresh water of all sizes throughout the interior of the continent during migration and winter. Individuals and even small flocks are even more prone than scoters to turn up in odd locales for a "sea duck": anywhere from golf course ponds to inland rivers and reservoirs. Long-tailed is one of the most vocal diving ducks, and males often give an unusual but pleasant *un-unh-AH,* a deft mix of a grunt and a squawk.

SIZE: Marginally smaller than Greater Scaup and Black Scoter. Larger than Lesser Scaup and Harlequin Duck. Similar to Razorbill.

STRUCTURE: Potbellied appearance is so pronounced that the belly seems to envelop the chest and gives the underparts an evenly rounded shape. The neck is thick and joins the rounded head seamlessly, giving the bird the feeling of a round thing with wings. The wings are extremely long and slender, and swept back slightly at the wrist. Female is smaller, with a distinctly smaller head and neck. Adult male has a long tail that trails behind the body, though this is difficult to see at a distance.

FLIGHT AND FLOCKING: Extremely distinctive. Rapid wingbeats drive the swift flight, which is slightly faster than that of scoters. Flocks display several subtle but distinctive traits that make them unmistakable once learned. Typical flock structure is a loose line, and individuals in the line bob up and down completely out of sync with one another. From a distance these movements appear to be strictly vertical, so at any time any member of the line can pop up for a second or two before settling back into the line. In addition, flocks tend to undulate slightly, flying just over the water, then rising noticeably for a short period, then sinking back down to the waves. Finally, they regularly rock from side to side as if they are shifting their weight from shoulder to shoulder. Within a flock, these rocking motions are rarely in sync, so some members of the flock may be twisted toward the observer while others are twisted away. Once learned, each one of these motions can be distinctive individually. Combined, they allow identification of Long-tailed Duck from ridiculous distances.

APPEARANCE: Basic Adult Male: All males have a dark bill with a large pink ring. Mostly white below with a large brown spot on the neck and a dark brown "shield" that stretches across the chest and extends down to the upper belly. Above, the scapulars are pale and create two white slashes on the otherwise brown back. The wings and tail are completely chocolate brown. **Basic Adult Female:** Pale below with a brown cap that extends in some birds down to connect to the large circular brown spot behind the cheek. There is a dusky tan wash across the chest, and the back and wings are dark brown. **Alternate Adult Male:** Like basic male, but the neck, crown, and throat become dark brown whereas the face remains a stone gray color. **Alternate Adult Female:** Like basic female, but the head acquires a more extensive dusky brown wash, leaving only a small pale area around the eye. **First-cycle Male:** Like basic adult female but with variable white splotches on the scapulars and gray rather than brown flanks. **First-cycle Female:** Like basic adult female, but the crown, facial spot, and chest are paler brown. **Distant:** At moderate distances in fall and winter, birds look brown and white, the dark wings contrasting with the pale bodies, and the dark chest of the males clearly visible. At extreme distances the brown is lost and birds look like little white balls bobbing along the horizon. In late spring and summer the overall appearance is much darker, with brown rather than white coloration dominating.

SIMILAR SPECIES: Black Scoter: Immature females are superficially similar but are blackish rather than brown, with blunter, broader wings; a heavier overall structure; and steadier flight. **Bufflehead:** Smaller, with shorter wings and much faster wingbeats. Flocks fly in tight balls that lack the bounding appearance of Long-tailed Duck flocks. Males have brighter white plumage with large white wing patches; females are dark gray. **Alcids:** Eager observers can mistake female Long-tailed Ducks for an alcid. Alcids have more strongly contrasting black-and-white plumage, and their wingbeats are even faster, with the wings becoming a blur. Although alcids rock from side to side like Long-tailed Duck, they maintain a straight flight line without bobbing or undulating.

MICHIGAN, NOV. CORY GREGORY.
- Wings are long and slender for a diving duck, with a swept-back hand tapering to a sharp point.
- The dark wings stand out against the sky, whereas the pale portions of the body disappear.

TWO ADULT MALES AND THREE FEMALES. NEW JERSEY, DEC. KEVIN KARLSON.
- The female in the back illustrates how stocky and rounded this species appears when viewed in profile.
- Against water, the dark wings and back blend in but the white bellies are evident at tremendous distances—just the opposite of the effect when this species flies against the sky. The pale bellies may be blocked briefly by the wings but flash clearly once exposed again.

ONTARIO, APR. KEN BEHRENS.
- Flocks do not rise and billow like flocks of scoters. Usually they stay close to the surface of the water, though individuals continually make small adjustments to their height, so perfectly straight lines are rare.
- Spring flocks sport a variety of different plumages and thus have a mottled appearance.

(RIGHT) PAIR. ONTARIO, DEC. RAYMOND BARLOW.

ALTERNATE ADULT MALE. NEW JERSEY, APR. KEVIN KARLSON.
- In summer most males attain this darker plumage, though the molt timing among individuals varies drastically, leading to a great variety of appearances during spring and summer.
- Only males have the pink band on the bill. It begins to develop on first-cycle males in late fall.

WITH FOUR BLACK SCOTERS. NEW JERSEY, FEB. KEVIN KARLSON.
- The head and neck almost seem to merge with the body. At a distance the birds appear almost like round white blobs skimming above the surface of the water.
- The two birds at the rear of the flock are a first-cycle female (L) and a first-cycle male (R). The birds with the scoters are adults.

TWO MALES AND ONE FEMALE. MASSACHUSETTS, JAN. KEN BEHRENS.
- The body appears ridiculously stocky whereas the wings are slim.
- Although the long tail of the male draws attention away from the otherwise stocky silhouette, the tail disappears at long range.

ONE ADULT MALE AND TWO ADULT FEMALES. NEW JERSEY, DEC. KEN BEHRENS.
- Slender, dark wings contrast with rounded, pale bodies.
- The dark "shield" across the chest of the male is a diagnostic trait.

WITH TWO BLACK SCOTERS AND ELEVEN SURF SCOTERS. NEW JERSEY, NOV. FRANÇOIS DEWAGHE.
- Small groups of Long-tailed Ducks join scoter flocks, but large groups are usually monotypic.
- Slightly smaller than scoters, and their pale appearance makes them appear even smaller than they actually are.

TWO BASIC MALES AND ONE FEMALE. NEW JERSEY, FEB. KEVIN KARLSON.
- Its stunning appearance and weird, frequently given call make Long-tailed Duck a favored species at seawatches.
- Exceptionally deep belly creates a rounded appearance at a distance.

COMMON GOLDENEYE
Bucephala clangula
DIMENSIONS
L: 18.5 in.; WS: 26 in.; WT: 1.9 lb.

SPRING ARRIVAL

OH: mid-Mar.; s. MB: late Mar.;
w. Hudson Bay: early June

FALL ARRIVAL

SD: late Sept.; s. ON: mid-Oct.; KS: mid-Oct.; TX
coast: early Nov.; VA: mid-Nov.

Largest numbers winter
along coast from
New England to
Chesapeake Bay and
inland on Great Lakes and
on St. Lawrence and upper
Mississippi Rivers

Declining in parts of
southern portion
of winter range

This bulky diving duck earned the colloquial name "whistler" from the loud whistle that its wings produce in flight. Although technically a sea duck, this species prefers protected bays and large bodies of fresh water and is infrequently seen on unprotected coastlines. It is rarely seen as a diurnal migrant along the coast, though large movements are regular on the Great Lakes.

SIZE: Slightly smaller than Surf Scoter. About the size of Black Scoter.

STRUCTURE: Heavy, almost muscular appearance, with a large, blocky head and fairly short, broad wings. The neck is short and thick, but the head is so oversized that it overwhelms the neck, creating an appearance something like a mushroom cap on a short stalk. The wings are set far forward on the body, but the heavy chest and large head balance the appearance.

FLIGHT AND FLOCKING: Wingbeats are fairly fast and even. Although the species actually moves quickly, its flight appears to be slow and somewhat labored. Tends to fly at midheight. Small flocks fly in messy lines with wide but irregular spacing between individuals. Larger flocks form bunches but maintain distinct spacing, often forming flocks that slant upward, a distinctive structure. Typically seen in single-species flocks, though pairs and singles will join scoters or other large flocks of ducks.

APPEARANCE: Adult Male: The neck, breast, and belly are pure white. The head is glossy green, though it appears dark at a distance, and there is a white circular spot near the base of the bill. The back, tail, and wings are black, but there is an extensive white patch near the base of the wing. **Adult Female:** Chocolate brown head with a white neck ring. The bill is usually dark with a dull orange or yellow tip, and rare individuals have a completely orange bill. The body is mostly medium gray with a pale belly. The wings are also gray with large white patches on the inner wing separated by thin black lines. At a distance these lines disappear and the patches appear as a single large patch. **First-cycle Male:** Like female but

with slightly more white in the wing and an all-black bill. In the fall the white spot on the face begins to appear and can initially appear crescent-shaped, which can cause confusion with Barrow's Goldeneye. **First-cycle Female:** Like adult female but with a slightly paler brown head, an all-dark bill with the yellow tip developing during winter, and early in season, dark eyes. **Distant:** Males are bright white with a dark head and huge flashing white patches on the wings. Females are dull gray with a dark head and flashing white wing patches and belly.

SIMILAR SPECIES: Barrow's Goldeneye: Very similar in shape but with a slightly huskier build. Male has a crescent-shaped spot at the base of the bill and less white in the wings. Female has a glowing orange bill and less white in the wings. **Scoters:** Silhouette is similar, but scoters are sleeker with different head shapes. All scoters average darker than Common Goldeneye and lack the white wing patch extending onto the secondary coverts that is shown by both sexes of goldeneye. **Bufflehead:** Similar structure, but much smaller, with much faster wingbeats and shorter wings. Flocks tend to fly lower than goldeneye, and with tighter flock structure.

TWO ADULT MALES, TWO FIRST-CYCLE MALES (BOTTOM), AND TWO ADULT FEMALES. UTAH, JAN. KEN BEHRENS.

- Oversized head; short, broad wings; and heavy body give Common Goldeneye a blocky and powerful appearance.
- The huge patch of white on the inner wing flashes noticeably in both sexes.
- Small to medium-sized flocks form messy ovals or upward-slanted lines.

WITH NORTHERN SHOVELER (REAR). UTAH, JAN. KEN BEHRENS.

- Most diving ducks appear compact and heavy compared with dabbling ducks.
- Goldeneye wings are broad with fairly blunt wingtips, reinforcing the short-winged impression.
- Larger head, white chest, and all-black bill of the center bird indicate it is a first-cycle male. The lead bird is an adult female.

MASSACHUSETTS, JAN. KEN BEHRENS.
- Although many species of ducks sport extensive white markings, few match the blinding white color of male goldeneyes and Bufflehead.

UTAH, JAN. CAMERON COX.
- The contrast between the dark underwing and pale body is evident at great distances.
- *What is the species in the background?*

SWEDEN, APR. KEN BEHRENS.
- Vaguely oval-shaped flocks are a common formation for goldeneyes.
- Migrating flocks fly higher than most other diving ducks, though *Aythya* often fly at similar heights.

ADULT FEMALES. UTAH, JAN. KEN BEHRENS.

- Goldeneyes often form distinctive slanting flocks.
- Although goldeneye flocks often look disorganized, each bird largely holds its place, so the flock structure changes slowly. Flocks lack the chaotic feeling communicated by flocks of scoters or Bufflehead.

UTAH, JAN. KEN BEHRENS.

- Gives a muscular impression.
- The large head seems too large for the neck when viewed from a distance.

FIRST-CYCLE FEMALE (FRONT) WITH ADULT FEMALE. UTAH, JAN. CAMERON COX.

- Wing pattern can be useful for separating Common from Barrow's Goldeneye, but age must always be taken into account.

ADULT MALE (R) AND FIRST-CYCLE MALE. UTAH, JAN. KEN BEHRENS.

- In midwinter, the white spot on the lores of first-cycle males begins to appear. As this spot emerges, it can temporarily take on a crescent shape, leading to confusion with Barrow's Goldeneye.

BARROW'S GOLDENEYE
Bucephala islandica
DIMENSIONS
L: 18 in.; WS: 28 in.; WT: 2.1 lb.

SPRING ARRIVAL

cen. QC: late Apr.

FALL ARRIVAL

ON: mid-Oct.; ME: late Nov.;
MA: late Nov./early Dec.

Molt sites located well north of breeding range: on north coast of Labrador and Ungava Bay, and near Belcher Islands in e. Hudson Bay

Most eastern birds winter in St. Lawrence estuary and around Gaspé Peninsula

Total eastern population may not exceed 4000 birds

Very rare or casual outside mapped range

Records north to w. Hudson Bay and as far south as TX, NC

Barrow's is the sibling species to the widespread Common Goldeneye. It is largely western in distribution, though a small population nests in eastern Canada and winters along the Atlantic Coast. The eastern breeding areas are not well known but appear to be mostly in Quebec. The vast majority of these birds stay in Quebec for the winter, favoring the St. Lawrence Estuary. Elsewhere in the East, Barrow's is a treasured find, with small numbers wintering on the Atlantic Coast from the Atlantic Provinces to New Jersey.

SIZE: Slightly larger than Common Goldeneye. Virtually the same as Black Scoter.

STRUCTURE: Like Common Goldeneye but slightly larger and heavier with a more prominent peak to the forehead and a shorter bill.

FLIGHT AND FLOCKING: Almost identical to that of Common Goldeneye. Nearly all eastern sightings are with Common.

APPEARANCE: Adult Male: White neck, breast, and belly with a dark, glossy purple head and a crescent-shaped white mark at the base of the bill. The back and wings are black, and there is a large white patch on the inner wing, though this patch is less extensive than on male Common Goldeneye. **Adult Female:** Very similar to female Common Goldeneye but has a glowing orange bill. Dark chocolate brown head with a white neck ring, gray body, and white belly. Dark gray wings with variable white patches in the inner wing. Some show the same pattern as female Common Goldeneye, but most have reduced or absent white markings on the coverts, so the patch is restricted to the secondaries. **First-cycle Male:** Like adult female but with a black bill, whitish chest, and slightly more extensive white wing patches. **First-cycle Female:** Like adult female but with a slightly paler brown head, an all-dark bill changing gradually through winter to orange, and early in season, dark eyes. **Distant:** Like Common Goldeneye but marginally darker.

SIMILAR SPECIES: Common Goldeneye: Virtually identical in structure but slightly slimmer. Male Common Goldeneye is distinguished by the rounded rather than crescent-shaped white spot on the face, less pronounced peak to the forehead, more extensive white wing patch, and extensive white in scapulars extending well beyond the wing base. Most female Common Goldeneye have a black bill, though a small number have a bill that is half or even completely yellow-orange. Even these do not match the bright orange of most female Barrow's, though this is hard to judge in flight. Female Common Goldeneye are also slightly paler gray with a more mottled appearance to the breast and have a paler brown head that shows rusty tones, rather than the deep, even brown shown by female Barrow's. Like the male, female Common has a broader, more extensive white wing patch.

WITH A NORTHERN SHOVELER. UTAH, JAN. KEN BEHRENS.
- Barrow's Goldeneye is slightly stockier and more powerfully built than Common Goldeneye.
- Barrow's appears slightly darker than Common in all plumages.
- First-cycle birds (male second from R; female fifth from R) create identification headaches.

ADULT MALES. UTAH, JAN. KEN BEHRENS.
- Crescent-shaped loral spot is evident at fairly long distance.
- The high contrast between black and bright white plumage is characteristic of adult male goldeneyes.

ADULT MALE WITH AN ADULT MALE COMMON GOLDENEYE (L). UTAH, JAN. KEN BEHRENS.
• With good views, identification of adult males based on their facial patch is straightforward.
• Barrow's has smaller white wing patches in all plumages.
• Note the slightly broader wings and different head shape of Barrow's.

PAIR. ICELAND, APR. EINAR GUDMANN.
• Female Barrow's can show a partially black bill, heightening the importance of the wing pattern in separating it from Common Goldeneye.
• The bill tip is fairly blunt and curves up slightly. Common Goldeneye has a straight, thinner-tipped bill.

MALE AND FEMALE WITH FOUR COMMON GOLDENEYE. UTAH, JAN. KEN BEHRENS.

- Structures are quite similar, but Barrow's appears slightly heavier, with broader wings.
- Differences in structure are most apparent at medium distance; they are difficult to see at long distances and are often ignored at short distances.
- The brown on the head of female Barrow's extends farther down the neck than it does on female Common, creating a slightly longer-necked appearance.
- Female Common Goldeneye (top C) has three distinct patches of white on the wing separated by narrow black bars. Adult female Barrow's (top L) has two patches. At a distance, the exact wing pattern is difficult to determine, but the impression of more white on the wings of Common and less on Barrow's is still apparent.

MALE AND FEMALE WITH MALE AND FEMALE COMMON GOLDENEYE (TOP AND BOTTOM). UTAH, JAN. KEN BEHRENS.

- Both species have a heavy, muscular build and oversized head.

UTAH, JAN. CAMERON COX.

- Diving ducks require a running start to take off, whereas dabblers can spring directly off the water.

BUFFLEHEAD
Bucephala albeola
DIMENSIONS
L: 13.5 in.; WS: 21 in.; WT: 13 oz.

SPRING ARRIVAL

IA: mid-Mar.; s. MB: early Apr.

FALL ARRIVAL

s. ON: mid-Oct.; NJ: late Oct.; NC: early Nov.;
w. Gulf Coast: early Nov.

This tiny and compact diving duck is the smaller cousin of the goldeneyes. Like goldeneyes, it nests in tree cavities, an unexpected place to find this tiny "sea duck." Since it is able to exploit more habitats than most diving ducks, it is widespread and common. Remarkably hardy for such a small bird, Bufflehead can winter as far north as open water allows.

SIZE: Tiny. Although Green-winged Teal is virtually the same size, Bufflehead is the smallest duck on average.

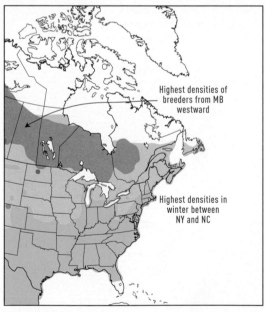

Highest densities of breeders from MB westward

Highest densities in winter between NY and NC

STRUCTURE: Compact and chubby with a large, puffy head. The head is typically lifted well above the body on a short, inconspicuous neck. The wings are centered on the body and are fairly broad-based but are surprisingly short for such a chunky bird.

They taper quickly, so the hand is short but very pointed. Bufflehead often gives the impression of a round thing with wings.

FLIGHT AND FLOCKING: Ultrafast whirring wingbeat causes the flight to look very swift and the wings to blur. Flies very low, typically just above the water, and entire flocks can be lost in ocean troughs. Flight has an unstable quality, as the birds constantly rock from side to side and frequently alter their course dramatically, even making wide, seemingly pointless circles. They seem to be in a frantic hurry to go nowhere. During migration, Bufflehead is rarely seen alone, more frequently in pairs, but most often in small flocks of 5–15. Flock structure is a tightly packed clump, much like that of Green-winged Teal, with some, but not extensive, reshuffling of individuals within the flock. Flocks will sometimes briefly spread into ragged lines, then quickly return to a tightly packed pod. Usually in single-species groups but will occasionally join goldeneyes, teal, or scoters.

APPEARANCE: Adult Male: The bright white breast and belly create the impression of an overwhelmingly pale bird. The head is dark with multicolored iridescent gloss, and white "earmuffs" that start just behind the eye wrap around the head. The back is black, as are the wings, though there is an extensive white wing patch that cuts all the way across the center of the inner wing. **Adult Female:** Dark gray overall with slightly paler belly. The head is brown with a small oval-shaped spot on the cheek. The wings are dark, with a small patch of white on the secondaries at the base of the wing. **First-cycle Male:** Like adult female, but the spot on the face is longer and thinner, almost touching the eye, and the neck and chest are paler, so there is no contrast with the belly. The white wing patch is slightly larger than on adult females but smaller than on adult males. **First-cycle Female:** Like adult female but has slightly paler head with smaller cheek patch and darker gray breast and belly. The wing patch is reduced and barely noticeable. **Distant:** Adult males look almost all white, whereas females look uniformly gray. Flocks that include both sexes look distinctly pied, showing a degree of contrast that is unusual in a monospecific flock. Some flocks are made up of only males or only females, so depending on their makeup, distant flocks may appear pied, bright white, or dull gray.

SIMILAR SPECIES: Alcids: With their whirring wingbeats, rocking flight, and tendency to hug the water, Bufflehead can momentarily give the impression of an alcid. Alcids, however, show no structural distinction between head and body. All except Black Guillemot lack the large white wing patch of male Bufflehead, and none have anything like its "earmuffs." Alcids are also more contrastingly black and white than female Bufflehead. Dovekie is smaller than Bufflehead; Razorbill and murres are larger; and Black Guillemot is similar but has a pale underwing and very different flight style and wing shape. **Common Goldeneye:** Larger, with more stable flight, more space between individuals in flocks, and a tendency to fly higher. Male has a white spot at the base of the bill; female has a more defined white belly and lacks the pale cheek spot. **Long-tailed Duck:** More fluid flight, with a tendency to form straight lines rather than bunches. Longer wings than Bufflehead, and though both rock in flight, Long-tailed Duck does so more smoothly and less frantically. Male Bufflehead is brighter white than Long-tailed Duck, and female Bufflehead is gray rather than brown and white.

WITH EIGHT GREEN-WINGED TEAL (C). NEW JERSEY, DEC. KEN BEHRENS.
- Bufflehead is smaller than Green-winged Teal but is significantly stockier.
- Both species have very rapid wingbeats and a tightly clumped flock structure, but Bufflehead tend to expand into lines and then contract back into a ball, whereas Green-winged Teal stay in their ball-like formation.
- Flocks of female Bufflehead are dark like teal but always show small flashes of white.

WITH GREEN-WINGED TEAL (TOP FRONT) AND TWO OTHER DUCKS. NEW JERSEY, NOV. KEN BEHRENS.
- Bufflehead beat their wings so quickly that they often appear to be blurred.
- *What are the two trailing ducks?*

ADULT MALE (BOTTOM) WITH TWO FEMALE COMMON GOLDENEYE. UTAH, JAN. KEN BEHRENS.
- These two species are closely related, but their different size and wingbeat speed separate them, even at a distance.

FIRST-CYCLE MALE (L), FEMALE, AND TWO ADULT MALES. ONTARIO, APR. KEN BEHRENS.
- Adult males are evident at greater distances than are females. The distant sight of one or two little white specks moving just over the surface of the water may resolve into an entire flock of Bufflehead through a scope.

WITH A MALE LESSER SCAUP (C). NEW YORK, APR. KEN BEHRENS.
- Bufflehead are tiny, with a stocky body, oversized head, and short, slender wings.
- First-cycle males (front) look much like females but often have a paler chest, more white in the wing, and a slightly different facial pattern.

- Bufflehead hug the surface and can disappear into wave troughs for extended periods.
- A tightly packed flock of tiny ducks that are dark overall with a few patches of bright white is a flock of Bufflehead.

MALE AND FEMALE. MASSACHUSETTS, JAN. KEN BEHRENS.

- The white cheek patch of the female is often difficult to see, but the small white wing patch is usually obvious.
- At a distance, Bufflehead look like tiny white or dark balls, depending on sex.
- On migration, singles or pairs often join other flocks of ducks rather than fly alone.

ADULT MALES. UTAH, JAN. KEN BEHRENS.

- Sharply contrasting pure white-and-black plumage is characteristic of male Bufflehead and males of both goldeneye.

THREE ADULT MALES AND ONE FEMALE. UTAH, JAN. CAMERON COX.

- Wings are tiny compared with the body.
- The gorgeous iridescent gloss on the head of males is a rarely seen treat.

COMMON MERGANSER
Mergus merganser
DIMENSIONS
L: 25 in.; WS: 34 in.; WT: 3.4 lb.

SPRING ARRIVAL

n. Great Lakes: late Mar.; MB: late Mar.

FALL ARRIVAL

OH: late Oct.; IA: early Nov.; VA: mid-Nov.;
AR: mid-Nov.

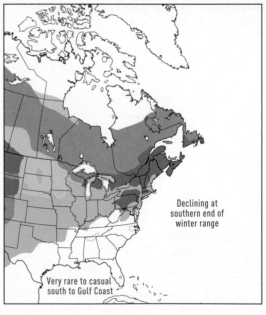

Declining at southern end of winter range

Very rare to casual south to Gulf Coast

This powerful diving duck is the largest of the piscivorous merganser clan. Unlike its smaller cousin, Red-breasted Merganser, Common Merganser spends most of its life in fresh water and is a regular sight on lakes and rivers.

SIZE: Quite large. Slightly larger than White-winged Scoter, though slimmer. About the size of Red-throated Loon.

STRUCTURE: Heavy but very long, with a sleek, aerodynamic silhouette that is somewhat reminiscent of a loon. The bill is long and thin, though broader-based than in the other mergansers. The head and neck are equally thick and are virtually indistinguishable, though sometimes the ruff of feathers on the nape of the female is flared, making the head more prominent. The head and neck projection is noticeably longer than in Red-breasted Merganser. The body is long and lean but bulges noticeably at the belly, giving the appearance of heavier "hips." The wings are centered on the body, and though the long neck makes the bird look slightly front-heavy, this is by far the most balanced-looking of the mergansers. The wings are broad-based and taper to a sharp point.

FLIGHT AND FLOCKING: Flight is fast and powerful, lacking the jerky quality of the two smaller mergansers. Wingbeats are mostly straight up and down, and the wings are only slightly swept back. Rarely forms large flocks, with 2–15 birds most typical. Smaller flocks form evenly spaced and slightly slanting lines that are fairly stable, whereas larger flocks become more disorganized. Flies at mid- or occasionally high altitudes when covering significant distance, as during migration. When commuting short distances, as between feeding areas, often flies low. Generally chooses higher flight lines than Red-breasted Merganser. The only frequent association is with Red-breasted Merganser, especially on the wintering grounds. Mixed flocks of migrants are rare.

APPEARANCE: Basic Adult Male: Beautiful pale cream breast and belly, dark iridescent green head, and a red bill. The lower back and tail are gray, and the upper back is black, as is the outer half of the wing; the inner half is marked with a bold white slash, and the underwing is white as well. The bright orange legs can be quite noticeable against the vent. **Female:** Mostly gray above and white below, with some gray along the flanks and sides of the breast. The head is rusty red with a small but sharply defined white chin. The bill is red like the male's but duller, and often has a black cutting edge. The inner half of the underwing is white and the outer half dark gray. The upperwing is tricolored: the secondaries are white, the secondary coverts gray, and the primaries and primary coverts black. **Alternate Adult Male:** Like female but paler gray with a white chest and much larger white wing patches. **First-cycle Male:** Like female but with more white on the upper wing and a paler chest with patches of white creeping in along the back and flanks during the winter. **Distant:** Males are overwhelmingly pale, with a dark head and flashes of black on the wing. Females are dark, but with flashes of white from the wing and belly in good light.

SIMILAR SPECIES: Red-breasted Merganser: Smaller and slimmer, particularly in the head and neck. The belly bulges far less noticeably. Wingbeats are faster and have a more twitchy appearance. Flocks are more tightly packed and less organized. Male is darker than male Common, with less extensive white wing patches. Female is very similar in plumage to female Common though has a duller red head and smaller, less-defined white chin, darker gray chest, and slightly smaller white wing patches. **Northern Pintail:** Much slimmer with a longer neck and slim wings set farther forward on the body. Male lacks the white wing patch, and female is tan rather than gray.

TWO ADULT MALES. MICHIGAN, FEB. ED POST.
- Adult males are truly striking!
- Length of Common Merganser approaches that of Common Eider, but the merganser has a long, lean shape that disguises its great size.
- Head is smoothly rounded, lacking the shaggy crest of male Red-breasted Merganser.

WITH A MALE RED-BREASTED MERGANSER (SECOND FROM R). ILLINOIS, DEC. KEN BEHRENS.
- In bright light, the white chins of female-plumaged birds glow noticeably.
- The bulk of Common Merganser separates it from the more slender Red-breasted.

ILLINOIS, DEC. KEN BEHRENS.
- Both Common and Red-breasted Mergansers tend to fly in fairly clean lines with little movement of individuals within the flock.
- Straight, pointed wings centered on the body contribute to an aerodynamic impression.
- The deepest point of the body is farther back than on Red-breasted Merganser, so Common appears "heavy-hipped."

FEMALE. ILLINOIS, DEC. KEN BEHRENS.
- More colorful and shows more contrast than female Red-breasted Merganser.

FEMALE WITH TWO RED-BREASTED MERGANSERS (BEHIND). ILLINOIS, DEC. KEN BEHRENS.
• Common is much larger, with broader wings and a longer neck.

ADULT MALE. MICHIGAN, MAY. KEN BEHRENS.
• Although males are quite pale, they rarely glow white as male goldeneyes do.

MICHIGAN, JAN. ED POST.
• They inhabit mainly freshwater rivers and lakes, often gathering in large rafts, with small flocks frequently flying in and out, providing an excellent situation for studying them in flight.
• *What species are in the background?*

RED-BREASTED MERGANSER
Mergus serrator
DIMENSIONS
L: 23 in.; WS: 30 in.; WT: 2.3 lb.

SPRING ARRIVAL

MO: late Feb.; MI: late Mar.;
Hudson Bay: late May

FALL ARRIVAL

WI: mid-Oct.; s. Great Lakes: mid-Oct.;
NJ: late Oct.; Gulf Coast: early Nov.

This striking, medium-sized merganser winters on coastal bays. Small lines winging their way between sheltered coves are an expected sight all along the Atlantic and Gulf Coasts. This species also congregates on the Great Lakes and on large lakes and reservoirs. Unlike the other two mergansers, it migrates diurnally, and movements of migrants are particularly conspicuous along the Atlantic Coast and on the Great Lakes.

SIZE: Often appears midsized but is actually quite large. Slightly larger than Common Goldeneye and

Thousands on Lake Erie during Nov.

Exceptional nesting records from as far south as the Carolinas

Some nonbreeders summer in winter range

Uncommon to rare migrant and winter visitor inland outside mapped range

Surf Scoter but appears smaller than both owing to its slim build.

STRUCTURE: Skinny overall, with an almost gangly appearance. The thin head and neck are usually held straight out from the body, though at times they are slightly drooped, and the narrow bill is often angled up slightly. The wings project stiffly straight out from the body, angling back slightly at the wrist and tapering to a sharp point. The body is long and lean, expanding only slightly at the belly.

FLIGHT AND FLOCKING: Fast and direct; the swiftest species of waterfowl, outstripped among waterbirds only by loons. The wingbeats are ultrafast and have a mechanical quality; each movement is identical and precise but with a slight jerkiness that creates an unmistakable cadence. Larger flocks generally fly at medium height; smaller groups may fly just above the water. At a given location tends to use a regular flight path as if it were delineated by road signs visible only to Red-breasted Mergansers. Flies in very straight lines, with distinct spacing between individuals—wider than in other species of similar size. Flocks may momentarily bunch up, especially during direction changes, but almost immediately re-form into meticulous lines. Very small flocks or singles may join other ducks, but the only regular association is with Common Merganser in shared wintering areas.

APPEARANCE: Basic Adult Male: The head is deep green, with a reddish bill and white neck ring. The back fades from blackish above to pale gray on the rump. The chest is a dull, mottled brown, and the belly is white. The wings have a large white patch on the inner wing, though it is not as extensive as that of Common Merganser. The hand is dark both above and below, and the underwing coverts are pale. **Female:** Largely dull gray with a dull red head and orange-red bill. The belly and underwing coverts are pale; a modest white wing patch consists of most of the secondaries and half of the greater secondary coverts. **Alternate Adult Male:** Like female but retains the extensive white wing patches of basic plumage. This is the plumage held by most adult males during fall migration. **First-cycle Male:** Virtually identical to basic adult female but begins to show greenish patches on the head in late winter. **Distant:** Dark gray overall with flashing white wing patches. Males look dark-headed and have more noticeable white wing patches.

SIMILAR SPECIES: Common Merganser: Larger, with a much heavier build. Significantly paler overall. See Common Merganser account for more information. **Northern Pintail:** Similar in forming precise lines and having direct flight but has longer wings, neck, and tail. It also has smooth wingbeats and an elegant bearing, quite different from the frantic twitchiness of Red-breasted Merganser. Generally flies higher than mergansers. **Red-throated Loon:** Similar in having rapid wingbeats, fast flight, and being overall dusky gray. However, loons never form precise lines, and they choose a great variety of flight lines. Their wings are longer and their wingbeats are slower, deeper, and more powerful.

NEW JERSEY, DEC. KEN BEHRENS.
• Although many species of ducks fly in lines, merganser flocks appear more organized, as most individuals in a flock coordinate their wingbeats.

WITH FOUR NORTHERN PINTAIL. NEW JERSEY, DEC. KEN BEHRENS.
• Northern Pintail also tends to fly in organized lines but has smooth, effortless wingbeats, whereas mergansers have a slight jerkiness to their wingbeats.

TEXAS, APR. KEN BEHRENS.

- Mergansers hold their slim, pointed wings virtually straight throughout the wingbeat.
- Exceptionally large flocks of all duck species tend to discard "typical" flock formations. Such flocks of all medium to large duck species often form wedges, though scoters rarely fly in wedges.
- Despite the colorful plumage of the males, flocks of Red-breasted Mergansers often look quite uniform. This is particularly true early in fall migration, as males undertake much of migration before attaining their bright basic plumage.

ADULT MALES. ONTARIO, APR. KEN BEHRENS.
- Skinny almost to the point of awkwardness.
- The deepest point in the body of Red-breasted occurs slightly farther forward than in Common Merganser. Red-breasted appears to have a slight bulging belly, whereas Common appears "heavy-hipped."

(BELOW) MALE AND FEMALE. ONTARIO, APR. KEN BEHRENS.
- From afar, Red-breasteds often look dull; up close and in good light, they are spectacular.

NORTH CAROLINA, FEB. KEN BEHRENS.
- Large flocks of mergansers are more organized than large flocks of scoters or scaup; they form multitiered groups, with several linear subflocks often stacked on top of each other.
- Most segments in this macroflock have formed very precise lines, a behavior typical of Red-breasted Mergansers.

UTAH, APR. PAUL HIGGINS.
- First-cycle male (R) has a smaller white wing patch than adult male, similar to that of female (L).
- In both first-cycle and adult males molting into basic plumage, the green of the head first begins to show as a dark area around the eye.

FEMALES WITH ONE FEMALE COMMON MERGANSER (SECOND FROM R). ILLINOIS, DEC. KEN BEHRENS.
- The dark head and white chin of the female Common Merganser are sharply defined, whereas the head pattern of the female Red-breasted Mergansers looks washed out.
- Because of their sharper definition and paler overall color, female Common Mergansers look "pretty" whereas female Red-breasteds appear dingy.

HOODED MERGANSER
Lophodytes cucullatus
DIMENSIONS
L: 18 in.; WS: 24 in.; WT: 1.4 lb.

SPRING ARRIVAL

s. ON: early Mar.; SD: late Mar.;
cen. QC: mid-Apr.

FALL ARRIVAL

s. Great Lakes: early Sept.; s. NJ: mid-Oct.;
Gulf Coast: early Nov.

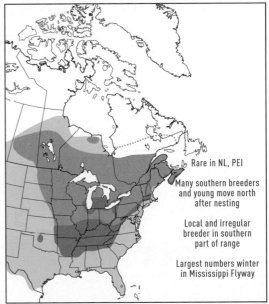

Rare in NL, PEI

Many southern breeders
and young move north
after nesting

Local and irregular
breeder in southern
part of range

Largest numbers winter
in Mississippi Flyway

This small merganser is unique in nearly every respect, from appearance to life history. Unlike the larger mergansers, which prefer open water and form large flocks, Hooded Merganser is typically found in small groups on tree-lined ponds, creek mouths, and open pools in coastal salt marshes. It is often seen flying at dawn and dusk, commuting between roosts and daytime feeding locations. While it typically avoids large bodies of open water, it does migrate over the ocean and along large rivers, though it flies high and hugs the shore.

SIZE: Distinctly smaller than Red-breasted Merganser. Larger than Bufflehead. About the same size as Lesser Scaup but appears smaller because of its slender build.

STRUCTURE: Distinctive, with an oddly flattened body. The wings are centered on the body and are quite short, wedge-shaped, and held very straight, which in combination with the long, pointed tail gives a balanced appearance. The head is held slightly above the body or slightly drooped, rarely level. Within a flock, individuals may alternately display both postures. Often looks awkward or hunched, particularly when the head is drooped. In flight, the manelike crest is held tightly against the neck, usually visible only as a slight tuft on the nape, though some birds may open the crest slightly, creating a distinctly square-shaped head.

FLIGHT AND FLOCKING: Wingbeats are extremely rapid, with a choppy feeling similar to that of Red-breasted Merganser. Flight is marked by a subtle rocking motion that contributes to an awkward and erratic appearance. Flocks are typically small, 12 or fewer, but may grow to 30 or more. Flocks typically form an oval shape, and have a cohesive and compact appearance despite the fact that individuals maintain wide spacing between each other. At times flocks will expand out into irregular lines, then quickly contract back into an oval-shaped ball. Occasionally a flock will hold a line formation for several minutes. Typically flies fairly high, choosing consistent flight lines at a given location. When commuting to roosts at dusk, flies just above the trees, often along streams.

APPEARANCE: Adult Male: Spectacular. Glossy black head with a white half-moon-shaped patch that spreads out behind the golden eye. When a bird is taking off or flying for short distances, this white patch is conspicuous, but in longer flights it is compressed down to a thin white streak. The back and most of the upperwing are black, and two black spurs jut down from the shoulder into the white breast. The belly is white, and the flanks are washed with bronzy orange. Both the secondaries and greater coverts are white, creating a double white bar across the arm. **Adult Female:** Rusty crown with gray cheek, breast, and flanks, slightly darker gray upperparts, and contrasting white belly. In flight generally appears uniformly dark and dingy. Has a white inner wing that is like the male's but more restricted. **First-cycle Male:** Like female, but the pale belly is brighter and extends farther up the chest. **First-cycle Female:** Like adult female but slightly paler gray with virtually no white on the inner wing. **Distant:** Males are strongly contrasting black and white; females are largely dark gray with the small but sharply defined pale belly visible in good light.

SIMILAR SPECIES: Bufflehead: Female is similar in plumage to female Hooded Merganser but is dumpy and large-headed rather than slim and narrow-headed. Bufflehead has deeper, faster wingbeats and tends to fly very low. **Ruddy Duck:** Rarely observed in flight over extended distances. When it does fly, it barely skims the water, and its wingbeats are faster and deeper below the body than Hooded Merganser's. Ruddy Duck imparts the impression that it is barely able to remain airborne. Structurally, it looks short and very stocky, with the whole body angled slightly upward.

ONE FEMALE AND THREE MALES. NEW JERSEY, NOV. CAMERON COX.
- Fairly small with a long, pointed tail and slightly drooped head.
- Teeters from side to side, which, combined with rapid and slightly jerky wingbeats, makes the flight appear erratic.
- Often commutes between roost locations at dusk and dawn, when shape is crucial to identification.

NEW JERSEY, DEC. KEN BEHRENS.
- Small, with short wings and a long, pointed tail.
- The pale belly stands out sharply on this dark species.

ADULT MALE. SOUTH CAROLINA, NOV. KEN BEHRENS.
- In flight, the large white cheek patch compresses to a narrow streak.

WITH BLACK SCOTERS. NEW JERSEY, NOV. KEN BEHRENS.
- Migrating Hoodeds often join scoter flocks, but they can be difficult to pick out.
- *Can you find the Hooded Merganser? There is also a single Surf Scoter in the flock. Where is it?*

FIRST-CYCLE FEMALE. ONTARIO, DEC. RAYMOND BARLOW.
- Head is usually lowered, giving a hunchbacked appearance.
- First-cycle females are particularly drab.

FLORIDA, DEC. KEN BEHRENS.
- Oval- or ball-shaped flocks are typical of Hooded Mergansers.
- This is a slightly above-average flock size for the species; flocks larger than this are rare.
- Within a flock, birds may display different head postures; some hold their head even or slightly above their body, whereas most droop their head.

ADULT MALE. BRITISH COLUMBIA, DEC. GLENN BARTLEY.
- The only duck that droops its head so drastically.

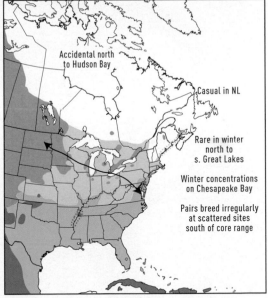

RUDDY DUCK
Oxyura jamaicensis
DIMENSIONS
L: 15 in.; WS: 18.5 in.; WT: 1.2 lb.

SPRING ARRIVAL

IA: mid-Mar.; ON: early Apr.; s. MB: late Apr.

FALL ARRIVAL

MO: late Sept.; VA: early Oct.;
Gulf Coast: mid-Oct.

Accidental north
to Hudson Bay

Casual in NL

Rare in winter
north to
s. Great Lakes

Winter concentrations
on Chesapeake Bay

Pairs breed irregularly
at scattered sites
south of core range

The distaste that Ruddy Duck has for flight is legendary; it barely belongs in a flight identification guide. It migrates at night, and only rarely flies for short distances diurnally, though flight occurs slightly more frequently on the breeding grounds. Despite the species' distinctiveness, it can puzzle observers who are unfamiliar with its appearance in flight. Although diurnal migration is rarely observed, this species can occasionally be spotted following coastlines south either in small monospecific flocks or, more often, in the company of scoters.

SIZE: Tiny. Only slightly larger than Bufflehead and Green-winged Teal.

STRUCTURE: Short and stocky with a heavy bill; large, square head; long, wedge-shaped tail; and stubby wings. The thick, bulging neck produces a silhouette that is unmistakable. In flight the head is raised above the body and the whole body is angled up slightly.

FLIGHT AND FLOCKING: With ultrafast, almost panicked wingbeats that are so fast they are completely blurred, Ruddy Duck typically barely clears the surface of the water. Generally seen as singles or pairs, but dense bunches of up to 15 all flying at the same height also occur at times. Migrants sometimes join scoter flocks.

APPEARANCE: In all plumages the underwing is dingy brown and the belly dirty white. **Alternate Adult Male:** Unlike in other ducks, the alternate plumage is the bright plumage: striking brick red with a black crown, white cheek, and powder blue bill. **Adult Female:** Gray-brown overall with darker crown, dull gray bill, and dirty gray cheek crossed with a single dark brown line. **Basic Adult Male:** Like adult female but with plain white cheek. **Distant:** Uniformly dark, dingy brown.

SIMILAR SPECIES: Bufflehead: Female is roughly similar in plumage to female Ruddy Duck. Both species have very rapid wingbeats, but Bufflehead is more fluid, with much stronger flight. Bufflehead rocks side to side, banks and circles, whereas Ruddy Duck always takes the shortest route to its destination. Bufflehead has a tiny bill, rounded head, and short tail, compared with the large bill, blocky head, and long, wedge-shaped tail of Ruddy Duck.

ALTERNATE MALE. NORTH DAKOTA, MAY. CAMERON COX.

- Flying is not Ruddy Duck's strongest talent, which is evident every time it awkwardly takes to the air. An almost exclusively nocturnal migrant, it is usually seen at seawatches only early in the morning.
- The heavy body seems far too large for the tiny wings.
- Wings beat furiously, giving the impression that effort and sheer panic are the only things keeping the bird aloft.

FEMALE WITH LESSER SCAUP (R). UTAH, JAN. KEN BEHRENS.

- Didn't you always wonder what a Ruddy Duck looks like from directly underneath?
- The wings are set bizarrely far back on the body.

WITH SURF SCOTERS. NEW JERSEY, OCT. KEN BEHRENS.

- With scoters, Ruddy Ducks seem so out of context that they may be difficult to place. However, their over-sized head, large feet, and panic-stricken flight give them away.

TWO FIRST-CYCLE MALES AND ONE ADULT MALE IN BASIC PLUMAGE (R). UTAH, JAN. KEN BEHRENS.

- Feet are enormous and are often noticeable in flight.
- Plumage is uniformly brown in fall and winter, including a dingy underwing.
- Sexing first-cycle Ruddy Ducks is very difficult in fall, but by early winter first-cycle males gain a white cheek. The cheek is usually flecked with brown, separating these two first-cycle males from the adult male.

CORMORANTS AND ANHINGA

Cormorants are large waterbirds in the family Phalacrocoracidae with long necks, long tails, and hooked bills. The species found in North America are largely dark in color with glossy plumage highlights. Anhinga is the only New World representative of the family Anhingidae, also known as "darters." Like cormorants, Anhinga is a large, long-necked, long-tailed waterbird that has mostly dark plumage with a glossy sheen. It differs from cormorants in possessing a long, sharply pointed bill adept at spearing fish, whereas the hooked bills of cormorants are suited to grabbing prey. We have lumped these two families together, taxonomy aside, because from a flight identification standpoint the similarities between them outweigh their differences. We cover three species of cormorants plus Anhinga.

Cormorants and Anhinga dive powerfully to catch fish. They also fly strongly. Cormorants use a powered flight in most situations, soaring rarely, whereas Anhinga uses powered flight to move short distances but prefers to soar for longer flights or during migration. Soaring cormorants can be misidentified as Anhingas by those who associate soaring with Anhinga and are unaware that cormorants occasionally soar as well. Cormorants usually fly in flocks, and during migration massive flocks of Double-crested Cormorants numbering in the thousands are a regular occurrence. Flocks of cormorants look like disorganized flocks of geese that no one taught to maintain a straight line; they constantly undulate, and the shape of the flock changes as birds shift places. Flocks of Anhinga, which also may number in the hundreds or even thousands of individuals, migrate like buteos by soaring upward in columns of hot air, then gliding down to the next

Double-crested Cormorants have adapted well to a landscape dominated by humans, and gangly cormorants in their characteristic disorganized flocks can be found on most bodies of water in eastern North America. New York, April. Ken Behrens.

thermal where they again gain altitude. Like American White Pelicans, Anhinga rise in a spiral in tight, organized squadrons, each bird mimicking the actions of the bird immediately in front of it.

The population of Double-crested Cormorant has exploded to the point that it has attracted the ire of fishermen and fish farmers, who see the birds as competitors. This has led to the killing of cormorants, both in government-sanctioned culls and impromptu massacres. Great Cormorant also seems to be increasing, and may actually be a fairly recent colonist from the Old World. Neotropic Cormorant has also greatly expanded its range in recent years and is venturing north as a rarity with increasing frequency. Anhinga populations remain fairly stable.

The sexes are similar in the three species of cormorants but differ in Anhinga. All species show decorative breeding plumes but whether this constitutes a true alternate plumage is debated. It takes several years to attain adult plumage in all species and differences between adults and immature birds are obvious in most cases.

Cormorants and Anhinga show broad similarities, but a close look reveals several differences. Note the long, sharply pointed bill and longer neck and tail of the Anhinga (L) compared with the shorter, hook-tipped bill; shorter, thicker neck; and shorter tail of the Double-crested Cormorant. Florida, Dec. (L), Utah, June (R). Ken Behrens.

DOUBLE-CRESTED CORMORANT
Phalacrocorax auritus
DIMENSIONS
L: 33 in.; WS: 52 in.; WT: 3.7 lb.

SPRING ARRIVAL

IA: late Mar.; ME: late Mar.;
MB: early/mid-Apr.; QC: mid-Apr.

FALL ARRIVAL

MO: late Aug.; MD: late Aug.;
Gulf Coast: early Sept.

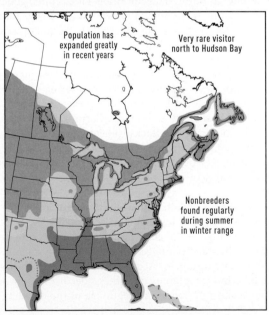

Population has expanded greatly in recent years

Very rare visitor north to Hudson Bay

Nonbreeders found regularly during summer in winter range

This large waterbird is widespread and common thanks to its ability to make use of a variety of different habitats. As its breeding range has expanded north and its numbers have increased, it has drawn the ire of fishermen and aquaculturists, who have successfully lobbied some states and provinces to enact cormorant control measures. Increased cormorant populations are a boon to seawatchers, however, who have the pleasure of watching immense flocks during migration. These flocks are visible for miles and can be confused with flocks of geese and, coastally, with distant lines of scoters.

SIZE: Larger than Brant. Smaller than Canada Goose. About the size of Snow Goose. Smaller than Great Cormorant but larger than Neotropic Cormorant.

STRUCTURE: Gives a heavy and awkward impression, with a potbellied body; broad, blunt wings; long slender neck; and medium-length, square tail. The hooked tip to the bill is visible from a moderate distance but not at long range. The neck is usually held in a distinct crook but rarely may be held almost straight. The wings are also slightly crooked, with the wrist thrust forward. The hand curves downward gently when gliding.

FLIGHT AND FLOCKING: Wingbeats are fairly quick and shallow, seeming to come mostly from the wingtip with the majority of the motion occurring below horizontal. Frequent short glides are the defining characteristic of cormorant flight, and these are most noticeable in the flight of Double-crested. This behavior is clearly discernible at long range and instantly sets cormorants apart from flocks of waterfowl. Most frequently seen in flocks, which usually range from 5 to 350, though on days of peak migration, flocks of many thousands may form. Flocks form lines or ragged Vs. Large flocks are made up of multiple layers of Vs that constantly undulate, waver, and re-form in a slow, hypnotic manner as birds change position. Flocks often glide in sections; a small group will glide briefly, followed by the group behind, so that the gliding action ripples through the flock. Usually flies at low to moderate heights over water but rises to greater heights when flying into light winds. Flies higher over land and occasionally soars on thermals. Flight lines often follow coastlines or rivers, but the birds do not hesitate to cross land. Cormorants usually form monospecific flocks, though cormorant species may mix where their ranges overlap. On rare occasions, Double-crested Cormorant will briefly flock with scoters or Brant.

APPEARANCE: Adult: Plumage is black but may show bronze or green highlights in good light. The brilliant orange of the gular pouch and lores contrasts with the dark plumage. The gray bill is visible at moderate distances. Acquires short black or black-and-white filoplumes on either side of the crown for a short period at the beginning of the breeding season, resulting in the "double crest" for which the species is named. First Cycle: Paler facial skin than adult with a largely pale orange bill. The face, throat, and breast are pale tan to light brown and may fade to a dirty whitish color. The crown, nape, and back are medium brown to blackish, and the flight feathers are blackish. Subadult: It takes several years for Double-crested Cormorant to gain full adult plumage. Second-, third-, and possibly some fourth-cycle individuals are intermediate between adults and juveniles. They usually have the brighter facial skin of an adult but the paler bill of a juvenile. The face and breast are dark brown to blackish, becoming darker each year, sometimes with a mottled appearance, lacking the glossy uniformity of adults. Distant: Flocks appear uniformly dark; the orange face of all plumages and pale chest of immatures are not evident at long range.

SIMILAR SPECIES: Great Cormorant: Larger and heavier, with a larger head and larger, more hooked bill. Adult has a white patch at the base of the bill, and first-cycle bird has a sharply defined pale belly. Neotropic Cormorant: Smaller and slimmer with a longer tail and straighter neck. Wingbeats are faster and weaker. Much smaller gular pouch is harder to see at a distance. Anhinga: Slimmer overall, with a very slender neck, longer and straighter wings, and much longer, narrow-based tail. Brant: At a distance the dark overall color and similarly irregular flock shapes can create confusion, but Brant flies faster and beats its wings constantly, never gliding as cormorants often do. Its wingbeats are even, above and below the body, and seem to emanate from the base of the wing rather than from the wingtips as in cormorants. Brant also has slimmer, more pointed wings; a thicker neck; and lacks the long tail of cormorants. Scoters: At extreme distances flocks of scoters appear very similar to flocks of cormorant. Both are dark waterbirds that form long irregular lines. Flocks of scoters, however, cover distance far more quickly, and they bunch up and then expand rapidly. The entire shape of the flock may shift almost instantly, whereas cormorant flocks appear to crawl across the horizon, shifting shape in slow motion. Canada Goose: Forms organized flocks that maintain a constant shape, typically fly higher than cormorants, and move across the sky at a significantly slower pace than cormorants. Has a longer neck, broader wings, and shorter tail than cormorants.

ONTARIO, APR. KEN BEHRENS.
- Broad, slightly crooked wings and long neck and tail are typical of cormorants.
- Although proportioned much like a goose, cormorants have a more gangly shape and clumsy flight.

NEW YORK, SEPT. CAMERON COX.
- Medium-sized flocks can temporarily form well-defined Vs but quickly break down into less-organized clumps.

PENNSYLVANIA, APR. KEN BEHRENS.
- Flocks of cormorants can resemble flocks of scoters or geese, but cormorants frequently pause to glide, and in a flock of this size, some gliding individuals will be evident almost immediately.

NEW JERSEY, OCT. FRANÇOIS DEWAGHE.
- Massive flocks are visible from tremendous distances and constantly change shape as they crawl across the sky, like a tormented macro-organism.

WITH SURF AND BLACK SCOTERS AND GREEN-WINGED TEAL (C). NEW JERSEY, NOV. FRANÇOIS DEWAGHE.
- Lone cormorants or small groups occasionally join flocks of scoters, usually near the back of the flock.
- *How many Green-winged Teal are in this flock?*

ONTARIO, SEPT. BRANDON HOLDEN.
- Although some birders dismiss cormorants, seawatchers appreciate them for their widespread abundance, which boosts count totals, and for the rustling sound created by the wings of close flocks, which once heard, can become an addiction!

NEW JERSEY, NOV. KEN BEHRENS.
- Flocks undulate in constantly shifting lines like flocks of scoters, but at much slower speeds and with wider spacing between individuals.
- At extreme distances, the speed with which flocks change shape is the best way to separate cormorants from scoters.

• Their gangly appearance and long tails separate cormorants from geese.

COMPOSITE SHOWING SHIFTING FLOCK. NEW JERSEY, OCT. CAMERON COX.

• Large flocks are continually in flux, writhing and undulating in slow motion. Notice how the flock in this series is V-shaped, rectangular, and almost linear at various times.

• There is always a section of the flock that is gliding, which immediately separates cormorants from geese.

• Large flocks of scoters can use formations like some of those shown here, but they shift and undulate at a much faster speed than cormorants.

• The spacing between individuals is slightly greater than in scoter flocks.

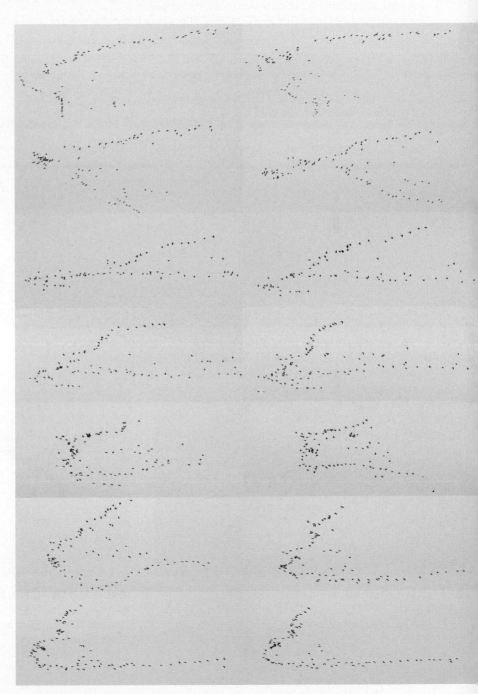

IMMATURES AND ONE ADULT (SECOND FROM R). NEW JERSEY, NOV. FRANÇOIS DEWAGHE.
• The neck and breast of immatures range from very pale tan to dull brown to black, creating a patchwork appearance in flocks at close and moderate ranges.
• At extreme distances, the pale breasts of immatures disappear and flocks look uniformly dark.

ONTARIO, APR. KEN BEHRENS.
• The crooked neck is evident at tremendous distances.

NEW JERSEY, NOV. KEN BEHRENS.
• Occasionally, small flocks or individuals will soar for extended periods.
• A large, black soaring waterbird may recall Anhinga, but close examination will reveal shorter, broader wings and tail, as well as a more relaxed cadence of the wingbeats if the birds flap.

FIRST-CYCLE BIRDS. FLORIDA, DEC. KEN BEHRENS.
• Among cormorants, the even, pale, tan color through the neck and breast is unique to immature Double-cresteds.
• Color varies individually and by age. Birds generally get darker as they age, though some first-cycle birds are also quite dark.

GREAT CORMORANT
Phalacrocorax carbo
DIMENSIONS
L: 36 in.; WS: 63 in.; WT: 7.2 lb.

FALL ARRIVAL

NY: late Sept.; VA: mid-Oct.; SC: late Oct.

In the region covered by this guide, this hulking cormorant inhabits the Atlantic Coast, mainly in the Northeast, but it is also widely distributed in the Old World and Greenland. Unlike the widespread Double-crested Cormorant, Great Cormorant is never abundant in North America and is almost entirely restricted to coastal regions, though vagrants occur on the eastern Great Lakes and other inland lakes in the Northeast.

SIZE: Slightly smaller than the largest Canada Goose. Significantly larger than most Double-crested Cormorants, though the smallest Great Cormorants may overlap large Double-cresteds.

STRUCTURE: Generally similar to Double-crested but with subtle differences. The wings are broader, particularly the hand. They also appear marginally straighter than those of Double-crested. The body is

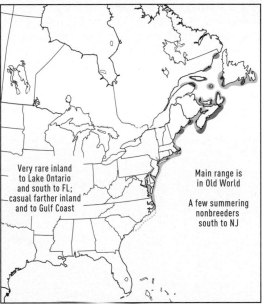

Very rare inland to Lake Ontario and south to FL; casual farther inland and to Gulf Coast

Main range is in Old World

A few summering nonbreeders south to NJ

bulkier but usually more evenly heavy, rather than potbellied, as in Double-crested. The bill is heavier with a more distinct hooked tip that is visible at greater distances. At times the head appears large and blocky, clearly discernible from the neck, but more often the head and neck merge seamlessly as in Double-crested. The neck is thick and held in a slight crook that is less obvious than that of Double-crested, perhaps disguised by its greater thickness.

FLIGHT AND FLOCKING: Wingbeats are slightly slower, heavier, and more gooselike than Double-crested's. They are shallow and evenly distributed above and below the body, differing subtly from the mostly below-horizontal wingbeats of Double-crested. Flocks are small even in the heart of the species' North American range. Singles and pairs are most common, and flocks of up to 10 are fairly common; those exceeding 20 are exceptional. Carefully examining single cormorants on the East Coast, particularly from Delaware Bay north, is an efficient way to find Great Cormorant. Regularly joins flocks of Double-crested, usually as singles or pairs. Rarely, small flocks are found in a flock of Double-crested, though groups larger than three or four are far more likely to form their own flock. In North America shows great reluctance to cross land, which is surprising since even the coastal subspecies in Europe is common inland.

APPEARANCE: Adult: All black with a small patch of bright orange facial skin surrounded by a large white throat patch. In the breeding season, acquires white "hip" patches and silvery filoplumes on the head, giving the crown and nape a frosted appearance. **First Cycle:** Largely blackish with a dingy brown head, neck, and upper breast; sharply defined pale belly; and small pale throat patch. A restricted patch of orange facial skin usually does not extend above the eye, and the bill is gray. **Subadult:** It can take several years for Great Cormorant to gain full adult plumage. Most subadults show

a pale belly that contrasts with the darker upper breast, but unlike in juveniles, the belly is mottled with dark spots. Older subadults are more blackish overall, and some birds lose the obviously pale belly. Some also show orange extending into the lores and, compared with adults, have a reduced white throat patch. **Distant:** Very dark overall, like Double-crested. The sharp white belly of juvenile is detectable at greater distances than the creamy breast and neck of juvenile Double-crested.

SIMILAR SPECIES: Double-crested Cormorant: Both species are quite variable in size and structure. This means that some individuals are easily differentiated by the characteristics mentioned below, whereas others are quite tricky. Double-crested is generally smaller and slimmer with a slimmer body, thinner wings, and a slimmer bill with a less obvious hooked tip. In all plumages, it has more extensive orange facial skin and lacks a white throat patch. During the breeding season, adults can easily be distinguished, as Double-crested lacks the white "hip" patch and frosted head of Great. Juvenile Double-crested is paler overall, tending to be palest on the throat and upper breast with a slightly darker belly—the opposite of the pattern shown by juvenile Great Cormorant. Subadults present the biggest challenge, as dark mottling may obscure the pattern shown by juveniles of both species. Usually a shadow of the juvenile pattern is discernible even on heavily marked individuals. Also, the overall color of subadult Great Cormorant is a bit colder than that of Double-crested, and subadult Double-crested has an orange lower mandible in addition to its more extensive orange facial skin.

ADULT AND FIRST CYCLE (L). SWEDEN, APR. KEN BEHRENS.

- Great Cormorant is larger than Double-crested Cormorant, with a bulkier body and neck, heavier bill, and broader wings.
- The sharply defined, clean white belly of the first-cycle bird is a key Great Cormorant trait.
- Flight identification of adults hinges on size and structure, as the diagnostic white patch at the base of the bill is usually difficult to see.

STRUCTURAL COMPARISON. GREAT CORMORANTS (BELOW) WITH DOUBLE-CRESTED CORMORANTS (ABOVE). KEN BEHRENS.
• Compare the structure of each Great Cormorant with the Double-crested Cormorant above it.

SUBADULT. NEW JERSEY, DEC. KEN BEHRENS.
• The species gives a bulky impression, being broad-winged and thick-necked.
• The belly is still paler than the neck on this subadult, a pattern Double-crested never shows, though the difference is less distinctive than in the first cycle.

SWEDEN, NOV. TOMAS SVENSSON.
• Flocks behave much like those of Double-cresteds, though flocks larger than 10 are rare in North America.
• Because the neck is thicker, the crook is less noticeable than in Double-crested.
• Shows enough size variation that smaller individuals can be mistaken for Double-crested.

WITH SEVEN DOUBLE-CRESTED CORMORANTS. NEW JERSEY, DEC. KEN BEHRENS.
• The larger size, broader wings, and thicker neck of the Great Cormorant (third bird from L) are noticeable but could easily be overlooked, particularly since all cormorants show variation in size and bulk.

TWO ADULTS AND TWO FIRST CYCLES (C). NEW JERSEY, NOV. KEN BEHRENS.
• The first cycles are useful reference points, as their white bellies makes them easy to identify. These two are the same size as the two adults; therefore all four are Great Cormorants.

ADULT. WALES, MAR. KEN BEHRENS.
• The decorative head plumes held for a short period in spring temporarily simplify identification of adults.
• Cormorant plumage appears uniformly black at a distance, but the intricate, scaly pattern is beautiful when seen at close range and in good light.

NEOTROPIC CORMORANT
Phalacrocorax brasilianus
DIMENSIONS
L: 25 in.; WS: 40 in.; WT: 2.6 lb.

SPRING ARRIVAL

cen. TX: early Mar.; OK: late Mar.

This small, lean cormorant was formerly restricted to the western Gulf Coast but has spread inland and appears poised to continue its range expansion. It is most common on fresh water but may also be found coastally. It has a strong tendency to wander and has been recorded widely in the Midwest and recently in Florida. Although the species is regularly reported in the Northeast, most of these reports appear to refer to small Double-crested Cormorants.

SIZE: Slightly smaller than Brant. Slightly larger than Mallard. Significantly smaller than Double-crested Cormorant.

STRUCTURE: Significantly leaner than the other eastern cormorants, lacking their heavy-bellied appearance. The small bill with weakly hooked tip is

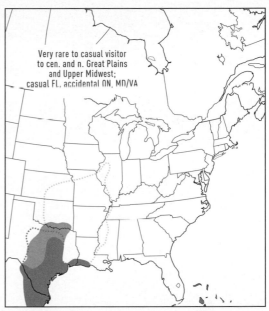

Very rare to casual visitor to cen. and n. Great Plains and Upper Midwest; casual FL, accidental ON, MD/VA

evident only at close range. The wings are slimmer and slightly more pointed than those of other eastern cormorants, and the tail is clearly longer. Unlike in other cormorants, the projection of the tail behind the body is equal to that of the head in front of the body, imparting a balanced impression. Neotropic holds its slender neck straighter than Double-crested does, and a bulging "Adam's apple" is usually more prominent at the base of the neck. Although Double-crested can show this look, it rarely does, perhaps because its thicker neck obscures this basal lump.

FLIGHT AND FLOCKING: Wingbeats are clearly faster and deeper than those of Double-crested. Despite this, Neotropic's flight appears weaker, as if the bird is batting feebly at the air. It flaps almost continuously with fewer and shorter glides than in Double-crested. Typically forms small flocks of fewer than 20, rarely larger than 100. Flocks tend to form roughly oval-shaped clumps rather than the ragged Vs or lines of Double-crested.

APPEARANCE: All plumages show a small dull orange gular pouch that extends farther behind the eye than in Double-crested and tapers to a point. **Adult:** All black with the gular pouch outlined in a crisp white V during the breeding season. **First Cycle:** Blackish to dark brown neck, chest, and belly that may fade to a dirty tan. The bill is usually gray and

the lores dark, but these areas become pale yellow late in the first cycle. **Subadult:** Second- and third-cycle birds are blackish overall with a dark brown throat and upper breast. The bill and lores are often dull yellow-orange. **Distant:** The most uniformly dark cormorant among the eastern species. Flocks are uniformly black even at moderate distances, as the juveniles are darker than juvenile Double-crested and their small gular pouches are inconspicuous.

SIMILAR SPECIES: Double-crested Cormorant: Larger and heavier with a deeper belly; shorter tail; broader, blunter wings; and more obviously hooked bill. Also has stronger wingbeats and glides more frequently. Immature has a paler head and breast than immature Neotropic. At close range, the details of the face pattern are useful for separating adults. **Anhinga:** Larger, with a longer and more pointed bill, slimmer neck, longer wings, and longer, narrow-based tail. Its flight style is almost opposite that of Neotropic, consisting of long periods of soaring or gliding broken by short bursts of flapping.

TEXAS, APR. KEN BEHRENS.
- Small, spindly cormorant with a significantly longer tail than Double-crested.
- Typically found in small monospecific flocks.
- Although most frequently found on fresh water, also moves along the Gulf Coast.

WITH TWO DOUBLE-CRESTED CORMORANTS. KENTUCKY, JAN. DAVE ROEMER.
- Although size is a useful trait for separating these species, cormorants show considerable size variation.
- Neotropic's longer tail and narrower wings are clinching characteristics.
- Neotropic also has weaker wingbeats, giving the impression of batting at the air.
- *Which bird is the Neotropic?*

ADULT. TEXAS, MAY. KEN BEHRENS.
- The distance that the head and neck project in front of the wing is almost identical to the projection of the tail behind the wing.
- At close range, the small gular pouch with pointed white border is diagnostic.

FIRST CYCLE. TEXAS, JULY. KEN BEHRENS.
- Neotropics are extremely lean and have a small, weak bill.
- First-cycle birds are darker and more evenly colored than immature Double-cresteds.

WITH ONE DOUBLE-CRESTED CORMORANT (LOWER L). TEXAS, JAN. KEN BEHRENS.
- Neotropic has a slimmer neck and wings than Double-crested.
- These species occasionally fly together, and vagrant Neotropics are often found with flocks of Double-cresteds.
- Note how the individual postures of the Neotropics affect perception of the ratio of head and neck to tail.

WITH IMMATURE DOUBLE-CRESTED CORMORANT (L). FLORIDA, NOV. TOM DUNKERTON.
- Although an undersized Double-crested can be confused with a Neotropic, typical individuals are distinctive.
- The tail length equals the head and neck length in Neotropic, whereas Double-crested is shorter-tailed.

ANHINGA
Anhinga anhinga
DIMENSIONS
L: 35 in.; WS: 45 in.; WT: 2.7 lb.

SPRING ARRIVAL

LA: late-Mar.; AR: early Apr.; NC: early Apr.

An observer seeing the snakelike head of this odd bird emerge from a murky swamp, with a fish speared on its long bill, might think it an unlikely aerialist. But this bird is an accomplished flier, capable of extended soaring and long migrations. Anhinga is cormorant-like in some aspects of appearance and behavior, but it is different enough that confusion should rarely be an issue. Southern wetlands with slow-moving fresh water are the heart of the species' range, but it has a strong tendency to wander.

SIZE: Larger than Neotropic Cormorant. Slightly smaller than Double-crested Cormorant. Its lanky, attenuated appearance makes it appear larger than it actually is.

STRUCTURE: So long and lean as to look almost emaciated. Has a long, sharply pointed bill; long,

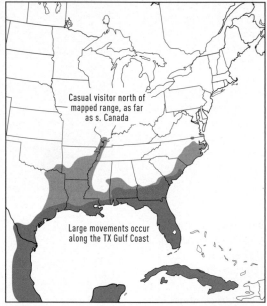

Casual visitor north of mapped range, as far as s. Canada

Large movements occur along the TX Gulf Coast

straight, slightly pointed wings; and a long tail that is pinched at the base and flares to a fan shape. The head projection is equal to the tail projection, and the wing length is similar as well, so Anhinga can have the appearance of an even-armed cross. The neck is slightly hunched at the base, creating a small hump in front of the chest.

FLIGHT AND FLOCKING: Flight style can vary drastically. Often soars effortlessly or glides for extended periods, though this relaxed flight can be punctuated by sudden, *Accipiter*-like bursts of wingbeats. Unlike in cormorants, the wings are held almost flat when gliding. Whereas movements of any distance are accomplished by soaring, local movements are powered by slow, labored wingbeats. During migration usually gathers in flocks ranging from several individuals to dozens. At concentration points in south Texas, these flocks may grow to hundreds of birds. Flocks gain altitude on thermals like some raptors do, but unlike raptors, they turn in tight, synchronized spirals similar to those formed by American White Pelicans.

APPEARANCE: Adult Male: Blackish overall with dark green iridescent highlights and a bright yellow bill. The greater coverts are white, the median and lesser coverts flecked white, and the scapulars and tertials white-striped, creating a silvery panel on the upperwing. The tail has a broad buff tip. **Adult Female:** Like adult male, but the upper breast and throat are tan, and the crown and nape are dark brown instead of black. **First Cycle:** Like adult female but with a dull brown (rather than black) body and wings, lack of any white markings on the upperwing, and a tail that lacks a pale tip. Male has a darker, typically dull gray, crown and nape. **Subadult:** Plumage progression is complex and not well known, taking 3–4 years to reach maturity. Subadults are much like adults but with fewer white markings on the wing. Each year they gain more white markings until they achieve adult plumage. **Distant:** Males look like a jet-black cross. The pale head and chest of females often disappear against pale backgrounds, creating the appearance of a flying black T.

SIMILAR SPECIES: Double-crested Cormorant: Significantly bulkier with a shorter and heavier neck, shorter and broader-based tail, and hooked bill. The wings are broader with blunter tips and are held in a slight crook. Beats its wings for longer stretches and glides far less. Although it doesn't do so frequently, Double-crested Cormorant does soar and has been confused with Anhinga by those who are unaware that cormorants can soar. The structural traits that separate these species are still evident when they are soaring high overhead, and this error can be easily avoided. **Neotropic Cormorant:** Smaller with a short, hooked bill and shorter neck and tail. Beats its wings rapidly and for extended periods, making only short glides.

ADULT MALE. FLORIDA, DEC. KEN BEHRENS.
- Although superficially similar to a cormorant, Anhinga has longer wings and tail, and its body is exceptionally slender.
- The pale patches in the wings and at the tip of the tail are identical in both sexes and take several years to fully develop.

FLORIDA, DEC. KEN BEHRENS.
- The long, incredibly slender neck earns Anhinga the colloquial name "snake bird."
- The long, sharply pointed bill is utterly unlike the heavier, hook-tipped bill of cormorants.
- *What are the birds in the background?*

MEXICO, SEPT. JEFF BIREK.
- As in American White Pelicans, soaring flocks rotate in unison, tracing elegant spirals through the air.
- At a distance the slender neck can disappear (particularly the female's tan neck), creating the appearance of a flying T rather than a flying cross.

TEXAS, SEPT. GREG LAVATY.
- Tail is very narrow at the base, then flares into a distinctive fan shape.
- Wings are very long and are held straighter than are those of cormorants.

ADULT MALE. FLORIDA, DEC. KEN BEHRENS.
- Note this adult male's fully developed wing pattern and broad pale tip to the tail.
- Unlike cormorants, Anhingas replace all of their flight feathers at once (thus becoming temporarily flightless), so their wings always appear even, avoiding the ragged appearance that cormorants acquire from having feathers of different ages.
- Flapping Anhingas share the explosive flap-flap-flap-glide cadence of *Accipter* and Black Vultures.

LOONS AND GREBES

Loons, family Gaviidea, and grebes, family Podicipedidae, are both small families of medium-sized to large waterbirds found primarily in northern temperate regions. We have placed them together not because they are closely related—the relationship between the two families is unclear—but because they have similar structure and behaviors and from a seawatching standpoint are comparable. For loons, we cover two regularly occurring species and one regular vagrant to eastern North America, Pacific Loon; we exclude a much rarer vagrant, Yellow-billed Loon. We include two regular species of grebes but exclude one regular species, Pied-billed Grebe; one regular vagrant to eastern North America, Eared Grebe; and the two rare *Aechmophorus* grebes, Clark's and Western Grebes. We exclude Pied-billed and Eared Grebes because both migrate almost exclusively at night. Even when disturbed,

they prefer to dive rather than fly and therefore do not belong in a guide to birds in flight.

Members of both families are accomplished diving birds; in fact in Europe loons are called "divers." As graceful as loons and grebes are in the water, they are extremely awkward on land and have difficulty taking flight. They sometimes mistake wet asphalt parking lots or roads for bodies of water and crash-land on them, becoming stranded because of their inability to take flight without an aquatic "runway." Once airborne, loons fly easily and with great speed and power, whereas most grebes fly weakly. Loons may fly at heights from just over the water to hundreds of feet in the air, whereas grebes tend to barely clear the surface of the water in diurnal flight. Both groups show a strong tendency to follow shorelines and a hesitation to fly over land during the day. Loons form extremely loose flocks that can hardly be called a "flock." Grebes form slightly tighter flocks, though these are still looser than those formed by most waterfowl species. Loons and

Grebes tend to appear awkward in flight, and most species fly weakly and reluctantly, in contrast to loons, which are strong fliers. We have excluded several species of grebes found regularly in eastern North America, including the widespread Pied-billed and the diminutive Least Grebe shown here, because they are so rarely seen in flight. Most birders are probably unaware that Least Grebes have a largely white wing, because they have never seen it! Texas, July. Ken Behrens.

This small, widely spread group of Red-throated Loons cutting past a flock of Black and Surf Scoters is a typical sight at a Mid-Atlantic seawatch in mid- to late fall. On good migration days, Red-throated Loons can fill the sky, flying from just above the water to hundreds of feet in the air, though they avoid crossing land as much as possible. New Jersey, Nov. Ken Behrens.

grebes almost always occur in monospecific flocks. Associations with other species and groups are only incidental. Loons can be vocal in flight, especially in spring.

There are no real identification challenges among the eastern grebes, though basic plumaged and first-cycle Red-necked Grebes can be momentarily confused with Red-throated Loons. Clear differences in structure and the overall dingy appearance of Red-necked Grebe should quickly end any confusion with the trimmer, neatly attired Red-throated Loon. Identification of loons is a bit more challenging. In particular, the rare Pacific Loon falls between the two common species in size and can potentially be confused with either. Cadence of the wingbeats, the structure of the head and neck, the way the head and neck are held, the size of the feet, and the overall color are important traits to assess when identifying loons. Common and Red-throated Loons are quite different, and though occasional odd individuals can cause some waffling, these species can be separated at great distances with some experience.

The sexes appear similar in all species covered here, and they all have distinctive alternate plumages. Differences between first-cycle birds and adults are subtle in most species and may not be apparent at a distance. They acquire adult appearance in the second or third cycle.

The pointed bill, long and slender wings, and projecting feet of this Common Loon are typical of all loons. Loons struggle to take flight because of their heavy body, but once in the air they fly powerfully and with great speed. South Carolina, Nov. Ken Behrens.

RED-THROATED LOON
Gavia stellata
DIMENSIONS
L: 25 in.; WS: 36 in.; WT: 3.1 lb.

SPRING ARRIVAL

s. Great Lakes: mid-Mar., Hudson Bay: late May

FALL ARRIVAL

NJ: mid-Oct., s. Great Lakes: late Oct.,
GA: early Dec.

This is a small, dainty loon with a strong preference for coastal regions, though it is also numerous on the eastern Great Lakes and occurs in small numbers on inland lakes. During migration it vastly outnumbers Common Loon along much of the Atlantic Coast, and its peak migration days in the late fall are among the most extraordinary of seawatch spectacles. Flocks are very loose, and there are many solo birds, meaning that a big Red-throated Loon day fills the sky with birds in a manner quite unlike that of any other migrating waterbird.

SIZE: Slightly larger than Red-breasted Merganser. Slightly smaller than Brant. Significantly smaller than Common Loon.

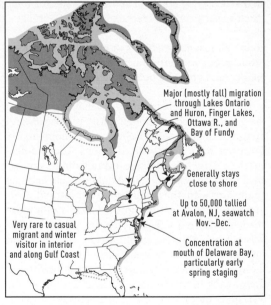

Major (mostly fall) migration through Lakes Ontario and Huron, Finger Lakes, Ottawa R., and Bay of Fundy

Generally stays close to shore

Up to 50,000 tallied at Avalon, NJ, seawatch Nov.–Dec.

Very rare to casual migrant and winter visitor in interior and along Gulf Coast

Concentration at mouth of Delaware Bay, particularly early spring staging

STRUCTURE: Slender, almost delicately built. The slim neck is usually drooped in flight so that the head is slightly below the body, and the tiny bill is held slightly upturned. This combination creates a distinctive silhouette, though the bill is small enough that it virtually disappears at a distance. The wings seem slightly farther back on the body, and the wings angle back more at the wrist, than on other loons. The feet are significantly shorter and smaller than those of Common Loon, and the toes

COMMON LOON
Gavia immer
DIMENSIONS
L: 32 in.; WS: 46 in.; WT: 9 lb.

SPRING ARRIVAL

MO: mid-Mar.; s. Great Lakes: late Mar.;
Hudson Bay: late May/early June

FALL ARRIVAL

NJ: early Sept.; TX: mid-/late Sept.; GA: early Oct.

This is the most widespread and widely recognized loon, familiar to birders and nonbirders alike. Its striking plumage and haunting wail are almost as emblematic of boreal lakes as loon curios are of north country gift shops! Common Loon winters mostly along the Atlantic and Gulf Coasts, often well offshore, but it also winters on large reservoirs in the southern states and is widespread during migration. There are some odd differences in timing between Common Loons migrating coastally

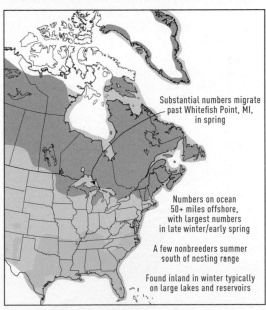

Substantial numbers migrate past Whitefish Point, MI, in spring

Numbers on ocean 50+ miles offshore, with largest numbers in late winter/early spring

A few nonbreeders summer south of nesting range

Found inland in winter typically on large lakes and reservoirs

in the Mid-Atlantic in fall compared with those seen at concentration points farther west. Common Loons peak more than a month earlier along the Mid-Atlantic coast, and occur in much smaller numbers. Over the past two decades the numbers of Common Loons counted at the Avalon Seawatch in New Jersey have declined drastically, whereas the numbers at the Cayuga Lake Loonwatch in western New York, and farther west on the Great Lakes, have shown much less change.

SIZE: Variable. Significantly larger than Red-throated and Pacific Loons. The largest are the size of Canada Goose. Smaller individuals are more similar in size to Snow Goose.

STRUCTURE: Bulky and powerful, with a deep belly that gives a "paunchy" impression while still managing to appear sleek. The neck is thick, and the large, blocky head has a slight peak above the eye. The bill is heavy, dagger-shaped, and visible from great distances. It is often held open in flight, particularly on warm days, a distinctive trait that is surprisingly obvious.

The slender wings are centered on the body, so that the head and neck extension in front of the wings is almost equal to that of the body and feet behind. The balanced appearance that this creates is distinctly different from the unbalanced, forward-leaning appearance of Red-throated Loon. A defining characteristic of Common Loon is the large paddlelike feet that trail behind the body. Most migrating Common Loons hold their toes open, enhancing this impression, though birds in shorter flights or in very cold weather keep the toes closed.

FLIGHT AND FLOCKING: Wingbeats are steady, even, and fairly shallow. The outer portion of the hand flexes slightly with each wingstroke, giving a "soft" look to the wingbeats, different from the stiff wingbeats of Red-throated. Flight is deceptively rapid, and birds rarely check their progress. Flocks typically number 1–15 birds, rarely more. They are so loose as to stretch the bounds of what can be called a "flock," with birds often 100 yards or more apart, though still seeming to move through the sky in an established order. Pairs sometimes fly together in tighter formations, a behavior rarely displayed by Red-throated. Most often flies at moderate heights but can fly very high, particularly over land, or skim low over the water.

APPEARANCE: Alternate Adult: Blackish head and bill with a bold white throat strap. Back is black with an impressive checkerboard pattern of white squares. Belly and underwing are white. This striking alternate plumage is worn by most northbound migrants. **Basic Adult:** Blackish above, white below with an uneven border between the white throat and black nape. This plumage is worn by fall migrants. **First Cycle:** Like basic adult but slightly paler with a less stark division between the dark nape and white throat. Shows subtle pale fringes to the back feathers, though this is difficult to see in flight. **Distant:** Contrasting blackish and white at moderate distance. At even greater distances, just blackish.

SIMILAR SPECIES: Red-throated Loon: Usually noticeably smaller. Much smaller bill; thinner head and neck, which are often drooped below the body; and much smaller feet. Wingbeats are faster and deeper and appear choppier because of the stiffly held hand. At great distances, Red-throated Loons look like shapeless gray specks, whereas Common Loons have the appearance of loon-shaped blackish specks. **Pacific Loon:** Smaller, with a less gangly appearance. The bill and neck are shorter and the crown is gently rounded, not peaked. The belly is smoothly rounded, lacking the hanging paunch of Common, and the feet are smaller and held flat so are less obvious. In basic plumage has a distinctly dark-hooded appearance, often with a silvery nape. At close range, basic birds also show a clean "chin-strap" across the throat, quite different from Common's smudgy neck markings.

CALIFORNIA, OCT.
BRIAN SULLIVAN.
- Sleek but powerful shape and deep belly recall a weightlifter with a beer belly.
- Darker above than Red-throated Loon, so even at a distance appears black and white, whereas Red-throated Loon appears dull gray.
- Bill is heavy with a formidable daggerlike shape.
- Feet are large and obvious.

**NEW JERSEY, NOV.
KEN BEHRENS.**
- Form smaller flocks than Red-throated Loons, with greater spacing between individuals and more frequent obvious pair associations.

**ALTERNATE ADULT. TEXAS, APR.
KEN BEHRENS.**
- When migrating on warm days, Common Loon often "pants" with its bill open. Calling in flight is also common on spring migration and occasionally in fall.
- The toes are usually spread, enhancing the large-footed appearance. On short-distance flights or on cold days, the toes may be held closed, significantly altering the silhouette.

ALTERNATE ADULT. MICHIGAN, MAY. KEN BEHRENS.
- Even at great distances maintains an unmistakable black-and-white loonlike silhouette, whereas Red-throated Loon melts into a shapeless gray dot on the horizon.

ALTERNATE ADULTS. MICHIGAN, MAY. KEN BEHRENS.
- Breeding pairs may fly much closer together than do individuals in migrating flocks.
- With the toes closed, the feet still look large but are less obvious at a distance.

ALTERNATE ADULT. WASHINGTON, JULY. ROBERT WHITNEY.
- A truly stunning bird!
- The long, slender wings seem at odds with the bulging paunch and heavy bill.
- Often shows a moderately to distinctly peaked forehead.

MICHIGAN, MAY. KEN BEHRENS.
- Silhouette looks balanced but not particularly graceful thanks to the bulging belly, peaked forehead, and prominent feet.

STRUCTURAL COMPARISON: COMMON LOON (L) WITH RED-THROATED LOON (R).

- Common Loon typically holds the neck straight in flight. Red-throated frequently droops the neck so the head is lower than the body.
- The larger head, bill, and feet of Common Loon allow identification by silhouette alone.
- The bulging lower belly is a trait shown only by Common Loon and the vagrant Yellow-billed Loon.
- Although still prominent, the larger feet of Common Loon are less obvious when the toes are closed. The large bill and broader wings are still obvious.
- Wingbeats of Common Loon are shallower, with more flex to the wingtips. Those of Red-throated Loon are deeper and less flexible.

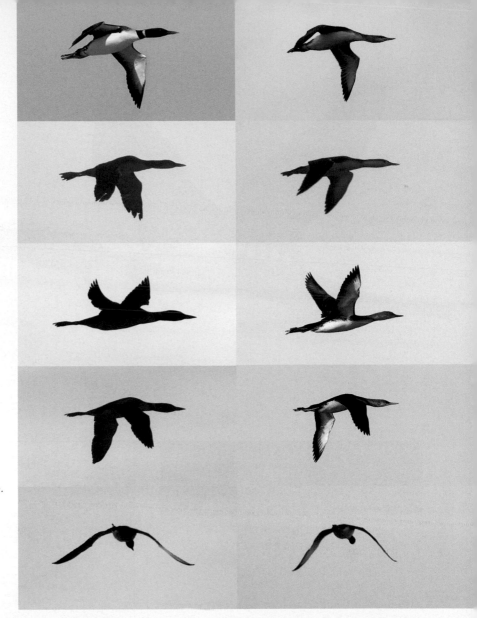

ALTERNATE ADULT WITH THREE RED-BREASTED MERGANSERS. MICHIGAN, MAY. KEN BEHRENS.

- Size and the bulk of Common Loon prevent it from being confused with Red-breasted Merganser, whereas Red-throated Loon is close enough in size and overall color to the merganser to create momentary confusion.
- Note the loon's bulging belly and peaked forehead.

PACIFIC LOON
Gavia pacifica
DIMENSIONS
L: 25 in.; WS: 36 in.; WT: 3.7 lb.

SPRING ARRIVAL

Hudson Bay: late May/early June

Although this midsized loon breeds in the Arctic as far east as Hudson Bay, the vast majority of its population winters along the Pacific Coast. Small numbers regularly spend the winter on large reservoirs in the south-central U.S. and along the western Gulf Coast. The species becomes progressively less common farther east and is rare on the Atlantic Coast, though there has been a recent increase in records, particularly from the New England coast.

SIZE: Slightly larger than Brant. Slightly smaller than Snow Goose. Clearly smaller than Common Loon.

STRUCTURE: Compact, with balanced proportions and smoothly rounded lines. Not bulky and gangly like Common Loon or skinny and pitched forward like Red-throated Loon. The bill is usually short but fairly thick-based, and the neck appears slightly

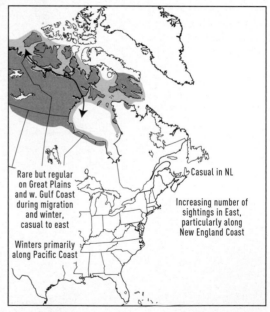

Rare but regular on Great Plains and w. Gulf Coast during migration and winter, casual to east

Winters primarily along Pacific Coast

Casual in NL

Increasing number of sightings in East, particularly along New England Coast

shorter than on other loons. The head merges into the neck so evenly that they are often indistinguishable, though some birds have a larger, more noticeable head. The forehead rises out of the bill and continues through the crown in a slight and smoothly rounded curve. The belly is also smoothly rounded without the hanging paunch of Common Loon. The feet are of moderate size but held straight, with the toes closed, so they are less obvious than those of Common Loon.

FLIGHT AND FLOCKING: Wingbeats are steady and powerful, as in other loons, but faster than in Common and with less flexibility in the wingtips. However, they are not as deep or choppy as in Red-throated. Forms large flocks on the Pacific Coast, but in eastern North America is usually seen singly or accompanying Common or Red-throated Loons.

APPEARANCE: Alternate Adult: Medium gray head with a silvery nape and dark iridescent purple throat that usually looks black, bordered by a series of thin vertical white lines. Back and upperwing are black with a white-checkered pattern that is less extensive than in Common Loon, limited to the scapulars. **Basic Adult:** Black above, darker than Common Loon, and white below. Has a distinctly dark-hooded appearance, as the blackish crown and nape extend farther down, encompassing the eye, much of the face, and the sides of the neck. The division between the dark crown and neck and the white throat is sharp and straight. The dark crown extends so far down the neck that the white throat is barely visible except on high-flying birds. Most adults have a narrow dark "chinstrap" across the throat and a dark vent strap, but both are difficult to see in flight. **First Cycle:** Like basic but slightly paler above with a paler nape and subtle

pale fringes to the back feathers, though these are difficult to see in flight. Most first-cycle birds lack the dark chinstrap shown by basic adults. **Distant:** Alternate birds are dark with a white belly, blackish throat, and silvery nape. Basic birds are very starkly black and white with a more distinct dark hooded appearance than other eastern loons.

SIMILAR SPECIES: Common Loon: Usually significantly larger, but the occasional small individual can create confusion. Even small Common Loons have more of a bulging belly; larger, more obvious, protruding feet; and slightly slower wingbeats with more flexible wingtips. Basic Common Loons are slightly paler above than Pacific Loon and show a jagged division between the white throat and dark nape. Appears less hooded than Pacific as the dark markings do not extend as far down onto the neck. **Red-throated Loon:** Usually easily separated, though some first-cycle birds have an extensive dark wash on the neck and throat that can approximate the hooded appearance of Pacific Loon. Red-throated Loon is smaller and slimmer, with a skinny neck that is usually drooped below the body with the bill angled upward. It appears less balanced, as the wings are set farther back on the body. The wings angle back more distinctly at the wrists, and wingbeats are slightly faster. Even dark first-cycle birds are not as black as Pacific and have an ill-defined division between dark and light on the neck, lacking the crisp border of Pacific.

FIRST CYCLE. CALIFORNIA, DEC. BRIAN SULLIVAN.
- Similar in structure to Common Loon but is smaller, more compact, and lacks a peaked forehead.
- Bill and feet generally appear smaller than those of Common Loon, though there is some overlap.
- Strikingly dark-headed in basic plumage, with the diagnostic black "chinstrap" visible at extremely close range.

ALTERNATE ADULTS. MANITOBA, JUNE. TOM JOHNSON.
- Short, stocky neck and smaller head and bill differentiate Pacific Loon from Common Loon.
- In alternate plumage, the silvery nape is a unique trait of Pacific Loon.

COMPARISON: PACIFIC LOON WITH COMMON LOON (TOP). COMMON, CALIFORNIA, SEPT.; PACIFIC, CALIFORNIA, DEC. BRIAN SULLIVAN.
- The belly of Pacific Loon is slim compared with the bulging paunch of Common Loon.
- Pacific has a darker face and cleaner neck pattern.
- Pacific's feet are smaller and do not extend as far behind the bird.
- Pacific appears more compact overall than Common.

RED-NECKED GREBE
Podiceps grisegena
DIMENSIONS
L: 18 in.; WS: 24 in.; WT: 2.2 lb.

SPRING ARRIVAL

s. Great Lakes: late Mar.;
w. Great Lakes: early Apr.

FALL ARRIVAL

Lake Superior: late Aug.; Lake Erie: late Oct.;
Atlantic Coast and St. Lawrence River: Oct.

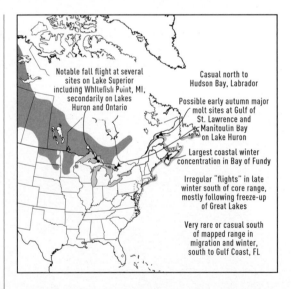

Notable fall flight at several sites on Lake Superior including Whitefish Point, MI, secondarily on Lakes Huron and Ontario

Casual north to Hudson Bay, Labrador

Possible early autumn major molt sites at Gulf of St. Lawrence and Manitoulin Bay on Lake Huron

Largest coastal winter concentration in Bay of Fundy

Irregular "flights" in late winter south of core range, mostly following freeze-up of Great Lakes

Very rare or casual south of mapped range in migration and winter, south to Gulf Coast, FL

This distinctive species is the only large grebe that occurs regularly in eastern North America. Because of its size, it is more likely to be confused with loons than with other grebes. It breaks the grebe mold by regularly migrating diurnally as well as nocturnally. Breeding occurs on northern freshwater lakes and ponds, while the majority of the birds wintering in eastern North America are found in the Atlantic Provinces and eastern Great Lakes. Impressive numbers are recorded in active migration on the Great Lakes, particularly eastern Lake Superior in fall and Lake Ontario in spring. After large numbers move over Lake Superior in early fall, the majority of the population disappears for more than a month to molt. Molt sites are thought to be in the eastern Great Lakes, specifically Lake Huron, but only a small percentage of the population can be located at this time.

SIZE: Slightly smaller than Red-throated Loon. Clearly larger than Horned Grebe. About the size of Gadwall.

STRUCTURE: Oddly and somewhat awkwardly proportioned. The heavy body often shows a Common Loon–like bulging belly, whereas the neck is long and skinny. The modestly peaked head blends into the neck in flight and does not stand out. The large feet project past the tail and are so oversized that they appear to be covered in heavy gloves. Both the neck and feet are slightly drooped, creating a hunchbacked appearance. The wings are located slightly ahead of center on the body and are long and slim, like a loon's, but they angle back more at the wrist and have blunter tips.

FLIGHT AND FLOCKING: Steady flight is driven by wingbeats that are fairly even and shallow. Although the beats may actually be slower than those of loons, they have an awkward twitching quality that makes them seem frantic. In this respect, Red-necked Grebe flies more like a Red-throated Loon than like the other loons, but the frantic quality of its wingbeats exceeds even that of Red-throated Loon. Flight speed exceeds that of Horned Grebe but is slower than in loons. Usually seen as singles or small flocks of 2–6, though flocks of up to 20 occur during big movements on the upper Great Lakes. Usually flies just above the water. Avoids flying over land diurnally.

APPEARANCE: Alternate Adult: Black crown and nape contrast sharply with the bold white face and chin; the neck and upper breast are rust colored. The back is blackish and the flanks are gray, fading to a dirty white belly. The secondaries and the leading edge of the wing are white, as are the axillaries and most of the underwing. **Basic Adult:** Dark gray above and dingy white below with a darker throat and faintly paler ear patch. Wing pattern is same as in alternate. **First Cycle:** Like basic, but pale underparts are more heavily washed with gray. Lacks the pale leading edge of the wing shown by adult. **Distant:** Appears dark gray to paler dirty gray. Rarely looks black, and always gives a dingy impression. The white patches on the wing can disappear at a distance, giving the wings an oddly slender appearance.

SIMILAR SPECIES: Red-throated Loon: Larger and more streamlined with a less pronounced hunchbacked appearance. The feet are much smaller and project almost straight behind the body rather than dangling downward. Loons' wingbeats are faster and stiffer, and their flight is swifter. The overall appearance is cleaner, with paler gray upperparts and brighter white underparts lacking white patches on the upperwing. **Horned Grebe:** Smaller, with much faster wingbeats and shorter wings. Sharply contrasting black and white in basic plumage, and lacks the white face of Red-necked Grebe in alternate plumage.

ALTERNATE ADULTS. ONTARIO, APR. KEN BEHRENS.
• Unmistakable because of their large size, gangly shape, and dingy coloration.
• Both the neck and feet are drooped below the body, a distinctive Red-necked Grebe trait.
• Silhouette is quite loonlike but stockier and shorter-winged.
• Red-necked Grebe is particularly distinctive in alternate plumage; white-cheeked and rusty-necked, it appears cleaner and more colorful than it does in its drab basic plumage.

ALTERNATE ADULTS. ONTARIO, APR. KEN BEHRENS.

- The white secondaries and leading edge of the wing can disappear, giving the wings a misshapen appearance.
- Flight is much stronger than that of Horned Grebe, but still seems labored.

FIRST CYCLE. WASHINGTON, NOV. ROBERT WHITNEY.

- Similar to a basic adult in most respects.
- The amount of white in the wing is variable; some first cycles nearly lack white in the wing. The pale cheek of adults is also less apparent, or nonexistent, on first cycles.

MICHIGAN, MAY. KEN BEHRENS.

- Flocks are loose and usually small. Individuals are more widely spaced than in duck flocks, though much closer together than in loon flocks.

ONTARIO, APR. KEN BEHRENS.

- Although loonlike in structure, lacks the sleek elegance of loons and always retains some of the awkwardness that characterizes grebes in flight.

HORNED GREBE
Podiceps auritus
DIMENSIONS
L: 14 in.; WS: 18 in.; WT: 1 lb.

SPRING ARRIVAL

OH: early Mar.; NE: late Mar.;
Hudson Bay: mid-/late May

FALL ARRIVAL

s. Great Lakes: mid-Oct.; NJ: mid-Oct.;
e. Gulf Coast: early Nov.

Despite being almost comically awkward in flight, Horned is by far the most likely small grebe to be observed in flight. It is remarkable that although this species seems barely able to fly during the day, it undertakes lengthy nocturnal migrations. Horned Grebe breeds on lakes and ponds and moves south into coastal bays, estuaries, freshwater lakes, and reservoirs during migration and winter.

SIZE: Slightly smaller than Lesser Scaup. Slightly larger than Bufflehead. About the size of Blue-winged Teal.

STRUCTURE: Disjointed and awkward. The slim neck is either drooped below the body or, more frequently, stretched upward so the head is elevated above the body. Even with the neck elevated, the small and rounded head is held level so the bill points straight forward. This peculiar posture recalls that of a turtle craning its neck to evaluate its

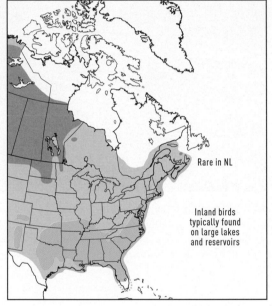

Rare in NL

Inland birds typically found on large lakes and reservoirs

surroundings. The short, heavy body is vaguely oval in shape and tilts up slightly. The wings are short and narrow, seeming too small for the bird. The legs and feet hang down behind. As in all grebes, the feet are oversized and almost seem to be wearing mittens; they are either drooped downward or cocked at an awkward upward tilt.

FLIGHT AND FLOCKING: Horned Grebe beats its wings in a furious blur, seeming just able to maintain a heavy, inelegant semblance of flight. During the day it strictly avoids flying over land and skims just above the water. Rarely flies more than a few hundred yards before flopping back down for a rest. Migrating birds often land when they see other Horned Grebes sitting on the water. Eventually the newly enlarged flock will take flight again after a clumsy running takeoff. Flocks usually number 2–6 but can grow to 12, and rarely larger. Flocks have a loose, horizontal structure, and there are often distant trailing birds that seem to be trying to keep up with the main group.

APPEARANCE: **Alternate Adult:** The black head is bisected by a golden band that runs from behind the eye to the nape. The neck and flanks are rusty, the back gray, and the belly white. The upperwing is largely gray, but the secondaries are bright white, and often there is a small white patch on the leading edge of the wings near the body. **Basic Adult:** Sharply contrasting black and white: a black crown with a white face and throat. The belly and underwing are white, whereas the back and upperwing are dark gray except for the large white secondary patch. **First Cycle:** Like basic adult but shows some dusky clouding on the throat and reduced white in the secondaries. **Distant:** Alternate birds are mostly dark with obvious white wing patches. Basic birds are stark black and white.

SIMILAR SPECIES: **Eared Grebe** (not included in this guide): Generally rare in eastern North America except along the western Gulf Coast and virtually never seen in extended flight as it is a strictly nocturnal migrant. Much slimmer than Horned with a shorter, slimmer neck and thin bill. Darker in all plumages. In basic it shows a strong gray wash to the neck that obscures the division between the dark crown and nape and the paler face and throat. **Pied-billed Grebe** (not included in this guide): Rarely seen in flight. Slightly larger than Horned with a longer neck and longer legs. This gives it a lankier appearance, and although its posture in flight is similar to that of Horned Grebe, it appears even more awkward. Pied-billed is darker than Horned overall, brown above with a dingy white belly. **Bufflehead:** Similarities include very rapid wingbeats, overall black-and-white plumage, and small flocks that fly just above the water. Nonetheless, Bufflehead is easily separated, as it is far more fleet and agile. It is also more compact than grebes, lacking the long neck and dangling feet.

BASIC ADULT. FLORIDA, JAN. DANNY BALES.
- Combination of small size, compact but awkward shape, furious but weak wingbeats, and black and white color makes it easy to identify.
- Clean white throat and black cap separate it from Eared Grebe.

ALTERNATE ADULT. NORTH DAKOTA, JUNE. KEN BEHRENS.
- The feet are so large that they appear to be wearing mittens. They trail behind the body and usually droop downward.
- Adults have more extensive white in the wings than first-cycle birds.

FLORIDA, FEB. STEPHAN MANN.
- Wings are broad but fairly short.
- Flocks tend to form tight bunches, often with one or two birds slightly separated from the rest of the flock.
- Flocks this size are rare, usually found only in staging areas. Groups of 2–12 are more typically seen in flight.

ALCIDS

Alcids are stocky, small to medium-sized seabirds of Arctic and temperate seas. The name "alcid" is an abbreviation of the family name, Alcidae; "auks" is another name for this group. We cover six species in this guide. The three large black-and-white species—Common Murre, Thick-billed Murre, and Razorbill—can be very difficult to tell apart at a distance. The three smaller species are all distinct: the widely recognized Atlantic Puffin; Black Guillemot; and the tiny Dovekie, known as Little Auk in Europe.

All of the Atlantic alcids have a northern distribution, with the southernmost breeding species reaching their southern limit in northern New England. Most species are poorly known and seldom seen by most birders and are therefore highly prized, particularly the charismatic Atlantic Puffin and the tiny elusive Dovekie. However, several of these species are extremely numerous in their core Arctic range. Dovekie, for example, is one of the most numerous birds in the world with a population estimated in the tens of millions. All alcids are primarily pelagic in the winter, except Black Guillemot, which stays close to rocky shorelines or humanmade structures like docks and jetties year-round.

Alcids are often compared to the better-known penguins of the Southern Hemisphere, mainly because of their shared manner of swimming. Both groups use their short, stiff wings to propel themselves underwater with great speed and agility, a sort of "flying underwater." Alcids are unlike penguins in that they have maintained their ability to fly, though their frantic flight would suggest that they only just maintain their ability to fly! They have extremely fast wingbeats that blur the short wings, which in most species appear too small for the body. The wingbeats are continuous, and unlike in many species in this guide, they show almost no variation in cadence under varying weather condition, although many species rock from side to side as they fly.

Alcids need the ability to fly because of the presence of terrestrial predators, such as Arctic fox, in the Northern Hemisphere. Many species nest colonially on steep cliffs inaccessible to foxes and other terrestrial predators. When visiting a colony of murres, it is easy to see which sections of the cliff face are accessible to predators, as they are empty. Where suitable ledge space is inaccessible to predators, murres will occupy every available inch. Puffins defeat predators by digging burrows for their nest. The smaller Atlantic alcids, Black Guillemot and Dovekie, nest in cracks in cliff faces or in crevices among boulders and scree on beaches.

The sexes appear similar in all six species covered here, and they all have distinctive alternate plumages. They also show differences between first-cycle birds and adults. They acquire adult appearance in the second cycle.

Alcids, like this Common Murre, use their short, stiff wings as a primary source of propulsion to "fly" underwater. B&C Alexander/Arcticphoto.

RAZORBILL
Alca torda
DIMENSIONS
L: 17 in.; WS: 26 in.; WT: 1.6 lb.

SPRING ARRIVAL

St. Lawrence Estuary: mid-Apr.;
Greenland: late Apr.

FALL ARRIVAL

offshore NL: mid-Oct.; s. ME: late Oct.;
MA: mid-Nov.

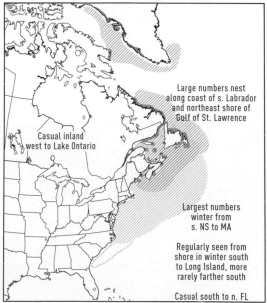

Large numbers nest along coast of s. Labrador and northeast shore of Gulf of St. Lawrence

Casual inland west to Lake Ontario

Largest numbers winter from s. NS to MA

Regularly seen from shore in winter south to Long Island, more rarely farther south

Casual south to n. FL

Razorbill is the most widespread and regularly encountered Atlantic alcid, and it serves as a good starting point for comparing the large alcids. It is regularly seen from shore between fall and early spring, from the Atlantic Provinces to North Carolina and occasionally farther south under the right conditions. Some years are exceptional and Razorbills are sighted from shore all along the Atlantic Coast and seen in large numbers on winter pelagic trips. In other years they are scarce south of Long Island. The trio of Razorbill and the two murres forms a complex of large black-and-white alcids that are difficult to differentiate in flight. A large alcid spotted in flight at a distance often cannot be narrowed to species.

SIZE: Slightly smaller than Thick-billed and Common Murres, though the large bill can trick an observer into thinking Razorbill is bigger. About the same size as Lesser Scaup, though structure is very different.

STRUCTURE: Bulky and potbellied but with a long, sleek body. The bill is large and deep, though smaller in the first cycle, and is typically held tilted slightly upward, unlike in murres. The head is large and blocky and the neck is thick, merging smoothly with the body. The wings are centered on the body; the deepest point in the body falls level with or slightly behind the trailing edge of the wing, creating a potbellied appearance. The wings are slender and often appear short because of the ultrafast wingbeats, but they are actually fairly long. The tail is long and pointed, unlike that of murres, and extends past the feet, usually obscuring them, and often curls up slightly at the tip.

FLIGHT AND FLOCKING: Typically flies very low to the water with whirring wingbeats that blur the outline of the wing. At times flight is steady but usually rocks side to side slightly. In a flock, individuals rock completely out of sync with one another. At times they bob the head up and down. Small groups fly in near-perfect lines, usually with generous and distinct spacing between birds. As flocks get larger they become messier and more tightly packed and may take on a shape similar to a flock of *Aythya* ducks. All three species of large black-and-white alcids fly together where their ranges overlap. Razorbill may join waterfowl, particularly scoters, usually at the back of a flock, as it has trouble keeping up with the ducks.

APPEARANCE: **Alternate Adult:** Very dark, almost black above, though at close range some brown tones are visible, particularly on the wings. The dark color cuts straight down in front of the wings to encompass the throat. The large bill is also black, set off by two thin white lines that are not visible at a distance. The belly is entirely white, as are the underwing coverts, which contrast with the dark undersides of the wing feathers. As in Thick-billed Murre, but unlike Common Murre, the white from the belly wraps around the flanks extensively, so on a bird flying directly away the lower back looks like a thin blackish stripe hemmed with white. This mark is difficult to gauge from most angles, and without lots of comparative experience. **Basic Adult:** Like alternate but with a white throat and area of white behind the eye. Also has a partial thin, dark collar that extends down in front of the wings. **First Cycle:** Like basic adult but with a duskier face and smaller bill that lacks the white lines of adult and is therefore more similar to that of Thick-billed Murre. **Distant:** Black and white.

SIMILAR SPECIES: **Thick-billed Murre:** Slightly larger and clearly bulkier, with a much shorter tail that exposes the feet. The bill is significantly smaller than that of adult Razorbill but similar to that of first-cycle Razorbill, and is held angled slightly downward. In basic plumage has a much darker head than Razorbill, with black behind and underneath the eye. **Common Murre:** Longer and skinnier with a slim, pointed bill and a shorter tail that exposes the feet. Significantly paler than Razorbill: dark gray-brown, showing faint dusky markings on the underwing and flanks.

SCOTLAND, SEPT. JOHN ANDERSON.
- Stark plumage and a heavy, football-like shape characterize all three large black-and-white alcids.
- The long tail obscuring the feet and the heavy, blunt bills identify these as Razorbills.
- Small flocks are carefully ordered, but large flocks of Razorbills become less organized and can recall a flock of ducks, though they never adopt the tight ball-shaped formations of similar-sized ducks such as Bufflehead.

RAZORBILL. MAINE, JULY. KEN BEHRENS.
- Tail covers feet.
- Blunt bill tilts slightly upward.
- Blackish upperparts.

THICK-BILLED MURRE. NORWAY, JUNE. HUGH HARROP.
- Feet exposed.
- Heavy, pointed bill tilts down.
- Black upperparts.

COMMON MURRE. WALES, APR. KEN BEHRENS.
- Feet exposed.
- Slender, pointed bill is usually straight.
- Blackish brown upperparts.

BASIC BIRDS. NORTH CAROLINA, FEB. KEN BEHRENS.
- Unstable in flight, often banking from side to side; white bellies flash brightly as they catch the sun.

ALTERNATE ADULTS WITH TWO ALTERNATE ADULT COMMON MURRES. MAINE, JULY. CAMERON COX.
- Razorbills often look slightly larger than Common Murres because of their heavier bill and overall build.
- *Can you find both Common Murres?*

FIRST CYCLE. SWEDEN, SEPT. TOMMY HOLMGREN.
- Much smaller bill than adult.
- Unlike both murres, Razorbill has a long, pointed tail.
- First-cycle Razorbill can be told from Thick-billed Murre by the extensive white behind the eye and the slightly upward-tilted bill.

ALTERNATE ADULTS WITH ONE ALTERNATE ADULT ATLANTIC PUFFIN (R). MAINE, JULY. CAMERON COX.
• Much larger and longer than Atlantic Puffin, Razorbill is the next largest Atlantic alcid besides the two murres.

NEW JERSEY, JAN. TOM JOHNSON.
• Along most of the U.S. Atlantic Coast, flocks this size are rare and typically indicate an exceptional event caused by weather or a food shortage.
• Large flocks are similar in structure to flocks of *Aythya* ducks but with more space between birds.

ALTERNATE ADULTS. WALES, APR. KEN BEHRENS.
• In alternate plumage, the completely dark head enhances the blocky appearance.
• Large alcids with such distinctly upward-tilted bills are always Razorbills.

(LEFT)
ALTERNATE ADULT. MAINE, JULY. KEN BEHRENS.

THICK-BILLED MURRE
Uria lomvia
DIMENSIONS
L: 18 in.; WS: 28 in.; WT: 2.1 lb.

SPRING ARRIVAL

s. Greenland: early Apr.; Baffin Bay: early May

FALL ARRIVAL

off ME: mid-Aug.; off MA: mid-Nov.;
off NY: late Nov.

This hearty alcid thrives in frigid northern seas, where it forages along ice edges year-round. Although the species deserts the most northern part of its breeding range in winter, most birds still remain very far north. Thick-billed Murre is not normally seen in large numbers on the Atlantic at locations easily accessible to humans, though huge flights have been witnessed from sites in Atlantic Canada during strong onshore winds.

SIZE: Slightly larger than Razorbill. Almost identical to Common Murre but often appears larger. About the same size as Black Scoter.

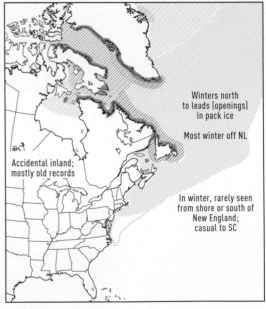

Winters north
to leads (openings)
in pack ice

Most winter off NL

Accidental inland;
mostly old records

In winter, rarely seen
from shore or south of
New England;
casual to SC

STRUCTURE: Strikingly bulky and powerful with a slightly rounded back and deep, rounded belly, imparting a football-like shape. The bill is short but fairly deep and slightly decurved, the head is large and blocky, and the thick neck is virtually indistinguishable from the body. The body seems thicker throughout its length than that of Razorbill, but the deepest point is located in roughly the same place, about level with the trailing edge of the wing. The wings are slightly broader than those of the other large alcids and are centered on the body; they appear fairly short in flight, as the speed of the wingbeats blurs the wing profile, but they are actually quite long. The tail is short, barely noticeable in flight, and the feet stick out well beyond the tail. When murres first take off, the feet are very obvious, instantly separating them from Razorbill, but in longer flights the feet are held tightly closed and are less noticeable.

FLIGHT AND FLOCKING: As in Razorbill.

APPEARANCE: Alternate Adult: Dark blackish above, slightly paler than Razorbill with a slightly more noticeable brownish tint. The black bill is marked with a strong white line running down the gape, referred to as a tomial stripe. The throat is also dark; the belly and underwing are clean white. Like in Razorbill, but unlike in Common Murre, the white from the belly wraps around the flanks extensively, so on a bird seen flying directly away the lower back looks like a thin blackish stripe hemmed with white. **Basic Adult:** Like alternate but with a small white throat that is often obscured by dark mottling and can appear completely dark on a bird flying close to the water. Some birds keep a fully dark throat throughout the winter. Also has a thick, dark band extending down from the shoulder across the base of the throat; it usually does not go all the way across, though often appears to in the field. Overall looks distinctly dark-headed. **First Cycle:** Like basic adult but with a smaller bill with a less distinct tomial stripe and often an even duskier throat. **Distant:** Black and white.

SIMILAR SPECIES: Razorbill: Slightly smaller, with a sleeker silhouette, slimmer wings, and a longer tail that obscures the feet. The bill of adult is large and blunt-tipped, though first-cycle birds have a bill similar to Thick-billed Murre's. At all ages the bill of Razorbill is typically held with a slight upward angle, not downward as in Thick-billed Murre. Basic adult Razorbill has a more extensive, cleaner white throat and white extending behind the eye. These white marks are clearly visible at long range, unlike those of Thick-billed. First-cycle Razorbill is the most similar to Thick-billed but still appears paler-headed with some white behind the eye. The appearance of the head plus the differences in structure should allow a well-seen bird to be identified, but distant birds often must be left as "large alcid species." **Common Murre:** Longer and leaner. Although the same size or slightly larger than Thick-billed, it often appears smaller because of its slimmer build. Has a slimmer, more pointed bill; smaller head; and longer neck, which combine to make it look very pointed in front. The wings are slightly slimmer and set slightly farther forward, so there appears to be more bird behind the wings than in front. Paler than Thick-billed and can be picked out by color in mixed flocks, though the color is hard to judge on a single bird. Common has faint dusky markings on the flanks and duskier underwings. Some individuals are extremely similar to Thick-billed and are best left unidentified without excellent views or good photos.

BASIC ADULT. MASSACHUSETTS, DEC. JEREMIAH TRIMBLE.
• Stocky and powerful; more compact than Razorbill.
• In winter has a darker head than Common Murre or Razorbill, and the pale throat is often invisible.
• The feet project beyond the short tail.

ALTERNATE ADULT. NORWAY, MAR. HUGH HARROP.
• The pale tomial stripe on the bill is very difficult to see in flight but is visible in photos.

WITH COMMON MURRE (FRONT). NORWAY, MAR. HUGH HARROP.
- Longer neck and bill of Common Murre give it a more pointed appearance.
- Thick-billed Murre is stockier and broader-winged.
- Common has darker wingpits and dark-streaked flanks, giving these areas a dirty appearance, whereas the flanks and underwing of Thick-billed appear cleaner. The darker axillaries of this Common Murre are particularly striking, while the flank streaking is lighter than normal.

ALTERNATE ADULTS. NORWAY, JUNE. JAMES LOWEN.
- They angle their bill downward slightly, a characteristic that is more noticeable at a distance than at close range.
- Large alcids regularly form mixed flocks, so check each individual with care.

ALTERNATE ADULT WITH FIVE ALTERNATE ADULT COMMON MURRES. NORWAY, MAR. HUGH HARROP.
- Bulky build, darker mantle, and white tomial stripe identify the Thick-billed Murre (second from R), but lighting and angle can play tricks on your eyes. Notice that the Common Murre directly behind the Thick-billed looks quite similar from this angle.

COMMON MURRE
Uria aalge
DIMENSIONS
L: 17.5 in.; WS: 26 in.; WT: 2.2 lb.

FALL ARRIVAL

off MA: early Dec.; off NY: mid-Dec.

Common Murre breeds at slightly lower latitudes than its Arctic-nesting cousin Thick-billed Murre, making it a bit more accessible as a breeder. It regularly breeds as far south as Maine in small numbers. Recent winter pelagic trips have discovered some interesting facts about the distribution of the two murres along the New England and Mid-Atlantic coasts. Most Common Murres seem to stay in a fairly narrow band starting 3–5 miles offshore and extending out to about 15 miles offshore. Thick-billed Murres are more pelagic and are found farther out, though a few are found inshore, closer than most Common Murres. Outside Atlantic Canada, where both species may be found in good numbers at prime seawatching locations, both species are rare from shore, though at the seawatching mecca of Cape Ann, Massachusetts, Common Murre has become fairly common in recent years, far more regular than Thick-billed Murre.

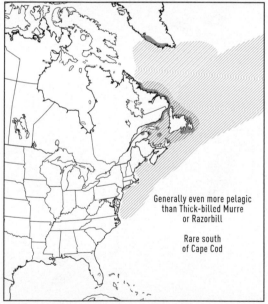

Generally even more pelagic than Thick-billed Murre or Razorbill

Rare south of Cape Cod

SIZE: Technically the largest of the three large alcids by a tiny margin. Virtually the same size as Thick-billed Murre but often appears slightly smaller in the field. Most are clearly larger than Razorbill.

STRUCTURE: Longer-bodied than the other large alcids, with a long, narrow bill; small head with a flat forehead; and longer, thinner neck. The fact that the bill, head, and neck are all slightly longer and narrower than those of the other large alcids makes the front of the bird look attenuated whereas the rear is still fairly stocky. The bill points straight ahead, accentuating this impression. Although it is still heavy-bodied and deepest near the rear, Common Murre appears slimmer than the other large alcids; in particular its chest appears less robust. The wings are thin, like Razorbill's, but set farther forward, so more of the body falls behind the wings than in front of them. The tail is short, barely noticeable in flight, and the feet stick out well beyond it. When murres first take off, the feet are obvious, instantly separating them from Razorbill, but in longer flights the feet are held tightly closed and are less noticeable.

FLIGHT AND FLOCKING: As in Razorbill.

APPEARANCE: Alternate Adult: Dark brown above and across the throat. Some, called "Bridled" Murres, have a thin white eye-ring and line running behind the eye. The belly is all white, but the axillaries are heavily mottled and the underwing coverts are slightly dusky, so the underwing is not clean white as in the other large alcids. The flanks are lightly marred with brown streaking, and they do not wrap around to the back extensively, so the dark back looks broader on a bird flying away than it does on the other large alcids. **Basic Adult:** Like alternate but with a clean white throat and extensive amounts of white behind the eye extending up to the sides of the nape. A few may remain dark-headed throughout the winter. **First Cycle:** Like basic adult but with a shorter bill and slightly duskier face and flanks. **Distant:** Black and white.

SIMILAR SPECIES: Thick-billed Murre: Stockier, with a shorter, thicker bill; larger, blockier head; and fuller chest. Slightly darker above and much darker-headed in basic plumage with cleaner white underwings and flanks. See Thick-billed Murre account for more. **Razorbill:** Slightly smaller, with a sleeker silhouette, larger bill, and longer tail. Darker-backed with cleaner white underwings and clean white flanks. See Razorbill account for more information.

ALTERNATE ADULTS. MAINE, JULY. KEN BEHRENS.
- Longer and slimmer than the other large alcids.
- Whereas other large alcids have a boxy-headed appearance, Common Murre has a longer, slimmer neck and appears pointed at the front.
- Any large alcid with a distinct dark wingpit like that of the top bird is a Common Murre.

ALTERNATE ADULTS WITH ALTERNATE ADULT RAZORBILL (TOP). WALES, APR. KEN BEHRENS.
- In good light the color difference between Common Murre and Razorbill is obvious; Thick-billed Murre falls between the two.
- The feet of murres are exposed. Those of Razorbill are hidden beneath the long tail.

BASIC ADULT. SCOTLAND, SEPT. JOHN ANDERSON.
- Long and lean for an alcid.
- Bill is usually held perfectly level.
- In basic plumage, the extensive white behind the eye separates Common from Thick-billed Murre.

ALTERNATE ADULTS. GREENLAND, MAY. B&C ALEXANDER/ARCTICPHOTO.
- In the Atlantic, both species of murres are birds of high latitudes, often foraging right at the edge of the pack ice. The vast majority of Atlantic murres spend all of their lives far north of the vast majority of North American birders!

BASIC ADULT WITH TWO COMMON GOLDENEYE. SWEDEN, NOV. THOMAS SVANBERG.

- Singles of all three large alcid species readily join flocks of ducks, blending in surprisingly well.
- Stray alcids are often near the rear of scoter flocks.
- The projecting feet of murres can be easily overlooked but provide an instant means for separating them from the similar Razorbill.

ALTERNATE ADULTS. WALES, MAR. KEN BEHRENS.

- A typical line of large alcids. Such lines are most often observed low over the water.
- The sharply pointed appearance shown by these birds is unique to Common Murre.

ALTERNATE ADULT. MASSACHUSETTS, JAN. TOM JOHNSON.

- This bird has already begun its molt into alternate plumage in January, months ahead of the same molt in Thick-billed Murre.
- At close range, the dark streaking on the flanks provides an excellent ID character.

WITH RAZORBILL (TOP). MAINE, JULY. KEN BEHRENS.

- Diagnostic differences in shape and overall color easily distinguish these species at close to moderate distances, but identification can be difficult or impossible at long distances. "Large alcid species" is a good designation for birds that cannot be pinned down.

ATLANTIC PUFFIN
Fratercula arctica
DIMENSIONS
L: 15 in.; WS: 23 in.; WT: 1.4 lb.

SPRING ARRIVAL

off NL: early Apr.; Gulf of St. Lawrence:
mid-Apr.; n. Greenland: mid-May

FALL ARRIVAL

off MA: late Oct.; off NY: early Dec.

This striking medium-sized alcid is widely recognized even by nonbirders for the distinctive and slightly bizarre adornments worn by adults in the breeding season. This appearance has been characterized as comical by some and solemn by others; in Newfoundland, puffins are known by the colloquial name "sea-parrot." Birders most often see this species on its breeding grounds, as it is highly pelagic when not breeding. As such, it is rarely seen from shore, even a short distance south of its breeding range, and is highly prized at seawatches.

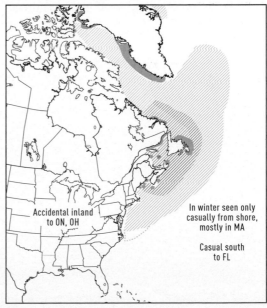

Accidental inland
to ON, OH

In winter seen only
casually from shore,
mostly in MA

Casual south
to FL

SIZE: Medium-sized. Clearly larger than Dovekie. Significantly smaller than Razorbill. About the size of Black Guillemot.

STRUCTURE: Compact and stocky with a very blunt front. The oversized, wedge-shaped bill is held angled downward, the upper mandible curving up to merge smoothly with the oversized, blocky head. The body is heavy and even throughout its length but angles upward to meet the almost nonexistent tail, giving the rear of the bird a chopped-off or abbreviated appearance. The wings are narrow and appear blunt-tipped. Overall gives more the appearance of a flying loaf of bread than of a "flying football," the description often given to the larger alcids.

FLIGHT AND FLOCKING: Flight is strong and direct, with whirring wingbeats that blur the outline of the wing. Birds rock constantly from side to side, more noticeably than in the large alcids. Flocks form lines that are fairly straight when they include only a few individuals but that become messy and uneven when more than five or six birds fly together. Usually flies in monospecific flocks but will join flocks of Razorbill and murres.

APPEARANCE: Alternate Adult: Glossy black above with a complete black throat strap separating the pale gray face from the white belly. The bill is ornate: bright orange at the tip, blue-gray at the base, and separated by a curving yellow band that rings the blue-gray base. A bright orange fleshy rosette at the gape provides a further flourish. The underwing is largely black but shows a faint silvery lining in bright light. The feet are bright orange and easily visible at moderate distances. **Basic Adult:** Like

alternate, but the face darkens, particularly in front of the eye, and the bill becomes smaller and duller. **First Cycle:** Like basic adult but with a smaller bill. **Distant:** Fairly uniformly dark, particularly in winter when the face is dark; however, flight is unstable, rocking side to side, and as birds turn away their pale bellies are visible, creating a noticeable white flash. In good light, the pale cheek of alternate adults is visible and may even appear pure white.

SIMILAR SPECIES: Razorbill: Significantly larger with a longer, sleeker body. Flight is more stable, with less side-to-side rocking. In all plumages has extensive white underwings, a white trailing edge to the wing, and white extending high up the rear flanks. In alternate plumage has a darker head than Atlantic Puffin, and in basic plumage has much more white on the face than puffin. In dark conditions, however, can appear to have all-dark underwings, and this may trip up observers who fail to look for additional traits. **Black Guillemot:** Similar in size but with broader wings, a thinner neck, a smaller head, and a thin, pointed bill. In alternate plumage, black with a huge white patch on the upperwing and with contrasting white underwings. In basic, much paler than puffin, with a mottled pale gray body, white underwings, and white patches on the upperwing. First-cycle bird has smaller pale patches on the upperwing but is still much paler than first-cycle Atlantic Puffin.

ALTERNATE ADULTS WITH A COMMON TERN. MAINE, JULY. CAMERON COX.

- A striking alcid in alternate plumage, unlikely to be confused with any other species on the Atlantic.
- The large multicolored bill, obvious at close range, tilts downward slightly.
- At a distance, the bill is less obvious and the head appears squared off.
- On the Atlantic, the solid black underwing is shared only with Dovekie, though bright sunlight may cause the underwing to appear paler, as in the top bird.

ALTERNATE ADULTS. MAINE, JULY. KEN BEHRENS.
• The gray face can look surprisingly dark in poor light.

ALTERNATE ADULT. MAINE, JULY. KEN BEHRENS.
• One of the most widely recognized Atlantic seabirds. The spectacular breeding adornments have earned it the colloquial name "sea-parrot."

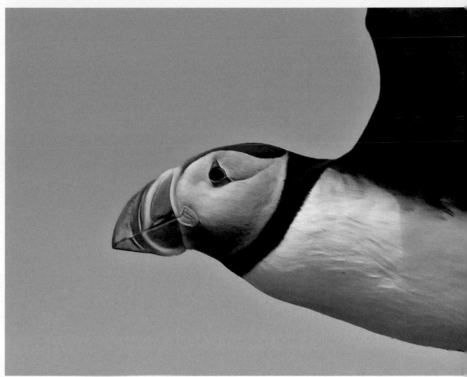

ALTERNATE ADULT. MAINE, JULY. KEN BEHRENS.
• Alcids have ultrafast wingbeats that cause their wings to appear blurred.
• The puffin's bright orange feet separate it from other Atlantic alcids.

ALTERNATE ADULTS. MAINE, JULY. KEN BEHRENS.
• Identification purists look away—this photo serves no purpose but to add some color and interest!

- Puffins are smaller, shorter-bodied, and more compact in appearance than the large alcids.
- Birders seeing their first puffins are often surprised by their small size.
- Basic-plumaged Atlantic Puffins have a darker gray face and much smaller bill.

ALTERNATE ADULT WITH TWO RAZORBILLS (R). MAINE, JULY. CAMERON COX.
- Puffins are much shorter-bodied but almost as stocky as Razorbills.
- The large head of puffins appears very blunt at a distance.

THREE ADULTS AND ONE FIRST CYCLE (R). MAINE, JULY. KEN BEHRENS.
- In winter, adults look very similar to the first-alternate bird: darker on the face and with a smaller bill.

BLACK GUILLEMOT
Cepphus grylle
DIMENSIONS
L: 13 in.; WS: 21 in.; WT: 15 oz.

SPRING ARRIVAL

Gulf of St. Lawrence: Apr.; n. Greenland: Apr.

FALL ARRIVAL

MA: late Oct.; NY: early Dec.

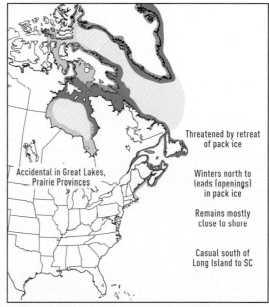

Threatened by retreat of pack ice

Winters north to leads (openings) in pack ice

Remains mostly close to shore

Casual south of Long Island to SC

Accidental in Great Lakes, Prairie Provinces

This attractive, medium-sized alcid is distinctive in both appearance and behavior. Whereas other alcids are pelagic for at least part of the year, Black Guillemot spends its time close to shore, often in sheltered coves around rocky coasts. When it can't find rocky coasts, it may use human-made jetties, where it is inconspicuous and easily overlooked until it takes flight, flashing its distinctive white wing patches. Black Guillemot is infrequently observed as a vagrant south of New England, but it sometimes stages "mini-invasions" in which a handful turn up in the Mid-Atlantic or even farther south.

SIZE: Medium-sized. Clearly larger than Dovekie. Significantly smaller than Razorbill. About the size of Atlantic Puffin or Bufflehead.

STRUCTURE: Rather squat, with an evenly rounded belly; small head; thin, pointed bill; and short, broad, rounded wings. The head is held raised above the body, emphasizing the rounded belly. Looks a bit like a bowling pin tipped over on its side.

FLIGHT AND FLOCKING: Wingbeats are fast, blurring the wings, but are weak and fluttering; birds always look like they are about to fall out of the air. Flies directly, low over the water, and tends to rock slightly from side to side. Usually flies singly or in pairs, occasionally in small flocks of four or five in a loose line. Virtually never flies with any other species, including other alcids.

APPEARANCE: Alternate Adult: All black except for large oval-shaped patches in the center of the wing, white underwings, and bright red feet. **Basic Adult:** Very pale, with the white head smudged with gray and a white belly and rump. The back is dull gray; the wings are black with large white oval-shaped patches and a white underwing. **First Cycle:** Like basic adult but with smaller wing patch that is heavily mottled. By summer looks like alternate adult but with the same small mottled wing patch. **Distant:** In alternate plumage, mostly black with small flashes of white coming from both the upper- and under-wing, depending on the position of the wings. In basic looks almost completely pale but with a slight dinginess.

SIMILAR SPECIES: Atlantic Puffin: Stockier, with a larger head, more evenly thick body, and narrower wings. Has dark wings and lacks the white upperwing patch and underwings of Black Guillemot in all plumages. **Bufflehead:** Surprisingly similar in both size and shape. Bufflehead has stronger, swifter flight and flies in tighter flocks. Male is brighter white than a basic-plumaged Black Guillemot and has a dark forehead and throat and a more extensive white wing patch that crosses the entire inner wing. Female is darker than basic Black Guillemot, but not as dark or as even as alternate guillemot, and has a dark head with a white spot in the center, and much smaller white wing patches that are only on the trailing edge of the wing, not in its center.

ALTERNATE ADULTS. QUEBEC, JUNE. GERRY DEWAGHE.
- Striking in alternate plumage: all black except for distinctive oval-shaped white wing patches and white underwings.
- Less gregarious than other species of alcids. Singles and pairs are far more common than flocks. Groups of 4–5 are occasional, and groups in flight of 10 or more are exceptional.
- Often very close to shore; this is the least-pelagic Atlantic alcid.

ALTERNATE ADULT WITH TWO RAZORBILLS. MAINE, JULY. KEN BEHRENS.
• Black Guillemot is broad-winged and distinctly potbellied.
• Has a completely different structure and flight style than other alcids.

BASIC ADULT. NEW JERSEY, DEC. KEVIN KARLSON.
• Very pale in basic plumage, but the bold white wing patches and odd shape remain distinctive.

FIRST CYCLE. NEWFOUNDLAND, JAN. BRUCE MACTAVISH.
• Like basic adult but has dark markings through the white wing patch.

ALTERNATE ADULT. MAINE, JULY. CAMERON COX.
• Bright white under-wings flash clearly as the wings are raised.
• Adults have glowing red feet.
• Body is oddly shaped, reminiscent of a bowling pin tipped on its side.

DOVEKIE
Alle alle
DIMENSIONS
L: 8.25 in.; WS: 15 in.; WT: 6 oz.

SPRING ARRIVAL

n. Greenland: early May

FALL ARRIVAL

off NL: Oct.; off ME: late Oct.;
off MA: early Nov.; off NY: mid-Nov.

By far the smallest Atlantic alcid as well as the most abundant, Dovekie breeds by the millions in the far North Atlantic and into the Arctic Ocean. This species is difficult to see from shore in most places, though it is regular from several sites in Massachusetts in the fall, particularly during storms with strong onshore winds. It can also be common from shore in Atlantic Canada from late fall through winter, usually during an onshore wind.

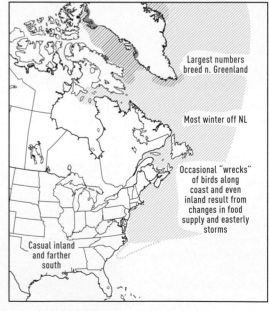

Largest numbers breed n. Greenland

Most winter off NL

Occasional "wrecks" of birds along coast and even inland result from changes in food supply and easterly storms

Casual inland and farther south

Dovekie is somewhat irruptive, and an event called a "wreck" occurs in years when large numbers of weakened individuals are found near shore or even inland. These events are probably caused by crashes in food resources, and many of the individuals involved die. Winter pelagic trips off the Mid-Atlantic have proven one of the best ways to see this species in numbers. A lucky trip may find Dovekies by the hundreds well offshore.

SIZE: By far the smallest Atlantic alcid. Smaller than American Robin. About the same size as Red Phalarope.

STRUCTURE: Small yet stocky, with no discernible break between the head and body. The bill and tail are too insubstantial to be noted in most conditions, so the basic appearance is a dumpy little oval sporting wings. The wings themselves are quite long and sharply bent back at the wrist, placed near the center of the body. They flap so quickly that they usually appear as a blur, and it is hard to perceive their exact structure in flight.

APPEARANCE: Has a solid dark underwing in all plumages. **Alternate Adult:** Unique among alcids in having a solid black upper breast and throat as well a black head and upperparts. The belly is bright white, contrasting with dark upperparts, so the overall appearance is similar to that of the large alcids. **Basic Adult:** The breast, throat, and a small area behind the eye become white. A dark band extends from the shoulder and forms a partial collar. **First Cycle:** Like basic but duller, as black areas soon fade to dark brown and the pale areas on the head show faint dusky mottling. **Distant:** Blackish, but the bright white belly flashes frequently as birds bank and twist.

FLIGHT AND FLOCKING: Flight is rapid and direct, skimming low over the water with whirring wing-beats. Usually looks slightly unsteady as birds often rock side to side and may also bob up and down, particularly to clear large waves. Typically seen singly or in small groups. Flocks may recall a small flock of sandpipers, particularly those of Purple Sandpiper. "Large" flocks (five or more) look less like shorebirds and more like small ducks, as they lack the coordinated efficiency of shorebird flocks and, though tightly packed, often retain discernible subflocks of three to six within the larger flock structure. On the breeding grounds, where Dovekie is abundant, it often forms dense, oval-shaped flocks.

SIMILAR SPECIES: Atlantic Puffin: First-cycle puffin is vaguely similar to Dovekie but is much larger and stockier, with a larger bill and blockier head that gives it a blunt-fronted appearance. At all times of the year at least a hint of orange is visible on the bill of Atlantic Puffin. Alternate-plumaged Atlantic Puffin has a large pale face; basic-plumaged puffin has a darker head than basic Dovekie. **Razorbill:** Sometimes confused with Dovekie by excitable observers. Razorbill dwarfs Dovekie and has a longer body, larger and more distinct head and bill, and pale underwings. Wingbeats are fast, but the flight is steadier, with less up-and-down movement than in Dovekie.

SWEDEN, NOV. TOMAS SVENSSON.

• Tiny size and unstable, constantly bouncing and twisting flight easily separate Dovekies from other Atlantic alcids. Because of their small size and tendency to drop into wave troughs, the real problem is seeing them!
• There is no discernible break between the head and body, so distant Dovekies look like winged, oval-shaped blobs.

(NEXT TWO PAGES) SWEDEN, NOV. TOMAS SVENSSON.

ALTERNATE ADULTS. NORWAY, MAY. B&C ALEXANDER/ ARCTICPHOTO.
- Flocks can appear very similar to those of sandpipers.
- Flocks this large and dense are typical on the high-northern breeding grounds.
- Some birds here are twisted with their belly facing the camera while others are twisted away. *How would that affect the appearance of the flock against a dark ocean?*

NORTH CAROLINA, FEB. KEN BEHRENS.
- Small flocks form vague, messy lines with individuals frequently shifting within the flock.
- Among Atlantic alcids, the dark underwing is shared only with Atlantic Puffin.

ALTERNATE ADULTS WITH TWO THICK-BILLED MURRES (R). NORWAY, JUNE. JAMES LOWEN.
- Dovekie is very similar in plumage to the murres and Razorbill, but in alternate plumage the black on its head extends onto the upper breast.
- Medium to large flocks often break into subgroups of two to six that are discernible within the greater flock structure.

TUBENOSES

Tubenoses include four families of birds worldwide, two of which we cover in this guide: the shearwaters and petrels, family Procellariidae; and the storm-petrels, family Hydrobatidae. These are true pelagic seabirds that come to shore only to breed. The name "tubenose" refers to the naricorns—two raised tubes on the top of the bill. There is ongoing debate about the taxonomy of many species and groups of tubenoses. We have followed the American Ornithologists' Union taxonomy, though we acknowledge that on both the species and family levels, the taxonomic landscape for tubenoses is likely to change in the future.

The shearwater and petrel family is complex and includes four groups, three of which we cover in this guide: the shearwaters, with five species found in these pages; the fulmarine petrels, represented by Northern Fulmar; and the gadfly petrels, represented by Black-capped Petrel.

From the storm-petrel family, we cover three species: one "southern" species, Wilson's Storm-Petrel; and two "northern" species, Leach's and Band-rumped Storm-Petrels. "Northern" storm-petrels have a longer "arm" and shorter legs than the "southern" storm-petrels, and some authors have suggested that they represent different families. Band-rumped Storm-Petrel presents another thorny taxonomic issue. European authorities have split Band-rumped Storm-Petrel into three species, though the number of Atlantic Band-rumped Storm-Petrel taxa may actually be four, at least two of which have occurred off North Carolina.

In addition to the species covered here, there are about 15 other tubenoses that have occurred in eastern North America. Some are extreme vagrants that have been reported only a few times. Others are almost annual in small numbers but are primarily seen far offshore and rarely if ever from shore. This guide focuses on species that are regularly seen from shore, albeit in some cases mainly after hurricanes or tropical storms.

Across the board, from tiny storm-petrels to massive albatrosses, tubenoses display impressive abilities of flight and undertake long migrations. Tubenoses use several different flight styles but are most associated with a style in which they arc up and down just above the waves, known as "dynamic soaring." Most simply, they use their wings like a sail, twisting so the underside of the wings catches the wind to rise, then tipping the wings so air flows over the top and the birds glide back down toward the water. The height and frequency of these arcs depend on the strength of the wind and also on the species. Tubenoses can even use the updrafts from

We do not cover albatrosses in this guide because of their rare occurrence in eastern North America, but there is no denying the charisma of these huge tubenoses. However unlikely it may be, it never hurts to hope for an "Atlantic" Yellow-nosed Albatross to sail past your local seawatching site on a day with howling winds. There have been a handful of records from shore in eastern North America. South Africa, Oct. Ken Behrens. *What is the non-albatross in this photo?*

waves to generate lift, a unique adaptation to their oceanic environment. The dynamic soaring flight of each species has unique characteristics. Identifying these characteristics and learning how different weather conditions alters them are among the most important aspects of tubenose identification, especially at the long ranges typical of a seawatch. In strong winds, dynamic soaring can be used by gulls, jaegers, and sulids as well as by shearwaters and petrels.

In calm conditions, gadfly petrels and shearwaters lose their dynamic flight style and glide low over the water using regular bursts of wingbeats to keep aloft; this flight style is similar to that of hawks in the genus *Accipiter*. In all conditions, Storm-petrels beat their wings much more frequently than the larger tubenoses, but they do glide, and some species employ an arcing, dynamic soar at times. The cadence of the wingbeats and the shape of the wings play a key role in the often challenging identification of storm-petrels. Since significant differences exist in flight style depending on whether a storm-petrel is actively foraging or traveling from one point to another, it is important to assess what a bird is doing before judging flight style.

The sexes appear similar in all ten species covered here. Differences between first-cycle birds and adults are very difficult to detect at a distance.

CORY'S SHEARWATER
Calonectris diomedea
DIMENSIONS
L: 18 in.; WS: 44 in.; WT: 1.8 lb.

SPRING ARRIVAL

off NC: early May; off NJ: late May; off NY:
mid-June; off MA: early July; off TX: early July

Cory's Shearwater is one of the largest shearwaters in the world, and this is evident in its every
movement. Unlike the other shearwaters in this
guide, Cory's shows marked size dimorphism between the sexes, with males significantly larger.
Additionally, there are two distinct subspecies, *C.
d. diomedea* and *C. d. borealis*, both of which occur
regularly in our waters. These two subspecies vary in
size, contributing to the wide array of sizes of Cory's
seen in the field. North of Long Island, Cory's is irruptive, being numerous in some years and scarce in
others. It is also scarce in the Gulf of Mexico, though
it is also the most expected shearwater there.

SIZE: Slightly larger than Great Shearwater. About
the same size as Ring-billed Gull and Royal Tern,

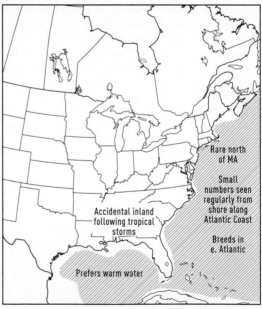

Rare north
of MA

Small
numbers seen
regularly from
shore along
Atlantic Coast

Accidental inland
following tropical
storms

Breeds in
e. Atlantic

Prefers warm water

but looks larger than all three of these species because of its heavier build.

STRUCTURE: Bulky, with a heavy chest, large head,
broad wings, and deep-based bill. The wings are
held slightly crooked, and the hand is curved down-

ward when gliding—a very different wing profile than that of the Great Shearwater, which holds its wings quite straight and almost perfectly flat.

FLIGHT AND FLOCKING: Wingbeats are deep and ponderous and usually rather slow. Smaller individuals can show a snappier wingbeat, whereas the largest individuals have a lethargic, almost albatross-like wingbeat. In windy conditions the flight becomes faster, and birds arc and shear in a manner more similar to that of the larger *Puffinus* shearwaters. Compared with other shearwaters, however, Cory's flight appears a bit flat even in the windiest conditions. It is social, often feeding or resting on the water in large unstructured flocks, though birds tend to stay widely spaced once they take to the wing. Loosely associates with other tubenoses, particularly Great Shearwater.

APPEARANCE: Uniquely warm brown above, with darker flight feathers. The brown on the head extends down almost to the throat, creating a hooded appearance. Clean white below with blackish wingtips. Most show a narrow, irregular pale band across the uppertail coverts that can be pronounced in some individuals. The yellow bill is unique among shearwaters. **Distant:** Dull brown above. The hooded appearance is obvious on high-arcing birds silhouetted against the sky. Uniformly pale below, cleaner than Great Shearwater but not blindingly white like Black-capped Petrel. The heavy bill is usually visible and angled down slightly.

SIMILAR SPECIES: Great Shearwater: Slimmer build with narrower, more pointed wings that are held straighter. Wingbeats are typically faster and stiffer. Overall color is colder, with the black cap contrasting with the paler back. Lacks the hooded appearance of Cory's. The dark-flecked underwings and gray-washed belly give the underparts a dirty appearance that is unlike the clean white of Cory's.

SUBSPECIES: Two subspecies, *C. d. diomedia* and *C. d. borealis*. The true status of the Mediterranean Sea–breeding *C. d. diomedea*, sometimes referred to as "Scopoli's" Shearwater, is still being worked out, but it is certainly more numerous in our area than previously recognized. See Taxonomic Notes (p. 591) for more information.

NORTH CAROLINA, AUG. CHRIS SLOAN.
• White veins extending well into the primaries on the top bird suggest the Mediterranean-breeding *diomedea*, or "Scopoli's," Shearwater, whereas the blackish primaries of the bottom bird indicate *borealis*, the more expected, Atlantic-breeding subspecies. See Taxonomic Notes for more information.

MASSACHUSETTS, JULY. KEN BEHRENS.
• Heavy, broad-winged, and heavy-billed; the largest shearwater in the North Atlantic.
• The bill is often angled down slightly. *Puffinus* shearwaters hold their bill straight.

WITH TWO GREAT SHEARWATERS AND A WILSON'S STORM-PETREL. MASSACHUSETTS, JULY. KEN BEHRENS.
- Cory's has a hooded appearance in contrast to the clean black cap of Great Shearwater.

MASSACHUSETTS, JULY. KEN BEHRENS.
- The only shearwater with a yellow bill.
- In both subspecies, males have a longer, heavier bill than females. Atlantic breeders also have a larger bill than Mediterranean breeders.

MASSACHUSETTS, JULY. KEN BEHRENS.
- Cory's significant bulk is evident in flight. Even as a bird arcs up and down in strong wind, it seems heavy, controlled, and less agile than *Puffinus* shearwaters.
- The hooded appearance is visible at most angles, from great distances, and in poor light.

WITH GREAT SHEARWATER (BELOW) AND HUMPBACK WHALE. MASSACHUSETTS, JULY. KEN BEHRENS.
- Differences in coloration can be masked by bad lighting or distance, but the greater bulk and broader wings of Cory's are still effective identification traits.

WITH GREAT SHEARWATER (R). NORTH CAROLINA, AUG. CAMERON COX.
- Compare the wing posture of these two large shearwaters—relaxed in Cory's, rigid in Great.
- Any shearwater that rises to the apex of an arc with a distinctly downward-curved hand is a Cory's.
- Cory's has a clean belly and underwing, whereas Great has a dirty appearance.

MASSACHUSETTS, JULY. KEN BEHRENS.
- Sandy brown upperparts and yellow bill are diagnostic.

WITH TWO GREAT SHEAR-WATERS (BOTTOM AND L). MASSACHUSETTS, JULY. KEN BEHRENS.
- Individual size variation, due to sex and subspecies differences, is often apparent in Cory's, whereas *Puffinus* shearwaters show little individual variation in size.

GREAT SHEARWATER
Puffinus gravis
DIMENSIONS
L: 18 in.; WS: 42 in.; WT: 1.8 lb.

SPRING ARRIVAL

off NC: early May; off ME: late May;
off NJ: late May

This large and well-marked shearwater occurs in huge numbers in the North Atlantic but is a transient species making a brief visit to our region as part of a long journey. It breeds in the Tristan da Cunha islands in the South Atlantic and spends the nonbreeding season, the Northern Hemisphere summer, in the North Atlantic, some individuals traveling almost 18,000 miles. The species is particularly apparent off New England from midsummer to early fall and frequently can be observed from shore. Farther south it is less common and more difficult to see from shore, and sightings in the Gulf of Mexico are rare.

SIZE: Larger than Laughing Gull and Black-capped Petrel. Smaller than Cory's Shearwater.

May linger into early Dec. off New England

Small numbers seen from shore, particularly from Cape Cod and Long Island

Breeds in S. Atlantic

Very rare to casual in Gulf of Mexico

STRUCTURE: Large and powerful but trim, with long, sleek lines that give an athletic impression. The wings are broader-based than those of the other eastern *Puffinus* shearwaters but still appear slim, tapering gradually to sharp points. The body is long, slim, and even, almost cigar-shaped. When gliding, the wings are held rigidly, straight out from the body, but when arcing in and out of troughs the wings relax and become slightly crooked. The overall impression is very balanced, with the head projection in front of the wings similar to that of the tail projection behind.

FLIGHT AND FLOCKING: Flight is an endless series of smooth arcs interspersed with quick, stiff wingbeats. In high winds the flight becomes more dynamic, with higher arcs and sharper twists and tacks. It is generally similar to that of other medium to large *Puffinus* shearwaters but slightly more ponderous, as this is the largest member of the genus found in the area. In prime areas, loose flocks feed in the same vicinity with other tubenoses, particularly Cory's Shearwater.

APPEARANCE: Dark gray above with a blackish cap and a black bill. Most have a narrow, pale collar and a pale band across the uppertail coverts, though both are almost absent on some birds. The underparts are mostly pale, with a variable, dusky belly patch and black undertail coverts. There is a fairly complex mottled pattern on the underwing; the upperwing is plain dark gray with a faint scaly pattern when fresh. **Distant:** Appears dark above but rarely black, except as a silhouette; usually some hint of gray is visible. Likewise, rarely looks clean white underneath except when strongly lit. Usually looks pale with an indistinct dusky wash or slight mottling.

SIMILAR SPECIES: **Cory's Shearwater:** Larger and heavier with more ponderous flight; broader, more arched wings; slower wingbeats. Also has a distinctive yellow bill that is much heavier than that of Great Shearwater, visible at greater distances, and often held angled slightly downward, almost as if the bird were peering at the water. Cory's has warmer brown upperparts than Great and cleaner underwings and belly. Despite these differences, observations of these two species at extreme distances are often best left as "large shearwater species," particularly for observers with little comparative experience.

MASSACHUSETTS, JULY. CAMERON COX.
- Typical *Puffinus* shearwater shape: very streamlined with long, pointed wings that are held very straight.
- Glides most of the time, with wingbeats coming in short, explosive bursts.
- The largest *Puffinus* on the Atlantic, with broader wings and slightly slower wingbeats than all other shearwaters on the North Atlantic except Cory's.

WITH TWO SOOTY SHEARWATERS (R AND SECOND FROM L). MASSACHUSETTS, JULY. KEN BEHRENS.
- In strong wind Great Shearwaters arc high above the horizon.
- Note how the dark cap disappears on the bird with the ocean behind it, whereas it is obvious on the birds against the paler background of the sky.

SOUTH AFRICA, OCT. KEN BEHRENS.
• The dark wash on the belly is diagnostic and, combined with dark markings on the underwing, gives the underparts a slightly dingy cast that is evident at a distance.

SOUTH AFRICA, JAN. KEN BEHRENS.
• In poor light it appears evenly dark above, but the contrast created by the black cap and white throat is still apparent.

WITH CAPE GANNET. SOUTH AFRICA, OCT. KEN BEHRENS.
• Unlike Cory's Shearwater, Great holds its wings rigidly, straight out from the body.
• Other *Puffinus* shearwaters hold their wings in a similar manner, but those found in North Atlantic waters are smaller and have slimmer wings.

(RIGHT) SOUTH AFRICA, JAN. KEN BEHRENS.

SOOTY SHEARWATER
Puffinus griseus
DIMENSIONS
L: 17 in.; WS: 40 in.; WT: 1.7 lb.

SPRING ARRIVAL

off NC: mid-May; off NY: mid-May;
off ME: late May

What this species lacks in bright colors it more than makes up for with its stunning mastery of the air. Even in a family of wanderers, Sooty Shearwater stands out; its annual migration is among the longest of any creature. Birds in the Pacific are known to cover more than 40,000 miles in a single year. Breeding in the Southern Hemisphere, Sooty Shearwater spends its nonbreeding season, our summer, traversing the oceans of the Northern Hemisphere. It seems to circumnavigate northern oceans with a clockwise rotation and is found off eastern North America from May through early September. It tends to arrive earlier in the year than other shearwaters but is usually outnumbered by Great Shearwater in the north and Cory's in the south.

SIZE: Slightly larger than Long-tailed Jaeger and Black-legged Kittiwake. Smaller than Great Shearwater. About the size of Laughing Gull.

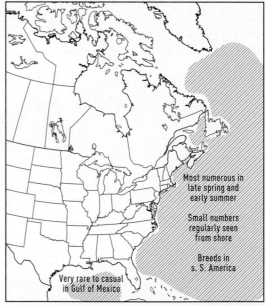

Most numerous in late spring and early summer

Small numbers regularly seen from shore

Breeds in s. S. America

Very rare to casual in Gulf of Mexico

STRUCTURE: Very lean, with extremely long, slender wings that taper to a sharp point. The bill is long and thin, and the tail tapers to a point, so the body is pointed in all directions.

FLIGHT AND FLOCKING: Flight is very rapid, with sudden bursts of stiff wingbeats followed by extended gliding. The body is often tilted drastically to one side or the other so that one wing points up and the other down. Even in moderate wind, it arcs up and down, in and out of the troughs, twisting its body so one wingtip after the other points down. In higher wind these undulations become more dramatic, gaining incredible speed as a bird cruises down from a high arc, disappears into a trough, then blasts back up, pausing only slightly at the apex of the next arc. In calm conditions, unlike other shearwaters, Sooty maintains a rapid, effortless flight, though it loses the arcing action and flaps more frequently. This species is a joy to watch and imparts an appearance of supreme control beyond that of any other eastern shearwater. Flocking seems incidental, but Sooties are often side by side with other tubenoses.

APPEARANCE: Sooty brown overall; the only dark-bellied eastern shearwater. Silver linings to the underwing coverts are usually conspicuous, though a few have almost solidly dark underwings. **Distant:** Uniformly dark, often appearing black, but the silvery underwing coverts flash when banking.

SIMILAR SPECIES: Great Shearwater: Larger and heavier, with broader wings, slower wingbeats, and less explosive flight. Pale underneath, unlike the all-dark Sooty, so likely to be confused only at great distances or in poor light. **Trindade Petrel** (not included in this guide): The dark morph of the rare Trindade Petrel (formerly considered conspecific with Herald Petrel) is the only other eastern tubenose that has a color scheme similar to Sooty Shearwater. Trindade Petrel has smaller measurements but looks larger because of its heavy body, broad wings, and shorter, heavier bill. It has a powerful flight that is even more dynamic than Sooty's in high winds but that stagnates in calm conditions.

WITH GREAT SHEARWATER (ABOVE). SOUTH AFRICA, OCT. KEN BEHRENS.
• Smaller and slimmer than Great, and flies with an easy speed and control unmatched by Great.

MASSACHUSETTS, JULY. KEN BEHRENS.
• Medium-sized with extremely slender, sharply pointed wings.
• The only all-dark shearwater in the Atlantic.

WITH FOUR GREAT SHEARWATERS AND A WILSON'S STORM-PETREL (CENTER L). MASSACHUSETTS, JULY. CAMERON COX.
• Dark and sleek. Significantly smaller than Great Shearwater. Huge compared with the tiny storm-petrel.
• Moves quickly without ever appearing to exert much effort.
• Tail is more pointed than that of any other eastern shearwater.

**SOUTH AFRICA, OCT.
KEN BEHRENS.**
- Underwing has an extensive silvery lining, almost invisible at times but flashes brightly when struck by the sun.

MASSACHUSETTS, JULY. KEN BEHRENS.
- When not shearing the water, Sooties shear the air with ease.

WITH TWO GREAT SHEARWATERS (R). MASSACHUSETTS, JULY. KEN BEHRENS.
- Evenly dark coloration identifies Sooty at any distance, except in very poor light.
- The pale wing lining varies greatly among individuals.

(LEFT) BRITISH COLUMBIA, SEPT. GLENN BARTLEY.

MANX SHEARWATER
Puffinus puffinus
DIMENSIONS
L: 13.5 in.; WS: 33 in.; WT: 1 lb.

SPRING ARRIVAL

Bermuda: Feb.; NC: Mar.; New England: Apr.

FALL ARRIVAL

Mid-Atlantic: Oct.; e. South America: Nov.

Breeds mainly in Old World, also probably in Atlantic Provinces, New England

Accidental in MI, Lake Ontario

Most likely nesting areas

Substantial fall flight through waters off Bermuda

Rare in winter in U.S. waters

Most winter off e. S. America

This fast and elusive little shearwater is often glimpsed only as a black-and-white blur knifing though salty troughs. Manx is at home in chilly waters, breeding farther north than any other species of shearwater in the world. The majority of Manx Shearwaters breed in Europe, but there is one regular colony in North America, on Middle Lawn Island in Newfoundland. Manx Shearwater has also bred once in Massachusetts, and breeding has been suspected from other locations in New England and the Atlantic Provinces. Manx seems willing to forage closer to shore than most shearwaters, but as it is generally scarce, it is still rarely seen from shore. Although it winters mostly off West Africa and northern South America, a handful stick it out on the North Atlantic and are sometimes glimpsed on winter pelagic trips.

SIZE: Slightly larger than Audubon's Shearwater. About the same size as Bonaparte's Gull.

STRUCTURE: Small, lithe shearwater with long, narrow, sharply pointed wings and a slender body. The wings are almost perfectly centered on the body, unlike those of the longer-tailed Audubon's Shearwater, imparting a balanced appearance. As in most *Puffinus* shearwaters, the wings are held rigidly and almost straight out from the body. The bill is long and thin, basically disappearing at a distance.

FLIGHT AND FLOCKING: Appears to fly very quickly, competing with Sooty Shearwater for the title of fastest shearwater in the East. Flight is fairly dynamic, far more so than that of Audubon's, typically consisting of medium-length glides interspersed with short, explosive series of wingbeats that notably increase the velocity of the bird. Banks frequently and sometimes vigorously enough that the wings are aligned vertically, a behavior never exhibited by Audubon's Shearwater. Overall there is a direct and hurried appearance to the flight that is missing from that of all other eastern shearwaters. In North America typically solitary, occasionally in pairs, except around breeding colonies or locations being scouted for potential breeding sites, where small groups may fly together.

APPEARANCE: Blackish above, slightly darker than Audubon's, and white below, including the undertail coverts. The underwing is largely white with a narrow, dark trailing edge. The dark primaries have silvery inner webs, lessening the contrast with the white coverts. A narrow finger of white wraps around behind the auriculars but is visible only at close range. **Distant:** Starkly black and white.

SIMILAR SPECIES: Audubon's Shearwater: Slightly smaller with slightly shorter, broader, more rounded wings and a longer tail. Typically stays close to the water and rarely banks hard or turns vertically as Manx often does. Wingbeats are spaced between medium-length glides, just as with Manx, but are weaker, and flight is much slower. The most telling plumage characteristics of Audubon's are usually the much broader dark trailing edge to the underwing and the sharp contrast between primaries and underwing coverts. Audubon's also typically shows a bit of white above the eye but lacks the pale finger wrapping around the auriculars, though both marks can be difficult to see in the field. Likewise, its dark undertail coverts are difficult to see, particularly given the species' tendency to fly close to the water. **Sooty Shearwater:** Unlike Manx, has an all-dark body, but these species can be confused at great distances or in poor light as they both have narrow wings and fly swiftly. Sooty is significantly larger and has a proportionally longer neck and tail, which appears more pointed. These differences of size and structure translate to significant differences in the way the two species fly. Sooty's flight is smooth and casually controlled, whereas Manx's always seems hurried. Sooty seems able to maintain its fluid flight style even in light winds, whereas Manx clearly labors in calm conditions.

MASSACHUSETTS, JULY. KEN BEHRENS.
- Small and slender with long, pointed wings.
- Wings are centered on the body, creating a balanced impression, unlike the longer-tailed Audubon's Shearwater.
- Flight is fast, with wingbeats coming in sudden, rapid series.
- The white wedge behind the auriculars can be difficult to see in the field but is discernible in photos.

WITH CORY'S SHEARWATER (L). FLORIDA, NOV. BOB WALLACE.
- Dwarfed by the much larger and more powerfully built Cory's.
- Notoriously sneaky. Views of Manx are often just a small black-and-white shape streaking past or going directly away. Flies low and easily disappears into troughs.

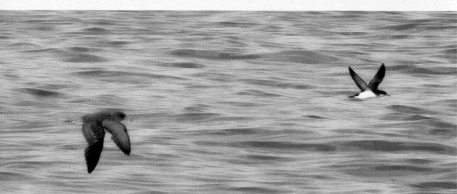

WITH CORY'S SHEARWATER (L). MASSACHUSETTS, JULY. KEN BEHRENS.
- Manx is long-winged but compact—not as rangy as the large shearwaters.
- Wings are more pointed than in Audubon's Shearwater.

SWEDEN, SEPT. TOMMY HOLMGREN.
- In all conditions, but particularly in strong wind, the flight style is faster and more aggressive than in Audubon's. Frequently twists the wings fully vertical, something Audubon's never does.

WITH "EUROPEAN" HERRING GULL. SCOTLAND, SEPT. JOHN ANDERSON.
- Truly a tiny shearwater!
- Blacker above than Audubon's and Sooty Shearwaters.
- Frosty color and dark tail band separate this "European" Herring Gull from "American" Herring Gull, but both of these taxa are variable.

AUDUBON'S SHEARWATER
Puffinus iherminieri
DIMENSIONS
L: 12 in.; WS: 27 in.; WT: 7 oz.

SPRING ARRIVAL

off NC: mid-Mar.; off TX: mid-Apr.;
off NJ: mid-July; off MA: late July

This small black-and-white shearwater is strictly confined to warm waters, often in association with floating *Sargassum* seaweed. Audubon's is rarely seen from land except when lines of *Sargassum* are pushed onshore or during tropical systems. Bridled Tern also frequently forages along lines of *Sargassum,* and following a flock of Bridled Terns at sea will often lead to observations of Audubon's Shearwater.

SIZE: Smallest regularly occurring North American shearwater. Slightly larger than Black Tern. Smaller than Bonaparte's Gull. About the same size as Black-bellied Plover.

STRUCTURE: Gives a petite impression, with a tiny head and bill, slim body, and long tail for a shearwa-

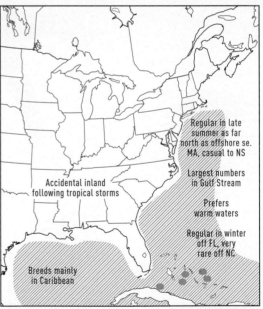

Regular in late summer as far north as offshore se. MA, casual to NS

Largest numbers in Gulf Stream

Prefers warm waters

Regular in winter off FL, very rare off NC

Accidental inland following tropical storms

Breeds mainly in Caribbean

ter. The wings are fairly short and slightly broader and blunter than those of speedsters such as Manx and Sooty Shearwaters, and may appear paddle-shaped when banking.

FLIGHT AND FLOCKING: Glides smoothly, usually just above the surface with the wings parallel to the water and wingtips bent downward slightly. In strong wind it may assume a moderately arcing flight, but it never rotates the body so that the wings align vertically, as other shearwaters often do. Wingbeats come in short, quick series, like those of other shearwaters, but lack the speed and the snap displayed by Manx and Sooty Shearwaters. After each series of wingbeats, Audubon's alters its course slightly. A typical flight series includes a series of wingbeats, a glide that drifts right, a series of wingbeats, a glide that drifts left, and so on. The overall course is straight, but the flight has a subtle zigzagging quality. It also appears slightly slower than in similar shearwaters, particularly Manx. Will occasionally adopt a quicker and more direct flight style, but this is rare. Unlike other shearwaters, which rarely form flocks in flight, Audubon's is often found flying in small groups, one after another spaced 10–30 feet apart. Pairs or groups of three are regular, and the rule in prime habitat.

APPEARANCE: The upperparts are evenly blackish brown; the underparts from the throat to the vent are white and contrast with the dark undertail coverts. The underwing coverts are mostly white and contrast sharply with the blackish flight feathers which form a broad, slightly irregular dark trailing edge. The legs are dusky pink, a potentially useful characteristic for separating Audubon's from the vagrant Barolo Shearwater (not covered in this guide), which has bluish legs, though this is visible only at close range. **Distant:** Strikingly black and white. In good light the brownish tint to the plumage may be visible. Because of Audubon's habit of flying just over the water, the dark undertail coverts are usually not discernible even at moderate distance.

SIMILAR SPECIES: Manx Shearwater: Prefers colder water than Audubon's, and the two species are seldom seen in close proximity. Manx's flight is swifter and more dynamic, on longer, thinner, more pointed wings. It tends to maintain a straight course, whereas Audubon's constantly makes slight shifts in direction. The dark secondaries form a narrower trailing edge to the underwing than on Audubon's, and the underside of the primaries is silvery gray, not contrasting sharply with the underwing coverts. **Great Shearwater:** Much larger and heavier, with longer, pointed wings; slower, more powerful wingbeats; and a tendency to wheel and bank, unlike Audubon's, which skims just above the surface. Great Shearwater has a stronger pattern both dorsally and ventrally, including a belly that is smudged with gray.

NORTH CAROLINA, JUNE.
MICHAEL O'BRIEN.

• Small shearwater with broad, somewhat paddle-shaped wings.
• Very long-tailed for a shearwater; distinctly longer-tailed than Manx.
• Often the most easily visible plumage difference from Manx is Audubon's broader dark trailing edge of the wing.
• Undertail coverts are black, not white as in Manx, but this can be difficult to see clearly.
• Rarely seen from land.

COMPARISON: AUDUBON'S SHEARWATER (L) WITH MANX SHEARWATER (R).

- Audubon's has shorter, broader wings and a wider black trailing edge.
- Audubon's usually appears to have more white on the face.

- Audubon's has blunter wingtips.
- In most postures Audubon's holds the wings straighter than Manx does.
- The broad dark trailing edge of the wing is the most obvious plumage trait on Audubon's at a distance.

- Audubon's has dark undertail coverts; Manx has white undertail coverts.
- Audubon's has a paler face than Manx.

- In Audubon's, the underwing coverts contrast sharply with the dark primaries. In Manx, pale vanes extend onto the primaries so there is no clean division between underwing coverts and primaries.
- Audubon's averages browner above, but light conditions can make this challenging to judge, and heavily worn Manx can appear brown.

NORTH CAROLINA, AUG.
KEN BEHRENS.

- Flight is less dynamic than that of larger shearwaters; tends to skim low over the water, with one wing held slightly higher than the other. Wingbeats have a fluttering quality, lacking power.
- When gliding, shows slightly more arched wings than Manx does.

NORTHERN FULMAR
Fulmarus glacialis
DIMENSIONS
L: 18 in.; WS: 42 in.; WT: 1.3 lb.

SPRING ARRIVAL

Canadian Arctic: late Apr./early May

FALL ARRIVAL

off ME: late Sept.; off NY: late Sept.;
off NC: mid-Oct.

This stocky seabird is unique among North American tubenoses in breeding on open ledges on steep cliffs rather than in crevices or burrows. It is also the only tubenose in this guide that shows multiple color morphs. These are traditionally called light and dark (or "blue") morphs, but there is enough variation to seriously blur these categories. In most of our area, Northern Fulmar is rarely seen from shore except in late fall or winter nor'easters, though it can be seen from shore, sometimes in large numbers, at some promontories in eastern Canada.

SIZE: Slightly larger than Laughing Gull. Almost identical to Great Shearwater but appears stockier and shorter-winged.

Possibly rare but regular in fall in offshore Hudson Bay

Recent expansion of numbers in nw. Atlantic

Small numbers regularly summer south to Gulf of Maine

Very rarely seen from shore in winter

Mostly north of MA

Numbers in southern part of winter range vary substantially from year to year

Casual south to FL

Accidental inland

STRUCTURE: Extremely stocky body with a large head and short, stout bill. The wings are fairly short and very broad for a tubenose, jutting straight out from the center of the body. The tail is more like a gull's than a shearwater's: short, broad, and slightly rounded. The heavy build is often the best identification feature, especially when comparing with similar species.

FLIGHT AND FLOCKING: Wingbeats are stiff, shallow, and almost entirely below the horizontal, coming in quick bursts spaced by long glides. Overall, flight appears heavy and is noticeably steadier and less buoyant than that of large shearwaters. In calm conditions struggles to maintain flight; bursts of wingbeats occur more frequently and are more extended, and glides become shorter. More dynamic, arcing soar is employed in strong winds, with extended glides, but series of wingbeats still occur more frequently than in most shearwaters. Even at top speed, the flight appears controlled, and a bird often pauses momentarily at the apex of a loop before gliding back toward the surface. Rarely flocks except incidentally around concentrations of food.

APPEARANCE: Variable. Very pale gray and white to solidly gray-brown with a full range of intermediates. **Pale Morph:** White head and underparts with a pale gray mantle, resulting in an appearance that is very similar to that of a pale-mantled gull. Distinctive, variably sized pale patch at the base of the primaries. The outer portion of the hand is slate gray to blackish; the rump and tail are very pale gray to white. **Dark Morph:** Medium brown overall with a greatly reduced or absent pale inner primary patch.

Distant: Pale morph looks much like a gull but is always strikingly pale-headed, and the white inner primary patches are obvious. Dark morph looks uniformly blackish. Intermediate birds appear mottled.

SIMILAR SPECIES: Pale-mantled gulls: Pale morph shares some similarities with gulls, but gulls have deeper, more fluid wingbeats with much of the wing action above the body, and the wings are also arched. Gulls' bodies are also proportionally slimmer, the head is smaller, and they lack pale inner primary windows. **Sooty Shearwater:** Darker than dark-morph Northern Fulmar but Northern Fulmar can appear quite dark at a distance. Much slimmer, with slimmer wings, a thin bill, and pointed tail. Sooty's flight is far more agile and buoyant, which is particularly noticeable in calm conditions. Sooty has strongly contrasting pale underwing linings, which fulmars lack.

SUBSPECIES: Three subspecies are recognized. *F. g. glacialis* is found in the Atlantic high Arctic. *F. g. auduboni* is an Atlantic low-Arctic breeder but is difficult to separate from *glacialis*. The Pacific *F. g. rodgersii* clearly differs from Atlantic forms but does not occur in the area covered by this guide.

LIGHT-MORPH. MARYLAND, FEB. CAMERON COX.
- Medium-sized and stocky, with a thick neck and large head.
- Most individuals are superficially similar to a pale-mantled gull, but with a white patch in the inner primaries. Each individual is different, though; some are entirely medium gray, others very pale with an extensive inner primary patch.

LIGHT-MORPH. WALES, APR. KEN BEHRENS.
• Head-on, the wings appear oddly razor-thin and too short for the ponderous body.

DARK-MORPH WITH THREE LITTLE GULLS. SWEDEN, JAN. JOHAN STENLUND.
• Dark-morph birds in the Atlantic are sometimes called "Blue" Fulmar due to their smoky blue-gray color. They are never as dark as the dark-morph birds found in the Pacific.
• *What ages are the Little Gulls?*

LIGHT-MORPH. SCOTLAND, MAY. JOHN ANDERSON.
• Relatively short, extremely stocky body is unlike that of any other North American tubenose or gull.

LIGHT-MORPH WITH HERRING GULL (L). MARYLAND, FEB. CAMERON COX.
• Fulmar's shorter, more rigid wings; stocky, bull-necked appearance; and more explosive flight alleviate confusion with large gulls, though their plumage may be similar.

LIGHT-MORPH. WALES, APR. KEN BEHRENS.
- Short, square tail is more similar to that of gulls than that of other large tubenoses.
- White head contrasts with the gray mantle, but unlike in gulls, the tail is the same color as the mantle or slightly paler and creates little contrast.

LIGHT-MORPH WITH BLACK-LEGGED KITTIWAKE (L). WALES, MAR. KEN BEHRENS.
- Unlike the buoyant flight of kittiwakes, the flight of Northern Fulmar appears distinctly heavy.
- Sluggish in calm weather, fulmars move with great speed in windy conditions, with an arcing, shearwater-like flight.

LIGHT-MORPH. WALES, APR. KEN BEHRENS.
- Northern Fulmar's unique structure can be seen from all angles.

BLACK-CAPPED PETREL
Pterodroma hasitata
DIMENSIONS
L: 16 in.; WS: 37 in.; WT: 1 lb.

SPRING ARRIVAL

off s. FL: early May

Black-capped Petrel is the only member of the celebrated genus *Pterodroma*—favored by seabird watchers for their high-speed, high-arcing, high-octane flight—that occurs frequently in eastern North America. The habits of Black-capped Petrel are not well known, and the only location where nesting is still known to occur is on cliffs high in the mountains of Hispaniola in the Caribbean. Once a widespread breeder in the West Indies, the species has declined dramatically, though it is probably breeding at locations yet to be discovered. Its occurrence in North America is almost completely restricted to the Gulf Stream. It is virtually never seen from shore under normal conditions, but tropical storms may bring it close to land, and

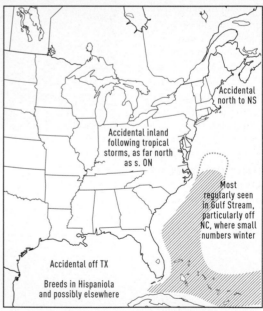

Accidental north to NS

Accidental inland following tropical storms, as far north as s. ON

Most regularly seen in Gulf Stream, particularly off NC, where small numbers winter

Accidental off TX

Breeds in Hispaniola and possibly elsewhere

even to interior bodies of water. It is most regularly found off North Carolina, typically from early May through October, but likely ranges widely in the Gulf Stream.

SIZE: Slightly smaller than Laughing Gull. Larger than Franklin's Gull. Smaller than Great Shearwater.

STRUCTURE: Stocky and powerfully built, with a large head; short, powerful bill; and long, wedge-shaped tail. Unlike in most shearwaters, the broad-based wings are held in a slight crook and slant downward when gliding. The appearance is front-heavy, unlike that of shearwaters, which appear relatively sleek.

FLIGHT AND FLOCKING: In high winds maintains a dynamic, arcing flight style that exceeds that of any shearwater. It arcs higher, climbs faster, and drops down more sharply than even the most aggressive shearwater, covering distance with incredible speed. Wingbeats come in infrequent bursts that are noticeably deeper and more powerful than those of large shearwaters. In calm conditions normally sits on the water, and when it does fly, is out of its element, with heavy, labored wingbeats and short glides.

APPEARANCE: The chest and belly are blindingly white, the back and upperwing are dark gray, and marked with a weakly contrasting darker M pattern. The rump is bold white, the tail black. When low against the water, the upperparts largely blend into the background, but the bright white rump is easy to follow, at times appearing to be a disembodied white square bounding across the waves! The

white underwings are crossed by a black bar that varies in intensity among individuals. The characteristic black cap also varies greatly, as does the white collar that borders the cap. Some individuals are paler, with the black cap restricted to the crown, and thinner black bars on the underwing. Others are darker and may have a reduced white collar. It is possible that some of this variation is due to birds coming from different breeding colonies, and multiple species may even be involved. **Distant:** Dark with a glowing white breast and rump.

SIMILAR SPECIES: Great Shearwater: Vaguely similar color scheme. Slightly larger but much lankier, with a slimmer body and thin bill. Holds its wings almost perfectly straight, whereas Black-capped Petrel juts its wrists forward, creating an angular silhouette. Great's white collar and rump patch are much narrower than those of Black-capped, its white chest is not as bright, and its belly sports a dusky wash. Although the flight of Great is dynamic, almost effortless, Black-capped Petrel puts it to shame in all but the calmest weather conditions. **Fea's Petrel** (not included in this guide): Very rare. Smaller, lacks the white collar, and has mostly dark underwings and a pale gray rump and tail. **Bermuda Petrel** (not included in this guide): Very rare. Smaller and lacks the white collar, creating a unique dark-cowled look. Has a thicker black bar on the underwings and a very restricted white rump patch.

NORTH CAROLINA, SEPT.
CAMERON COX.

- Powerful, heavy-billed seabird with a swept-back hand and sharply pointed wingtips.
- Massive white rump patch is a key trait, though both the rump patch and white collar vary significantly.
- The short, heavy bill is unlike that of shearwaters, but it is held at a downward tilt that is often more apparent at a distance than its structure.
- In high winds, powerful arcing flight shows a dynamism exceeding that of any shearwater, covering distance with ease. In calm conditions, sits on the water or flies with heavy, labored wingbeats.

COMPOSITE WITH GREAT SHEARWATER (R). NORTH CAROLINA, JULY. KEN BEHRENS.
- Slightly shorter-winged than the shearwater. Heavier-bodied, more compact, and with more angular wings.
- Belly is blindingly white, not dingy like Great Shearwater's.

NORTH CAROLINA, AUG. KEN BEHRENS.
- The angular wing shape and white rump are all one needs to identify this bird.
- The rump patch is the most easily discernible feature against a dark ocean.

NORTH CAROLINA, AUG. KEN BEHRENS.
- Short, heavy bill and bull-necked appearance are distinctly different from any shearwater.
- Some lack the distinct white collar and have a dingy gray collar instead.

NORTH CAROLINA, SEPT. CAMERON COX.
- The black border to the underwing is narrower on this bird than on many Black-capped Petrels.
- Variations in plumage, molt, and size may indicate that "Black-capped Petrel" refers to more than one species.

WILSON'S STORM-PETREL
Oceanites oceanicus
DIMENSIONS
L: 7.25 in.; WS: 18 in.; WT: 1.2 oz.

SPRING ARRIVAL

off NC: early May; off NJ: mid-May;
off ME: late May

The typical view of this abundant tubenose is of a tiny dark shape fluttering just above the water, dancing in and out of shimmering summer heat waves. This is the most abundant storm-petrel in eastern North America, and one of the most abundant birds in the world. It is by far the most frequently observed storm-petrel from shore along the Atlantic Coast, and may even invade large bays. At some coastal locations it is not unusual to observe hundreds of these active little "sea swallows" pattering over the waves. Although the species is somewhat regular in the deepwater portions of the Gulf of Mexico, it is never seen there in the numbers found in the Atlantic and is rarely observed from shore there. Wilson's breeds on subantarctic islands and crosses the equator to spend the nonbreeding season, the boreal summer, in the Northern Hemisphere—a stunning migration for such a tiny bird.

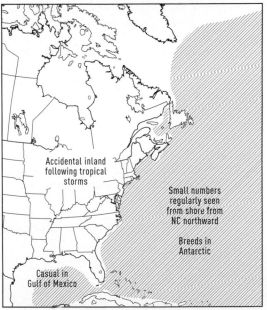

Accidental inland following tropical storms

Small numbers regularly seen from shore from NC northward

Breeds in Antarctic

Casual in Gulf of Mexico

It generally occurs in eastern North America from late May to early September.

SIZE: Smaller than American Robin. Slightly smaller than Purple Martin. About the size of White-rumped Sandpiper. Smallest regular eastern storm-petrel, though some individuals overlap with some Band-rumped and Leach's Storm-Petrel

STRUCTURE: Slightly built, with a short body; stubby, triangular wings; square tail; and tiny bill. The arm is significantly shorter than in Leach's and Band-rumped Storm-Petrels, and the hand often appears shorter as well, though measurements of this portion of the wing do not differ significantly from those of larger storm-petrels. Although it is difficult to see at a distance, the long legs cause the feet to protrude beyond the tail, a trait unique in eastern North America to Wilson's.

FLIGHT AND FLOCKING: Most often seen foraging, fluttering above the water on stiff, shallow wingbeats. Spends extended periods foraging in the same location, hovering and foot-pattering, then tucking into a glide and skimming low over the water, pulling up suddenly and beginning the process again. In this manner it covers very little distance, in contrast to Leach's and Band-rumped, which appear to always be coursing over the water, pausing only briefly to hover or pick from the surface before continuing on. The wings are typically held angled slightly above the body, with long legs dangling. Traveling flight is swift and effortless, and strikingly different from feeding flight, with quick bursts of wingbeats interspersed with short glides. This flight style is much more difficult to observe, as it often occurs deep in the troughs of waves. Storm-petrels, particularly Wilson's, form loose flocks when foraging in areas of abundant food. Typical configurations are irregular clumps of 4–30 birds stretched over 10–40 feet in roughly oval-shaped squadrons. Sometimes these flocks will form fairly clean lines, though these usually dissolve back into disorder quickly. When resting, flocks sit on the water, shoulder to shoulder, in tight balls.

APPEARANCE: Blackish with an extensive white rump patch that wraps around the undertail coverts. The upperwing is dark gray, with a strong pale ulnar bar that fades just before meeting the wrist. Often shows a faint pale band running up the center of the underwing, a unique feature among the storm-petrels covered here. The webbing of the feet is bright yellow, a diagnostic feature though it is difficult to see. **Distant:** Mostly black, though those portions of the bird can disappear against the waves, whereas the white rump is usually conspicuous, flashing and disappearing as a bird dances and turns.

SIMILAR SPECIES: Band-rumped Storm-Petrel: Larger and longer-winged, with direct, powerful flight on stiff, punctuated wingbeats, unlike the weak flight of Wilson's. The most notable wing shape difference between Band-rumped and Wilson's is the length of the arm: distinctly longer in Band-rumped and with a more prominent wing bend. Band-rumped is slightly paler and browner overall, and its ulnar bar shows less contrast. It also has shorter legs that do not project beyond the tail. **Leach's Storm-Petrel:** Strikingly larger with longer, more angular wings and a distinctive, bounding flight. Has a longer and much more forked tail and shorter legs than Wilson's. Also slightly paler than Wilson's, with a strong ulnar bar that extends all the way to the wing bend. The white on the rump is more restricted, extending only marginally to the undertail coverts, and is usually bisected by a dusky central line. **Purple Martin:** Adult male is all dark and similar in size. At times, particularly during migration, this species may be seen far out over the ocean. Although its structure and behavior differ significantly from that of any tubenose, observers seeing a martin out of context often try to force it into a seabird mold, and Wilson's Storm-Petrel is the most similar. Adult male Purple Martin lacks white in the plumage, whereas female has much more white than Wilson's. Martins also have broader wings, slower and deeper wingbeats, and an overall smoother and more casual flight style.

ADULT. NORTH CAROLINA, AUG. KEN BEHRENS.
- Tiny, with a short-winged appearance; short, square tail; and feet that extend beyond the tail.
- The white rump patch is prominent.
- A faint pale stripe is often visible along the underwing. Larger storm-petrels do not show this, while the vagrant European Storm-Petrel has a much stronger white stripe.
- The advanced stage of primary molt (P10 is the only remaining old primary) indicates this is an adult. First-cycle birds at this date will have only begun primary molt.

WITH TWO LEACH'S STORM-PETRELS. MASSACHUSETTS, SEPT. JEREMIAH TRIMBLE.

• *Which are the Leach's? How can they be identified?*

MASSACHUSETTS, JULY. KEN BEHRENS.

• Yellow toe webbing is diagnostic but difficult to see.

• Exceptionally long legs are characteristic of Southern Hemisphere–breeding storm-petrels of the genus *Oceanites*. Northern-breeding storm-petrels have shorter legs.

MASSACHUSETTS, JULY. KEN BEHRENS.

• Traveling flight is swift and direct; quite unlike the aimless foraging flight. Observers only familiar with foraging behavior are apt to mistake a Wilson's in traveling flight for one of the larger storm-petrels.

• Compared with the two larger storm-petrels, Wilson's has a much shorter arm (inner wing).

• The pale diagonal band across the wing is broad and easy to see but fades away before reaching the leading edge of the wing.

WITH TWO GREAT SHEARWATERS. MASSACHUSETTS, JULY. KEN BEHRENS.
- Wilson's is one of the smallest waterbirds—tiny compared with the hefty shearwaters.
- The short, fat, diagonal wingbars are clearly visible at moderate distance.
- Note the short inner wing.

NORTH CAROLINA, SEPT. CAMERON COX.
- Wilson's often spend extended periods pattering and picking over the same small area. The larger storm-petrels tend to course back and forth over a much larger area, and to patter only briefly.

MASSACHUSETTS, JULY. KEN BEHRENS.
- Large flocks often sit on the water in tight balls, flushing simultaneously when approached by a boat.
- Large white rump patch stands out clearly at a distance.

(RIGHT) MASSACHUSETTS, AUG. IAN DAVIES.
- The diagonal wingbar is short, thick, and obvious, though it fades before reaching the carpal bend.
- Feet project beyond the tail, unlike in the two larger storm-petrels. At a distance this can be difficult to see, and Wilson's will occasionally not display projecting feet, so this trait should be used with caution.

LEACH'S STORM-PETREL
Oceanodroma leucorhoa
DIMENSIONS
L: 8 in.; WS: 20 in.; WT: 1.4 lb.

SPRING ARRIVAL

off Bermuda: early Apr.; MA: early May;
ME: early May; off NC: early May

FALL ARRIVAL

Bermuda: early Oct.

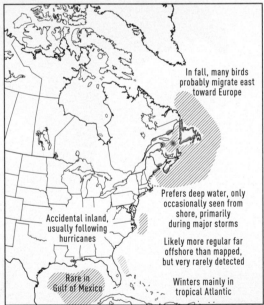

In fall, many birds probably migrate east toward Europe

Prefers deep water, only occasionally seen from shore, primarily during major storms

Likely more regular far offshore than mapped, but very rarely detected

Accidental inland, usually following hurricanes

Rare in Gulf of Mexico

Winters mainly in tropical Atlantic

Leach's is the largest regularly occurring eastern storm-petrel. It is also one of the few tubenoses that nests in the region covered by this guide. Although breeding colonies are scattered from Massachusetts up through the Atlantic Provinces, the nocturnal habits of this species make it almost impossible to see in these places. Boats are the best bet to encounter this species, but even at sea Leach's can be difficult, as it is wary and, unlike Wilson's, rarely lingers at chum slicks. Leach's prefers cooler waters than Band-rumped Storm Petrel, and they rarely overlap. Leach's is most often observed from April to October, though stragglers may overwinter on the North Atlantic. From late September through early April, any storm-petrel observed in North America is likely to be this species.

SIZE: Larger than Purple Martin. Smaller than Black Tern. About the same size as Pectoral Sandpiper. Similar to Band-rumped Storm-Petrel but often appears larger.

STRUCTURE: Large and angular, with long, slender wings. The long and sharply pointed hand is swept back at the wrist so the wing bend juts out prominently. The head and chest are prominent and heavy, but the body quickly tapers to a long, forked tail.

FLIGHT AND FLOCKING: Flight is distinctive, bounding erratically on deep, powerful wingbeats that cover distance with ease. This flight is often compared to a nighthawk's, but it is swifter and more unpredictable, with quicker wingbeats than a nighthawk. Nonetheless, the way the wings are held, with arm raised and hand flattened, does recall a nighthawk. Leach's typically does not pause much when feeding; it bounces along, dropping suddenly to pick food from the surface. In strong wind it will forage by facing the wind and picking from the surface while foot-pattering constantly to maintain its position. It is less prone to flocking than other storm-petrels, and groups larger than six are rarely seen, with sightings of single birds the most frequent.

APPEARANCE: Cold blackish gray with the most limited white rump patch of any eastern storm-petrel. This area of white fails to wrap around to the rump and is usually divided by a faint dusky central line that is difficult to see. The pale ulnar band is distinct and reaches the wrist. **Distant:** Mostly blackish to black, with a white rump that is far less conspicuous than that of other eastern storm-petrels and that may disappear completely.

SIMILAR SPECIES: Band-rumped Storm-Petrel: Rarely overlapping because of its preference for the warmer waters of the Gulf Stream. Flight is more direct and controlled than Leach's, flapping less and gliding more. Wingbeats are stiffer and shallower, mostly above the horizontal, though birds may briefly adopt a very Leach's-like flight. Slightly darker with a warmer brown cast to the plumage than Leach's, which has a cool gray tone to the body plumage. Band-rumped has a much weaker pale ulnar bar that does not reach the wing bend, and an all-white rump without the dusky dividing line shown by most Leach's. The tail is almost square or slightly forked, not deeply forked as in Leach's. **Wilson's Storm-Petrel:** Never shows the erratic, bounding flight that typifies Leach's; typical foraging flight is weak and fluttery, lingering over a small area for an extended period. The wings are shorter, lacking the prominent wing bend and long, pointed hand of Leach's. Additionally, the tail is short and squared off, and the feet project beyond the tip of the tail. Shows much more white on the rump and undertail, the body is blacker, and the ulnar bar does not reach the leading edge of the wing.

NORTH CAROLINA, SEPT. CAMERON COX.
- Long, angular wings.
- Strongly forked tail is diagnostic but can be difficult to see.
- Almost no white wraps around from the rump to the undertail coverts.
- The palest and grayest eastern storm-petrel.

WITH WILSON'S STORM-PETREL (R). MASSACHUSETTS, JULY. LUKE SEITZ.
- Leach's is paler and larger, with longer wings that are pushed forward at the wrist.
- Wilson's is darker and smaller, and the white rump patch is brighter white.
- Since the two species breed in opposite hemispheres, molt timing is different, though immature Leach's may molt in the summer like Wilson's does.

MASSACHUSETTS, JULY. KEN BEHRENS.
• A large flock displaying several characteristic postures.
• Note how far several individuals' wings are lifted high above the body.

**MASSACHUSETTS, JUNE.
JEREMIAH TRIMBLE.**
• The pale band across the wing is distinct and reaches the wing bend.
• The rump patch is longer than it is wide and usually divided by a faint dark line.
• In eastern North America, the very gray color is unique to Leach's.
• The angular wings are characteristic.

WITH THREE WILSON'S STORM-PETRELS. NEW HAMPSHIRE, AUG. ERIC MASTERSON.
• Foraging Leach's (L) often blend into flocks of Wilson's more readily than do birds in point-to-point flight.
• Leach's larger size, paler color, and limited white under the tail are apparent.
• The forked tail is less obvious on some Leach's, particularly heavily worn birds.
• Compare the short legs of Leach's to those of the Wilson's to its right.

BAND-RUMPED STORM-PETREL
Oceanodroma castro
DIMENSIONS
L: 9 in.; WS: 19 in.; WT: 1.5 oz.

SPRING ARRIVAL

FL: late Apr.; Gulf of Mexico: mid-May;
NC: late May

Long considered a single species, it seems that Band-rumped Storm-Petrel may actually be a group of very similar species rather than a single species. The Band-rumped Storm-Petrels breeding in the northeast Atlantic are now thought to represent four different species with different breeding schedules, vocalizations, and minor morphological differences. They also all seem to be separate from the Band-rumped Storm-Petrels in the Pacific, though Pacific birds have not yet received the same level of scrutiny. All four Atlantic taxa are found in warm water and breed on islands off the coasts of Spain and North Africa. These taxa are quite difficult to separate in the field, so Band-rumped Storm-Petrel remains a convenient term for the group as a whole even if the group is split in the future. Although our knowledge is still evolving, it seems that at least two taxa occur in North American waters. These birds are found in the warm Gulf Stream waters from April to late August. They are most regularly

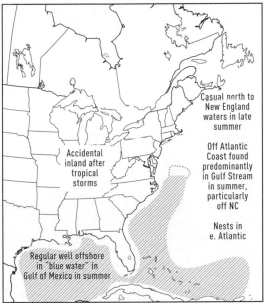

observed off North Carolina, though there are records from Florida to Massachusetts. Band-rumped Storm-Petrel is rarely seen from shore, though tropical storms occasionally drive it onshore or even inland.

SIZE: Slightly larger than Purple Martin. About the same size as Pectoral Sandpiper. Averages intermediate between Wilson's and Leach's Storm-Petrels but can overlap both.

STRUCTURE: Medium-sized, slightly chunky storm-petrel with a heavy bill. It has a noticeably longer arm and more pronounced wing bend than Wilson's, with shorter legs that do not extend beyond the tail. The wings are broader, slightly shorter, and less angular than those of Leach's. The tail is also shorter than Leach's and is squared off or slightly concave.

FLIGHT AND FLOCKING: Traveling flight is the most direct of the eastern storm-petrels. Wingbeats are smooth and fairly shallow, with long glides on slightly arched wings. In strong winds glides more, and flight begins to take on the appearance of a tiny *Pterodroma* petrel, bounding along on set wings. Forages by quickly picking from the surface or pausing to hover or foot-patter briefly, preferring to make repeated looping passes over a prime foraging location rather than hover in one spot for an extended period. At times adopts a more erratic flight style that is very similar to that of Leach's Storm-Petrel, with the wings held up in a dihedral and jerky wingbeats. Flocks loosely around concentrations of food, and readily joins large flocks of Wilson's Storm-Petrels.

APPEARANCE: When well lit, dark brown plumage appears warmer toned than that of Wilson's and Leach's. The white rump wraps partially around to the undertail coverts, though not as extensively as on Wilson's. The pale ulnar bar is fairly weak and fades out just before reaching the wrist. **Distant:** Blackish to dull brown depending on the light. The white rump may be visible but is often inconspicuous.

SIMILAR SPECIES: Wilson's Storm-Petrel: Noticeably smaller, with shorter and more triangular wings, and longer legs that extend past the tail. Flight is weaker, with faster wingbeats, rarely gliding for extended periods, and never bounding with wings motionless. Also shows a stronger silvery ulnar bar, more extensive white rump with the white wrapping around to the undertail coverts, faint pale stripe up the middle of the underwing, and slightly darker, glossier plumage. **Leach's Storm-Petrel:** Similar in size but often looks larger. The wings are narrower and more pointed, with a jutting wing bend, and tail is forked. Flight is erratic, with sharp, snappy downstrokes and infrequent glides with the wings held above horizontal. The ulnar bar is narrow but clearly defined and extends all the way to the wing bend, unlike Band-rumped's. The white rump is often divided by a narrow dark line, and the white does not wrap around to the undertail coverts.

SUBSPECIES: See Taxonomic Notes (p. 591) for more information.

COMPOSITE WITH WILSON'S STORM-PETREL (R). NORTH CAROLINA, AUG. CAMERON COX.
- Band-rumped gives an angular-winged impression like Leach's, but the wings are slightly broader and the hand a bit shorter and less pointed than on Leach's.
- Inner wing is longer than on Wilson's, with a prominent wing bend. Wilson's has an evenly curved leading edge to the wing, though at a distance their wing has a triangular appearance.
- Band-rumped is slightly paler than Wilson's but lacks the cold gray tones of Leach's.

WITH NINETEEN WILSON'S STORM-PETRELS. MASSACHUSETTS, SEPT. JEREMIAH TRIMBLE.
- The Band-rumped (L side of flock) is identified by its larger size and broader wings.
- A Band-rumped sitting in a flock of Wilson's is often the first bird to flush when a boat approaches.

MASSACHUSETTS, AUG. JEREMIAH TRIMBLE.
- The pale band across the wing does not contrast as strongly as in Leach's and often fades before reaching the wing bend.
- The white rump patch is wider than it is long, the opposite of Leach's.
- As in Leach's, the inner wing is longer than Wilson's, but Band-rumped tends to hold its wings straighter than Leach's does.
- Most birds seen in eastern North America have a square tail, but some populations of this species show a notched tail, and these birds are seen occasionally in eastern North America.

NORTH CAROLINA, AUG. KEN BEHRENS.
- Occasionally flies with erratic wingbeats like a Leach's, but more typically the wingbeat is stiff and does not extend as far above the body as in Leach's. Band-rumped also frequently banks and glides on set wings, like a miniature *Pterodroma* petrel.

FRIGATEBIRDS

Frigatebirds are a small group of large, highly distinctive seabirds in the family Fregatidae. Their lightweight bodies and long wings allow them to soar for hours with an effortlessness that could be envied even by vultures! We cover the only regularly occurring species of frigatebird in North America, Magnificent Frigatebird. There is a record of Lesser Frigatebird from Maine and of a Great Frigatebird from Oklahoma, which indicate the potential that frigatebirds have for long-distance vagrancy. Although their slim, angular wings and forked tail ensure that frigatebirds are impossible to mistake for other types of birds, separating the different species of frigatebirds from each other is extremely challenging. Given the challenges of identification, the birds' ability to wander long distances, and the tendency for observers to assume that all the frigatebirds are the expected Magnificent, it seems likely that non–Magnificent Frigatebirds are more regular than the handful of records suggests at present.

Although Magnificent Frigatebird ranges widely in the Gulf of Mexico and can be quite numerous, there is only one breeding colony in the U.S., on the Dry Tortugas in the Florida Keys. It can be 6 to 10 months from the time the single egg is laid until the young fledge. Even after fledging, young frigatebirds are dependent on their parents for at least a year and a half. For this reason most frigatebirds do not breed every year; every other year is typical, though the time between broods can be as much as 4 years. Frigatebirds wait 5 to 11 years before they begin nesting, and this time is spent in nomadic wandering. They do not have clear migrations but use trade winds to carry them long distances. Frigatebirds usually do not fly at night but return to a roost location each evening.

Frigatebirds are kleptoparasitic, stealing fish from boobies, gulls, and even other frigatebirds. They are impressively agile when attacking other birds, using their long, forked tail to execute sharp twists and turns. They also fish for themselves, specializing in flying fish. The long, hooked bill of frigatebirds is ideally suited for grasping flying fish as well as for plucking items from the water's surface that are dropped by other birds.

Frigatebirds are sexually dimorphic and also have a complex series of immature plumages before reaching the adult plumage cycle. Careful attention to the pattern on the breast, throat, and axillaries as well as bare-part coloration is important for aging frigatebirds and for separating Magnificent Frigatebird from potential vagrants.

The sexes differ in frigatebirds but their appearance does not change seasonally. They mature slowly and it may take 8–10 years to attain full adult plumage.

Frigatebirds are skilled aerialists that show a variety of different shapes and postures in flight. Ken Behrens.

(RIGHT) Characteristic parasitic behavior, with a Laughing Gull the unlucky victim. Texas, Aug. Mark B. Bartosik.

MAGNIFICENT FRIGATEBIRD
Fregata magnificens
DIMENSIONS
L: 40 in.; WS: 90 in.; WT: 3.3 lb.

SPRING ARRIVAL

TX: late Apr.; GA: late Apr.; NC: late May

This incredible aerialist is a specialty of the Gulf Coast and southern Florida. It can be seen soaring effortlessly high overhead or aggressively swooping on other waterbirds, forcing them to drop their prey. Its graceful wheeling has a hypnotic quality, and watching frigatebirds doing almost nothing can be incredibly addictive. Magnificent Frigatebird frequently wanders far north of its normal range, usually along the Atlantic Coast but occasionally deep into the interior as well. Often these vagrants are associated with tropical storm systems in the summer or fall, but in recent years there has been an increase in the number of frigatebird occurrences that are not clearly linked to powerful storms.

SIZE: Similar in length to Northern Gannet but with much longer wings. Also much longer-winged than Brown Pelican and slightly shorter-winged than American White Pelican, though structure is utterly unlike a pelican's.

STRUCTURE: Unmistakable. Extraordinarily long, slender wings jut forward sharply at the wrist, ex-

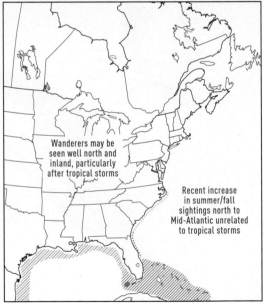

Wanderers may be seen well north and inland, particularly after tropical storms

Recent increase in summer/fall sightings north to Mid-Atlantic unrelated to tropical storms

tending beyond the tiny head and long, hooked bill. The arm is raised, but the long hand is tilted downward. Head-on this gives a crooked wing profile similar to that of Osprey, only more exaggerated. The body is slim, tapering into a long, forked tail. The tail is typically held closed or partially closed, giving the appearance of a long spike trailing behind the bird. However, when a frigatebird chases other birds, it spreads its tail, allowing it to maneuver with great agility to follow the twists and turns of its smaller victims.

FLIGHT AND FLOCKING: Typically soars effortlessly, rising thousands of feet high at times, with the wings held almost motionless, steering with tiny movements of the rudderlike tail. When it does beat its wings, the wingbeats are extremely slow, flexible, and exaggerated. The impression is of rowing through Jell-o rather flapping through air. Particularly when foraging, tends to be solitary. As in gulls, though, a horde may descend where there is food. Sometimes gangs of two or three mercilessly pursue one gull or tern or even another frigatebird in order to steal its food. In areas where Magnificent Frigatebird is abundant, soaring birds form small to medium-sized kettles, much like those of some raptors, which may drift about aimlessly without flapping for hours.

APPEARANCE: Adult Male: All black but showing a faint purple gloss at close range. The fleshy red throat patch is typically retracted into the throat and difficult to see but occasionally is inflated or partially inflated in flight, even far from breeding areas. **Adult Female:** Black with a white band across the chest, isolating the black head. A dull brown or dirty white ulnar bar runs across the arm from the wrist to the body. At close range some white mottling may be visible in the axillaries. **Juvenile:** Black with a white head and chest. Broad black spikes extend from the sides of the chest, like the beginnings of a chest band, but the center of the chest is always white. Like female, has a whitish ulnar bar and some white mottling in the axillaries. **Subadult:** Extremely variable, as birds take several years to reach adult plumage. Initially like juvenile but lacking the black spikes on the sides of the breast. By the third cycle shows a dark strap across the throat and has black mottling on the chest that begins to hint at the sex of the bird, males becoming dark across the breast and females showing more mottling on the lower belly. **Distant:** Adult appears uniformly black; the white chest of female is not apparent except in good light. The white head of first-cycle birds is often visible.

SIMILAR SPECIES: Utterly distinctive, except for other frigatebirds, which are extremely rare. **Great Frigatebird** (not included in this guide): Very unlikely in eastern North America as populations in the Atlantic are small. Despite its name, Great Frigatebird is noticeably smaller than Magnificent, though subtly stockier and slightly shorter-tailed. Male has a pale bar running through the upperwing coverts that may be whitish when fresh or dull brown when worn, whereas male Magnificent has a completely black upperwing. At close range, male Great Frigatebird shows pink feet and often has a pale scalloped pattern in the axillaries. Female has a dull gray throat and dark head, appearing hooded, and tends to have a rounded division between the white breast and black belly; in female Magnificent this dividing line is wedge-shaped. At close range the pink orbital ring of female Great Frigatebird is noticeable. First-cycle Great has a significant cinnamon wash to the head and chest, separating it easily from first-cycle Magnificent, which is white in these areas. Subadult birds are much more difficult, but Great tends to have a faint cinnamon wash somewhere on the head or chest and a rounded division between the black and white on the lower belly, whereas this division tapers almost to a point in Magnificent. Dull pink feet are diagnostic for all immature Great Frigatebirds but are difficult to see. **Lesser Frigatebird** (not included in this guide): Much smaller. Male has small white oval patches on the flanks extending into the axillaries. Adult female has much more white extending into the axillaries than female Magnificent does. First-cycle bird has a dull cinnamon-washed head and large pale spurs extending into the axillaries, a trait shared with subadult.

BAJA CALIFORNIA, MEXICO, JULY.
STEVE MLODINOW.

- Long, angular wings and long tail create an unmistakable silhouette.
- Where common, they gather in large numbers and swirl hypnotically for hours.
- Juvenile's white head and female's white chest tend to disappear at a distance.
- Tail can either be spread in a distinct fork or held closed to look like a long trailing spike.

ADULT FEMALE. FLORIDA, MAY. CAMERON COX.
- Adult female has a dark head and throat and white chest.
- The infrequent wingbeats are slow and exaggerated and appear to pull the wingtips toward the body.

ADULT MALE. FLORIDA, MAY. CAMERON COX.
- Away from the breeding grounds, adult males usually hide their inflatable throat sacs, but they are sometimes partially exposed as in this individual.
- The forked tail is usually held closed so it resembles a long spike.

GALAPAGOS, ECUADOR. NOV. MIKE DANZENBAKER.

SULIDS

"Sulids," a commonly used abbreviation for birds in the family Sulidae, form a small group of large, long-winged seabirds with distinctive torpedo-shaped bodies. There are two branches of the family, the gannets, found primarily in cold water, and the boobies, which prefer tropical and subtropical climes. We cover the only gannet found in the Northern Hemisphere, Northern Gannet, and the two boobies most regularly found in the southeastern U.S.: Brown Booby and Masked Booby. We do not cover Red-footed Booby, a species found rarely in south Florida and exceptionally elsewhere in the area covered by this guide.

All sulids plunge-dive to catch fish or squid. They drop out of the sky, lay their wings flat against the body at the last moment, and disappear with as little splash as an Olympic diver. It is this spectacular diving behavior that gains Northern Gannets many fans at Atlantic seawatches. When schools of baitfish are driven to the surface by predatory fish, flocks of scores or hundreds of gannets gather above them, with dozens diving at any one moment, though staggered slightly so that each bird strikes the water a split second after the bird before it. The seawatcher knows immediately that it is a good day for gannets if, when scanning the horizon at first light, the water is pockmarked with dozens of tiny white splashes. Plunge-dives may take place from heights of over 300 feet, and Northern Gannet has been recorded diving to depths of 50 feet. Once underwater, sulids chase down prey by swimming, using their wings like paddles for propulsion. Sulids do not spear fish with their dives as folklore holds. Most often, they dive beneath a school of fish and grab one as they return to the surface.

This Brown Booby displays the traits typical of sulids: long, pointed wings; rounded head with sharp bill; and long tail. Brazil, Oct. Tony Gálvez.

Northern Gannet is a medium-distance migrant, usually moving within sight of shore, making it easy to observe at many locations along the Atlantic Coast. Promontories provide concentration points where hundreds or even thousands can be seen. Fall counts at the Avalon Seawatch in New Jersey have surpassed 100,000 in several years. Brown and Masked Boobies do not have a well-defined migration. They are somewhat nomadic, and in the U.S. can be found reliably only in the Dry Tortugas, where both species breed in small numbers. They are also regular in the waters surrounding the outer Florida Keys. Both species, Masked in particular, range widely in the Gulf of Mexico and along the southern Atlantic states but are sparsely distributed. They often associate with offshore oil platforms, buoys, and other human-made structures that provide perches. Sulids are found almost exclusively along the coast or in pelagic regions far from shore, but Northern Gannet occurs regularly on the eastern Great Lakes, and a booby will occasionally create a sensation by showing up on an interior lake.

Northern Gannet takes 6 or more years to reach adult plumage, moving slowly through several distinct but variable plumages. During the fall there are some vague differences in migration timing between the different age classes: second-cycle and older immature birds move south first, followed by juveniles, whereas adults are last to move south. During midfall, though, all age classes overlap. Many immature gannets oversummer in the winter range, and they can be confused with boobies by those who associate boobies with warmer temperatures. Boobies mature faster than Northern Gannet, in 3 or 4 years, but still display several distinct plumages.

Sexes appear similar in all three species covered here, and they do not change their appearance seasonally. Immature birds differ significantly from adults and adult plumage is not attained until at least the third or fourth cycle.

Northern Gannets are striking and beautiful whether they are 10 feet or 1 mile away. South Carolina, Jan. Cameron Cox.

NORTHERN GANNET
Morus bassanus
DIMENSIONS
L: 37 in.; WS: 72 in.; WT: 6.6 lb.

SPRING ARRIVAL

ME: early Mar.; QC: mid-Apr.

FALL ARRIVAL

ME: late Aug.; NJ: late Sept.; NC: early Oct.;
w. Gulf Coast: mid-Oct.

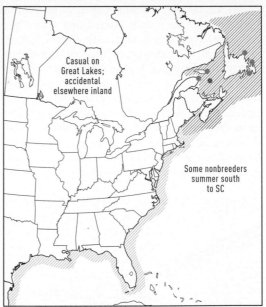

Casual on Great Lakes; accidental elsewhere inland

Some nonbreeders summer south to SC

Northern Gannet is one of the marquee species of the Atlantic seawatch. Its striking appearance and spectacular, torpedo-like plunge-dives make it a huge crowd pleaser. Except for pelicans, it is the largest species regularly seen from shore in eastern North America. The distinct appearances of different age classes are easily discernible, allowing observers to track these classes throughout a season and note temporal patterns. The species is almost exclusively coastal but is seen rarely but regularly on the eastern Great Lakes.

SIZE: The largest sulid, clearly larger than Masked Booby. Wings are slightly shorter than those of Brown Pelican but longer than those of Tundra Swan. Although the wing length is that of a swan, the body is shorter, even shorter than that of an average Canada Goose.

STRUCTURE: Extremely large with an unmistakable shape. The body is long, slender, and tubelike, tipped with a daggerlike bill. Unlike boobies, Northern Gannet usually holds its bill angled downward at an approximately 25°–35° angle. The exceptionally long wings are centered on the body and are slim and even throughout their length, ending in sharply pointed tips. The tail is also long, and shaped like a slender wedge with a sharply pointed tip. A simple trick for remembering the structure of gannet is to think of it as the compass bird, pointed in all four directions.

FLIGHT AND FLOCKING: Wingbeats are strong and fairly stiff but with flexible wingtips. Flight behavior varies tremendously even within a single day, depending on weather. Often flies well above the water and gives a series of wingbeats of variable number followed by a short to medium-length glide, then another series of wingbeats, and so on. Progress is punctuated by sudden vertical dives when fish are available, followed by periods of sitting on the water. Regaining flight requires an awkward flurry of heavy wingbeats. With this combination of flying, foraging, and resting, birds usually make slow progress on migration. When behaving like this, they can trickle by singly or in a veritable river, with thousands of individuals passing a single point in just a few hours. In more determined migratory flight, flies low to the water in carefully spaced, short lines of 5–30 birds. On exceptional days forms larger, narrow, V-shaped flocks, though unlike in most such waterbird flocks, the two arms of the V often are not level, with one side higher than the other, and the sides swapping high position frequently. In this sort of flight uses faster, choppier wingbeats with shorter glides, and travels at significantly faster speeds. In high winds uses a dynamic soar, making long arcs, with the wingbeats coming in short, hurried series. In windless conditions it is lethargic, with slow, deep wingbeats and long periods spent resting on the water. The bane of a seawatch counter is a day that starts with gannets mainly foraging and not really going anywhere, but then being launched back into migratory mode by a subtle shift in wind direction. Instead of meandering back and forth while foraging, the birds begin to move steadily south while continuing to make regular plunge-dives. A counter who is not on alert for such a shift may let hundreds of gannets slip by uncounted before noticing the change in behavior.

APPEARANCE: Adult: Bright white with black primaries and a dull golden wash covering the head and neck. A small number of individuals, likely aberrant fourth-cycle or delayed fifth-cycle birds, have adult plumage except for solid black secondaries. Observers unaware of this variation have been known to call such birds Masked Boobies or even the Southern Hemisphere resident, Cape Gannet. Don't do that! **First Cycle:** Dull brown wings with paler gray body and a narrow white band crossing the uppertail coverts. **Subadult:** Northern Gannets take several years to mature, and from the beginning of the second cycle until they become adults their appearance is constantly changing. We describe the most typical appearances for each cycle, but there is much variation. On average, second-cycle individuals attain paler body plumage than juveniles, often with a distinct pale collar, but maintain largely brown wings. In the third cycle, birds gain largely white body plumage and a significant amount of white speckling in the wings and begin to show the golden color on the head. Fourth cycles are largely like adult but with black central tail feathers and variable numbers of black secondaries that may be spaced evenly in a "piano key" pattern or may occur in irregular blocks. **Distant:** Adults appear cleanly black and white or, at extreme distances, like glowing white specks. Adults and the palest subadults may be identified from extraordinary distances, many miles away on exceptionally clear days, particularly if you have a vantage above the ocean or if the birds are flying high. First-cycle birds look dull dark brown and are not visible at such incredible distances. Subadults look mottled, and distant flocks of gannets often include multiple ages and have a mottled appearance as well.

SIMILAR SPECIES: In most areas covered by this guide, Northern Gannet will be the only likely sulid. Along the southern Atlantic Coast and Gulf Coast, boobies may rarely be seen from shore. Northern Gannet is much larger than any of the boobies and typically holds its bill angled downward, whereas boobies hold theirs straight. Boobies have rounded patches of bare facial skin with little feathering extending in front of the eye. **Masked Booby:** First cycle has a strong white collar, pale underwings, and a strong white band across the base of the tail that is unlike the thin white band on the tips of the uppertail coverts of first-cycle gannet. The mask, secondaries, greater coverts, and tail are all completely black on adult. **Brown Booby:** First-cycle is darker and more uniform than first-cycle gannet and has solid brown uppertail coverts. Subadult birds show strong contrast between the pale belly and brown chest. Adult has even more strongly contrasting white belly and solid brown upperparts. **Other Large Waterbirds:** Both Great Black-backed Gull and Brown Pelican can briefly be mistaken for gannets, particularly when gliding. Both can approximate the overall color shown by one of the age classes of gannet, but both are so unlike gannet in structure and wingbeats that any confusion should be fleeting.

ONE ADULT (L) AND TWO SECOND CYCLES. NEW JERSEY, NOV. KEN BEHRENS.
- Largest sulid in North America, with a long but bulky body.
- Bill is typically angled down slightly.
- Second-cycle birds can resemble first-cycle Masked Booby but are dingy gray with heavily marked underwings.

NEW JERSEY, NOV. KEN BEHRENS.
- Migrating gannets frequently stop to forage and may gather in large groups over schools of fish. Although the number of birds in such a flock may not change noticeably, a trickle of new birds usually continues to join the flock while other birds leave to continue migration or join the next feeding flock.

SUBADULTS WITH SURF, BLACK, AND WHITE-WINGED SCOTERS. NEW JERSEY, DEC. KEN BEHRENS.
- It is easy to "tune out" gannets when large numbers of other species are on the move, but a brief period spent carefully watching them usually reveals that they are moving in greater numbers than a casual look would suggest.
- *How many Surf Scoters are in this flock?*

ADULT. FLORIDA, JAN. CAMERON COX.

• Although distant adults are little more than white dots on the horizon, gannets are striking at close range.

• The bright white color, speed with which they move across the horizon, and mere fact that they are still visible at distances of up to several miles are the traits used to identify gannets at extreme distances.

• *What gull species are in this photo?*

NEW JERSEY, DEC. KEN BEHRENS.

• Flocks this large and well organized are rare and occur only on days when gannets are moving by the thousands.

THIRD CYCLE. NEW JERSEY, DEC. KEN BEHRENS.

• Immatures with black secondaries are similar to adult Masked Booby, but note the yellow wash on the head and the largely white greater coverts.

FIRST CYCLE. FLORIDA, JAN. CAMERON COX.

• Although they look uniformly dark in bad light, first-cycle birds show a pale belly when well lit.

• As the first cycle progresses, the belly becomes dingy gray.

(LEFT) SCOTLAND, JULY.
JOHN ANDERSON.

WITH TWO HERRING GULLS.
NEW JERSEY, DEC.
KEN BEHRENS.

- Head, tail, and wings are all sharply pointed. No other North Atlantic seabird has such a shape.
- Bill is subtly angled downward. Smaller sulids tend to hold their bill straight.

THIRD-CYCLE TYPE WITH SECOND-CYCLE GREAT BLACK-BACKED GULL (L). NEW JERSEY, APR. TONY LEUKERING.
- Gliding Great Black-backed Gulls can look similar to a gannet but have blunter, arched wings.
- Great Black-backed is a huge gull!

NEW JERSEY, DEC. KEN BEHRENS.
- Scenes like this are why seawatchers get up early on bone-chilling mornings and spend the day watching distant birds.

FLORIDA, APR. CAMERON COX.
• Since Northern Gannet takes at least 5 years to mature, it displays a diversity of plumages, which often gives distant flocks a mottled black-and-white appearance.

ADULT. NORTH CAROLINA, FEB. KEN BEHRENS.
• The long tail is wedge-shaped but is held closed most of the time and from a distance appears pointed.
• The gape line extends well behind the eye in gannets. In boobies it stops at the eye.

FIRST CYCLE. SWEDEN, SEPT. TOMMY HOLMGREN.
• On windy days the set-winged arcing flight and stiff wingbeats of immatures can cause confusion with a large shearwater or even an albatross. However, the gannet's wings are more sharply pointed, and the tail is too long for a tubenose.

MASKED BOOBY
Sula dactylatra
DIMENSIONS
L: 32 in.; WS: 62 in.; WT: 3.3 lb.

SPRING ARRIVAL

off TX: late Mar.

This striking sulid resembles Northern Gannet in appearance but is mainly tropical in distribution, with only a small colony in the U.S., on Hospital Key in the Dry Tortugas of Florida. Masked is the most pelagic of the sulids, most often observed in the deep blue water of the Gulf of Mexico and the Gulf Stream off the southern Atlantic Coast. It is rarely observed from shore away from breeding areas, except during tropical storms.

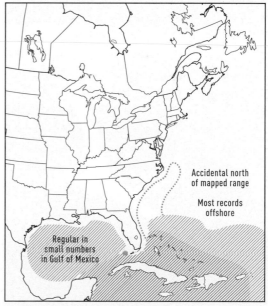

Accidental north of mapped range

Most records offshore

Regular in small numbers in Gulf of Mexico

SIZE: Significantly smaller than Northern Gannet. Slightly larger than Brown Booby. Fairly similar to Double-crested Cormorant but longer-winged.

STRUCTURE: A cut-down version of Northern Gannet. The head and neck projection in front of the wings is similar to the tail projection behind the wings. The bill is typically pointed straight forward or tilted downward slightly, unlike that of Northern Gannet, which tilts distinctly downward. The wings are long and pointed, clearly slimmer than those of Northern Gannet.

FLIGHT AND FLOCKING: Wingbeats are somewhat slow and stiff and appear to emanate largely from the hand. Although the wingbeats are slow for a booby, they are still faster than those of Northern Gannet and tend to be slightly shallower as well. In the area covered by this guide, Masked Booby is rarely numerous, except around the Dry Tortugas, and usually solitary; occasionally seen in pairs.

APPEARANCE: Adult: Black and white overall, in a pattern similar to that of Northern Gannet but with a yellow bill and black "mask." There is black on the secondaries, greater secondary coverts, and tail, unlike in gannet. **First Cycle:** Sports an olive to dull yellow bill and dark facial skin like adult but has a brown head, strong pale collar, gray-brown back and upperwings, broad pale band across the rump, and dark brown tail. The belly and underwing are largely dull white with faint dusky markings. **Second Cycle:** Similar to adult but appears dirtier, with a mix of brown and black flight feathers, variable dark mottling in the upperwing coverts, and dusky smudging on the lower back. The bill is brighter yellow. **Distant:** Adults are sharply contrasting black and bright white, with the black secondaries clearly evident at great distances. Juveniles and subadults are dark brown and dull white, and the contrast is less distinct, though the clean pale underwings are evident with a good view.

SIMILAR SPECIES: Northern Gannet: Clearly larger, with a thicker body, broader wings, and a bill angled distinctly downward. Adult lacks the black secondaries and secondary coverts of Masked, though a gannet that otherwise looks like an adult may rarely show black secondaries. These aberrant birds lack the black greater secondary coverts of Masked and typically have a white or black-and-white tail rather than the all-black tail of Masked. Second-cycle gannet can be confused with juvenile Masked Booby but has distinctly dirtier-looking underwings, a white U across the tips of the uppertail coverts rather than a straight band across the rump, and typically has some dirty gray markings on the belly and head. **Red-footed Booby** (not included in this guide): Smaller, with a more active flight style and a longer tail. Adult has white greater secondary coverts, so the black trailing edge to the wing is narrower than in Masked Booby. The primary underwing coverts are boldly marked with black. The bill is gray rather than yellow. Juvenile has solidly dark underwings.

ADULT WITH ADULT BROWN BOOBY (L). CARIBBEAN, JAN. COLIN SCOTT.
• Larger and heavier than Brown Booby, with broader wings, shorter tail, and deeper bill, though still distinctly smaller than Northern Gannet.

FIRST CYCLE. TEXAS, JULY. MARY GUSTAFSON.
• Broad, pale collar over the top of the neck eliminates both immature Northern Gannet and Brown Booby.
• The gape line stops at the eye, whereas it continues well past the eye in Northern Gannet.

FIRST CYCLE. FLORIDA, AUG. STAN CZAPLICKI.

- Even first-cycle Masked Boobies have clean a white belly and largely white underwings. First- to third-cycle Northern Gannets have a dingy belly and underwings.
- The dark facial skin is already apparent, and the bill is a dull yellowish color.

SUBADULT. NORTH CAROLINA, JULY. CAMERON COX.

- Has black secondaries as well as black greater coverts, so there is much less white on the upperwing than on Northern Gannet.
- Not as slender as Brown Booby but, like it, holds the bill virtually straight, so its entire body appears straighter than that of a gannet.

ADULT (R) WITH FOURTH-CYCLE TYPE NORTHERN GANNET (L).

- A few subadult Northern Gannets have a complete black trailing edge to the secondaries, like adult Masked Booby, but they lack the solid black greater coverts.

BROWN BOOBY
Sula leucogaster
DIMENSIONS
L: 30 in.; WS: 57 in.; WT: 2.4 lb.

Brown Booby is a small and agile sulid well suited to catching its favorite prey item, flying fish. Like Masked Booby, it has a tentative breeding toehold in the Dry Tortugas of Florida but is mainly tropical in distribution. Unlike Masked Booby, which ranges widely in the Gulf of Mexico and the Gulf Stream but is rarely found outside its normal range, Brown Booby has a small area of distribution in southern Florida, but vagrants occur widely. It tends to be a nearshore booby, whereas Masked is very pelagic, which may account for this difference.

SIZE: Slightly smaller than Masked Booby. Only slightly larger than Herring Gull.

STRUCTURE: Gannet-like but much more slender, with significantly slimmer wings and a slightly longer tail. As in Masked Booby, but unlike in Northern Gannet, the bill is held almost perfectly straight or angled downward only slightly.

FLIGHT AND FLOCKING: Wingbeats are faster but weaker than those of Masked Booby and appear to emanate from the shoulder rather than the hand,

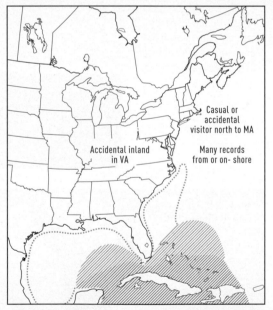

Casual or accidental visitor north to MA

Accidental inland in VA

Many records from or on- shore

giving a somewhat floppy impression. At times can look quite similar to Cory's Shearwater, arcing up slowly with a quick series of wingbeats when gliding down into the trough of a wave. Tends to flap more frequently and glide less than Masked Booby.

APPEARANCE: Adult: Dark brown head, chest, back, and upperwings contrast sharply with a clean white belly. A wedge of dirty white underwing coverts extends out to the wrist; the wingtips are solidly dark brown. The bill and feet are bright yellow. **Juvenile:** Almost uniformly brown with slightly paler belly and underwing coverts. **Subadult:** Like adult, but the white belly is marred with variable amounts of light brown mottling, reducing the contrast between chest and belly, and the bill is duller yellow. **Distant:** Often uniformly dark, though the contrasting white belly of adult can be evident at great distances in good light. The color tends to be warmer and browner than that of immature Masked Booby or Northern Gannet, which give a colder, grayish impression.

SIMILAR SPECIES: Northern Gannet: Significantly larger, imparting a sense of greater bulk with wing-beats that are slower, stiffer, and shallower than those of Brown Booby. Gannets typically hold the bill angled downward at a noticeable angle, whereas boobies hold it virtually straight. Juvenile Northern Gannet is slightly paler overall than juvenile Brown Booby, is a colder gray color, and has a bold white band across the uppertail coverts. **Red-footed Booby** (not included in this guide): Slightly smaller and slimmer, with faster wingbeats, creating the impression of more agile flight. Juvenile is paler overall and shows contrast between the tan upperwing coverts and the dark hand, and also between the solid brown underwings and pale gray-brown chest. In comparison, Brown Booby has a uniform upperwing, and first-cycle bird shows little contrast between the body and underwing.

ADULT. BRAZIL, OCT. TONY TANOURY.
• White belly set off by sharply defined dark head and bright yellow bill make identification of adults straightforward.
• Slimmer overall and slightly longer-tailed than Masked Booby and Northern Gannet.

FIRST CYCLES. FLORIDA, JULY. ANGEL ABREU.
• Similar in pattern to first-cycle Northern Gannet but brown rather than dingy gray.
• Build is slender. In particular, the bill and neck are very slim for a sulid.

ADULT WITH THREE SUBADULT NORTHERN GANNETS. FLORIDA, APR. CAMERON COX.
• The gannets appear powerful and heavy, whereas the Brown Booby (bottom R) is slender with narrower wings.
• The head and bill of the booby are held slightly straighter than those of the gannets.

PELICANS

Pelicans form a small family of distinctive waterbirds that includes some of the largest flying birds in the world. Their combination of long and pouchlike bill, bulky body, and broad wings with

Both of North America's pelicans: American White Pelicans on the sandbar and smaller Brown Pelicans in flight. Texas, Nov. Clay Taylor.

"multifingered" wingtips makes them so distinctive that they are widely recognized by nonbirders. Two species of pelicans are found in North America, and we cover both in this guide. Brown Pelican is primarily a coastal species, best known for its spectacular manner of catching fish: headfirst plunge-dives often made from great heights. Brown Pelican was among the species hardest hit by DDT and was federally listed as endangered in 1970. Since then, the species has made an impressive comeback, and it was removed from federal protection in 2009. American White Pelican is substantially larger than Brown Pelican, among the largest flying birds in North America, with a wingspan that approaches 10 feet. It is primarily a freshwater species that hunts by paddling across the surface of the water and using its huge bill to scoop up fish, amphibians, and invertebrates. Large groups of American White Pelicans often work in concert to herd fish into shallow water or encircle them, concentrating the prey.

Pelicans generally do not mix with other species of birds in flight or during migration, and mixed groups of American White and Brown Pelicans are rarely seen in flight. Brown Pelicans usually migrate in small flocks that often form lines and glide over the surface of the ocean, and more rarely soar in loose, disorganized kettles. Along the Gulf Coast where the species is resident, larger flocks form, and long lines follow the dunes or glide just above the waves off the beaches. In contrast, American White Pelicans migrate almost exclusively by soaring, rising to great heights in organized groups that may number hundreds of individuals. These migrant flocks often follow major river corridors. Unlike kettles of raptors, flocks of American White Pelicans turn in unison in tight spirals. The coordination these massive birds display when gaining altitude on a rising thermal is truly impressive. Using turn after perfectly coordinated turn, they gradually climb, flashing bright white when they catch the light.

Pelican are easy to identify and do not show differences in appearance between the sexes, but they do vary somewhat seasonally and have a slow and complex plumage progression to reach adult plumage. Brown Pelican in particular shows significant age-related variation, and flocks of Brown Pelicans often include several age classes, giving the flock a strongly mottled appearance. Because American White Pelican is largely white, the plumage differences it shows in different age classes are much more subtle than those of Brown Pelican, but this does not mean its plumages are less complex, as it also takes American White Pelican 3 to 5 years to reach adult plumage.

Sexes are similar in both species but they show subtle seasonal changes in appearance.

AMERICAN WHITE PELICAN
Pelecanus erythrorhynchos
DIMENSIONS
L: 62 in.; WS: 95–120 in.; WT: 16.4 lb.

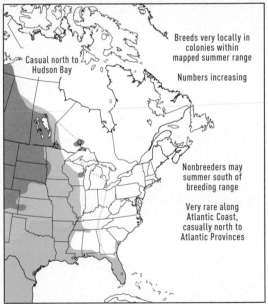

Breeds very locally in colonies within mapped summer range

Numbers increasing

Casual north to Hudson Bay

Nonbreeders may summer south of breeding range

Very rare along Atlantic Coast, casually north to Atlantic Provinces

SPRING ARRIVAL

IA: late Mar.; s. MB: mid-Apr.

FALL ARRIVAL

MO: mid-Aug.; Gulf Coast: mid-Sept.

Watching flocks of this massive black-and-white pelican swirl overhead is almost hypnotic. American White Pelican is one of the largest birds in North America, and it seems almost miraculous that it can even take flight, let alone with the grace and precision it displays. It is primarily a western species, though large numbers winter on the Gulf Coast. It has a strong tendency to wander and can turn up just about anywhere in eastern North America, particularly during the warmer months of the year.

SIZE: Massive. Dwarfs Brown Pelican. Longer-winged than Trumpeter Swan but not as heavy.

STRUCTURE: Bulky and awkward, with a very long bill held at a slight downward angle; a massive, somewhat oval-shaped body; and long, very broad wings. The wings are held in a more modest arch than those of Brown Pelican and are often almost straight, with the hand angled down slightly. As in Brown Pelican, the wing is tipped with long, finger-like primaries.

FLIGHT AND FLOCKING: Slow, ponderous wingbeats come in short series followed by a short glide.

Tends to flap more regularly and glide for shorter periods than Brown Pelican except when catching a thermal, when it may soar on set wings for hours. Even more gregarious than Brown Pelican; flocks of hundreds occur regularly. In powered flight, small flocks form lines, larger flocks line up wing to wing in shallow U- or V-shaped formations, and the largest flocks contain a jumble of Vs and lines that devolve into a shapeless mass. For long-distance flights uses thermals, rising in well-organized flocks with each bird following the bird in front of it, spiraling up in slow, synchronized circles, then gliding to the next rising pocket of air. Tends to fly at medium heights or higher, rarely skimming low over the water as Brown Pelican often does, except when flushed off a roost site.

APPEARANCE: Adult: Bright orange bill and facial skin, all-white body, and jet-black primaries, primary coverts, and secondaries. During the breeding season there is a knob on top of the bill. Acquires a black-spotted crown or full blackish cap for a short period from midsummer to early fall.

Whether this truly represents an additional plumage or is a delayed acquisition of alternate plumage in not known. **First Cycle:** Like adult, but the head, neck, and back are marked with a variable dusky gray wash and the bill is duller. Although it takes 3–5 years for American White Pelican to acquire full adult plumage, the intervening cycles do not differ greatly. **Distant:** Strongly contrasting black and white. When riding a distant thermal, catches the light and flashes bright white at certain angles only to disappear as the flock continues to rotate. Some flocks are large enough that some portion of the flock is always catching the light, causing white flashes to dance through the flock.

SIMILAR SPECIES: Wood Stork (not included in this guide): Similar in pattern but smaller, with a gray or dull yellow bill and legs that project well beyond the tail. Unlike American White Pelican flocks, large flocks of Wood Stork rising on thermals usually swirl in chaotic, every-bird-for-itself kettles like raptors, though small groups may circle in synchronized bunches like American White Pelicans.

FLORIDA, FEB. CAMERON COX.
- Soaring birds turn in unison, unlike soaring raptors.
- At a distance, flocks can disappear as they turn wing-on to the observer and then flash bright white as they rotate and catch the light again.

TEXAS, JAN. KEN BEHRENS.
- One of the largest birds in North America. The sheer bulk, nearly 10-foot wingspan, and distinctive structure are the primary identification characteristics.

WITH TWO BROWN PELICANS (R). TEXAS, JAN. KEN BEHRENS.
• Brown Pelican is large but is still dwarfed by the colossal American White Pelican.

TEXAS, JAN. KEN BEHRENS.
• Massive, scooplike bill is a highly effective foraging tool and also serves as a conspicuous identification trait.

TEXAS, JAN. KEN BEHRENS.
• When not soaring, flocks form lines that undulate slightly as they alternate between short periods of slow, heavy wingbeats and long glides.

FLORIDA, JAN. CAMERON COX.
• They tend to be more gregarious than Brown Pelicans, forming massive flocks (see background).

TEXAS, JAN. KEN BEHRENS.
• Large flocks that are not soaring sometimes form boxy constructions of parallel, undulating lines. Such flocks can be identified at great distance.

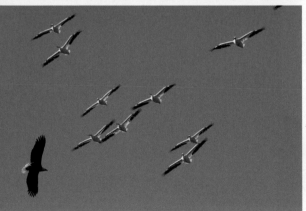

WITH WOOD STORK (TOP) AND BALD EAGLE (BOTTOM). FLORIDA, JAN. CAMERON COX.
• Flocks soar on fixed wings for long periods, and are sometimes joined by other soaring birds.

OKLAHOMA, SEPT. JIM ARTERBURN.
• Huge size, black-and-white plumage, and long, downward-angled bill make this one of the easiest waterbirds to identify at any distance.

BROWN PELICAN
Pelecanus occidentalis
DIMENSIONS
L: 51 in.; WS: 79 in.; WT: 8.2 lb.

SPRING ARRIVAL

MD: mid-Apr.; NJ: mid-May; NY: early June

This massive waterbird has made a phenomenal comeback after being devastated by DDT in the late twentieth century. The hordes of Brown Pelicans that are now found along the Gulf and southern Atlantic Coasts are a testament to the resilience of nature. This is a highly conspicuous species, often observed making spectacular plunge-dives into the water in pursuit of fish—among pelicans, a behavior shared only with South America's Peruvian Pelican. Brown Pelican disperses well north of its breeding range in late summer and fall, when it occurs on Long Island and, rarely, even farther north. It is occasionally found inland on lakes or rivers, often in conjunction with powerful storms, but sometimes for no discernible reason.

SIZE: Significantly smaller than American White Pelican. Only slightly longer-winged but significantly bulkier than Northern Gannet.

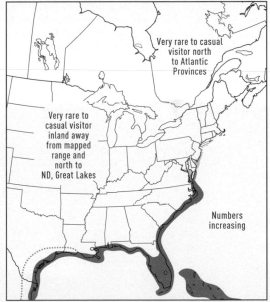

Very rare to casual visitor north to Atlantic Provinces

Very rare to casual visitor inland away from mapped range and north to ND, Great Lakes

Numbers increasing

STRUCTURE: Bulky and awkward, with a very long bill held at a distinct downward angle. The neck is curled back toward the body and is rarely noticeable. The body is chunky, broad, and somewhat oval shaped (especially when viewed from below), the wings are long and broad, and the tail is short and rounded. The wings are held in a moderate downward arch and are tipped with fingerlike primaries reminiscent of an eagle's.

FLIGHT AND FLOCKING: Wingbeats are slow and deliberate, usually coming in a series of four or five to several dozen followed by an extended glide. In most conditions glides more than it beats its wings, but the number and frequency of wingbeats increase in very calm or very windy conditions. May soar on thermals to great heights, but only a few individuals at a time and never in the highly organized flocks formed by soaring American White Pelicans. Regularly skims just above the water with impressive precision, disappearing amid ocean swells. Flocks usually include 3–25 birds, though some flocks grow to more than 100. May fly in tight synchrony, side by side, with wingtips almost touching, or in loose strands with several yards between each bird. Smaller flocks form lines or horizontal Vs. Larger flocks usually form twisting, vaguely U-shaped formations. The largest flocks comprise multiple Us that combine into messy globs. Flocks most often move parallel to coastlines, ranging from well out over the water to inside the beach, gliding above sand dune ridgelines.

APPEARANCE: **Alternate Adult:** Pale yellow crown fades into a buff strip running down to the throat. The nape and belly are rich brown—distinctly darker than the silvery brown back and wing coverts which also contrast with the blackish primaries. Just as the chicks hatch, adult acquires a pale crown with variable dark spotting, often referred to as the "chick-feeding plumage." Whether this truly represents an additional plumage or is a delayed acquisition of alternate plumage is not known. **Basic Adult:** Same as alternate adult, but most of the head and neck become white, sometimes with some dull yellow around the base of the bill. **First Cycle:** Dull brown head, chest, back, and upperwing coverts with moderately contrasting dark brown flight feathers. The belly is pale. The underwing is largely brown with a strong white stripe running down its center. **Subadult:** The maturation process is slow and complex, taking 4–6 years. Overall becomes darker with each successive year until adulthood is attained. Second-cycle birds look like first cycle but have a darker head, bill, and back. Third cycle are darker still, with the breast pattern of an adult, a more restricted pale belly often with some brown mottling, and no white stripe on the underwing. **Distant:** Dull brown with two-toned wings. In distant flocks containing multiple ages, adults appear darker and consequently larger than pale-bellied juveniles, and the whole flock may take on a mottled appearance owing to varying shades of brown.

SIMILAR SPECIES: **American White Pelican:** Much larger, with slower wingbeats and striking black-and-white plumage. **Northern Gannet:** Juvenile can be confused with Brown Pelican when gliding close to the surface of the water, as both are large, dark seabirds. Gannet, however, is slim and pointed on all ends, whereas pelican has blunt, many-fingered wingtips, a short and rounded tail, and a long, oddly shaped bill.

FIRST CYCLE WITH A WHITE IBIS AND A BLACK-BELLIED PLOVER. FLORIDA, DEC. KEN BEHRENS.
- Combination of large size, distinctive structure, and dark plumage makes Brown Pelican unlikely to be confused with any other North American bird.
- This individual can be aged by the clean appearance of its wings, lacking any molt, and its immaculate white belly.

FIVE FIRST CYCLE AND ONE SECOND CYCLE. TEXAS, APR. KEN BEHRENS.

- Older immatures show a darker head and back and more dark mottling on the belly.
- The second-cycle bird (bottom R) lacks a white underwing stripe.

FLORIDA, AUG. CAMERON COX.

- Long, downward-angled bill; broad, "multifingered" wings; and short tail make a pelican silhouette unmistakable.
- Unlike American White Pelican, Brown Pelican often beats its wings almost continuously in calm conditions, pausing to glide only briefly.

FIRST CYCLE. GEORGIA, OCT. CAMERON COX.

- The remarkable plunge-diving is a behavior American White Pelican never exhibits.
- Spotless white belly, broad white stripe on the underwing, and lack of molt indicate that this is a first-cycle bird.

FLORIDA, JAN. KEN BEHRENS.

- Best known for its impressive size, bearing, and behavior, Brown Pelican is also beautiful and intricately patterned, with subtle seasonal plumage changes.
- The white nape of this adult indicates it is in basic plumage. Breeding birds have a brown nape.

TEXAS, MAY. KEN BEHRENS.
- Found in a variety of coastal habitats alongside several other species, but their bulk and dark color set them apart.
- *What are the other species in this photo?*

TEXAS, APR. KEN BEHRENS.
- Migrating or commuting flocks form small- to medium-sized lines that hug coastlines and fly low, often cruising just above sand dunes.

WITH BLACK SKIMMERS AND A ROYAL TERN. GEORGIA, OCT. CAMERON COX.
- Brown Pelicans attain maturity in 4–6 years. The even flight feathers on the lead bird mark it as a first cycle. The complex wing pattern on the second bird indicates it is a third or fourth cycle.

(RIGHT) TEXAS, MAY. KEN BEHRENS.
- Alternate-plumaged adults.

SKUAS AND JAEGERS

The word *jaeger* has a magical effect at sea-watches. When it's uttered, every observer is keenly focused in one direction, there are appreciative *oooh*s and *aaahh*s, terse directions are muttered to the frantic few who have not located the bird, and the scene often ends with some debate over the identification. The word *skuu* has the same effect magnified 10 times. Why are members of this group such seawatch favorites? In most locations, jaegers are uncommon, and skuas are rarely seen from shore anywhere in eastern North America. The flight of skuas and jaegers is unmistakably powerful while still appearing supremely effortless, almost arrogant; it's a joy to watch them move through the air. What's more, these birds often engage in breathtaking pursuits of gulls or terns, the hapless victim pulling out every trick in the book before giving up and surrendering a tasty morsel for the jaeger or skua to pluck from the air. They are the avian equivalent of the fearless honey badger!

In this guide we cover five species in the family Stercorariidae: the European-breeding Great Skua, the Antarctic-breeding South Polar Skua, and the three Holarctic-breeding jaegers. The overall structure of skuas and jaegers is very similar to that of gulls (family Laridae), and they were considered part of the Laridae family until 2006, when they were split into their own family. The larger skuas were separated from jaegers in the genus *Cathar-acta* until 2000, when they were merged into the genus *Stercorarius* with jaegers. Although similar to jaegers, skuas are larger, with broader wings, shorter tails, and larger white areas at the base of the primaries, called the white "flash." Jaegers are smaller, have protruding central tail feathers (particularly the alternate-plumaged adults), and are polymorphic.

Skuas and jaegers are in the same genus, and share a basic shape and overall brown color, but they differ in size and precise structure, as shown by this Long-tailed Jaeger and the Great Skua that is attempting to kleptoparasitize it. Newfoundland, Sept. Bruce Mactavish.

Flocks of jaegers are rarely seen in eastern North America, which is unfortunate, as this flock of Long-tailed Jaegers is a stunning sight. Scotland, May. Steve Duffield.

Skuas and jaegers are often referred to as the pirates of the avian world, as they engage in kleptoparasitism—stealing food from other birds. All members of the family kleptoparasitize for at least part of their food, and some do so almost exclusively. Some species have favorite victims. For example, Great Skuas prefer Northern Gannets, and often breed close to gannet colonies so they can steal food that adult gannets attempt to bring back to their young. Long-tailed Jaegers haunt the migratory footsteps of Arctic Terns, following them straight across the center of the Atlantic, which means that neither species is frequently seen from the Atlantic Coast as a migrant. These parasitic habits can often be turned into a useful identification trait for distant skuas or jaegers attacking prey. It is often easier to identify the bird being parasitized, at least to a broad group such as medium-sized tern, small gull, or large gull, than it is to identify the jaeger or skua. Once you've identified the victim, you can use that information to judge the size and build of the unknown skua or jaeger.

Like large gulls, skuas and jaegers take 3 or 4 years to reach adult plumage. The appearance of skuas tends not to vary greatly with each successive immature plumage, but the appearance of jaegers changes significantly. In general, the adult and juvenile plumages are well known, and the identification traits relevant for identifying jaegers in these plumages are well documented. Subadult birds can be significantly more challenging. Although large gulls also go through a complex series of plumages, it is much easier to work out the aging and identification criteria for immature gulls, as they allow close approach and extended viewing. Immature jaegers spend most of their time at sea, where they are much harder to study. In the case of Long-tailed Jaeger, they are completely absent from the Northern Hemisphere for much of the year. In general, juvenile jaegers start out brown or gray, with barring on the underwings and the tail coverts. As they age they become more similar to adults; characteristics such as the dark cap and dark breast band develop and become more defined. With each successive plumage cycle, the underwing loses more of its barring, becoming solidly dark. Given the distant views of fast-moving jaegers typical at a seawatch or lakewatch, it is difficult to accurately age many of the jaegers that pass by.

On top of their age variation, the jaegers are polymorphic, making them among the most variable of all birds. Their morphs are usually labeled "light morph" and "dark morph" in guides, but there is a range of variation, with intermediates common. Although Long-tailed Jaeger lacks a dark-morph adult, it has dark and intermediate morphs as juveniles and occasionally as older birds as well. The darkest dark-morph jaegers often lack any of the plumage characteristics that are critical for identification, and if their structural characteristics are ambiguous, they must be left unidentified.

One of the most challenging aspects of jaeger and skua identification is the difficulty of judging their size. Because of their powerful and dark appearance, they often appear much larger than they actually are, particularly to those who have little experience with this group. Pomarine Jaeger is only roughly the size of Ring-billed Gull but often gives the impression that it is much larger; skuas look enormous but are only about the size of Herring Gull. The polymorphism in the jaegers only adds to the problem. All jaegers tend to look very dark at a distance, but against a dark background such as the ocean, the white belly of a light-morph bird will stand out more clearly and make the bird appear larger. A dark-morph bird of the same size will blend into the dark background and appear smaller in relation to the light-morph bird; against a pale background such as the sky, the reverse is true. Additionally, although average size differences do exist among all the members of this group, the largest individuals of each species overlap the smallest individuals of the next larger species. So although it is essential to try to evaluate the size of an unknown skua or jaeger, do so with caution.

Along most of the Atlantic Coast, jaegers are seen singly, in pairs, and rarely in small flocks. Large flocks of Pomarine and Parasitic Jaegers sometimes form along the northeast coast of Florida in the fall, and it is likely that significant flocks can also be seen in Arctic Canada, as such flocks have been observed during migration in Scandinavia. When flocks do form, they have a loonlike appearance, with widely spaced individuals forming a vaguely defined shape. Most often, jaeger sightings are of single birds cruising quickly just above the waves. Once a savvy seawatcher has sighted a jaeger, he or she will check a few hundred yards in front and behind it for additional jaegers, as pairs and even trios often fly and hunt together.

Sexes appear similar in all five species, and they have an alternate plumage that changes the appearance of the three jaegers but does not affect the overall appearance of the two skuas appreciably. Likewise, the immature plumage of skuas are similar to those of adults while jaeger show distinct age-related differences. Adult plumage is attained in 3–5 years.

MASSACHUSETTS, JULY. KEN BEHRENS.
• When skuas and jaegers attack other birds, like these Common Terns, knowing the identity of the victim can help you identify the attacker, but size can also be misleading. This Long-tailed Jaeger (rear) and dark-morph Parasitic Jaeger (front) are almost exactly the same size.

GREAT SKUA
Stercorarius skua
DIMENSIONS
L: 23 in.; WS: 55 in.; WT: 3.2 lb.

SPRING ARRIVAL

off Greenland: May

FALL ARRIVAL

ME: mid-Sept.; MA: mid-Oct.; NC: early Dec.

This imposing ocean predator breeds exclusively in European waters and is the only skua that breeds in the Northern Hemisphere. Its huge size is hinted at by its ability to bully Northern Gannets. Great Skuas often nest near colonies of gannets and make their living stealing fish meant for gannet chicks. In fall and winter this species disperses into the North Atlantic, including small numbers in North American waters, though most are far offshore. Even on winter pelagic trips, Great Skua is

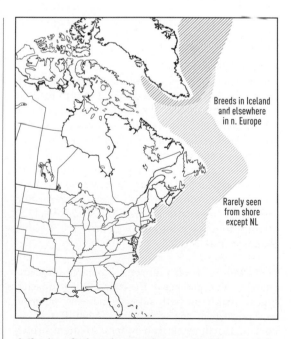

Breeds in Iceland and elsewhere in n. Europe

Rarely seen from shore except NL

difficult to find, and any sighting is highly prized. In recent years the only place it has been found regularly is off North Carolina. Sightings from shore are even rarer, though they are somewhat regular from the Atlantic Provinces in late summer and fall, and there are a handful of U.S. Atlantic Coast records, mostly from New England. In most skua sightings from shore, it is difficult to be certain of the species involved. An assumption based on likelihood at a given time of year is unlikely to be compelling given that any skua seen from shore in eastern North America is a vagrant. Also, the challenge of separating Great from South Polar Skuas should not be the only consideration. Brown Skua, a bird that has not been documented in North America but has occurred in Europe, should also be eliminated.

SIZE: Clearly larger than Pomarine Jaeger. Slightly larger than South Polar Skua. Herring Gull–sized but usually appears much larger.

STRUCTURE: Built like a stovepipe with wings. The body is broad and deep-chested. Appears bull-necked with a large head and heavy, hooked bill. The wings are very broad, and unlike in jaegers, the hand is quite short, though still distinctly pointed. The tail is strikingly short and slightly wedge-shaped, and the distance between the trailing edge of the wing and the tip of the tail is distinctly shorter than the breadth of the wings. The short-tailed appearance is further enhanced by the tail projection beyond the trailing edge of the wing being shorter than the projection of the head and bill in front of the wings. The distinctly short-tailed, broad-winged appearance is a key trait for separating distant skuas from large jaegers.

FLIGHT AND FLOCKING: Wingbeats appear very heavy, slow, and continuous, with some similarities to the wingbeat of a large gull but with the easy power of the smaller Pomarine Jaeger. In strong wind intersperses short stints of dynamic soaring with periods of heavy flapping. Unlike jaegers, soars regularly while at sea and does so with ease and skill. When actively chasing prey, its bulk and heavy flight disappear and it is surprisingly agile and acrobatic, flashing moves even a Parasitic Jaeger would admire. If the victim is small, the skua is likely to attempt to drive it into the water and kill it rather than just steal its catch.

APPEARANCE: In all plumages has large crescent-shaped white patches at the base of the primaries, highly visible on both sides of the wing, tapering to a point near the secondaries. **Adult:** Rarely occurs in North American waters. Medium brown overall, with a blackish mask or full blackish cap. The cheeks and neck are often finely streaked with buff. The wing coverts are also streaked and blotched with buff, making them contrast with the flight feathers and giving the wings a two-toned appearance. In summer, adults are paler and look quite messy, covered with uneven pale streaking. In winter they are darker with a cleaner appearance, though the wings still appear two-toned. Most lack the "pale blaze" surrounding the base of the bill that is typical of South Polar Skua, though heavily worn individuals can approximate it. **First Cycle:** Dark brown. Darker and cleaner-looking than adult, usually with reduced but still prominent white wing patches. In good light the entire head appears slightly darker than the body. The body has a reddish or warm brown tone and contrasts slightly with the darker underwing coverts; the back is almost uniform in color with the upperwings. The wing coverts contrast slightly with the darker flight feathers, creating a subtle two-toned appearance. Additionally, the leading edge of the wing is often noticeably rusty brown. By late winter may have a blotchy, uneven appearance, and the two-toned quality of the wings is more noticeable because of wear. **Subadult:** Like adult with a dark cap or mask, but usually lacks buff streaking on the neck. The white wing-flashes are larger, and the two-toned quality of the wings is more apparent than on first-cycle birds. **Distant:** Very dark overall with large white wing-flashes. The two-toned appearance to the upperwing may be apparent in excellent light.

SIMILAR SPECIES: South Polar Skua: Slightly smaller with a smaller head and bill and slightly slimmer, more pointed wings. Plumage appears quite cold, with blackish wings that contrast with a grayer body. Adult has a strong "pale blaze" around the bill and a pale nape, very different from the dark mask and cap of Great Skua, but the differences are hard to see at a distance. South Polar Skua has a paler back that contrasts with the blackish wings, unlike the uniform back and two-toned wings of Great Skua. First-cycle birds are cold-toned and usually lack strong patterning other than very slight contrast between the blackish wings and dark gray body. **Pomarine Jaeger:** Distinctly smaller, with a smaller head, slimmer body, and longer tail. White wing-flash is smaller, less obvious, and restricted to the underwing. The black-and-white barred rump and undertail coverts show up as contrastingly pale areas, whereas these areas are dark on Great Skua. Lacks the extensive pale mottling on the upper back and wing coverts typical of Great Skua, appearing more evenly dark across the mantle.

SOUTH POLAR SKUA. CALIFORNIA, OCT. BRIAN SULLIVAN.
- Structure is clearly that of a skua, but it is a bit trimmer than Great Skua, with a smaller head and bill and slimmer wings.
- Darker and more uniform than Great Skua.
- The white flash is much smaller on this individual than is typical, but it varies in both skua species.

GREAT SKUA. NEWFOUNDLAND, SEPT. BRUCE MACTAVISH.
- Heavy build, broad wings, and very short tail are typical skua traits.
- Extensively mottled back and wing coverts separate it from South Polar Skua.
- The faint dark cap is another useful ID trait.

WITH FIRST-CYCLE GREAT BLACK-BACKED GULL. SWEDEN, OCT. MÅRTEN MÜLLER.
- Based purely on its size compared with the Great Black-backed Gull, this has to be a skua. In addition to its large size, the broad wings, short tail, and extensive white flash in the wings firmly establish the identity as a skua.
- The specific identity as Great Skua is much more difficult. The location and date strongly suggest that Great Skua is correct, but at this distance it is often best to leave it as "skua sp."

SOUTH POLAR SKUA
Stercorarius maccormicki
DIMENSIONS
L: 21 in.; WS: 52 in.; WT: 2.5 lb.

SPRING ARRIVAL

off NC: mid-May; off NJ: late May;

off MA: late May; off ME: mid-June

Athough it does not have the same aura of rarity as Great Skua, thanks to its regular occurrence off the West Coast, along the Atlantic Coast South Polar Skua is almost as elusive as Great Skua. Immatures and adults of this Antarctic-breeding species display astoundingly different migratory patterns. Adults remain fairly close to their breeding territories after gaining maturity, whereas juveniles and subadults embark on one of the longest migrations in the world. Most circumnavigate the Pacific Ocean clockwise, while much smaller numbers do the same on the Atlantic. Most pass through the waters off the Eastern Seaboard between late spring and fall, unlike Great Skua, which occurs primarily in fall and winter. The two species overlap in the Atlantic Provinces in fall, where they are seen rarely but regularly from shore in some locations.

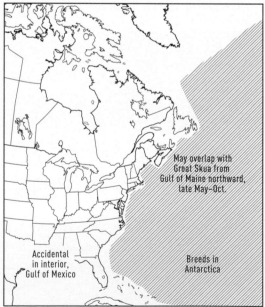

May overlap with Great Skua from Gulf of Maine northward, late May–Oct.

Accidental in interior, Gulf of Mexico

Breeds in Antarctica

SIZE: Very large. Most are clearly larger than Pomarine Jaeger and average slightly smaller than Great Skua. However, there is overlap with both species: extensive overlap with Great Skua and limited overlap with Pomarine Jaeger. Slightly smaller than Herring Gull but usually appears much larger.

STRUCTURE: Much like Great Skua, with an unmistakably heavy body, large head, and heavy, hooked bill. The wings are broad with a short but pointed hand and a very short tail. Skuas have slightly projecting central rectrices, giving the tail a wedge-shaped appearance when seen up close, though this usually isn't obvious at a distance. Like in Great Skua and unlike in the jaegers, the length from the trailing edge of the wing to the tip of the tail is distinctly shorter than the width of the wings, and also less than the head and neck projection in front of the wings. Most birds have a slightly smaller head and smaller, less hooked bill than Great Skua, but these differences are slight and rarely useful for identification of distant birds.

FLIGHT AND FLOCKING: Much as in Great Skua, though South Polar Skua has marginally faster wingbeats and appears slightly more agile in normal flight. Unlike Great Skua, it survives primarily by fishing for itself, and any skua observed plunge-diving is probably a South Polar. It also steals from other seabirds, particularly large shearwaters, though its attacks on other birds tend to be much shorter in duration than those of Great Skua, lacking the drama of an extended chase.

APPEARANCE: In all plumages has large crescent-shaped white patches at the base of the primaries, highly visible on both sides of the wing, tapering down to a point near the secondaries. **Adult:** Rarely seen in the Northern Hemisphere. The body ranges from dark brown to pale gray: distinctly cold-toned and averaging paler than in any other species of skua. Extremely pale birds are absolutely distinctive but are rare in North America. Most individuals sport a strong pale blaze at the base of the bill and have a pale band across the nape. The wings are uniformly dark, and all but the darkest birds show contrast between the paler body and blackish underwing coverts. **First Cycle:** Usually medium to dark gray with a cold-toned and fairly uniform appearance. The wings are uniformly blackish, causing the underwing to contrast clearly with the flanks. Above, the upperwing contrasts slightly with the paler back, creating a subtle pale saddle. Sometimes has a faint pale band across the nape or a distinctly paler head than body. **Subadult:** Very similar to adult. May show a bicolored bill. **Distant:** Very blackish overall with obvious white wing-flashes. A paler head may be noticeable on some. Very rare light-morph adults have a strikingly pale body that contrasts sharply with the blackish wings.

SIMILAR SPECIES: Great Skua: Slightly larger and bulkier with a blockier head and heavier bill. Typically shows clear contrast between the wing coverts and flight feathers and little between the wings and body, whereas South Polar has uniformly blackish wings that contrast with a paler body. First-cycle Great Skua shows warm tones to the body and in the wings, particularly along the leading edge, and the head is darker than the warm brown body, creating a hooded appearance. **Pomarine Jaeger:** Distinctly smaller with a smaller head, slimmer body, and longer tail. The white wing-flash is restricted to the underwing and is smaller and less obvious than that of South Polar Skua. The black-and-white barred rump and undertail coverts show up as contrastingly pale areas, whereas these areas are dark on South Polar Skua.

CALIFORNIA, SEPT.
BRIAN SULLIVAN.

- Heavy body and broad wings are clear indications of a skua.
- Gray body and strong contrast with the underwings are typical of South Polar Skua.
- Although they lack the extravagant tail streamers of jaegers, skuas have slightly projecting central rectrices, giving the tail a wedge-shaped appearance.

WITH WILSON'S STORM-PETRELS. NORTH CAROLINA, MAY. BOB FOGG.
- The head and body of the upper bird are much paler than that of any Great Skua.
- The bird hidden behind the wave has uniformly dark wing coverts, lacking the mottled coverts that give a two-toned appearance to the wings in Great Skua.
- South Polar Skuas often hover and plunge-dive for fish, whereas Great Skuas rarely fish for themselves.

CALIFORNIA, SEPT. BRIAN SULLIVAN.
- Tail is very short in relation to the width of the wings.
- Head and body are cold gray, lacking the dark cap and mottled upper back of Great Skua.
- Like many extreme long-distance migrants, South Polar Skua molts primaries in large blocks. Great Skua and Pomarine Jaeger molt primaries individually.

WITH CORY'S SHEARWATER. NORTH CAROLINA, MAY. BOB FOGG.
- The contrast between the skua's body and underwings is obvious.
- Large shearwaters are a favored target of South Polar Skuas off the East Coast.

POMARINE JAEGER
Stercorarius pomarinus
DIMENSIONS:
L: 18.5 in.; 23 in. with adult tail streamers; WS: 52 in.; WT: 1.5 lb.

SPRING ARRIVAL

off VA: late Apr.; off ME: mid-May;
Davis Strait: mid-May

FALL ARRIVAL

off MD: late Aug.; Great Lakes: late Sept.;
Gulf of Mexico: late Sept.

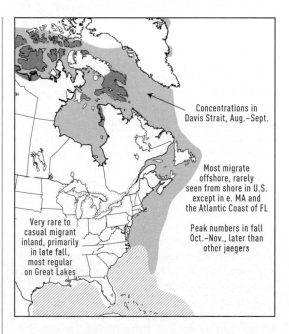

Concentrations in
Davis Strait, Aug.–Sept.

Most migrate
offshore, rarely
seen from shore in U.S.
except in e. MA and
the Atlantic Coast of FL

Peak numbers in fall
Oct.–Nov., later than
other jaegers

Very rare to
casual migrant
inland, primarily
in late fall,
most regular
on Great Lakes

An adult Pomarine Jaeger bearing full streamers is a sight to behold, both beautiful and brutish. This large jaeger bridges the gap between the smaller jaegers and the larger skuas. It is the latest migrant of the three jaegers and winters the farthest north. In most locations it is infrequently seen from shore, though it is significantly more frequent from shore than is Long-tailed Jaeger. It prefers deeper water than does Parasitic Jaeger; on pelagic trips, Parasitic Jaegers are often encountered first, in the waters close to shore, whereas the jaegers in offshore waters are mostly Pomarine and Long-tailed.

SIZE: Large. Larger than Parasitic Jaeger, though there is overlap. Most are clearly smaller than the skuas, though the largest overlap with small skuas. Only slightly larger than Ring-billed Gull but gives an impression of size closer to Herring Gull.

STRUCTURE: Appears quite formidable, with a stout body, broad wings, and a tail that usually appears short. However, the tail streamers of adult are broader and more obvious at a distance than those of other jaegers and can create the illusion of a long tail. The head is large, rounded, or at times quite blocky, with a sturdy neck. The body is usually deepest at the belly or near the front of the wing, but the entire belly appears deep and moderately rounded. Often it is the width of the body that is most striking, not the depth. Especially when a bird is flying head-on, the chest appears very broad, and the entire body seems slightly oversized. Whereas the skuas easily eclipse Pomarine Jaeger in this respect, neither of the smaller jaegers can match Pomarine's girth. The wings are broader than those of the smaller jaegers, and the hand is shorter, tapering quickly to a sharp point. Although not as stub-tailed as skuas, the tail appears shorter than those of the other jaegers, and when the tail streamers are excluded, the distance from the trailing edge of the wing to the tip of the tail is usually slightly shorter than the width of the wings. The tail appears significantly broader than those of the smaller jaegers. The broad, spoon-shaped tail streamers of adults are distinctive, particularly in alternate plumage when they are typically longer and twisted so that much of their surface area is exposed in profile. Sometimes the streamers break, leaving behind a jagged point or no streamer at all. Basic adults and subadults have shorter streamers that are slightly less noticeable but still distinctive. First-cycle birds have very short streamers, causing the tail to appear slightly wedge-shaped.

FLIGHT AND FLOCKING: Flight typically appears slower, more direct, and steadier than Parasitic Jaeger's. Pomarine is far less likely than Parasitic to interrupt its flight to chase other birds, but when it does, it makes short, aggressive attacks to the head and body of its victim and is far less acrobatic than Parasitic. Wingbeats are steady and powerful, only occasionally interrupted by short glides. Overall its flight is much like that of a Herring Gull but gives an impression of supreme ease and power that is unmatched by any gull. At any speed, Parasitic Jaeger tends to give the impression that it is going as fast as it can, whereas Pomarine gives the opposite impression, and no matter how fast it is traveling, it always looks like it is holding back a little. It uses a dynamic soar flight style less than other jaegers and

only in strong wind. Large flocks are rare in most places in eastern North America but do occur occasionally, particularly on the northeast coast of Florida. Such flocks resemble those of Red-throated Loon in structure, with birds loosely spread out at a variety of heights, with little discernible structure or cooperation among members.

APPEARANCE: All ages show a bicolored bill and three to eight pale primary shafts. In addition to the white wing-flash, most show a subtle second pale crescent along the bases of the primary underwing coverts, creating a "double flash" that is most obvious in Pomarine Jaeger, though other jaegers can show it to a lesser degree. **Alternate Adult Light Morph:** About 90 percent of adults are light. Dark brown above and pale below with a black cap that extends down below the bill, giving a "heavy-jowled" appearance. Male often lacks a breast band or has an indistinct mottled breast band. Female has a complete or mottled breast band. The vent and undertail coverts are solidly dark, and the flanks may be dark or dark-barred as well. **Basic Adult Light Morph:** Like alternate but appears messier, some extensively so and others only marginally more than alternate. The face is duskier, and most show a mottled breast band and flanks that are mottled or smudged. May show barring on the rump and undertail, though not as crisply as first cycle, and often these areas are dark as on alternate. **Adult Dark Morph:** Uniformly dark brown throughout the year. **First Cycle:** Juvenile plumage is retained at least through fall migration. Most juveniles (90 percent or more) are medium to dark brown; a few have a slightly paler gray head and belly. The upper- and undertail coverts are barred crisply black and white and, along with the pale-barred underwings, are noticeably paler than the brown body. Birds with a paler head often show a dark streak through the eye, giving the face an angry expression. Undergoes a complete preformative molt late in the first cycle; the first prealternate molt occurs soon after or overlaps the preformative molt. Following these two molts, often shows some adultlike traits, particularly on the head and body, though some do not change markedly from juvenile plumage. **Subadult:** Variable; molts and plumages not well understood. Pomarine Jaeger is thought to take at least 4 years to reach adult plumage. Second-cycle birds look much like first cycle but have a pale belly and more developed tail streamers. Older subadults tend to look like messy adults and have variable amounts of pale barring on the underwing. **Distant:** Even light-morph birds tend to look dark, while dark morph birds simply look black. The white flash on the underwing is visible at great distance only in good light.

SIMILAR SPECIES: Skuas: Larger, heavier, and shorter-tailed. Have much larger white wing-flashes that are visible on the upper- and underwing. Also lack the protruding spoon-shaped tail streamers shown by many Pomarine Jaegers and the pale barring on the rump shown by first-cycle birds and some basic adults. **Parasitic Jaeger:** Smaller and slimmer, particularly across the chest, with slimmer wings, a longer hand, and longer tail projection behind the wings. Has a quicker wingbeat and typically seems more hurried, though it glides more frequently than Pomarine Jaeger. Frequently breaks off to pursue other birds in extended, aerial battles, unlike Pomarine, which tends to make short, direct attacks. Adult and subadults often have medium-length, pointed tail streamers. Light-morph adult is similar to that of Pomarine Jaeger but is slightly paler overall and has a cleaner and neater appearance than most Pomarine Jaegers. Its dark cap does not extend below the bill as on Pomarine, and the bill is uniformly gray, not two-toned. First-cycle birds tend to be more uniform than first-cycle Pomarines, with less contrasting tail coverts and underwings. They also tend to show warm tones on the body, including a rusty nape and leading edge to the wing. Many juvenile Parasitic Jaegers have a noticeable white flash on the upperwing as well as the underwing, whereas the flash is restricted to the underwing in Pomarine Jaeger. Some Parasitics have slightly paler bases to the primary coverts and show a weak "double flash," but this is never as clear as on most Pomarine Jaegers. Some individuals, particularly very dark birds, may be unidentifiable. **Long-tailed Jaeger:** Significantly smaller, with looser and more buoyant wingbeats. Tends to look very long-tailed, even without tail streamers, whereas Pomarine Jaeger typically looks short-tailed. Long-tailed has a meandering flight style and often hovers, plunge-dives for fish, and engages in shallow, arcing, dynamic soar even in light winds. Pomarine does none of these things. First-cycle Long-tailed can appear quite similar to first-cycle Pomarine, though Long-tailed tends to be paler and colder gray and is far more likely to show a distinct pale head. Careful attention to structure and flight style should separate these two species in all plumages.

BASIC LIGHT-MORPH ADULT. NEW JERSEY, SEPT. ERIC MASTERSON.

- Fairly broad-chested and broad-winged, though not as formidable as a skua.
- Broad, rounded protruding central tail feathers are diagnostic.
- Most basic adults in winter and subadults have shorter streamers than alternate adults.
- Dark cap extends well below the bill, creating a unique "heavy-jowled" appearance.
- Pale bases to the primary coverts as well as to the primaries create the well-known "double flash." Unfortunately, it is typically too faint to be visible at a distance.

WITH LONG-TAILED JAEGER (R). FLORIDA, AUG. BOB WALLACE.

- While the difference in bulk is striking, also notice how the weight is distributed. Pomarine has a deep belly, whereas Long-tailed has a heavy chest but lean body.
- Compare the width of the wings on both species to the distance from the trailing edge of the wings to the tip of the tail. Pomarine is skua-like in having broad wings and a short tail, whereas Long-tailed has narrower wings and a much longer tail.

DARK-MORPH ADULT. CALIFORNIA, SEPT. MIKE DANZENBAKER.
- Dark morphs are greatly outnumbered by light morphs. Intermediates are also rare.
- This individual has a relatively small head and delicate bill, whereas some Pomarines have a much larger head and bill and give a more massive impression.
- Bill has a pale gray base, whereas Parasitic has an all-dark bill.
- The white wing-flash is reduced in dark morphs, and the "double flash" is barely evident.

DARK- AND LIGHT-MORPH ALTERNATE ADULTS. SCOTLAND, MAY. MARK DARLASTON.
- Flocks are loose and disorganized, sometimes recalling the flock structure of Red-throated Loons, though this flock is more compact.
- Streamers are shorter than those of other jaegers, but since the streamers are also broader, they can be seen at greater distances, creating the impression of a long tail.
- The dark morph in the middle appears larger since its silhouette can be seen more clearly. The bellies of the light morphs break up the silhouette and cause them to appear smaller.

FIRST CYCLE. CALIFORNIA, SEPT. TONY LEUKERING.

- Jaeger identification is often very challenging, but some Pomarines are so obviously broad-chested and broad-winged that there can be no question of their identity.
- Short tail streamers are typical in fall and winter.

DARK-MORPH ADULT. MASSACHUSETTS, JULY. KEN BEHRENS.

- Hand is slightly shorter than the inner wing, unlike in the two smaller jaegers.
- The deep, powerful body is striking on this individual, but in some it is much less obvious.

COMPARISON: POMARINE JAEGER (TOP AND BOTTOM L) WITH PARASITIC JAEGER (TOP R) AND LONG-TAILED JAEGER (BOTTOM R).

- Carefully compare structure.
- Despite the size difference, Long-tailed is frequently confused with Pomarine. Although the "double flash" is associated with Pomarine, Long-tailed can also show a noticeable "double flash." Parasitic Jaeger never shows this mark strongly.

LIGHT-MORPH ADULT. NORTH CAROLINA, MAY. MIKE DANZENBAKER.
- The black cap extends below the bill, giving the face a menacing expression and setting off the two-toned bill.
- This is a bruiser of a Pomarine, with a massive head and heavy bill.

WITH THIRD/FOURTH-CYCLE HERRING GULL. ONTARIO, SEPT. BRANDON HOLDEN.
- Hand is slightly shorter than the inner wing.
- Any interaction between a jaeger and a victim provides a perfect size comparison.
- Although Pomarine Jaeger is slightly smaller than Herring Gull, its dark color and powerful build can make it appear as large or larger.

JUVENILE. ONTARIO, NOV. BRANDON HOLDEN.
- This is a lightly built Pomarine, but it still has the broad wings and short hand typical of the species.
- On this juvenile the black-and-white-barred undertail and lack of rusty tones, particularly on the leading edge of the wing, eliminate Parasitic Jaeger.

SUBADULT. NORTH CAROLINA, SEPT. CAMERON COX.
- Sheer bulk often serves as the primary identification trait.
- The large size is evident in flight, when the bird often looks heavy and lethargic compared with the smaller jaegers.

PARASITIC JAEGER
Stercorarius parasiticus
DIMENSIONS
L: 16.5 in.; 20 in. with adult tail streamers; WS: 46 in.; WT: 1 lb.

SPRING ARRIVAL

NC: early Apr.; NJ: mid-May;
Hudson Bay: late May

FALL ARRIVAL

St. Lawrence Estuary: late Aug.;
Great Lakes: late Aug.; VA: late Aug.;
Gulf of Mexico: early Sept.

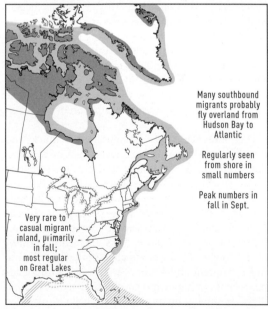

Many southbound migrants probably fly overland from Hudson Bay to Atlantic

Regularly seen from shore in small numbers

Peak numbers in fall in Sept.

Very rare to casual migrant inland, primarily in fall; most regular on Great Lakes

Along most of the Atlantic Coast, Parasitic Jaeger is the jaeger most frequently observed from shore, and therefore the key jaeger to learn well. Conveniently, it is also the midsized jaeger and serves as a natural comparison with the other two species. While the sighting of any jaeger is an instant seawatching highlight, a Parasitic Jaeger often provides additional spice by engaging in spectacular aerial duels with terns or small gulls in order to pirate a hard-won catch. If when watching such an encounter you root for the jaeger, you might be a seawatcher!

SIZE: Although the midsized jaeger, Parasitic does overlap somewhat with the generally smaller Long-tailed and the larger Pomarine, and falls between Laughing and Ring-billed Gulls in size. Although it gives a slightly larger impression, it does not appear substantially larger than its true size, as Pomarine Jaeger often does.

STRUCTURE: Sleek, athletic, and very long winged. May approximate a medium-sized gull in size and basic shape but is more extreme in every detail, primed for speed and agility. Adults and subadults have medium-length, sharply pointed tail streamers that are diagnostic if present but are difficult to see at a distance and are prone to breaking off. The most striking aspect of structure at a distance is the long, slender wings. The hand, in particular, is strikingly long and tapers to a fine point. Unlike in Pomarine Jaeger, the width of the arm and the inner portion of the hand are almost equal, whereas the outer portion of the hand tapers dramatically. The bill is long but slim, and the head is small, with a slightly longer neck than in Long-tailed Jaeger. At a distance the head has a pointed, triangular shape. The body shape is an oft-heralded field mark but varies greatly in all three jaeger species. In general, Parasitic has the most neutral shape of the three, typically lacking the expanded chest and flat belly of Long-tailed Jaeger and the deep, rounded "beer belly" of Pomarine. Most Parasitic Jaegers look lean and even. There is slight expansion at the chest, with the deepest point falling just behind the leading edge of the wings, and the belly is slightly rounded. Some individuals closely resemble one of the other two species in this aspect of structure, so caution is warranted. The wings are centered on the body, enhancing an overall impression of balance.

FLIGHT AND FLOCKING: Wingbeats are quick and powerful, and flight is fast—faster than in any similar-sized gull. Typical flight style involves extended series of wingbeats broken irregularly by a few seconds of gliding on bowed wings. Head-on, the glide profile is very similar to that of Peregrine Falcon. Usually gives the impression of being in a serious hurry to get someplace. Less frequently, cruises more slowly with fewer wingbeats in each series and more frequent glides, but even this slower flight appears swift. In high wind employs a dynamic soaring flight, bouncing up and down in shallow arcs often hidden behind waves. This flight is largely executed on set wings with occasional bursts of deep, powerful wingbeats. Parasitic is so proficient at this type of flight that it can easily be mistaken for a Sooty Shearwater, though shearwaters hold their wings straight whereas Parasitic Jaeger performs this flight with its wings angled back sharply at the wing bend.

At any time it can break into "attack mode," displaying deep wingbeats and a marked increase in speed, closing on a victim spotted at a distance with ease. It often starts low over the water, then rises at a shallow angle to attack from underneath. It accelerates right up to the moment of contact, unlike jaeger-mimicking gulls, which typically break off at the last moment in hopes that the threat of an attack is enough to cause the victim to release its catch. Once a Parasitic locks onto a victim, it is relentless, engaging in incredible aerial shootouts that are far more extended and acrobatic than those of other jaegers. No matter the length of the engagement, it typically ends with the unfortunate tern or gull dropping some morsel of food and the jaeger plucking it neatly from midair. Parasitic Jaeger is usually solitary, though two or three may fly and hunt in tandem at times. Large flocks are rare in most places but do occur occasionally on the northeast coast of Florida during fall. Such flocks resemble those of Red-throated Loon in structure, with birds loosely spread out at a variety of heights with little discernible structure or cooperation among members.

APPEARANCE: Alternate Adult Light Morph: Uniformly gray-brown above, paler than Pomarine Jaeger, and lacking the contrast between wing coverts and mantle shown by Long-tailed Jaeger. They have a small black cap, white underparts, and may have a smooth gray breast band, though many have a broken breast band or lack a band entirely. When present, the breast band is paler than the dark cap—a smooth gray that matches the dark vent. **Basic Adult Light Morph:** Like alternate but not as crisp and clean, with dark mottling on the flanks and black-and-white barred upper- and undertail coverts. **Adult Dark Morph:** Dark brown overall, often tinged gray, with a slightly darker cap and paler vent. **First Cycle:** Juvenile plumage is retained at least through fall migration. Shows tremendous color variation overall, though most individuals are quite uniform. Most are medium brown, often with strong rusty tones, including a rusty nape and leading edge to the wing. Some are much darker, and others have a pale head and belly. All show less contrast between the underwing and the body than the other two jaegers in the first cycle. Both the upper- and undertail coverts appear to have rusty or buff barring on a brown background, contrasting less with the body than the black-and-white barred tail coverts of the other jaegers do. Many juveniles have white wing-flashes on the upperwing as well as the underwing. Other juvenile jaegers have white wing-flashes only on the underwing. Late in the first cycle undergoes a complete preformative molt; the first prealternate molt occurs soon after or overlapping the preformative molt. Following these two molts, often shows some adultlike traits, particularly on the head and body, although some do not change markedly from juvenile plumage. **Subadult:** Variable; molts and plumages are not fully understood. By the second cycle, most light morphs are much paler than in the first cycle, with a more defined dark cap and extensively barred underwings. Late in the second cycle, after the second prealternate molt, and until they reach full adult plumage, they tend to look like basic adults but with some barring on the underwings and heavier markings on the body. **Distant:** Dark brown to blackish, much darker than a first-cycle Laughing Gull. The pale body of light-morph birds is often not apparent when they fly low. The white wing-flash can sometimes be seen but is usually not obvious.

SIMILAR SPECIES: Long-tailed Jaeger: Slightly smaller and more buoyant than Parasitic Jaeger. Wingbeats are looser, usually without the precise, snappy downstroke of Parasitic Jaeger. The body bounces slightly with every wingbeat, as in a medium-sized tern, whereas Parasitic Jaeger is more stable. Long-tailed has a more meandering flight, whereas Parasitic seems to be in a hurry. Long-tailed often hovers and plunge-dives for fish and is more likely to use a dynamic soar in light wind. Its wings are slightly thinner than those of Parasitic Jaeger and are farther forward on the body, not centered as on Parasitic. It tends to have a deep chest and an athletic impression, whereas Parasitic has a more neutral body shape. Even excluding the longer tail streamers, Long-tailed also has more tail projecting behind the trailing edge of the wing than does Parasitic Jaeger, giving it a long-tailed appearance at all ages. Adults are slightly paler and grayer than adult Parasitic, and lack a white wing-flash, but show distinct contrast between the upperwing coverts and the darker primaries and secondaries. First-cycle birds are cold-toned, and the black-and-white barred rump contrasts with the body, as do the finely barred underwings. At close range, Long-tailed Jaeger has two bright white primary shafts to the two outermost primaries; Parasitic Jaeger has three or more obvious bright white shafts. A few first-cycle birds cannot be identified in the field.

Pomarine Jaeger: Larger and heavier with a fuller chest, broader wings, and shorter hand. The head is larger and blockier and the neck thicker, so it lacks the triangular head shape of Parasitic Jaeger. Tends to look short-tailed, whereas Parasitic has balanced proportions. Wingbeats are slower and more continuous, rarely pausing to glide. Tends to fly even more directly than Parasitic, rarely chasing other birds during migratory flight. When it does chase birds, it goes directly at the head and body of the victim, trying to overpower it quickly, instead of using the more acrobatic and drawn-out chases frequently made by Parasitic. Light-morph adults tend to look blacker and messier than Parasitic, with a darker and more "menacing" face and distinctly two-toned bill. The tail streamers are rounded, often twisted, and even when partially broken off are broader than the streamers of Parasitic. First-cycle Pomarine Jaegers lack the warm tones of first-cycle Parasitics and have contrasting black-and-white barred rumps and finely barred underwing coverts. In addition to the white flash at the base of the primaries, the base of their primary coverts is pale, creating a subtle "double flash."

LIGHT-MORPH ADULT. SCOTLAND, MAY. JOHN ANDERSON.

- Has a balanced, lean shape with long, angular wings.
- The width of the wings is equal to the distance from the trailing edge of the wing to the tip of the tail (excluding the streamers). Pomarine Jaeger has broader wings and a shorter tail. Long-tailed Jaeger has narrower wings and a longer tail.
- The neck is longer than that of Long-tailed Jaeger, and the bill is long and slender. From a distance this creates the appearance of a triangular or bullet-shaped head.

DARK-MORPH ADULT. NORWAY,
JULY. HUGH HARROP.

WITH A FIRST-CYCLE HERRING GULL. ONTARIO, SEPT. BRANDON HOLDEN.

- Many juveniles have a white flash on the upper-side of the wing; juveniles of the other two jaegers lack this trait.
- Attacks on prey are often extended and highly acrobatic, though attacks on larger birds, like this Herring Gull, tend to be much briefer.

DARK-MORPH SUBADULT WITH GREAT CRESTED TERN. SOUTH AFRICA, OCT. KEN BEHRENS.

- Has a rather long neck and small head, unlike Pomarine Jaeger, which appears bull-necked, or Long-tailed Jaeger, which has a short neck and rounded head.
- Subadults often have shorter tail streamers.

WITH POMARINE JAEGER (R). NEW YORK, OCT. BRYAN TARBOX.

- Most adults have a small pale area of feathers just above the bill that Pomarine Jaegers lack.
- The dark wash on the vent does not extend up onto the belly as it does on Long-tailed Jaeger.
- The bull-necked appearance and contrasting pink-based bill are visible on the Pomarine Jaeger.

PALE-MORPH ADULT WITH PALE-MORPH ADULT POMARINE JAEGER (R). NORTH CAROLINA, MAY. BOB FOGG.

- Compare where the deepest point of the body falls on each bird.
- There is significant size variation in all three jaegers. The size difference between these two species is not always this dramatic.

FIRST CYCLE. MASSACHUSETTS, JULY. KEN BEHRENS.
- The buffy irregular markings on the underwing create little contrast with the belly. First-cycle Pomarine and Long-tailed Jaegers have neat white barring that is more noticeable at a distance.
- Body has an even, tubular shape, not distinctly broad-chested as in Pomarine.

LIGHT-MORPH ADULT WITH ONE ROYAL TERN (R) AND THREE LAUGHING GULLS. TEXAS, NOV. CAMERON COX.
- At a distance, even light-morph birds look dark.

JUVENILE. KENTUCKY, SEPT. DAVE ROEMER.
- Juveniles have a distinctly warm appearance, with extensive rusty or buffy barring and scalloping.
- The buff-and-brown barring on the undertail coverts contrasts less with the body than do the paler undertail coverts of the other jaegers, so the overall appearance is more uniform.

ADULT. SWEDEN, SEPT. TOMMY HOLMGREN.
- Graceful and agile in flight and gives the impression of being built for speed.
- Tail averages longer and narrower than that of Pomarine.

(RIGHT) WITH FORSTER'S TERN. NEW JERSEY, OCT. BRANDON HOLDEN.

LONG-TAILED JAEGER
Stercorarius longicaudus

DIMENSIONS

L: 15 in.; 23 in. with adult tail streamers; WS: 43 in.; WT: 11 oz.

SPRING ARRIVAL

off MA: late May; Greenland: late May;
Hudson Bay: late May/early June

FALL ARRIVAL

off ME: late July; off MA: mid-Aug.;
off NC: mid-Aug.

Wished for far more often than it is seen, Long-tailed is the smallest of the jaegers and the most coveted. It typically migrates off the continental shelf, shadowing the migration path of Arctic Tern, and is rarely seen from shore, though it does occasionally occur during extended onshore winds. Small numbers, particularly of juveniles, migrate through the interior, and birders on the Great Lakes and in other landlocked areas have started to find Long-tailed Jaeger regularly in recent years by looking for it in late summer and early fall, particularly in late August and early September.

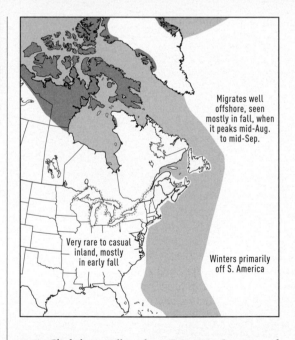

Migrates well offshore, seen mostly in fall, when it peaks mid-Aug. to mid-Sep.

Very rare to casual inland, mostly in early fall

Winters primarily off S. America

SIZE: Slightly smaller than Parasitic Jaeger and Laughing Gull but often appears larger than its true size.

STRUCTURE: Slender, round-headed, and long-winged, giving a light but powerful impression. The neck is short and the wings are pushed forward on the body rather than being centered. Even excluding the projecting tail feathers, the distance between the trailing edge of the wing and the tip of the tail is noticeably longer than in the other two jaegers. The body is deepest at the chest, usually right along the leading edge of the wing, whereas the belly is flat and tapers smoothly into the long tail. The expanded chest and flat belly give an athletic appearance, and also contribute to the impression that most of the weight is carried in front. The wings are slim, and the hand appears even longer and more pointed than Parasitic's. Adults have incredibly long central tail feathers that flap like a trailing ribbon when they fly. In fall, however, the streamers may have broken off and be missing. First-cycle birds have the longest projecting tail feathers among jaegers of this age, sometimes extending an inch or more beyond the rest of the tail. These feathers are sometimes visible even at a distance.

FLIGHT AND FLOCKING: While still powerful, flight is noticeably lighter and more buoyant than that of other jaegers. In typical flight the wingbeats appear weaker than Parasitic Jaeger's and the movements of the hand are less crisp and precise than Parasitic's, appearing somewhat loose. The body bounces slightly with each wingbeat, adding to the appearance of lighter flight. When Long-tailed really wants to move, it moves quickly, but more often it seems unhurried and is frequently described as "playful," whereas Parasitic Jaeger is all business all the time. Steals from other birds, particularly medium-sized terns, but its attacks are not as aggressive or persistent as those of Parasitic Jaeger and seem impulsive. As a tern nearby catches something, a Long-tailed may try to steal it, whereas a Parasitic will mark a victim from a distance, track it down, and pummel it. Long-tailed Jaeger also forages in the manner of a small gull, hovering over the water and dipping down to pluck small fish from the surface. A jaeger displaying this behavior is almost certainly a Long-tailed. In general, Long-tailed glides more and flaps less than Parasitic. It uses a dynamic soar more often than any other jaeger, even in light wind, dipping up and down on swept-back wings.

APPEARANCE: In all plumages, the outer two primary shafts are bright white. This is diagnostic if seen well, but several of the shafts adjacent to the outer shafts are pale and can appear white in bright light. Adult: Gray-backed and white-breasted, with a small, clean black cap and black bill. The vent, much of the belly, and the flanks are washed smoothly with ashy gray. The lead gray mantle contrasts clearly with the blackish flight feathers, a trait unique to Long Tailed among adult jaegers. Long-tailed lacks the white patch on the underside of the primaries clearly shown by the two larger jaegers. It also apparently lacks a dark-morph adult. First Cycle: The

preformative molt occurs after Long-tailed Jaeger has left North America, so this description applies to juvenile plumage. The majority are dark morph, blackish to cold medium gray overall with a slightly paler nape, slightly darker chest band, and paler gray belly. The wings and mantle are cold medium gray. The uppertail coverts are crisply barred black-and-white, the underwing is finely barred with black and white, and there is a small to moderate white wing-flash at the base of the primaries on the underwing. The rare light morph has a stark, cold appearance with a dull white head, faint gray breast band, and paler belly. The uppertail coverts and wing pattern are like dark morph's, but the white flash is often slightly larger. Subadult: Like adult but with shorter tail streamers, dark smudging on the underparts, and barred underwing. Distant: Usually very dark. On adults the contrast between the mantle and flight feathers can sometimes be seen in excellent light and the throat may look pale, but the rest of the underparts are quite dark. Juveniles are uniformly dark, though the pale barring on the rump may be faintly visible. A small number of juveniles have a strikingly pale head.

SIMILAR SPECIES: Parasitic Jaeger: Slightly larger, with a more direct flight style and crisper, more powerful wingbeats. Appears more balanced, as the wings are centered on the body, and the deepest point of the body is slightly farther back than on Long-tailed. The wings are slightly broader, and the width of the wings is about equal to the amount of tail that projects behind the trailing edge of the wings. Adult is slightly darker and more uniform than Long-tailed, usually displaying a noticeable dark breast band. Parasitic lacks the contrast between mantle and flight feathers and has a strong pale flash on the underwing that is lacking in adult Long-tailed. First-cycle Parasitic is often very rusty or warm-toned, instantly separating it from first-cycle Long-tailed, which invariably has a cold-toned appearance. In first-cycle Parasitic Jaeger this rusty coloration is most noticeable on the nape and leading edge of the wing; the barred rump varies from warm buff and brown to cinnamon and brown. It also has larger white wing-flashes, which are often present on the upper- and underwing of fresh juveniles. Pomarine Jaeger: Usually separated by size and flight style alone, though large juvenile Long-tailed Jaegers have been misidentified as Pomarine Jaegers, primarily because of similar plumage patterns. Pomarine Jaeger has slower, steadier wingbeats and rarely uses dynamic soaring, whereas Long-tailed does so frequently. Pomarine's wings are much broader, broader than the length between the trailing edge of the wings and the tip of the tail; the opposite is true for

Long-tailed. Pomarine also has a shorter hand and blunter wingtips. Adult light-morph Pomarine is uniformly blackish all the way across the wings and mantle and generally has a dark breast band. To an even greater extent than first-cycle Long-tailed Jaeger, first-cycle Pomarine tends to be very dark and never has a contrasting white head like some Long-taileds do. It tends to be dull dark brown, not as gray or cold as Long-tailed. First-cycle Pomarine usually lacks visible tail streamers, whereas first-cycle Long-tailed has noticeable streamers. **Sooty Tern:** First cycle is a dark seabird whose flight style is somewhat similar to that of Long-tailed Jaeger, but it is smaller and shorter-winged. The head and breast are dark, but the underwing and vent are white, easily separating it from Long-tailed Jaeger.

IMMATURE WITH ARCTIC TERN (L). CALIFORNIA, AUG. PETER LATOURRETTE.
- The smallest jaeger, often described as ternlike in build and flight style.
- Often kleptoparasitizes medium-sized terns.
- Wings are very slender and narrower at the base than in other jaegers.
- Any time a jaeger attacks another bird, use the opportunity to compare the size and shape of the jaeger to that of the species being attacked. This can greatly simplify identification.

ALTERNATE ADULTS. ENGLAND, MAY. STEVE DUFFIELD.
- Migrating flocks are loose and disorganized, almost like a loon flock, though not quite that widely spaced.
- Flocks like this are likely to be seen only at high latitudes.
- Silhouette is thin-winged and ternlike even at a distance.

SECOND-CYCLE LIGHT MORPH (R) AND THIRD-CYCLE INTERMEDI-ATE MORPH (L). CALIFORNIA, JULY. BRIAN SULLIVAN.
- The second cycle has bold black-and-white barring on the underwing and undertail coverts. Parasitic Jaeger never shows such contrasting barring.
- The white flash in the wings is almost absent on both birds.

JUVENILE. NORTH CAROLINA, SEPT. CAMERON COX.
- Juveniles are often quite dark and this is the hardest plumage to separate from dark Parasitic.
- Faint white barring is evident on the tail coverts, causing the rump to appear paler than the rest of the body.
- Note the short neck, rounded head, and long tail.

ALTERNATE ADULT. ALASKA, JULY. CAMERON COX.
- Adults lack a dark morph, but the vent and lower belly are heavily washed with gray.
- Adults completely lack a white flash at the base of the primaries on the underwing, unlike the two larger jaegers, which both have a distinct white flash as adults.

SUBADULT WITH SUBADULT POMARINE JAEGER (L). CALIFORNIA, AUG. PETER LATOURRETTE.
- It is often difficult to judge the size of a jaeger in the field, but when seen with another jaeger, the difference between species can be obvious.
- Note the large number of pale primary shafts on the Pomarine vs. only two on the Long-tailed.

IMMATURE WITH A WILSON'S STORM-PETREL. MASSACHUSETTS, JULY. JEREMIAH TRIMBLE.
• The small head, slender build, and long tail are very striking on this individual.
• Even lacking the long central tail feathers, Long-tailed appears distinctly long-tailed in relation to other jaegers.

(BELOW) ALTERNATE ADULTS WITH ADULT IVORY GULL. GREENLAND, AUG. BRUCE MACTAVISH.
• Adults have two-toned wings: gray coverts with blackish flight feathers, which create a dark trailing edge that other adult jaegers lack.

JUVENILE. CALIFORNIA, SEPT. MIKE DANZENBAKER.

- The crisply barred axillaries and undertail coverts lack the rusty tones expected on a juvenile Parasitic.
- The delicate build of this individual is striking.
- A faint dusky indentation extends from the primaries into the white flash. Although diagnostic, this trait is not present on all juvenile Long-taileds.
- The hand is longer and more pointed than on the two larger jaegers.

GULLS

Gulls, family Laridae, are a large and diverse group of birds whose members range in size from the tiny Little Gull to the hulking Great Black-backed Gull, and in habits from the parking lot–loafing Ring-billed Gull to the near-mythical Arctic-haunting Ivory Gull. We cover 18 species of gulls, which can be broken into two broad groups: "ternlike" gulls and "typical" gulls, though additional subdivisions can be made within these groups. Ternlike gulls are fairly small gulls with dainty bills that tend to have an agile and tern-like flight style. The ternlike gull group includes the small hooded gulls, kittiwakes, Sabine's Gull, and Ivory Gull. The typical gull group includes the medium-sized hooded gulls—Franklin's Gull and Laughing Gull—and all other medium-sized and large gulls. The typical gulls are larger, heavier-bodied, heavier-billed, broader-winged, and have a more labored flight style than the ternlike gulls.

Gulls, large gulls in particular, have a reputation among birders for being incredibly challenging to identify. For the most part the reputation is over-blown, and with a little time and good views, the overwhelming majority of gulls in eastern North America can be identified with relative ease. In flight, however, good and long views are rare, so a different identification strategy is required. The first and foremost trait is size, as deduced by the speed of the wingbeats, the flight style and by comparisons with nearby known species. It is followed

This first-cycle Black-headed Gull (L) is a member of a group of smaller gulls known as ternlike gulls. The third-cycle "European" Herring Gull in front of it is a typical gull. Ternlike gulls are smaller and slimmer-winged than typical gulls. They mature more quickly than larger gulls, usually in 2 years. Typical gulls are more heavily built, broader-winged, and have a heavier bill. Depending on the species, they mature in 3–4 years. Wales, March. Ken Behrens.

in importance by the flight style itself. These pieces of information should allow any gull to be narrowed down to a few possibilities. Next look for structure to continue to narrow the list of suspects. If size could not be pinned down well enough to place an unknown gull into either the ternlike or typical gull categories, carefully evaluating the structure of a given bird should allow you to do so even at great distances. The dainty bills, small rounded heads, and more pointed wings of the ternlike gulls create a silhouette totally unlike that of the bulky, heavy-billed, blunt-winged typical gulls.

Overall color is the next step after structure. You should know at this point whether you are looking at a typical or ternlike gull, and the overall color may be the only additional piece of information needed to identify the bird. At closer range, more specific details can be seen. The amount and distribution of black on the wings and how strongly it contrasts with the rest of the wings are generally the most important plumage characteristics. Depending on the group or specific species involved, there may be other visible plumage traits that are helpful. The specific flight line the gull uses may also serve as an identification aid, though gulls tend to establish new flight lines with every change of the weather, so it's best to ascertain what specific species are doing at the beginning of each period of observation and be prepared for it to shift as the weather changes.

Flight style in gulls varies significantly, more so than in any other group covered in this guide. It varies with wind speed and direction as well as depending on what the bird is doing. A gull that is actively migrating will have a slightly different flight style than a bird in a short-distance flight, and an actively feeding gull will have still another flight style. A bird flying into the wind will fly more slowly and have a heavier wingbeat than a bird sailing along with a tail wind. In high wind, many species will adopt the up-and-down arcing flight style of shearwaters, though most do so clumsily and tend to beat their wings as they descend toward the water. Flight style is essentially determined by the size and structure of a bird, so once you are familiar with the flight style of a species in one set of conditions, it is not terribly difficult to pick up the variations that occur as conditions change. If you are unfamiliar with a certain species, it is very helpful to watch it in flight for an extended period to absorb the flight style and observe how it changes in different conditions.

Mantle color is a key trait, particularly when looking at large gulls that are perched. Unfortunately, mantle color can be very difficult to judge in flight. It varies depending on light conditions, the color of the background a bird is viewed against,

Gulls freely mix when feeding. This diverse flock includes three Bonaparte's Gulls, two Ring-billed Gulls, a Herring Gull, a Great Black-backed Gull, and a Lesser Black-backed Gull. New Jersey, Feb. Cameron Cox. *Can you locate and age all members of all five species?*

and the angle of viewing. Low light or heavily overcast conditions make mantles look much darker than they actually are. Bright conditions wash out mantle colors. Even worse, slight shifts in the position of the bird relative to the observer can have a surprisingly strong effect on how the mantle color is perceived; a possible Lesser Black-backed Gull can alter its course slightly and transform into a typical Herring Gull! Our brain can adjust to many of these differences and compensate for them, but problems arise when observers are looking for rare species and fail to consider more common species because the mantle color seems wrong. Mantle color can be just as useful for flight identification as when watching gulls loafing at a dump, but take caution not to base identifications solely on mantle color.

All gulls take at least two plumage cycles—roughly 2 years—to attain adult plumage, and large gulls take four cycles or more. All the ternlike gulls are two-cycle gulls, except for Black-legged Kittiwake, which is a three-cycle gull. Typical gulls are either three- or four-cycle gulls, though some individuals take longer. When identifying gulls in

flight at a distance, overall color and broad patterns are more important than plumage and aging minutiae, but it still is helpful to understand the plumage progression in gulls, particularly large gulls, as they show the most variation.

AGING AND APPEARANCE OVERVIEW FOR A FOUR-CYCLE GULL

First Cycle: Largely mottled brown or gray with darker wingtips and a dark tail band or fully dark tail. The eye starts out dark in all species but lightens somewhat by spring in species with pale eyes as adults. The bill also starts out black but may rapidly develop a pink base in some species. First-cycle birds have slightly more pointed wingtips than birds in other cycles.

Second Cycle: Still largely mottled brown or gray, though the head, body, and rump may be less heavily mottled and lighter in color. The back acquires the adult mantle color while the wings are typically still mottled, so birds have the appearance of wearing a light gray to blackish saddle, depending on the species. Light eyes are usually apparent in species that show light eyes as adults. Most species

Three first-cycle Herring Gulls and one first-cycle Ring-billed Gull (top C). By spring many gulls, particularly first-cycle birds, show significant feather wear and fading. Notice how brown the primaries and secondary bars on these birds have become and how each of these birds has an individual pattern of wear. Birds that have spent the winter on sunny southern beaches are particularly worn and faded, with some becoming almost white-winged. Texas, April. Ken Behrens.

show moderate to extensive amounts of pink on the bill. Some individuals mature more slowly and look much like a first-cycle bird during their second cycle, but have blunter wingtips.

Third Cycle: The wings attain extensive amounts of adult mantle color but still retain some brown mottling. The black on the primaries is much more extensive than on adults and includes the primary coverts. The underparts are mostly white with variable amounts of brown mottling. The color of the bare parts may be similar to what was seen in the second cycle or may be almost as in an adult. This is the most variable cycle.

Fourth Cycle: Some are inseparable from adults. Others retain black markings on the tail, traces of brown smudging on the mantle, black marks on the primary coverts, reduced white mirrors on the outer primaries, and additional black marking on the bill.

The sexes appear similar in all species covered here, and they all have distinctive alternate plumages.

(LEFT) TURKEY, JAN. KEN BEHRENS
• Unlike many species of birds, gulls like these Yellow-legged and Black-headed Gulls frequently exploit human waste and thrive even in major cities and other heavily altered environments.

This flock includes four Ring-billed Gulls, two Herring Gulls, an adult California Gull, and a Franklin's Gull. Gulls fly powerfully and frequently wander far outside their normal ranges and this is one of the main attractions of the group. Gulls from Europe, Asia, South America, and western North America have occurred in the area covered by this guide. Some species like California and Little Gulls do so regularly, while vagrants like Black-tailed and Slaty-backed Gulls are much rarer. Kentucky, Oct. Dave Roemer.

RING-BILLED GULL
Larus delawarensis
DIMENSIONS
L: 17.5 in.; WS: 48 in.; WT: 1.1 lb.

SPRING ARRIVAL

s. QC: early Mar.; NE: early Mar.; MB: late Mar.

FALL ARRIVAL

NJ: early July; MO: early Aug.;
w. Gulf Coast: late Aug./early Sept.

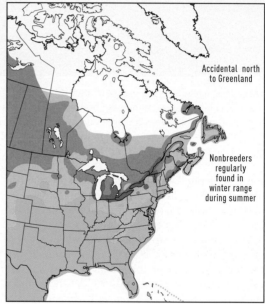

Accidental north
to Greenland

Nonbreeders
regularly
found in
winter range
during summer

This is the most widespread and common medium-sized gull, as likely to be seen scavenging for French fries in a parking lot as soaring over the ocean. Strong fall cold fronts can trigger massive migratory movements of Ring-billed Gulls along coastlines and interior lakes and rivers. Although gull migration is often subtle and difficult to distinguish from local movements, these impressive events cannot be mistaken for anything other than migration. In contrast, spring migrants slip by more stealthily.

SIZE: Slightly larger than Laughing Gull. Much smaller than Herring Gull. Slightly smaller than Caspian Tern.

STRUCTURE: Both the body and wings are distinctly slimmer than in Herring Gull. The arm is roughly the same length as the hand, and the wing bend comes to a sharp point. This is a clear difference between Ring-billed and larger gulls, which generally show a rounded wing bend, and this difference is easy to see on soaring birds. The wings are slightly more pointed than on Herring Gull but less pointed than on small gulls.

FLIGHT AND FLOCKING: In normal flight the wingbeats are shallow, with a powerful downstroke and quick, easy upstroke. Wingbeats are clearly quicker and lighter than those of the larger gulls but not as fast or emphatic as those of small gulls. Frequently soars, flapping occasionally with only the tips of the wings. In high winds often uses a dynamic soar style punctuated by occasional bursts of deep, powerful wingbeats. Migrants tend to follow consistent flight lines at a given location. Frequently these flight lines are quite high, rather than just above the water as in most other gulls. On peak migration days forms large high-flying kettles of dozens or hundreds of birds, much like some species of migrating raptors.

APPEARANCE: Alternate Adult: Clean white head and body with a yellow bill that has a distinctive black subterminal ring. As in Herring Gull, the mantle is pale gray with an extensive black patch in the outer primaries, though on Ring-billed this patch is larger, with mirrors on both P9 and P10. **Basic Adult:** Like alternate but with gray streaking on the head and neck, that is generally darker and better defined than that on Herring Gull, like pencil marks applied with great force. **First Cycle:** Juvenile is mottled gray-brown overall, paler than first-cycle Herring Gull, with a contrasting pale rump, white base of the tail, and black tail band that is usually quite narrow. Most acquire a clean pale gray back like the adult's early in fall and lose the mottling on the belly, becoming nearly clean white underneath. The wings have a fairly bold pattern, with pale gray-brown secondary coverts and a large pale inner primary window contrasting sharply with black outer primaries and a black secondary bar. The bill has a bubblegum-pink base and a sharply defined black tip. **Second Cycle:** Like adult but with more black in the primary tips and primary coverts, reduced or absent white mirrors on the outer primaries, and more extensive head streaking. Often shows remnants of a black tail band. **Distant:** Adults are pale with very large black wingtips. First-cycle birds are also quite pale with a bold, pale gray-and-black upperwing pattern and whitish underwings. The white rump flashes even paler than the rest of the upperparts and makes the narrow black tail band more noticeable.

SIMILAR SPECIES: Herring Gull: Clearly larger, broader-winged, and thicker through the body. The most distinctive traits at a distance are the slower wingbeats and blunter wingtips. The more rounded wing bend typical of large gulls is often obvious. Adult shows far less black on the outer primaries, and in the interior of the continent Herring Gull lacks the mirror on P9 possessed by adult Ring-billed. **Mew ("Common") Gull:** Slimmer and shorter-bodied with narrower wings. After the first cycle, the wings have blunter tips than those of Ring-billed. The mantle of adults is slightly darker than that of Ring-billed with a broader, more distinctly contrasting white trailing edge to the secondaries. The mirrors on the outer primaries are noticeably larger than in Ring-billed Gull. The thinner bill has a narrower, less sharply defined black band near the tip. First-cycle "Common" Gull has a more sharply defined black tail band, more uniform upperwings, and more extensive brown mottling on the underwing than Ring-billed. **Mew ("Short-billed") Gull:** Structure is like "Common" Gull, smaller and slimmer than Ring-billed. The mantle of adults is clearly darker gray than that of Ring-billed with a broader white trailing edge and larger white mirrors on P9 and P10. The head streaking is smudgier than that of Ring-billed and often much more extensive. First-cycle birds are browner overall than first-cycle Ring-billed Gulls with a mostly brown tail and heavily brown-barred rump that does not contrast conspicuously with the tail.

BASIC ADULT. UTAH, JAN. KEN BEHRENS.
• Clearly larger than all other small and medium-sized gulls, but slimmer and smaller-headed than large gulls.
• Adults have two large mirrors on the outer primaries.
• Wing bend is sharply pointed, unlike in larger gulls.

JUVENILE. WASHINGTON, AUG. CAMERON COX.
• Has a gray-brown body, though most become largely white by early fall.
• Wing pattern is similar to that of a first-cycle Herring Gull, but the pattern is slightly stronger and the underwing is paler.

TWO FIRST CYCLES (LOWER L AND R) AND TWO SECOND CYCLES (UPPER L AND C). FLORIDA, DEC. KEN BEHRENS.

- The stereotypical "parking-lot gull."
- Second-cycle birds look like adults but have more extensive black in the primaries, lack the large white mirrors on the outer primaries, and may have remnants of a black tail band.
- First-cycle birds vary in the degree of brown mottling they retain on the body and are separated from first-cycle Herring Gulls by the narrow black tail band and mostly pale underwings.

FLORIDA, DEC. KEN BEHRENS.

- Silhouette is distinctive: the basic shape is that of a large gull, but the body is more slender and the wings more narrow. It does not quite fit with either small gulls or large gulls, therefore it must be a Ring-billed.
- Large gulls do not usually show a sharp angle to the wing bend.

WITH TWO LAUGHING GULLS (RIGHT C). FLORIDA, JAN. KEN BEHRENS.

- Distinctly larger than Laughing Gull and built more like a large gull.

(RIGHT) FIRST CYCLE. ILLINOIS, DEC. KEN BEHRENS.

- Dull pinkish-based bill and pale gray overall color are typical during the first cycle.

BASIC ADULT. ILLINOIS, DEC. KEN BEHRENS.
- Despite being bold and obvious, the ring on the bill does not show up well enough at a distance to be a useful identification trait at a seawatch.
- Head streaking is finer than that of Herring Gull.

LOUISIANA, JAN. KEN BEHRENS.
- Away from the coast and Great Lakes, Ring-billed is the most common and widespread gull in winter.
- Large white primary mirrors are visible even at a distance. Herring Gulls on the Atlantic Coast may have two mirrors that rival those of Ring-billed, but most Herring Gulls in the interior have only a single smaller mirror.

BASIC ADULT WITH BASIC ADULT HERRING GULL (L). KENTUCKY, JAN. DAVE ROEMER.

- Note the pointed carpal bend and narrower wings than in Herring Gull.
- Smaller head and bill and slimmer body create a more delicate silhouette when viewed at great distances.
- The larger black wingtips of Ring-billed are the main plumage difference between these two species, which are otherwise very similar in color and pattern.

WITH ONE SECOND-CYCLE HERRING GULL (NEAR C). LOUISIANA, JAN. KEN BEHRENS.

- Although still quite variable, Ring-billeds do not display as much variation as four-year gulls, such as Herring Gull.

TWO FIRST CYCLES (SECOND AND THIRD FROM L) WITH THREE FIRST-CYCLE HERRING GULLS. TEXAS, APR. KEN BEHRENS.
- First-cycle birds are variable but have a consistently paler, grayer body than first-cycle Herring Gulls and a whitish rump that contrasts with the rest of the body.

**NEW JERSEY, NOV.
CAMERON COX.**

- Migrates by soaring in kettles more frequently than any other gull except Franklin's.
- Large movements are often triggered by strong fall cold fronts.

ALTERNATE ADULT. NEW YORK, APR. KEN BEHRENS.

- Extensive black primary tips separate Ring-billed from Herring Gull at long distances.

MEW GULL
Larus canus
DIMENSIONS
L: 16 in.; WS: 43 in.; WT: 15 oz.

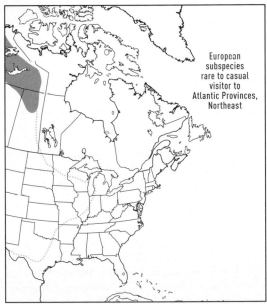

European subspecies rare to casual visitor to Atlantic Provinces, Northeast

The Mew Gull complex is made up of four taxa, none of which breeds in eastern North America. The two members of the complex covered in this account, *L. c. canus,* or "Common" Gull, originating in Europe, and *L. c. brachyrhynchus,* or "Short-billed" Gull, from western North America, are both regular vagrants to the East. These two taxa are considered separate species by European authorities, whereas the American Ornithologists' Union considers them conspecific. They are fairly distinct visually, so in this account the name "Short-billed" Gull refers to *brachyrhynchus* and "Common" Gull to *canus,* while we use the name Mew Gull to refer to both collectively.

SIZE: Only slightly smaller than Ring-billed Gull but appears much smaller. About the same size as or slightly larger than Laughing Gull.

STRUCTURE: Slender and delicate for a medium-sized gull. Slimmer than Ring-billed Gull with a shorter, thinner bill and narrower wings. First-cycle birds have sharply pointed wingtips, but after the first cycle they have slightly blunter wingtips than Ring-billed. The head is small and rounded, and there is less head and neck projecting in front of the wings than in Ring-billed.

FLIGHT AND FLOCKING: Flight style is closer to that

of a small gull than to Ring-billed Gull, quick and agile with fast wingbeats. When foraging often hovers low over the water on rapid wingbeats like a Bonaparte's Gull. In eastern North America typically found with Ring-billed or Herring Gulls.

APPEARANCE: Alternate Adult "Common" Gull: Clean white head and body with a greenish yellow bill. The mantle is pale gray, slightly darker than in Ring-billed and Herring Gulls. The white trailing edge of the wing is broad through the secondaries but narrows when it reaches the inner primaries. The black on the outer primaries is extensive, particularly on P8–P10, creating a rectangular black block. P10 has a large white mirror; the mirror on P9 is medium-sized to large. Small to medium-sized white tongue-tips are present on the middle primaries but not on P8, forming a short, weak "string of pearls." **Alternate Adult "Short-billed" Gull:** Like alternate adult "Common" Gull but with slightly darker mantle that is obviously darker than that of Ring-billed and Herring Gulls. The white trailing edge to the wing is broad through the secondaries and inner primaries before breaking into a series of large white tongue-tips in the middle primaries, usually including P8, that form a prominent "string of pearls." The black on the outer primaries is not as extensive as in "Common" Gull. Only P10 and to a lesser degree P9 are extensively black, and P8 shows significantly less black than in "Common" Gull. The net effect is more like that of a black spike along the leading edge of the hand rather than of a black rectangle. Both P9 and P10 have large white mirrors. **Basic Adult:** Like respective alternate adult of its taxa but with variable brown streaking on the head and neck, sometimes extending to the chest. In "Short-billed" Gull the streaking is more smudgy and extensive enough to create a dark-hooded impression, often merging into a nearly solid brown band across the hindneck in many individuals. The head markings in "Common" Gull are less smudgy, made up of better-defined streaks, and usually less extensive. Most "Common" Gulls have an irregular dusky subterminal band across the bill that is sometimes broken but is quite distinct in some individuals. "Short-billed" Gull tends to lack this mark or have a very faint band. **First-cycle "Common" Gull:** Juvenile has a brown back with crisp, pale scalloping and underparts extensively washed with gray. The brown on the back is replaced with clean gray by early fall, and the underparts become much paler, almost white, with small to moderate amounts of gray streaking on the head, breast, and flanks. The rump and base of the tail are clean white and contrast with the sharply defined black tail band. The upperwing coverts are grayish brown with a paler inner primary window and blackish outer primaries and secondary

bar. The underwings are mottled with pale brown, though some individuals have fairly whitish underwings. **First-cycle "Short-billed" Gull:** Juvenile is brownish gray overall with a light brown back covered with buff scalloping. The brown on the back is replaced with medium gray by early fall. The underparts tend to be darker and smudgier brown than those of first-cycle "Common" Gull, though the face and breast tend to lighten. By the end of the first cycle they may have faded considerably. Most have a nearly solid brown hindneck and often nearly solid brown flanks. The base of the tail is moderately to heavily barred, reducing the contrast with the brown tail. The upperwing pattern is much like that of "Common" Gull's, though the pale inner primaries may have more prominent dark spots near the tip of each feather. The underwing is liberally washed with brown. **Second Cycle:** Like adult but with brownish smudges in the wing coverts, more black in the outer primaries and primary coverts, and a duller bill. Traits for separating "Common" Gull from "Short-billed" Gull at this age are not well known. The wing pattern is highly variable, but birds with a large white tongue-tip on P8 can safely be assigned to "Short-billed" Gull. "Short-billed" Gull also tends to show a variable black tail band, whereas "Common" Gull tends to have a pure white tail. **Distant:** The slightly darker mantle of adult compared with that of Ring-billed Gull causes it to shine less in the sun and allow its broader white trailing edge to the secondaries (extending onto the inner primaries in "Short-billed" Gull) to stand out clearly. The wings show large black tips, and the large mirrors on the outer primaries form a small patch of white that is visible even at long distances. First-cycle "Short-billed" Gull is fairly brown and uniform looking, a bit like a miniature Thayer's Gull. First-cycle "Common" Gull looks much like first-cycle Ring-billed Gull but has a mottled brown underwing.

SIMILAR SPECIES: Ring-billed Gull: Distinctly larger and broader-winged with a larger head and longer, heavier bill. Has a slower, more measured wingbeat that is more like that of a large gull, whereas Mew Gull is more agile, with a wingbeat reminiscent of a small gull. Adult Ring-billed has a paler mantle than do "Common" and "Short-billed" Gulls, narrower white trailing edge to the secondaries, smaller mirrors on P9 and P10, and a brighter yellow bill with a bolder, broader black ring near the tip. Compared with first-cycle "Common" Gull, first-cycle Ring-billed has more dark marks on the rump and the base of the tail and more white in the outermost tail feathers, so the black tail band is not as clean, contrasting, or extensive. On average, Ring-billed also has a slightly paler back, slightly more contrasting wing pattern, and paler underwings on average.

FIRST-CYCLE "SHORT-BILLED" GULL (TOP L). WASHINGTON, FEB. CAMERON COX.
- Body heavily mottled with brown and often appears dark. Brown wash is heaviest on hindneck and flanks.
- Little contrast between mottled rump and all-brown tail.

BASIC ADULT "SHORT-BILLED" GULL (BOTTOM L). WASHINGTON, FEB. CAMERON COX.
- Usually has more extensive head streaking than basic adult "Common" Gull.
- Usually lacks a dark ring on the bill.
- White trailing edge to the wing is broad along the secondaries and inner primaries.
- Has a strong "string of pearls" on the middle primaries and much less black on P8 than is found on adult "Common."

FIRST-CYCLE "COMMON" GULL (TOP R). TURKEY, FEB. KEN BEHRENS.
- Body is lightly mottled with gray-brown but appears pale overall.
- Mostly white rump contrasts sharply with broad black tail band.

BASIC ADULT "COMMON" GULL (BOTTOM R). TURKEY, FEB. KEN BEHRENS.
- Little head streaking in winter.
- Noticeable dark ring on the bill.
- White trailing edge to the wing is broad through the secondaries but narrow on the inner primaries.
- Extensive black on P8 creates a larger, more rectangular block of black on the outer primaries than it does in adult "Short-billed" Gull.

BASIC ADULT "SHORT-BILLED" GULL WITH
BASIC ADULT RING-BILLED GULL (R). UTAH, JAN.
KEN BEHRENS.
- Extensive, cloudy brown head
  streaking of some adult "Short-billed"
  Gulls instantly separates them from
  both Ring-billed and "Common" Gulls.
- "Short-billed" Gull has a much
  broader white trailing edge to the wing
  than Ring-billed, and the white is set
  off by the darker gray mantle color.
- Mantle color of "Common" Gull is only
  slightly darker than Ring-billed Gull,
  and not obviously darker like this
  "Short-billed" Gull.

TWO "COMMON" GULLS WITH YELLOW-LEGGED
AND BLACK-HEADED GULLS. TURKEY, FEB.
KEN BEHRENS.
- Clean white rump and base to the tail
  on the first-cycle bird (bottom R, above
  Two Black-headed Gulls) are obvious
  at a distance and contrast strongly
  with the black tail band.
- Adult (lead bird) clearly shows
  extensive black primary tips with very
  noticeable white mirrors on the outer
  primaries.

FIRST-CYCLE "COMMON" GULL. WALES, MAR.
KEN BEHRENS.
- The adult gray of first-cycle "Common"
  Gull, present on the back and scapulars by
  fall, is paler than that of "Short-billed" Gull
  and only slightly darker than that of
  Ring-billed Gull.
- Some first-cycle "Common" Gulls have a
  very broad tail band, but the band is black,
  not brown as in first-cycle "Short-billed"
  Gull, and the tail is edged in white.

BASIC ADULT "SHORT-BILLED" GULL. WASHINGTON, FEB. CAMERON COX.
- The gray mantle bleeds through the wing, creating a faint
  dusky band on the underwing, unlike in Ring-billed Gull.
- On the upperwing, the broad white trailing edge transi-
  tions into a strong "string of pearls." "Common" Gull has
  a narrow white trailing edge on inner primaries and an
  indistinct "string of pearls."
- Head streaking is not as heavy on this individual as it is in
  some basic adults, but it still forms a strong brown band
  on the hindneck.

CALIFORNIA GULL
Larus californicus
DIMENSIONS
L: 21 in.; WS: 54 in.; WT: 1.3 lb.

SPRING ARRIVAL

NE: late Mar.; MB: mid-Apr.

FALL ARRIVAL

NE: late July

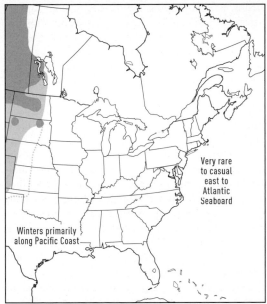

Very rare to casual east to Atlantic Seaboard

Winters primarily along Pacific Coast

This large gull is widespread and common over much of western North America, and strays are regularly found in the East. There are two subspecies: *L. c. californicus* and *L. c. albertaensis*, both of which have occurred in eastern North America, but the differences between the two taxa are slight. Vagrants are most regular in the Midwest, western Gulf Coast, and Great Lakes, and most rare from New England north.

SIZE: Slightly smaller than Herring Gull. Larger than Ring-billed Gull. About the same size as Lesser Black-backed Gull.

STRUCTURE: Long-winged and exceptionally slender for a large gull, with a long, thin bill. Similar in structure to Lesser Black-backed Gull, but the wings are slightly slimmer, the arm and the hand are almost equal in length, and the hand does not look as tapered or as pointed as in Lesser Black-backed. Somewhat short-tailed compared with its close relatives, though this is rarely striking. California Gull swells slightly at the breast but has a flat belly. It is more similar to Ring-billed in structure than any other large gull is, but with a longer bill and wings and a lankier overall appearance.

FLIGHT AND FLOCKING: As in Herring Gull, but wingbeats are slightly faster and deeper. In eastern North America typically found singly within flocks of Herring or Ring-billed Gulls.

APPEARANCE: Alternate Adult: Clean white head and body with a yellow bill, yellow legs, and a dark eye. The bill has both a faint dark ring and a red spot. The mantle is medium gray, clearly darker than that of Ring-billed or Herring Gull, and the white trailing edge of the wing contrasts sharply. The black area on the outer primaries is very large, and there is a large mirror on P10 and a small mirror on P9. The gray mantle bleeds through to the underwing, forming a dusky gray band across the base of the secondaries and inner primaries below. **Basic Adult:** Like alternate but with brown streaking on the head and neck, often concentrated on the hindneck. California Gull is known for having both black and red on the tip of the bill, and the black area is more developed in winter, often forming a complete ring. This trait is difficult to judge in flight, however, and winter Herring Gull can also have a variable black mark on the tip of the bill in addition to a red spot. **First Cycle:** Juvenile is medium to dark brown with strong pale scalloping on the back and wing coverts. The bill is initially solidly black, but most acquire a sharply bicolored bill by early fall. The pale fringes on the back are replaced by mottled grayish feathers; the pale fringes to the coverts wear and become less obvious. The hand is largely blackish, and there is little to no pale inner primary window. There is both a dark secondary bar and a fairly distinct dark greater covert bar, and the underwing is fairly even brown throughout. During the winter the body fades from brown to pale gray-brown; the throat and chest become whitish in many individuals while the hindneck is still heavily washed with brown. As in Herring Gull, the tail is mostly brown, but the rump averages paler than in Herring, creating greater contrast. By midwinter tends to have a rather shabby appearance, more so than in first-cycle gulls that are common in eastern North America. During the first prealternate molt, late in the first cycle, often acquires some adult gray on the back, and the head and body become whiter. **Second Cycle:** Variable. The body is often much paler than in the first cycle, whitish with variable gray smudging. The face is also paler, though the neck is usually heavily streaked and washed with brown. Some are extensively brown below, more like first-cycle birds. The bill has a pale pink base with a small, sharply defined black tip. The back and occasionally some of the upperwing coverts gain the medium gray color worn by adult, while the remainder of the coverts are mottled brown. The outer primaries are extensively blackish, sometimes with a small white mirror on P10. Unlike in the first cycle, there is often a contrasting inner primary window. The underwing is significantly paler than in the first cycle. The tail is largely black with variable white speckling. In the second prealternate molt, late in second cycle, gains more adult gray upperwing coverts and a cleaner white head and body. **Third Cycle:** Very similar to adult but with a duller bill and legs, slight brown smudging in the wing coverts, a slightly more extensive black area in the outer primaries that often extends into the primary coverts, and a variable broken black tail band. **Distant:** Adult appears medium gray above, slightly darker than it appears when sitting, but clearly not blackish in most conditions. The white trailing edge to the wing is more obvious than in Herring Gull, and the contrast between the extensive black wingtips and the mantle is not as obvious as at close range but is still visible. Unlike in Lesser Black-backed Gull, the light dusky band on the underwing is difficult to see. First-cycle birds are evenly gray-brown to brown overall and may resemble first-cycle Herring Gulls but have slightly darker wings, and many have a noticeably pale chest while much of the head is still brown. This pattern is never seen in Herring Gull.

SIMILAR SPECIES: Herring Gull: Larger overall with a thicker body and broader wings. Wingbeats tend to be slightly slower and shallower. Adult has a slightly paler mantle than California Gull, which does not bleed through the underwing as on California Gull. From a distance the most obvious difference is that adult Herring Gull has far less black in the outer primaries. First-cycle Herring Gull is usually paler than first-cycle California Gull, but both species vary greatly in overall color. Herring Gull tends to be browner than the colder-toned, gray-brown first-cycle California Gull. It also has a large, pale inner primary window and tends to have a paler underwing. Second-cycle birds of both species are variable and best identified by structure, though Herring Gulls tend to have even head streaking whereas California Gulls often show a more concentrated band of streaking across the nape, which creates a messy half-collar. **Lesser Black-backed Gull:** Slightly larger and more heavily built with broader-based wings. Both Lesser Black-backed and California Gulls look slender, but Lesser Black-backed Gull looks slender in an athletic, aerodynamic way, whereas California Gull looks almost spindly. Adult Lesser Black-backed has a distinctly darker gray mantle than California Gull, a smaller white mirror on P10, and an inconspicuous mirror or no mirror at all on P9. The darker mantle color is also useful for separating third-cycle birds. First-cycle birds are similar, but Lesser Black-backed Gulls tend to have a very cold gray appearance at this age with noticeably darker wings; first-cycle California Gulls tend to be more brownish and often have a messy, uneven appearance. Lesser Black-backed Gulls have a narrower black tail band and show greater rump contrast than first-cycle California Gulls. Second-cycle Lesser Black-backed Gulls have evenly dark upperwings, whereas California Gulls of this age tend to show some paler coverts and a contrasting inner primary window. When present, the darker back color of second-cycle Lesser Black-backed Gulls is quite different from that of California Gull. Finally, Lesser Black-backed Gulls have distinctly darker underwings than second-cycle California Gulls, contrasting sharply with their whitish belly. **Ring-billed Gull:** Smaller, with thinner wings, a shorter bill, and a smaller head. Wingbeats are faster and slightly deeper, and the wing bend is more sharply pointed. Adult's mantle is paler gray than that of California Gull, and they have a narrower and less contrasting white trailing edge to the wing, and slightly less black in the outer primaries. First-cycle Ring-billed Gulls can be confused with second-cycle California Gulls but have sparser, paler streaking on the hindneck, a paler gray back, and a narrower, cleaner black tail band. Second-cycle birds differ from California Gulls in the same ways as do adults.

ALTERNATE ADULT. CALIFORNIA, MAR. CAMERON COX.

- Slender and trim for a large gull, with long slim wings.
- Bill is long and slender.
- Mantle is medium gray—darker than in Ring-billed and Herring Gulls but much paler than in Lesser Black-backed Gull.
- Black primary tips are extensive and tend to create a square-looking block.

BASIC ADULT (TOP L) WITH RING-BILLED GULLS. UTAH, JAN. KEN BEHRENS.

- Mantle of adult California Gulls is noticeably darker than that of Ring-billed Gulls, but very bright light or low light may minimize the differences.
- Both species have extensive black tips to the primaries, but in California Gull the black has a squared-off shape, whereas the black on the upperwing of Ring-billed Gull forms a rough 7.

FIRST CYCLE. CALIFORNIA, OCT. BRIAN SULLIVAN.

- First cycles are similar to first-cycle Herring Gulls but tend to be a slightly paler and colder gray-brown overall, with more uniformly dark under-wings like a Lesser Black-backed Gull.
- They also lack the pale inner primaries window of first-cycle Herring Gulls.
- Bill becomes sharply two-toned early in fall.

SECOND CYCLE. CALIFORNIA, MAR. CAMERON COX.

- For a large gull, head is extremely small and bill is very slender.
- This bird has attained much of the adult medium-gray mantle color, clearly darker than the mantles of Ring-billed and Herring Gulls.
- Inner primaries show a faint pale window, though the entire hand appears dark at a distance.

SUBADULTS AND ADULTS UNDERGOING PREBASIC MOLT. UTAH, JUNE. KEN BEHRENS.

- Very lean, long-necked, and long-billed.

UTAH, JAN. KEN BEHRENS.

- Long lines and V-shaped flocks are most often formed by large gulls commuting to and from roost locations but can also occur during peak migrations days.

(RIGHT) BASIC ADULTS. UTAH, JAN. KEN BEHRENS.

- The gray mantle bleeds through to the under-wing, creating a faint dusky band that's lacking in Ring-billed and Herring Gulls.

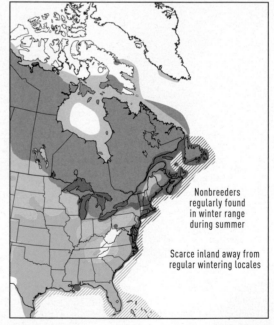

HERRING GULL
Larus argentatus
DIMENSIONS
L: 25 in.; WS: 58 in.; WT: 2.5 lb.

SPRING ARRIVAL

s. MB: early/mid-Mar.; Hudson Bay: mid-May

FALL ARRIVAL

w. Gulf Coast: mid-Sept.; MO: late Sept.;
s. FL: early Oct.

Nonbreeders regularly found in winter range during summer

Scarce inland away from regular wintering locales

This most widespread and common large gull in eastern North America is infamous for its variable appearance. Although no distinct subspecies have been described in the region, significant geographic variation combines with extensive individual variation to make for a bewildering array of plumages in the species. Most notably, adults along the Atlantic Coast typically have mirrors on the two outermost primaries (P9 and P10) and reduced black in the wingtips, whereas adults in the Great Lakes and the interior of the continent have a mirror only on P10 and more black in the wingtips. Another interesting aspect of Herring Gull variability is that some populations are fairly sedentary whereas others undertake long migrations.

SIZE: Distinctly larger than Ring-billed Gull. Slightly larger than Lesser Black-backed Gull. Distinctly smaller than Great Black-backed Gull.

STRUCTURE: The middle-of-the-road large gull. Clearly sleeker and has slimmer wings than the hulking Great Black-backed and Glaucous Gulls but is more powerfully built and broader-winged than Lesser Black-backed and California Gulls. Overall it is large but lean and balanced with a long, slim bill. The hand and arm are of almost equal length, and the wing bend is thrust forward slightly but is gently rounded, not coming to a distinct point as in Ring-billed Gull.

FLIGHT AND FLOCKING: Typical flight is steady, on measured, fairly shallow wingbeats. In strong winds may employ a dynamic soar, but does so clumsily, making only shallow arcs. May soar during migration but does so less frequently than Ring-billed Gull and forms smaller, looser kettles. Typical migratory behavior is flying at medium height in singles, pairs, or small strung-out flocks. It is usually difficult to distinguish this from the casual movements of local birds, making Herring Gull migration very easy to overlook, though seasonal changes in numbers at given locations, including the winter withdrawal from large parts of its range, indicate that the species is highly migratory. The majority of the migration of Herring Gull and other large gulls may occur at night, though this is not known definitively.

APPEARANCE: Alternate Adult: White head and body, pale gray mantle, and yellow bill with a red gonydeal spot. The color of the mantle is almost identical to that of Ring-billed Gull. The bright yellow eyes can be detected at moderate distances. The exact pattern of the primaries varies greatly, both geographically and individually, though the former seems more important. Along the Atlantic Coast has less black in the primaries, a very large mirror on P10, and a medium-sized mirror on P9. Elsewhere has significantly more black in the outer primaries, a large mirror on P10, and no mirror on P9. In winter, Atlantic-type birds are frequent on the eastern Great Lakes in modest numbers, and interior-type birds can be seen on the Atlantic Coast, particularly in the Southeast, but overall these types remain quite faithful to their respective regions. **Basic Adult:** Like alternate but with varying amount of brown streaking on the head and neck and occasionally the breast. Usually the streaking is evenly distributed and of moderate intensity, only occasionally heavy enough to create a hooded appearance. The streaking is strong enough to be visible at moderate distance but not heavy enough to coalesce into a solid brown wash on any one part of the head. **First Cycle:** Juveniles are uniformly brown, ranging from dark brown to frosty gray-brown. The wings are brown with large, obvious, pale inner primary windows contrasting with dark brown outer primaries. The tail is usually completely dark brown like the outer primaries, contrasting little with the brown rump. Some show extensive white barring on the outer tail feathers or, rarely, an extensive dark tail band rather than a fully dark tail. During the first winter, the back, scapulars, and many of the body feathers

are replaced, but this does not greatly affect appearance at a distance. In most the head becomes distinctly paler, usually by late fall. The bill starts out all black, but most acquire a sharply contrasting pink base by late fall though a narrow band of black is often retained along the cutting edge of the bill and a few maintain a solid black bill throughout the first cycle. Individuals from the more northern part of the breeding range tend to replace fewer feathers in the first-cycle and do so more slowly so they often appear more uniform. **Second Cycle:** Like first cycle but with a pale gray back, blacker primaries, and paler head and belly. The eye is usually dingy yellow and the bill sharply two-toned, with a pink base and black tip. Retains a large inner primary window, and the tail is largely black. Highly variable; some gain no gray on the back and can appear much like first cycle. **Third Cycle:** Like adult but with more black in the outer primaries, which may extend onto the primary coverts, and the tail has a variable ragged black band. The head streaking is heavier than in adults, the adult gray of the mantle is broken up by mottled brown patches, and the white breast may sport some brown patches. Highly variable; some individuals are more advanced, looking more like adults, whereas others have slower plumage progression and look more like second-cycle birds. **Distant:** Adults are very pale with fairly small to medium-sized black wingtips. The wingtips can blend with a dark background creating the appearance of a white-winged gull. A few have enough head streaking in winter to create a hooded appearance, but this streaking is not visible at a distance in most individuals. First-cycle birds often look uniformly muddy brown throughout. The pale inner primary window does not stand out strongly but is usually visible. The whitish head that many first-cycle birds acquire during winter often stands out strongly, and the contrast between head and body becomes the most visible plumage characteristic at a distance. Immatures generally appear messier and with more dark coloration than other immature gulls that are common in eastern North America so that, in the East, dark, messy gulls are virtually certain to be Herring Gulls.

SIMILAR SPECIES: Ring-billed Gull: Smaller and slimmer-bodied with narrower, more pointed wings and with faster, snappier wingbeats. Adult has the same mantle color as adult Herring Gull but has significantly more black on the outer primaries and always has white mirrors on both P9 and P10, though the mirror on P9 may be small. First-cycle Ring-billed Gull is most likely to be confused with second-cycle Herring Gull but has a narrower black tail band, less mottled underwings, and crisper gray markings on the head and body. **Lesser Black-backed Gull:**

Slightly smaller with distinctly longer and more pointed wings. Adult has a significantly darker mantle and more black on the outer primaries. First-cycle birds are the most similar to Herring Gull but are still darker above than Herring, lacking the pale inner primary windows, and typically have a whiter body that contrasts clearly with the dark wings. Lesser Black-backed Gull also has more contrast, usually showing a black tail band, white tail base, and pale rump that contrasts sharply with the rest of the upperparts. **Thayer's Gull:** Structurally very similar but has a smaller head, a shorter bill, and averages slightly broader-winged with blunter wingtips. The dark primary tips on adult are never truly black as in Herring Gull, but range from blackish to silvery gray. The dark area on the outer primaries is not as extensive as on Herring Gull, and the underside of the primaries is almost pure white. Second- and third-cycle birds can be difficult to separate from Herring Gulls of the same ages but tend to have brownish rather than black outer primaries, and the underside of the hand tends to be almost fully white. First-cycle Thayer's is more even and "prettier" than first-cycle Herring Gull, lacking the pale head even late in the first cycle. The uppersides of the outer primaries are medium brown with a two-toned pattern of dark outer webs and pale inner webs, not evenly dark brown like those of first-cycle Herring Gull. The underside of the primaries is whitish with a silvery sheen. Unlike most Herring Gulls, Thayer's has an all-black bill through most of the first cycle.

FIRST CYCLE AND ADULT. NORTH CAROLINA, FEB. KEN BEHRENS.
- Large and powerfully built. Generally common, and serves as a reference standard for all large gulls.
- Adult has a pale gray mantle, identical in color to that of adult Ring-ringed Gull.
- Uniform brown coloration is the hallmark of first-cycle Herring Gulls.
- In large gulls, first-cycle birds typically have a slightly longer, more pointed hand than older birds.

MASSACHUSETTS, JAN. KEN BEHRENS.
- Large but fairly lean and balanced.
- A flock like this is more typical of a group commuting to a roost than a migrating flock. During migration large gulls form lines similar to this, but individuals are usually spaced more widely.

BASIC ADULT. NORTH CAROLINA, FEB. KEN BEHRENS.
- Staring yellow eye is typical but difficult to see at a distance.
- Head streaking is heavier and more diffuse than on Ring-billed Gull.
- Mantle color does not bleed through to the underwing.

WITH SECOND-CYCLE LESSER BLACK-BACKED GULL (BOTTOM L) AND FIRST-CYCLE GREAT BLACK-BACKED GULL (BACKGROUND). MARYLAND, FEB. CAMERON COX.
- Many first-cycle Herring Gulls, like the right-hand bird, develop a sharply defined pink-based bill by midwinter, separating them from Thayer's and Lesser Black-backed Gulls.
- Third- and fourth-cycle Herring Gulls (top front) have more black in the outer primaries and smaller white mirrors than adults.
- Even before they gain the adult mantle color, first- and second-cycle Lesser Black-backed Gulls have darker upperwings than Herring Gull.

WITH A SECOND-CYCLE GREAT BLACK-BACKED GULL (BOTTOM R). NORTH CAROLINA, FEB. KEN BEHRENS.
- Distant flocks often have a mottled appearance due to tremendous age-related and individual variation.
- Great Black-backed Gulls are noticeably larger, broader-winged, and less agile than Herring Gulls.

FIRST CYCLE. NEW JERSEY, NOV. KEN BEHRENS.
- Among common eastern gulls, only first-cycle Herring are so uniformly dark brown.
- Translucent inner primary windows combined with the muddy brown plumage clinch the identification.

FIRST CYCLE WITH SECOND-CYCLE GREAT BLACK-BACKED GULL (R). NORTH CAROLINA, FEB. KEN BEHRENS.
- Herring Gull is one of the largest gulls in North America but is dwarfed by Great Black-backed.
- The pale window stands out clearly on the left wing of this first-cycle Herring Gull.

MAINE, JULY. KEN BEHRENS.
- The black wingtips can disappear against a dark background.
- Along most of the Atlantic Coast, Herring is the dominant large gull and takes advantage of every food resource.

FIRST CYCLE. MASSACHUSETTS, JAN. CAMERON COX.
- Uniformly brown, like first-cycle Thayer's Gull, but is slightly darker brown, lacks the "frosty" appearance of Thayer's, and tends to be longer-billed.

TEXAS, APR. KEN BEHRENS.
- Although they appear distinctly large and powerful, the flat belly ensures that they still look lean.
- Atlantic-type Herring Gulls, with large white mirrors on both P9 and P10, do occur on the Gulf Coast but tend to be far less numerous than interior-type Herring Gulls, which have a single mirror on P10.

COMPARISON: INTERIOR-TYPE HERRING GULL (L) AND ATLANTIC-TYPE HERRING GULL (R).
- Interior-type has more extensive black wingtips and only a single mirror on P10.
- Atlantic-type has smaller black wingtips, a larger mirror on P10, and an additional mirror on P9.
- In winter these two types mix, but Atlantic-type birds dominate the Atlantic Coast, whereas birds found on the Great Lakes, interior, and Gulf Coast are primarily interior-type birds.

THAYER'S GULL
Larus thayeri
DIMENSIONS
L: 23 in.; WS: 55 in.; WT: 2.2 lb.

SPRING ARRIVAL

s. MB: late Apr.; Hudson Bay: mid-May;
n. Canadian Arctic: mid-May

FALL ARRIVAL

n. Great Lakes: mid-Oct.; Niagara River:
mid-Nov.; IA: mid-Nov.

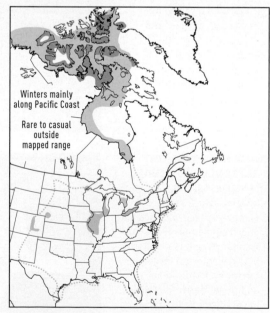

Winters mainly
along Pacific Coast

Rare to casual
outside
mapped range

Thayer's Gull can aptly be described as an enigma wrapped in a misidentification. Formerly considered a subspecies of Herring Gull, it was given full species status in 1972 by the American Ornithologists' Union. Since then, some who have studied Thayer's Gull have sought to include it as part of the Iceland Gull complex, while others have argued emphatically for its status as a full species. For the moment, Thayer's Gull lives on despite the contro- versy. Most Thayer's winter along the Pacific Coast of North America, though small numbers winter east through the Great Lakes. The Great Lakes are also a hotbed of confusing birds that show characteristics intermediate between Thayer's and "Kumlien's" Iceland Gulls. Whether such birds are hybrids or extreme examples of variation in these two highly variable species is unknown.

SIZE: Slightly smaller than Herring Gull. Very similar to Iceland Gull but averages slightly larger.

STRUCTURE: Nearly identical to Herring Gull, but the wings appear slightly broader with blunter tips. The head is marginally smaller than that of Herring, the bill is shorter, and the tail also tends to look shorter. Small and slightly built Thayer's Gulls will stand out from Herring Gulls, but large Thayer's closely resemble Herring in all aspects of structure.

FLIGHT AND FLOCKING: As in Herring Gull. In eastern North America usually found with Herring or Iceland Gulls.

APPEARANCE: Alternate Adult: Clean white head and body with an eye that is typically dark and yellow bill with a red gonydeal spot. In some the eye is paler; the most extreme have pale yellow eyes, but never bright gold like those of Herring Gull. The mantle is light gray, marginally darker than in Herring Gull, and the white trailing edge to the wing is slightly broader than in Herring Gull. The dark areas in the outer primaries are never truly black but range from blackish to slate gray and are restricted largely to the outer webs of the outer primaries and connect to dark subterminal bands. This creates a pattern of blackish and pale gray stripes above that is sometimes referred to as the "Venetian blinds effect." There are large mirrors on P9 and P10 and small white tongue-tips on the middle primaries. From underneath the wings are mostly white with dark tips to the outer primaries. **Basic Adult:** Like alternate but with a duller bill, often with a greenish yellow base and variable brown streaking on the head, neck, and breast. The streaking is more diffuse than in Herring Gull and often more extensive. The hindneck and breast in particular tend to be more heavily marked than in Herring Gull, often with circular dark blotches on the chest and a solid brown wash across the hindneck. **First Cycle:** Juveniles have a very neat appearance ranging from soft medium brown to dark brown with slightly darker brown primaries. The overall effect is very even, and they lack the obviously paler head shown by most first-cycle Herring Gulls. The precise pattern of the outer primaries is similar to the "Venetian blinds" pattern of adult, with darker outer webs and dark tips with contrasting paler inner webs. From underneath the primaries are silvery pale with a faint dark trailing edge. The tail tends to be mostly dark, slightly darker than the outer primaries and contrasting modestly with the rump. A dark brown secondary bar is usually present, though it often fades as it extends out the wing. The bill is solidly black through most of the first cycle, beginning to show a pale base only in late winter. **Second Cycle:** Like first cycle but tends to have a predominately gray rather than a predominately brown appearance and tends to look messy. Most have a paler head and breast, but the belly is still quite brown. The bill has a pink base and a large black tip. The adultlike gray back is well developed in some, but many have a mostly dull brown back. The upperwing coverts appear more mottled than in the first cycle. The pale inner primary window is large, and the outer primaries are medium brown to gray-brown; the underside of the primaries is silvery and pale. The tail is largely blackish and contrasts with the pale rump. Late in the second cycle the gray back becomes more developed, the wing coverts paler, and the head and body more whitish with less gray mottling. **Third Cycle:** Like adult but often with a black tip to the bill, heavier brown streaking on the head and breast and sometimes the belly, brown smudging in the upperwing coverts, and a variable black tail band. The dark areas on the outer primaries are more extensive, with a more Herring Gull–like pattern. However, these dark areas are never black, and more often tend toward the slate gray end of the scale, whereas the outer primaries on most adults tend toward the blackish end of the scale. There is a large mirror on P10 but little to no mirror on P9, and the pale tongue-tips on the middle primaries may be reduced or absent. **Distant:** Adults are pale, but the broad white trailing edge to the secondaries is bold enough to be noticeable in favorable conditions. In basic plumage many have heavy head streaking, creating a hooded appearance. The dark areas on the outer primaries are far less noticeable than at closer distances, and birds can appear entirely white-winged. First-cycle birds are evenly brown like Herring Gull but have a smoother, somewhat frosty appearance. The darker wingtips are often difficult to discern, but the dark tail band can often be distinguished. The silvery underside of the primaries often contrasts slightly with the rest of the underwing, unlike in Iceland Gull.

SIMILAR SPECIES: Herring Gull: Averages larger with slightly more pointed wings. Adult has more extensive black on outer primaries, which is visible on both the upper and lower surfaces of the wing. Be aware that Herring Gulls molting P9 or 10 show significantly less black in the primaries and can be confused with Thayer's. The bright yellow eyes of adult Herring Gull can be seen at moderate distances, whereas Thayer's has dull yellow or dark eyes. **Iceland Gull (kumlieni):** Adult typically has dark markings on the outer primaries that are much less extensive than on Thayer's. However, the wingtip pattern is variable, ranging from entirely white to almost as dark as that of Thayer's Gull, making the separation of dark extreme "Kumlien's" Gull from Thayer's Gull a significant challenge. The mantle color of adult Iceland Gulls tends to be slightly paler than in Herring Gull, whereas that of Thayer's is typically slightly darker than in Herring. Subadult birds are extremely variable and without excellent views or photos often need to be left without a definitive label. Likewise, many first-cycle birds are very challenging in flight. First-cycle Iceland Gulls are paler than first-cycle Thayer's and many have nearly white wingtips, lack the strong dark secondary bar shown by Thayer's, and have a tail that is fairly similar in color to the rump, whereas Thayer's has a brown tail and paler rump.

BASIC ADULT WITH A BASIC ADULT CALIFORNIA GULL (TOP). UTAH, JAN. KEN BEHRENS.

- Pattern of very limited dark markings on the outer primaries is referred to as the "Venetian blinds effect."
- The dark wing markings are never truly black; they range from medium gray to blackish but often look black in the field.
- Underwing, visible on the right wing, is almost completely pale.
- White trailing edge of the wing is broader than in Herring Gull.
- Head streaking of basic adults averages more extensive than on Herring Gull, and often extends onto the chest.
- Mantle color is slightly darker than Herring Gull's but paler than California Gull's.

FIRST CYCLE WITH SECOND-CYCLE HERRING GULL (R). KENTUCKY, JAN. DAVE ROEMER.

- First-cycle Thayer's is clean-looking, with attractive "frosty" tones to the plumage, whereas first-cycle Herring generally looks messy. Thayer's lacks the contrasting white head shown by many first-cycle Herring.
- Underside of the primaries on Thayer's has the silver sheen typical of a white-winged gull.
- Thayer's is slightly smaller and more compact than Herring and tends to have a slightly pudgy appearance.

FIRST-CYCLE THAYER'S GULL (R) WITH FIRST-CYCLE ICELAND GULL (L). MASSACHUSETTS, JAN. KEN BEHRENS (L); WASHINGTON, FEB. CAMERON COX (R).

- First-cycle Iceland and Thayer's Gulls are both variable, but average individuals such as these two are easily separated. Iceland shows paler primaries, lacks a contrasting secondary bar, and has a much paler tail with noticeable internal barring.
- Iceland averages smaller overall, and usually has a smaller bill than Thayer's, but there is overlap.
- Darker first-cycle Thayer's Gulls are more similar to first-cycle Herring Gulls than to first-cycle Iceland Gulls. Compared with Herring, they have brown, not blackish, outer primaries and a neater, "frosty" appearance.
- The pale base on Thayer's bill develops slowly and is rarely noticeable in the first cycle; even in the second cycle, many birds retain a mostly black bill.

BASIC ADULT. CALIFORNIA, JAN. BRIAN SULLIVAN.

- The "Venetian blinds effect" may not be visible when the wings are not fully extended, but the blackish wingtips are still more restricted than in Herring Gull, particularly on the underwing.
- The gray mantle color bleeds through slightly, creating a faint gray band on the underwing.
- Dull coloration at the base of the bill with a slightly brighter tip, dull eye, and blotchy head streaking that extends far down the breast are all good supporting features for Thayer's Gull.

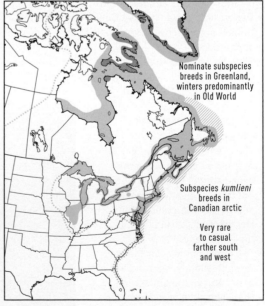

ICELAND GULL
Larus glaucoides
DIMENSIONS
L: 22 in.; WS: 54 in.; WT: 1.8 lb.

SPRING ARRIVAL

Hudson Bay: late May

FALL ARRIVAL

Niagara River: early Nov.; ME: early Nov.;
VA: mid-Dec.

Even those who foolishly consider all large gulls "ugly" should be struck by the frosty beauty of an Iceland Gull. The American Ornithologists' Union recognizes two subspecies, nominate *L. g. glaucoides,* which breeds in Greenland, and *L. g. kumlieni,* or "Kumlien's" Gull, which breeds in northeast Canada. Except in Greenland, "Kumlien's" Gull makes up the overwhelming majority of the Iceland Gulls in North America. Although problems with separating these very similar taxa cloud the status of nominate *glaucoides,* it seems to be uncommon to rare in eastern Newfoundland, and exceptionally rare elsewhere in North America. Typical *glau-*

coides are slightly smaller and more petite than "Kumlien's," with a light gray mantle, pure white wingtips, and a clear yellow eye. Away from eastern Canada, Iceland Gull is rare to uncommon and most sightings are of immature birds.

SIZE: Distinctly smaller than Glaucous Gull. Slightly smaller than Herring Gull. Very similar in size to Thayer's Gull but averages slightly smaller.

STRUCTURE: Compact and relatively petite for a large gull. The head is small and rounded, with a short bill and short neck, which creates less head projection in front of the wings than in Herring or Glaucous Gulls. The body is short, with a gently rounded undercarriage, often slightly heavier at the breast. The wings are broad-based and fairly broad through the arm to the inner portion of the hand before tapering quickly to the wingtip. Compared with Herring Gull, the hand looks longer and more pointed in first-cycle Iceland Gull. Adult Iceland Gull, however, often gives the impression of having a shorter hand relative to Herring Gull, and Iceland's wingtip often looks slightly blunter.

FLIGHT AND FLOCKING: As in Herring Gull but with slightly faster, stiffer wingbeats that give the impression of being crisper and more purposeful. Outside eastern Canada, flocks of Iceland Gulls larger than a few individuals are rare and they are usually found in large groups of Herring Gulls.

APPEARANCE (*KUMLIENI*): Alternate Adult: Clean white head and body with a yellow bill. The mantle is pale gray, usually slightly paler than that of adult Herring Gull. The primary pattern is highly variable. Most have medium to dark gray stripes on the outer primaries, often connected to dark subterminal bands. This pattern can be dark and obvious, approaching that of Thayer's Gull, or much lighter and less extensive so that the wingtips appear completely white. Somewhere near the middle of these extremes is the normal pattern. A small number of "Kumlien's" Gulls do have pure white wingtips like nominate *glaucoides* but have the darker mantle and darker eye of "Kumlien's." Basic Adult: Like alternate but with a duller greenish yellow bill and variable amounts of smudgy gray streaking on the head, nape, and breast. First Cycle: Juveniles are highly variable but tend to be very pale overall with extensive gray streaking and smudging on the body. The wing coverts are pale and coarsely marked with pale-gray checkering and barring. The primaries are very pale, almost white, but many have slightly darker outer webs to the outer primaries. Most lack a noticeable secondary bar, but a few show a modest to fairly obvious dark secondary bar. The tail is pale and either heavily barred and uniform in color with the rump or solidly washed with gray so that it is modestly but noticeably darker. During the first cycle the color fades considerably, becoming paler and more uniform; by late winter most are whitish. Juveniles have a black bill, but by the end of the first cycle most have a bicolored bill: a pale inner two-thirds and a black outer third. Second Cycle: Most have the smooth pale gray back of adult but with medium gray to light brown smudging and vermiculations throughout the wing coverts. The primaries range from medium brown to completely white. The body is mainly pale, though unevenly smudged with gray. The bill is bicolored, with a pale base and black tip. Third Cycle: Like adult but with a dull bill, usually with a complete black subterminal ring, more extensive gray in the outer primaries, and brown smudging in the wing coverts. Distant: Adults are extremely pale and usually look entirely white-winged since the gray markings on the outer primaries are very difficult to detect in all but the darkest individuals. First-cycle birds appear uniformly whitish to pale tan, rarely showing any discernible markings.

SIMILAR SPECIES: Glaucous Gull: Much larger and bulkier but with a rangier appearance because of its longer head and neck projection in front of the wings. The wings are broader and blunter. It has substantially slower, more rolling wingbeats that betray its larger bulk and that are clearly different from the swift, crisp wingbeats of Iceland Gull. At all ages Glaucous Gull has pure white primaries, lacking the dark markings in the outer primaries shown by most "Kumlien's" Gulls. Adult Glaucous has a paler gray mantle than "Kumlien's" but is similar to *glaucoides* Iceland Gull. Thayer's Gull: Confusion is possible only with "Kumlien's" Gull, not with the paler *glaucoides*. Thayer's has on average a larger and longer bill and a marginally longer hand than "Kumlien's." Adult Thayer's also usually has more extensive and darker markings on the outer primaries and a slightly darker mantle than adult "Kumlien's." However, separating adult Thayer's from dark "Kumlien's" Gulls based on a brief flyby view is challenging or impossible. Because of the huge degree of variability shown by second- and third-cycle Thayer's and "Kumlien's" Gulls, flight identification is often not possible without extended views from close range. In both ages, however, extensive dark outer primaries that contrast noticeably with the rest of the wing or a bold blackish tail are characteristics strongly in favor of Thayer's Gull. Likewise, first-cycle birds that have a solid, contrasting brown tail, bold secondary bars, and distinctly dark brown outer primaries can safely be called Thayer's Gulls.

FIRST CYCLE WITH FIRST-CYCLE HERRING GULL (ABOVE). MARYLAND, DEC. CAMERON COX.
- First-cycle Iceland is very pale, with cold, frosty plumage tones.
- Slightly smaller than Herring Gull with smaller head and shorter bill.
- Hand is distinctly pointed, far more so than in first-cycle Glaucous Gull.

ADULT *GLAUCOIDES* ICELAND GULL. ICELAND, FEB. STÉPHANE AUBRY.
- Status of the Greenland-breeding nominate subspecies, *L. g. glaucoides*, is uncertain in North America since it is difficult to separate from the pale extreme, *L. g. kumlieni*. Adult *glaucoides* has a slightly paler gray mantle than *kumlieni* and lacks any dark markings on the outer primaries, but pale *kumlieni* are very similar.

BASIC FOURTH/FIFTH-CYCLE *KUMLIENI* ICELAND GULL. MASSACHUSETTS, JAN. KEN BEHRENS.
- Has slightly darker gray mantle than *glaucoides* and dark markings on the outer primaries. The degree to which the primaries are marked varies greatly. Most are similar to this individual, but some virtually lack dark pigment, whereas others approach or overlap pale Thayer's Gulls.

FIRST CYCLE. MASSACHUSETTS, JAN. KEN BEHRENS.
- Compact with a small head, short neck, and broad-based wings tapering to a distinct point.

SECOND CYCLE. MASSACHUSETTS, JAN. CAMERON COX.
- All second-cycle white-winged gulls tend to have a messy appearance with patches of dark smudging.

BASIC ADULT WITH HERRING GULLS AND A GREAT BLACK-BACKED GULL (TOP L). ONTARIO, DEC. BRANDON HOLDEN.
- The gray marks on the outer primaries are difficult to see at a distance on all but the darkest Iceland Gulls, and the underwings always appear entirely white. To separate Iceland from Glaucous Gulls, concentrate on the wingbeat: it is faster and snappier in Iceland Gull. Iceland also shows narrower wings, smaller head, and shorter neck.

GLAUCOUS GULL
Larus hyperboreus
DIMENSIONS
L: 27 in.; WS: 60 in.; WT: 3.1 lb.

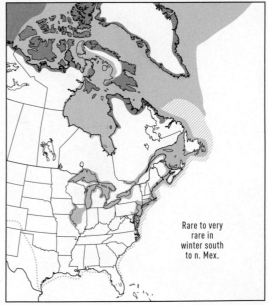

Rare to very rare in winter south to n. Mex.

SPRING ARRIVAL

Canadian Arctic: late Apr.

FALL ARRIVAL

off NL: early Oct.; NS: early Nov.; NJ: mid-Nov.; VA: late Dec.

In North America this hardy resident of the great frozen north is second only to Great Black-backed Gull in size. The vast majority of Glaucous Gulls found outside the Arctic and subarctic regions of North America are immature birds, since most adults migrate only a relatively short distance from their breeding territories.

SIZE: Only slightly smaller than Great Black-backed Gull but usually does not give the same overwhelmingly massive impression as that species. Tends to show more variation in size than Great Black-backed Gull, and small Glaucous Gulls may be close to Herring Gull in size.

STRUCTURE: Powerfully built with a large head; long, thick neck; and long bill. The body is thick throughout but often heaviest at the chest. The wings are exceptionally broad and somewhat blunt-tipped with a short hand.

FLIGHT AND FLOCKING: Wingbeats are slow, leisurely, and powerful, similar to those of Great Black-backed Gull. Like Great Black-backed, often halts its wingbeats to glide heavily for short distances on almost flat wings. In most regions it is found individually or in twos or threes, often in the company of Herring Gulls.

APPEARANCE: Alternate Adult: Clean white head and white body with a bright yellow bill. The mantle is pale gray, noticeably paler than in Herring Gull. The bases of the primaries are pale gray like the mantle but fade to pure white at the tips. **Basic Adult:** Like alternate but with variable brownish streaking on the head and neck. **First Cycle:** Juveniles are very pale and washed with pale tan on the head and body. The wing coverts are finely barred with pale gray or tan, and the flight feathers are whitish with faint gray vermiculations, strongest on the tail. Most birds quickly fade, becoming largely or entirely white by midwinter. The bill has a sharply defined black tip while the remainder is soft pink. **Second Cycle:** Like first cycle but often has a messier appearance. Very white overall with irregular gray mottling on the body. Usually does not gain much adult gray in the back until late in the second cycle. The eyes are dull yellow but often look dark at a distance. **Third Cycle:** Like adult but with white smudges on the upperwing coverts, completely white primaries, and black smudges near the tip of the bill. **Distant:** The clean white wingtips and extremely pale gray mantle of adult tend to be obvious, but beware that the black wingtips of pale-mantled gulls can sometimes disappear against dark backgrounds, making them look white-winged. First-cycle birds usually appear pure white but may be pale cream-colored early in the winter.

SIMILAR SPECIES: Iceland Gull (*kumlieni*): Wingbeat and structure are often the best way to separate these two species, as both tend to look white or whitish at a distance. Iceland is substantially smaller than Glaucous Gull with narrower, more pointed wings and significantly faster, snappier wingbeats. It has a small head and shorter neck and bill, so there is less head projection in front of the wings. Glaucous never shows noticeable amounts of dark pigment on the outer primaries as many "Kumlien's" Gulls do. Adult "Kumlien's" also has a slightly darker mantle than adult Glaucous. For much of the first cycle, "Kumlien's" has an all-black bill, and when the bill is bicolored it differs from that of first- and second-cycle Glaucous Gulls in having a more extensive dark tip, about one-third to one-half of the bill.

FIRST CYCLE (L) AND BASIC ADULT. ONTARIO, FEB. BRANDON HOLDEN.
- Large, bulky gull with very broad wings and a relatively short, blunt-tipped hand.
- Mantle color of adults is significantly paler than that of Herring Gull; at a distance Glaucous Gulls of all ages appear to have entirely white wings.
- Both first- and second-cycle birds have a pink-based bill with a sharply defined black tip.

NEWFOUNDLAND, FEB.
BRANDON HOLDEN.

- Glaucous is a bird of the far north, the dominant large gull over much of the Arctic and subarctic. Adults rarely venture very far south once they have begun breeding. The vast majority of Glaucous Gulls observed in the Lower 48 are first- and second-cycle birds.
- Note the powerful build and heavy bill of these birds.

FIRST CYCLE. INDIANA, DEC.
KEN BEHRENS.

- There are no solid field marks separating Glaucous from Iceland Gull at a distance, so identifications must be based on wing shape and flight style. Fortunately, the broad wings are noticeable, and the slow, heavy wingbeats give a powerful but lethargic impression distinctly different from that given by the more agile Iceland Gull.

FIRST CYCLE WITH FIRST-CYCLE HERRING GULL (R). MARYLAND, FEB. CAMERON COX.

- Obviously larger than Herring Gull but usually does not appear to dwarf it as does Great Black-backed Gull.
- This is a dark first-cycle Glaucous. Most individuals quickly fade to whitish.

SECOND CYCLE. ALASKA, JUNE. CAMERON COX.

- Heavy chest and long, heavy bill help separate Glaucous from Iceland Gull at a distance.
- Mottled, uneven appearance is typical of the second cycle.

LESSER BLACK-BACKED GULL
Larus fuscus
DIMENSIONS
L: 21 in.; WS: 54 in.; WT: 1.8 lb.

SPRING ARRIVAL

Greenland: Apr.

FALL ARRIVAL

NJ: early Sept.; s. ON: mid-Sept.; TX: mid-Sept.

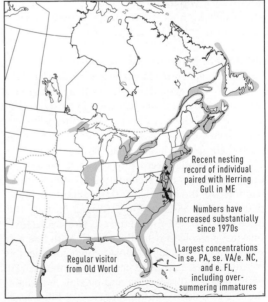

Recent nesting record of individual paired with Herring Gull in ME

Numbers have increased substantially since 1970s

Largest concentrations in se. PA, se. VA/e. NC, and e. FL, including over-summering immatures

Regular visitor from Old World

This Old World visitor was first documented in the U.S. in 1934 and has dramatically increased since the early 1980s. It is now regular over much of the continent, particularly in coastal areas and on the Great Lakes, and occurs regularly in the interior as well. Eastern Pennsylvania and northeastern Florida host notable concentrations; groups of several hundred sometimes occur at both locations. There is one confirmed breeding record in eastern North America outside Greenland: a single bird paired with a Herring Gull for several years on Ap-pledore Island in southern Maine. Hybrids with Herring Gulls are increasing, creating a new gull identification challenge. It is unknown whether these are hybrids with North American Herring Gulls occurring at undiscovered locations or with European Herring Gulls. This taxon forms a complicated complex in the Old World, with several subspecies described and discussion about whether some of them are distinct species. Although there have been some in North America that pertained to another subspecies, *intermedius* which has a noticeably darker-mantled, approaching the color of Great Black-backed Gull, the overwhelming majority of New World birds are of the *graelsii* subspecies, so it is that subspecies we treat in this account.

SIZE: Slightly smaller than Herring Gull. Distinctly smaller than Great Black-backed Gull. Distinctly larger than Ring-billed Gull. Only slightly larger than Caspian Tern.

STRUCTURE: Much like Herring Gull but slimmer overall with a smaller head. The wings are longer and narrower than in Herring with a slender, sharply pointed hand. The body is almost evenly slim with a slightly rounded belly. Slimmer than Herring Gull and not as heavy in the chest as Great Black-backed Gull.

FLIGHT AND FLOCKING: Flies with an easy, controlled grace that is unusual in a large gull. Wingbeats are slightly faster and snappier than Herring Gull's and clearly faster than Great Black-backed's. In strong winds employs a dynamic soar style, rising quickly and easily in moderate arcs, occasionally mixing in a few quick wingbeats as it glides down. Migrants are usually seen as singles or mixed with Herring Gulls low over the water.

APPEARANCE (*GRAELSII*): Alternate Adult: Clean white head and body with a bright yellow bill and legs. The mantle is slaty gray, dark enough to appear almost black in poor light but pale enough to show clear contrast with the black area on the outer primaries when seen well. There is a large mirror on P10 and about half of birds have a small white mirror on P9. The dark mantle bleeds through to the underside of the primaries and secondaries, creating a dusky band across the underwing. **Basic Adult:** Like alternate but with variable gray streaking on the head, often concentrated around the eye. **First Cycle:** Juveniles have a cold gray head and body with fine pale streaking and speckling. Most lighten considerably by midwinter, becoming largely pale underneath with coarse gray streaking and barring, but maintain a very cold overall appearance. The bill is black throughout the first cycle. The upperwings are very dark with fine gray barring in the secondary coverts and a blackish hand; they exhibit a dark greater covert bar in addition to the dark secondary bar but lack a pale inner primary window. The underwing is quite dark: dusky gray with faint pale barring. The tail has a broad black band. The whitish rump, which is flecked with black, contrasts strongly with both the black tail band and the back. **Second Cycle:** The head and body are largely white with variable brownish smudging and streaking. The bill is black with a small pale tip. Some begin to develop some yellow on the bill during the second cycle. Most gain at least some slaty gray adultlike back feathers, whereas some attain a fully adult gray back. The upperwing is fairly uniformly dark with some gray flecking and barring in the secondary coverts and a very blackish hand. Likewise, the underwings are fairly uniformly dark and contrast with the whitish belly. Most birds have a largely black tail with variable white flecking, but some have much more white on the tail with a broken, black tail band. During the second prealternate molt, late in the second cycle, they may acquire additional adult gray in the secondary coverts and whiter body plumage. **Third Cycle:** Like adult but with variable brownish smudging in the upperwing coverts, a reduced or absent white mirror on P10, brownish blotches on the body and underwing, more streaking on the head, and a variable jagged black tail band. Lesser Black-backed Gulls develop slowly and are extremely variable, and there is significant overlap between second- and third-cycle birds. **Distant:** Adults look very dark above. The contrast between the black outer primaries and the rest of the mantle is often difficult to see, and no white mirrors are visible. The thin white trailing edge to the wing may be visible. The dusky band on the underside of the primaries and secondaries contrasts modestly with the white underwing coverts. On first-cycle birds, the most noticeable features are the cold, dark gray or whitish head and body, uniformly dark wings, and pale rump.

SIMILAR SPECIES: Great Black-backed Gull: Much larger and heavier with broader and blunter wings. Wingbeats are slower, and its massive bulk is revealed by every movement. Adult has a much blacker mantle than Lesser Black-backed Gull and significantly larger white mirrors in the outer primaries. First-cycle birds are paler and more mottled than first-cycle Lesser Black-backed, particularly on the upper surface of the wings. **Herring Gull:** Slightly larger and heavier, with broader wings and a shorter, blunter hand. From the second cycle on, has a distinctly paler back than Lesser Black-backed. First-cycle birds are uniformly brown, often appearing fairly warm-toned, with a pale inner primary window, whereas first-cycle Lesser Black-backed Gulls have uniformly dark wings that contrast with a cold gray body. **California Gull:** Slightly smaller and slimmer with a perfectly flat belly. Adult has a paler mantle and larger white mirrors on the outer primaries than Lesser Black-backed.

First-cycle birds have a bicolored bill with an extensive pink base. Their tail is almost completely dark brown and contrasts only modestly with their paler rump, whereas first-cycle Lesser Black-backed have a broad blackish tail band that contrasts sharply with a whitish rump. First-cycle Californias tend to be more brownish overall, whereas first-cycle Lesser Black-backed are whitish or cold gray. Second-cycle birds have more contrasting wings with paler underwings than shown by Lesser Black-backed.

FIRST CYCLE. MARYLAND, FEB. CAMERON COX.

- Sleek, large gull with slender body and long, distinctly pointed wings.
- Overall color in first cycle is a very cold gray.
- Underwing is uniformly dark, lacking noticeable pale inner primary windows.
- This individual has a darker body than most first-cycle Lesser Black-backed and gives a fairly uniform impression, like a first-cycle Herring Gull, but the plumage has a colder appearance and the body has a crisp, coarse pattern of mottling, whereas first-cycle Herring Gull is more evenly washed with brown.

WITH "EUROPEAN" HERRING GULLS AND COMMON SHELDUCKS. WALES, MAR. KEN BEHRENS.

- The dark mantle bleeding through to the underwing creates an obvious dusky band.
- The bright yellow legs of adults may be visible at moderate distance under optimal light conditions.
- Wings appear slightly longer, slimmer, and more pointed than those of Herring Gull.

FIRST CYCLE WITH FIRST-CYCLE HERRING GULL (BEHIND). NORTH CAROLINA, FEB. KEN BEHRENS.

- Evenly dark underwings contrasting with a paler body are typical of first-cycle Lesser Black-backed. First-cycle Herring may have a contrasting pale head, but the body is uniformly brown.
- Lesser Black-backed's long hand tapers to a distinct point.

BASIC ADULT WITH FIRST-CYCLE GREAT BLACK-BACKED GULL (L). NORTH CAROLINA, FEB. KEN BEHRENS.

- Lesser Black-backed is dwarfed by the massive and broad-winged Great Black-backed.
- Adult shows discernible contrast between the gray mantle and black primary tips, unlike adult Great Black-backed.

ALTERNATE ADULT. WALES, MAR. KEN BEHRENS.

- Small head, slim bill, and slender body are distinctly different from the bulky and powerfully built Great Black-backed Gull.
- Outer primaries may have one or two white mirrors, but the mirrors are always small and usually not visible at a distance, unlike the large, conspicuous white mirrors shown by Great Black-backed.

FIRST CYCLE WITH THREE FIRST-CYCLE GREAT BLACK-BACKED GULLS. NEWFOUNDLAND, SEPT. BRUCE MACTAVISH.

- First- and second-cycle birds are similar to immature Great Black-backed in overall appearance but tend to have a grayer body and darker wings, which are very angular and are slimmer and more pointed than those of Great Black-backed.
- *Which bird is the Lesser Black-backed Gull?*

GREAT BLACK-BACKED GULL
Larus marinus
DIMENSIONS
L: 30 in.; WS: 65 in.; WT: 3.6 lb.

SPRING ARRIVAL

QC: early Apr.

FALL ARRIVAL

Lake Erie: late Aug.; GA: late Aug.;
IL: early Nov.

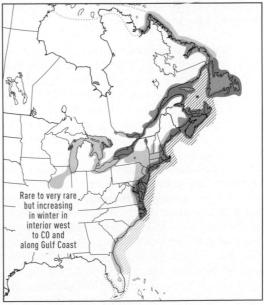

Rare to very rare but increasing in winter in interior west to CO and along Gulf Coast

This hulking gull is primarily a coastal species, rare inland except on the Great Lakes where modest numbers reside. Its aggressive nature and large size make it an effective predator. It raids waterbird nesting colonies, often with devastating effects, and regularly tries to drive migrant passerines into the water when presented with the opportunity. It also frequently bullies birds up to the size of Osprey and Bald Eagle into giving up their prey. In short, Great Black-backed Gull is a perfect, adaptable avian predator.

SIZE: The largest gull. Clearly larger than Herring Gull. Slightly larger than Glaucous Gull. Approaches Northern Gannet in body length.

STRUCTURE: Massive and powerful. Overall shape is typical of a large gull, but the tremendous size and bulk can cause an observer to reject the idea of a gull and substitute something larger, such as a gannet or pelican, while the ambitious subconscious may suggest an albatross! The bill is long and heavy, with a noticeably swollen tip. Sandwiched between the massive bill and a bulging chest, the head appears small, whereas the neck is long and thick at the base. The head tapers into the bill so that, at a distance, the front of the body has a wedge-shaped appearance. The long neck and relatively short tail make the wings appear to be set too far back on the body. The wings are exceptionally broad, the arm and hand are even, and in all but first-cycle birds, the wingtips are fairly blunt. First-cycle birds typically have a longer, more pointed hand and a smaller bill and are more likely to be mistaken for a Lesser Black-backed Gull but first-cycle birds have a long neck and broad-based wings like older birds.

FLIGHT AND FLOCKING: Typical flight is relaxed, with slow, shallow wingbeats that have a slightly arthritic quality. Frequently glides short distances on slightly bent wings. In strong wind may use a dynamic soar but appears slow and heavy, lacking the easy grace of Lesser Black-backed Gull. Its migratory behavior—singles and small flocks trickle along low to the water—allows it to slip by almost unnoticed. Like other gulls, it may be a mainly nocturnal migrant, though this has not yet been proven. Most often found in single-species flocks but will flock with other gulls, particularly Herring Gull.

APPEARANCE: Alternate Adult: Clean white head and body and a yellow bill with a large red gonydeal spot. The mantle is the darkest of any regularly occurring North American gull, almost black with only slight contrast with the black outer primaries. The mirror on P10 is often merged with the feather's white tip, creating an extensive white tip matched by few other gulls; there is also a large mirror on P9. The mantle bleeds through to the underside of the primaries and secondaries, creating a strong sooty band on the underwing. **Basic Adult:** Like alternate but with a slightly duller bill and dark streaking on the head and neck. The streaking is usually pale and sparse, invisible at a distance. **First Cycle:** Juveniles have a black bill and whitish head and body, though the head, breast, and flanks are variably marked with fine gray streaking and speckling. The upperwing coverts have a distinctive coarse gray-and-white checkered pattern. The hand is blackish with a faintly paler inner primary window and dark secondary bar sometimes fringed with white. The rump and base of the tail are white but extensively flecked with black, and the black tail band is broken up by white mottling, particularly on the outer tail feathers. **Second Cycle:** Like first cycle but with an irregular pink base and small pink tip to the bill, a more whitish body with sparser and blurrier gray markings, and some blackish feathers appearing on the back, particularly late in the cycle. **Third Cycle:** Quite variable. Most birds develop more slowly than Herring Gulls of the same age. The back and upperwing coverts are usually a blotchy mix of adultlike blackish feathers and mottled gray-brown feathers. The head and body are white with some streaking on the head and neck. Some show dusky patches along the sides of the breast and a variable black tail band. They often have a white mirror on P10. The bill is pink- or yellow-based with a black subterminal ring or black tip. Some are quite adultlike, but the mantle is several shades paler than that of adults. **Distant:** Adults look black above with a noticeably broad white trailing edge to the secondaries and white mirrors that are large enough to be visible much of the time. The sooty band on the underwing contrasts strongly with the white underwing coverts. First-cycle birds are cold pale gray overall with blackish outer primaries.

SIMILAR SPECIES: Herring Gull: In most cases the smaller size, slimmer wings, significantly weaker bill, and quicker wingbeat allow for immediate separation. From the second cycle on, the pale gray back and mantle of Herring Gull are the most definitive plumage trait. First-cycle Herring Gulls are darker than first-cycle Great Black-backed Gulls, being medium to dark brown overall, whereas first-cycle Great Black-backed are paler gray and cold-toned with a contrasting white rump and black tail band and a smaller inner primary window. After midwinter most first-cycle Herring Gulls show a pale head that contrasts with the dark body, whereas first-cycle Great Black-backed Gulls have an evenly gray head and body. **Lesser Black-backed Gull:** Significantly smaller with faster wingbeats and more agile flight. Has more balanced proportions, a much smaller bill, smaller head, shorter neck, slimmer wings, and a long, tapered hand with a pointed wingtip. Although adult Lesser Black-backed Gulls of the regularly occurring subspecies *graelsii* have a noticeably paler gray mantle than adult Great Black-backed Gulls and show contrast between the mantle and the black outer primaries, mantle color can be difficult to judge in flight and varies somewhat in both species so additional traits should be used in addition to mantle color. Adult Lesser Black-backed has smaller mirrors on the outer primaries than adult Great Black-backed. It also has heavier gray streaking on the head in winter. First-cycle birds are similar, but Lesser Black-backed typically has a darker upperwing with little to no inner primary window, broader and darker tail band, and heavier gray streaking on the body.

SECOND CYCLE (L) AND PROBABLE FOURTH CYCLE. NEW JERSEY, SEPT. CAMERON COX.

- Massive bird with a massive bill; it can be identified solely by size.
- Heavy chest accentuates the small head and long, tapered forehead, which gives a wedge-shaped appearance at a distance.

ALTERNATE ADULT. DELAWARE, JULY. KEN BEHRENS.

- Its formidable appearance starts with its formidable bill.
- Gull identification usually hinges on the examination of details such as the precise color of the eye, orbital ring, and bill. These details are rarely visible to a seawatcher, for whom an approach based on overall structure, overall color, and wingbeat is more effective.

WITH ALTERNATE ADULT BONAPARTE'S GULLS. ONTARIO, APR. KEN BEHRENS.

- Great Black-backed is the largest gull in the world, and the tremendous difference in size and structure between it and Bonaparte's Gull highlights the group's diversity.

FIRST CYCLE. NEW JERSEY, SEPT. CAMERON COX.
- First-cycle birds have a fairly pointed hand. In subsequent cycles the hand has a blunter tip but still appears very long.
- Compared with the huge bill and bulging chest, the head is quite small.

WITH HERRING GULL (R). MASSACHUSETTS, JULY. KEN BEHRENS.
- Great Black-backed often raises its head slightly, causing the chest to bulge and creating a distinctively awkward silhouette.
- Great Black-backed Gull appears two-toned, whereas Herring Gull appears uniformly dark brown.

SUBADULT (C) AND A FIRST- OR SECOND CYCLE (LOWER R) WITH HERRING GULLS. NORTH CAROLINA, FEB. KEN BEHRENS.
- The large white mirrors on P9 and P10 are clearly visible on adults, even at a distance.
- The blackish mantle bleeds though the wing, creating a distinct dark band on the underwing.

SECOND-CYCLE TYPE. WALES, APR. KEN BEHRENS.
• Aging Great Black-backeds is difficult, as they are slow to mature. This bird is probably in its second cycle but shows more black on the back than most second-cycle birds. Note that the wingtip is blunter than that of a first-cycle bird.

WITH THREE LESSER BLACK-BACKED GULLS AND TWO HERRING GULLS (PARTIALLY OUT OF FRAME). NORTH CAROLINA, FEB. KEN BEHRENS.
• Bright light can bleach out the differences in mantle color between Great Black-backed and Lesser Black-backed Gulls; structure and wingbeat can still separate the two.
• Notice the narrower wings, shorter neck, and shorter, weaker bill of the Lesser Black-backed.
• *What other separating characteristics can you see?*

FIRST CYCLE. SWEDEN, OCT. THOMAS SVANBERG.
• Has much paler wings than first-cycle Lesser Black-backed Gull, as well as a less distinct dark tail band.
• Compared with first-cycle Herring Gull, has a much whiter body, paler rump, and a colder, frostier appearance.

LAUGHING GULL
Larus atricilla
DIMENSIONS
L: 16.5 in.; WS: 40 in.; WT: 11 oz.

SPRING ARRIVAL

s. NJ: early Mar.; MA: mid-Apr.; ME: late Apr.

This handsome gull is a loquacious summer resident of coastal regions from New England through the Gulf Coast, retreating from the northern part of its range in winter. Laughing Gull is generally an early migrant in both spring and fall, though a few may linger in northern latitudes into December. It is normally restricted to coastal locations but is among the species most likely to be pushed inland by large storms, particularly tropical systems.

SIZE: Slightly smaller than Ring-billed Gull. Slightly larger than Franklin's Gull but often appears significantly larger. Slightly smaller than Royal Tern.

STRUCTURE: Long and lean. The body is slender, and the slim impression is enhanced by the long neck, sloping forehead, and long, slender bill. The wings are very long and pushed forward at the wrist with a long, tapered hand and sharply pointed wingtip. Overall quite angular and somewhat jaegerlike.

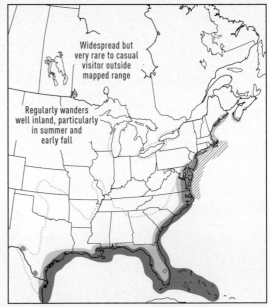

Widespread but very rare to casual visitor outside mapped range

Regularly wanders well inland, particularly in summer and early fall

FLIGHT AND FLOCKING: Wingbeats are powerful and fluid, starting from the inner portion of the wing and rolling out toward the tip. Shows an astounding variety of flight styles, which can lead observers to confuse it with a range of other species, including jaegers, shearwaters, and other gulls. Wingbeats may be very deep or quite shallow, depending on the wind and the bird's activity. May fly quickly and powerfully just above the waves or hover lazily overhead. In strong wind often uses an elegant dynamic soar, arcing up and down with ease. Migrants or birds commuting to roosts often fly in small flocks that may form ovals or tightly spaced lines. They may also trickle by singly or in pairs along a consistent flight path. After strong cold fronts, sometimes migrates in kettles, often mixed with other gulls and hugging coastlines.

APPEARANCE: Alternate Adult: The most striking feature is the complete blackish hood. The bill is dull red. The mantle and most of the wing are medium gray, with extensive black wingtips. The underparts and tail are white. The dark eye is set off by modest white eye crescents. **Basic Adult:** Most of the black hood is lost, though smudgy gray remnants of it are visible behind the eye, extending back toward the nape. The bill becomes black, and the eye crescents remain but are less obvious. **First Cycle:** Juveniles have a sandy brown back with a solid brown wash across the head and breast. By early fall the back is medium gray and the face and throat become paler. The nape, hindneck, and breast are still heavily washed with gray-brown, and the dark breast band hems in the white belly. The secondary coverts are mostly brownish gray, though some birds may already show the clean medium gray color of adults, whereas the hand and secondary bar are blackish. There is also a narrow but bright white trailing edge on the secondaries. The underwing is heavily washed with gray; the rump is clean white and contrasts sharply with the back and black tail. By spring some may look much like basic adults but with

brown patches in the secondary coverts and worn primaries. **Second Cycle:** Like adult but with more extensive black wingtips and with a heavy gray wash across the nape and sides of the breast. Often shows remnants of a black tail band. **Distant:** Adults look very dark in all but the best light. As it catches the light, the white tail will flash, eliminating any possibility of a jaeger. First-cycle birds are also quite dark, with a contrasting white rump.

SIMILAR SPECIES: Franklin's Gull: Has a shorter hand with rounded wingtips, a more rounded head, and a shorter bill. Holds its wings straight and has stiff wingbeats, unlike the powerful, rolling wingbeats and more angular wings of Laughing Gull. Adult Frankin's shows far less black on the wingtip and a subterminal white crescent across the outer primaries. First-cycle Franklin's has more black on the nape, forming a more distinct half-hood, and its underparts are clean white. Except during migration on the western Gulf Coast, Franklin's and Laughing Gulls are never common in the same location. **Ring-billed Gull:** Can be confused at long distance, particularly during migration when it often mixes with Laughing Gull. Both are medium-sized, but Ring-billed has a heavier body and broader-based wings. Its hand is shorter and its wingtips blunter than those of Laughing Gull. Additionally, its wingbeats are slower and more rigid than Laughing Gull's. Ring-billed has paler gray upperparts as an adult and shows large mirrors on the outer two primaries. First-cycle Ring-billed is also distinctly paler than first-cycle Laughing Gull, with large inner primary windows and pale underwings.

BASIC ADULT. FLORIDA, JAN. CAMERON COX.

- Medium-sized, slim-bodied gull with extremely long, slender wings and a long, drawn-out hand ending in a sharply pointed wingtip.
- Adults are sharply patterned, attractive gulls with extensive black undersides to the primaries.

FIRST CYCLE WITH SECOND-CYCLE RING-BILLED GULL (R). FLORIDA, JAN. CAMERON COX.

- Approaches Ring-billed Gull in both wing and body length but has a slimmer body, narrower wings, and faster wingbeats. Usually this would mean Laughing Gull would appear much smaller at a distance; however, Laughing Gull is also much darker than Ring-billed, and under many conditions this causes it to look larger than it actually is, increasing the potential for confusion with Ring-billed and occasionally with Lesser Black-backed.

ALTERNATE ADULT. NEW JERSEY, JULY. KEN BEHRENS.

- This bird is molting its inner primaries, changing the wing profile. Primary molt in gulls occurs slowly and affects the profile in different ways depending on which part of the wing is undergoing molt. Molt also affects the wingbeat.

ALTERNATE ADULTS. MASSACHUSETTS, JULY. KEN BEHRENS.

- Flocks frequently form long tight lines, and less frequently tight bunches of birds; they are more cohesive than flocks of large gulls without approaching the densely clumped, ternlike structure of Bonaparte's Gull flocks.

WITH BASIC ADULT RING-BILLED GULL (R). FLORIDA, JAN. CAMERON COX.
- The extensive black underside of the hand is noticeable in good light, even at a distance.
- The contrast between the black primary tips and medium-gray mantle is distinct in good light, but in poor light the mantle appears much darker and the contrast is difficult to see, causing Laughing Gull to look more like Lesser Black-backed Gull in coloration.

FIRST CYCLE. TEXAS, APR. KEN BEHRENS.
- First-alternate plumage, shown here, differs significantly from the dingy appearance shown by first-cycle Laughing Gulls during fall and winter.
- Wing bend is thrust forward and the long, pointed hand is distinctly angled back, creating an angular, almost jaegerlike wing profile.

ALTERNATE ADULT. MASSACHUSETTS, JULY. KEN BEHRENS.
- Attractive and distinctly patterned gull, particularly in alternate plumage.
- Larger and longer-winged than other hooded gulls in North America.

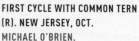

FIRST CYCLE WITH COMMON TERN (R). NEW JERSEY, OCT. MICHAEL O'BRIEN.

- Laughing Gulls frequently attempt to steal food from terns and other gulls.
- First cycle looks very dark at a distance, and when chasing other birds, can be mistaken for a jaeger. However, the attacks are not as direct as jaeger attacks, and Laughing Gulls lack the agility and power that are evident as jaegers attack prey.

WITH ADULT RING-BILLED GULL. TEXAS, APR. KEN BEHRENS.

- Fly in long, staggered lines, frequently with tighter spacing between individuals than in larger gulls, so flocks have a more cohesive appearance.
- At a distance, the long wings are the most noticeable aspect of structure; the slender body almost disappears.

ALTERNATE ADULTS. NORTH CAROLINA, JULY. KEN BEHRENS.

- Exceptionally long wings allow Laughing Gulls to adapt their flight style to the changeable conditions they encounter in their coastal environment. Their highly variable flight can create problems for seawatchers, particularly in poor light.

FIRST CYCLE. FLORIDA, JAN. CAMERON COX.

- The extensive gray wash on the body and underwing give first-cycle birds a dark and dingy appearance in fall and winter compared with the neat, very pale appearance of first-cycle Franklin's Gulls in fall.

FRANKLIN'S GULL
Larus pipixcan
DIMENSIONS
L: 14.5 in.; WS: 36 in.; WT: 10 oz.

SPRING ARRIVAL

IA: late Mar.; CO: early Apr.; MB: mid-Apr.

FALL ARRIVAL

CO: late July; MO: late Aug.;
w. Gulf Coast: early Oct.

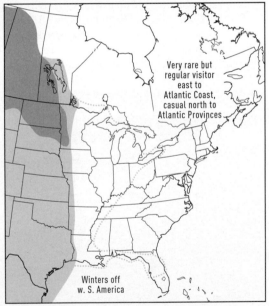

Very rare but regular visitor east to Atlantic Coast, casual north to Atlantic Provinces

Winters off w. S. America

Franklin's Gull can be described as a smaller, prettier Laughing Gull that has abandoned the coast to breed in interior prairies. It is a long-distance migrant that travels in large, densely packed flocks and often rises in kettles using thermals like some raptors. It winters along the coasts of Peru and Chile, though a few may linger in the Northern Hemisphere into December and sometimes later. This is the only gull, and one of the few bird species in the world, that has two complete molts per year.

SIZE: Slightly smaller than Laughing Gull. Slightly larger than Bonaparte's Gull.

STRUCTURE: Compact, with a short bill, rounded head, short and slightly pudgy body, and relatively short wings. The wings have fairly round tips and are held stiffly almost straight out from the body, completing a distinctive profile. Although the plumage resembles that of Laughing Gull, the structure is very different.

FLIGHT AND FLOCKING: Wingbeats are noticeably stiff, with all the motion coming from the shoulders while the rest of the wing is held rigidly. As it gains altitude, it groups its wingbeats into short, quick series vaguely reminiscent of *Accipiter*. During migration forms flocks that may grow to hundreds or even thousands of individuals. They rise in kettles to great heights before gliding on in a continuous stream, then repeating the process, taking advantage of thermals in the same manner of some raptors. Although other gulls may also form kettles in migration, no other species use thermals with the frequency or proficiency of Franklin's Gull; this is probably an energy-saving behavior, considering their very long migration. Vagrants in the East usually join groups of Laughing or Ring-billed Gulls.

APPEARANCE: **Alternate Adult:** Extremely pale, almost appearing to glow in bright conditions. Early in spring most individuals show a moderate to intense pink flush on the breast. The mantle is medium gray, slightly paler than in Laughing Gull, and has a slightly silvery sheen. The head has a complete dark hood set off by very strong white eye crescents that can be seen up to moderate distances. Has a small amount of black on the outer primaries, separated from the gray mantle by a narrow white crescent. **Basic Adult:** Like alternate, but the full hood is replaced with a partial dusky gray hood that extends from the eyes around the nape. The eye crescents are still obvious. Most birds lack the rosy pink flush. **First Cycle:** Juvenile has a largely white body and brown back and wing coverts that are replaced with medium-gray by early fall. The nape and breast are much cleaner than on first-cycle Laughing Gull,

and the partial dark hood is more extensive and more sharply defined. Unlike in first-cycle Laughing Gull, the underwings are clean white. The black tail band does not extend completely across the tail, leaving clean white edges. Prior to migrating north in spring it goes through an extensive molt, so that in its first spring it looks much like basic adult, though lacking the white subterminal wing crescent and having more black in the primaries. The outer primaries are usually not replaced and are old and worn. **Distant:** Adult looks surprisingly pale at a distance. Its subterminal white wingtip crescents glow, and the small black primary tips are often invisible, making this already fairly short-winged gull look even shorter-winged. First-cycle bird also looks fairly pale and clean, and the dark half-hood is often visible.

SIMILAR SPECIES: **Laughing Gull:** Larger and longer-winged, with sharply pointed wingtips and a leaner overall impression. Adult has far more black on the primaries and lacks the subterminal white wing crescent of adult Franklin's. First-cycle Laughing Gull is dingier than first-cycle Franklin's: washed with gray along the sides, across the breast, and around the base of the neck, with heavily mottled gray underwings. The partial hood tends to be less extensive and less sharply defined than in Franklin's, and the eye crescents are less noticeable.

ALTERNATE ADULTS. TEXAS, APR. BILL SCHMOKER.
• Medium-sized with a compact body shape and fairly short, blunt-tipped wings.
• Limited black in the primaries and odd white crescents create an unmistakable wing pattern.
• In spring, adults often sport a strong pink wash to the underparts.

FIRST CYCLE. FLORIDA, DEC. MICHAEL BROTHERS.
• Has very adultlike plumage by its first fall, unlike first-cycle Laughing Gull.
• White body and underwing and extensive, sharply defined black hood with strong white eye crescents give first cycle a neat, attractive appearance.

NORTH DAKOTA, MAY. CAMERON COX.
- Frequently migrate in well-defined kettles.
- When soaring, flocks appear extremely pale and often flash brightly as they rotate and catch the sun.
- The white wing crescents glow translucently, and the black wingtips are difficult to see.

FIRST CYCLE. FLORIDA, NOV. TOM DUNKERTON.
- The narrow black tail band is distinctly different from the all-dark tail of first-cycle Laughing Gull.
- Has pale inner primary windows, whereas first-cycle Laughing Gull has an all-dark hand.
- The half-hood tends to be very distinct.

BASIC ADULTS. TEXAS, NOV. KEVIN KARLSON.
- Rounded head and body are distinctly different from the leaner build of Laughing Gull.
- Extensive, sharply defined half-hood highlights the eye crescents.
- Black wingtips are far more restricted than in basic-plumaged Laughing Gull.

FRANKLIN'S GULL (L) WITH LAUGHING GULL (R). UTAH, JUNE. KEN BEHRENS (L); FLORIDA, MAY. CAMERON COX (R).
- The Laughing Gull appears lean and stretched out, whereas Franklin's looks compact and slightly pudgy.
- Franklin's Gulls look short-tailed.
- The difference in the pattern of the primaries is visible at great distances.

BONAPARTE'S GULL
Chroicocephalus philadelphia
DIMENSIONS
L: 13.5 in.; WS: 33 in.; WT: 7 oz.

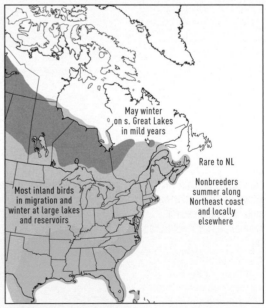

May winter on s. Great Lakes in mild years

Rare to NL

Nonbreeders summer along Northeast coast and locally elsewhere

Most inland birds in migration and winter at large lakes and reservoirs

SPRING ARRIVAL

Lake Erie: late Mar.; NE: early Apr.

FALL ARRIVAL

s. Great Lakes: late July/early Aug.;
NY: early Sept.; MO: early Oct.

Bonaparte's is the only regularly occurring small gull in most of eastern North America. In its flight style and behavior, it shares some similarities with terns. As a migrant and during the winter, it may gather on rivers and lakes in the interior, often in impressive numbers. The largest concentrations are found on the eastern Great Lakes, where flocks of thousands are regular. It is always worthwhile to sift through milling throngs of Bonaparte's for rarer species such as Little and Black-headed Gulls.

SIZE: Slightly larger than Forster's Tern. Significantly smaller than Black-legged Kittiwake.

STRUCTURE: Slender and delicate in build; decidedly ternlike in many respects. The tiny head and dainty bill swell into a short but relatively thick body. The wings are broad through the arm, but the hand tapers quickly to a sharply pointed wingtip. Even for a gull, it looks short-tailed.

FLIGHT AND FLOCKING: Flight is quite variable, but is generally agile and buoyant. Frequently makes sudden jerky movements, changes altitude, or dips down to pick food off the surface. The speed of the wingbeats can change suddenly, depending on the bird's current activity or flight mode. Typical flight style in migration is direct, a quick wingbeat with a strong, snappy downstroke. May also fly slowly with loose, languid wingbeats interspersed with quick pauses and short glides. When Bonaparte's is actively foraging, the wingbeats are very fast and frantic, similar to those of medium-sized terns, and it often hovers. It doesn't use the dynamic soar employed by many other gulls in high wind. Quite social; most migratory flocks number 10–45, but winter groups may grow much larger. Migrants often form long irregular lines low over the water or tight oval-shaped bunches with stragglers trailing out behind. Migrants over the interior may form looser, high-flying ovals much like those of medium-sized terns. Less frequently, migrates like other gulls in widely spaced singles or pairs.

APPEARANCE: Alternate Adult: Very pale overall, with a pale gray mantle, white underparts, and black hood. The outer primaries are white, forming a narrow wedge. This wedge is translucent in strong light and contrasts with the rest of the wing, particularly the narrow black trailing edge to the wing. **Basic Adult:** Lacks the black hood of alternate plumage but has a large dark spot behind the eye and an extensive light gray wash to the nape. **First Cycle:** Fresh juvenile is soft brown on the back and scapulars, with a small brown cap. The brown plumage is quickly lost, however, and by fall the back is clean pale gray, whereas the body and underwing are clean white. A mottled dark band crosses the arm;

the hand has the same white leading [edge as] adult but is broken up by black spots a[nd a] narrow black band forms the trailing e[dge of the] wing and the tail also sports a narrow bla[ck band]. There is an obvious dark spot behind the ey[e and] the bill is black. In spring, a poorly defined, [par-] tial black hood is acquired. **Distant:** Adults are e[x-] tremely pale overall, but even so, the white leading edge to the hand stands out sharply, flashing bright white and glowing translucently when struck by the sun. First-cycle birds also look quite pale; the dark bands and trailing edge of the wing do not stand out as strongly as might be expected. Flocks are often identified by the white flashes in the wings of adults, and once the identification of Bonaparte's Gull has been established, first-cycle birds in the flock can be recognized by their slightly darker, messier appearance.

SIMILAR SPECIES: Black-headed Gull: Larger overall, longer- and broader-winged, with slower wingbeats. Flies more like a "typical" gull. Adult has a large black patch on the underside of the primaries, restricting the white wedge on the underside to the outer few primaries. Adults also have a deep red bill and feet that are visible up to moderate distances. In winter also has a more whitish nape than adult Bonaparte's. First-cycle Black-headed has a broader black trailing edge to the wing and a more distinct white wedge on the hand. **Little Gull:** Much smaller, with a more compact, pudgy appearance and disproportionally broad wings compared with Bonaparte's. Flight is more erratic than Bonaparte's and often includes distinctive deep, stiff, batlike wingbeats. Adult has obvious dark underwings. First-cycle bird has a bold, extensively black upperwing pattern and dark cap.

BASIC ADULT. NEW JERSEY, DEC. KEN BEHRENS.

- Small ternlike gull with a small head, slender bill, and sharply pointed wings.
- Typical wingbeat of a migrating Bonaparte's is quick and shallow with a sharp, powerful downstroke and looser upstroke.
- Very pale, and distant birds flash much more brightly when struck by the sun than any of the large gulls do.

TEXAS, APR. KEVIN KARLSON.

- The white leading edge to the primaries on adults stands out sharply at a distance. Although this mark is more subdued on first-cycle birds, any adults in a flock can help suggest the identity of associated first-cycle birds based on similar size and wing action.

BASIC ADULTS. NEW JERSEY, FEB. CAMERON COX.

- Small and agile. They often hover for extended periods when foraging.
- Wings are fairly broad-based, and both the body and tail appear short.
- Note extensive gray wash on the nape.

(RIGHT) FIRST CYCLE. FLORIDA, JAN. TOM DUNKERTON.

- The dark trailing wing edge is narrower and better defined than that of first-cycle Black-headed Gull.

ALTERNATE ADULTS WITH LITTLE GULLS, SABINE'S GULLS, AND ARCTIC TERNS. MANITOBA, JUNE. TOM JOHNSON.

- Carefully checking large flocks of Bonaparte's Gulls is often rewarding, as scarcer small gulls may be found within them.
- *How many Sabine's and Little Gulls are in this flock?*

WITH BASIC ADULT LAUGHING GULL (C) AND FORSTER'S TERN (R). TEXAS, JAN. CAMERON COX.
- Bonaparte's will plunge into the water headfirst after food, unlike larger gulls, and will also pluck food items from the surface while still in flight.
- Forster's Tern is superficially similar but is smaller and slimmer, with faster wingbeats.

FIRST CYCLE (JUVENILE). INDIANA, AUG. PETE GRUBE.
- The brown markings on the back, nape, and crown are lost by late fall.
- First-cycle Black-headed Gull shows more white in the outer primaries.

BONAPARTE'S GULLS. MICHIGAN, MAY. KEN BEHRENS.
- In the interior, migrating flocks form ovals or messy wedges and fly much higher than they do along the Atlantic Coast.

BASIC ADULTS. NEW JERSEY, NOV. TONY LEUKERING.
- Typical flock formation for migrating Bonaparte's on the coast or Great Lakes.
- The only gull regularly seen in such tightly bunched flocks in eastern North America.

BLACK-HEADED GULL
Chroicocephalus ridibundus
DIMENSIONS
L: 16 in.; WS: 40 in.; WT: 9 oz.

SPRING ARRIVAL

(vagrants): MD: early Mar.; NY: early Mar.

FALL ARRIVAL

(vagrants): ME: early Sept.; NJ: early Sept.

This Old World species is slightly larger than Bonaparte's Gull but very similar to it in most respects. It is a vagrant to North America, found most frequently in the Atlantic Provinces, Great Lakes, and New England, but has the potential to show up anywhere.

SIZE: Clearly larger than Bonaparte's Gull. Slightly smaller than Laughing Gull.

STRUCTURE: Similar to Bonaparte's Gull, but the wings are longer and broader. In particular, the hand is broader and does not taper down as quickly, displaying a shape more like that of Ring-billed Gull. In flight appears closer in size to Ring-billed than to Bonaparte's. The bill is longer and heavier than that of Bonaparte's, and the head does not ap-

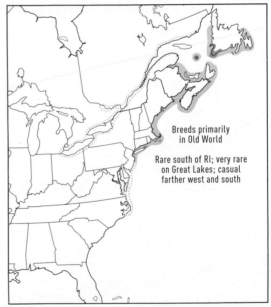

Breeds primarily in Old World

Rare south of RI; very rare on Great Lakes; casual farther west and south

pear as conspicuously small in comparison with the body as in Bonaparte's.

FLIGHT AND FLOCKING: Wingbeats are slightly slower and more powerful than those of Bonaparte's wingbeats, making Black-headed appear to fly more like a "normal" gull than the slim-winged and ternlike Bonaparte's does. In North America usually found in flocks of Bonaparte's, though it occasionally also mixes with Ring-billed Gull. In most cases, observations of Black-headed Gull will be of a single individual, but pairs and small flocks can be found together in Atlantic Canada and coastal New England.

APPEARANCE: Alternate Adult: Like Bonaparte's Gull but with a brownish rather than black hood, bill and feet strikingly red, and the underside of the middle primaries being black, which is usually the best identification trait. Tends to acquire the dark hood earlier in the spring than Bonaparte's. **Basic Adult:** Like Bonaparte's, but the dark spot behind the eye tends to be smaller and the gray wash across the nape is much lighter, causing the nape to look whitish. The red on bill and feet can be obvious. The black underside on the middle primaries contrasting with the white wedge on the outer primaries remains distinctive. **First Cycle:** Juvenile is extensively washed with brown across the back and scapulars, but this is quickly replaced with pale gray. The wing pattern is much like that of first-cycle Bonaparte's Gull, but the dark trailing edge of the wing is much broader and the white along the leading edge of the primaries is more extensive because the primary coverts are entirely white, unlike the mottled coverts of Bonaparte's. The underside of the primaries is dusky gray. In spring acquires a partial dark hood. The base of the bill is pale orange, but this is difficult to see. **Distant:** Adults are extremely pale, slightly paler than Bonaparte's Gull. They have a white wedge on the wing like Bonaparte's, but it contrasts less and is not as translucent. The dark patch on the underside of the primaries is still the best distinguishing feature, but it is difficult to discern. First-cycle birds are similar to Bonaparte's, but the broader dark trailing edge and additional white along the leading edge of the wing create a stronger wing pattern that is obvious at greater distances.

SIMILAR SPECIES: Bonaparte's Gull: Noticeably smaller with faster, shallower wingbeats. Adult lacks the large black patch on the underside of the primaries shown by adult Black-headed. The bill is black and the feet are pink, whereas both are deep red in Black-headed. First-cycle Bonaparte's has a narrower dark trailing edge to the wing and less white along the leading edge of the hand. The white underwing of Bonaparte's is quite different from that of Black-headed, which always shows a contrastingly dark underside to the primaries, which vary from dusky gray on a first cycle to blackish on an adult.

BASIC ADULT WITH BASIC ADULT BONAPARTE'S GULL (BOTTOM). NEW JERSEY, FEB. MICHAEL O'BRIEN.
- The black underside of the primaries is the most reliable trait for separating Black-headed from Bonaparte's in flight, but the bright red feet are often visible as well.
- Black-headed has a much whiter hindneck than Bonaparte's in winter.
- At a distance the deep red bill of Black-headed appears black.

FIRST CYCLE. WALES, MAR. KEN BEHRENS.
- Has a broader dark trailing edge to the wing and shows more white along the leading edge of the hand than first-cycle Bonaparte's.
- Compared with Bonaparte's, Black-headed Gull has longer, broader wings; a larger head; and a longer neck.

TURKEY, FEB. KEN BEHRENS.
- Flock formation is that of a small gull, but birds appear closer to Ring-billeds than to Bonaparte's in size.
- The broad, dark trailing edge to the wing on first-cycle Black-headed Gull is evident at long distances.

ALTERNATE ADULT. WALES, MAR. KEN BEHRENS.
- Actually has a dark brown hood that develops earlier in the spring than the black hood of Bonaparte's Gull. Also note the broad wings.

ALTERNATE ADULT. SWEDEN, APR. KEN BEHRENS.
- In silhouette, similar to Bonaparte's but has noticeably longer and broader wings and a longer, heavier bill.

BASIC ADULT WITH BASIC ADULT BONAPARTE'S GULL (L). NEW JERSEY, FEB. CAMERON COX.
- Black-headed has slower wingbeats than Bonaparte's and appears steadier in flight, lacking the jerky twists and abrupt changes that characterize the flight of Bonaparte's.
- The bright red feet can be seen on Black-headeds flying directly away.

LITTLE GULL
Hydrocoloeus minutus
DIMENSIONS
L: 11 in.; WS: 24 in.; WT: 4.2 oz.

SPRING ARRIVAL

NJ: late Feb.; s. Great Lakes: late Apr.;

St. Lawrence River: mid-May;

Hudson Bay: early June

This well-named species is the smallest gull in the world. It is primarily an Old World species but breeds in small numbers in North America as well. Most Little Gulls in North America are found in the company of Bonaparte's Gull so it is a good idea to carefully search wintering groups of Bonaparte's for Little Gulls.

SIZE: The smallest gull. Slightly larger than Black Tern. Clearly smaller than Bonaparte's Gull and Common Tern.

STRUCTURE: Stocky, with a large head and short tail. The wings are broad and, after the first cycle, distinctly rounded. First-cycle birds still have broad

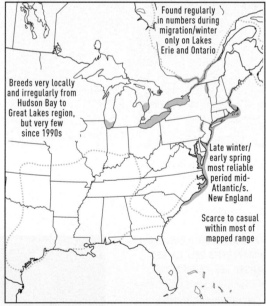

Found regularly in numbers during migration/winter only on Lakes Erie and Ontario

Breeds very locally and irregularly from Hudson Bay to Great Lakes region, but very few since 1990s

Late winter/ early spring most reliable period mid-Atlantic/s. New England

Scarce to casual within most of mapped range

wings, but the wingtips are more pointed, and consequently they appear to have a longer hand.

FLIGHT AND FLOCKING: Flight is buoyant, bounding, and erratic, with quick, somewhat stiff wingbeats. Normal flight is often punctuated by periods of foraging in which a bird courses back and forth on distinctive, deep, batlike wingbeats. In North America sightings are usually of single individuals in the company of Bonaparte's Gulls, though small flocks do occur. During migration, single individuals unaccompanied by Bonaparte's occur at coastal locations.

APPEARANCE: Alternate Adult: White body and very pale gray mantle set off the black hood. The underwings are almost entirely blackish and contrast sharply with the narrow bright white trailing edge of the wing that extends all the way to the wingtips. **Basic Adult:** Lacks the black hood but has a dusky cap and a dark spot behind the eye. The large, dark eye is more noticeable than in alternate, and clearly larger than the eye of Bonaparte's Gull. **First Cycle:** Full juveniles are fairly rare in the U.S. and Canada but are striking: almost entirely black above with a strongly contrasting white base to the tail. The dark back and scapulars are replaced early in the fall with pale gray, but the dark cap, broad diagonal dark bar across the inner part of the wing, and almost entirely black hand remain. In spring some attain a partial dark hood. **Second Cycle:** Like adult, but the dark underwing is often less extensive and dusky gray rather than blackish and there are small black spots on the tops of the outer primaries. **Distant:** In adults the distinctive dark underwings are unmistakable. In first-cycle birds the bold black bars across the wings are obvious whereas the pale triangle on the trailing edge is dull, with poorly defined borders.

SIMILAR SPECIES: Bonaparte's Gull: Larger, slightly leaner, and longer-winged. Adult has more pointed wings and lacks the dark underwing of Little Gull. First-cycle bird has a largely pale rather than largely dark upperwing pattern. **Ross's Gull:** Clearly larger, with angular, pointed wings and a long tail. Adult has a paler underwing than most adult Little Gulls. Immature Little Gulls with paler underwings are more similar, but adult Ross's has a broader white trailing edge to the wing that does not extend all the way up the primaries. First-cycle birds are distinguished from first-cycle Little Gull by the bolder Sabine's Gull–like triangular pale patch on their upperwing, lack of a dark cap, and dusky gray underwing.

BASIC ADULTS. SWEDEN, JAN. LASSE OLSSON.
- The smallest gull in the world, and adults have a very distinctive structure and plumage.
- Blunt-tipped, paddle-shaped wings of adults are unique. First-cycle birds have sharper wingtips.
- The main plumage identification trait for adults at a distance is the striking black underwing.
- Secondarily, the white trailing edge to the wing that wraps all the way around the tip of the wing is also unique.

BASIC ADULT WITH BASIC ADULT BONAPARTE'S GULL (R). NORTH CAROLINA, FEB. KEN BEHRENS.
- Smaller than Bonaparte's but has a much stockier build.
- Underwing color varies from almost pure black to medium gray, but at a distance shadowing usually makes it appear black.

ALTERNATE ADULT. SWEDEN, JULY. TOMMY HOLMGREN.
- The white trailing edge glows brightly when backlit and sets off the dark underwing.
- Flight is generally fluttery and erratic with quick wingbeats. At times flies with deep, stiff, bounding wingbeats that recall the flight of a giant butterfly!

SECOND CYCLE WITH BASIC ADULT BONAPARTE'S GULL (L). NEW YORK, APR. TOM JOHNSON.
- Second-cycle Little Gulls often have black markings on the outer primaries and primary coverts.
- Little Gulls are really small!

FIRST CYCLE. ONTARIO, NOV. BRANDON HOLDEN.
- Wing pattern can be confused with that of Sabine's Gull at long distances but is not as sharply defined. Sabine's is also much bigger.
- The faint, dark secondary band is surprisingly evident at moderate distances.

ROSS'S GULL
Rhodostethia rosea
DIMENSIONS
L: 13.5 in.; WS: 33 in.; WT: 6 oz.

SPRING ARRIVAL

Hudson Bay: early June

Ross's is not *a* gull, it is *the* gull; more legend than actual being! It breeds primarily in northeast Siberia, though a tiny disjunct population near Churchill, Manitoba, is famous among North American birders. Ross's migrates north into the Arctic Ocean in fall and is thought to spend the winter feeding along the edges of the pack ice, though much is still unknown about its wintering habits. The first record in the Lower 48, in Newburyport, Massachusetts, during the winter of 1974–1975, caused a sensation, but more recently one or more Ross's Gulls have been found outside the Arctic regions of North America almost annually.

SIZE: Clearly larger than Little Gull. About the same size as Bonaparte's Gull or Sabine's Gull but often appears slightly smaller than either.

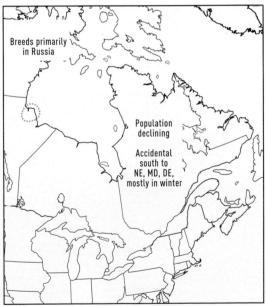

Breeds primarily in Russia

Population declining

Accidental south to NE, MD, DE, mostly in winter

STRUCTURE: Body has a compact, slightly chubby appearance with a large, rounded head tipped with a tiny bill. The unique long, wedge-shaped tail gives the body an attenuated appearance. An angular impression is imparted by the slender, pointed wings that are thrust forward sharply at the wing bend.

FLIGHT AND FLOCKING: Flight is buoyant and agile with quick wingbeats that, unlike those of Bonaparte's Gull, are usually quite deep. The upstroke is loose, but the downstroke is crisp and emphatic, giving the flight a more powerful appearance than that of Bonaparte's. Like Bonaparte's, Ross's may dip suddenly to pick food from the surface of the water at any moment. Unlike Bonaparte's or Little Gull, in strong winds it arcs high above the water on set wings in a dynamic soaring flight style; among gulls only Black-legged Kittiwake is more proficient at this manner of flight. Vagrants are often seen singly or with flocks of Bonaparte's Gulls.

APPEARANCE: Alternate Adult: Very pale, with the head and body washed with a pink flush. A narrow black ring encircles the head from the throat around the nape. The upperwing is very pale gray with a broad white trailing edge and a very narrow black leading edge to the hand. The underwing is dusky gray, appearing quite dark much of the time, with a sharply contrasting white trailing edge. **Basic Adult:** Like alternate, but the pink flush is reduced or absent and the black neck ring is lost, though traces may still be visible, particularly just behind the eye. A dusky area develops around the large dark eye, accentuating its large size even further. A pale gray wash on the hindneck that wraps around to the breast creates contrast with the clean white head. **First Cycle:** Juvenile is rarely seen but is heavily washed with brown across the crown, neck, sides of the breast, and entire back. The face is mostly white, with a dark patch around the eye and another behind the ear coverts. Early in fall the brown juvenile plumage is replaced with pale gray, and the amount of dark on the face is reduced. Throughout the first cycle, the wing pattern remains the same. There is a broad black band that extends diagonally across the arm to the wing bend and continues down the leading edge of the hand. The trailing edge of the wing displays a large white triangle. The underwing is pale dusky gray with a bold white trailing edge. The central tail feathers are tipped in black. During the prealternate molt, late in the first cycle, acquires a body plumage that looks much like that of alternate adult, complete with the pink flush and narrow black neck ring. The wings, however, maintain their bold black band and white triangle. **Distant:** Adults are extremely pale overall. The dusky gray underwing with a broad, bright white trailing edge remains distinctive. First-cycle birds look like first-cycle Little Gulls but have a crisper, cleaner upperwing pattern and dusky underwings with a broad and sharply contrasting white trailing edge.

SIMILAR SPECIES: Little Gull: Distinctly smaller and shorter-tailed. A basic adult with paler underwings can be separated from basic adult Ross's Gull by its narrower white trailing edge to the wing, which extends all the way around the tip of the rounded wingtip. In winter, first cycle has a wing pattern somewhat similar to that of first-cycle Ross's, but the pale triangle on the trailing edge of the wing is not as bright or as clearly defined and there is often a faint, dark secondary bar. The underwing of Little Gull lacks the dusky wash of Ross's, and it has a small black cap.

BASIC ADULT. CALIFORNIA, NOV. BRAD SCHRAM.
- Has a stocky body, long and angular wings, and a long, wedge-shaped tail.
- In basic plumage the crown and neck are broadly washed with gray, and traces of the black neck ring of alternate plumage may remain.
- Underwing is smoky gray with a broad white trailing edge.
- Dark smudges around the eye in basic plumage emphasize the large black eye.

(RIGHT) ALTERNATE ADULT. NUNAVAT, JUNE. MARK MAFTEI.

BASIC ADULT. ALASKA, OCT. JOHN PUSCHOCK.
- Hand is long and sharply pointed.
- The white trailing edge of the wing contrasts sharply with the gray underwing and can be seen at long distances.
- Note the tiny bill and steep forehead.

FIRST CYCLES. ALASKA, OCT. DECLAN TROY.
- The bold white triangle on the wings is not as distinct as that of Sabine's Gull, but is paler and more sharply defined than that of first-cycle Little Gull and also lacks that species' dark secondary bar.
- The elongated tip of the tail is black, but first-cycle Ross's Gull lacks a complete black tail band.

BASIC ADULTS WITH FIRST-CYCLE IVORY GULL (C). ALASKA, OCT. MARK MAFTEI.
- The pink wash for which this beautiful gull is known varies among individuals; some are intensely pink, others have only a light wash. The perception of the pink flush can be influenced by light conditions, being washed out and difficult to see in bright sunlight but obvious in cloudy conditions.

IVORY GULL
Pagophila eburnea
DIMENSIONS
L: 17 in.; WS: 37 in.; WT: 1.4 lb.

SPRING ARRIVAL

n. Greenland: early June

FALL ARRIVAL

e. Greenland: early Sept.; Baffin Bay: mid-Oct.

Ivory Gull is one of the most mythical and sought-after birds in North America. Nesting in a few remote areas of the high Arctic, it spends most of its life in the vicinity of the Arctic icepack. A few show up in the subarctic regions of North America during a typical winter, and in some recent years there have been invasions of dozens or even hundreds in the Atlantic Provinces and smaller numbers in the northeastern U.S.

SIZE: Significantly larger than Forster's Tern. Slightly smaller than Laughing Gull. Distinctly smaller than Iceland Gull.

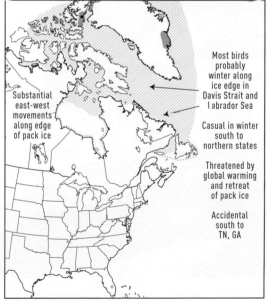

Most birds probably winter along ice edge in Davis Strait and Labrador Sea

Substantial east-west movements along edge of pack ice

Casual in winter south to northern states

Threatened by global warming and retreat of pack ice

Accidental south to TN, GA

STRUCTURE: Compact and deep-chested, with a short, heavy body. The head is small and appears wedge-shaped in flight, the bill is short and pointed, and the tail is short and slightly rounded. The wings are broad-based, with a long and sharply pointed hand. At times looks very similar to a Rock Pigeon, and sometimes lets its legs dangle.

FLIGHT AND FLOCKING: Flight is powerful and direct with quick, somewhat stiff wingbeats. Appears more stable than other small gulls and glides easily on high-arched wings. Away from the high Arctic usually found singly and does not associate closely with other gulls.

APPEARANCE: Adult: Very bright white broken only by the large black eye and gray-based bill tipped with dull yellow. **First Cycle:** Still very white but with black tips to the wings, tail feathers, and wing coverts, and a dark face. The extent of these dark markings is variable. Some individuals are more heavily marked, though the black tips wear significantly on first-cycle birds so that late in the first cycle they are paler than when fresh. **Distant:** Adults

are pure shining white. First-cycle birds are also bright white, but dark smudges may be visible.

SIMILAR SPECIES: Iceland Gull: Much larger and bulkier, with a heavier bill and blunter wingtips. Adult is very pale but has a pale gray mantle rather than the pure white of Ivory Gull. Adult Iceland also has a bright yellow bill, yellow eyes, and often has gray bands on the outer primaries. Subadult differs from subadult Ivory Gull in many of the same ways that the adults differ, but it also has dark markings on the body, wings, and tail. The pale overall color of a first-cycle Iceland Gull covered in coarse gray or brown markings is distinctly different from the bright white color and neat lines of black dots that typify a first-cycle Ivory Gull. However, at a distance or when heavily worn, Iceland can appear completely white. Careful attention to structure and wingbeats should still easily separate it from Ivory Gull.

FIRST CYCLE. NEWFOUNDLAND, FEB. BRANDON HOLDEN.

- Ivory Gull is the avian gem of the Arctic. Its glowing white plumage belies its grisly role as a scavenger at polar bear kills.
- First cycles are virtually all white with a dark-smudged face and dark flecking on the wings and tail.
- Body is short and chunky with a low center of gravity, and the wings are very broad-based.
- One of few things that could be confused with Ivory Gull would be a leucistic gull, but leucistic gulls typically have a smudgy or cloudy appearance to the wings, whereas even first-cycle Ivory Gulls appear bright white.

FIRST CYCLE (L) AND ADULT. NEWFOUNDLAND, FEB. BRANDON HOLDEN.
- Adults are pure white. First-cycle birds vary considerably in the extent of dark smudging on the face and the size of the flecking on the wings and tail. The dark feather tips wear, so all first-cycle birds become paler late in the first cycle.

ADULT. MASSACHUSETTS, JAN. CAMERON COX.
- Wings are broad-based but taper to sharply pointed wingtips.

(NEXT TWO PAGES) ADULT IVORY GULLS. NEWFOUNDLAND, FEB. BRANDON HOLDEN.
- They have a seemingly fearless demeanor, allowing close approach from humans, and squabbling viciously with neighbors when picking over a carcass.

SABINE'S GULL
Xema sabini
DIMENSIONS
L: 13.5 in.; WS: 33 in.; WT: 6 oz.

SPRING ARRIVAL

off NL: late May; Greenland: early June;
Baffin Is.: early/mid-June

FALL ARRIVAL

off NL: mid-Aug; off ME: mid-Aug.

This stunningly beautiful and highly pelagic small gull is generally rare in eastern North America. Most Sabine's Gulls in eastern North America leave their breeding areas in the Canadian Arctic Archipelago and Greenland and strike out across the middle of the Atlantic to their wintering areas off the western coast of Africa and reverse along a similar path in the spring. This bold migration route keeps the species far from coastal regions where it could likely be seen by birders. Lost Sabine's Gulls are found on interior lakes as often, or perhaps more often, than along the Atlantic Coast. Sabine's

Most migrate offshore

Most birds migrate southeast to w. European waters and then to off w. Africa

Very rare but regular fall migrant through interior and off Atlantic Coast south to FL (casual in spring)

Accidental in winter

Winters mostly in S. Hemisphere (e.g., off w. Africa)

Gulls maintain their juvenile plumage until they reach their wintering areas, and the vast majority of individuals found out of range are juveniles.

SIZE: Much smaller than Black-legged Kittiwake. Slightly larger than Forster's Tern. Similar to Bonaparte's Gull.

STRUCTURE: Neat, trim appearance with a small head and a long, slightly forked tail. The wings seem oversized in comparison with the body and are broad through the arm, whereas the hand is tapered and sharply pointed. The wing bend is thrust forward aggressively, creating a highly angular wing shape, and throughout the wing each line is straight and clean as if it were cut out with a razor.

FLIGHT AND FLOCKING: Wingbeats are typically deep and buoyant but still powerful and purposeful. Flight is more direct than that of Black-legged Kittiwake or Bonaparte's Gull, and Sabine's generally cuts through high winds with strong wingbeats rather than using the arcing dynamic soaring style favored by Black-legged Kittiwake. In eastern North America usually found singly and does not associate closely with other gulls, though it will temporarily join feeding flocks of gulls or terns. In places where it's common, Sabine's often forms small flocks, though this rarely occurs in eastern North America.

APPEARANCE: Alternate Adult: Black-hooded with black-based, yellow-tipped bill. The wing pattern is utterly distinctive even at great distances: a huge white triangle, black outer primaries, and medium gray inner wing. **Basic Adult:** Like alternate but lacks the black hood and instead has a broad black collar on the nape. **First Cycle:** Juvenile has the same unmistakable tricolored wing pattern as adult but instead of a gray mantle has a finely barred gray-brown back and inner wing. This gray-brown coloration extends forward to the head and wraps around behind the eye, creating a dark-cowled appearance. The forked tail sports a narrow black band. After migration acquires a clean gray back, white head, and black collar like basic adult but keeps the brownish inner wing. In spring undergoes a complete molt, acquiring a fully gray back and inner wing like adult, losing the black tail band and dark collar, and gaining a partial dark hood. **Distant:** In all plumages the large white triangle on the wing allows for instant identification. No other regularly occurring gull species has such a bold, sharply defined pattern.

SIMILAR SPECIES: Black-legged Kittiwake: Distinctly larger with longer, slightly straighter wings and shorter tail. First-cycle kittiwake has a vaguely similar wing pattern but has a black band that extends across the inner wing to the body, a duller and less-defined pale triangle across the wing, and lacks the dark-cowled appearance. **Ross's Gull:** Slightly smaller and more delicate, with thinner wings. Looks long-tailed like Sabine's, but the tail is wedge-shaped, not forked. First cycle has a vaguely similar wing pattern but has a broad black band that extends across the inner wing to the body, a duller and less-defined pale triangle across the wing, a pale back, and a white cap.

OREGON, AUG. TOM JOHNSON.
- Beautiful small pelagic gull with striking, sharply defined white triangles on the wing, visible on both the upper- and underwing in all plumages.
- Adults migrate in alternate plumage, and juveniles (far L) head south in full juvenile plumage, so these two plumages account for the majority of Sabine's Gulls seen in North America.

FIRST CYCLE. SOUTH AFRICA, JAN. KEN BEHRENS.

- First-cycle birds in the midst of the preformative molt, like this bird, are rare in North America, as the preformative molt does not begin until after migration. Occasionally Sabine's Gulls winter off the southeastern U.S. and can be seen in this plumage.
- Basic adults are similar but are slightly more crisply patterned.
- Even in light winds the wings are rarely held straight. Instead the wing posture is aggressive and angular, with the wing bend thrust forward, but the wings are broader than those of Black-legged Kittiwake, particularly through the hand.

JUVENILE. SWEDEN, SEPT. TOMMY HOLMGREN.

- At virtually any seawatch in eastern North America this distinctive sight will create absolute pandemonium, screaming, and cursing. *Sab's Gull moving left; get on this bird!*

WITH BONAPARTE'S GULLS. MANITOBA, JUNE. TOM JOHNSON.

- Only slightly larger than Bonaparte's Gull, but its broad wings and heavier chest make it appear larger and more powerfully built.
- Sharply defined white triangles in the wing are diagnostic at any distance.

JUVENILE WITH BONAPARTE'S GULLS AND EARED GREBES. UTAH, NOV. PAUL HIGGINS.

- The brown hindneck and crown create a dark-cowled appearance in juvenile plumage.
- The bright white triangles in the wings of first-cycle birds appear as clean and sharply defined as those of adults when viewed from a distance.
- The vast majority of vagrant Sabine's Gulls found in the interior of the continent are juveniles.

BLACK-LEGGED KITTIWAKE
Rissa tridactyla
DIMENSIONS
L: 17 in.; WS: 36 in.; WT: 14 oz.

SPRING ARRIVAL

Greenland: late Mar.; Baffin Is.: mid-May

FALL ARRIVAL

ME: late Aug.; MD: late Oct.; NC: late Oct.

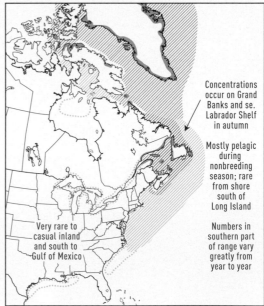

Concentrations occur on Grand Banks and se. Labrador Shelf in autumn

Mostly pelagic during nonbreeding season; rare from shore south of Long Island

Numbers in southern part of range vary greatly from year to year

Very rare to casual inland and south to Gulf of Mexico

This smartly patterned gull possesses aerial mastery unmatched among other gulls. One of the great pleasures of seawatching is watching Black-legged Kittiwakes migrate on bright, windy days—bird after bird gleaming brilliantly as it reaches the apex of a high, effortless arc. Unfortunately, this sight is rarely seen away from the northeast U.S. and Canada, as this gull is highly pelagic away from its breeding grounds. Many seawatchers can only hope to get lucky during strong onshore winds, though this kind of anticipation is just the sort of spice that makes seawatching so engaging and addictive! Even more exciting are the rare sightings of Black-legged Kittiwake on the Great Lakes and elsewhere inland.

SIZE: Clearly larger than Bonaparte's and Sabine's Gulls. Clearly smaller than Ring-billed Gull.

STRUCTURE: Oddly proportioned, with an oversized head, thick neck, slim and sharply pointed wings, and short tail. The wings are angular but fairly broad-based, tapering down to a very slender hand with a sharply pointed tip. The wing bend is prominently thrust forward and sharply pointed, particularly in strong winds.

FLIGHT AND FLOCKING: Flight is generally loose and buoyant. In calm winds wingbeats are stiff and fairly shallow, and birds frequently tilt from side to side. In stronger winds flies more directly on deep, powerful wingbeats or adopts a dynamic soar. A kittiwake's skill at manipulating the wind in this dynamic flight style is unmatched among larids. It can arc high above the water and plummet down at great speed. Occasionally forms dense oval-shaped flocks, but loose, staggered strings or singles are much more typical.

APPEARANCE: Alternate Adult: Very pale overall. White below and pale gray above, with an unmarked yellow bill. The pale gray mantle fades to a paler silvery gray on the upper surface of the primaries, which form an almost translucent panel. At the tip of the wingtips is a small and clean-cut patch of black, almost as if the wings hads been dipped in black ink. **Basic Adult:** Same as alternate but with dusky markings on the nape. **First Cycle:** The wing has a large, Sabine's Gull–like, whitish triangle outlined with strong black bars that form a shallow black M pattern across both wings. A broad black collar crosses the nape, and a smaller dusky spot lies just behind the eye. Otherwise quite pale with a black bill and narrow black tail band. Late in the first cycle the collar is lost, the bill becomes yellow, and the black markings on the wings and tail become more muted. **Distant:** Adults are extremely pale and strongly reflect sunlight. The hand is subtly but distinctly paler than the inner wing, and the small black wingtips are difficult to see. On first-cycle birds the strong black bar and dull whitish triangle on the wing create a distinctive pattern and the clean white underwing flashes brightly.

SIMILAR SPECIES: Ring-billed Gull: Under normal conditions, its comparatively languid flight style makes confusion with Black-legged Kittiwake unlikely. However, in strong winds Ring-billed Gull can achieve a dynamic flight style that might create confusion at great distances. Ring-billed Gull is significantly larger, with broader, less pointed wings. And even at its most acrobatic it is no match for a kittiwake. Adult Ring-billed also has far more black on the wingtip than adult Black-legged Kittiwake. **Bonaparte's Gull:** Clearly smaller, with a smaller head and shorter hand. Flight is less direct and powerful. Adult has a distinctive white leading edge to the hand. First-cycle has narrow black bars across the upperwing that resemble the M-shaped pattern of first-cycle Black-legged Kittiwake, but the pattern is far duller, and it also has a complete black trailing edge to the wing and lacks the black collar.

- Small, agile, mainly pelagic gull with angular wings and a narrow, sharply pointed hand.
- Adults are very pale with black "dipped-in-ink" wingtips.
- In strong wind the wings are drawn in toward the body, making them appear very angular, with a sharply pointed wing bend.
- The wing grows paler as it approaches the black wingtips, becoming translucent.

FIRST CYCLE. SWEDEN, OCT. THOMAS SVANBERG.
• The whitish triangles inside the black M are reminiscent of Sabine's Gull, though not as clearly defined. The shallow black M catches the eye, whereas on Sabine's Gull the crisp white triangles are the most notable feature.

ALTERNATE ADULT. ICELAND, JUNE. SNÆVARR ÖRN GEORGSSON.
• Oddly proportioned for a gull, with an oversized head, fairly short tail, and wings that are broad at the base but narrow through the hand.
• Kittiwakes are versatile flyers that often twist and tip in flight, sometimes rotating the wings almost vertically.

BASIC ADULT WITH BONA-PARTE'S GULLS. UTAH, NOV. PAUL HIGGINS.
• Although primarily pelagic, Black-legged Kittiwake is rare but regular on the Great Lakes and in the interior of the continent.
• Noticeably larger and broader-winged than Bonaparte's Gull, the species with which interior strays often associate. Kittiwake also has a sleeker, more athletic silhou-ette.
• The black spot behind the eye and gray wash to the hindneck are typi-cal of basic-plumaged adults but are rarely noticeable at a distance.

ALTERNATE ADULTS. WALES, MAR. KEN BEHRENS.

- Gregarious on the breeding grounds, forming tightly packed flocks near breeding colonies.
- During migration they are mainly solitary. Migrating kittiwakes often follow well-defined flight lines on windy days, with birds passing one after the other.

ALTERNATE ADULT (L) WITH ADULT "EUROPEAN" HERRING GULLS. WALES, MAR. KEN BEHRENS.

- The wings of adults fade from gray to pale silver, a unique and surprisingly obvious characteristic.

FIRST CYCLE. FLORIDA, JAN. TOM DUNKERTON.

- Sharply patterned and unmistakable.
- Late in the first cycle, the bold black M fades to medium gray and the black collar is lost.
- Bill is stout for a small gull.

TERNS AND SKIMMERS

Terns make up the widespread Sternidae family of waterbirds. Their basic shape is similar to that of gulls, and the two families often share the same habitat, but whereas most gulls are generalists, terns are specialists. They forage in flight and plunge-dive to catch fish or pluck items from the surface with sharply pointed bills. In this guide we cover 13 species of terns. They can be broken into several well-known groups: the "crested" terns, Royal and Sandwich, of the recently formed genus *Thalasseus;* the "medium-sized" terns, Common, Arctic, Forster's, and Roseate Terns, all in the genus *Sterna;* the "marsh" terns of the genus *Chlidonias,* of which Black Tern is the only regularly occurring species in North America; the "tropical" or "dark-backed" terns, Sooty and Bridled, of the recently formed genus *Onychoprion;* and the noddies, genus *Anous,* represented by Brown Noddy. The remaining terns do not fall into any particular group, usually because they have no similar species with which to be grouped.

Considered closely related to terns is the Black Skimmer, the only New World representative of the small, highly distinctive family Rynchopidae. Skimmers are the only birds with a lower mandible longer than the upper mandible. When foraging, the lower mandible knifes through the water, and when it come in contact with a fish, the bill snaps shut. Unlike in terns, male skimmers are significantly larger than females, with a much deeper bill. The difference is great enough that the sexes can be differentiated at a glance. Skimmers have exceptionally long wings, and their wing action is almost entirely above the plane of the body. This enables them to fly close to the water so they can employ their skimming foraging strategy, and also creates a highly distinctive flight style that can be recognized at distances where plumage traits cannot be resolved. Skimmers are the only birds that can, like a cat, compress their pupils down to vertical slits protecting their eyes when they are active at night. This allows them to forage during favorable tidal conditions regardless of the time of day.

Terns use a variety of migration strategies, from that of Brown Noddy, which apparently disperses into the pelagic waters surrounding its breeding islands, to the well-known, world-champion migrant Arctic Tern, which may travel nearly 25,000 miles each year, spending most of the year in near-continual sunlight at one pole of the globe or the other. Some species migrate mainly nocturnally, so the migration of terns is surprisingly inconspicuous considering the large numbers breeding in North America. There is still some opportunity to see di-

This composite shows a Common Tern using the preferred method of feeding for most terns: plunge-diving to capture fish. They usually hover momentarily before diving, though they can make sudden dives as well. Maine, July. Ken Behrens.

urnal migration in most of the terns covered here, the exceptions being Arctic and Roseate Terns, whose migratory routes take them far from shore, and the pelagic tropical terns and Brown Noddy. More careful examination of tern migration, particularly in the southeastern U.S., may reveal new points of concentration and produce daily numbers that easily eclipse the high counts that have so far been recorded.

When flying in flocks, smaller species of terns alternate between flying in tight, ball-like flocks and spreading out in loose lines low to the water. Large species are more apt to move individually or in small, widely spaced flocks. In many species the young are dependent on the parents for an extended period, so the sight of a first-cycle tern following one of its parents and giving incessant begging calls is not unusual. The most conspicuous tern migrations occur in the waters immediately adjacent to the Atlantic and Gulf Coasts, but the major rivers in the interior also concentrate the migration of several species. Movements of Caspian Tern are particularly apparent along major rivers. Some immature Royal and Sandwich Terns move up the Atlantic

In this comparison of adult (L) and first-cycle Royal Terns, notice that both show strong contrast between the fresh inner primaries and older outer primaries. Several terns show this pattern in spring and summer. Texas, April (L); Georgia, Oct. (R). Cameron Cox.

Coast to areas north of the breeding range during spring, probably searching for new locations for nesting. They are joined in late summer by a number of adults with recently fledged young in tow.

An oddity found in many species of terns is the pale, powdery "bloom" on the upper surface of the primaries. It is created by tiny, elongated white barbules that are densest when the feathers are fresh, but it gradually wears off. The underlying feather color is typically black, so as the pale bloom wears away it exposes the dark feather underneath. So the primaries of many terns become *darker as they wear,* whereas in most gulls the outer primaries start out black and, as they wear, gradually fade to brown or, in extreme cases, to white.

Molt in terns—particularly the unique strategies seen in the molt of the primaries—is complex, puzzling, and utterly fascinating. Adults of most species molt a variable number of inner primaries, up to eight or nine in some species, in the late winter or early spring as part of the prealternate molt, while the remaining outer primaries are older feathers retained from the previous prebasic molt. In some species a second molt of the inner primaries, called a presupplemental molt, follows slightly later in spring, replacing several of the same inner feathers attained in the prealternate molt! Whether a presupplemental molt takes place or not, the prealternate molt ensures there will be at least two generations of primaries during the spring and summer. Because the outer primaries have received several additional months of wear compared with the inner primaries acquired in spring, much of the pale bloom will have already worn off the outer primaries. As the feathers continue to wear, the dark base color begins to emerge, contrasting with the clean white inner primaries. Since primaries are replaced sequentially from the innermost to the outermost, the newest feather will always lie alongside the oldest feather, heightening the contrast. The best-known example of this is in Common Tern, which sports a "dark wedge" that develops as the outer primaries wear; it is a key identification trait for separating Common Tern from Arctic and Forster's Terns. The rate at which the pale bloom on the primaries of adult Common Terns wears off varies individually, so the time frame when the dark wedge appears varies greatly. It is present on some birds by April, whereas a few may begin to show a dark wedge only in July. This trait is particularly scrutinized in Common Tern, but several other terns show a similar effect caused by the same phenomenon. The examples mentioned here provide only a taste of the intricacies of molt in terns; a complete overview of the subject is beyond the scope of this book. We recommend Steve Howell's *Molt in North American Birds,* which provides a readable starting point for exploring this subject.

Calls do not play a major role in the flight identification of most species covered in this guide, as many species rarely call in flight, or their vocalizations do not carry long distances. However, this is not the case with terns. They vocalize frequently in flight, their calls carry well, and in most cases the calls are distinct and definitive. Particularly in the large species, first-cycle birds continue to give begging calls to adults well into fall, and though these calls are quite different from those of adults, they are still distinctive. We have included phonetic representations for the calls of many species. Capital letters indicate emphasis or volume, spaces indicate pauses between syllables, and hyphens between syllables indicate very brief pauses or hesitations in the call.

The sexes appear similar in all species covered here, and all have distinctive alternate plumages. They show distinct age-related differences in appearance and adult plumage is attained in the second or third cycle.

(Next page) Least, Black, Sandwich, and Royal Terns, plus a Semipalmated Plover. Florida, Aug. Cameron Cox.

BLACK SKIMMER
Rynchops niger
DIMENSIONS
L: 18 in.; WS: 44 in.; WT: 11 oz.

SPRING ARRIVAL

VA: mid-Apr.; MD: mid-Apr.; NY: early May

This odd and highly distinctive species is thought by many to be most closely related to terns, though the exact relationship is uncertain. It has an extremely long lower mandible that it uses to knife through the water and snag fish, and vertical pupils that allow it to see well at night and to forage during the most favorable tidal conditions. Along the Gulf and southern Atlantic Coasts, Black Skimmer makes short migrations or is resident. It is an exclusively summer resident from Virginia to New England, often massing in huge flocks for weeks before fall migration. Very vocal species that frequently gives a repeated, nasal *yep-yep*.

SIZE: Appears slightly larger than Royal Tern, though Royal Tern is bulkier. Slightly smaller than Ring-billed Gull. The difference in size between the sexes is far more evident than in any of the terns and is often obvious in the field.

STRUCTURE: Extremely prominent, laterally compressed bill is held angled downward, with the

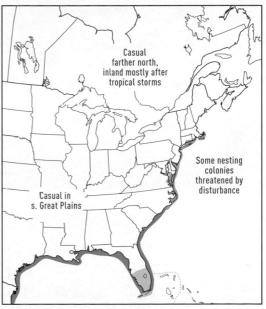

Casual farther north, inland mostly after tropical storms

Some nesting colonies threatened by disturbance

Casual in s. Great Plains

long lower mandible projecting beyond the upper mandible. The body is slim and the tail short. The wings are extremely long and broad-based, slowly tapering along the length of an extended hand. The wing bend is thrust forward sharply, and the hand appears to curve back, creating a scimitar-shaped silhouette.

FLIGHT AND FLOCKING: Distinctive wingbeats are slow and almost completely above the body, an adaptation that allows skimmers to skim just over the surface of the water. May fly alone, in pairs, or in small to medium-sized tightly packed groups or messy lines. Low over the water, these flocks fly with nearly coordinated wingbeats, though a few members are always out of sync. As flocks rise to greater heights, much of this coordination is lost and individuals become more widely spaced. Almost never flies with other species except when flushed from a shared roost.

APPEARANCE: **Alternate Adult:** Blackish above with white on the forehead, a white outer tail, and a broad white trailing edge to the secondaries. The underparts, including the underwing, are white, though the chest may be washed with faint yellow. The bill has an orange base and a black tip. **Basic Adult:** Like alternate adult but with a white nape that isolates the black cap. **First Cycle:** Juvenile is mottled gray above with strongly pale-edged wing coverts and darker primaries. During the first winter, the back and upperwing coverts acquire black feathers in patches. **Distant:** Appears largely black, but the underparts can suddenly flash white. As flocks often move in close coordination, an entire flock may bank together, creating a distinctive white flash low over the water, which quickly disappears, then appears again the next time the flock twists.

SIMILAR SPECIES: Appearance and flight style are utterly distinctive.

TEXAS, APR. KEN BEHRENS.
- Unmistakable in both structure and plumage.
- Skimmers are the only birds in the world with a lower mandible that is longer than the upper mandible.
- Extremely slim and long-winged.
- Males are larger than females and have a significantly larger bill.

NEW JERSEY, NOV. CAMERON COX.
- Flocks are surprisingly tightly packed for such a long-winged bird, and they twist and writhe in slow-motion synchrony.
- Wingbeats extend high above the body but go barely below the body, an adaptation necessary for their skimming method of feeding.

NEW JERSEY, SEPT. CAMERON COX.
- Wings are broad and angular, with an exceptionally long hand.
- With the wings raised, skimmers flash white, but they can disappear against a dark background when the downstroke exposes the black upperwing.

NORTH CAROLINA, JULY. KEN BEHRENS.
- The distinctive bill is used to capture small fish, which are snapped up reflexively upon contact with the lower mandible.
- Skimmers are extremely vocal and are often located by their yapping call, which sounds almost like an obnoxious small dog!

WITH SANDWICH AND COMMON TERNS. TEXAS, APR. KEN BEHRENS.
- When Black Skimmers fly significant distances, they form single-species flocks, but they readily mix with other species near foraging and roosting locations.
- The unmistakable appearance of Black Skimmer makes it a useful species to use as a size comparison when sorting out a distant mixed flock of terns.

TEXAS, JULY. KEN BEHRENS.
- A skimmer's long lower mandible knifes through the water, and the bill snaps shut when it comes into contact with a fish.
- Skimmers are always distinctive in flight, and are doubly distinctive when engaged in this unique skimming behavior!

NEW JERSEY, SEPT. CAMERON COX.
• The bill is always angled downward in flight, and this is visible at great distances.

LOUISIANA, JAN. KEN BEHRENS.
• Skimmers forage based on tidal conditions, and they are often active at dawn, dusk, and even during the night.

CASPIAN TERN
Hydroprogne caspia
DIMENSIONS
L: 21 in.; WS: 54 in.; WT: 1.4 lb.

SPRING ARRIVAL

VA: mid-Apr.; IA: late Apr.; ON: late Apr.;
MA: late Apr.; MB: mid-May

FALL ARRIVAL

NJ: late July; VA: mid-Aug.; MO: early Sept.;
LA: mid-Sept.

This massive tern, the largest tern in the world, possesses an unmistakably powerful, almost gull-like appearance. It is the only large tern that prefers fresh water. Although it usually avoids open ocean, it does frequent sheltered coastal bays. Observers are often alerted to its presence by its loud and frequent call: a rough and explosive *KE-OUW*.

SIZE: The largest tern in the world. Clearly larger than Royal Tern. Falls between Ring-billed and Lesser Black-backed Gulls, though at times appears as large as Herring Gull.

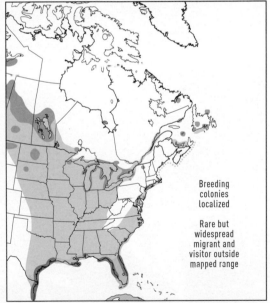

Breeding colonies localized

Rare but widespread migrant and visitor outside mapped range

STRUCTURE: Silhouette is strikingly bull-necked and front-heavy. The head is large and blocky with a flat crown. The bill is extraordinarily broad-based for a tern, tapering to a sharp tip; the combination gives a lethal appearance reminiscent of a spearhead. The bill is often held pointed downward, making it even more obvious and creating the appearance that the bird is peering downward. The thick neck merges smoothly with the heavy body, which swells slightly at the chest and then tapers, appearing to end prematurely in a very short, shallowly forked tail. The wings are broad-based for a tern, with a moderately prominent wing bend and a long, pointed hand.

FLIGHT AND FLOCKING: Wingbeats are slow and fairly shallow but with the powerful appearance of a large gull. Despite its bulk and powerful flight, Caspian maintains a grace that is unmistakably that of a tern, and it is unlikely to be mistaken for a gull for more than a moment. Flocks larger than three are unusual despite the fact that large numbers often roost together. Migratory behavior is a constant trickle of widely spaced singles or pairs that follow a nearly identical flight path and altitude. Often follows inland lakes and rivers on migration, and is one of the most likely tern species to be seen in active migration. Flight associations with other species are rare and seem purely incidental.

APPEARANCE: Alternate Adult: Extremely pale gray above and white below with a bright orange-red bill, solid black cap, and mostly black undersides of the primaries. Unlike in Royal Tern, the bill has a dusky tip. **Basic Adult:** Like alternate but the cap is flecked with white. **First Cycle:** Like basic adult but with a paler orange bill, dark gray upper surface to the primaries that wears to jet-black by spring, and a faint secondary bar. **Distant:** Extremely pale with a faint silvery sheen. The black undersides of the primaries flash like signal flags when the wings are raised.

SIMILAR SPECIES: Royal Tern: Has a trimmer and more athletic appearance with faster, deeper, and more fluid wingbeats. The bill is paler orange, and except for a short period in spring, the forehead is clean white; the black markings on the head are restricted to a thin strip behind the eye to the nape. Often shows a dark wedge on the upperside of the outer primaries, like Common Tern, whereas the underside of the wing is largely pale. Additionally, Royal holds its bill straight in point-to-point flight, occasionally dropping it to glance downward briefly, whereas Caspian Tern frequently points its bill downward in any kind of flight. **Ring-billed Gull:** Similar in size, often found in the same habitat, and like Caspian, appears very pale at a distance. Ring-billed, however, has faster wingbeats, slightly slimmer wings set farther forward on the body, no black on the head, and a significantly smaller, yellow bill.

WITH FIRST-CYCLE RING-BILLED GULL. PENNSYLVANIA, APR. KEN BEHRENS.

- Powerful build and broad wings suggest a gull, but the long tapered hand is unmistakably that of a tern.
- The bill is heavy enough to be obvious at a distance.
- Clean white upperwing and extensive black underside to the primaries are distinctive.
- Significantly larger than Ring-billed Gull.

ALTERNATE ADULT WITH COMMON TERNS, ROYAL TERNS, AND ONE SANDWICH TERN. TEXAS, APR. KEN BEHRENS.
- Caspian is the largest tern in the world, dwarfing all other terns in direct comparison.
- Often appears stub-tailed.
- *Where is the Sandwich Tern?*

FLORIDA, DEC. KEN BEHRENS.
- Combination of broad wings, heavy bill, and short tail create a distinctive silhouette.

ADULT WITH FIRST-CYCLE ROYAL TERN (L). GEORGIA, OCT. CAMERON COX.
- Bull-necked appearance is unique among terns.
- Even in winter, Caspian maintains a nearly complete black cap, unlike Royal Tern.

ALTERNATE ADULTS WITH BONAPARTE'S GULLS. ONTARIO, APR. KEN BEHRENS.
- The short tail makes the wings appear to be set too far back on the body.

COMPARISON: CASPIAN TERN (L) WITH ROYAL TERN (R).
- Compare the beefy Caspians to the slimmer, sleeker Royals.
- The wings of Caspian are wider throughout their length but are particularly broad-based.
- Caspian's bill is no longer than Royal's but is distinctly heavier.
- Caspian usually flies with the bill down (as in top L).
- Royal usually has limited black on the underwing, whereas Caspian has a large black wedge.

WITH LESSER BLACK-BACKED GULLS. GHANA, FEB. KEN BEHRENS.
- The hefty Caspian is the only tern that will easily blend into a flock of large gulls.

ALTERNATE ADULTS. ONTARIO, APR. KEN BEHRENS.
- Extensive black underside to the primaries contrasts sharply with the white wing lining and is obvious when the wing is raised.

BASIC ADULT. GEORGIA, OCT. CAMERON COX.
- From late summer through winter, Caspian has a dark cap with pale streaking; Royal Tern has a white crown and forehead.
- Worn Caspians can show dark on the upperwing.

ROYAL TERN
Thalasseus maximus
DIMENSIONS
L: 20 in.; WS: 41 in.; WT: 1 lb.

SPRING ARRIVAL

VA: late Mar.; MD: mid-Apr.; NJ: mid-Apr.

FALL ARRIVAL

MA: late June

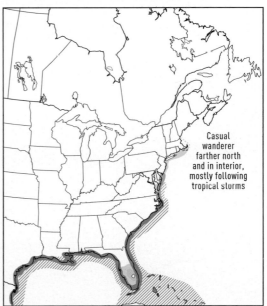

Casual wanderer farther north and in interior, mostly following tropical storms

This large and vocal tern is one of the most dominant species in the warm coastal waters of the southern Atlantic states and the Gulf Coast, challenged only by Laughing Gull and Brown Pelican for the title of most conspicuous species in this habitat. Royal Tern is almost strictly coastal, though it is one of the most likely species to be blown inland by a tropical system. In late summer and early fall, large numbers move north along the Atlantic Coast, with some reaching Massachusetts. The loud, rolling *kerrrr* vocalization given by adults in flight makes them easy to pinpoint. In the fall, juveniles often trail behind adults, giving an incessant piping whistle.

SIZE: Distinctly smaller than Caspian Tern. Clearly larger than Sandwich Tern. Slightly smaller than Ring-billed Gull.

STRUCTURE: Gives an athletic impression, long and lean but unmistakably powerful. The smooth transition between the long, moderately deep bill and the head creates a missile-like shape similar to that of Northern Gannet. The chest swells moderately whereas the belly is flat, tapering abruptly into a medium-length forked tail. The long, slender wings are pushed forward at the wrist and sport a long, tapered, sharply pointed hand. The wings are centered evenly on the body, enhancing an overall appearance of balance.

FLIGHT AND FLOCKING: Wingbeats are smooth and moderately deep, with a casual, athletic grace. In light wind wingbeats are steady and regular; in stronger wind they become slightly irregular and pause momentarily for brief glides. Most frequently seen in pairs, but small, loose groups of 5–15 also occur and sometimes include Sandwich Tern.

APPEARANCE: Alternate Adult: Very pale gray mantle, white underparts, bright orange bill, and black cap. The black cap is held briefly, from spring to early summer, and is replaced with a white forehead and crown in late summer. The wings have a Common Tern–like blackish wedge in the outer primaries that darkens over the summer. **Basic Adult:** Retains the pale crown and lores of late summer. Like alternate, but the bill is often paler orange and the primaries are uniformly pale for a brief period in midwinter. **First Cycle:** Like basic adult, but the bill is dull orange, the upper side of the hand is dark gray to blackish, and a dark secondary bar is clearly visible. **Distant:** Large and very pale, though usually not gleaming white. The dark wedge on the upperside of the primaries in adults may be evident but more often is not. The all-dark hand of first-cycle birds is quite discernible.

SIMILAR SPECIES: Caspian Tern: Larger and bulkier, with a heavier bill; shorter, thicker neck; deeper chest; broader wings; and shorter tail. The slower wingbeats have a deliberate air that imparts a sense of weight that is lacking in the flight of Royal Tern—something that is apparent even at great distances. Adult Caspian has extensive black undersides to the primaries and uniformly pale upperwings, whereas the upperwings of Royal have a distinct dark wedge and the underside of the wingtip is largely pale. **Sandwich Tern:** Slimmer, with a thinner black bill, slimmer wings, and quicker wingbeats that appear slightly jerky, unlike the fluid wingbeats of Royal. The body lacks the powerful appearance of Royal's, being so slender it almost seems emaciated. The outer primaries tend to be a bit paler than those of Royal, and the dark wedge less extensive and less obvious, but there is overlap. The secondaries are translucent on Sandwich but not on Royal, a trait that is particularly obvious on birds overhead.

ALTERNATE ADULT WITH ALTERNATE ADULT SANDWICH TERN (R). TEXAS, MAY. KEN BEHRENS.
• Large tern with a lean, athletic appearance. Wings are long and centered on the body, creating a balanced appearance. Bill is slimmer than Caspian's and is orange, not reddish.
• Sandwich is smaller, with slimmer body and wings.

BASIC ADULT. NEW JERSEY, SEPT. CAMERON COX.
- In this plumage, distinguished from Caspian by the white crown, extensively dark hand, and white underside of the primaries.

JUVENILE. FLORIDA, AUG. CAMERON COX.
- Juvenile terns often fledge before their flight feathers or bills are full length, drastically altering their silhouette and flight style for a short period in the summer.
- The gray wings of juveniles quickly become black.

ALTERNATE ADULTS WITH FIVE SANDWICH TERNS AND FIVE LAUGHING GULLS. FLORIDA, MAY. CAMERON COX.
- Royal Tern is large, about the same size as Laughing Gull, and clearly larger than Sandwich Tern.
- The Sandwich Terns are slightly paler above, causing them to shine more at a distance.
- From late spring through midfall, individual terns show significant variation in the amount and intensity of dark coloration in the outer primaries.

WITH A LAUGHING GULL AND AN UNIDENTIFIED *STERNA* TERN. TEXAS, APR. KEN BEHRENS.
- Flocks of this size are uncommon. They occur mainly near roosting or breeding sites.
- Many terns form loose, linear flocks, particularly when commuting short distances.
- There are several first-cycle Royal Terns in the flock, distinguished at a distance by the extensive dark upper surface to the primaries.

FLORIDA, DEC. KEN BEHRENS.
- Silhouette is lean and balanced but powerful. In comparison, Caspian Tern is stout and blocky, and Sandwich Tern looks petite and undernourished. The prominent wing bend and longer hand give Royal's wings a more angular appearance than those of Caspian.

ALTERNATE ADULTS WITH FIVE SANDWICH TERNS AND A BLACK SKIMMER. TEXAS, APR. KEN BEHRENS.
- The closely related Royal and Sandwich Terns occupy almost the same range and habitat. Although distinctive at close range, they can be confused at a distance, when they are best separated by wingbeat: quick and choppy in Sandwich, slower and with a deeper downstroke in Royal.

(RIGHT) ADULT (TOP) AND FIRST CYCLE. TEXAS, APR. KEN BEHRENS.
- First-cycle birds often have a paler bill than adults. Also note upperwing pattern.

SANDWICH TERN
Thalasseus sandvicensis
DIMENSIONS
L: 15 in.; WS: 34 in.; WT: 7 oz.

SPRING/SUMMER ARRIVAL

NC: early Apr.; VA: late Apr.; MD: early June;
NJ: late July

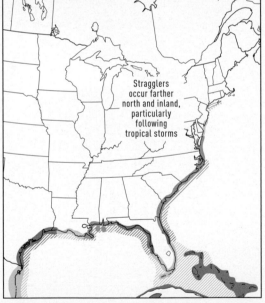

Stragglers occur farther north and inland, particularly following tropical storms

A sleek, exclusively coastal tern, Sandwich is similar in many ways to its larger cousin and frequent cohort, Royal Tern. Generally it is far less conspicuous than Royal Tern, being less common and less vociferous. Sandwich Tern is rarely found inland after tropical storms or hurricanes. It is often located by its call: a rolling *ker-rik,* which is shorter and less ringing than the call of Royal Tern, and has a harsher quality.

SIZE: Slightly larger than Gull-billed Tern and Bonaparte's Gull. Clearly smaller than Royal Tern.

STRUCTURE: Gives the impression of being long and very lean, almost emaciated, with long, slender wings and balanced proportions. The head is fairly small but the neck is quite long so the head extends farther in front of the wings than in the Sterna terns. The body swells slightly at the chest before tapering smoothly to a medium-length, strongly forked tail. Often the longer outer tail feathers are difficult to see or broken off, creating a very short-tailed appearance. The wing bend is moderately thrust forward and the hand angles back sharply, so the whole wing has an angular appearance. The yellow-tipped bill is long and thin, though the tip disappears at a distance, creating the illusion that the bill is shorter and heavier than it actually is. Often in flight the bill is pointed straight down as they search the water for prey, a behavior not shown by *Sterna* terns.

FLIGHT AND FLOCKING: Wingbeats are quick and powerful but lack the fluidity of Royal Tern's and instead appear slightly jerky. In some conditions wingbeats are shallow, in others moderately deep. Whether deep or shallow, wingbeats are even above and below the body, unlike those of Royal Tern, which has more wing action below the body. Most often in pairs, but also flies in flocks of 3–25, sometimes in mixed flocks with Royal Tern.

APPEARANCE: Alternate Adult: Virtually all white with a black cap, black bill with a small yellow tip, and dusky outer primaries. The black cap is held for only a short period in spring; by midsummer the forehead and crown have returned to white. Many show a slight pink flush early in spring. **Basic Adult:** Retains the pale crown and forehead of late summer. The outer primaries darken from midsummer through fall, when the outer third of the hand can be quite dark. By midwinter the primaries have

all been replaced and the wing is uniformly pale. **First Cycle:** Like basic adult but with dusky tertial centers, a moderately distinct gray secondary bar, dusky leading edge of the wing, black outer primaries, and an overall messy, disheveled appearance. **Distant:** Bright white, slightly paler than Royal Tern. First-cycle birds and basic adults in fall have a blackish wedge on the outer primaries.

SIMILAR SPECIES: Gull-billed Tern: Heavier overall build with broader-based wings and slower wingbeats that are smooth and elegant compared to the quick, choppy wingbeats of Sandwich Tern. The bill is shorter and much heavier than Sandwich's, though Sandwich's bill can appear surprisingly similar when the yellow tip is not visible. Gull-billed acquires the black cap earlier in the year and retains it longer than Sandwich, which only have the full black cap for a short time in the spring. In basic plumage, Gull-billed has an almost totally white head with a small dark patch behind the eye, whereas Sandwich retains an obvious black band that wraps behind the eye and joins at the nape. **Royal Tern:** Larger and heavier with fluid wingbeats that are deeper below the body. Has a much heavier bright orange bill, darker gray mantle, and typically shows blacker outer primaries.

ALTERNATE ADULTS. FLORIDA, APR. CAMERON COX.
- Extremely slim with long, narrow wings.
- Bill looks very long and slender, but the yellow tip disappears at a distance, which can create the illusion that the bill is much stouter than it actually is.

SANDWICH TERNS WITH AN ADULT COMMON TERN (LOWER R) AND A FIRST-CYCLE FORSTER'S TERN (UPPER L). TEXAS, MAY. KEN BEHRENS.
- Wings and body are longer than those of medium-sized terns, but the body is not significantly heavier nor the wings significantly broader, which creates an oddly lanky silhouette.

ALTERNATE ADULTS WITH TWO ROYAL TERNS AND A COMMON TERN. TEXAS, APR. KEN BEHRENS.
- Both Royal and Sandwich Terns have a balanced silhouette, but notice how the Sandwich Terns look spindly in comparison with the Royals.
- Royals never show a noticeable translucent patch in the wings like the Sandwich Tern in the center does.

WITH ROYAL TERNS. GHANA, FEB. KEN BEHRENS.
- The yellow tip of the bill disappears at middle and long distances, and the bill takes on a heavier appearance.
- Both species have different subspecies in the Old World, but they are similar to those found in North America.

FIRST CYCLE. FLORIDA, MAY. CAMERON COX.
- A first-cycle bird with an extensive black hand, tiny yellow tip to the bill, head pattern like a basic adult, and dusky secondaries.

FLORIDA, AUG. LAUREN DEANER.
- Silhouette is strikingly slim.
- Could almost be mistaken for a medium-sized tern, but the long, thin bill and attenuated head are unique.

WITH THREE ROYAL TERNS AND A LAUGHING GULL. TEXAS, NOV. CAMERON COX.
• The posture of the bird coming in to land is similar to the typical hunting posture: bill pointed down searching for fish.

ALTERNATE ADULTS WITH BLACK SKIMMERS. TEXAS, APR. KEN BEHRENS.
• Distinctive birds such as Black Skimmer can be identified at great distances, and serve as a reference with which to establish the size of species near them. Here, in comparison with the skimmers, these terns are clearly too large to be medium-sized terns, and too small to be Royal Terns. So even if this flock were seen at a distance, the possible choices could be reduced to Gull-billed or Sandwich Tern based solely on size in relation to the skimmers.

GULL-BILLED TERN
Gelochelidon nilotica
DIMENSIONS
L: 14 in.; WS: 34 in.; WT: 6 oz.

SPRING ARRIVAL

NC: mid-Apr.; VA: late Apr.; NJ: early May

This beautiful tern has adapted to capturing small crabs and large insects as its primary food, and fish—which are the primary food of other terns—form only a supplement to its diet. This adaptation has allowed Gull-billed Tern to become far less bound to water than other terns, and it is often observed coursing over sand flats or even upland fields. Although its breeding range is extensive, the species is thinly spread over much of its range, locally common in some areas but numerous only along the western Gulf Coast. Gull-billed Tern is mostly quiet during migration and winter, but on the breeding grounds it often utters two calls: a distinctive three- or four-part laugh that trails off at the end and a more extended cackling laugh.

SIZE: Slightly larger than Forster's Tern. Marginally smaller than Sandwich Tern but often appears slightly larger because of its heavier build.

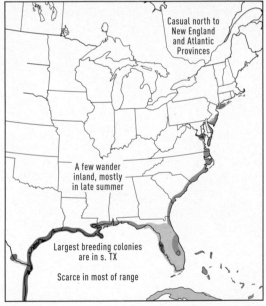

Casual north to New England and Atlantic Provinces

A few wander inland, mostly in late summer

Largest breeding colonies are in s. TX

Scarce in most of range

STRUCTURE: Heavyset, with a stout bill, thick neck, and short, moderately forked tail. The wings are broad-based and tend to be held straight out from the body but can also be bent back to give a sickle-shaped appearance. Holds the head steady with the bill pointed forward in point-to-point flight, but while foraging shows the most head movement of any tern, swiveling the head around constantly.

FLIGHT AND FLOCKING: Flight is elegant, with deep, deliberate wingbeats that impart an impression of controlled power. On the upstroke the wings appear to fly up loosely, whereas the downstroke is crisp and emphatic; together they create an unmistakable cadence unlike that of any other tern. Frequently seen coursing over open flats or fields, generally 10–40 feet high, and occasionally swooping down in a shallow dive to pick prey off the surface. Most often observed in pairs or individually, though large numbers concentrate at prime foraging and breeding locations. Rarely associates with other species. Limited observation of migrants suggests that it flies close to the water in small groups, as do other terns, but this species is rarely noted during active migration.

APPEARANCE: Alternate Adult: Extremely pale with a narrow black cap and all-black bill but otherwise virtually all white. **Basic Adult:** Very pale with a dark patch on the face that ranges from a nearly Forster's Tern–like eye patch to a small dusky spot behind the eye. **First Cycle:** Like basic adult but with almost no eye patch. Late in the first cycle, the outer primaries may wear to almost jet-black. **Distant:** All white, but a flat white that rarely glints or flashes in the manner of other mostly white terns.

SIMILAR SPECIES: Sandwich Tern: Much leaner, with slimmer wings and a longer tail. Wingbeats are jerky and fairly quick, whereas the flight of Gull-billed appears elegant and unhurried with slower, deeper wingbeats. Sandwich maintains a black cap for only a short period in spring, but in winter it has more black on the head than Gull-billed. **Forster's Tern:** Similar in overall color but substantially smaller, with weaker wingbeats, a smaller head and bill, and a longer tail.

ALTERNATE ADULT. NEW JERSEY, MAY. KEVIN KARLSON.
- Moderate size and somewhat gull-like proportions, with heavy body, large head, strong bill, short tail, and fairly broad wings.
- Unlike other terns, often seen singly or in pairs coursing over dry fields or open sand flats, swooping down with elegant, shallow dives to snatch crabs or large insects.
- Extremely pale, but maintains the black cap from early spring until fall, much longer than Sandwich Tern.

ALTERNATE ADULT. TEXAS, APR. KEN BEHRENS.
- Unlike other terns, infrequently feeds on fish but uses its heavy bill to capture crabs and large insects.

JUVENILE. FLORIDA, AUG. KEVIN KARLSON.
- Has a pinkish area near the base of the bill and slight pale scaling on the wings, but otherwise is like basic adult.

ALTERNATE ADULTS WITH TWO ALTERNATE ADULT FRANKLIN'S GULLS. TEXAS, APR. KEN BEHRENS.
- Like Franklin's Gull, more likely to be seen feeding in fields than on open beaches.
- Head is large, body stocky, and tail quite short.
- Forages by flying back and forth about 10–40 feet off the ground at a steady pace, occasionally hovering or swooping.

WITH TWO FORSTER'S TERNS (BOTTOM L AND TOP R). TEXAS, JAN. KEN BEHRENS.

- Very pale like Forster's Tern but larger with broader wings, a heavier body, and a thicker bill.
- In winter some Gull-billed Terns have a large dark spot surrounding the eye, similar to Forster's, but most are white-headed.

**ALTERNATE ADULT.
NEW JERSEY, JULY.
MIKE DANZENBAKER.**

- Stout black bill is unique among terns.
- Similar in size to Sandwich Tern but substantially bulkier and broader-winged.
- For a tern, has a short tail, only moderately forked.
- When foraging for food over a marsh or field, the head constantly swivels from side to side.
- Flight has a smooth, floating quality; Gull-billeds rarely seem hurried.

COMMON TERN
Sterna hirundo
DIMENSIONS
L: 12 in.; WS: 30 in.; WT: 4.2 oz.

SPRING ARRIVAL

NC: mid-Apr.; NJ: late Apr.; s. MB: late Apr.;
w. Great Lakes: early May

FALL ARRIVAL

Lake Erie: late July; MO: early Aug.;
GA: early Aug.; w. Gulf Coast: early Aug.

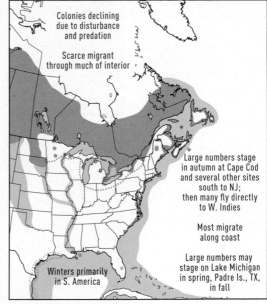

Colonies declining due to disturbance and predation

Scarce migrant through much of interior

Large numbers stage in autumn at Cape Cod and several other sites south to NJ; then many fly directly to W. Indies

Most migrate along coast

Large numbers may stage on Lake Michigan in spring, Padre Is., TX, in fall

Winters primarily in S. America

This adaptable, medium-sized tern is equally at home in coastal regions and on freshwater lakes. Its versatility has made it the most widespread tern in North America and the best starting point for understanding the difficult *Sterna* group of midsized terns. Common Tern is a long-distance migrant, with virtually all individuals vacating the U.S. and Canada for the winter, though a few stragglers may linger along the Gulf Coast into early January, leading to the misconception that they are overwinter-ing. Common Tern is quite vocal, particularly on its breeding grounds. The most common call is a loud, slightly two-syllabled *kee-yaa*.

SIZE: Slightly larger than Roseate Tern. Slightly smaller than Bonaparte's Gull and Forster's Tern. Similar to Black-bellied Plover but not as stocky.

STRUCTURE: Silhouette is neutral with an even distribution of weight and a very balanced appearance. The small head, flat crown, and longish bill create a wedge-shaped front. The body is slightly deeper at the chest, where the leading edge of the wing joins the body, and the belly is flat. The wings are centered on the body with a fairly long hand that is moderately swept back at the wrist. The adult tail streamers are the shortest among the *Sterna* terns, though they often break off on *Sterna*s, so short streamers do not necessarily point to Common Tern.

FLIGHT AND FLOCKING: Wingbeats are fast, steady, and fairly deep in standard flight; faster and steadier than Forster's Tern but not as deep or powerful as Arctic Tern. Typically more gregarious than larger terns, often moving in tightly packed flocks of 30 or more. Migrants sometimes travel one at a time, each following an identical course to the preceding bird, like many gull species, and birds may be spaced out every 3–4 seconds or there may be 30 minutes or more between individuals. Migrants may also form high-flying U- or V-shaped flocks, particularly in spring when flying over land. Mixes readily with other *Sterna* terns, particularly when foraging and, to a lesser degree, when migrating.

APPEARANCE: Alternate Adult: The typical *Sterna* tern: black cap; red-based, black-tipped bill; and gray body. The cheek is whitish, and the breast and belly are pale gray. The line dividing the white cheek from the rest of the body is usually diffuse but can be distinct in some individuals. The upperwing is also pale gray. Although the entire wing often looks uniform in spring, by midsummer most birds show an obvious wedge-shaped block of darker outer primaries that contrasts with the paler gray inner primaries. The underwing is pale and there is a dark trailing edge to the primaries that is usually broad and diffuse, though some show a narrower, crisper trailing edge more like that of Arctic Tern. In strong light, a large block of inner primaries may appear translucent. **Basic Adult:** The bill becomes black; forecrown and lores are white. The underparts are white, and the outer primaries continue to darken and contrast sharply with the inner primaries until they are replaced after fall migration. **First Cycle:** Juvenile is initially heavily washed with brown, but this fades quickly; by fall it has a blackish V extending from behind the eye to the nape, leaving the area below the eye and most of the crown whitish. The lesser coverts and much of the hand are dark gray to black, and there is a noticeable black secondary bar. By the following summer birds look much as they did during the winter but display a dark wedge on the hand like that of adults. **Second Cycle:** Like alternate adult but with white forehead and lores, making the black cap incomplete. The underparts are white or white with gray blotches rather than solidly gray. **Distant:** Depending on the light, may appear very pale or almost black. Both the isolated patch of translucent inner primaries and the dark wedge on the outer primaries are visible at great distances in good light. Even in strong light, Common Tern never appears as pale as Forster's or Roseate Terns.

SIMILAR SPECIES: Forster's Tern: Slightly larger, with marginally wider wings, longer tail, and bulkier chest. Paler overall; the flight feathers often appear to shine silvery white, paler than the coverts. During much of the year, lacks a black cap and instead wears a distinctive black eye patch. See Forster's Tern for additional differences. **Arctic Tern:** Slightly smaller but with a more compact appearance. Slimmer wings, with a longer hand and slightly smoother, deeper, more emphatic wingbeats. In all plumages the translucent flight feathers are more obvious and include the outer primaries. The wing is uniformly pale gray, lacking the dark wedge of Common Tern, and the black trailing edge is longer, thinner, and more sharply defined. Breeding adult is darker gray below than Common and has a thin white line across the cheek that is usually better defined than the pale cheek of Common. First-cycle bird has more dark on the head than first-cycle Common Tern and has paler, uniformly gray flight feathers and clean white secondaries.

TEXAS, MAY. KEN BEHRENS.
- The most typical medium-sized tern, Common serves as the ideal species to compare with the other *Sterna* terns.
- The weight distribution is very balanced and there are few striking structural features.

ALTERNATE ADULTS AND FIRST CYCLES. MASSACHUSETTS, JULY. KEN BEHRENS.

- Flocks are never homogenous. The amount of dark markings on the wing, pattern of the bill, and presence or absence of a black cap all vary. Learning this variation is key to being able to pick out rarer species from Common Tern flocks.
- *There are two individuals of one other species in this photo. What species are they, and where are they?*

(TOP) ALTERNATE ADULT WITH LAUGHING GULL (R). TEXAS, MAY. KEN BEHRENS.

- Slimmer and slightly smaller than the gull.

(BOTTOM) COMMON TERNS. COLORADO, SEPT. BILL SCHMOKER.

- When migrating over land, small and medium-sized terns fly in shallow U- or V-shaped flocks, somewhat like a flock of shorebirds, and move with remarkable speed.
- As Common Terns are gray underneath, even a slight shadow can cause them to appear black.

ALTERNATE ADULTS WITH FIRST-CYCLE ARCTIC TERN (L). MASSACHUSETTS, JULY. KEN BEHRENS.
• Arctic has a shorter neck and more rounded body than the two Common Terns. Also notice the narrow dark trailing edge to the primaries of the Arctic compared with the broad edge on the Common.

ALTERNATE ADULT WITH ROYAL TERNS AND A SANDERLING. TEXAS, APR. KEN BEHRENS.
• Paler inner primaries contrast with darker outer primaries, creating a dark wedge. This trait is subtle on this spring individual but becomes more apparent as the white bloom wears off the outer primaries.
• On the near wing, the dark trailing edge is broad but not sharply defined.
• Throat and belly are pale gray, not as dark as on Arctic Tern, and the white cheek does not contrast sharply as it does on Arctic.

SOUTH AFRICA, JAN. KEN BEHRENS.
• Migrating birds in coastal areas often form tightly packed bunches that fly low over the water.

WITH ONE ALTERNATE ADULT LAUGHING GULL (C). MASSACHUSETTS, JULY. KEN BEHRENS.
- When not in a tightly packed flock, Common Terns spread out into lines.
- At a distance against a dark background, the dark primary wedge may be difficult to see.

ALTERNATE ADULTS WITH ALTERNATE ADULT ROSEATE TERN (L). MASSACHUSETTS, JULY. CAMERON COX.
- Even in bright light, Common Terns have a dull appearance, whereas Roseates glow bright white.

JUVENILE. NEW YORK, JULY. KEVIN KARLSON.
- Initially has fairly pale wings, but quickly becomes darker.
- The dark secondary bar is a key trait of first-cycle Common Tern.

WITH AN ALTERNATE ADULT FORSTER'S TERN (L). TEXAS, APR. KEN BEHRENS.
- Forster's Tern has a slightly heavier body and thicker neck than Common Tern.
- In spring the dark wedge on the upperwing of Common Tern is poorly defined or invisible. It is just beginning to show on the middle primaries of these three birds.
- At their palest in early spring, Common Terns have uniformly pale wings. They are still different from Forster's Terns, as spring Forster's have pale silvery primaries that are slightly paler than their pale gray wing coverts.

WITH FOUR ALTERNATE ADULT SANDWICH TERNS AND THREE FORSTER'S TERNS. TEXAS, MAY. KEN BEHRENS.

- The Common Terns have a slightly duller appearance than the other two species.
- Sandwich Terns can show a dark wedge like Common, but they are larger, leaner, and paler overall.

WITH ONE FORSTER'S TERN. NEW JERSEY, SEPT. CAMERON COX.

- Broad, poorly defined dark trailing edge to the primaries is typical of Common Tern, but a few in this photo do show a better-defined trailing edge.
- Several individuals here are replacing their inner primaries, altering their wing shape.
- Common Terns replace their inner primaries both in spring and fall but replace their outer primaries only in fall. The contrast between fresher inner primaries from spring and worn outer primaries from the prior fall creates the dark wedge in summer.
- *Can you find the Forster's Tern?*

ARCTIC TERN
Sterna paradisaea
DIMENSIONS
L: 12 in.; WS: 31 in.; WT: 3.9 oz.

SPRING ARRIVAL

ME: mid-May; Hudson Bay: late May;
s. Greenland: late May;
high Canadian Arctic: mid-June

Although it's called Arctic Tern, this species
spends its nonbreeding season in the southern polar
region, making it one of the world's most accomplished avian travelers. Migration typically occurs
in pelagic waters far from shore and is therefore
rarely observed. Fall records south of the breeding
grounds in North America are scarce, as most Arctic Terns seem to head east into the Atlantic, then
cut south across the open ocean or follow the coasts

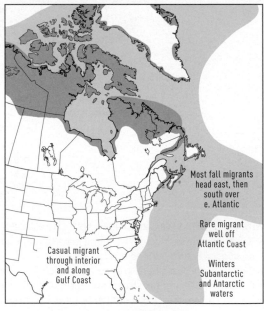

Most fall migrants
head east, then
south over
e. Atlantic

Rare migrant
well off
Atlantic Coast

Winters
Subantarctic
and Antarctic
waters

Casual migrant
through interior
and along
Gulf Coast

of western Europe and West Africa south to the wintering grounds. Northbound migration occurs closer to the coasts of the Americas, making spring sightings south of the species' breeding range far more regular than fall sightings, particularly during strong east winds. Subadults continue to trickle north into early summer and are regularly observed in southern New England and the Mid-Atlantic. The call, heard regularly on the breeding ground, *Keeee-Y-a-a-a-a*, is rougher than Common's, with the later part of the call sounding drawn-out.

SIZE: Same as Common Tern. Slightly smaller than Sabine's Gull.

STRUCTURE: A cursory look suggests it is identical to that of Common Tern, but a more detailed examination shows several subtle differences, which add up to a significantly different bird. The head is smaller and more rounded, the neck is shorter, the body is slightly stockier throughout its length, and the tail is longer. The wings appear to be placed farther forward on the body, and are slimmer overall with a slightly shorter arm and a longer, more attenuated hand than Common Tern's, creating the impression that Arctic Tern is longer-winged.

FLIGHT AND FLOCKING: Much as with structure, the flight style of Arctic Tern seems quite similar to that of Common Tern, but on close examination there are subtle differences that add up to a different way of flying. In fact the structural differences and flight differences seem intimately related. The wings farther forward on the body, thicker neck, and more compact head all contribute to a tense, forward-leaning, and powerful look to Arctic Tern's flight. The longer hand, shorter arm, and slimmer wing also create a more powerful flight style, making the wingbeats appear deeper and more liquid than those of Common. As in most gulls and terns the flight of Arctic Tern is highly variable, but this variability is even more pronounced with Arctic. On the breeding grounds the flight is usually delicate and smooth, much like Common's but with an elegant impression. At sea, particularly during migration, Arctic adopts a strikingly powerful, aggressive flight that allows it to cut through a headwind with ease. In this flight it appears clearly more powerful than Common Tern, with deeper wingbeats. Flocking tendencies are much like Common Tern's.

APPEARANCE: Alternate Adult: Solidly bright red bill, black cap, and pale dusky gray body and wings. The gray of the body is slightly darker than that of Common Tern and extends higher up the face so only a narrow, well-defined pale stripe across the cheek separates the gray body from the black cap. In the Northern Hemisphere, the primaries are always uniformly pale gray, as Arctic Tern typically molts flight feathers only once per year, in the Southern Hemisphere. In contrast, Common Tern shows contrast between fresher inner primaries and worn outer primaries for most of its time in the Northern Hemisphere. Arctic's primaries are extensively translucent, a trait best observed on the underside of the wing, and most noticeably when backlit. The primaries also have a narrow, sharply defined black trailing edge. **First Cycle:** Throughout the first cycle, Arctic Tern sports a more extensive dark hood than Common Tern, often covering much of the crown and extending below the eye. The scaly juvenile plumage is quickly lost, and during their first fall birds have slightly darker dusky gray primaries and duskier lesser coverts than adults. In the following spring the primaries look much like those of adults, and the lesser coverts are only faintly darker than the rest of the wing. **Second Cycle:** Birds returning north for their second spring resemble adults but have variable amounts of pale mottling in the lores and forehead, causing the cap to be incomplete. White blotches mar the gray belly, and many birds show faint dusky lesser coverts. **Distant:** The darkest of the *Sterna* terns, Arctic often appears black at a distance, but when the sun shines through the translucent flight feathers it gives a distinctive two-toned appearance to the wing, the illuminated flight feathers contrasting with the darker opaque wing coverts.

SIMILAR SPECIES: Common Tern: In all plumages the longer neck and bill and flatter crown are useful traits at close range but are difficult to judge at a distance. The differences in flight style can be striking, but the variability of both species' flight styles can make this tricky. Overall, Common's wingbeats are usually shallower and look less smooth and powerful than Arctic's. Common also looks more balanced and not quite as front-heavy as Arctic. In all plumages Common has a small isolated area of translucent inner primaries and a broader black trailing edge to the primaries that is less defined than in Arctic. Most alternate adult Commons show a distinct dark wedge on the outer primaries unlike the evenly gray primaries of Arctic. First-cycle Common has more restricted black on the head, usually just a V of black extending behind the eye to the nape, whereas the more extensive black on the head of first-cycle Arctic gives it a hooded look. First-cycle Common also tends to have darker lesser coverts and a darker hand than first-cycle Arctic, and a blackish, not white, secondary bar.

FIRST CYCLE WITH ADULT COMMON TERN (L). MASSACHUSETTS, JULY. CAMERON COX.
- Slightly narrower wings and more rounded head than Common Tern.
- Leading edge of the wing is not as black as on a first-cycle Common Tern, and there is no black secondary bar.

PROBABLE SECOND CYCLE. MASSACHUSETTS, JULY. KEN BEHRENS.
- Neck is significantly shorter than Common Tern's.
- Arctic Tern has extensively translucent primaries. Only the inner primaries are translucent in Common Tern.
- White speckling on the forehead and belly suggest this is a second-cycle bird.

ALTERNATE ADULTS. SCOTLAND, JUNE. JOHN ANDERSON.
- Wings are set far forward on the body, and the hand is extremely long and attenuated.
- Unlike Common Terns, Arctics molt flight feathers only once a year, on their Southern Hemisphere wintering grounds after fall migration. Consequently, their wings are uniform during summer in the Northern Hemisphere, lacking contrasting dark outer primaries.
- As in Common Tern, the gray body of Arctic ensures that even a modest amount of shadow causes it to look nearly black.

ALTERNATE ADULT WITH AN ALTERNATE ADULT COMMON TERN (L). MASSACHUSETTS, JULY. KEN BEHRENS.

- Arctic has a shorter bill and neck and a rounded crown.
- Upperwing of the Arctic is uniformly pale, whereas Common shows a dark wedge.
- White cheek of the Arctic is narrower and contrasts more with the gray throat.

FINLAND, MAY. HUGH HARROP.

- Often looks heavy-chested.
- When unbroken, the tail streamers are significantly longer than those of Common Tern.

COMPARISON: ARCTIC TERN (L) WITH COMMON TERN (C) AND FORSTER'S TERN (R). MASSACHUSETTS, JULY (ARCTIC AND COMMON); UTAH, JUNE. KEN BEHRENS.

- Arctic has the smallest bill, darkest underparts, and narrowest dark trailing edge to the primaries.
- Common has a medium-sized bill, medium-dark underparts, and is the only *Sterna* with a dark secondary bar.
- Forster's has the largest bill, palest underparts, and heaviest body, which often looks flat.

FORSTER'S TERN
Sterna forsteri
DIMENSIONS
L: 13 in.; WS: 31 in.; WT: 6 oz.

SPRING ARRIVAL

NJ: late Mar.; KS: mid-Apr.; n. IL: late Apr.;
s. MB: late Apr.

FALL ARRIVAL

s. IL: mid-July; NC: late July; n. FL: late July

This is the largest of the *Sterna* terns as well as
the hardiest; it is the only member of the group to
overwinter in North America. Forster's is known
for its distinctive "bandit's mask," though observers can be confused during the brief period in
spring and early summer when Forster's attains a
full black cap and suddenly looks surprisingly similar to Common Tern. Although it can be observed
side by side with Common Tern, in most areas
where overlap occurs Forster's cedes the open water and sandy beaches to Common and instead uses
marshy channels and back bays. Its call is like Common's, a harsh *Keeeaa*, but is slightly lower-pitched,
rougher, and usually just a single syllable.

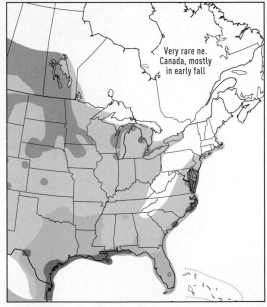

Very rare ne.
Canada, mostly
in early fall

SIZE: Slightly larger than Common Tern. Slightly
smaller than Gull-billed Tern and Bonaparte's Gull.

STRUCTURE: Extremely similar to Common Tern.
Differences may not be immediately apparent,
but with experience they can be useful. Forster's is
slightly bulkier overall with a marginally heavier
body, broader wings, longer neck, and thicker-

based bill. In spring, adults sport an incredibly long tail, though it is prone to breaking off.

FLIGHT AND FLOCKING: Wingbeats are quick and fairly powerful, similar to those of Common Tern but with a slight hitch that gives Forster's a subtle jerkiness to its flight that Common lacks. This difference is apparent only in point-to-point flight; there is no discernible difference in the faster wingbeats employed by both species when actively foraging. Forster's greater weight compared with Common Tern allows it to maintain a steady course even in strong wind, but it seems less maneuverable and graceful than Common. Forster's is quite gregarious, often forming flocks of 3–40 during migration and when commuting to and from roost locations. Flock structure is variable. Most often, flies low to the water in long drawn-out bunches, but may also fly higher in a tight clump, or in very loose aggregations with individuals spread at various altitudes, often with some foraging occurring as they travel. May join Common Tern in mixed flocks. Associations with other terns are less common but do occur. Often forages alongside Bonaparte's Gull when migrating and in winter.

APPEARANCE: Alternate Adult: The black cap contrasts with the pale gray mantle and white body. The inner wing is pale gray, fading into silvery white primaries. When lit by the sun, the primaries gleam and flash with a silvery sheen that heightens the contrast between the pale gray arm and paler hand. Unlike other *Sterna* terns that possess modest (Common) to extensive (Arctic and Roseate) patches of translucent primaries, Forster's Terns show translucency in just a few of the innermost primaries; this is rarely obvious in the field but can appear in photos. The bill is orange-based with a black tip. By late summer most birds have lost the full black cap,

and the outer primaries darken to pale gray. **Basic Adult:** Like alternate but with a striking rectangular black "bandit mask" surrounding the eye and a completely black bill. **First Cycle:** Very similar to basic adult, sporting a full "bandit mask," but with dusky centers to the tertials and dusky gray primaries. Over the first winter and spring these primaries gradually darken, and by the time the bird is almost a year old, at the end of the first cycle, the primaries may be almost black, the only period in the life cycle of a Forster's Tern when it shows fully black primaries. **Second Cycle:** Like basic adult but with slightly darker outer primaries. In spring some may acquire a partial black cap. **Distant:** Gleaming white. The hand flashes silvery in sunlight and can appear paler than the inner wing.

SIMILAR SPECIES: Common Tern: Slightly smaller with a more balanced, less front-heavy appearance. Has slightly slimmer wings and body and shorter neck and tail. Wingbeats are smoother, and flight is more graceful but less stable. From midspring through fall migration, usually shows a distinct dark wedge in the outer primaries, unlike the uniformly pale wings of Forster's. **Roseate Tern:** More slender build with slimmer wings and a longer tail. Wingbeats are faster and shallower, with a distinctly choppy appearance recalling Least Tern. Whereas Forster's is quite pale and its wings gleam in the sun, Roseate's flight feathers are strikingly transparent, and in almost any light conditions it is extremely pale and almost seems internally lit. **Gull-billed Tern:** Although it is only marginally larger than Forster's, its heavier build creates the appearance of significantly larger size. Wingbeats are significantly slower in most conditions and are the most useful identification criterion at great distance. Additionally, the wings are broader, the bill much heavier, and the tail shorter.

BASIC ADULTS. TEXAS, JAN. KEN BEHRENS.

- Very pale tern that sports a distinctive rectangular black eye patch for much of the year.
- Has a husky build for a medium-sized tern.
- The only medium-sized tern likely to be seen in winter in eastern North America.

TWO BASIC ADULTS WITH TWO BASIC ADULT BONAPARTE'S GULLS. TEXAS, JAN. CAMERON COX.

- Forster's Tern and Bonaparte's Gull have similar foraging techniques and often feed together in winter.
- These two species are sometimes confused as they are similar in color and form similar flocks.
- Forster's Tern is smaller, with faster wingbeats, and tends to fly more erratically than Bonaparte's Gull.

TEXAS, JAN. CAMERON COX.
- Migrating and commuting birds often form vaguely oval-shaped flocks.

(RIGHT) ALTERNATE ADULT. UTAH, JUNE. KEN BEHRENS.

BASIC ADULT. NEW JERSEY, NOV. CAMERON COX.
- Uniformly pale but with an unusual flat quality, lacking the strong reflective or glowing appearance of Roseate Tern, though not as dull as Common Tern.

FIRST CYCLE. FLORIDA, JAN. CAMERON COX.
- The well-defined eye patch is diagnostic.
- First cycle looks much like basic adult but is slightly duller. The flight feathers gradually become darker throughout the first winter.

COMPARISON: FORSTER'S TERN (L) WITH COMMON TERN (R).

- Forster's has slightly broader-based bill, more prominent forehead causing the head to appear larger, slightly broader wings, and slightly heavier body with a flat belly.
- The primaries on Forster's have a pale, silvery appearance.
- On Common, the inner primaries are paler than the outer primaries, creating a dark wedge.
- Forster's has a slightly shorter hand.

FIRST CYCLE (C) WITH TWO COMMON TERNS. TEXAS, APR. KEN BEHRENS.

- Combination of heavier body, broader wings, and larger bill compared with Common Tern is subtle, but once learned it is effective at greater distances than the differences in head pattern.
- The retained juvenile flight feathers on the Forster's are beginning to show wear and will become darker over the next few months. Only late in the first cycle does Forster's ever have blackish primaries.

WITH THREE LAUGHING GULLS. TEXAS, JAN. CAMERON COX.

- Flocks of this size are unusual but occur in some locations along the Gulf Coast in winter, particularly as birds gather to roost.

ROSEATE TERN
Sterna dougallii
DIMENSIONS
L: 12.5 in.; WS: 29 in.; WT: 3.9 oz.

SPRING ARRIVAL

s. FL: mid-Apr.; se. MA: early May;
Long Island: mid-May

FALL ARRIVAL

off NC: late Aug.; West Indies: Sept.;
ne. South America: Oct.

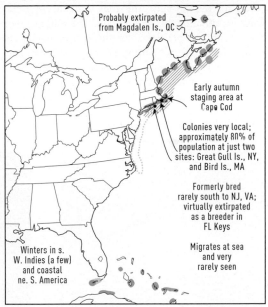

Probably extirpated from Magdalen Is., QC

Early autumn staging area at Cape Cod

Colonies very local; approximately 80% of population at just two sites: Great Gull Is., NY, and Bird Is., MA

Formerly bred rarely south to NJ, VA; virtually extirpated as a breeder in FL Keys

Migrates at sea and very rarely seen

Winters in s. W. Indies (a few) and coastal ne. S. America

In a family of beautiful and elegant birds, Roseate Tern is among the most beautiful and elegant. Its mystique is enhanced by its scarcity and fragmented range, which have led some people to speculate that the species was once far more common and widespread but now persists only in a few former strongholds. Roseate is primarily a pelagic migrant that is rarely seen in North America away from its breeding range. It is often located by its distinctive call, a two-syllabled *CHI-vit*, quite different from the calls of other *Sterna* terns.

SIZE: About the same size as Common Tern but appears smaller because of its slim build.

STRUCTURE: Slimmer than the other *Sterna* terns with thinner, proportionally shorter wings that are held straighter than those of other *Sternas*. It has exceptionally long tail streamers that bounce and quiver noticeably with every wingbeat. At a distance these steamers are often difficult to detect, and they are also prone to breaking off; in these instances, Roseate Tern appears strikingly short-tailed rather than long-tailed. The bill is long, slim, sharply pointed, and slightly decurved. It differs noticeably from the bills of other *Sterna* terns at close range, but its distinctiveness melts away at a distance.

FLIGHT AND FLOCKING: Flight style is totally distinct from that of other *Sterna* terns. Wingbeats are quick, shallow, and stiff. To some degree they recall the wingbeats of Least Tern but are more measured and never appear frantic. Tends to patrol and forage at greater heights than other *Sterna* terns, 20–30 feet above the water. Usually observed singly or in pairs but readily joins flocks of other *Sterna* terns. Limited observation of migrants suggests that they fly in small, tightly packed flocks low over the water. Probably because of the scarcity of the bird, solo migrants are also frequent.

APPEARANCE: Alternate Adult: Extremely pale, with a black cap and a faint rosy flush to the underparts. The bill is almost totally black, though it briefly develops a reddish base during the breeding season. The feet are bright red, brighter than on any other *Sterna* tern. The gray of the mantle is clearly paler than that of Common Tern, and Roseate reflects light in such a manner that it almost appears to glow when hit by the sun. The fully translucent flight feathers enhance this impression. The outer two or three primaries are dark, creating a thin, dark strip unlike the wedge of Common Tern. **First Cycle:** Distinctive, with an almost fully dark cap and upperparts heavily marked with dark V-shaped markings, a pattern completely unlike that of any other juvenile *Sterna* terns. By fall the markings have largely faded and the forehead and crown are pale with fine dark streaking, and a darker V extends from behind the eye to the nape. The wing pattern is like that of a washed-out first-cycle Common Tern, with faint, smudgy lesser coverts, pale dusky hand, and faint gray secondary bar. Thin, silvery tips to the secondaries and inner primaries form a faint pale trailing edge that is difficult to detect in flight but diagnostic if noted. **Distant:** Bright white even in dark conditions. Almost appears to be illuminated from within.

SIMILAR SPECIES: Common Tern: Slightly heavier build with more angular wings, and deeper, more fluid wingbeats. Whereas Roseate Tern is strikingly pale with fully translucent flight feathers, Common Tern is darker and duller, often with a strong dark wedge on the outer three to five primaries. The translucent patches in the wing are restricted to the inner primaries. **Forster's Tern:** Can be mistaken for Roseate by those unfamiliar with both species, as both share very pale overall coloration and long tail streamers. Forster's is slightly, but distinctly, larger than Roseate with a blockier head, deeper chest, and heavier bill. It also has deeper, slightly slower wingbeats and broader wings. Unlike in Roseate, the flight feathers show only a tiny translucent patch in the inner primaries, and the hand is paler than the arm. Forster's also lacks the narrow strip of dark outer primaries shown by adult Roseate Tern in summer. Forster's has a strong orange base to the bill and lacks a rosy wash on the chest. Although both species are quite pale, Forster's Tern seems to reflect light in the same way a mirror does, whereas Roseate Tern almost seems to glow like a light bulb.

ALTERNATE ADULT. MASSACHUSETTS, JULY. KEN BEHRENS.

- Has the slimmest wings and body of any medium-sized tern.
- Bill is long and slender. The amount of red at the base in summer varies but is usually modest. Some lack red entirely.

ALTERNATE ADULT WITH TWO COMMON TERNS. MASSACHUSETTS, JULY. CAMERON COX.

- Has a beautiful and distinctive "luminous" quality, unlike any other medium-sized tern. Blindingly white in bright light, and even in shadow maintains a slight pale glow.
- Tail streamers are exceptionally long and flutter with every wingbeat.

ALTERNATE ADULTS WITH TWO ALTERNATE ADULT COMMON TERNS. MASSACHUSETTS, JULY. TOBY SACKTON.

- Note how the head and bill profile differs from that of Common Tern.
- Roseate has a white body, whereas Common in summer has a noticeably gray body and contrasting white cheek.

ADULTS WITH FIVE LESSER CRESTED TERNS. MADAGASCAR, NOV. KEN BEHRENS.

- Their bills are very slender and sharply pointed.
- The bottom right bird (out of focus) is still in alternate plumage.
- In alternate plumage, Roseate has much brighter red feet than other *Sterna* terns, visible at moderate distance, including on birds flying directly away.

JUVENILE (BOTTOM) AND ADULT. MASSACHUSETTS, JULY. KEN BEHRENS.

- Terns and many other large waterbirds fledge before their wings and bills are fully grown, altering their structure and flight style for several weeks. Note the short, blunt wings and short bill of the juvenile.

JUVENILE. MASSACHUSETTS, JULY. KEN BEHRENS.

- Among medium-sized terns, the scaly pattern of dark V-shaped markings is unique to juvenile Roseate. They also have much more extensive dark markings on the head than other juvenile *Sterna* terns.

ALTERNATE ADULT. MASSACHUSETTS, JULY. KEN BEHRENS.
• Can show a dark wedge in the primaries like Common Tern, but it is usually narrower, restricted to just a few outer primaries.

ALTERNATE ADULTS (TOP L AND BOTTOM R) WITH TWO ALTERNATE ADULT COMMON TERNS. MASSACHUSETTS, JULY. KEN BEHRENS.
• Roseate has stiff, shallow wingbeats unlike those of any other *Sterna* terns.
• Translucent patches in the wings are larger and more obvious than those shown by Common Tern.

ALTERNATE ADULT WITH COMMON TERN (BOTTOM). MASSACHUSETTS, JULY. KEN BEHRENS.
• Roseate Terns are noticeably slimmer and paler than Common.

ROSEATE TERN.
- Most slender and slimmest-winged of the medium-sized terns.
- So pale it seems to glow.
- Long tail bounces with every wingbeat.

COMMON TERN.
- Appears lean and rangy, but still more heavily built than Roseate.
- Larger-headed than Roseate; longer-necked than Arctic.
- Typically the shortest-tailed of the medium-sized terns.

FORSTER'S TERN.
- Heavy-billed and large-headed.
- Chest often looks flat.
- Clean, pale overall appearance but does not glow like Roseate.

MASSACHUSETTS, JULY. KEN BEHRENS.
- Lacks the dark trailing edge to the primaries shown by the other Sterna terns.
- The long tail streamers break off easily, and even when present they easily blend into pale backgrounds, which can make Roseate Terns look abnormally short-tailed.

LEAST TERN
Sternula antillarum
DIMENSIONS
L: 9 in.; WS: 20 in.; WT: 1.5 oz.

SPRING ARRIVAL

TX: late Mar.; n. FL: early Apr.; NE: late Apr.; VA: late Apr.; ME: mid-May

This tiny tern is slightly smaller than look-alikes from the Old World—Little Tern and Saunder's Tern—making it the smallest tern in the world. It is a summer visitor to sandy beaches along the southern Atlantic and Gulf Coasts and major rivers and lakes in the central U.S. Its preference for open, sandy habitat makes it vulnerable to flooding and predation. The additional human pressures of development, dams, and beachgoers have caused the species to decline to the point that it is recognized as endangered in the majority of its range. Least Tern is pugnacious and very vocal, challenging trespassers with an explosive *Kadee-Kadee*.

SIZE: The smallest tern. Clearly smaller than Black Tern. About the size of Sanderling.

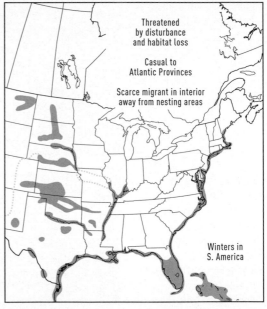

Threatened by disturbance and habitat loss

Casual to Atlantic Provinces

Scarce migrant in interior away from nesting areas

Winters in S. America

STRUCTURE: Stocky and neckless, with a disproportionally large head and very thin wings. The wings are thrust slightly forward and curved back at the wrist, creating a scimitar-shaped silhouette. The bill is small, thin, and frequently pointed down but can be difficult to see at a distance as it blends easily into most backgrounds. The tail is of moderate length and strongly forked, though it too disappears at a distance, creating a remarkably short-tailed appearance.

FLIGHT AND FLOCKING: Wingbeats are deep and rapid, the body bobbing up and down with each wingbeat. Flight appears slightly jerky and unstable as the bird is often tossed about by the wind. Rarely maintains a constant speed; it checks and accelerates, pauses and hovers, dives, and hovers some more. Has almost hummingbird-like abilities to move vertically. It is not unusual to see a Least Tern skimming the surface of the water one moment, then bounce 10 feet straight up in the air, hover, and plunge-dive straight back down, striking the water with a splash. Gregarious, often found in tightly packed flocks, though only flies with other tern species incidentally.

APPEARANCE: Alternate Adult: Extremely pale gray above and white below, with a black cap and black outer primaries. The black cap is broken by a triangular white forehead. The bill is bright yellow with a small dark tip. **Basic Adult:** Like alternate but with a black bill, and the white forehead expands to include most of the crown. Most birds have moved south before molting into this plumage, though in the Gulf states many attain this plumage right before they migrate. **First Cycle:** Striking. The wings display a muted Sabine's Gull–like pattern with gray inner wings, a blackish hand, and contrastingly bright white secondaries and greater coverts. A black line runs through the eye, and the crown is mostly pale with faint dark streaking. The back is initially covered with dark U-shaped markings, but these are quickly lost and replaced with a pale gray mantle. **Distant:** Gleaming white with a faint silvery sheen, like Forster's Tern. Like Forster's Tern, shows only a tiny patch of translucent inner primaries that are rarely discernible in the field.

SIMILAR SPECIES: No truly similar species in North America. **Black Tern:** Slightly larger. Much darker in all plumages, with broader wings and a smooth, floating flight style. ***Sterna* Terns:** Any medium-sized tern can briefly be confused with Least, but the very rapid, slightly jerky wingbeats of Least should be sufficient to separate it from the four *Sterna* terns, which have slower, more powerful wingbeats. Roseate Tern is somewhat similar to Least in having an odd, slightly jerky wingbeat, but the wingbeats of Roseate are shallow and the flight steadier.

WITH TWO COMMON TERNS, A FORSTER'S TERN, A BLACK TERN, AND A SANDERLING. TEXAS, APR. KEN BEHRENS.
• Tiny and short-tailed, with a fairly large head and very slender wings.
• Flocks can be quite large and tightly packed, like a flock of shorebirds but not as cohesive.
• Only slightly smaller than Black Tern, but the pale color and narrower wings make it appear much smaller.
• Half the size of a *Sterna* tern, with much faster, stiffer wingbeats.

ALTERNATE ADULTS. TEXAS, APR. KEN BEHRENS.
- Tiny size in combination with the white V on the forehead, yellow bill, and narrow black leading edge to the primaries makes them unmistakable.
- Flocks sit on beaches in close groups and, when disturbed, take flight in unison with a noisy, aggressive chatter, quickly settling back on the beach one by one after the threat has passed.

JUVENILE. NEW JERSEY, AUG. CAMERON COX.
- Dark U-shaped markings on the back and extensive dark head markings are similar to those on juvenile Roseate Tern, but Least Tern's wings are darker, with a Sabine's Gull–like pale trailing edge that is unique among terns.

WITH TWO BLACK TERNS (BOTTOM R). FLORIDA, JULY. CAMERON COX.
- Notice how the Least Terns' tails seem too short and their heads too large.
- A bird that looks like a basic adult or first alternate individual is in the upper-left corner. First-cycle birds are rarely seen in spring, but a few appear in fall when they are over a year old. See the next page for a bird late in the first cycle.

(RIGHT) FIRST CYCLE. NEW JERSEY, SEPT. CAMERON COX.

ALTERNATE ADULT. TEXAS, JULY. KEN BEHRENS.
• Hovers frequently and often for long periods and dives vertically for fish.

ALTERNATE ADULTS AND FIRST CYCLES WITH TWO COMMON AND FOUR BLACK TERNS. NORTH CAROLINA, JULY. KEN BEHRENS.
• Least Terns look short-winged.

WITH A BLACK TERN (SECOND FROM L). OKLAHOMA, SEPT. JIM ARTERBURN.
• Northern-breeding Least Terns leave their breeding territories in alternate plumage, though a few will lose their black crown, like the bottom-right bird.
• Along the Gulf Coast, many adult Leasts progress well into prebasic body molt before departing for their wintering grounds.
• Note the two juveniles in the background.

BLACK TERN
Chlidonias niger
DIMENSIONS
L: 9.75 in.; WS: 24 in.; WT: 2.2 oz.

SPRING ARRIVAL

TX: late Mar.; MO: late Apr./early May;
ME: mid-May; MB: mid-May

FALL ARRIVAL

DE: mid-July; GA: mid-July; TX: mid-July

This striking species is the only native "marsh tern." This charismatic group has two additional representatives in the Old World (White-winged and Whiskered Terns), both of which have occurred as vagrants in eastern North America. A Black Tern bounding over its breeding territory with its butterfly-like flight is a thing of beauty; however, during migration it tends to have a shabby appearance with variable amounts of black blotching. It is usually silent but in large flocks gives a high, scratchy *KEK*.

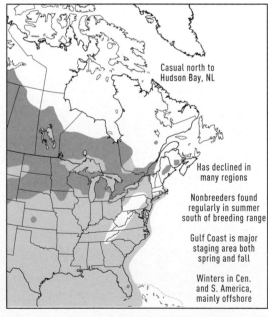

Casual north to Hudson Bay, NL

Has declined in many regions

Nonbreeders found regularly in summer south of breeding range

Gulf Coast is major staging area both spring and fall

Winters in Cen. and S. America, mainly offshore

SIZE: Slightly larger than Least Tern. Significantly smaller than Common Tern. Only slightly smaller than Little Gull.

STRUCTURE: Appears petite, with a compact, slightly pudgy body. The small, round head is held slightly raised, and the bill tilts down slightly. The wings are broad but proportionally short for a tern, consisting of a short broad arm and a long hand that is initially quite broad but tapers to a sharp point. The tail is also short and slightly forked.

FLIGHT AND FLOCKING: Their completely distinctive and mesmerizingly beautiful way of flying is unlike that of any other North American tern. Standard flight is erratic, with deep wingbeats, often hesitating and changing altitude. Foraging flight is even more erratic, with the wings tucked in toward the body. Tentative, shallow wingbeats are sporadically interspersed with deep, rowing wingbeats. Unlike in medium-sized terns, the body does not bounce up and down with the wingbeats. The whole bird moves up and down, almost giving the impression of floating through the air. As a migrant, typically seen in flocks of 3–200 but occasionally forms much larger flocks. These flocks may be loosely spread over a large area in loonlike fashion or in tightly packed knots. Sometimes even forms well-defined U-shaped flocks, rather like those of some ducks. This type of flock structure is sometimes shown by other tern species as well and seems characteristic of high-flying flocks that are migrating toward the breeding grounds.

APPEARANCE: Alternate Adult: All-black head and underparts extend down to the bright white vent. The wings and back are medium gray, the underwings pale dusky gray. **Basic Adult:** Black cap with partial "earmuffs" that extend down behind the eyes.

White underneath with a variable smudgy dark bar that extends down onto the sides of the breast, and medium gray above. Blotchy-looking transitional birds are commonly seen during spring and fall migration. **First Cycle:** Much like basic adult but usually slightly paler with a cleaner appearance. Gray cap with darker "earmuffs." Medium gray above, often washed heavily with brown in the late summer and early fall and with a darker leading edge of the wings and paler rump. White underneath with pale gray underwings. **Distant:** Alternate adults are strikingly black and gray with pale underwings, but migrants often have a shabby appearance, dingy gray with variable black patches. Even the palest first-cycle birds have a lackluster appearance, being dull gray and dingy white.

SIMILAR SPECIES: White-winged Tern (not included in this guide): This vagrant from the Old World seems to be occurring in eastern North America far less frequently than formerly. When it does occur, it should be easily separated from Black Tern if seen well. Alternate adult is unmistakable, with bold white patches on the upperwing and jet-black underwing coverts. Basic adult is far paler than Black Tern, with restricted black markings on the crown, a paler mantle, and white underparts and rump, lacking the smudgy gray sides of the breast of basic Black Tern. **Little Gull:** Juvenile shares some similarities with basic and juvenile Black Terns but is stockier with broader and blunter wings, paler underwings, and a white tail with a black tail band.

TEXAS, APR. KEN BEHRENS.
- Small, dark tern with broad, curved wings.
- On the breeding grounds they are birds of shallow freshwater pools, but in spring and fall they stage and migrate along the Gulf Coast in huge numbers.

BASIC ADULT. NORTH CAROLINA, AUG. CAMERON COX.
- During migration, most Black Terns are molting and have a messy appearance.

JUVENILE. NORTH CAROLINA, AUG. CAMERON COX.
- Brown back is typical of juveniles in early fall but wears away quickly. Even without the brown back, juveniles are distinctive because of their neat appearance.
- The medium gray color causes Black Terns to look very dark in poor light.

ALTERNATE ADULTS. NORTH DAKOTA, MAY. KEN BEHRENS.
- On the breeding grounds there is no trace of the messy, patchwork appearance seen during migration. Black Terns are absolutely stunning and unmistakable.

ALTERNATE ADULT WITH NINE COMMON AND FOUR ARCTIC TERNS. MASSACHUSETTS, JULY. KEN BEHRENS.

• Their small size can make them difficult to pick out from flocks of larger terns, despite their drastically different coloration.
• *Can you find all five Arctic Terns?*

OKLAHOMA, AUG. JIM ARTERBURN.

• They hover like other terns but make controlled dives and snatch prey delicately off the surface rather than plunge headfirst into the water.

ALTERNATE ADULT. NORTH DAKOTA, MAY. KEN BEHRENS.

• When you can see the pink gape you are really seeing a Black Tern!
• Notice the contrast created by the bright white undertail.

ONE FIRST CYCLE AND THREE ADULTS WITH A SANDWICH TERN. TEXAS, APR. KEN BEHRENS.

• Note the messy, mottled appearance of several individuals. At a distance, flocks take on this same patchy aspect.

SOOTY TERN
Onychoprion fuscatus
DIMENSIONS
L: 16 in.; WS: 32 in.; WT: 6 oz.

SPRING ARRIVAL

Dry Tortugas, FL: late Dec.; TX: mid-Apr.; off NC: mid-May

Sooty Tern is a truly pelagic species, and some individuals may spend years on the open ocean, coming to shore only to breed. In the U.S. the species breeds primarily on the Dry Tortugas in the Florida Keys but may be found regularly during the summer and early fall in the deep waters of the Gulf of Mexico and warm Atlantic offshore waters north to North Carolina, with small numbers following the Gulf Stream all the way up to Massachusetts. Although rarely seen from shore during normal conditions, Sooty Tern is often observed from land or even on inland bodies of water in association with tropical storms. Call is loud, raucous *wide-a-awake* or *KERR-wacka-wack*.

SIZE: Slightly larger than Bridled Tern. About the same size as Sandwich Tern but appears larger because of its dark color.

May be found well north and inland following tropical storms

STRUCTURE: Powerful, athletic build; long wings; and a long, forked tail. The chest is notably deeper than the rest of the body, which tapers into the long tail. The wings are set far forward on the body and are long and angular with sharply pointed tips.

FLIGHT AND FLOCKING: Deep, powerful wingbeats cover distance with supreme ease; the swift flight may almost recall a jaeger at times. Unlike Bridled Tern, often soars to great heights, hanging in the air much like a frigatebird. Often seen in pairs or small groups of 3–12 but may form huge feeding flocks where fish are abundant. May forage and flock with Bridled Tern and occasionally with Sandwich Tern.

APPEARANCE: Adult: Glossy black above with extensively white forehead and white outer tail feathers. The underparts are bright white, as are the underwing coverts, which contrast strongly with the blackish flight feathers. **First Cycle:** Lives up to the species' name, being sooty black overall with pale but dingy underwing coverts and vent. The upperwing coverts have small pale tips, but these are rarely visible in flight. **Distant:** Adults look jet-black but show flashes of the white belly and underwing coverts. In particular, the underwing contrast can be evident at great distances. First-cycle birds appear matte black, their paler vent and underwings invisible.

SIMILAR SPECIES: Bridled Tern: Often difficult to separate at the distances and conditions typical of tropical tern observations. Slightly smaller with more elegant, less powerful flight. Has a paler gray mantle than Sooty, so that the black cap contrasts with the back, though this trait is difficult to judge at a distance. The underwing is more extensively pale, but the contrast between the primaries and underwing coverts, which is usually obvious on Sooty Tern, is reduced.

JUVENILE. NORTH CAROLINA, AUG. CAMERON COX.
- Lanky tern with an exceptionally long hand and long, forked tail.
- Readily soars, an unusual behavior among terns.
- Juvenile is quite unlike other juvenile terns: sooty overall with pale but dingy wing linings.

ADULT AND JUVENILE WITH SANDWICH (LOWER L) AND BLACK TERNS (UPPER R). FLORIDA, SEPT. BOB WALLACE.
- Noticeably larger and more powerfully built than Sandwich Tern, and dwarfs Black Tern.

ADULTS WITH TWO BROWN NODDIES (R). FLORIDA, APR. CAMERON COX.
- Bright white underwing contrasts sharply with the black wingtip. In Bridled Tern, white bleeds into the wingtip, significantly reducing the contrast between the wing lining and primaries. This aspect of plumage is visible at greater distances than other plumage traits.
- Brown Noddies look a bit like juvenile Sooty Terns but have a longer tail and lack the pale wing lining.

- The black head does not contrast noticeably with the blackish back, and there is no pale collar.
- Raucous feeding flocks quickly form when predatory fish drive smaller fish to the surface.

ADULT WITH BRIDLED TERN (R). NORTH CAROLINA, AUG. KATE SUTHERLAND.

- In close comparison the difference in mantle color is obvious; however, Bridled Terns appear darker at a distance, making this trait less reliable.
- Bridled Tern has a shorter, slightly blunter hand.
- The white triangle on the forehead of Sooty Tern is short and fat, extending only to the eye. Adult Bridled Terns have a longer but fairly narrow white triangle, extending behind the eye. However, many Bridled Terns seen in the Gulf Stream have a largely white head, like the bird shown here.

BRIDLED TERN
Onychoprion anaethetus
DIMENSIONS
L: 15 in.; WS: 30 in.; WT: 3.5 oz.

SPRING ARRIVAL

off FL: late Mar.; off NC: mid-May;
w. Gulf of Mexico: late June

FALL ARRIVAL

off VA: mid-Aug.; off NJ: mid-Aug.

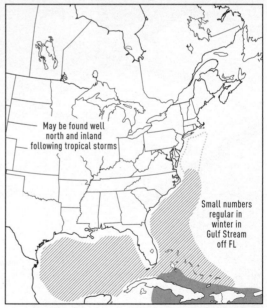

May be found well north and inland following tropical storms

Small numbers regular in winter in Gulf Stream off FL

Like Sooty Tern, Bridled Tern is pelagic and some individuals may spend years at sea before returning to land, though unlike Sooty, they often rest on floating debris or even passing sea turtles. This species forages most frequently around mats or lines of *Sargassum* weed, unlike Sooty, which usually feeds on marine life driven to the surface by tuna and other large predatory fish. Only a few Bridled Terns nest in the Florida Keys, the only breeding location in the U.S., but the species is regular in the warmer months in the Gulf of Mexico and the Gulf Stream north to North Carolina, and rarely farther north. Like Sooty, it is often found close to shore or even inland during tropical weather systems, whereas away from the breeding grounds, observations from shore not related to tropical systems are rare. Call is a soft *weep*, rarely heard away from the breeding grounds.

SIZE: Slightly smaller than Sooty Tern. About the same size as Common Tern but may appear larger and heavier because of its darker color.

STRUCTURE: Similar to Sooty Tern but slimmer, with a touch of the emaciated look of Sandwich Tern. The body is marginally deeper just before the wings but lacks the expanded chest of Sooty, and the entire body tapers gradually to the long, forked tail, creating the impression of a longer, more drawn-out body than those of the *Sterna* terns. The hand is slightly shorter and broader than that of Sooty, with the arm and hand being almost equal in length, causing the wingtips to appear slightly blunt—a minor difference compared with Sooty but distinctly different from the *Sterna* terns, which have longer hands.

FLIGHT AND FLOCKING: Wingbeats are typically unhurried and buoyant with an elastic quality that is unlike the powerful, driving flight of Sooty Tern. Does not soar as Sooty often does. Regularly seen in pairs or flocks of three to eight, but in excellent foraging areas much larger groups may gather. Will flock with Sooty Tern and occasionally with Sandwich Tern.

APPEARANCE: Alternate Adult: Black cap with a narrow white triangle on the forehead that extends behind the eye. A very pale gray band across the nape emphasizes the contrast of the black cap. The remainder of the upperparts is medium gray-brown with slightly darker flight feathers. The underparts are almost fully white with the darker flight feathers contrasting moderately with the wing coverts. A diffuse pale area extends up the shaft of each primary feather so that the white coverts appear to fade into the darker wingtip, unlike the sharp contrast between these areas on Sooty Tern. The tail is almost all white except for the gray central feathers. **Basic Adult:** Like alternate but with extensive pale forehead and crown. **First Cycle:** White forehead and crown, with the nape and upper back washed with pale gray, darkening to medium gray farther down the back. The wings are medium brown and clearly darker than the back and nape. The underparts and underwing pattern are similar to those of adult. **Distant:** A hint of the paler back may be visible on adults. First-cycle birds often have an obvious pale head that contrasts with the dark upperwings.

SIMILAR SPECIES: Sooty Tern: Larger, with a stockier appearance and more direct and powerful flight. The nape is the same color as the back, lacking the contrast of Bridled. On the underwing of Sooty there is a sharp dividing line between the white primary coverts and the dark primaries that is often visible at great distances. **Black Tern:** Much smaller and more compact, with a plump body, shorter wings, and short tail. Wingbeats are weaker, and flight is more buoyant and aimless than Bridled's. In all plumages the underwing is plain gray.

JUVENILE. NORTH CAROLINA, JULY. CAMERON COX.

- Like Sooty Tern, Bridled is large and long-winged, but it is slimmer than Sooty, with a shorter hand.
- In all plumages, white vanes extend onto the underside of the primaries, reducing the contrast between dark primaries and pale underwing coverts.
- This bird can be aged as a juvenile by the fine pale fringes to the upperparts and the weak head pattern.
- Juvenile Bridled is utterly different from juvenile Sooty, but is fairly similar to adult Bridled.

ADULT AND JUVENILE (L). NORTH CAROLINA, AUG. CAMERON COX.
- The underside of the primaries is largely pale on both birds, whereas Sooty Terns have dark primaries that contrast sharply with the white underwing coverts.
- Bridled lacks the expanded chest of Sooty Tern.

ADULT. NORTH CAROLINA, AUG. CHRIS SLOAN.
- The black crown contrasts clearly with the pale gray upper back, unlike in Sooty Tern.
- The white area on the forehead is narrower than on adult Sooty but extends farther behind the eye.

NORTH CAROLINA, AUG. KEN BEHRENS.
- Even at this angle, the paler back is apparent.
- Wings are slightly paler than those of Sooty Tern, with obvious gray tones.
- On the underwing, the white vanes extending into the primaries are clearly visible.
- Many Bridled Terns seen in the Gulf Stream in late summer have a largely white head, like this bird.
- The dark oval on the right wing is a growing primary (P10).

BROWN NODDY
Anous stolidus
DIMENSIONS
L: 15.5 in.; WS: 32 in.; WT: 7 oz.

Brown Noddy is an odd, ternlike tropical seabird. In the area covered by this guide it is found regularly only in the Dry Tortugas of Florida, where several thousand breed. Away from the Dry Tortugas it is found occasionally in the Florida Keys and rarely off the Florida peninsula. Elsewhere it is very rare in the Gulf of Mexico and in the Gulf Stream north to North Carolina and is accidental farther north, usually only after a tropical system. Call is a harsh, croaking *Karrk*.

SIZE: About the same size as Sooty and Sandwich Terns. Slightly smaller than Laughing Gull.

STRUCTURE: Slender and long-winged like Sooty Tern, but the wings are slightly broader, shorter, and blunter-tipped. The head is small and slopes into the long, slightly drooped bill. The long tail is the most distinctive aspect of the structure; depending on

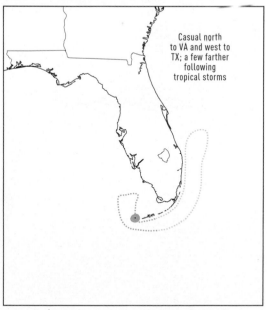

Casual north to VA and west to TX; a few farther following tropical storms

how it is held, it can appear wedge-shaped, lobed, pointed, or blunt-tipped. No matter how it is held, it looks odd and completely unlike the deeply forked tail with long outer tail feathers of most terns.

FLIGHT AND FLOCKING: Fairly swift and powerful, as in Sooty Tern, but with deeper wingbeats that are slightly slower than Sooty's and that give the appearance of being looser and less controlled. Because of this, the flight appears less direct and purposeful than Sooty's, an impression that is heightened by Brown Noddy's tendency to rock side to side with each wingbeat. Often flies in pairs or in small loose flocks of up to 10. Sometimes flies with Sooty or Bridled Terns.

APPEARANCE: Adult: Warm medium brown overall with slightly darker flight feathers and a white forehead that fades into a gray nape. **First Cycle:** Like adult but with very restricted white forehead and no gray nape. Late in the first cycle, the wing coverts become very tattered and faded and may look like a paler brown streak running down the center of the wing. **Distant:** Uniformly brown. In good light, contrast between pale head, paler brown back, and darker brown flight feathers may be visible.

SIMILAR SPECIES: Sooty Tern: Slightly sleeker, with thinner, more sharply pointed wings and a very different tail shape. Adult has bright white underparts and underwing coverts. First cycle also has a pale vent and underwings, but they are far less obvious than those of adult, and the bird can appear all dark at a distance, like a Brown Noddy, but tends to have a colder appearance. Differences in flight style and structure are also useful for separating first-cycle Sooty Tern from Brown Noddy. **Black Noddy** (not included in this guide): Extremely rare away from the Dry Tortugas, where it is scarce. Slightly smaller and slimmer than Brown Noddy, with a longer, thinner bill. Typically darker with a sharply defined white cap; however, worn birds may appear similar to Brown Noddy. Chances are, if you are anywhere in the eastern U.S. or Canada other than the Dry Tortugas, the bird you are looking at is likely not a Brown Noddy and definitely not a Black Noddy.

ADULTS. FLORIDA, APR. CAMERON COX.

- Slender shape and long, wedge-shaped tail, which appears pointed when closed, create a striking silhouette.
- Uniformly brown plumage, including the underwing, eliminates all regularly occurring terns. The similar Black Noddy is extremely rare away from the Dry Tortugas; it is smaller, thinner-winged, shorter-tailed, and has darker, colder-toned plumage.
- Potential confusion with a dark-morph jaeger should be eliminated by the long, slender bill and very different flight style.
- Differences between first-cycle and adult Brown Noddies are subtle and not noticeable at a distance.

WHERE TO WATCH

WATCH SITES

1 L'ANSE AUX MEADOWS
2 CAPE SPEAR
3 CAPES RAY AND ANGUILE
4 EAST POINT
5 CAPES NORTH AND ST. LAWRENCE
6 CHEBUCTO HEAD AND HARTLEN POINT
7 WESTERN HEAD AND BACCARO POINT
8 BRIER ISLAND
9 QUODDY HEAD
10 DYER POINT, CAPE ELIZABETH
11 CAPE ANN
12 CAPE COD
13 MONTAUK POINT
14 SANDY HOOK
15 AVALON
16 DELAWARE BAY
17 CAPE HENLOPEN STATE PARK

18 ASSATEAGUE ISLAND
19 CHESAPEAKE BAY
20 BACK BAY NATIONAL WILDLIFE REFUGE
21 OUTER BANKS
22 FORT FISHER
23 HUNTINGTON BEACH STATE PARK
24 TYBEE ISLAND
25 NORTHEAST FLORIDA
26 DRY TORTUGAS
27 FORT PICKENS
28 CAMERON PARISH
29 EAST BEACH, GALVESTON
30 SOUTH PADRE ISLAND
31 MISSISSIPPI RIVER
32 LAKES KENTUCKY AND BARKLEY
33 OHIO RIVER

34 MILLER BEACH
35 WHITEFISH POINT
36 SARNIA/PORT HURON
37 BRUCE PENINSULA
38 PRESQUE ISLE STATE PARK
39 NIAGARA RIVER
40 VAN WAGNER'S BEACH
41 CONEJOHELA FLATS
42 HAMLIN BEACH STATE PARK
43 CAYUGA LAKE
44 HUDSON RIVER
45 LAKE CHAMPLAIN
46 OTTAWA RIVER
47 ST. LAWRENCE WATERWAY

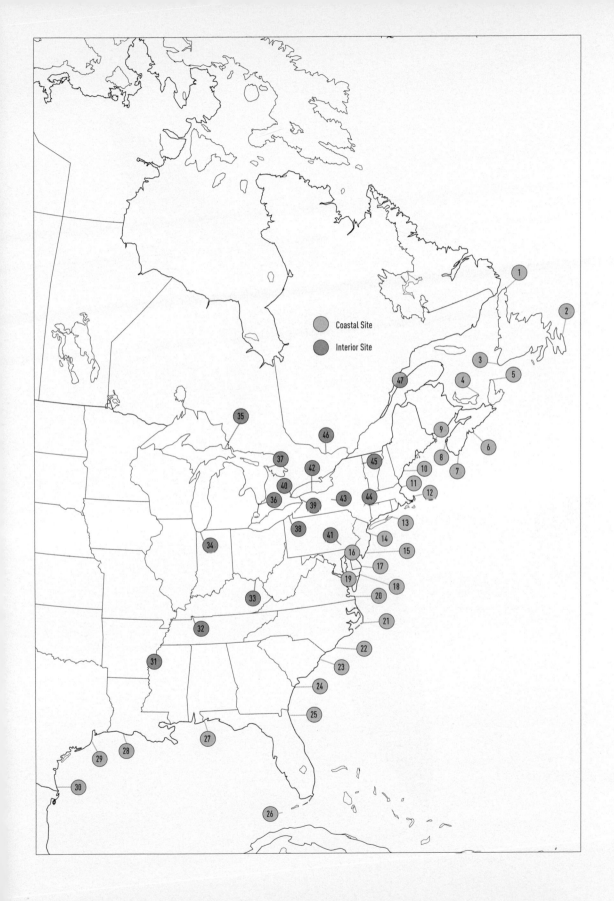

Coastal Site

Interior Site

INTRODUCTION

This section is designed both to direct readers to established migration watch points and to suggest areas for further exploration. The pages that follow describe 47 sites scattered all across eastern North America. This is not intended to be a complete listing of good watch points, but rather covers a diverse, and we hope representative, set of sites. In addition to providing information for potential visitors to these sites, these accounts should give you some idea of what can be expected at migration watches in different parts of eastern North America. Even if we do not cover the site nearest you, reading the accounts for adjacent areas should give you an idea of what to expect at your local site. The longer accounts cover places frequently visited for seawatching. The shorter accounts cover a mix of established, though generally less known, sites and suggested areas for further exploration. We are grateful to the many people who provided information for, and in some cases even wrote, several of the accounts; you will see their names listed after the name of the relevant watch site.

The sites covered here are only the tip of the iceberg; the potential for discovery is almost endless. Even most of the "well-known" sites mentioned here have been covered only sporadically. Since the boom in popularity of hawk watching, hundreds of sites with good raptor migrations have been discovered, many of which now record numbers carefully. We believe the potential for discovery of waterbird migration concentration points is just as great, and that there would be great value in conducting widespread counts. Hawk counting has proved a valuable tool in monitoring the status of raptor populations and overall environmental health. Seawatching has just as much potential, both as an enjoyable pursuit and as something valuable to conservation and ornithology.

It is worth noting here that hurricanes and other tropical storms can push birds far inland, making a "seawatch" on almost any body of water potentially productive. Places hundreds of miles inland have hosted oceanic birds under these circumstances.

Where possible, we have included sidebars with numbers in the accounts that follow. Some accounts mention only a few exceptional counts, whereas others feature more comprehensive numbers, such as top 10 species counts and even seasonal averages. Some of the numbers reflect precise counts, and others reflect estimates; both types of data are useful and all too rare! We hope these numbers will help observers to understand the dynamics of waterbird migration in eastern North America. Some of these sites have been visited and counted by many different observers, without the data ever being compiled in one place. In some such cases, we include the numbers of one observer with whom we corresponded, but we do so without meaning disrespect to data that might have been gathered by others. We would be grateful to receive additional data from any watch point, whether included below or not. In the text of the site accounts, we often use vague language to describe numbers. Unfortunately this is necessary in the absence of consistent, comparable numbers for many seawatch sites.

Seawatchers who want to quantify their observations face the same challenge faced by raptor counters: differentiating local movements from long-range movements. Few counters want to count the same birds every day under the illusion that they are counting fresh migrant birds. Most seawatchers will find something inherently different about tame Mallard dallying about a lakefront versus fully wild birds that are flying high and headed south. At some sites, particularly those without much to offer feeding birds, it is easy to count passing migrants. At others, blessed with rich feeding areas, it is much harder to distinguish between locally commuting birds and long-distance migrants. Some species are more challenging than others. When a Common Loon rockets down a lakeshore in October, it is almost certainly migrating, whereas it is much more difficult to know what is intended by a Herring Gull following the same trajectory. There are no easy answers when it comes to how one should count birds; ultimately the distinction between local movement and long-distance movement is a bit artificial. In any case, more observers counting more birds in more places will shed light on the dynamics of North American waterbird migration, making the differentiation of migrants from local birds easier.

Few birders set out for a day of pure seawatching, and few birders while scanning the sea could fail to be amazed by the sight of songbirds flying in off the waves, so the accounts in this section also include some general birding information. We will be disturbed and disappointed if this book inspires a cadre of observers who care for nothing beyond flyby waterbirds!

SEAWATCH RECORDS

The following table includes the top three single-day counts for 75 of the 112 species covered in this guide. Some species were excluded because of their general rarity or a lack of established counts in places where they commonly occur. Chief among the latter are several tern species, which could probably be counted in impressive numbers at certain places on the Gulf or southeastern Atlantic Coasts.

Compiling comprehensive seawatch records for eastern North America would have been a massive and almost impossible project, given the scattered whereabouts of such records. Instead, we have included data from well-established and frequently counted watch sites (where hundreds of watches have been conducted). We only had access to data for seven such sites in our area: Cape Ann, Massachusetts; Avalon, New Jersey; Lake Champlain, Vermont; Hamlin Beach, New York; Presque Isle, Pennsylvania; Miller Beach, Indiana; and Whitefish Point, Michigan. In the "Other Exceptional Counts" column we highlight some impressive numbers that

have been counted at other sites. Again, this is not intended as a comprehensive listing of such numbers, but is rather a smattering of interesting numbers that we have encountered while preparing this table.

Despite the non-comprehensive nature of the table, we believe it is useful for several reasons. The chief one is as an inspiration for future observers to carefully record data and to try to break the records presented here. Another is to help birders fit their local observations into the continental picture. Finally, the dates and locations associated with the record numbers should be another useful tool—in addition to the maps and fall and spring arrival dates in the species accounts—in understanding the flow of waterbird migration in our region.

SPECIES	#1 SINGLE-DAY COUNT	#2 SINGLE-DAY COUNT	#3 SINGLE-DAY COUNT	OTHER EXCEPTIONAL COUNTS
Tundra Swan	**PI** 794–Nov. 1998	**CM** 382–Nov. 12, 1998	**PI** 227–Nov. 1997	
Mute Swan	**HB** 50–Nov. 4, 2003	**CM** 8–Nov. 22, 1998	**CM** 7–Oct. 26, 1995	
Canada Goose	**CM** 20,325–Dec. 9, 2010	**CM** 17,238–Dec. 8, 2005	**LC** 6,684–Oct. 11, 2004	
Cackling Goose	**HB** 47–Oct. 27, 2008	**WP** 41–Sept. 30, 2005	**WP** 19–Sept. 20, 2006	
Snow Goose	**LC** 16,100–Nov. 16, 2002	**LC** 14,000–Dec. 15, 2001	**LC** 13,000–Nov. 23, 2005	
Brant	**HB** 4,302–Oct. 18, 1999	**CM** 3,915–Oct. 30, 1995	**LC** 2,630–Oct. 16, 2003	
Wood Duck	**CM** 563–Nov. 3, 2005	**CM** 257–Oct. 17, 1995	**CM** 249–Oct. 30, 2010	
Northern Pintail	**HB** 1,041–Oct. 17, 1997	**CM** 876–Nov. 2, 2005	**PI** 745–Oct. 1, 2011	East Beach, TX: 6,455–Feb. 24, 2012
Mallard	**LC** 2,760–Nov. 23, 2007	**HB** 1,100–Jan. 23, 1994	**HB** 739–Nov. 20, 1993	
American Black Duck	**LC** 800–Nov. 23, 2007	**CM** 647–Oct. 30, 1995	**CM** 532–Nov. 18, 1998	
Gadwall	**MB** 226–Oct. 26, 2008	**MB** 118–Oct. 24, 1995	**MB** 109–Oct. 18, 1996	East Beach, TX: 370–Feb. 24, 2012
American Wigeon	**WP** 636–Sept. 27, 2004	**WP** 483–Oct. 1, 1998	**WP** 384–Sept. 18, 2010	
Northern Shoveler	**MB** 326–Oct. 24, 1995	**MB** 225–Oct. 31, 2009	**MB** 177–Oct. 26, 2008	East Beach, TX: 912–Feb. 24, 2012
Blue-winged Teal	**MB** 3,900–Sept. 23, 1993	**WP** 1,488–Sept. 12, 2010	**WP** 1,212–Sept. 6, 1998	East Beach, TX: 4,180–Feb. 24, 2012
Green-winged Teal	**CM** 3,197–Oct. 27, 1996	**CM** 2,445–Nov. 9, 2005	**CM** 2,127–Oct. 31, 1995	East Beach, TX: 5,908–Feb. 24, 2012
Canvasback	**PI** 574–Dec. 8, 2008	**PI** 550–Dec. 6, 2005	**PI** 280–Dec. 29, 2004	
Redhead	**HB** 1,350–Jan. 18, 1996	**HB** 1,178–Nov. 28, 1998	**PI** 980–Dec. 14, 2010	
Greater Scaup	**HB** 10,543–Nov. 28, 1998	**HB** 10,000–Jan. 2, 1994	**HB** 8,000–Jan. 2, 1997	
Lesser Scaup	**PI** 14,526–Dec. 3, 2010	**PI** 2,456–Nov. 7, 2005	**PI** 2,074–Nov. 1993	
Scaup species	**PI** 16,900–Nov. 26, 2008	**PI** 15,000–Nov. 1997	**LC** 5,000–Dec. 2, 2006	

CA	CAPE ANN, MA		**MB**	MILLER BEACH, IN
CM	CAPE MAY (AVALON), NJ		**PI**	PRESQUE ISLE, PA
HB	HAMLIN BEACH, NY (1993–1999 DATA)		**WP**	WHITEFISH POINT, MI
LC	LAKE CHAMPLAIN, VT			

SPECIES	#1 SINGLE-DAY COUNT	#2 SINGLE-DAY COUNT	#3 SINGLE-DAY COUNT	OTHER EXCEPTIONAL COUNTS
Ring-necked Duck	**CM** 211–Oct. 31, 2006	**CM** 201–Nov. 14, 1994	**WP** 168–Oct. 11, 2001	
Common Eider	**CA** 8,020–Nov. 4, 2003	**CA** 6,360–Oct. 26, 1990	**CA** 4,650–Nov. 7, 1997	
King Eider	**HB** 9–Dec. 2, 1999	**CM** 7–Dec. 9, 1997	**HB** 5–Nov. 12, 1997	Cape Spear, NL: 17–Mar. 1, 1987
White-winged Scoter	**HB** 8,631–Dec. 9, 1997	**HB** 7,324–Dec. 14, 1998	**HB** 5,523–Dec. 1, 1999	
Surf Scoter	**CM** 69,928–Oct. 25, 2007	**CA** 58,670–Oct. 27, 2011	**CM** 42,522–Oct. 28, 1999	
Black Scoter	**CM** 74,998–Oct . 25, 2007	**CM** 42,507–Oct. 26, 1998	**CM** 38,284–Oct. 23, 2008	
Harlequin Duck	**CA** 76–Nov. 25, 2008	**CA** 34–Feb. 23, 2007	**CA** 15–Nov. 4, 2010	
Long-tailed Duck	**WP** 16,231–Oct. 31, 2004	**WP** 10,782–Oct. 27, 2009	**WP** 8,376–Oct. 24, 2007	
Common Goldeneye	**WP** 2,132–Nov. 10, 2000	**WP** 1,392–Nov. 5, 1994	**WP** 1,327–Oct. 25, 1998	
Bufflehead	**WP** 2,129–Nov. 12, 2005	**WP** 2,116–Nov. 3, 1989	**CM** 1,432–Nov. 13, 1998	
Common Merganser	**HB** 699–Nov. 30, 1995	**LC** 588–Dec. 24, 1999	**HB** 391–Dec. 27, 1998	
Red-breasted Merganser	**MB** 23,000–Oct. 24, 1959	**PI** 16,065–Nov. 29, 2004	**PI** 11,685–Dec. 10, 2002	
Hooded Merganser	**MB** 168–Nov. 3, 1991	**CM** 113–Nov. 13, 1997	**MB** 84–Nov. 7, 2003	
Ruddy Duck	**PI** 40–Nov. 1998	**CM** 24–Nov. 21, 2005	**CM** 19–Oct. 31, 1995 & Oct. 30, 1996	
Double-crested Cormorant	CM 24,637–Nov. 12, 2008	**CM** 24,078–Oct. 21, 2004	**CM** 23,317–Nov. 2, 2003	
Great Cormorant	**CA** 32–Oct. 19, 2004	**CA** 30–Nov. 1, 1997	**CM** 24–Oct. 27, 1999	
Red-throated Loon	**CM** 16,851–Nov. 21, 2011	**CM** 15,787–Nov. 22, 2011	**CM** 11,214–Nov. 21, 2010	Sandy Neck Beach, MA: 8,200–Nov. 17, 2002
Common Loon	**HB** 2,982–Nov. 7, 1997	**HB** 2,602–Oct. 16, 1993	**WP** 2,094–May 7, 1996	Cayuga Lake, NY: 6,064 on Nov. 10, 1997 & 3,338 on Nov. 23, 1995; Beverly Shores, IN: 2,270–Nov. 20, 2005. Although these may pertain to locally wintering birds, a tremendous movement of 8,000+ was observed from Cape Hatteras Point, NC, on Feb. 1, 1998
Red-necked Grebe	**WP** 6,789–Aug. 22, 2003	**WP** 5,665–Aug. 19, 2002	**WP** 5,079–Aug. 18, 1992	
Horned Grebe	**PI** 1,927–Nov. 1998	**HB** 554–Nov. 14, 2003	**HB** 347–Nov. 4, 1999	
Razorbill	**CA** 3,760–Mar. 2, 2007	**CA** 2,920–Dec. 15, 1999	**CA** 1,410–Dec. 7, 2004	Cape Hatteras, NC: 8,875–Feb. 15, 2004; Brier Island, NS: 8,600–Dec. 19, 2000; Head of the Meadow Beach, Cape Cod, MA: 5,850–Dec. 5, 2012
Thick-billed Murre	**CA** 2,300–Dec. 17, 1976	**CA** 485–Mar. 7, 2001	**CA** 400–Dec. 24, 1976	Brier Island, NS: 20,000–Dec. 20, 1973; Cape Spear, NL: 3,000–Mar. 19, 1983 & Nov. 3, 2007
Common Murre	**CA** 420–Dec. 12, 2002	**CA** 288–Nov. 28, 2004	**CA** 233–Jan. 15, 2007	Cape Spear, NL: 1,200–Nov. 3, 2007

SPECIES	#1 SINGLE-DAY COUNT	#2 SINGLE-DAY COUNT	#3 SINGLE-DAY COUNT	OTHER EXCEPTIONAL COUNTS
Atlantic Puffin	**CA** 104–Oct. 12, 2002	**CA** 16–16 Oct 2002	**CA** 8–Nov. 3, 2007	Cape Spear, NL: 400–Oct. 17, 2004; L'Anse aux Meadows, NL: 250–Oct. 9, 1981
Black Guillemot	**CA** 31–Apr. 16, 2007	**CA** 24–11 Dec 1992	**CA** 24–Nov. 3, 1999	Cape Spear, NL: 300–Apr. 14, 1991
Dovekie	**CA** 18,000–Nov. 30, 1957	CA 10,000+–multiple times in 1950s	**CA** 340–Nov. 25, 2008	Cape Spear, NL: 25,000–Jan. 13, 1996; Cap-d'Espoir, QC: 20,300–Dec. 14, 2003
Cory's Shearwater	**CA** 432–Aug. 29, 2009	**CA** 127–Aug. 23, 2009	**CA** 36–Aug. 21, 1997	Provincetown, Cape Cod, MA: 2,700–July 7, 2009
Great Shearwater	**CA** 35,000–Sept. 28, 2002	**CA** 6,150–Nov. 3, 1999	**CA** 3,060–Aug. 29, 2009	Provincetown, Cape Cod, MA: 19,000–July 7, 2009; Cape Spear, NL: 14,000–Sept. 19, 1999; Brier Island, NS: 10,000–Sept. 4, 2007
Sooty Shearwater	**CA** 1,710–Aug. 29, 2009	**CA** 162–June 28, 2009	**CA** 47–Aug. 23, 2009	North Carolina coast: 8,000–May 27, 1972; Cape Spear, NL: 6,000–Sept. 19, 1999; Brier Island, NS: 5,000–Sept. 19, 2009; Race Point, Cape Cod, MA: 3,875–July 9, 2009
Manx Shearwater	**CA** 115–Aug. 29, 2009	**CA** 64–Aug. 12, 1998	**CA** 61–July 26, 2001	Cape Spear, NL: 134–Sept. 6, 1999; Race Point, Cape Cod, MA: 87–Oct. 17, 2009
Northern Fulmar	**CA** 830–Oct. 16, 2002	**CA** 816–Dec. 9, 2009	**CA** 390–Oct. 28, 2008	L'Anse aux Meadows, NL: 12,000–Oct. 9, 1981; Cape Spear, NL: 5,000–Apr. 11, 1987; Race Point, Cape Cod, MA: 380–Oct. 29, 2009; Brier Island, NS: 300–Dec. 18, 1990
Wilson's Storm-Petrel	**CA** 1,050–Aug. 15, 1999	**CA** 1,040–Aug. 15, 2004	**CA** 355–June 6, 2000	Race Point, Cape Cod, MA: 2,000–June 20, 2009; Brier Island, NS: 500–Aug. 1, 2009; Cape Hatteras, NC: 150–May 23, 1987
Leach's Storm-Petrel	**CA** 285–Oct. 12, 2005	**CA** 66–Apr. 16, 2007	**CA** 25–May 24, 2005	Cape Spear, NL: 15,000–Sept. 23, 1999; First Encounter Beach, Cape Cod, MA: 350–Aug. 13, 1979
Northern Gannet	**CM** 16,946–Nov. 11, 2008	**CM** 9,717–Nov. 10, 2010	**CM** 9,437–Nov. 10, 2009	Corporation Beach, Cape Cod, MA: 12,000–Oct. 19, 2009
Brown Pelican	**CM** 189–Oct. 12, 2009	**CM** 94–Sept. 29, 2010	**CM** 76–Oct. 2, 2007	

CA	CAPE ANN, MA	**MB**	MILLER BEACH, IN
CM	CAPE MAY (AVALON), NJ	**PI**	PRESQUE ISLE, PA
HB	HAMLIN BEACH, NY (1993–1999 DATA)	**WP**	WHITEFISH POINT, MI
LC	LAKE CHAMPLAIN, VT		

SPECIES	#1 SINGLE-DAY COUNT	#2 SINGLE-DAY COUNT	#3 SINGLE-DAY COUNT	OTHER EXCEPTIONAL COUNTS
Pomarine Jaeger	**CA** 107–Nov. 17, 2002	CA 77–Nov. 6, 2002	CA 61–Nov. 3, 1999	Canaveral National Seashore, FL: 2,226–Nov. 9, 1992; L'Anse aux Meadows, NL: 429 on Sept. 13, 1978 & 425 on Sept. 13, 1979
Parasitic Jaeger	**CM** 37–Oct. 14, 2011	CM 36–Nov. 4, 1999	CM 27–Nov. 13, 2003	L'Anse aux Meadows, NL: 300–Sept. 13, 1979; Race Point, Cape Cod, MA: 85–Oct. 2, 2011
Long-tailed Jaeger	**CA** 2–June 15, 2002	CA 2–May 24, 2005	LC 2–Sept. 10, 2004	Cape Hatteras, NC: 12–May 28, 1987; L'Anse aux Meadows, NL: 12–Sept. 3, 1986; Race Point, Cape Cod, MA: 5–June 27, 2009
Ring-billed Gull	**LC** 30,000–Nov. 23, 2005	**LC** 25,000–Nov. 18, 2008	**LC** 20,500–Nov. 19, 2008	
Herring Gull	**CM** 8,309–Nov. 5, 1996	**CM** 7,070–Dec. 11, 1999	**CA** 5,000–Sept. 28, 2002	
Great Black-backed Gull	**CA** 900+–Aug. 29, 2006	**CA** 800–Oct. 28, 2008	**CM** 500–Oct. 13, 1998	Herring Cove Beach, Cape Cod, MA: 1,500–Nov. 2, 2008
Laughing Gull	**CM** 6,603–Oct. 12, 2000	**CM** 5,787–Oct. 19, 2007	**CM** 4,423–Oct. 19, 1999	Provincetown, Cape Cod, MA: 2,500–Oct. 12, 2008
Franklin's Gull	**MB** 598–Nov. 8, 2008	**MB** 477–Nov. 12, 1998	**MB** 78–Nov. 9, 1998	
Bonaparte's Gull	**HB** 5,750–Dec. 2, 1997	**WP** 4,441–May 11, 2002	**HB** 3,308–Dec. 1, 1999	Race Point, Cape Cod, MA: 8,000–Nov. 9, 2008
Little Gull	**HB** 22–Nov. 20, 1997	**HB** 8–Nov. 6, 1999	**HB** 6–Dec. 9, 1997	Outer Banks, NC: 91–Feb. 5, 1994
Sabine's Gull	**MB** 28–Sept. 16, 2005	**MB** 11–Sept. 18, 2001	**MB** 9–Sept. 11, 2001	
Black-legged Kittiwake	**CA** 4,300–Nov. 3, 1999	**CA** 4,260–Oct. 21, 1996	**CA** 2,425–Dec. 9, 2009	L'Anse aux Meadows, NL: 125,000–Sept. 13, 1979; L'Anse aux Meadows, NL: 100,000–Sept. 13, 1978; Brier Island, NS: 48,000–Dec. 27, 1978; Cape Spear, NL: 25,000–Apr. 11, 1987
Caspian Tern	**HB** 105–May 12, 2009	**HB** 48–Aug. 15, 1995	**HB** 26–Sept. 1, 1994	Pittsburgh, PA: 37–Apr. 11, 2008
Royal Tern	**CM** 1,520–Oct. 18, 1996	**CM** 1,027–Oct. 17, 2006	**CM** 186–Oct. 15, 2003	
Forster's Tern	**CM** 3,284–Nov. 5, 1996	**CM** 1,606–Oct. 6, 2001	**CM** 1,441–Oct. 27, 2007	
Common Tern	**MB** 5,700–Sept. 24, 1996	**MB** 4,000 –22 Sep 2001	**MB** 3,500–Sept. 11, 2002	Michigan City, IN: 7930– Sept. 24, 1996
Arctic Tern	**CA** 400–May 25, 2005	**CA** 75–May 14, 2006	**CA** 18–May 24, 2005	
Roseate Tern	**CA** 225–Aug. 24, 2005	**CA** 89–Aug. 29, 2009	**CA** 22–Sept. 2, 2003	
Black Tern	**MB** 1,265–Aug. 25, 2007	**MB** 563–Sept. 3, 2002	**MB** 363–Aug. 4, 2005	
Black Skimmer	**CM** 160–Oct. 11, 2008	**CM** 150–Oct. 11, 2004	**CM** 144–Oct. 8, 2009	

1. L'Anse aux Meadows, Newfoundland

Information from Bruce Mactavish

This site at the northern end of Newfoundland lies almost equidistant from Cape Cod and Greenland. It is a magnificent spot for seawatching; limited watching has revealed incredible flights of waterbirds. Days in late August and early September have had multiple Long-tailed Jaegers and Great Skuas, while September and October are the prime months for flights of thousands of Northern Fulmars, Black-legged Kittiwakes, and Red Phalaropes and hundreds of Pomarine and Parasitic Jaegers. On one early October day, an estimated 250 storm-driven juvenile Atlantic Puffins flew by. Perhaps most incredible of all, three different watches in January and February produced more than 100 flyby Ivory Gulls! L'Anse aux Meadows gives a hint of what might await a seawatcher in Labrador and elsewhere in northern Canada.

2. Cape Spear, Newfoundland

Information from Bruce Mactavish

Excluding Greenland, Cape Spear is the easternmost point in North America, and one of its best seawatching locations. The numbers of alcids, Black-legged Kittiwakes, Northern Fulmars, shearwaters, and Leach's Storm-Petrels here are mind-boggling for those accustomed to birding farther south. Cape Spear is utterly soaked in seabirds throughout the year. It lies in the heart of the breeding range of many species, and vast numbers can be seen commuting to feeding sites throughout the summer. Spring and fall see big migrations during the right conditions, while winter brings large numbers of eiders and white-winged gulls.

LOCATION

The cape is only a few miles southeast of St. John's, the capital of Newfoundland and Labrador. The entire point lies in a national historic site. From the main parking lot, walk a few minutes out to the point. The rocks on either side of the point provide shelter from the wind, except on days of straight east winds. Cape Spear is the best-known and most frequently visited seawatch in Newfoundland, but almost any point along Newfoundland's coast can offer good watching.

TIMING

Regardless of weather, there will always be waterbirds to see from Cape Spear. Certain conditions, however, can produce exceptional flights. September and October storms with northeast winds can bring huge numbers of migrating shearwaters and Leach's Storm-Petrels. Late-summer and fall hurricanes can also produce onshore winds and tubenoses. Birds such as alcids and eiders often move by irrespective of the winds.

BIRDS

DIVING DUCKS Scoters, Long-tailed Ducks, Greater Scaup, Red-breasted Mergansers, and Harlequin Ducks occur in small numbers. Common Eider is present year-round, with migrations in both fall and spring and lots of local movement in winter; these winter movements are larger than those in fall, sometimes approaching 10,000 birds per day. King Eider is rare but sometimes seen in flocks of Commons.

CORMORANTS Great Cormorant is present except during summer, but large migrations have not been observed.

LOONS AND GREBES Common and Red-throated Loons are scarce. Red-throated occurs mainly in October.

ALCIDS All six eastern species are common. Thick-billed Murres are present year-round, though in much larger numbers in winter. From May to August, thousands of Common Murres and Atlantic Puffins, and hundreds of Razorbills and Black Guillemots, can be seen daily, thanks to nearby breeding colonies. Late fall and early spring see movements of these species that seem to correspond to longer-distance migration. In fall there are often big southward movements of Dovekies, sometimes totaling many thousands. Winter may see movements of Dovekies in either direction, depending on weather.

TUBENOSES This is one of the best places in North America to see large numbers of tubenoses from shore. The best season is June to October, with peak numbers in August and September during northeast winds. Great Shearwater is most common, with daily counts exceeding 10,000. Sooty also occurs in the thousands, whereas Manx is much less common. Leach's Storm-Petrel can also occur by the thousands in the same period.

SULIDS A large nearby breeding colony means that Northern Gannets can be seen from spring to fall. Migration seems to occur in a steady trickle, with few big movements noted.

JAEGERS AND SKUAS Pomarine Jaeger is frequent, especially from June to October. Parasitic is less common, and Long-tailed Jaeger is rare. This may be the best place in North America to see skuas from

Newfoundland's Cape Spear is the easternmost point in North America (excluding Greenland). Bruce Mactavish.

shore. Both South Polar and Great Skuas are rare but regular, though they are often difficult to separate. Most records come from northeast storms in September and October.

GULLS Large numbers of Iceland and Glaucous Gulls are present in winter. More than 1,000 Iceland Gulls and 300 Glaucous Gulls can be seen on a good day.

TERNS Common and Arctic Terns occur but have not been noted migrating in large numbers.

TOP 10 SPECIES	SINGLE-DAY HIGH COUNT
1. Black-legged Kittiwake	25,000 on Apr. 11, 1987
2. Dovekie	25,000 on Jan. 13, 1996
3. Leach's Storm-Petrel	15,000 on Sept. 23, 1999
4. Great Shearwater	14,000 on Sept. 19, 1999
5. Sooty Shearwater	6,000 on Sept. 19, 1999
6. Northern Fulmar	5,000 on Apr. 11, 1987
7. Thick-billed Murre	3,000 on Mar. 19, 1983 & Nov. 3, 2007
8. Common Murre	1,200 on Nov. 3, 2007
9. Razorbill	700 on Nov. 3, 2007
10. Black Guillemot	300 on Apr. 14, 1991

Numbers courtesy of Bruce Mactavish. These numbers reflect only his counts and not those of other observers.

3. Cape Ray and Cape Anguile, Newfoundland

These twin capes pin down the southwestern corner of Newfoundland. Although neither is well known as a seawatch site, the proximity of rich feeding grounds and vast seabird colonies should make for excellent year-round watching. The mix of birds is similar to that at Cape Spear.

4. East Point, Prince Edward Island

Information from Eric Mills

The rich marine waters and excellent geographical situation of this point can produce excellent seawatching. As at other sites in the Atlantic Provinces, eiders, Northern Gannet, Black-legged Kittiwake, jaegers, and alcids are on offer.

5. Cape North and Cape St. Lawrence, Nova Scotia

By Eric Mills

Both of these capes are rarely birded because of their remoteness (no road access), but they likely offer great seawatching, thanks to their locations at the south side of Cabot Strait, which gives access to the Gulf of St. Lawrence, and to the deep water of the Laurentian Channel nearby. Fall shearwater movements and fall and winter passages of Black-legged Kittiwakes, white-winged gulls, and alcids are to be expected. Reaching either cape requires a hike across private land, though public access is allowed. The 3-mile hike to Cape North is quite demanding.

6. Chebucto Head and Hartlen Point, Nova Scotia

By Eric Mills

These points are located, respectively, at the southwest and southeast entrances to Halifax Harbor, just south of the city of Halifax. Both are best in fall and winter. There are occasional passages of jaegers in fall and regular occurrences of murres and the occasional Atlantic Puffin in late fall and early winter. Shearwaters occasionally come close to shore, most commonly Great and Sooty but also Cory's, especially in late fall.

7. Western Head and Baccaro Point, Nova Scotia

By Eric Mills

Both of these sites are located on the South Shore of the province, the first near Liverpool and the second not far from Shelburne. Both face a broad continental shelf, but despite this, Sooty and Great Shearwaters are regular in small numbers. Northern Gannets pass by in large numbers in spring and fall. Black-legged Kittiwakes are scarce but are regular throughout the year, and Black Guillemots are also a year-round feature. Murres and a few puffins can be expected from October through April. Harlequin Ducks frequently pass both points in small numbers from November into April.

8. Brier Island, Nova Scotia

By Eric Mills

With abundant rocky coastlines populated by huge numbers of breeding seabirds and a rich marine environment, the Atlantic Provinces are made for seawatching. Brier Island is one of the best sites in this exceptional region, and it is good year-round. It lies at the western extremity of Nova Scotia, at the junction of the Bay of Fundy and Gulf of Maine. This is a staging area for Red-necked and Red Phalaropes from mid-July to September, when it is sometimes possible to see tens of thousands of these birds that are rarely seen from seawatches elsewhere in east-

ern North America. It is also one of the premier places in eastern North America to see large movements of alcids.

LOCATION

A ferry gives access to the island from the mainland. The best sites are Western Light and Northern Point, about 4 miles apart.

TIMING

Brier Island is good year-round but best from midsummer to early winter. Some of the best flights occur in fall, when there are west or northwest winds, particularly on rising tides. When food is abundant near the island, the watching can be good even in calm conditions.

BIRDS

DIVING DUCKS All three scoters occur on passage in April and May and between September and November. Harlequin Duck is uncommon as a migrant and wintering bird. Common Eider is common year-round, and flights of hundreds occur in April. King Eider is rare but always possible with Common Eider.

CORMORANTS Constant passage of Double-crested occurs in September and October, with some days seeing hundreds of birds. Great Cormorant occurs from November through winter in small numbers.

LOONS AND GREBES There is a steady passage of Common Loons from late winter through May and from August into December. Good flights of Red-throated Loons have occurred in May and November.

ALCIDS Black Guillemots and Atlantic Puffins are regular year-round. Razorbills are a constant presence from fall to spring because of a large wintering group nearby. The other alcids are variable from year to year, though large numbers often occur during gales in fall and winter. Both murres are regular and often abundant in winter, but Thick-bills usually outnumber Commons by 10 to 1 or more. Dovekies are often abundant, frequently appearing with the first gale in early November.

TUBENOSES Northern Fulmar is occasional in summer, becoming regular in low numbers from November through winter. Great and Sooty Shearwaters occur in thousands or tens of thousands in years when the food supply is abundant, from early July into early November, usually peaking in August. Although Sooty arrives first, Great usually outnumbers Sooty 10 to 1, though in some years Sooty inexplicably far outnumbers Great. Manx

The Northern Point lighthouse on Brier Island, Nova Scotia. Eric Mills.

Shearwater is regular in low numbers from early August into early November. Wilson's Storm-Petrels are regular and sometimes abundant within sight of shore. There were hundreds per day seen during the summer of 2009. Leach's Storm-Petrels breed on a nearby island but are seldom seen because they feed far offshore.

SULIDS Northern Gannet is absent only in winter. Spring and fall migrations of hundreds have been seen.

JAEGERS AND SKUAS Pomarine and Parasitic Jaegers occur in late summer and fall; Pomarine outnumbers Parasitic roughly 10 to 1. Great Skua is occasional in winter. South Polar Skua is occasionally seen from shore from late July into October.

GULLS Black-legged Kittiwake is present year-round, with big numbers in late fall and winter, especially during strong northwest winds, when tens of thousands have been counted. Iceland Gull is frequently seen from late fall to spring among the huge numbers of local Herring and Great Black-backed Gulls.

TERNS There is a trickle of migrating Common Terns and even fewer Arctic Terns in August and September.

TOP 10 SPECIES	SINGLE-DAY HIGH COUNT
1. Red Phalarope	50,000 on Sept. 8, 2005
2. Black-legged Kittiwake	48,000 on Dec. 27, 1978
3. Thick-billed Murre	20,000 on Dec. 20, 1973
4. Great Shearwater	10,000 on Sept. 4, 2007
5. Razorbill	8,600 on Dec. 19, 2000
6. Sooty Shearwater	5,000 on Sept. 19, 2009
7. Dovekie	3,346 on Dec. 14, 2006
8. Red-necked Phalarope	2,000 on Aug. 22, 2002
9. Wilson's Storm-Petrel	500 on Aug. 1, 2009
10. Northern Fulmar	300 on Dec. 18, 1990

Rarities: There have been reports of Bulwer's Petrel, Balearic Shearwater, and Audubon's Shearwater.

Numbers courtesy of Eric Mills.

9. Quoddy Head, Maine

Information from Louis Bevier, Lysle Brinker, Derek Lovitch, and Bill Sheehan

Quoddy Head is the easternmost point in Maine, lying right on the Canadian border. The best viewpoint is the lighthouse at Quoddy Head State Park. Black-legged Kittiwake is particularly common here and can be seen even in summer. Good shearwater flights have occurred, with Great most common, followed by Sooty and Manx. Alcids are common, with Razorbill and Black Guillemot most

Herring and Great Black-backed Gulls on Quoddy Head, Maine. The ocean here is rich, and high concentrations of waterbirds can be seen throughout much of the year. Derek Lovitch.

likely. Common Eider, Great Cormorant, and jaegers can also be seen for much of the year. Limited watching here has turned up rarities such as Little and Sabine's Gulls, and the potential of this spot is enormous. The passage of birds into and out of the extensive inland waterways here might disguise long-distance migrants, but it also means there are birds to be seen in flight throughout the year.

10. Dyer Point, Cape Elizabeth, Maine

Information from Derek Lovitch

The rocky and seabird-rich coast of Maine is blessed with countless places to seawatch. Dyer Point is one of the best sites close to the population centers of southern Maine and New Hampshire. Like the watches in Massachusetts, this is a year-round watch worth a stop almost any time. Although the site has never been systematically counted, local birders are watching with increasing frequency. Along with offering good chances to see a variety of diving ducks, tubenoses, and alcids, this is probably the best site covered in this book for significant movements of Great Cormorants.

LOCATION

Cape Elizabeth lies 10 miles south of Portland and is one of the most prominent headlands on the southern Maine coast. Dyer Point is on the south-

eastern corner of the cape, near Two Lights State Park. Access the point by driving to the end of Two Lights Road, where there is a parking lot and the famous Lobster Shack Restaurant (open from March to October). What better way to celebrate a successful watch than to devour a lobster roll!

TIMING

Seawatching can be good all year. One problem that plagues this watch is fog, which can obliterate otherwise promising days. Fall features diverse flights of diving ducks, loons, cormorants, grebes, Northern Gannets, and gulls. Best conditions at this time of year are when there are northeast winds. Summer is excellent for tubenoses, especially with onshore winds. Flyby terns are also abundant throughout the summer, though most sightings probably pertain to local movements. Spring sees diverse flights similar to those of fall; one problem with spring, however, is that the same southeast winds likely to produce a good flight are also likely to produce fog. Days with east winds are also likely to have birds, and more likely to be clear. Winter is the best season for alcids and white-winged gulls.

BIRDS

DABBLING DUCKS American Black Duck is seen in moderate numbers, with smaller numbers of Mallard, although local "commuters" make migrant estimation tough. All other dabblers are scarce.

DIVING DUCKS Common Eider, Long-tailed Ducks, Red-breasted Mergansers, and the three scoter species make up the bulk of spring and fall flights. Smaller numbers of Greater Scaup, Bufflehead, Common Goldeneye, and Harlequin Ducks also pass by.

CORMORANTS Double-crested can number in the thousands on a good fall flight, and as the season progresses, Greats begin to mix in, starting with ones and twos and increasing to hundreds on some days, with pure flocks of Greats becoming common in November, usually in smaller flocks than Double-crested. Northbound movements of both species are smaller in spring.

LOONS AND GREBES Both loons are fairly common. Although there are more Commons than Red-throateds overall, the passage of Red-throateds tends to be concentrated into a few larger flights, which can be quite impressive. Horned and Red-necked Grebes occur in good numbers.

ALCIDS Razorbill is fairly common from late fall to spring. Strong onshore winds in winter can produce Thick-billed Murre and Dovekie. Black Guillemot can be seen year-round, though obvious and significant migrations have not been observed.

TOP 10 SPECIES	SINGLE-DAY HIGH COUNT
1. Double-crested Cormorant	1,508 on Oct. 23, 2006
2. Northern Gannet	1,449 on Oct. 25, 2005
3. Common Eider	1,001 on Oct. 25, 2004
4. Black Scoter	886 on Apr. 3, 2005
5. Long-tailed Duck	310 on Apr. 24, 2005
6. White-winged Scoter	302 on Oct. 8, 2005
7. Common Tern	224 on May 26, 2005
8. Great Shearwater	200+ on Nov. 5, 2004
9. Surf Scoter	195 on Oct. 23, 2006
10. Laughing Gull	193 on Sept. 7, 2008

Rarities: Barrow's Goldeneye, Dovekie, Atlantic Puffin, and Least Tern.

Numbers courtesy of Derek Lovitch. These numbers reflect only his counts and not those of other observers.

TUBENOSES Wilson's Storm-Petrel is the most common tubenose from late spring through summer. Great Shearwater is also common, while Sooty Shearwater is fairly common and Cory's and Manx Shearwaters are occasional. Leach's Storm-Petrel is rarely seen from shore in the U.S. but has been seen here.

The rocky coastlines of Maine offer abundant seawatch sites, such as Dyer Point on Cape Elizabeth. Derek Lovitch.

SULIDS Northern Gannet occurs year-round, with largest numbers during good fall and spring migrations. The numbers in midwinter and midsummer are highly variable.

JAEGERS AND SKUAS Parasitic and Pomarine Jaegers are regular, with highest numbers in fall. Parasitic outnumbers Pomarine two to one.

GULLS Flights of Ring-billed and Bonaparte's Gulls have been noted. Black-legged Kittiwake is a fairly common migrant in both fall and spring, often seen during onshore winds. It is also regular in winter during these conditions.

TERNS The presence of large numbers of locally breeding terns confuses the situation. However, definite migrations of Common Terns, mostly juveniles, have been observed in late August and September.

11. Cape Ann, Massachusetts

Information from Richard Heil

Massachusetts is favored with deep waters that lie close to the shore, abundant rocky coastlines, and a prime position on the migration paths of Common Eider, Northern Gannet, alcids, and tubenoses. It's not surprising that the state's two largest promontories, Cape Ann and Cape Cod, offer superlative seawatching. Cape Ann is closer to major roads and population centers, and its seawatching potential has been well documented, largely through the efforts of Richard Heil, who has been carefully observing and recording here for decades.

LOCATION

The cape lies about 50 miles northeast of Boston. The best seawatching is from the town of Rockport, on the northeast corner of the cape. The best sites here are Halibut Point State Park and, just to the east, Andrew's Point. The former offers a spectacular setting but requires a half-mile walk from the parking areas. Dead-end streets around Andrew's Point may allow observation from your vehicle, but prime viewing areas can become crowded on good days, so be sure not to trespass or block access to local residences.

TIMING

This is one of the best year-round seawatches on the East Coast, though fall is the best time. The peak occurs between mid-October and early November, though good eider flights can occur well into December, which is also a good time for big alcid movements. Winter watches can be good for alcids and Black Kittiwake, with rocky-shore species such as Harlequin Duck and Black Guillemot always

present. Cape Ann is not well positioned for good spring migration, though small flights can occur at this time of year. In summer it is an excellent place to look for tubenoses. Occasional incursions of thousands of Great, Cory's, and Sooty Shearwaters have occurred. Late summer sees tern flights that include Arctic and Roseate Terns.

A northeast storm during the peak of fall migration can produce an incredible spectacle, with almost the entire gamut of species present in good numbers. Throughout the year, strong onshore winds, particularly east or northeast, can make for good seawatching. The occurrence of tubenoses, alcids, jaegers, and Black-legged Kittiwake is especially tied to these winds. A storm that stalls offshore and produces days of such winds can bring in rarities such as Great Skua and Leach's Storm-Petrel. Sometimes storms with south winds occur, causing many birds to take shelter behind Cape Ann. The day after such winds end, large numbers of birds are sometimes seen rounding the cape and heading back to sea. Strong winds from any direction are good for pelagic species, which seem to disappear on calm days. Fall loon and sea-duck flights predictably occur on cold, clear days with northwest winds, after the passage of a cold front.

BIRDS

DABBLING DUCKS Small numbers of Wood Ducks, Northern Pintail, American Black Ducks, American Wigeon, Gadwall, and Green-winged Teal fly by in fall, usually in scoter flocks.

DIVING DUCKS Common Eider flights numbering into the thousands can occur anytime between October and December, with much smaller flights in spring. King Eider is a regular wintering bird but is rarely seen in flight. Scoter migration peaks in October and early November, with Surf abundant and Black and White-winged common. There are small spring scoter flights. Long-tailed Duck is a common migrant in both fall and spring, with peak movements between late October and December and again in April. Harlequin Ducks can be seen throughout the winter, but they don't stage conspicuous migrations.

CORMORANTS Double-crested is uncommon, with its main migration routes west of the cape. Great is regular in small numbers from fall to spring.

LOONS AND GREBES Flights of hundreds of Red-throated Loons occur through most of the fall, with a November peak. Common Loon occurs in smaller numbers. No spring loon migration has been observed. Pacific Loon is a rare but regular flyby. Red-

Cape Ann, Massachusetts, is one of North America's premier seawatching sites. Richard Heil.

necked Grebes migrate past in small numbers in fall and spring.

ALCIDS All six eastern species occur, sometimes in remarkable numbers, though their occurrence is poorly understood. Razorbill is the most common, present from October to March. December and March seem to hold peak migrations. Formerly rare, Common Murre has become fairly common in recent years, peaking at the same time as Razorbill. Thick-billed Murre is more pelagic than other alcids and is uncommon at Cape Ann, occurring between December and March, with exceptional high counts in the hundreds. Black Guillemot is a common wintering bird seen migrating past in small numbers. Huge "wrecks" of thousands of Dovekies occurred into the 1950s, but the species has become much more rare since. It occurs primarily in November and December, with smaller numbers in February. Atlantic Puffin is the rarest alcid here, though nearby breeding colonies mean that it is possible year-round.

TUBENOSES Much like alcids, tubenoses are sometimes abundant but are unpredictable. Great Shearwater is the most common species, occurring mostly between July and December, with fre-

quent daily counts of hundreds and exceptional counts of thousands. Cory's Shearwater occurs in the same period in much smaller numbers. It was historically rare but has become fairly common in recent years. Sooty Shearwater moves by in small numbers mainly between May and September. Small numbers of Manx are seen between May and November. Northern Fulmar occurs regularly during onshore winds in both fall and spring, with high counts exceeding 200. Wilson's Storm-Petrel can often be seen in the summer, though there are higher numbers elsewhere in Massachusetts, particularly Cape Cod.

SULIDS Cape Ann is one of the prime places to see a spectacular Northern Gannet migration. Although present year-round, this species is most common in fall, peaking from October to mid-November, when high counts of thousands occur. There is a much smaller spike of spring migrants.

JAEGERS AND SKUAS Pomarine and Parasitic Jaegers are present between midsummer and midwinter, with sightings usually occurring during onshore winds. Pomarine is more common, with daily high counts of dozens in November. Long-tailed is very rare. There are a few records of Great and South Polar Skuas.

GULLS Bonaparte's is a common fall migrant, with smaller numbers in winter and spring. Black-legged Kittiwake is common in fall and winter. The peak of southbound kittiwake migration is late October to mid-November, when thousands may be tallied in a day.

TERNS Common Tern is an uncommon migrant in late summer, early fall, and spring, whereas Roseate and Arctic Terns are rare. Black Tern is regular in August and September.

TOP 10 SPECIES	SINGLE-DAY HIGH COUNT
1. Surf Scoter	58,670 on Oct. 27, 2011
2. Great Shearwater	35,000 on Sept. 28, 2002
3. Black Scoter	20,660 on Oct. 27, 2011
4. Dovekie	18,000 on Nov. 30, 1957
5. Northern Gannet	8,600 on Nov. 3, 1999
6. Red-breasted Merganser	8,570 on Nov. 5, 1983
7. Common Eider	8,020 on Nov. 4, 2003
8. Long-tailed Duck	5,900 on Nov. 5, 1983
9. Herring Gull	5,000+ on Sept. 28, 2002
10. Razorbill	3,760 on Mar. 2, 2007

Rarities: Ancient Murrelet (2 records), "Atlantic" Yellow-nosed Albatross, Black-capped Petrel, South Polar Skua, Great Skua, Franklin's Gull, Black-headed Gull, Little Gull, and Royal Tern.

Numbers courtesy of Richard Heil.

12. Cape Cod, Massachusetts

By Marshall Iliff and Blair Nikula

Cape Cod stretches so far into the Atlantic that birding here should almost be considered a pelagic trip rather than seawatching! This is one of the premier seawatching sites in North America. From June to November in recent years, it has become almost routine to see four species of shearwaters, sometimes in huge numbers, the two most common jaegers, several terns including Roseate, and Wilson's Storm-Petrel. From December to April one can expect at least Black-legged Kittiwake and Razorbill, sometimes in the hundreds or even thousands, and occasionally several other species of alcids. This is a remarkably dynamic area, governed by a complex mix of tides, currents, and winds. It is hard to understand and predict but is almost always exciting. Large feeding concentrations can develop spontaneously almost anywhere. Something rare is always possible on the cape, with past records including Black-capped Petrel, Yellow-nosed and Black-browed Albatrosses, both skuas, and Sooty and Bridled Terns.

LOCATION

Much of the cape offers good seawatching, but there are a few sites that have historically offered excellent viewing. All cape beaches require a permit or fee during the summer months, usually late June through Labor Day, but at most locations these fees can be avoided early (before 9:00 A.M.) or late (after 5:00 P.M.) in the day. We describe six of the best areas here.

PROVINCETOWN. The tip of Cape Cod provides the most reliable year-round seawatching. Good feeding grounds and rip tides off Herring Cove and Race Point Beaches regularly produce feeding frenzies that include gulls, terns, shearwaters, Wilson's Storm-Petrels, jaegers, alcids, cormorants, Northern Gannets, and often many thousands of Red-breasted Mergansers, depending on the season. There is always something interesting going on here, and the best strategy is to check the three main viewing areas (Race Point Beach, Herring Cove, and Provincetown Harbor) at several different tides and times of day, since the conditions can change hourly. Herring Cove is better for viewing from the car, whereas the opportunities for car-based viewing at Race Point are little or none depending on the height of the dunes and the height of your car. At Race Point Beach the seawatching is often good right from the parking lot, but if you feel so inclined you can walk the mile or more through soft sand to the tip of the point, which is probably the best spot, though it's unsheltered and takes more time to access. On days after nor'easters, there can be a significant phenomenon of birds exiting Cape Cod Bay that is best seen from Herring Cove Beach, although First Encounter Beach

The waters around Cape Cod sometimes support incredible concentrations of waterbirds and marine mammals. This photo shows Sooty and Great Shearwaters, Herring and Laughing Gulls, and humpback whales. Ken Behrens.

(see below) is almost always much better under these conditions. Be sure to check Provincetown Harbor from MacMillian Pier, where alcids (typically Razorbill, Thick-billed Murre, and Dovekie) can sometimes be seen on the water at point-blank range, especially after winter storms. Under certain conditions, shearwaters can even get trapped in the harbor here, and in 2011 a Brown Booby spent the entire fall roosting on the breakwater with cormorants! Reaching the Provincetown area from Boston takes at least 2 hours, much longer in weekend traffic.

EASTERN CAPE BEACHES. The entire stretch from East Orleans to Truro can provide superb seawatching even under calm conditions. June and July feeding frenzies that include gulls, terns, and humpback and fin whales sometimes attract four species of shearwaters, Wilson's Storm-Petrels, and summering immature Parasitic and Pomarine Jaegers. Winter at these same beaches is great for sea ducks, loons, grebes, and gulls, with Black-legged Kittiwakes usually in view and often hundreds or thousands of Razorbills commuting north or south to good feeding. In winter be sure to check Marconi Station and Nauset Beach, which have shoals and can be particularly good. Most of these beaches provide elevated views, and many provide views right from the car (marked with an asterisk): Nauset Beach, Coast Guard Beach, Nauset Light, Marconi Beach, Marconi Station, LeCount Hollow*, Cahoon Hollow*, Ocean View Drive*, Pamet Road, and Head of the Meadow Beach*. Try a few of these and space them out to try different stretches of coast. But be aware that under rainy nor'easter conditions, seawatching at these beaches can be difficult, with rain, salt spray, and sand blowing in your face, plus high seas obscuring any birds that may be present. Access in summer, generally late June through Labor Day, is either expensive or impossible (residents only), but access in winter months is unrestricted and free.

CHATHAM LIGHT. The parking lot at the Chatham lighthouse provides an elevated view over a natural inlet, and it is possible to seawatch from your car. At times, concentrations of seabirds (especially the four shearwaters) can be seen from here, and rarely they are even feeding right inside the inlet. Although the rip tides around the inlet can attract feeding birds, the problem here is that the birds flying along the outer beach are at least a mile away, if not more. Nonetheless, this can be a good spot to check. There is a 30-minute parking limit in summer, and it is sometimes difficult to find a spot. The overlook just off the trail at the Monomoy National Wildlife Refuge headquarters on Morris Island a mile south of

Chatham Light provides a similar vantage and is a bit closer to the ocean.

SOUTH SHORE OF CAPE COD. Although good for some sea ducks, the south shore of Cape Cod from South Chatham to Falmouth is comparatively very poor for seabirds. Only in very strong southeasterlies (in advance of a hurricane) have birders had much success here. One famous seawatch from South Chatham did score a White-tailed Tropicbird in advance of a hurricane. Sooty and Bridled Terns have also been recorded several times during or just after hurricanes.

SANDWICH, BARNSTABLE, AND DENNIS. Under nor'easter conditions, beaches at the base of Cape Cod can have the best seawatching, as seabirds are blown into Cape Cod Bay and concentrated on the bay's southwest end. This usually means looking into the wind and rain, but somewhat sheltered viewing can be found at Scusset Beach, beaches in East Sandwich, and Sandy Neck in Barnstable, though the last may require a beach permit.

FIRST ENCOUNTER BEACH, EASTHAM. Truly epic seawatching occurs on the Cape Cod Bay side near the "elbow" of Cape Cod when conditions are just right: strong northwesterly winds following on the heels of a day (or better, several days) of northeasterly winds. The northeasterly winds seem to pile seabirds into Cape Cod Bay, where they essentially get trapped. When the winds shift to westerly (northwest is best), the seabirds move east along the south shore of the bay, and when the shoreline bends northward, they often come quite close to shore, providing excellent looks from First Encounter Beach. These northbound seabirds often get trapped inside Wellfleet Harbor by Great Point and circulate back to the south, and then pass northward again along the beach—it's good for viewing though confounding for those trying to count the birds. On good days, the seawatching here is nothing short of spectacular, and there have been numerous counts of thousands of shearwaters, phalaropes, alcids, and Black Kittiwakes, tens of jaegers (often right over the beach), regular sightings of Sabine's Gulls from late August to mid-October, and multiple records of Great and South Polar Skuas, Long-tailed Jaeger, Sooty and Bridled Terns, and even a Yellow-nosed Albatross. The parking lot here can provide sheltered viewing from your car, though it still often entails wind blowing sand and rain right in your face. Play with the angle of your vehicle and keep only one window open! Once conditions calm, the good seawatching can continue for many hours, so it is often worth waiting it out. Skaket Beach in Orleans, a couple of miles to the southwest and visible from First Encounter Beach, can be equally productive, and depending on the wind direction, may be slightly more sheltered when viewing conditions are severe.

TIMING

Cape Cod is probably the best year-round sea-watching site on the East Coast of the U.S. A visit anytime could be interesting. The period from late June to October (sometimes into November) sometimes has major shearwater incursions. Fall offers the highest diversity, especially during nor'easters. A winter watch can reveal thousands of alcids, primarily Razorbills, along with Black-legged Kittiwakes and a chance for lingering tubenoses or jaegers. Spring and early summer are more subdued but always have potential. The northbound migration of Northern Gannets from late March through early May can be spectacular.

Not surprisingly, storms make the seawatching even better, but unlike most of the East Coast, Cape Cod can be good on both easterly and westerly winds. On easterly winds, seawatching from Race Point or one of the outer beaches (including Marconi Station, Nauset Light, and Chatham Light) is your best bet. Some of the north-facing beaches along the inner cape (such as Sandwich and Sandy Neck) can be good under nor'easter conditions, whereas the "elbow" of the cape (especially First Encounter Beach) offers some of the best seawatching in eastern North America on northwesterly winds.

BIRDS

The birding here is generally similar to that on Cape Ann, with some differences noted below. Cape Cod lies so close to deep water and to major feeding areas for a variety of species that it is often difficult to tell migrating birds from staging or wintering birds. Many of the movements observed here are likely the results of local shifts in feeding grounds rather than long-distance migrations. In any case, this is a great place to watch waterbirds.

DABBLING DUCKS A few, especially Green-winged Teal, accompany flocks of migrating scoters in fall. Most migrating dabblers that are following the Atlantic Coast probably cut across the base of Cape Cod.

DIVING DUCKS Common Eider occurs in even greater numbers than at Cape Ann, particularly in late fall and early winter. There are spring movements as well, but they are much smaller. The complex dynamics here of feeding, commuting, and roosting make it difficult to discern long-distance migrants. All three species of scoters are common and can be seen in hundreds or thousands, especially from late

October to November. White-winged is the most common on the east side, whereas Surf and Black are more common as migrants in Cape Cod Bay.

LOONS AND GREBES Cape Cod sees even larger fall Red-throated Loon flights than does Cape Ann, with the highest daily totals in the thousands. In spring, reduced flights have been seen moving north along the eastern shore, mainly in April. The significance of the area as a staging and feeding ground for Red-throated Loons often obscures the status of true migrants. In spring, 50–100 Common Loons are routinely counted crossing the middle of the cape in a day, whereas crossings by Red-throated Loon are rare.

ALCIDS Although large alcid numbers at Cape Ann seem to occur only with onshore winds, at Cape Cod they are a permanent fixture from late fall to early spring, probably because of the feeding grounds that lie closer to shore here. It is not uncommon to scan from Race Point and see 1,000 or more Razorbills, with Common and Thick-billed Murres and Dovekies also always possible. Atlantic Puffin is rare, and Black Guillemot much less common than at Cape Ann. Following nor'easters, all alcid species can be seen at First Encounter Beach, with Black Guillemot perhaps the least likely.

TUBENOSES In some recent years, an incredible phenomenon has been observed in mid- to late summer. Vast numbers of Great, Cory's, and Sooty Shearwaters circulate daily past the cape, particularly Provincetown, joined by smaller numbers of Manx Shearwaters. Their movements are not fully understood, but it appears that ocean conditions have produced excellent feeding conditions close to shore. The daily movements of birds may pertain to commuting between roost and feeding sites or between different feeding grounds. It remains to be seen how long this phenomenon will continue, though surely it has produced some of the most spectacular seawatching spectacles ever observed from the East Coast. There are often small numbers of Wilson's Storm-Petrels as well, and in years without shearwater incursions, Wilson's is often the most common tubenose visible from land. Black-capped Petrel has been recorded twice from Cape Cod.

SULIDS Concentrations of Northern Gannets feed offshore almost year-round. Huge numbers sometimes occur during spectacular spring and fall migrations, mainly from April to May and September to December.

JAEGERS AND SKUAS Cape Cod is an excellent place to see jaegers year-round, excepting January to

SPECIES	NOTABLE SINGLE-DAY COUNT	LOCATION
Great Shearwater	40,000 on Sept. 25, 1977	Provincetown
Northern Gannet	20,000 on Nov. 16, 2002	Herring Cove Beach, Provincetown
Surf Scoter	19,500 on Oct. 16, 2009	Corporation Beach, Dennis
Black-legged Kittiwake	15,000 on Jan. 28, 1979	Race Point, Provincetown
Large alcid sp.	10,100 on Dec. 28, 2009 & Feb. 28. 2010	Head of the Meadow Beach/Race Point Beach, Provincetown
Leach's Storm-Petrel	10,000 on May 10, 1977	Aggregate from multiple locations
Red-throated Loon	10,080 on Nov. 17, 2002	Corporation Beach, Dennis
Common Tern	8,800 on Aug. 28, 2007	Provincetown
Razorbill	8,400 on Jan. 28, 2006	Head of the Meadow Beach
Bonaparte's Gull	8,000 on Nov. 9, 2008	Race Point, Provincetown
Wilson's Storm-Petrel	7,000 on July 19, 2002	Wellfleet
Northern Gannet	6,000 on Nov. 17, 2002	Race Point, Provincetown
Sooty Shearwater	3,875 on July 9, 2009	Race Point, Provincetown
Cory's Shearwater	2,700 on July 7, 2009	Provincetown
Laughing Gull	2,500 on Oct. 12, 2008	Provincetown
Red Phalarope	2,500 on Dec. 13, 1992	First Encounter Beach
White-winged Scoter	2,100 on Dec. 31, 2008	Herring Cove Beach
Great Black-backed Gull	1,500 on Nov. 2, 2008	Herring Cove Beach
Dovekie	1,270 on Dec. 7, 2003	First Encounter Beach
Pomarine Jaeger	1,100 on Oct. 31, 1991	First Encounter Beach
Northern Fulmar	380 on Oct. 29, 2009	Race Point, Provincetown
Red-necked Phalarope	375 on Sept. 4, 2010	First Encounter Beach
Manx Shearwater	120 on Aug. 12, 1979	Sandy Neck Beach, Barnstable
Parasitic Jaeger	100 on Sept. 21, 1977	First Encounter Beach
Atlantic Puffin	24 on Nov. 29, 2004	First Encounter Beach
Sabine's Gull	11 on Sept. 19, 1996	First Encounter Beach
Long-tailed Jaeger	5 on June 27, 2009	Race Point, Provincetown

Numbers from Blair Nikula and eBird, courtesy of contributing observers (see Acknowledgments). Some numbers may include birds sitting on the water.

March. Parasitics are most often found around large concentrations of terns from August through October. The recent summer shearwater phenomenon has been accompanied by good numbers of jaegers, mostly Pomarine and Parasitic and even a few Long-tailed.

GULLS Flights of hundreds or thousands of Black-legged Kittiwakes occur in fall, with smaller numbers in spring. First Encounter Beach is one of the best places to observe good kittiwake movements. Sabine's Gull is probably more regular on Cape Cod than anywhere else on the East Coast, with several sightings each year in the Provincetown area and, after storms, at First Encounter Beach.

TERNS Thousands of Common Terns, a substantial proportion of the northwestern Atlantic population of Roseate Terns, and a few Arctic Terns gather on Cape Cod in mid- to late summer. Common Terns feed offshore all along the cape, with huge roosting and bathing groups at Hatch's Harbor (Herring Cove Beach) and Nauset Marsh, although these groups shift location somewhat from year to year. Common Terns undertaking long-distance migrations may cut across the base of the cape.

13. Montauk Point, New York

Information from Shai Mitra

Montauk Point forms the eastern end of Long Island. This is an exceptionally pelagic place in a generally landlubbing state, and it lies in a hotbed of activity for staging, wintering, and migrating waterbirds. Depending on the time of year, it can offer large numbers of Black-legged Kittiwakes, Common Eider, shearwaters, scoters, and gulls and is the best place in New York to see certain species, such as Thick-billed Murre and King Eider.

LOCATION

Reaching the easternmost point in New York State from New York City can take hours, especially when traffic is bad. There is a lighthouse at the point, and the restaurant just north of it makes an excellent observation point, offering some shelter from wind and rain. The bluffs at Camp Hero can also be good but offer no shelter. Both locations are worth checking, as tide and wind shift the birds around the point.

TIMING

Montauk can be good year-round. Late November to late December offers the biggest numbers of birds, particularly Razorbills, scoters, eiders, loons, and Northern Gannets. This area is such a busy feeding area that it is often difficult to know what birds are actively migrating. Winter is good for rare alcids. Spring is generally slow, though late spring sees the arrival of Roseate Terns, which remain throughout the summer. Summer can be great for tubenoses and jaegers.

BIRDS

GEESE Brant occurs in small numbers from fall to spring.

DABBLING DUCKS Small numbers regularly mix with migrating scoters. Green-winged Teal and Wood Duck are the most common, but the full range of species occurs.

DIVING DUCKS Greater Scaup is common in fall to spring, and sometimes during the winter as well. All other *Aythya* are scarce. Many thousands of all three scoters and low thousands of Common Eider sometimes occur between late fall and early spring, with variable numbers through the winter. The complex dynamics of feeding and staging at this spot make it difficult to discern long-distance migrants. Smaller numbers of Common Goldeneye, Bufflehead, Red-breasted Merganser, and Long-tailed Duck occur with the same timing.

CORMORANTS Modest migrations of Double-crested occur, mainly in October, while small numbers of Greats are seen throughout the winter.

LOONS AND GREBES Common and Red-throated Loons are present from midfall to early spring, with Red-throated less common. Pacific Loon has been recorded. Horned Grebe is fairly common and Red-necked rare but regular.

ALCIDS Montauk is a great place to see alcids from late fall to early spring. Razorbill vastly outnumbers other species, all of which are rare but regular.

TUBENOSES Sooty and Manx Shearwaters and Wilson's Storm-Petrel occur mainly in June. Cory's and Great Shearwaters predominate in July and August and sometimes later. Northern Fulmar is very rare.

SULIDS Northern Gannets are possible year-round, with huge numbers in late fall and early winter.

JAEGERS AND SKUAS Parasitic Jaegers first appear in June, increasing to peak numbers in September and October when there are big flocks of gulls and terns present. The other jaegers are much less common. Great Skua is one of the excellent rarities that has been seen from Montauk.

GULLS Laughing Gull is seen from spring to fall, peaking in late fall with huge numbers that have reached 10,000 in a day. Herring Gull is common year-round, and Lesser Black-backed is uncommon. Bonaparte's is seen sporadically from fall to spring, sometimes in big numbers. Little, Black-headed, and Franklin's Gulls have been recorded.

TERNS Roseate Terns are present from late spring through summer. Common Terns stage in fall, with some September counts exceeding 1,000. All other species are rare. The most exceptional species recorded have been Sooty and Sandwich Terns.

14. Sandy Hook, New Jersey

Information from Scott Barnes

Sandy Hook forms a protrusion from the New Jersey coast that lies directly south of New York City. The New Jersey Audubon spring hawk-watch conducted here usually records nonraptor migrants, making this one of the few places in the region with significant spring waterbird migration data. Good numbers of Red-throated and Common Loons, Northern Gannets, and Double-crested Cormorants pass through, mainly in late March and early April. In May, strong storms may bring large numbers of terns to shore, mostly Commons, with Roseates and Arctics occasional. Fall watching here is not as good as at Avalon, in southern New Jersey, though excellent scoter flights have been observed. One problem with seawatching here is that the hook lies in a sheltered corner of the coastline, and the birds tend to be very far away, especially in fall. Sandy Hook has enjoyed some great rarities such as Brown Booby, Pacific Loon, Sooty Shearwater, Sabine's Gull, Common and Thick-billed Murres, Dovekie, Black Guillemot, and Long-billed Murrelet. Island Beach State Park, about halfway between Sandy Hook and Avalon, is another good Jersey seawatching locality. Limited observations there have closely paralleled those from Avalon. Yet another good site is Barnegat Light, south of Island Beach, good for migrating scoters, other ducks, and loons, along with wintering Harlequin Ducks, Common and King Eiders, and scoters.

15. Avalon, New Jersey

Cape May is one of the best-known and most storied sites in North American birding, famous for spectacular migrations, particularly of passerines and raptors. Just north of the cape lies Avalon, which is not as well known but enjoys waterbird migrations that are every bit as remarkable as Cape May's terrestrial bird movements.

New Jersey lies at a significant crux of waterbird migration. It is far enough south to catch birds such as many dabbling ducks and Surf and Black Scoters, which seemingly cut across the continent from the Arctic, and it's far enough north to get good numbers of species such as White-winged Scoter and Common Eider, which come only partway down the coast in winter. Although there are no other full-time counts for comparison, few other sites on the East Coast could match the more than 1 million birds tallied at Avalon in a good year.

Avalon's situation on the coast plays a role in its remarkable counts. It projects into the Atlantic nearly 1 mile, creating an obstacle for southbound birds, many of which come close to shore as they round this corner. At the same time, Avalon is still firmly part of the mainland, keeping it on the migration path of birds such as swans, geese, dabbling ducks, and Double-crested Cormorant, which follow the coastline but might cut across a projection such as Cape Cod or follow the inland waterways at the Outer Banks. One interesting aspect of Avalon is that southbound birds can commonly be seen over both the ocean to the east and the Intracoastal Waterway to the west.

This count was started in the late 1970s by seawatching pioneer Dave Ward. In 1993 it was adopted by Cape May Bird Observatory and New Jersey Audubon Society, which hire counters and interpreters to staff the watch in most falls. This is the only seawatch on the East Coast where there is a full-time fall counter.

LOCATION

The town of Avalon lies on a barrier island about 20 miles north of Cape May. Once you cross the causeway and are on the island, drive to the northeast corner of Avalon. The seawatch is at the eastern end of 7th Street, where the street dead-ends at the seawall. The official watch runs from dawn to dusk from September 22 to December 22. For more information on Avalon and all other aspects of Cape May Birding, visit www.birdcapemay.org.

Cape May Point, less than an hour's drive south of Avalon, can also be good for seawatching. In fall, huge feeding flocks of terns and gulls attract jaegers. All of the species seen migrating past Avalon occur here, mostly in reduced numbers, though Cape May Point may get more Double-crested Cormorants and Common Loons, since southbound birds following the Delaware Bay and Atlantic shores converge here.

TIMING

Fall is the best time of year, with peak numbers and diversity occurring between late October and mid-November. The "big day" of up to 100,000 scoters is usually during the last week of October. By early January there is little migration occurring, though winter is a good time to look for Razorbills. Spring sees modest flights of scoters, Northern Gannets, and others, with the peak in late March. In summer, Avalon is a good place to watch for Wilson's Storm-Petrel and occasionally other tubenoses.

Despite the vast amount of data gathered from this site, the timing of big migrations remains largely mysterious, although a few things have been learned. The passage of a cold front and the clear skies and northwest winds that follow consistently produce migrations of Tundra Swan, Snow and Canada Geese, Double-crested Cormorant, and Ring-billed Gull. The huge scoter and Red-throated Loon flights that are the outstanding features of Avalon are difficult to predict. These species seemingly prefer inclement weather and will not normally stage big flights on clear, warm days. Some wind seems essential for scoters, which are strong fliers that effortlessly cut through a southern headwind. Farther north (in Massachusetts, for exam-

The official seawatch counter at New Jersey's Avalon Seawatch uses a variety of "clickers" to keep track of the migrants flying by. Louise Zemaitis.

ple), onshore winds make for interesting days, but that is rarely the case here. Such winds may serve to bring birds such as Northern Gannet, scoters, and jaegers closer to shore, but they rarely produce alcids or tubenoses.

BIRDS

SWANS Late fall sees the passage of hundreds of Tundra Swans. The mainly sedentary Mute Swan is rare.

GEESE The main migration routes of Canada and Snow Geese seem to lie inland, but west winds can bring big movements of these species. More than 15,000 have been counted on exceptional early December days. Brant are common from midfall onward; migrants usually follow the Intracoastal Waterway.

DABBLING DUCKS The numbers are but a small fraction of each fall's total, but dabblers furnish much of the challenge and enjoyment of seawatching at Avalon. They can appear anywhere, from the Intracoastal Waterway to directly overhead to the ocean, though the majority "hitch a ride" with scoter flocks. Green-winged Teal is the most common and oceanic, though the full range of species occurs. Mallard and American Black Ducks move through in large flocks in late fall.

DIVING DUCKS Scoters are the heart of the seawatch. A "big day" of up to 100,000 scoters is one of the more remarkable sights here. Surf and Black Scoters predominate, with a late-October to mid-November peak. Much smaller numbers of White-winged Scoters move through, mostly later. Scoter flocks are the engine driving the coastal duck migration, and almost every other diving duck species will join them, from Redhead and Ring-necked Duck to Hooded Merganser, and from Bufflehead to Common Eider. Red-breasted Merganser and Lesser and Greater Scaup are the most common non-scoter divers, with thousands counted every fall, and are the species most likely to be found in autonomous flocks. Common Eider is on the increase, with recent fall totals exceeding 100, whereas King Eider is rare but regular.

CORMORANTS The first big days on the watch are in early to mid-October when Double-crested Cormorants start to move in large numbers, with good days easily topping 10,000. Great Cormorant is uncommon, mainly later in fall, with annual totals of only dozens.

LOONS AND GREBES Moderate movements of hundreds of Common Loons in early to midfall are a prelude for the mass movements of Red-throated Loon that come later. The big loon days in late November fill the sky with loons, with daily counts sometimes exceeding 10,000. Horned Grebe is uncommon, with about 150 counted in an average fall, and Red-necked Grebe is rare.

ALCIDS A handful of Razorbills come past in late fall and winter, often in scoter flocks. All other alcids are extremely rare.

TUBENOSES Summer is the best time for tubenoses. Wilson's Storm-Petrel is the most frequent, while Great, Sooty, and Cory's Shearwaters are occasionally seen.

SULIDS Northern Gannet migration runs throughout the fall, starting with juveniles in late September and progressing through the December movements consisting nearly entirely of adults. Numbers seem to be on the increase, with more than 100,000 counted in some recent falls. There is a day in which more than 10,000 are counted nearly every fall. Northbound spring movements are much smaller.

PELICANS Brown Pelicans are occurring later and in larger numbers every year. When the count started, the annual average was about 100 birds, but 300 or more has been more typical in recent years.

JAEGERS AND SKUAS Parasitic Jaeger is the most common species and is seen on about two-thirds of the days of the fall watch. The average fall total is 150 birds. Pomarine is rare and Long-tailed extremely rare.

GULLS Although Ring-billed Gulls generally migrate inconspicuously, perhaps nocturnally, Avalon sees some obvious and spectacular migrations. These usually occur in late November, after the passage of a cold front. The gulls form kettles that slowly wheel south like gray-and-white Buteos. The fall average is over 10,000, though more than 30,000 were counted one year. Bonaparte's Gull stages large movements, mostly in mid- and late fall, with a fall average of about 4,500. Thousands of Herring and Great Black-backed Gulls are present and move around a lot, but they do so in a manner that makes it difficult to separate local from long-distance movements. Numbers vary hugely depending on the philosophy of the main counter each year. Glaucous, Iceland, Black-headed, and Little Gulls and Black-legged Kittiwake are rare.

TERNS The early days of the official watch in late September are sometimes livened by movements of hundreds of Common Terns. By mid-October,

Forster's Tern has largely taken over, with large movements sometimes totaling thousands of birds and sometimes mixing with Bonaparte's Gulls. The fall average for Forster's Tern is about 6,000. Good movements of Common Terns have been observed in spring, along with smaller numbers of other spe-cies. Hundreds, sometimes more than 1,000, Royal Terns are counted each fall. Many of these are pairs made up of an adult and a juvenile bird. Significant late-summer and early-fall movements of more southern tern species might be expected but have not yet been noted.

TOP 10 SPECIES	FALL SEASONAL AVERAGE	SINGLE-DAY HIGH COUNT
1. Double-crested Cormorant	185,789	24,637 on Nov. 12, 2008
2. Surf Scoter	146,893	69,928 on Oct. 26, 2007
3. Black Scoter	139,775	74,998 on Oct. 26, 2007
4. "Dark-winged" scoter	67,625	27,762 on Nov. 12, 2008
5. Northern Gannet	63,279	21,627 on Nov. 12, 2008
6. Red-throated Loon	56,745	16,851 on Nov. 21, 2011
7. Laughing Gull	16,339	6,603 on Oct. 12, 2000
8. Ring-billed Gull	13,993	9,081 on Dec. 10, 1995
9. Herring Gull	9,357	8,309 on Nov. 5, 1996
10. Canada Goose	9,026	20,325 on Dec. 9, 2010

Rarities: Greater White-fronted Goose, Ross's Goose, "Black" Brant, Barrow's Goldeneye, Pacific Loon, Thick-billed Murre, Atlantic Puffin, Black Guillemot, Northern Fulmar, Manx Shearwater, American White Pelican, Long-tailed Jaeger, California Gull, Sabine's Gull, Arctic Tern, Bridled Tern, White Ibis, Wood Stork, and Sandhill Crane.

Numbers courtesy of Cape May Bird Observatory.

16. Delaware Bay and River

Information from Vince Elia and

Nick Pulcinella

With Avalon and its spectacular waterbird migrations just across the Cape May peninsula, it's easy to ignore Delaware Bay as a migration corridor. Nonetheless, it attracts migrating birds in large numbers. In fact, it is often surmised that many southbound Black and Surf Scoters cut across the continent from the Arctic and then follow the Delaware down to the Atlantic. This migration probably occurs at great altitude or nocturnally, though it should still provide impetus for closer examination of this waterway. The Cape May Bird Observatory fall "dike count," on the bayshore on Cape May, is primarily interested in passerines but has noted dabbling ducks, scoters, Double-crested Cormorant, Common Loon, and even jaegers that appear to be migrating along the bay rather than the Atlantic.

The Delaware can be amazing after a tropical storm or hurricane. All three jaegers, Black-capped Petrel, Band-rumped and Leach's Storm-Petrels, White-tailed Tropicbird, and Arctic, Sooty, and Bridled Terns have all been seen exiting the bay after a storm has subsided. Even a minor storm can be enough to produce birds, particularly tropical terns. The most productive storms are ones in which the eye passes directly over the bay or slightly inland. The eye itself and the area to its northeast seem to hold most of the pelagic birds. Storms that pass to the east rarely produce much unless the eye is very close to the coast. Sunset Beach on the western side of the tip of Cape May has proven an excellent viewpoint for these post-storm movements. Further explorations elsewhere would undoubtedly turn up more good places to watch.

Farther up the Delaware, in southeast Pennsylvania, where the bay becomes a river, this body of water is still a significant corridor for waterbird migration. Double-crested Cormorant is an abundant migrant, and huge numbers of Ring-billed and Herring Gulls can sometimes be seen, though it is hard to know which movements are local and which are long distance. Less-common migrants include Snow and Canada Geese, a range of ducks, Red-throated and Common Loons, Bonaparte's Gull, and Caspian and Common Terns. Rarities on the river have included Little Gull and Gull-billed Tern. Storms have pushed coastal and pelagic birds such as Audubon's Shearwater, Black-legged Kittiwake, and Royal and Sooty Terns all the way up to Delaware County, Pennsylvania. Market Square Park at the southern tip of Delaware County is a good vantage point for riverwatching.

17. Cape Henlopen State Park, Delaware

By Forrest Rowland

The position of this park at the mouth of Delaware Bay makes it a good place to look for jaegers, gulls, terns, and waterfowl as they undertake long-distance migrations or move shorter distances in and out of the bay. Fall is the best season for sea-watching. As early as mid-October, thousands of cormorants, loons, and most species of waterfowl native to the continent are observed. Cormorants are the most numerous migrants. High day counts of Double-crested Cormorant range between 25,000 and 40,000. Most of the diving ducks are scoters (all three species), while Green-winged Teal is the predominant dabbler. High day counts of scoters number in the tens of thousands. Small numbers of other ducks, including coveted species such as both eiders and Harlequin Duck, also pass by. Brant are frequently seen in skeins of hundreds. Parasitic Jaegers are seen almost daily between mid-October and mid-November. Pomarine Jaegers also occur, though only a handful of individuals are recorded each fall. Rare gulls, mainly seen from late autumn through winter, include Sabine's, Iceland, Thayer's, and Black-headed. Black-headed Gulls are seen almost weekly in November and December. As is the case at any coastal promontory after a hurricane or strong easterly wind, Cape Henlopen can be great for storm birds. Leach's and Band-rumped Storm-Petrels, Great Shearwater, Sooty and Roseate Terns, and Magnificent Frigatebird have all been reported in or near the state park. The best viewing points are the hawk-watch platform and Herring Point.

18. Assateague Island and Ocean City, Maryland

By Bill Hubick

Assateague Island is, without question, the top birding destination in Maryland. Famous among the general public for its population of feral horses, the island is beloved among local birders for hosting exceptional migration events, especially in fall. Assateague is a 37-mile-long barrier island that lines much of the Maryland coastline south to Virginia. Ocean City occupies a similar landmass to the north, with the two separated by the Ocean City Inlet. The inlet is the access point of Sinepuxent Bay, which supports large numbers of waterbirds at all seasons. Maryland lacks full-time seawatching coverage, but anecdotal evidence suggests that timing and relative abundance of waterbirds here are very similar to those of Avalon, New Jersey.

LOCATION

Maryland birders concentrate their seawatching efforts between the Ocean City Inlet and locations on Assateague Island. You can access the Ocean City Inlet via a parking lot at the end of 2nd Street, which is at the south end of the famous boardwalk. When conditions allow, the far end of the north jetty pro-

vides the closest view of migrant waterbirds, but other spots can be chosen based on a given day's conditions. Concentrations of feeding gulls, terns, and shorebirds will almost always keep you entertained while you're scanning for migrant seabirds.

To access Assateague Island, cross the Verrazano Bridge, and immediately upon reaching the island, you will see a parking area for one of Assateague State Park's most popular seawatching spots. Cross over the dunes at one of the obvious cutovers to scan from the beach. The national seashore also offers good seawatching, and any access to the beach on the island will provide similar views of the ocean.

TIMING

Although all seasons can be productive, late fall is the most exciting time of year for seawatching. Peak numbers for many species occur between late October and mid-November, when major flights of scoters, loons, and Northern Gannets can be impressive. Winter bird movements are generally reduced, but winter is perhaps the best-covered season for seawatching in Maryland. Early January is a traditional time for Maryland birders to visit in search of alcids, eiders, white-winged gulls, and other rarities. Spring migration mirrors fall, with anecdotal evidence suggesting that numbers are significantly reduced. Summer is the best time to target tube-noses and to hope for pelagic mega-rarities.

BIRDS

SWANS Migrant flocks of Tundra Swans are common in November and are possible through March. They are more common inland and along Sinepuxent Bay but are regularly seen along the coast as well. Mute Swan is rare.

GEESE Large flocks of migrant Snow and Canada Geese are often observed in fall migration along the coast, though they are more common over Sinepuxent Bay and the coastal salt marshes. Such flocks should be checked for "Richardson's" Cackling Goose and Ross's Goose, which are uncommon but consistently present in small numbers during migration and winter. Brant arrive in numbers in October and November, sometimes supplemented by another December push from the north. Sinepuxent Bay is a major wintering area for "Atlantic" Brant, and they are easily detected through March, with decreasing numbers lingering through April and May. "Black" Brant has been recorded, and Greater White-fronted Goose is rare.

DABBLING DUCKS Fall dabbler migration is similar to that at other East Coast seawatching areas, with small flocks readily detected over both the ocean and inland sides of the barrier islands. Flocks are often mixed, and nearly any species can fall in with the abundant flocks of scoters. As at other sites along the coast, Green-winged Teal is the most common, but Wood Duck, Northern Pintail, American Black Duck, Mallard, and American Wigeon are also frequent.

DIVING DUCKS As described for Avalon, New Jersey, scoter migration here is a natural spectacle that should draw seawatchers to the coast. Even without having a formal seawatch, Maryland birders have often tallied several thousand scoters during brief watches in late fall. Surf and Black Scoters are abundant, especially during the late October to mid-November migration peak. White-winged Scoters are regular but slightly later and far less common. Red-breasted Mergansers, Greater and Lesser Scaup, Bufflehead, and Long-tailed Ducks are common. Redhead and Ring-necked Ducks come through but are probably often overlooked. Common Mergansers, Canvasback, and Common Goldeneye are very rarely detected on the coast. Common Eider is consistently present in winter, with record numbers at the Ocean City Inlet in recent years. Harlequin Duck is annual at the Ocean City Inlet in single digit numbers. King Eider is rare but regular.

CORMORANTS The huge flocks of Double-crested Cormorants along the coast are impossible to miss in October and November. Diligent observers can easily tally counts of several thousand individuals in a day. Great Cormorant is uncommon but is regularly detected during peak migration. Small numbers winter in the area, most reliably at the Ocean City Inlet.

LOONS AND GREBES Loons and grebes occur here in a pattern similar to that seen at Avalon, New Jersey, and other sites on the East Coast. Common and Red-throated Loons are common from late fall to spring, with peak movements occurring in November. There are records of Pacific Loon. Horned Grebe is regular, but numbers are small compared with those of loons. Red-necked Grebe is rare but regular, occurring in larger numbers during irruption years.

ALCIDS Most of the alcids here are seen on the water, though further observations would likely turn up more flybys. A few Razorbills are typically spotted at the Ocean City Inlet in January and February. Dovekie occurs less regularly. Atlantic Puffin and the two murre species are rarely observed from land, but Common Murre is increasing on the East Coast, including in Maryland. Black Guillemot has not yet been recorded in Maryland.

TUBENOSES Summer is the best time for tubenoses. Wilson's Storm-Petrel is easily detected in small numbers during July and August seawatches. Great, Sooty, and Cory's Shearwaters are occasional. There is one record of Yellow-nosed Albatross.

SULIDS Northern Gannets are abundant fall migrants, and the spectacle of hundreds of gannets streaming by the coast is a consistent highlight for late-fall seawatchers. Numbers are variable during midwinter, but spring sees a major spike in northbound birds. Small numbers of Northern Gannets summer in the area and should be carefully scrutinized for Brown Boobies. Maryland's first Brown Booby was documented on Assateague Island in July 2009, and additional records are expected.

PELICANS Brown Pelicans are common and easily detected throughout the summer months. Fall and spring spikes of migrating birds are to be expected but haven't yet been noted, as the abundant presence of local birds tends to obscure longer-range movements. American White Pelican is very rare.

JAEGERS AND SKUAS Jaegers are infrequently detected from land, probably because of lack of coverage during peak fall migration. Parasitic is the species most frequently seen. Pomarine is rare, and Long-tailed is extremely rare.

GULLS Laughing Gulls are common from spring to fall but very rare in January and February. Ring-billed Gulls are common winter residents that begin returning from the breeding grounds in August, with peak migration occurring in late fall. Bonaparte's Gulls are most numerous in November and December, and again in late March and early April. When large flocks are present, look for Little and Black-headed Gulls, which are rare but regular. Herring and Great Black-backed Gulls are abundant residents, making true migration difficult to detect. Lesser Black-backed Gulls are a fascinating phenomenon here, having become an increasingly common summering species in recent years. Glaucous, Iceland, and Thayer's Gulls and Black-legged Kittiwake are all rare but regular in season. Franklin's and Black-tailed Gulls are extreme rarities.

TERNS Least, Common, Forster's, and Royal Terns breed locally, arriving in April, and are easily observed in summer. Least Terns depart early, with a few individuals continuing into late August and early September. Peak fall migration for Common Tern is September, with large Forster's movements continuing later in the season. Caspian Terns are regular in small numbers during fall migration in August and September but are surprisingly uncommon in spring migration. Black Skimmers are low-density local breeders and are scarce but regular commuters from spring through fall. Migrant Black Terns are easily detected by dedicated seawatchers in July and August, as are small numbers of post-breeding Sandwich Terns, which often move through with begging juveniles. Gull-billed Terns are rare but annual and are a coveted find for Maryland birders during the July and August dispersal window. Arctic and Roseate Terns are very rare migrants, and Sooty, Bridled, and Roseate Terns are extreme rarities.

19. Chesapeake Bay, Maryland and Virginia

Information from Bill Hubick and
Ned Brinkley

This vast bay is well known as a waterbird staging and wintering area and is also a conduit for active migration. This is a very important area for waterfowl, particularly in winter, with scaup, Bufflehead, and Canvasback being particularly abundant. Point Lookout State Park in Maryland is an excellent baywatching area, situated at the point where the Potomac River empties into the bay. Huge numbers of waterbirds pass by the park, including many that appear to be actively migrating. These include scaup, scoters, both loons, Northern Gannet, Bonaparte's and Ring-billed Gulls, and Common Terns. Other species such as Double-crested Cormorant and Brown Pelican fly around a lot, but many of their flights may pertain to local movements. Rarities here have included both Common and King Eiders and Harlequin Duck, and Eared Grebe has been annual in recent years. Brown Pelican is present even in winter except in the most severe conditions. Northern Gannets are common in season. Inside the bay, alcids, tubenoses, and jaegers are rare, though recent summer boat trips have documented the consistent presence of Wilson's Storm-Petrels in July and early August.

The Chesapeake Bay Bridge-Tunnel, at the bay's mouth, is good for a surprising number of pelagic birds. Unfortunately, free access is currently restricted to One Island, which is not ideally situated for seawatching. The Bridge-Tunnel is a fantastic place to do "storm-watching" after a big hurricane or tropical storm pushes birds up the bay. Rarities that have been recorded here include Northern Fulmar, Herald and Black-capped Petrels, Manx Shearwater, Leach's and Band-rumped Storm-Petrels, Magnificent Frigatebird, Franklin's, Black-tailed, Mew, California, and Sabine's Gulls, numerous Bridled and Sooty Terns, Arctic Tern, Dovekie,

and Common Murre. The majority of these records were in the wake of hurricanes.

20. Back Bay National Wildlife Refuge, Virginia

Information from Ned Brinkley

The Mid-Atlantic coast has lots of good seawatch sites, and almost any vantage point can be productive when fall scoter migration hits full swing. Back Bay NWR is one of the best-known seawatching sites along Virginia's limited coastline. The flights here are generally similar to those at Avalon, New Jersey, and Assateague Island and Ocean City, Maryland, in terms of the numbers and mix of species. Shearwater and jaeger flights have been observed in spring and fall, and some winters see alcid incursions. Exceptional records include Pacific Loon, Thick-billed Murre, Dovekie, Black Guillemot, and perhaps the ultimate East Coast seawatching prize, a Yellow-nosed Albatross seen in November 1981. Post-hurricane storm-watching might be excellent, but the open beach offers little shelter, so few people have braved the weather to watch from here.

21. Outer Banks, North Carolina

Information from Ricky Davis

At their farthest point, near Cape Hatteras, these skinny barrier islands are more than 30 miles from the mainland! The Outer Banks are certainly one of the premier seawatching sites on the East Coast. In fall there are massive movements of scoters, cormorants, and loons that rival those at Avalon, New Jersey, but that have never been systematically counted for comparison. In spring and early summer, shearwaters, terns, and Northern Gannets pour by on their northward migrations. Pelagic species such as South Polar Skua and Audubon's Shearwater, which are rarely seen from shore elsewhere in the country, are occasionally seen during this period. It is also worth noting that the Outer Banks serve as the springboard for some of the most productive pelagic birding boat trips in North America, offering the chance to see species that are rarely seen from shore on the East Coast.

LOCATION

Cape Hatteras Point is the best all-around seawatch site in North Carolina. The point itself is sometimes closed, but the beaches on either side still offer good viewing. There are plenty of other good places to seawatch, including the Currituck County beaches, both sides of Oregon Inlet, and the Rodanthe and Avon piers. South of the Outer Banks, Cape Lookout and Cape Fear are great for seawatching, though access can be difficult.

TIMING

The Outer Banks can be interesting year-round, though fall tends to be the best, and late summer the slowest. Fall sees large movements of scoters and other diving ducks, loons, Northern Gannets, and cormorants, along with small numbers of other waterbirds. Winter can be good for loons, grebes, gulls, and sometimes alcids. Early spring sees Red-breasted Mergansers, scoters, loons, and gannets moving by in smaller numbers than in fall. Late spring and early summer sometimes have outstanding movements of terns, gulls, jaegers, gannets, and shearwaters at close range.

Different spots are best at different times of year. The Currituck County beaches, at the northern end of the Outer Banks, are best during spring migration. The middle beaches, from Nags Head to Rodanthe, are best during fall migration. The southern leg of the Outer Banks, with its east-to-west orientation from Ocracoke to Cape Hatteras, is good in spring and early summer during east to south winds.

Year-round, onshore winds can bring oceanic species closer to shore. Northerly winds are good during fall migration, though almost any day can be good. Big flights sometimes occur with moderate north or northeast winds the day after a cold front. In winter, west winds are ideal because they calm the water and allow visibility out to the horizon. Big movements in early spring often occur in conjunction with south winds. Best viewing in late spring and early summer is in east or southeast winds, which bring northbound birds close to shore.

The birding the day after the landfall of a hurricane can be amazing, though access may be difficult. The inlets are good places to watch for pelagic birds returning to the ocean.

BIRDS

GEESE Brant are uncommon on the east side of Pamlico Sound (which separates the Outer Banks from the mainland) but scarce along the ocean. Wintering birds are concentrated in the sound near Ocracoke and Hatteras Inlets.

DABBLING DUCKS Many species are seen in small numbers, mostly with scoters in the fall; Green-winged Teal is the most common.

DIVING DUCKS In fall, a large scoter migration runs from late October to December. Observers estimate daily totals of 50,000–100,000, but these exceptional days have never been formally counted. The vast majority are Black and Surf, with small numbers of White-winged. Spring sees a much reduced scoter migration. A few Common Eider are seen from late fall to early spring.

Lesser and Greater Scaup are the other species most often seen in scoter flocks. Limited observations suggest that the migrations of non-scoter diving ducks on the Outer Banks are not as large or diverse as those seen farther north, as at Avalon, New Jersey.

CORMORANTS Large numbers of Double-cresteds come through in fall, with peak days often coinciding with big scoter movements.

LOONS AND GREBES Migrant Common Loons have been observed in fall, though they seem sporadic. Impressive movements of Red-throated Loons occur in late November and December.

ALCIDS Razorbill is the most common alcid, usually appearing in small numbers. Dovekie is rare and sporadic, and Thick-billed and Common Murres are extremely rare. Invasions of hundreds or thousands of alcids, mostly Razorbills, have occurred in February. An incredible 8,875 Razorbills were counted from Cape Hatteras on February 15, 2004!

TUBENOSES Large northbound movements of shearwaters have been seen in late spring and early summer. Although they're far from predictable, the peak days have been in the last week of May and first week of June. The majority are Sooty Shearwaters, with smaller numbers of Great and Cory's and a handful of Manx. Audubon's Shearwater is very rare from shore from late spring through summer. Storm-petrels are also seen sporadically from shore. Wilson's is most common, but Leach's has also been noted.

FRIGATEBIRDS Magnificent Frigatebird is rare from spring to fall.

SULIDS Northern Gannets surge through in big numbers in spring and fall, with good numbers present throughout the winter. Brown Booby is very rare but has been seen from shore.

PELICANS Although some leave in winter, Brown Pelican is present year-round, which obscures whatever migration may be occurring.

JAEGERS AND SKUAS Parasitic and Pomarine Jaegers both occur year-round, though late spring and early summer see peak numbers. Long-tailed Jaeger is very rare, but this is one of the best places on the East Coast to see one from shore.

GULLS Most gull species seem to trickle through, with no perceptible surges in migration. Bonaparte's does occur in huge numbers in February and March, with estimates exceeding 40,000 in some years. These seem to be birds staging for their spring migration. Sabine's Gull and Black-legged Kittiwake are occasionally seen from shore.

TERNS Spring sees a strong tern migration, though the tendency of these birds to feed while migrating can disguise their long-range movements. Common Tern is the most common but occurs alongside a full range of other species: Royal, Caspian, Sandwich, Forster's, Gull-billed, Black, and Least. Roseate Tern is extremely rare but has been seen between late spring and summer.

22. Fort Fisher, North Carolina

By Ricky Davis

Fort Fisher offers the best seawatching in southeastern North Carolina. The main vantage point is the shore right across from the Fort Fisher Museum. There is a parking lot on the beach that gives great viewing with considerable elevation. The best time for seawatching is from fall through winter, sometimes into spring. Summer can be good for locally nesting Brown Pelicans and terns that feed offshore.

Fall movements are similar to those at other East Coast sites, with good scoter and Double-crested Cormorant migrations that can top thousands of birds in a few hours. Other waterfowl species become common in early November, often mixed with the scoter flocks. Northern Gannets start appearing in late October and can occur in large numbers. Jaegers, mostly Parasitic, are possible from November into January. Winter is good for waterfowl, grebes, gannets, and gulls, and there is usually an impressive flock of Red-throated Loons (averaging 500 birds) wintering off Fort Fisher. By late December, alcids are possible, with Razorbill by far the most common. Spring sees northward-moving loons, gannets, and some waterfowl (such as Red-breasted Mergansers). After several days of strong southeasterly winds, pelagics such as shearwaters and Wilson's Storm-Petrel are possible, especially from late May to mid-June.

This area is unique in North Carolina because of the Coquina Rock formation that is exposed on the beach and extends out onto the hard bottom just offshore. This formation is probably the reason that scoters, Bufflehead, scaup, and Long-tailed Ducks are often found near shore here. The best weather conditions for productive seawatches are fairly typical: northerly winds after fronts for fall and winter, and southeasterly winds from late winter to early

summer. As on the Outer Banks, westerly winds can flatten the ocean, providing optimal conditions for viewing birds sitting on the water or flying just above the surface.

23. Huntington Beach State Park, South Carolina

Information from Ricky Davis

Huntington Beach State Park is often considered the best all-around birding site in South Carolina, and solid seawatching is definitely on offer. The long rock jetty at the northern end of the park serves as an excellent seawatching platform. It also attracts interesting species of sea ducks, loons, and grebes, and even the rare alcid or two, which can be seen on the water even if no active migration is occurring. If the seawatching is slow, an alternative is to search the marshes and mudflats immediately behind the dunes for sparrows and shorebirds.

LOCATION

The park is 20 miles southeast of Myrtle Beach; an entrance fee is charged. Once inside, drive to the north parking lot. Although the watching can be good from here, the best spot is the long jetty a mile farther north, which is reached by walking along the beach.

TIMING

Fall and early winter are best and feature strong movements of scoters, both scaup, loons, Double-crested Cormorants, and Northern Gannets. Big flights sometimes occur with moderate north or northeast winds the day after a cold front. Winter offers the best chance of an alcid sighting, usually on the water around the jetty. Spring and summer are less interesting, though good for terns. Although the park is not very good for truly pelagic species, the best time to look for them is after an extended period of southeast winds or a hurricane.

BIRDS

DABBLING DUCKS Seen in small numbers, mostly with scoters in the fall; Green-winged Teal is the most common.

DIVING DUCKS Peak scoter migration runs from late fall through early winter, with the vast majority being Black and Surf; White-winged is rare. Spring sees a much reduced scoter migration. A few Common Eider are seen in winter. Lesser and Greater Scaup are common migrants, often seen in scoter flocks. Red-breasted Merganser is also common.

Bonaparte's Gulls gather around the jetty at Ponce Inlet. Michael Brothers.

CORMORANTS Large numbers of Double-cresteds come through in fall, with peak days often coinciding with big scoter movements. Small numbers of Great Cormorants usually winter around the inlet.

LOONS AND GREBES Migrant Common and Red-throated Loons and Horned Grebes have been observed in fall, and the jetty is a good place to see these species in winter.

ALCIDS All alcids are rare, but irruptions have occurred, and the jetty seems to draw in stray birds. Razorbill is the most likely species.

TUBENOSES All species are extremely rare here. Observations of shearwaters and storm-petrels are likely only after hurricanes or extended periods of onshore winds.

FRIGATEBIRDS Magnificent Frigatebird is rare from spring to fall.

SULIDS Northern Gannet comes through in big numbers in spring and fall, with many present throughout the winter.

PELICANS Although some leave in winter, Brown Pelican is present year-round. Some of the groups passing in fall and spring are certainly migrants.

JAEGERS AND SKUAS Parasitic Jaeger is regular, mainly from midfall to midwinter. Pomarine is rare.

GULLS Strong Ring-billed Gull movements have been seen on the first day after the passage of a late-fall cold front. Migration of other species is generally inconspicuous.

TERNS Spring is good for terns, with Common being the most common. Migration is not usually obvious, and terns simply seem to "appear" in spring.

24. Tybee Island, Georgia

The geography of this island suggests that it has good potential as a seawatching location, likely the best place along the coast of Georgia. It has received minimal coverage, and the observations so far have produced few results. However, given its location, it should see movements of scaup, scoters (particularly Black Scoter), Northern Gannets, gulls, and terns. More coverage is needed to determine its significance as a seawatch location.

25. Northeast Florida

Information from Michael Brothers,
Matt Hafner, and Wes Biggs

Amid the condos and high-rise hotels that typify the northeastern Florida coast are several places that offer good seawatching. The sites mentioned here all share a similar set of birds, though this set is noticeably different from that which characterizes seawatching locations in states to the north. In particular, this area can enjoy remarkable flights of jaegers and storm-petrels.

LOCATION

The northeast coast of Florida has few features to concentrate migrating seabirds, and any place with a good view of the ocean can serve as a seawatching location. As you move south, the coastline bulges to the east, with the result that sites in the Titusville area, particularly Playalinda Beach on Canaveral National Seashore, may show slightly higher concentrations of birds than locations farther north. Covered below are several sites with at least some history of seawatch observation that also offer convenient access to the ocean.

HUGUENOT MEMORIAL PARK NEAR FT. GEORGE, DUVAL COUNTY. Watching from the North St. John's River jetty can be productive in both spring and fall. The nearby nesting colony of Royal, Sandwich, and Gull-billed Terns ensures that there is always something to observe. Storm-petrels and Arctic Terns have been recorded in the spring, and jaegers and waterfowl can be observed in the fall.

LIGHTHOUSE POINT PARK ON PONCE INLET, VOLUSIA COUNTY. This park offers excellent access to Ponce Inlet, famous among Florida birders for its propensity to host rare birds. The north jetty offers the best vantage point in good weather, though in poor weather a car parked on the beach just north of the jetty provides welcome shelter. Rarities associated with tropical storms and hurricanes have included Black-capped Petrel, Brown Noddy, Masked and Brown Boobies, as well as large numbers of Sooty Terns and smaller numbers of Bridled Terns. Ponce Inlet is one of the best places to observe the occasional late-spring influx of storm-petrels.

TURTLE MOUND, CANAVERAL NATIONAL SEASHORE, VOLUSIA COUNTY. This is probably the site where the most seawatching has occurred in the southeastern U.S. A flight of 2,226 migrating Pomarine Jaegers counted here on November 9, 1992, boggles the mind, and days of more than 1,000 Pomarines are not unusual. More than 100 storm-petrels, mostly Leach's, were visible at one time on May 4, 2001, during a huge spring storm-petrel flight. Other rarities have included Masked and Brown Boobies, South Polar Skua, Long-tailed Jaeger, Sabine's Gull, and Black-legged Kittiwake. One of the reasons this location has received more coverage than others in Florida is that there is a restroom pavilion providing a sheltered view of the ocean.

PLAYALINDA BEACH, CANAVERAL NATIONAL SEASHORE, BREVARD COUNTY. Some birders have speculated that

Playalinda is even better than Turtle Mound, but it has not received the same level of coverage since there is no sheltered location from which to watch. Limited observations have revealed excellent flights of jaegers in the fall and storm-petrels in the spring.

SEBASTIAN INLET STATE PARK, BREVARD AND INDIAN RIVER COUNTIES. A state park straddles this inlet, and the jetties on both sides can be good seawatch locations. Most of the coverage here has been in the past few years, and the site has proven to have much the same birds as the other north Florida locations. A single-day count of more than 1,500 Pomarine and Parasitic Jaegers hints at the potential of this site.

DAYTONA BEACH, VOLUSIA COUNTY. This is one of the best places in North America to observe gulls in winter, as Daytona sees a massive evening influx of gulls from a local landfill. This phenomenon culminates with all the gulls moving a short distance offshore to roost on the water for the night, which draws Pomarine and Parasitic Jaegers and allows for excellent study as they harass the gulls.

TIMING

The two most exceptional seawatching events in Florida, storm-petrels in the spring and jaegers in the fall, depend on a specific set of weather conditions and are therefore sporadic, not occurring every year. Storm-petrels occur close to shore in the late spring, particularly in late May and early June, after several days of strong east winds. If east winds do not occur during that period or are weak, then storm-petrels are not present or occur in small numbers. If strong winds occur for an extended period, then storm-petrels may be seen all along the coast. Jaeger flights are best from late October to mid-November. The conditions that produce good numbers of jaegers are slightly more complex than those for storm-petrels, but any time when northeast winds persist for several days in October or November is a good time to try your luck.

BIRDS

DIVING DUCKS Lesser Scaup predominate, but smaller numbers of Greater Scaup and Redhead also occur. All three species of scoters pass by, though Black Scoter is by far the most numerous, occurring in modest numbers in late fall, particularly off the more northern portions of the coast. Scarce species such as Common Eider, Long-tailed Duck, and Common Goldeneye have all been observed, and with greater coverage would likely prove to be annual or nearly so.

TUBENOSES Storm-petrels may be present in late spring during east winds. Most of them are Leach's, with smaller numbers of Wilson's and the occasional Band-rumped. Occasionally a Sooty Shearwater is observed in the spring during a storm-petrel incursion. Shearwaters are never numerous but are more reliable in late summer or early fall, when a few Cory's and Great and the odd Audubon's are often present. Some tropical systems have driven larger numbers of Audubon's Shearwaters close to shore, and there have also been two sightings of Black-capped Petrel associated with tropical disturbances.

FRIGATEBIRDS Frigatebird sightings are surprisingly scarce and usually occur during tropical systems.

SULIDS Northern Gannets are often numerous and close to shore, not only during migration but throughout the winter. Masked and Brown Boobies have been observed at most of the locations listed above, often in conjunction with tropical systems or during periods of strong onshore winds.

PELICANS Good numbers of migrating Brown Pelicans likely pass through this area, but Brown Pelicans are so ubiquitous that separating migrants from residents is a challenge.

JAEGERS AND SKUAS This is the best location in eastern North America to see migrating Pomarine Jaegers, and one of the few places in the region where flocks of jaegers are a regular occurrence.

GULLS Little information on gull migration at these sites exists, though there are records of rarities such as Sabine's and Franklin's Gulls and Black-legged Kittiwake for several of these locations. As mentioned above, Daytona Beach is one of the best locations in North America to observe wintering gulls.

TERNS Little information exists, but northeast Florida would likely be a great spot to see migrating Royal, Sandwich, and Common Terns. It might even be possible to see migrating Gull-billed Terns, a species rarely noted in active migration. During strong east winds in late spring, there are occasional records of Arctic Tern.

26. Dry Tortugas, Florida

These tiny islands lie well out to sea off the southern coast of Florida. Although interesting flybys are always possible, the focus here is on breeding waterbirds. In addition to Fort Jefferson, a huge and rather eerie historical landmark, the islands host a large breeding colony of Sooty Terns and Brown Noddies. In recent years a handful of Bridled Terns have also established a breeding toehold on Bush Key, where they melt into the madness created by the thousands of Sooty Terns and Brown Noddies. Patience and careful scrutiny of incoming birds are required to pick out a Bridled. Roseate Tern formerly nested on Bush Key, and it may still be seen as a migrant. A colony of boobies, mostly Masked with a small number of Brown, nests on Hospital Key and is visible in the distance from Fort Jefferson. Long Key hosts the only breeding colony of Magnificent Frigatebird in the U.S., and there is rarely a moment when these angular tropical seabirds are not visible. Scanning farther out might produce Audubon's Shearwater, White-tailed Tropicbird, or a jaeger. The boat ride to the islands holds potential as well. Audubon's Shearwater is almost expected, Band-rumped Storm-Petrel is occasionally observed, and Cory's Shearwater and Black-capped Petrel are extremely rare.

27. Fort Pickens, Florida

Information from Bob Duncan

Although the Gulf Coast of Florida lies in seabird doldrums, it is still a significant leading edge that does concentrate migrating birds. The best site is probably the Fort Pickens part of Gulf Islands National Seashore. In March and April, movements of thousands of ducks have been observed here. Most are Blue-winged Teal, with smaller numbers of Northern Shoveler, scoters, and Fulvous Whistling-Ducks. All are westbound, suggesting a Mississippi River convergence point with the eastbound spring migrants seen on the Texas Gulf Coast. Northern Gannets also move through this area in significant numbers from fall to spring. Although the Gulf of Mexico is not known for its pelagics, observations from Fort Pickens and other locations in the western Florida panhandle during gale-force south winds have turned up a surprising number of pelagic species in fall and early winter. Audubon's, Sooty, Cory's, and Great Shearwaters as well as Brown Noddy have all been observed in recent years. Tropical storms and hurricanes have pushed in Sooty and Bridled Terns and Masked Booby as well.

Elsewhere on the Florida Gulf Coast, tens of thousands of Common Terns sometimes stage near Tampa. Further observations from this area would surely reveal significant tern migrations.

28. Cameron Parish, Louisiana

Information from Justin Bosler and Steve Cardiff

This parish (Louisiana's version of a county) is located just down the gulf from East Beach, Texas, and offers similar seawatching. Any of the beaches here can be good, including Holly, East Jetty,

Broussard, and Rutherford. March duck flights are the highlight. More than 10,000 Lesser Scaup can be seen in a day, along with smaller numbers of Greater Scaup, Fulvous Whistling-Ducks, Blue-winged and Green-winged Teal, Northern Shoveler, Northern Pintail, and Surf and Black Scoters. As at East Beach (see the next account), there are also large numbers of migrating wading birds. Fall migration here is poorly known.

29. East Beach, Galveston, Texas

Although the Gulf Coast is usually neglected as a seawatching area, it offers an exciting and different sort of migration and warrants further exploration. Spring migration on a good day at East Beach can be excellent and can feature big numbers of teal, Northern Shoveler, Northern Pintail, Fulvous Whistling-Ducks, and scaup, often in large mixed flocks; skeins of Brown Pelicans skimming the surf; small numbers of scoters and loons; and Northern Gannets far offshore. The upper Texas coast is also bursting with non-waterbird migrants at this time of year, and the seaside observer is often treated to the sight of warblers and sparrows bouncing over the waves and eventually making landfall. Another feature of migration here is the excellent wader flights. The full range of North American egrets, herons, and ibis occurs, and they show a strong tendency to follow the coastline on migration. Although the woodlots and warblers of the Texas coast are irresistible, tear yourself away and spend a day seawatching, and you're sure to gain a new appreciation for the astounding size and scope of migration in this area. Less is known about fall migration, though good flights of several species, particularly Fulvous Whistling-Duck, Yellow-crowned Night-Heron, and Blue-winged Teal (albeit in smaller numbers than in spring), have been observed. Black Tern migration is likely very evident as well. More observation, particularly in the late fall, could clarify the situation. Determining if the hordes of Redhead that winter in south Texas move along the coast diurnally or are strictly nocturnal migrants would be especially important.

LOCATION

East Beach is located in the city of Galveston, at its far southeastern corner. There is a huge parking area that is clearly signed off the Bolivar ferry road. The best place for observation is on or near a rock

A stormy spring day at East Beach, Texas. Laughing Gulls and Brown Pelicans fish the lee side of the jetty while a variety of shorebirds shelter on the adjacent beach. Ken Behrens.

jetty that defines the eastern side of Galveston and protects the inlet. On the other side of this inlet lies Bolivar Flats, a famous site for shorebirds and also a promising seawatch location.

TIMING

Spring migration is best, March being the peak month, with large numbers of ducks headed east, up and around the Gulf Coast. April is also excellent, and a better time for terns. During the madness of spring migration, any time of day can be good. Unlike at most seawatching sites, good evening flights are common here. South or west winds produce the best flights.

Summer is generally slow, and though the wide and shallow marine ledge usually keeps boobies and tubenoses far offshore, they are always possible, especially with onshore winds. East Beach would be an excellent place to watch for storm-driven birds after a hurricane, though access would be difficult.

Fall migration is poorly known. Although the upper Texas coast is not as well situated for fall migration as for spring, recent observations have revealed impressive fall migrations of passerines, and seawatching at this time of year can be quite interesting.

BIRDS

DABBLING DUCKS Blue-winged Teal is very common, often occurring in flocks of hundreds and peaking in March. Green-winged Teal is also common, often occurring in mixed flocks with Blue-winged. Dozens of Cinnamon Teal can also occur on a good day. On some days Northern Pintail is the most common migrant, with thousands counted in a day. Northern Shoveler is another of the most common dabblers, and also is often mixed with Blue-winged Teal. Hundreds of Gadwall and American Wigeon have been counted in a day, making this one of the best known sites to see these species actively migrating. Fulvous Whistling-Duck commonly follows the gulf on its migration, with hundreds passing on a peak day. Seeing a flock of this odd duck out over the waves can be a highlight of a Gulf Coast seawatch.

DIVING DUCKS Scaup are abundant, particularly in March, when thousands may be seen in a day. Lesser predominates, though surprising numbers of Greater are mixed in. Redhead and Red-breasted Mergansers are fairly common. Surf and Black Scoters are rare but regular.

CORMORANTS Neotropic and Double-cresteds are present, providing a good comparison, though significant migratory behavior has not been noted in either species here.

LOONS AND GREBES Small numbers of northbound Common Loons occur in spring.

TUBENOSES Although pelagic explorations have shown that the gulf supports species such as Audubon's and Sooty Shearwaters and Band-rumped Storm-Petrel, they are usually far offshore, and only an exceptional wanderer or storm-driven bird would be visible from land.

FRIGATEBIRDS Magnificent Frigatebird is fairly common from late spring through late summer.

SULIDS Northern Gannet is present in moderate numbers from fall to late spring. Masked and Brown Boobies occur regularly in the gulf, and the occasional bird might wander near to the shore.

PELICANS Brown Pelican migration is a real feature of East Beach, occurring throughout the spring. Good days might see hundreds or thousands of pelicans flying along the surf or even right over the beach. It is an enjoyable seawatch experience to have your "quarry" migrating only feet above your head! Smaller numbers of American White Pelicans can be seen following the gulf as well, sometimes in huge flocks.

GULLS Although adjacent Bolivar Flats and East Beach are magnets for rare gulls, active gull migration is not usually apparent here.

TERNS Spring sees huge numbers of terns invade this area, although it is rare to see most species obviously migrating. In fall, Black Tern migration can be quite obvious, and thousands may be observed moving southwest along the coast.

30. South Padre Island, Texas

The mile-long jetty at the south end of the island makes an excellent place to scan for Gulf of Mexico rarities such as Brown and Masked Boobies and Sooty Tern. Like the upper Texas coast, South Padre is an excellent location to watch hordes of migrating Blue-winged Teal along with smaller numbers of Northern Shoveler, Northern Pintail, and Green-winged Teal. Virtually nothing is known about the migration of diving ducks at this location. However, it should be an excellent location to see big numbers of Lesser Scaup, impressive movements of Redhead, and a scattering of other species. One unique feature of South Padre Island is the mass movement of Franklin's Gulls that occur here. Spring counts exceeding 20,000 individuals in a day have been observed, and fall counts can be just as impressive.

31. Mississippi River

Despite being America's greatest river, and namesake of the great Mississippi flyway, the precise role of the Mississippi in waterbird migration is not well known. It certainly acts as a magnet for gulls and waterfowl year-round, and active migration has been observed in several places, including St. Louis and western Kentucky. This is one of the great frontiers of North American waterbird migration, and fascinating discoveries undoubtedly await.

32. Lake Kentucky and Lake Barkley, Kentucky and Tennessee

Information from Dave Roemer

The mid-twentieth-century damming of the Cumberland and Tennessee Rivers created huge parallel lakes across western Kentucky and Tennessee. Not surprisingly, these lakes act as conduits for waterbird migration, and some excellent waterfowl movements have been witnessed. These usually comprise huge numbers of Lesser Scaup and smaller numbers of Northern Shoveler, Ring-necked Duck, Canvasback, Common Goldeneye, and others. Birds are not usually simple flybys but form rafts, fly in and out, and drop in from the sky. Franklin's Gull is regular in October, particularly on the approach of a cold front. Other common migrants are Common Loon, American White Pelican, Double-crested Cormorant, herons and egrets, gulls, and terns.

Two features seem to produce big waterbird flights here: a front approaching from the north or south of the continent (depending on the season) that puts birds on the move, and foggy and rainy conditions in Kentucky and Tennessee that ground the birds. Such scenarios tend to cause birds to drop out of the sky and form large groups sitting on the water. Cold winter weather farther north also produces flights of birds escaping freezing northern waters; waterfowl and gulls are the main groups affected. During clear conditions, most waterbirds probably pass over this region at high altitude and are difficult or impossible to observe.

The best spots for observation are the dams and spillwaters of the two lakes and the Little Bear Creek boat ramp on the west side of Lake Kentucky. Kentucky birder Dave Roemer has done extensive river- and lakewatching in his state, and he's seen active movements of large numbers of waterbirds on both of these lakes and at several other sites, including the Long Point Unit of Reelfoot National Wildlife Refuge, Barren River Lake, and on the Ohio and Mississippi Rivers. His observations in Kentucky serve as an exciting example of what may remain undiscovered elsewhere.

33. Ohio River

Information from
Geoff Malosh and Dave Roemer

Recent observations at the Dashields Dam on the Ohio River near Pittsburgh, Pennsylvania, have supported the idea that this large river acts as a conduit for migrating waterbirds. Spring watches have revealed a brief but intense migration of Bonaparte's Gull during the second week of April. More than 1,000 Bonaparte's have been counted in a single day in an area where 10 would be exceptional during most of the year! Rare Little and Laughing Gulls have been seen with the Bonaparte's. Ring-billed Gull, Caspian Tern, and Double-crested Cormorant are also regular river migrants. May sees smaller numbers of Common and Forster's Terns moving through. One of the most fascinating aspects of the gull phenomenon is that all the Bonaparte's seen in Pittsburgh are flying west, whereas observers on the river in Ohio and West Virginia have seen only eastbound Bonaparte's. This suggests that the northernmost point on the river, which lies between the two areas of observation, acts as a jumping-off point for the gulls, which have been concentrated on the river during their flight across the interior. Birds seem willing to follow the river as long as it takes them on a slanting northerly course, but will leave it when it turns back to the south.

Watching the Ohio River from Kentucky has also proved productive. Waterfowl, loons, and gulls have been observed in active migration. Dave Roemer observed an incredible flight from the Markland Dam on February 18, 2007, when a cold snap seemed to drive birds south. He reported a constant stream of birds flying down the river, comprising waterfowl, Double-crested Cormorants, and gulls, including the rare Great and Lesser Black-backed Gulls. Other good spots along the Ohio River in Kentucky include Smithland Dam in Livingston County, McAlpine Dam at Louisville, and Meldahl Dam upstream from Louisville. Further observations on the Ohio and other large rivers are sure to reveal fascinating patterns of waterbird migration.

34. Miller Beach, Indiana

Information from Ken Brock

Miller Beach lies at the far southern tip of Lake Michigan, the most vertically oriented of the Great Lakes. In fall the lake acts as a funnel for south-

Miller Beach can draw a crowd on prime fall "lakewatching" days. Ken Brock.

bound migrant birds, and Miller Beach lies at its outlet. This is one of the premier inland places to see jaegers and Sabine's Gull, and indeed, the numbers seen here compete with those at many coastal watches. It is also an excellent place to spot vagrant gulls and terns, plus some of the biggest Common and Black Tern movements so far documented. This is an excellent site at which to watch active shorebird migration, and good numbers of species rare elsewhere in Indiana have been counted. Miller Beach also serves as a concentration point for migrating non-waterbirds. Late August and September counts of Chimney Swifts have run into the hundreds, and on one occasion topped 1,000.

LOCATION
This public beach is in the town of Gary, about 20 miles east of Chicago. There are two prime places from which to watch: the Marquette Park boat ramp, and the concession stand 0.5 miles east of the boat ramp on Oak Avenue. The boat ramp allows watching from a vehicle, though a fee is charged until Labor Day. The concession stand is free, offers good shelter, and is the favorite site of lakewatchers on peak fall days.

TIMING
Fall is the time to visit, as this is when Lake Michigan's funnel brings birds to Miller Beach. Peak migration and best chances at jaegers occur in October. The best conditions are northerly winds during or after the passage of a cold front, as the winds push birds south to this extremity of the lake. Winter and spring may offer abundant gulls, and large

rafts of staging diving ducks and loons, but offer little in the way of active migration.

BIRDS
SWANS Modest flights of Tundra Swan occur in late fall.

GEESE Geese are surprisingly scarce and don't seem to follow the lake in numbers during fall migration.

DABBLING DUCKS Blue-winged Teal occur in good numbers in September. Peak counts are among the highest ever tallied in eastern North America and can exceed 1,000 individuals. Other species occur mainly in late September and October, with significant counts of Northern Shoveler, Gadwall, and Northern Pintail. Gadwall is generally an inconspicuous migrant, with very low high counts from most watch sites; the top daily counts here of more than 100 far exceed those from elsewhere.

DIVING DUCKS Good numbers of *Aythya*, Bufflehead, and Common Goldeneye occur. Scoters are uncommon but regular, and King Eider occurs annually. Large movements of Red-breasted Mergansers have been witnessed, with the estimated 23,000 on October 24, 1959, being truly exceptional, and one of the highest counts ever tallied for this species in the world. Much smaller numbers of Common and Hooded Mergansers also fly by.

CORMORANTS Double-crested is a common migrant throughout the late summer and fall. More than 5,000 were counted on August 1, 2009, attesting to the early start of this species' fall migration.

LOONS AND GREBES Common and Red-throated Loons move through in mid- to late fall, with Red-throated much less common. Small numbers of Horned and Red-necked Grebes are seen.

JAEGERS AND SKUAS Miller Beach is one of the premier inland locations for viewing jaegers. Movements occur primarily from mid-September to mid-November, peaking in October. Only a quarter of the jaegers are identified to species, and of these, 75 percent are Parasitic, 17 percent Pomarine, and 8 percent Long-tailed. Although Long-tailed is far from common, this is probably the best inland spot in North America that has yet been discovered for this species.

GULLS Large numbers of Herring and Ring-billed Gulls are on Lake Michigan year-round, though significant Herring Gull movements have been observed after November cold fronts. If you want to see a Sabine's Gull without getting on a boat, Miller Beach is a good bet, as some of the best one-day counts in the East come from here. The species moves through in a long period, from late September to mid-November. Black-legged Kittiwake is also rare but regular, in November. Franklin's Gull moves through irregularly, perhaps in response to unusual weather to the west that brings gulls this far east. An amazing 598 were counted on September 8, 2008.

TERNS August sees excellent movements of Black Tern, sometimes totaling hundreds in a day. September features Common Tern migrations that can run into the thousands in a day.

SPECIES	NOTABLE SINGLE-DAY COUNT
Red-breasted Merganser	23,000 on Oct. 24, 1959
Common Tern	5,700 on Sept. 24, 1996
Double-crested Cormorant	5,650 on Aug. 1, 2009
Blue-winged Teal	3,900 on Sept. 23, 1993
Black Tern	1,265 on Aug. 25, 2007
Common Loon	1,038 on Nov. 19, 2006
Franklin's Gull	598 on Sept. 8, 2008
Northern Pintail	349 on Oct. 4, 2006
Northern Shoveler	326 on Oct. 24, 1995
Gadwall	226 on Oct. 26, 2008
Hooded Merganser	168 on Nov. 3, 1991
Black Scoter	142 on Nov. 1, 2008
Ring-necked Duck	137 on Oct. 26, 2008
Sabine's Gull	28 on Sept. 16, 2005
Parasitic Jaeger	14 on Sept. 4, 2003

Rarities: Western Grebe, Northern Gannet, Black-tailed Gull, Little Gull, Black Skimmer (2 records), Least Tern, Gull-billed Tern, and Roseate Tern.

Numbers courtesy of Ken Brock; counted by many different observers.

35. Whitefish Point, Michigan

Lying in far northern Michigan, surrounded by wolf-haunted boreal forest and the deep blue waters of Lake Superior, this is a migration watch unlike any of the others covered in this guide. A look at a North American map shows that the great bulk of the Arctic lies in the northwest of the continent, west of Hudson Bay. The Great Lakes, despite variation in individual orientation, create a huge, roughly diagonal conduit for the passage of birds between the Arctic and most of eastern North America. Looking at Lake Superior in more detail reveals that its eastern end tapers down to a funnel, which is further pinched by a bulging Canadian shoreline to the north and the jutting Whitefish Point to the south. This unique geography makes Whitefish Point perhaps the best waterbird migration watch point on all the Great Lakes and gives some idea of the vast scope of migration on these lakes. One further factor making Whitefish an ideal vantage point is that Whitefish Bay, southeast of the point, offers some shelter, attracting resting and staging birds. In spring many of these birds, such as Common Loons, spend the night, then depart at dawn, producing a strong morning spike in activity.

Whitefish Point and Avalon, New Jersey, share the distinction of being the only seawatch sites that usually have full-time counters in the fall. On top of that, Whitefish is the only watch with a full-time spring counter, as this is one of few sites where large spring waterbird movements have been documented. This is the best site in North America for Red-necked Grebe, with numbers that dwarf those counted at all other watch sites combined. It is also one of the prime spots for observing Common Loons heading north in spring. Diving ducks are seen in excellent numbers and variety, and rarities such as jaegers, Sabine's Gull, Black-legged Kittiwake, and Harlequin Duck occur regularly. This is one of the only watches covered in the book where Sandhill Cranes pass in good numbers. Although the official count focuses on waterbirds, the site is well situated for excellent raptor and songbird migrations as well. The sandy point is also highly attractive to shorebirds, which frequently fly by or drop in. There is rarely a dull moment during migration at the point, even when waterbird movement is slow.

LOCATION

Whitefish Point is on the eastern side of Michigan's Upper Peninsula, its location remote and pristine, with only small towns nearby. At the tip of the point and the end of the road lies a lighthouse, the Great Lakes Shipwreck Museum, and the small headquarters of Whitefish Point Bird Observatory.

The "shack" that gives shelter to the full-time counter is 300 yards east of the main parking lot. The official count starts at dawn and runs for 8 hours daily, from April 15 to May 31 and from August 15 to November 15. For more information, visit www.wpbo.org/node/10.

TIMING

Fall is the best time of year. Late August usually holds the peak movements of Red-necked Grebe, while September has excellent duck diversity and the best chances for jaegers and Sabine's Gull. The best duck movements occur in October, with good overall diversity and big numbers of *Aythya* and Long-tailed Ducks. The best days in fall are usually on northwest winds, though good flights happen in a variety of weather. Strong south winds usually shut down migration.

Spring averages about a fifth as many birds as fall, but Whitefish still ranks among the best spring watch sites that have yet been discovered. Migration peaks in late April and early May, when there is good overall diversity and the peak movements of Common Loon. Southeast winds are ideal in spring.

The vast majority of movement occurs in the first 2 hours of daylight, particularly in spring, perhaps because of birds departing Whitefish Bay. Significant afternoon migration occurs only on the best of days, and the official count usually ends at mid-afternoon.

BIRDS

SWANS Trumpeter, Tundra, and Mute Swans are occasional.

GEESE Spring and fall see good movements of Canada Goose, with thousands counted in both seasons.

DABBLING DUCKS A full range of species occurs, with much higher numbers in fall, when diversity peaks in September and early October. Mallard is the most common, with most other species fairly common and Wood Duck and American Black Duck rare. Early fall movements of Blue-winged Teal are among the largest yet documented in North America. Most dabbler migration seems to be concentrated into a few days with both good numbers and diversity.

DIVING DUCKS Diving ducks make up about half of the birds counted. Spring movements are diverse

The small booth shown here offers the official counter at Whitefish Point some shelter from northern Michigan's often fearsome weather. Ken Behrens.

but small, whereas fall movements are diverse and large. The spring peak is in late April and early May, the fall peak in October. Greater Scaup is abundant, with peak days in the thousands; all other *Aythya* occur in smaller numbers. Red-breasted Merganser is abundant in fall, with daily flights of thousands, and more than 8,000 counted on average; 3,000 is the seasonal average for spring. The peak daily flights of Common Merganser run into only the dozens, and Hooded Merganser is scarce. Bufflehead and Common Goldeneye are common, especially in fall when the seasonal count total normally tops 1,000. The fall migration of Long-tailed Ducks can be spectacular, with days of more than 5,000 (exceptionally 10,000) sometimes occurring in late October. Spring movements of Long-taileds are obvious but small. White-winged Scoter stages fairly large flights in both spring and fall, with seasonal averages at both seasons of just under 3,000 birds. Surf and Black Scoters occur in small numbers. King Eider is rare but regular in fall.

CORMORANTS Double-crested is a fairly common spring migrant, less common in fall; seasonal totals are usually below 1,000 birds.

LOONS AND GREBES The spring Common Loon migration is among the biggest in the country, with more than 5,000 counted on average. Fall also sees thousands of Common Loons, and both seasons have moderate numbers of Red-throated Loons. Undoubtedly, the most outstanding seawatch spectacle at Whitefish is the fall Red-necked Grebe migration, which tops 13,000 in an average year. Although grebes move throughout the season, the peak, comprising thousands of birds in one day, usually occurs in late August when the grebes are still in breeding dress. Red-neckeds move through in smaller numbers in spring, with fewer than 1,000 counted on average. Horned Grebe is also fairly common in both seasons.

JAEGERS AND SKUAS Jaegers occur from August to October, peaking in September. Parasitic is by far the most common, with Pomarine and Long-tailed rare. Any jaeger is unusual in spring. Many birds are distant, making identification to species difficult.

GULLS Gulls are a constant feature of the point but don't often stage obvious migrations. Bonaparte's Gulls are an exception in spring, when they can sometimes be seen in large high-flying flocks. Sabine's Gull is regular in September.

TERNS Small numbers of Common Tern occur in spring and fall. Arctic is rare but regular in fall. Caspian is fairly common in spring.

TOP 10 SPECIES	SPRING SEASONAL AVERAGE	SINGLE-DAY HIGH COUNT
1. Common Loon	5,856	2,094 on May 7, 1996
2. Canada Goose	3,395	1,936 on Apr. 18, 1994
3. Red-breasted Merganser	3,358	904 on May 17, 2004
4. White-winged Scoter	2,678	2,683 on May 23, 1997
5. Long-tailed Duck	1,511	1,430 on May 17, 2006
6. Red-necked Grebe	737	1,762 on May 5, 2002
7. Double-crested Cormorant	694	223 on May 9, 1999
8. Greater Scaup	559	664 on Apr. 28, 1991
9. Red-throated Loon	465	129 on May 14, 2003
10. Common Merganser	441	66 on May 7, 1996

TOP 10 SPECIES	FALL SEASONAL AVERAGE	SINGLE-DAY HIGH COUNT
1. Red-necked Grebe	13,772	6,789 on Aug. 22, 2003
2. Long-tailed Duck	12,896	16,231 on Oct. 31, 2004
3. Red-breasted Merganser	8,410	3,291 on Oct. 5, 1995
4. Greater Scaup	5,391	5,180 on Oct. 14, 2003
5. Canada Goose	5,140	3,311 on Sept. 12, 1996
6. Unidentified scaup	4,821	
7. Common Loon	3,336	1,361 on Sept. 23, 2004
8. White-winged Scoter	2,880	953 on Oct. 20, 1998
9. Common Goldeneye	2,535	2,132 on Nov. 10, 2000
10. Bufflehead	1,470	2,129 on Nov. 12, 2005

Rarities: Brant, King Eider, Harlequin Duck, Pacific Loon, Ancient Murrelet, Little Gull, Sabine's Gull, Black-legged Kittiwake, Arctic Tern, and Red Phalarope.

Property of Whitefish Point Bird Observatory.

Presque Isle's geography contributes to its excellence as a seawatch site. John Buffington.

36. Sarnia/Port Huron, Michigan and Ontario

By John Haselmayer

The southern outlet of Lake Huron is the St. Clair River, which is also the border between this portion of Canada and the U.S. Lake Huron functions much like Lake Michigan, funneling birds to its southern end during their southbound migration. The lighthouse in Sarnia, Ontario, and the adjacent section of the St. Clair River is an excellent location for watching waterbird migration, especially on November days with winds from the northwest. The main groups represented are ducks and loons (watch for the occasional Red-throated among the Commons), but Parasitic Jaeger is a regular migrant, and both Pomarine and Long-tailed are recorded occasionally. This location is also a hotspot for rarities, with Black-legged Kittiwake and Sabine's, Ross's, and Ivory Gulls all having been recorded.

37. Bruce Peninsula, Ontario

The Bruce Peninsula Bird Observatory and its volunteers have documented a strong waterbird migration along this large peninsula that divides Georgian Bay from the main body of Lake Huron.

Counts of birds sitting on the water in Dyers Bay have revealed several trends, which a formal count of flybys would likely parallel. Red-necked Grebe migration is the main feature, with thousands counted over the course of a fall. The grebes occur in a broad peak from September to October. Other prominent migrants include Long-tailed Ducks, White-winged Scoters, Common Loons, and Horned Grebes. Common Loons peak in the same time period as Red-necked Grebes; Long-tailed Ducks and Horned Grebes peak later; and most of the White-winged Scoters occur during a short window in late October and early November. For more information on this area, visit the bird observatory's website: www.bpbo.ca.

38. Presque Isle State Park, Pennsylvania

Information from Jerry McWilliams

This peninsula juts out into Lake Erie and offers excellent fall lakewatching, with large numbers of diving ducks, loons, and grebes; good dabbling duck and gull diversity; and chances for exciting species such as jaegers and eiders. The Presque Isle count has been conducted almost solely by Jerry McWilliams for more than 20 years, and all the information presented here comes from him.

Since this is the nearest regular count to Hamlin Beach on Lake Ontario in New York (see watch site 42), the two watches make an interesting comparison. Generally there are fewer birds at Presque Isle, with some species such as Brant and Red-throated Loon much rarer. At both sites the bulk of the birds are flying west and following the lakeshore. More birds at Presque Isle seem to head directly south from Canada: in particular Tundra Swan, Canada Goose, Common Loon, and Double-crested Cormorant.

LOCATION

Presque Isle is very close to Erie and about 3 hours north of Pittsburgh. Within the large state park, the best viewing is from Sunset Beach, located at the northeastern corner of the loop road. Jerry McWilliams frequently counts here and is often joined by other birders during the peak of the fall season.

TIMING

As at most watches, fall is by far the best season. November is the best month, with more dabbling ducks and better diversity early in the month, but larger numbers later in the month as the scaup and Red-breasted Merganser migrations hit their stride. Records of rarities such as jaegers and Little Gull are scattered through the fall, while eiders are more likely in late fall. Spring waterbird migration here is minimal, though sites on the north shore of Lake Erie should be interesting in the spring. The vast majority of movement occurs in the first 2 hours of daylight, and the lake is usually quiet by late morning.

The best conditions are north winds after a fall cold front, especially after several days of warm southern winds without a frontal passage. Extremely windy conditions may produce birds but also make them difficult to see among the troughs.

BIRDS

SWANS This is one of the best sites yet discovered for observing Tundra Swan migration. Flights of hundreds have occasionally been observed in mid- to late fall.

DABBLING DUCKS The full range of species passes through in small numbers, mostly in September and October.

DIVING DUCKS Diving ducks make up the vast majority of the birds counted here. Huge numbers of Red-breasted Mergansers move past the point, peaking with flights of thousands in late November and early December. Scaup are also very common, with similar timing. Canvasback, Redhead, Common Goldeneye, Bufflehead, and Common Mergansers are common. All three scoters occur regularly in small numbers.

CORMORANTS Good flights of Double-cresteds occur mainly in October. They tend to pass from north to south rather than follow the lakeshore.

LOONS AND GREBES Common Loon is sometimes common, though sporadic, with the best flights mostly in early November, while Red-throated Loon is regular in small numbers. Horned Grebe migrates past in remarkable numbers, with a count of 1,927 on a single day in November 1998 far eclipsing any count from any other watch site. A handful of Red-necked Grebes are counted each year.

JAEGERS AND SKUAS Jaegers are rare but annual, with Parasitic being the most common, though many jaegers are very distant and difficult to identify to species.

GULLS Bonaparte's is common, peaking in Octo-

TOP 10 SPECIES	FALL SEASONAL AVERAGE	SINGLE-DAY HIGH COUNT
1. Red-breasted Merganser	15,060	16,065 on Nov. 29, 2004
2. Lesser Scaup	2,855	14,526 on Dec. 3, 2010
3. Double-crested Cormorant	1,369	3,825 on Oct. 10, 2004
4. Common Loon	989	1,577 on Dec. 4, 2008
5. Horned Grebe	587	1,927 in Nov. 1998
6. Canvasback	532	574 on Dec. 8, 2008
7. Greater Scaup	420	367 in Dec. 1998
8. Common Goldeneye	297	110 in Nov. 1993
9. Bufflehead	274	393 in Nov. 1993
10. Tundra Swan	266	794 in early Nov. 1998

Rarities: Greater White-fronted Goose, King Eider (4 records), Harlequin Duck (2 records), Eared Grebe (3 records), Northern Gannet, Laughing Gull, Franklin's Gull (2 records), Black-legged Kittiwake (4 records), unidentified Plegadis ibis, Red Phalarope (4 records), Red-necked Phalarope.

Numbers courtesy of Jerry McWilliams.

ber, and rare gulls such as Little should be looked for among the Bonaparte's. Glaucous, Thayer's, and Lesser Black-backed Gulls seem much less common here on Lake Erie than on adjacent Lake Ontario.

TERNS Early and midfall can see good movements of Common and Forster's Terns, though their occurrence is irregular.

39. Niagara River, New York and Ontario

The Niagara River is one of the best places in the East to see large numbers of waterbirds. There are vast numbers of Bonaparte's, Herring, and Ring-billed Gulls as well as Long-tailed Ducks and other waterfowl. In addition to the common species, a full suite of less-common gulls occurs, and this may be the best gull-watching site in North America. Observers have tallied up to 12 gull species in a single day, usually in November. This is a great place to hone your gull flight-identification skills, as at most times the vast majority of gulls are in flight. Although the Niagara Falls and River are such active feeding and staging areas that it is difficult to differentiate local movements from long-distance ones, it is certain that this area acts as a conduit for migration.

Where the Niagara River spills out into Lake Ontario, a great spectacle occurs in the winter. Each evening from November through February at least and often later, huge numbers of Bonaparte's Gulls exit the river and fly out onto Lake Ontario to roost. This phenomenon has been dubbed the "flypast." These gulls fly in fast, tight flocks. The fun challenge is to pick out the rare but regular Little, Black-headed, and Franklin's Gulls, as well as Black-legged Kittiwake. Even Ross's Gull is never out of the question on the Niagara River. The best place to view the flypast is at Navy Hall National Historic Site on the New York side of the river. It has an excellent view of the river and a few benches to boot.

40. Van Wagner's Beach, Hamilton, Ontario

By Scott Watson

Van Wagner's Beach, at the extreme western end of Lake Ontario, is an excellent fall lakewatching site. The annual numbers of jaegers and rare gulls can rival those at some seawatching sites, and this is among the best freshwater locations for generally oceanic birds. Van Wagner's is surrounded by the heavily populated "golden horseshoe" of Lake Ontario, within a short distance of a large number of birders.

Lake Ontario is the headwaters of the St. Lawrence River, which runs into the Atlantic, and is bisected by the "James Bay migration route," which many Arctic-breeding birds travel on their way to and from their Atlantic wintering grounds. As such, it is no coincidence that many generally oceanic species find themselves at Van Wagner's Beach.

LOCATION

Very close to Hamilton, Burlington, and Toronto, this site is only a short drive for many birders. Take QEW Exit 88 to Centennial Parkway (Highway 20, Stoney Creek) to Van Wagner's Beach Road, then go west (toward Skyway Bridge) and park near Hutch's Restaurant. With a restaurant and an observation tower here, it is easy to spend a few hours in lake-scanning mode.

TIMING

Fall is when Van Wagner's is best; birding can be productive from late August into December. September and October are the best months for jaegers and Sabine's Gull. By November, Northern Gannets may arrive, and diving ducks remain until the water freezes.

A strong east wind is essential for success at this site. By September the east winds will have started to blow, pushing many birds to the west end of the lake. If a strong September or October storm arises from the east, almost anything can turn up from the Atlantic. A Manx Shearwater appeared in September 2006!

BIRDS

SWANS Good numbers of Tundra Swans pass through in fall.

DABBLING DUCKS All the northeastern North American species can be found in moderate numbers from mid- to late fall.

DIVING DUCKS A wide selection occurs here in late fall. All three scoters fly by, with White-winged the most common. Canvasback, Redhead, both scaup, Common Goldeneye, Bufflehead, Common Merganser, and Red-breasted Merganser are common. Harlequin Duck is rare but annual.

CORMORANTS A large population of Double-crested Cormorants nests close to this site in summer. Great Cormorant has occurred.

LOONS AND GREBES Common and Red-throated Loons peak in November. Both Horned and Red-necked Grebes are readily seen as well.

SULIDS November is the best time to look for

Northern Gannets, which typically "dead-end" at Van Wagner's beach after flying up the St. Lawrence River.

JAEGERS AND SKUAS Incredible numbers of jaegers can be seen here each fall. Parasitic is the most common, occurring mainly in September and October. There is also a smattering of Long-tailed and Pomarines. Daily counts of more than 30 Parasitics streaming by close to shore have occurred during east winds.

GULLS This is one of the best places on the Great Lakes to see Sabine's Gull and Black-legged Kittiwake. During east winds, watch for Sabine's Gull close to shore in September and October, and for Black-legged Kittiwake from October into December. Bonaparte's Gulls can be found among the Ring-billed, Herring, and Great Black-backed Gulls.

TERNS Common Terns move through in small numbers in the fall.

41. Conejohela Flats, Pennsylvania

Information from Jerry Book

This site is situated on the mighty Susquehanna River, about an hour south of Harrisburg and near the town of Columbia. It is best known among Pennsylvania birders for the shorebirds it attracts. However, the Susquehanna is also one of the few large rivers that has been carefully examined as a conduit for migration, mostly by local birder Jerry Book.

The most visible migrants are gulls and terns. From mid-March through early April there is a good movement of Bonaparte's Gulls. They are joined by a few Little Gulls, with 5–20 counted during this period each year. Limited observations in April have tallied hundreds of migrating Caspian Terns, whereas May is the peak month for Black, Common, and Forster's Terns, all of which occur in good numbers. Spring also sees small movements of ducks, Tundra Swans, and Double-crested Cormorants. Fall tern migration is more spread out, running from July through October. This season sees excellent numbers of Common and Black Terns; both species have been observed in flocks of more than 100 after the passage of a cold front. The Conejohela Flats are excellent for vagrant gulls, terns, and skimmers, with records of Sabine's Gull, Black-legged Kittiwake, Black Skimmer, and Arctic, Gull-billed, Sooty, and Royal Terns. Least Tern and Laughing Gull are also surprisingly frequent for a location so far inland.

Spring migrations occur in all kinds of weather. Strong northwest winds are best for Bonaparte's and Little Gulls and Caspian Terns. Rainy and windy weather is generally best, as it seems to force birds to stay low in order to see and follow the river. South winds can be productive, although many birds may simply leave the river and fly overland in these conditions. Northwest winds after the passage of a cold front are the best conditions in fall.

Although observations so far suggest that observable migration here is rather hit-and-miss, this site certainly merits further watching. The Conejohela Flats have been the focus of efforts so far, but there may be other good watch points to be discovered elsewhere along the Susquehanna. At Conejohela, the best observation point is the Blue Rock Road boat ramp. Reaching this spot is complicated, so check out the following link for directions and lots of good information about the flats: www.conejohelaflats.pbworks.com.

42. Hamlin Beach State Park, New York

Hamlin Beach is situated on the southern shore of Lake Ontario. This is one of the prime places in North America to observe waterfowl migration, particularly diving ducks, along with a smattering of more oceanic species such as Brant, King Eider, and jaegers.

A fall waterbird count was conducted here in the 1990s, and the data were summarized in a superb monograph written by Brett Ewald and Dominic Sherony. Thanks to their efforts, we know more about this site than almost any other eastern watch. Volunteers have even carried the count well into February in some years, providing insight on continuing "fall" migration and wintering dynamics.

The movements observed from Hamlin Beach are fascinating for several reasons. Being situated on Lake Ontario, this site lies on a horizontal rather than vertical geographical leading line, unlike most of the prime watch points. Despite being on what are simplistically understood as north-to-south migrations, the vast majority of birds here are flying east or west. Even more interesting is that westbound birds predominate, even among species such as jaegers that you would expect to be ocean-bound. Hamlin demonstrates just how complex and poorly understood bird migration really is. Several different phenomena seem to intersect here: birds migrating from the central Arctic and then through the Great Lakes to the East Coast, birds migrating from the eastern Arctic to the interior via the Great Lakes, wintering birds moving between shifting feeding grounds, and undoubtedly more.

LOCATION

The state park is located 25 miles west of Rochester. When there is a volunteer counter between September and December, the lakewatch takes place near parking area number 4. Winter watches usually occur at parking area number 1. Although Hamlin is well situated on a bluff that projects into the lake, lakewatching can be good almost anywhere along the Lake Ontario shore.

TIMING

Probably because of the diverse and complex dynamics at play on Lake Ontario, Hamlin enjoys an extended period of high activity in fall. The potential for large numbers of birds, including rarities, exists anytime between mid-October and late December, and in mild years large numbers of birds may be present through the winter. Although some of these may be wintering locally and making short-distance movements, there is also an overall Great Lakes dynamic that may bring in new birds throughout the winter.

The best bet is usually the second day after a cold front, which often sees a strong flight of Red-throated Loons, diving ducks, and a good chance at a rarity. Brant and Green-winged Teal peak the day after a front's passage, whereas Double-crested Cormorant, most of the dabbling ducks, Canvasback, White-winged Scoters, and Common Mergansers peak 3 or 4 days after a front.

BIRDS

GEESE Brant move through in a short, intense migration from mid-October through early November, with thousands passing annually. They are an exception to the generally westbound movement at Hamlin, as nearly all the Brant counted are flying east. Canada Goose is also common, while Snow Goose is uncommon and sporadic.

DABBLING DUCKS The biggest movements usually occur 3–4 days after a fall cold front. Blue-winged Teal migrate early, mostly in August and early September. Thousands of Northern Pintail, hundreds each of Green-winged Teal and American Wigeon, and dozens of Gadwall were counted in most falls, with the peak at midfall. The most common dabblers, Mallard and American Black Duck, migrate later and seem to move in response to cooling weather. The average annual total for both species in the 1990s was in the low thousands.

DIVING DUCKS This diverse group is the heart of the Hamlin lakewatch. Most species peak 2–3 days after a fall cold front. Redhead is common, with peak numbers from late December into January. Greater Scaup is abundant, with an annual average of more than 50,000 counted, peaking in December and early January, though the migration period is obscured by large numbers of locally wintering birds. Lesser Scaup is much less common and peaks earlier. Canvasback and Ring-necked Duck are uncommon. King Eider occurs with surprising regularity, mostly in November.

Black and Surf Scoters are fairly common, peaking from mid-October to early November. On November 7, 1997, there was an incredible flight of more than 12,000 scoters, mostly Black. Remarkably, White-winged Scoter is the most common bird of the lakewatch, averaging more than 60,000 per fall during the counts in the 1990s. It shows a double peak: an earlier and smaller one in conjunction with the other two scoters, and a larger one in December. Long-tailed Duck is abundant, with most birds seemingly wintering locally. Common Goldeneye is abundant, with thousands counted each season. Bufflehead and Common Merganser are common, with counts in the high hundreds and low thousands. Hooded Merganser is scarce, occurring mostly in November. Red-breasted Merganser is abundant, peaking in late fall, with annual totals that ranged between 10,000 and 30,000.

CORMORANTS A few thousand Double-cresteds were counted most years, mostly in October, and there are a few records of Great.

TOP 10 SPECIES	FALL SEASONAL AVERAGE	SINGLE-DAY HIGH COUNT
1. White-winged Scoter	60,600	8,631 on Dec. 9, 1997
2. Greater Scaup	54,900	10,543 on Nov. 28, 1998
3. Red-breasted Merganser	19,058	7,885 on Nov. 18, 1997
4. Bonaparte's Gull	14,438	5,750 on Dec. 2, 1997
5. Long-tailed Duck	12,213	4,582 on Dec. 2, 1997
6. Red-throated Loon	9,841	2,777 on Nov. 25, 1997
7. Common Goldeneye	9,203	1,156 on Nov. 7, 1997
8. Common Loon	7,721	2,982 on Nov. 7, 1997
9. Canada Goose	6,204	3,511 on Sept. 21, 1999
10. Mallard	5,660	788 on Nov. 20, 1993

Rarities: Ancient Murrelet, Black-capped Petrel, Northern Gannet, Ross's Gull, Sabine's Gull, Ivory Gull, Least Tern, and Sooty Tern.

All numbers are from September–December, 1993–1999, from Ewald and Sherony 2001 (see Bibliography).

LOONS AND GREBES Common Loon is common, with well over 10,000 counted in a good year. Single-day flights of more than 1,000 Red-throated Loons and annual totals sometimes exceeding 10,000 are another one of the exceptional aspects of the Hamlin lakewatch. Red-throated peaks in late November, later than Common. Remarkably, the vast majority of both loon species are flying west, bound for points unknown. Horned Grebe is common. Red-necked Grebe is uncommon and migrates later in the fall.

JAEGERS AND SKUAS Pomarine and Parasitic are regular rarities, most likely in midfall 1–2 days after a cold front. Parasitic is more common; more than 100 were counted in the fall of 1996. The vast majority of jaegers are juveniles flying west, away from the Atlantic Ocean. Long-tailed is extremely rare in early fall.

GULLS Counts in the 1990s averaged more than 10,000 Bonaparte's Gulls per fall, with a peak in late November to mid-December. Little Gull and Black-legged Kittiwake are regularly seen in small numbers, mostly with Bonaparte's in November and December. Great Black-backed Gull undertakes a regular westbound migration in late fall.

TERNS Small numbers of Common and Caspian Tern pass in late August and into September, with the bulk of migration probably occurring in late summer, prior to the lakewatch. Forster's Tern is rare.

43. Cayuga Lake, New York

Information from Ethan Kistler

Cayuga Lake is a long, thin, vertically oriented lake in central New York. Ithaca's Cornell University lies on its shores, and the area has received much ornithological study, but it wasn't until 1992 that a huge movement of Common Loons traversing the lake was discovered. Bill Evans first publicized this phenomenon, and stalwart volunteer Bob Meade staffed the watch point nearly every fall day for more than 10 years. The findings at Cayuga are exciting because they point to the possibilities for further discovery, even at inland locations that are well covered by birders.

The Cayuga Common Loon totals far surpass those of any other watch point, and probably represent a large portion of the Atlantic wintering population. The single-day high count here is an incredible 6,064 counted on November 10, 1997, while the annual totals range from a couple of thousand in some years to over 13,000 in 1995. Care-

ful observations have revealed a morning "double pulse" of loons, with a first, smaller pulse of birds that have spent the night on Cayuga Lake, and a second, larger pulse comprising birds coming from Lake Ontario. Other species, including Brant, Snow Goose, Greater and Lesser Scaup, Long-tailed Duck, scoters, and Double-crested Cormorant have also been observed following the lake. For more information on the loonwatch, see www.cayugabird club.org/Resources/loon-watch.

LOCATION
The official loon count takes place at Taughannock Falls State Park, about 10 miles north of Ithaca on the western side of Cayuga Lake. Once in the park, drive past the ticket booth and follow signs to the central picnic area. The count is a volunteer effort, so there is not always someone present.

TIMING
When conducted, the official count runs from mid- or late October to late November or early December. Within that period, the peak is usually in the second or third week of November. Ideal conditions are strong north or northwest winds, especially after a cold front. Several days of south winds preceding the cold front and associated northwest winds is best of all, as these conditions seems to bottle up birds on Lake Ontario, producing a big push with the advent of favorable winds. The vast majority of movement is in the first 2 hours of light, so arrive early.

BIRDS
SWANS Migrating Tundra Swans are sometimes seen in late fall.

GEESE Canada Goose is a common migrant, with hundreds of migrants commonly seen in a day. Thousands of Snow Geese can fly by in a peak day in late fall. Some of the best Snow Goose flights probably occur in December after the loon watch has ended. Brant sometimes stage conspicuous migrations, where hundreds or even thousands are counted in a day. Late October seems to be the peak for Brant, with most of the movement of this species concentrated into a couple of big days, similar to the pattern observed on Lake Champlain.

DABBLING DUCKS Species including Northern Pintail, Mallard, and American Black Duck have been seen on active migration, following the lake. Pintail movements can be especially striking, with daily totals of hundreds of high-flying southbound birds.

DIVING DUCKS All 3 scoters and Long-tailed Ducks are regular in small numbers. Large flocks of *Ay-*

thya ducks are regularly observed, particularly both Greater and Lesser Scaup, Ring-necked Duck, and Redhead. Modest numbers of Bufflehead and all 3 mergansers occur, though they are seen sitting on the lake more often than in active migration.

CORMORANTS Movements of hundreds of Double-crested are sometimes observed in early to mid-fall.

LOONS AND GREBES Common Loons occur in fantastic numbers, with peak mornings of thousands of birds. The legions of Commons are joined by a handful of Red-throated Loons. The peak loon days are always in November, usually in the middle of the month .

JAEGERS AND SKUAS Parasitic Jaeger is a rarity that has been observed during the watch.

44. Hudson River, New York

By Richard Guthrie

A look at a North American map shows the Hudson River as an aquatic link between the Atlantic Ocean and the Saint Lawrence River, the Great Lakes, and Lake Champlain, where big waterbird movements have recently been documented. As such, it is not surprising that this mighty river acts as a migratory conduit. Additionally, this river is well situated to host storm-driven oceanic birds that are swept upstate until the weather calms, when they follow the river back to the ocean. Another factor at play here is winter freeze-ups in rivers and lakes farther north, which drive large numbers of waterfowl south along the river.

New York birders have seen ducks, geese, cormorants, gulls, terns, and even pelicans following the Hudson. Some of the more common winter species include Mallard, American Black Duck, Canvasback, Common Goldeneye, Common Merganser, plus the occasional Barrow's Goldeneye. Snow Goose can be seen both spring and fall, when thousands fly by over the course of multiple flight days. In spring, especially in mid-May, thousands of Brant move northward, flying close to the water in loose flocks. The Hudson is a magnet for gulls, with the more common species being Ring-billed, Herring, Great Black-backed, and Bonaparte's. Rare gulls include Iceland, Glaucous, and Lesser Black-backed. Even the near-mythical Ivory has been sighted, as has a Slaty-backed Gull. In winter, concentrations of more than 100 Bald Eagles can be seen from the overlook at the Bear Mountain Bridge or Riverside Park in New York City. In severe winters, eagles can even be seen riding down the river on ice floes! The best places to watch the Hudson are the many public boat launch parks along the river.

45. Lake Champlain, Vermont and New York

Information from Ted Murin

In the late 1990s Vermont birders began noticing southbound flocks of Brant following Lake Champlain. This is a species that is virtually never seen on the water in Vermont, and its occurrence inspired a fall lakewatch on the eastern shores of this expansive body of water. What was discovered was astounding. Large numbers of Brant, scoters, Long-tailed Ducks, and loons were counted, along with a diverse selection of other waterbird species, including some remarkable rarities such as Barnacle Goose, Common Eider, Leach's Storm-Petrel, and Northern Fulmar. Lake Champlain is clearly one of the premier inland sites for waterbird migration, and the best site yet discovered away from the Atlantic Ocean, Gulf of Mexico, and Great Lakes.

This watch is staffed entirely by volunteers, including Ted Murin, who has kept careful records of the counts conducted here. These volunteers cover an average of 43 days per year, focusing their efforts when weather conditions seem optimal. This same corps of observers has also investigated spring migration and found very little observable migration. The disparity might be due to the St. Lawrence River, which funnels southbound birds to Lake Champlain in fall, whereas northbound birds are not concentrated in such a manner.

LOCATION

Lake Champlain is long and narrow, and several sites on the Vermont side offer good lakewatching. The official count is run at the Charlotte town beach for the first half of the fall, then on private property on Thompson's Point for the second half. The Charlotte beach offers good lakewatching, and better general birding than most other lakewatch sites, with good chances for shorebirds and migrating passerines. The only downside is that the breadth of the lake here means than many birds are far away. Although the official Thompson's Point count site is on private land, there is a publicly accessible site nearby. To reach it from the town of Charlotte, take Thompson's Point Road to the Thompson's Point community. Turn right here on North Shore Road immediately past some tennis courts on the right. In less than 0.1 miles there is a small lake access point on the left and very limited parking on the right.

Another good public access point is farther

Lake Champlain is probably the best seawatch site yet discovered in North America away from the Atlantic and Gulf Coasts and the Great Lakes. Ted Murin.

north, at the ferry landing in the town of Grand Isle. This site obviously sees a lot of traffic, but it offers conveniences such as bathrooms and a restaurant. Dar State Park, at Lake Champlain's far southern end, is another excellent place to watch. The scenery is good, and the distance across the lake is short here, so some birds pass at close range. Good viewpoints undoubtedly remain to be discovered on the New York side of the lake, though the Vermont side has the advantage of being well lit for the prime morning hours.

TIMING

Fall is by far the best season. Although peak numbers occur from late October through the end of November, good days occur throughout. Almost without exception, the best migrations happen on the day after a cold front passes. Another factor seems to be strong northeast winds on the St. Lawrence in preceding days, which might drive more pelagic species such as jaegers and Black Kittiwake toward Champlain. As at most inland sites, the first 2 hours of daylight are best for most birds. Geese provide an exception, often flying late in the day.

Lake Champlain hosts large numbers of winter-ing waterfowl, though migration seems to be over by early January. Spring watches have turned up only small numbers of migrating waterbirds.

BIRDS

GEESE Huge flights of Snow Geese are one of the outstanding features of Champlain. Passage down the lake begins in October, with a peak occurring in November or December. More than 10,000 Snows have been counted in a single day on several occasions. Big Brant migrations are another feature of the watch; the entirety of this species' fall migration here occurs in just a few days in October, consistent with what has been observed at Hamlin Beach, New York. Canada Goose is an abundant migrant through the fall, though, interestingly, the species shows a primary peak in mid-October and a secondary one in December.

DABBLING DUCKS American Black Duck and Mallard are the most common species, peaking in November. Most other species move through from early to midfall, peaking in late October or early November. Northern Pintail and Green-winged Teal are fairly common; all other species are uncommon.

DIVING DUCKS Scoters occur in remarkable numbers, especially in late October, when flights of thousands have been observed; Black and White-winged are more common than Surf. Scaup are common though irregular, with more Greaters than Lessers and with peak numbers passing in late fall. Long-tailed Ducks, Bufflehead, and Red-breasted Mergansers all occur in moderate numbers in mid- and late fall. Common Goldeneye and Common Mergansers are both common in late fall.

CORMORANTS Good movements of Double-crested are observed in October.

LOONS AND GREBES Loons peak in November, when hundreds are counted on some days. Common outnumbers Red-throated. Very few migrating grebes have been seen.

JAEGERS AND SKUAS Almost all of Vermont's jaeger records come from the lake. Parasitic is the most common species, with several records in most years. Pomarine is uncommon and not quite annual, and Long-tailed is seen every few years.

GULLS Lake Champlain receives some of North America's most obvious and spectacular movements of Ring-billed Gulls. In most years a flight of more than 10,000 occurs sometime between late October and the end of November; 30,000 were estimated passing on November 23, 2005! Bonaparte's Gull also stages obvious migrations through October. The other big gull species are common but don't undertake obvious migrations. Sabine's Gull is seen every year, making this one of the best inland locations for the species away from the Great Lakes.

TOP 10 SPECIES	SINGLE-DAY HIGH COUNT
1. Ring-billed Gull	30,000 on Nov. 23, 2005
2. Snow Goose	16,100 on Nov. 16, 2002
3. Canada Goose	6,684 on Oct. 11, 2004
4. Black Scoter	4,650 on Oct. 27, 2004
5. Mallard	2,760 on Nov. 23, 2007
6. Brant	2,631 on Oct. 16, 2003
7. Greater Scaup	2,383 on Nov. 30, 2008
8. Double-crested Cormorant	2,213 on Oct. 10, 2006
9. White-winged Scoter	1,086 on Oct. 21, 2002
10. American Black Duck	800 on Nov. 23, 2007

Rarities: Barnacle Goose, Eurasian Wigeon, Common Eider, Pacific Loon, Black Guillemot, Leach's Storm-Petrel, Northern Fulmar, Northern Gannet, Black-headed Gull, Sabine's Gull, Ivory Gull, and Black-legged Kittiwake.

Numbers courtesy of Ted Murin and a dedicated crew of volunteers.

46. Ottawa River, Ontario and Quebec

Information from Bruce Di Labio

The Ottawa is a large river that forms the boundary between southern Ontario and Quebec and eventually flows into the St. Lawrence River. Its vertical orientation makes it a natural conduit for birds passing from the Arctic to the Atlantic. The most common species that have been observed in active migration are Brant, Black Scoter, and Red-throated Loon. This is the only location in southern Ontario where Arctic Tern is regularly observed during spring migration, mainly from late May to mid-June. The overall peaks of migration are from late May to early June and from mid-October to mid-November. In spring, rainy weather with fog or a low cloud ceiling produces birds, as do clear nights with winds out of the north or northwest. In fall, best conditions are during or just after the passage of a cold front, particularly when it is rainy and foggy. Good watch points include Dick Bell Park, Britannia Pier, Britannia Point, and Shirley's Bay, all of which offer views of Lake Deschenes and the Deschenes Rapids.

47. St. Lawrence Waterway, Quebec

Information from François Grenon

The St. Lawrence Waterway is one of the greatest bodies of water in North America, stretching from the Great Lakes to the North Atlantic. Although the waterway's mainly east-west orientation may not be ideal for attracting migrants, observations on the Great Lakes have revealed huge waterbird movements that challenge a simplistic understanding of the interplay between geography and migration. Indeed, observations along the waterway have confirmed that it acts as a major conduit for waterbird migration. Some species, such as Red-throated Loon and jaegers, seem to follow it west on spring migration before leaving it to head north overland to the Arctic tundra. This is one of the most exciting bodies of water in eastern North America, and continued observations here can help advance our knowledge of continental waterbird migration.

LOCATION

The waterway can be roughly divided into its fluvial, estuary, and gulf portions. The fluvial portion acts as a river, the estuary portion is where the ocean tides mix with the river, and the gulf portion acts as part of the Atlantic Ocean. Along this stretch of more than 700 miles, there are countless places to observe waterbird staging and migration. Mentioned below are a few that have been known to offer good sea- or riverwatching. The ferries crossing the St. Lawrence also offer good chances to see waterbirds; the long-distance boats crossing the estuary and gulf can be particularly good.

LAC SAINT-PIERRE lies on the fluvial portion of the river, about 40 miles east of Montreal. This broad and lakelike portion of the river is a major staging area for waterfowl. It is one of the best places to observe migrating Snow Geese, a well-known feature of spring and fall along the St. Lawrence. The best observation points are Baie-du-Febvre on the south shore and Saint-Barthélémy on the north shore. Late March to mid-May is the peak season.

BEAUHARNOIS, LASALLE, ÎLE-DES-SOEURS, POINTE-AU-PLATON, NEUVILLE, BAIE DE BEAUPORT, AND HAWKIN'S POINT (between Cornwall, ON, and Massena, NY) are just a few of the numerous points from which active waterbird migration can be witnessed in spring and fall on the fluvial portion.

QUAI DE RIVIÈRE-OUELLE lies on the south shore, 85 miles east of Quebec City. This is a good point for observing migrating Red-throated Loons, jaegers, and sea ducks.

THE UPPER NORTH SHORE is a large area about 120 miles east of Quebec City. Here, deep, cold Atlantic water is forced to the surface by a subsurface ridge, attracting many waterbirds. Some of the best seawatch sites are at Tadoussac, Cap Bon-Désir, and Quai des Escoumins.

POINTE-DES-MONTS is 180 miles east of Tadoussac, at the junction between the estuary and the gulf. This point offers sweeping 200° views of water, making it a great place to observe migrating sea ducks, loons, phalaropes, jaegers, gulls, terns, and alcids.

THE GASPÉ PENINSULA is a fine seawatching area. Tartigou, Cap-des-Rosiers, and Cap-d'Espoir are all solid observation points.

ÎLES-DE-LA-MADELEINE is a beautiful archipelago, reached by ferry or plane, lying in the middle of the gulf, making it a natural seawatching site. Although it hasn't received much seawatching coverage, limited observations are very promising. This is one of the best places in Quebec to see shearwaters and storm-petrels from shore. All the eastern alcids except Dovekie breed on Rochers-aux-Oiseaux, 21 miles to the northeast. Grosse-Île and Old Harry make good observation points, though any sand dune can serve.

TIMING

In spring, April to mid-June can be good. Jaegers and Arctic Terns peak in a narrow window in late May and early June. In fall there is a long period of waterbird migration running from August into early December. Peak diversity occurs from late August to mid-September.

BIRDS

GEESE The spring and fall migrations of Snow Goose are conspicuous enough to have earned a firm place in local culture, with various activities celebrating the species' passage; the fluvial portion is the best place to observe this migration. Brant also follow the waterway, most commonly on the estuary and gulf but also on the fluvial portion.

DABBLING DUCKS The full range of dabblers is known to follow the waterway, and they can sometimes be seen in active migration. American Black Ducks stage large premigratory gatherings in fall, mainly in the estuary and gulf.

DIVING DUCKS The entire St. Lawrence is excellent for diving ducks. The estuary and gulf are very good for fall migrations of Common Eider, scoters, Barrow's Goldeneye, and Long-tailed Ducks, all of which also occur on the fluvial portion in small numbers. Huge movements of scoters, with White-winged and Surf being most common, have been witnessed; flocks of more than 7,000 scoters have been reported. Checking Common Eider and scoter flocks can turn up King Eider and Harlequin Ducks. Fall also sees impressive gatherings and movements of Long-tailed Ducks and Red-breasted Mergansers. Spring migration is more subdued but still noticeable.

CORMORANTS Significant numbers of migrating Double-crested Cormorants can be observed on all portions of the St. Lawrence, whereas noticeable movements of Great Cormorants are limited to the gulf.

LOONS AND GREBES Common Loon is common all along the St. Lawrence during migration. Red-throated is also common, though mainly on the estuary and gulf portions. The north shore of the estuary and gulf attracts large numbers of both species from late April to early June. Both species depart as the ice melts off their respective breeding grounds: boreal lakes and Arctic tundra. The departure of Common Loons tends to be gradual, whereas Red-throateds make a rapid exodus. Large flocks of Red-throateds are often seen flying west in spring, though they disappear from the St. Lawrence somewhere before Quebec City, probably cutting overland; groups of hundreds of Red-throateds are common. A watch at Rivière-Ouelle on May 22, 2010, tallied 4,052 Red-throated Loons, including 1,500 within 15 minutes! Pacific Loon is an occasional flyby.

ALCIDS Black Guillemot, Razorbill, Atlantic Puffin, and Common and Thick-billed Murres all nest in the gulf. Migration can be witnessed over a short period in the spring as the birds return to begin breeding. Fall migratory gatherings and movements are spread over a longer period of time. Although alcids quickly become rare away from the gulf, there have been records all the way up the fluvial portion of the waterway, particularly after strong northeasterly winds in fall. Razorbill and Atlantic Puffin are the most likely species on fresh water. In invasion years, impressive flights of Dovekies can be seen from shore in the gulf and estuary, such as the 20,300 birds estimated on December 14, 2003, at Cap-d'Espoir and the 20,000 birds on November 1, 2007, at Pointe-des-Monts. There is still much to learn about the causes of these massive movements.

SULIDS Northern Gannet is common in migration in the estuary and gulf, particularly in August and September. Since 2008, the Île Bonaventure colony, at the tip of the Gaspé Peninsula, has been the world's largest, with more than 121,000 birds; it is still expanding at a rate of 3 percent per year. Northern Gannet is rare in the fluvial portion of the waterway in fall, mostly occurring after extended periods of northeasterly winds.

JAEGERS AND SKUAS The gulf supports good numbers of all three species of jaegers, with smaller numbers in the estuary and even smaller numbers in the fluvial portion. East or northeastern winds increase the occurrence of jaegers in the estuary. Spring migration is concentrated in late May and early June, with many of these birds leaving the St. Lawrence to follow the Saguenay River northward, undoubtedly cutting overland to reach the tundra. Fall migration is more diffuse, from August to October. Parasitic is the most common jaeger here, followed by Pomarine. There may be significant numbers of immature Long-tailed Jaegers spending the summer well offshore in the gulf.

GULLS As elsewhere on the continent, it is difficult to discern the exact nature of gull migration here. Herring, Great Black-backed, and Ring-billed Gulls are common year-round, but a significant, though varying, proportion (especially of the last species) are not wintering. Iceland and Glaucous Gulls are present in large numbers in winter. Black-legged Kittiwake is a very common breeding bird in the gulf, while Bonaparte's Gull is a common and conspicuous migrant throughout. Flocks of kittiwakes or Bonaparte's Gulls sometimes contain Little, Black-headed, or Sabine's Gulls, especially during fall migration, from late August into October. Some very large flocks of kittiwakes gather in the estuary, as shown by the 30,000 birds reported on October 18, 1997, from Île-au-Basque. June sometimes sees a massive spawning of capelin (a species of fish) in the estuary and gulf. This glut of easy food attracts huge numbers of gulls and Northern Gannets, and such events provide a good opportunity to search for rare gulls.

TERNS Common Terns both nest and migrate through in large numbers. Arctic Terns consistently use the waterway on migration, especially in spring. They are more numerous in the gulf and estuary, but some can be seen on the fluvial portion as well. Sightings of Caspian Tern in active migration are surprisingly rare. Black Tern migrates and nests along the fluvial portion but in much smaller numbers than Common Tern.

LONG-TAILED DUCK. NEW JERSEY, FEB. KEVIN CARLSON

ACKNOWLEDGMENTS

The genesis of this book occurred in Cape May, New Jersey, where we both worked as counters for the Cape May Bird Observatory/New Jersey Audubon Avalon Seawatch. We'd like to offer our thanks to those organizations for the rare opportunity to be "professional" seawatchers. We'd also like to offer our profound thanks to several members of the Cape May birding community who offered advice, inspiration, and support in this project throughout its various stages. We were privileged to have the help of some of North America's best birders and most renowned birding authors: Kevin Karlson, Richard Crossley, and Michael O'Brien.

Thanks to those who provided various forms of inspiration and advice or acted as sounding boards for various ideas. These included but are not limited to Nick Athanas, Keith Barnes, Paul and Janet Behrens, Richard Crossley, Lauren Deaner, Doug Gochfield, Richard Heil, Steve Howell, Rojo Johnarson, Tom Johnson, Kevin Karlson, Tony Leukering, Derek Lovitch, Evan Obercian, Michael O'Brien, Tom Reed, and Louise Zemaitis.

During the years that it took us to complete this guide, many people provided us with places to stay while we worked on the book. Deep and sincere thanks to Shaun Bamford; Ken's parents, Paul and Janet Behrens; Ken's grandmother, Edith Behrens; Lauren Deaner; François "France" Dewaghe; Bob Fogg; Derek and Jeanette Lovitch; Becky Marvil; Keith Morlock (several months, at two different houses!); and Mamasoa Ramananarivo.

For the "Where to Watch" section of this book, we were particularly reliant on the help of local experts. Without the following folks, inclusion of this section would have been impossible: Tim Avery, Scott Barnes, Louis Bevier, Wes Biggs, Jerry Book, Justin Bosler, Lysle Brinker, Ned Brinkley, Ken Brock, Michael Brothers, Chris Brown, Adam Byrne, Steve Cardiff, Willy D'Anna, Ricky Davis, Bruce Di Labio, Bob Duncan, Vince Elia, Bill Evans, Michael Fialkovich, François Grenon, Richard Guthrie, Matt Hafner, John Haselmayer, Richard Heil, Paul Hess, Patrick Homier, Bill Hubick, Marshall Iliff, Tom Johnson, Ethan Kistler, Paul Lehman, Derek Lovitch, Nova Mackentley, Bruce Mactavish, Tom Magarian, Geoff Malosh, Jerry McWilliams, Matt Medler, Eric Mills, Shai Mitra, David Mizrahi, Ted Murin, Chris Neri, Blair Nikula, Nick Pulcinella, Peter Riley, David Roemer, Forrest Rowland, Bob Schutsky, Luke Seitz, Bill Sheehan, Dominic Sherony, Jack Solomon, Dave Tetlow, Ken Tracey, Jeremiah Trimble, Scott Watson, and Chris Wood.

Great thanks to the birders and organizations that allowed the use of their seawatching data. These included those birders whose eBird data were used in the Cape Cod account: Frederick Atwood, Peter Bono, Matthew Garvey, John Hutchison, Blair Nikula, Jeremiah Trimble, and Peter Trimble.

The photos are at the heart of this guide, so we owe a special thanks to the photographers who allowed the use of their images. We provide a complete list of them in Appendix 2.

Thanks to our agent, Russ Galen, who believed in and advocated for this project early on, and who provided excellent advice. Thanks also to Lisa White, our long-suffering Houghton Mifflin Harcourt editor, who also believed in the project and helped bring it to fruition, not to mention tolerating many delays in its completion. At Houghton Mifflin Harcourt, we also thank Beth Burleigh Fuller, Katrina Kruse, Brian Moore, Taryn Roeder, Jill Lazer, and Laney Whitt.

Many thanks to Paul Lehman and Larry Rosche, who created the range maps.

Thanks to Tony Leukering for his expert review of the book, which was both meticulous and insightful. Thanks also to Liz Pierson, who carefully copyedited the whole manuscript.

Ken thanks his family for their support, interest, and inspiration both in this endeavor and throughout his life.

Cameron Cox thanks Lauren Deaner for her help and support throughout the long process.

ANSWERS TO QUIZZES IN PHOTO CAPTIONS

Greater White-fronted Goose, p. 47, top: The two species of ducks are Northern Shoveler and Green-winged Teal.

Snow Goose, p. 51, bottom: There are two Greater White-fronted Geese, both on the middle of the right side of the photo.

Dabbling Ducks, p. 64: The first thing to look at is size. Most of the ducks in this flock look obviously large. This hunch is confirmed by comparison with the White Ibis that are part of the flock. The ibis are big birds, and they are only slightly larger than the ducks. The large size of most of these ducks means that the majority of the flock is likely to be Mallards, American Black Ducks, or Northern Pintails. A careful scan through with an eye to size will also pick up some obviously small ducks and some mid-sized ducks. The next step is to look at behavioral traits. This flock is made up of birds that were frightened into flight, so the strong (and useful for identification) tendencies of migrating birds unfortunately don't apply here. The flock is fairly widely spaced even in its disorder, which supports the idea that these are mainly large ducks. The third step is to look carefully at individual birds' structure. A glance at their structure shows that most of these birds have the slender and elegant shape of Northern Pintail. The long-tailed males are unmistakable, and the females are still quite distinctive. The handful of small ducks have the more slender shape of dabbling ducks rather than the heavier shape of diving ducks, meaning that they are teal. They are not as small or compact as Green-winged Teal, so given the Florida location, they are almost certain to be Blue-winged Teal. The large heads, round bodies, long tails, and slim wings of most of the handful of mid-sized ducks make them American Wigeon. By the time that these structural traits are clearly visible, you can usually make out confirming plumage traits like the large white oval on the upperwing of the male. At this point, we are only 3 steps into the suggested process for identifying dabbler flocks, and have already identified almost all the members of the flock. The stealth members of the flock are Gadwall, which would be very easy to miss. It might take a couple of careful scans and considerations of the various identification criteria to pick out the Gadwall. Often it is this species' very drabness and its generic shape that suggest an identification once more distinctive species have been eliminated.

Wood Duck, p. 76, center: The second Wood Duck is third from the left in the top row, overlapping a male Black Scoter in an odd way, so it is not easily distinguished.

American Wigeon, p. 101, bottom: The second bird from the right is an adult female that shows an extensive cloudy patch of white on the upperwing. This variant of adult female is uncommon and can be difficult to separate from a first-cycle male. Typically, the pale-winged adult females are more crisply marked than first-cycle males, and their white wing patch is quite clean with only faint gray smudges, whereas first-cycle males typically have noticeable pale brown smudges obscuring the white wing patch.

Eurasian Wigeon, p. 103, bottom: There are three Gadwall. Of the last four birds in the flock, the lower two are Gadwall and the upper two are Eurasian Wigeon. The third Gadwall is directly in front of those last two Eurasian Wigeon—it's the fifth bird from the right, with its head hidden by the wing of the American Wigeon. Thus the rightmost, third from right, and fifth from right birds are Gadwall.

Blue-winged Teal, p. 110: The left-hand bird is an adult male. Adult male Blue-winged Teal often migrate south while still in the female-like alternate plumage. The bold white greater covert, deeper blue color to the upperwing coverts, and rich green speculum age it as an adult male. The middle bird, which is slightly smaller than the adult male, with a thinner greater covert bar and slightly paler blue upperwing coverts, is an adult female. The right-hand bird, which lacks a greater covert bar, is a first-cycle female.

Cinnamon Teal, p. 115: One female Cinnamon Teal is directly below the male and above a male Northern Shoveler in the lower-right corner. The other female Cinnamon Teal is the second-highest bird in the upper-left corner, directly beneath a female Northern Shoveler. The female Blue-winged Teal is the third-highest bird in the upper-left corner, next to and slightly left of the second female Cinnamon Teal. Notice that the female Blue-winged Teal has a distinct pale area at the base of the bill, whereas the female Cinnamon Teal have plain faces.

Mixed Ducks, p. 122, center: The American Wigeon is the fourth bird from the left, on top. It is smaller and slimmer than the Mallard, with slimmer and more pointed wings, a raised head, and a more rounded belly.

Mixed Ducks, p. 124, top: The female Northern Shoveler is the fifth bird from the right, and the highest bird in the flock, somewhat isolated above the main flock. Its similar size to the Gadwall and American Wigeon, thick greater covert bar, and hint of a downward-angled bill identify it.

Mixed Ducks, p. 124, bottom: The third bird from the right is a Blue-winged Teal.

Redhead, p. 137, bottom: There are four Lesser Scaup. There is an adult male near the center of the photo. Another adult male is two birds in front of and slightly below the male in the center. The head just entering the frame on the left side of the photo is an adult female. The final Lesser Scaup is the lowest bird that is fully in the frame, on the lower-left side of the photo.

Greater Scaup, p. 140, top: The four Lesser Scaup are (from right) the third (adult male), fourth (female), seventh (adult female), and twelfth (probable first-cycle male) birds in the flock. Note the shorter, thinner wing stripe, size, and head structure of the Lesser Scaup compared with the Greater Scaup.

Lesser Scaup, p. 145, top: The other species is a female Common Goldeneye, second from the left, the lowest bird in the flock.

Ring-necked Duck, p. 151, bottom: All the birds in this flock show a large head. Also, the wings are held very straight with slightly blunter wingtips than Lesser Scaup would show. The bulging belly is a bit more exaggerated than that of Lesser Scaup.

Scoters, p. 185, top: Near the bottom left side of the flock is a female Bufflehead, at the front of the lowest line of birds and directly in front of a male

Surf Scoter. The bird in the lower right of the photo, slightly separated from the rest of the flock, is a female Hooded Merganser.

Common Goldeneye, p. 200, center: The smaller, brown duck in the background is a female Green-winged Teal.

Bufflehead, p. 208, top: The two birds trailing the flock are Hooded Mergansers.

Common Merganser, p. 213, bottom: The ducks on the water all appear to be Common Goldeneye. The gulls are Herring Gulls.

Hooded Merganser, p. 221, center: The female Hooded Merganser is at the top of the tight subflock of Black Scoters in the lower right of the photo, directly in front of the rightmost bird in the photo, a female Black Scoter. The Surf Scoter is in the subflock of five scoters in the center of the photo—the highest of the three birds leading the subflock and the second bird from the front of the subflock overall. It appears to be a first-cycle male.

Double-crested Cormorant, p. 230, top: There are six Green-winged Teal, all fairly close together. They are the small brown birds at the upper-right section of the densest part of the scoter flock, roughly underneath the last three scoters in the line at the upper right that leads the flock.

Neotropic Cormorant, p. 238, bottom: The Neotropic Cormorant is the lead bird, at the left side of the photo. Although the Double-crested Cormorants with it appear fairly slender, note how much broader their wings are.

Anhinga, p. 242, top: The hunched posture, heavy bodies, and short tails identify the birds in the background as Double-crested Cormorants.

Razorbill, p. 267, bottom left: One Common Murre is in the bottom left; the other is second from the top. Note the pointed appearance of the murres.

Dovekie, p. 288, top: The black upperparts would blend into a dark ocean background, and bright flashes of white would appear at random places in the flock as birds twisted and exposed their bellies.

Tubenoses, p. 289: The bird in the photo that is not an albatross is a Great Shearwater.

Northern Fulmar, p. 311, bottom: The Little Gull at the bottom of the photo is a first cycle; the one at the top is in its second cycle; and the one on the left is an adult.

Wilson's Storm-Petrel, p. 319, top: The Leach's Storm-Petrels are the two lead birds. The slightly grayer color and longer wings are the traits that stand out most prominently compared with the three Wilson's Storm-Petrels. On the lead Leach's, notice that the ulnar bar is longer and thinner than that of Wilson's Storm-Petrel, reaching the wing bend. On the second Leach's, notice how little white wraps around to the undertail coverts compared with the three Wilson's. The last two Wilson's appear to be different sizes, but the last bird has just dipped down farther behind a wave. Such illusions are common when observing birds close to the ocean surface.

Northern Gannet, p. 336, bottom: The two lead birds in the line of scoters are Surf Scoters.

Northern Gannet, p. 337, top: There are two fairly clear adult Laughing Gulls to the left of the gannet and one out-of-focus adult Laughing Gull to its right. The brown smudges on the left side of the photo are first-cycle Herring Gulls, identified by being the only gull species with uniform brown coloration likely at the location where the photo was taken.

Brown Pelican, p. 354, top: The photo shows off the diversity found on the western Gulf Coast. There are numerous American Avocets, four Royal Terns, one Laughing Gull, one Great Egret, one Snowy Egret, one Reddish Egret, and one White Ibis.

Gulls, p. 385: The bird in the upper-right corner is an adult Great Black-backed Gull. To its left is a smaller, slightly paler-mantled gull, a Lesser Black-backed. It has some black flecking on the tail and brown mottling in the wings and is in either its third or fourth cycle. The large pale-mantled gull below and slightly left of the Lesser Black-backed is a Herring Gull. It also shows black in the tail and dark markings on the wing and is a probable third cycle. The three small gulls, two beneath the Herring Gull and one farther right, are Bonaparte's Gulls. The middle Bonaparte's, partially obscured by the Herring Gull, is in its first cycle, and the other two are adults. In the bottom-right corner are two adult Ring-billed Gulls.

Lesser Black-backed Gull, p. 424, bottom: The Lesser Black-backed Gull is the farthest-right bird, just above a Great Black-backed Gull; it is the smaller bird with slimmer, more pointed wings.

Great Black-backed Gull, p. 429, top right: The first-cycle Lesser Black-backed on the right side of the photo clearly shows very dark, evenly colored wings, and a broad tail band. The first cycle Lesser Black-backed at the top of the photo is at a more difficult angle, but the suggestion of a small head and the solidly dark wings can still be seen.

Bonaparte's Gull, p. 440, bottom: There are two Little Gulls, one with the wings up (near the center of the flock) and one with the wings down (back of the flock), and three Sabine's Gulls, two with the wings down (one near the center and the other directly behind it toward the back) and one with the wings up (in a cluster of gulls near the back of the flock).

Caspian Tern, p. 475, top: The bird to the right and slightly above the Caspian Tern is a Royal Tern. The bird directly above the Royal Tern is a Common Tern. Directly above that Common Tern is the Sandwich Tern, the highest bird on the right side of the photo.

Common Tern, p. 492, left: There are two first-cycle Arctic Terns. Both are out of focus. One is the bird second from the bottom, which appears to be almost touching the Common Tern below it. The other is on the far right side of the photo just above center with the left wing out of the frame. Notice their more rounded heads, black underneath the eye, and translucent primaries.

Common Tern, p. 495, bottom: The Forster's Tern is just below and slightly behind the topmost bird in the flock, which is a Common Tern. The "bandit mask" of the Forster's Tern is less noticeable at this angle.

Black Tern, p. 518, top: The first Arctic Tern, a first-cycle bird, is in the upper-right corner with two Common Terns. The second Arctic Tern, an adult, is two birds beneath the first Arctic Tern, the lowest bird on the far right side of the photo, overlapping a Common Tern. The third Arctic Tern, a first-cycle bird, is directly to the right of the Black Tern at the center of the photo. The final Arctic Tern, a first-cycle bird, is in the bottom-left corner with its wing partially drawn into the body.

ADDITIONAL PHOTOGRAPH INFORMATION AND CREDITS

Tundra Swan, p. 25: Jan., UT. Ken Behrens.

Trumpeter Swan, p. 29: Jan., WA. Kevin Merchant.

Mute Swan, p. 31: Apr., ON. Ken Behrens.

Canada Goose, p. 36: Oct., MA. Myer Bornstein.

Cackling Goose, p. 42: Nov., CO. Bill Schmoker.

Greater White-fronted Goose, p. 43: Jan., LA. Ken Behrens.

Snow Goose, p. 49: Feb., NM. Cameron Cox.

Ross's Goose, p. 54: Jan., TX. Ken Behrens.

Barnacle Goose, p. 57: Apr., Sweden. Ken Behrens.

Brant, p. 59: Feb., NJ. Kevin Karlson.

Fulvous Whistling-Duck, p. 67: May, TX. Ken Behrens.

Black-bellied Whistling-Duck, p. 70: Sept., TX. Greg Lavaty.

Wood Duck, p. 73: Dec., TX. Justin Inman.

Northern Pintail, p. 77: May, ND. Ken Behrens.

Mallard, p. 82: Nov., CA. Jerry Ting.

American Black Duck, p. 86: Dec., NJ. Ken Behrens.

Mottled Duck, p. 90: Apr., TX. Ken Behrens.

Gadwall, p. 93: Jan., UT. Ken Behrens.

American Wigeon, p. 97: Jan., BC. Glenn Bartley.

Eurasian Wigeon, p. 102: Oct., Sweden. Tommy Holmgren.

Northern Shoveler, p. 105: May, ND. Ken Behrens.

Blue-winged Teal, p. 109: Dec., TX. Greg Lavaty.

Cinnamon Teal, p. 113: June, UT. Ken Behrens.

Green-winged Teal, p. 116: Feb., CA. Mike Danzenbaker.

Canvasback, p. 130: May, MB. Glenn Bartley.

Redhead, p. 134: Jan., TX. Nova Mackentley.

Greater Scaup, p. 138: Mar., BC. Ralph Hocken.

Lesser Scaup, p. 143: May, ND. Cameron Cox.

Ring-necked Duck, p. 148: Jan., NY. Colin Clement.

Tufted Duck, p. 152: Feb., Sweden. Tommy Holmgren.

Common Eider, p. 157: Nov., Scotland. John Anderson.

King Eider, p. 163: Mar., Norway. Hugh Harrop.

White-winged Scoter, p. 168: June, AK. Daniel Greene.

Surf Scoter, p. 172: Feb., NJ. Kevin Karlson.

Black Scoter, p. 178: Feb., NJ. Kevin Karlson.

Harlequin Duck, p. 189: Feb., NJ. Kevin Karlson.

Long-tailed Duck, p. 192: Feb., NJ. Kevin Karlson.

Common Goldeneye, p. 198: Dec., IL. Ken Behrens.

Barrow's Goldeneye, p. 202: Jan., UT. Ken Behrens.

Bufflehead, p. 206: Dec., BC. Glenn Bartley.

Common Merganser, p. 210: Jan., UT. Ken Behrens.

Red-breasted Merganser, p. 214: Feb., NJ. Kevin Karlson.

Hooded Merganser, p. 219: Nov., BC. Glenn Bartley.

Ruddy Duck, p. 223: Oct., CA. Mike Danzenbaker.

Double-crested Cormorant, p. 227: July, ME. Ken Behrens.

Great Cormorant, p. 233: Aug., Wales. Dave Williams.

Great Cormorant, p. 235 (left to right): (a) Apr., NY; (b) Dec., NJ; (c) May, MI; (d) Nov., SC; (e–h) Apr., Wales. Ken Behrens.

Neotropic Cormorant, p. 237: July, TX. Ken Behrens.

Anhinga, p. 240: Dec., FL. Ken Behrens.

Red-throated Loon, p. 246: Apr., Scotland. John Anderson.

Common Loon, p. 251: June, BC. Kevin Karlson.

Common Loon, p. 255 (left to right): (a) May, MI; (b) Dec., NJ; (c–d) Nov., NJ; (e) May, MI; (f) Nov., SC; (g) May, MI; (h) Nov., SC; (i–j) May, MI. Ken Behrens.

Pacific Loon, p. 256: June, MB. Glenn Bartley.

Red-necked Grebe, p. 259: Apr., ON. Ken Behrens.

Horned Grebe, p. 262: May, ND. Ken Behrens.

Razorbill, p. 265: July, ME. Ken Behrens.

Thick-billed Murre, p. 270: Aug., Arctic. Frank Todd, ©Ecocepts Intl/Arcticphoto.

Common Murre, p. 273: July, ME. Cameron Cox.

Atlantic Puffin, p. 277: July, ME. Ken Behrens.

Black Guillemot, p. 281: Mar., Norway. Hugh Harrop.

Dovekie, p. 284: Aug., Greenland. Frank Todd, ©Ecocepts Intl/Arcticphoto.

Cory's Shearwater, p. 290: May, NC. Bob Fogg.

Great Shearwater, p. 294: Oct., South Africa. Ken Behrens.

Sooty Shearwater, p. 298: Aug., WA. Greg Lavaty.

Manx Shearwater, p. 302: Aug., Northern Ireland. Craig Nash.

Audubon's Shearwater, p. 306: Aug., NC. Cameron Cox.

Audubon's Shearwater, p. 308 (left to right): (a) Aug., NC. Cameron Cox; (b) July, MA. Ken Behrens; (c) Aug., NC. Cameron Cox; (d) July, MA. Ken Behrens; (e) July, MA. Ken Behrens; (f) July, MA. Ken Behrens; (g) Aug., NC. Cameron Cox; (h) July, MA. Ken Behrens.

Northern Fulmar, p. 309: Apr., Wales. Ken Behrens.

Black-capped Petrel, p. 314: Sept., NC. Cameron Cox.

Wilson's Storm-Petrel, p. 317: June, NC. Brian Sullivan.

Leach's Storm-Petrel, p. 322: Oct., England. Steven Round.

Band-rumped Storm-Petrel, p. 325: Aug., NC. Ken Behrens.

Magnificent Frigatebird, p. 330: Apr., FL. Cameron Cox.

Northern Gannet, p. 334: Feb., MD. Cameron Cox.

Masked Booby, p. 341: Apr., St. Helena. Mike Danzenbaker.

Masked Booby, p. 343 (left to right): (a) Dec., NJ. Ken Behrens.
(b) Aug., NC. Cameron Cox.

Brown Booby, p. 344: Apr., Cape Verde Islands. Mike Danzenbaker.

American White Pelican, p. 347: Jan., FL. Cameron Cox.

Brown Pelican, p. 351: Mar., FL. Brandon Holden.

Great Skua, p. 359: Aug., MA. Luke Seitz.

South Polar Skua, p. 362: May, NC. Bob Fogg.

Pomarine Jaeger, p. 365: May, NC. Bob Fogg.

Pomarine Jaeger, p. 369 (left to right): (a) Jan., MD. Cameron Cox; (b) Oct., South Africa. Ken Behrens. (c) Sept., NC. Cameron Cox. (d) July, MA. Ken Behrens.

Parasitic Jaeger, p. 371: June, AK. Ted Swem.

Long-tailed Jaeger, p. 378: July, AK. Cameron Cox.

Ring-billed Gull, p. 388: May, MI. Ken Behrens.

Mew Gull, p. 395: Jan., UT. Ken Behrens.

California Gull, p. 399: June, UT. Ken Behrens.

Herring Gull, p. 404: Jan., SC. Cameron Cox.

Herring Gull, p. 409 (left to right): (a) May, MI. Ken Behrens.
(b) Jan., MA. Cameron Cox.

Thayer's Gull, p. 410: Jan., CA. Brian Sullivan.

Iceland Gull, p. 414: Feb., ON. Brandon Holden.

Glaucous Gull, p. 418: June, MB. Tom Johnson.

Lesser Black-backed Gull, p. 421: Feb., NC. Ken Behrens.

Great Black-backed Gull, p. 425: Feb., MD. Cameron Cox.

Laughing Gull, p. 430: Jan., SC. Cameron Cox.

Franklin's Gull, p. 435: May, ND. Cameron Cox.

Bonaparte's Gull, p. 438: Apr., ON. Ken Behrens.

Black-headed Gull, p. 443: Dec., Sweden. Tommy Holmgren.

Little Gull, p. 446: June, Sweden. Thomas Svanberg.

Ross's Gull, p. 449: June, NU. Mark Maftei.

Ivory Gull, p. 453: Feb., NL. Brandon Holden.

Sabine's Gull, p. 458: Aug., WA. Glenn Bartley.

Black-legged Kittiwake, p. 462: Mar., Norway. Hugh Harrop.

Black Skimmer, p. 469: Apr., TX. Oswald Pfenninger.

Caspian Tern, p. 473: June, UT. Ken Behrens.

Caspian Tern, p. 476 (left to right): (a) May, TX. Ken Behrens. (b) Oct., GA. Cameron Cox. (c–d) Apr., TX. Ken Behrens.

Royal Tern, p. 477: May, FL. Lauren Deaner.

Sandwich Tern, p. 482: Apr., TX. Ken Behrens.

Gull-billed Tern, p. 486: July, TX. Ken Behrens.

Common Tern, p. 490: July, NJ. Kevin Karlson.

Arctic Tern, p. 496: May, AK. Kevin Karlson.

Forster's Tern, p. 500: Oct., NJ. Cameron Cox.

Forster's Tern, p. 504 (left to right): (a) Oct., NJ. Cameron Cox. (b) Oct., South Africa. Ken Behrens. (c) June, UT. Ken Behrens. (d) July, MA. Ken Behrens.

Roseate Tern, p. 505: May, Madeira. Mike Danzenbaker.

Roseate Tern, p. 509 (left to right): (a–b) July, MA. Ken Behrens. (c) July, MA. Cameron Cox. (d) July, MA. Ken Behrens. (e) May, ND. Ken Behrens. (f) May, TX. Ken Behrens.

Least Tern, p. 510: Apr., TX. Kevin Karlson.

Black Tern, p. 515: June, WA. Ryan Shaw.

Sooty Tern, p. 519: Oct., Australia. Andrew Hardacre.

Bridled Tern, p. 522: Sept., NC. Chris Sloan.

Brown Noddy, p. 525: May, FL. Cameron Cox.

CONTRIBUTING PHOTOGRAPHERS

The majority of the photos in this book were taken by the authors. The book would not have been possible, however, without the generous contributions of many other fine photographers. A complete list of contributing photographers follows. Where available, their websites are included in parentheses.

Angel Abreu
Bryan and Cherry Alexander (www.arcticphoto.co.uk)
John Anderson (www.pbase.com/crail_birder)
Don Armstrong
Jim Arterburn (www.pbase.com/oklahomabirder)
Stéphane Aubry (www.pbase.com/stephaubry/gulls)
Danny Bales (www.flickr.com/photos/mudhen)
Raymond Barlow (www.raymondbarlow.com)
Glenn Bartley (www.glennbartley.com)
Mark B. Bartosik (www.pbase.com/mbb/root)
Jeff Birek (www.flickr.com/jeff83180)
Myer Bornstein (www.flickr.com/photos/photobee1)
Ken Brock
Michael Brothers
John Buffington
Colin Clement (www.colinclementphotography.com)
Stan Czaplicki
Mike Danzenbaker (www.avesphoto.com)
Mark Darlaston
Ian Davies (uropsalis.com/)
Lauren Deaner
François Dewaghe
Gerry Dewaghe (www.pbase.com/gdewaghe)
Steve Duffield (www.western-isles-wildlife.com)
Tom Dunkerton (www.pbase.com/boidpikchas)
Bob Fogg (www.keekeekerr.com)
Tony Gálvez (www.tonygalvez.info)
Snævarr Örn Georgsson (www.flickr.com/people/snaevarr)
Daniel Greene (www.danielgreene.com)
Cory Gregory
Pete Grube (www.flickr.com/photos/avocet07)
Einar Gudmann (www.gudmann.is)
Mary Gustafson
Andrew Hardacre (http://www.flickr.com/photos/29954808@N00/)
Hugh Harrop (www.hughharrop.com)
Richard S. Heil
Paul Higgins (www.pbase.com/phiggins)
Ralph Hocken (www.flickr.com/photos/23791322@N00)
Brandon Holden (www.PeregrinePrints.com)

Tommy Holmgren (www.pbase.com/njutaren/root)
Bill Hubick (www.Billhubick.com)
Justin Inman (www.flickr.com/photos/ainman12)
Tom Johnson (www.flickr.com/photos/bonxie88)
Kevin Karlson (www.kevinkarlsonphotography.com)
Peter LaTourrette (birdphotography.com)
Greg Lavaty (www.pbase.com/dadas115)
Tony Leukering (www.flickr.com/photos/tony_leukering)
Derek Lovitch (www.freeportwildbirdsupply.com)
James Lowen (www.pbase.com/james_lowen)
Nova Mackentley (www.nightflightimages.com)
Bruce Mactavish
Mark Maftei
Stephan Mann
Eric Masterson (www.flickr.com/photos/20225164@N05)
Kevin Merchant (www.kevinmerchant.com)
Eric Mills
Steve Mlodinow
Mårten Müller (www.pbase.com/m_muller)
Ted Murin
Craig Nash (www.flickr.com/photos/peregrinebirdphoto)
Chris Neri (www.nightflightimages.com)
Michael O'Brien
Lasse Olsson (www.birding.se)
David A. Palmer (www.flickr.com/photos/22207425@N05)
Oswald Pfenninger
Ed Post (www.flickr.com/photos/edpost)
John Puschock
Dave Roemer
Steven Round (stevenround-birdphotography.com)
Toby Sackton (www.flickr.com/photos/tsackton)
Bill Schmoker (schmoker.org)
Brad Schram (www.flickr.com/people/chaparralbrad)
Paul Schroeder (www.flickr.com/photos/monocat)
Colin Scott (www.flickr.com/photos/16185727@N07)
Luke Seitz (www.flickr.com/photos/grallaria)
Ryan Shaw (www.flickr.com/photos/shyalbatross)
Chris Sloan (www.chrissloanphotography.com)

Tom Smith (www.flickr.com/photos/tsmzth)
Johan Stenlund (www.pbase.com/johanstenlund)
Brian Sullivan (www.flickr.com/photos/oceanites)
   Kate Sutherland (www.patteson.com)
Thomas Svanberg (www.pbase.com/svanis)
Tomas Svensson (www.flickr.com/people/tomas_s)
Ted Swem
Tony Tanoury (www.flickr.com/photos/tanoury)
Bryan Tarbox (www.pbase.com/disx0d)
Clay Taylor

Jerry Ting (www.flickr.com/photos/jerryting)
Frank Todd (www.arcticphoto.co.uk)
Jeremiah Trimble (www.flickr.com/photos/jrtrimble)
Declan Troy
Bob Wallace
Robert Whitney (www.flickr.com/photos/rlw)
Dave Williams (www.pbase.com/davidwilliams
   photography)
Mike Yip (vancouverislandbirds.com)
Louise Zemaitis

TAXONOMIC NOTES

CACKLING GOOSE

There are four described subspecies, of which only the nominate race, *Branta hutchinsii hutchinsii,* also known as "Richardson's" Goose, is regularly found in eastern North America. The remaining subspecies, *B. h. minima,* or "Ridgway's" Goose; *B. h. taverneri,* or "Taverner's" Goose; and *B. h. leucopareia,* or "Aleutian" Goose, all breed in Alaska and winter primarily along the Pacific Coast.

There are a few records of "Ridgway's" Goose from scattered sites around eastern North America. Some of these likely represent true vagrants. However, as "Ridgway's" Goose is the most popular Cackling Goose subspecies among waterfowl collectors, questions of captive origins cloud the status of any vagrants. "Ridgway's" Goose is the smallest of the Cackling Goose subspecies, and the smallest individuals will stand out among "Richardson's" Geese. Comparing these two subspecies in flight, "Ridgway's" Goose tends to have a shorter neck, more rounded head, darker breast (often with a purplish or bronze cast), and straight rear border to the cheek patch, lacking the slight indention usually shown by "Richardson's" Goose. A classic, tiny, dark "Ridgeway's" Goose would likely be separable from "Richardson's" in flight, but many, particularly first-cycle birds, cannot be identified out of range if seen only in flight.

The wintering status of "Taverner's" Goose in the interior of the continent away from its core wintering range in the Pacific Northwest is uncertain because of the difficulty of separating it from "Richardson's" Goose and the *parvipes* subspecies of Canada Goose. There are several records of "Taverner's" Goose in eastern North America, and records in the western Great Plains suggest it is regular in small numbers just west of the region covered by this guide. "Taverner's" Goose averages slightly longer-necked and heavier-bodied than "Richardson's" Goose, usually with a dull tan breast, but definitive identification of a bird seen only in flight, even if photos were obtained, would be difficult.

"Aleutian" Goose has not been recorded in eastern North America but could potentially occur. It is darker-breasted than "Richardson's" Goose and

usually has a strong white neck collar with a distinct dark lower border. Virtually all individuals show a dark stripe down the throat, dividing the white cheek patch into two parts; only about 25 percent of "Richardson's" Geese show this trait. A typical "Aleutian" Goose might be identifiable in flight in eastern North America on the basis of good photos.

BRANT

The subspecies of Brant are complex. There are three subspecies plus two additional forms that have not been given subspecific designations. This account refers to *Branta bernicla hrota,* often called "Atlantic" Brant, which breeds in the Canadian Arctic and winters on the Atlantic Coast. *B. b. nigricans,* or "Black" Brant, is the western subspecies and is a rare but regular stray to the Atlantic Coast and very rarely the interior and Gulf Coast. It is slightly larger than "Atlantic" Brant with a white necklace that extends, unbroken, across the throat, a darker back, and an extensive sooty belly that contrasts with the bright white flanks. The nominate race, *B. b. bernicla,* hails from Eurasia and is an extremely rare though perhaps overlooked vagrant to the Atlantic Coast. It has a darker gray back than "Atlantic" Brant with an extensive dark gray belly and restricted pale flanks that create little contrast with the rest of the body. Two additional forms nest in the Canadian high Arctic and have not been definitively recorded on the Atlantic Coast.

COMMON EIDER

Six subspecies of Common Eider are recognized. Four of them are found in North America: three in eastern North America and one exclusively along the Alaskan and northwest Canadian coast. Two additional subspecies are found in Europe. The three eastern subspecies are *Somateria mollissima sedentaria,* or "Hudson Bay" Eider; *S. m. borealis,* or "Northern" Eider; and *S. m. dresseri,* or "Atlantic" Eider. "Hudson Bay" Eider is found in Hudson Bay and James Bay region year-round. "Northern" Eider breeds from northeast Nunavut to northwest Labrador and winters along the coast from Labrador south to New England. "Atlantic" Eider breeds from northeast Labrador south to Maine and winters south to the Mid-Atlantic states, occasionally reaching the Atlantic Coast of Florida.

Subspecific differences are subtle, variable, somewhat clinal, and difficult to distinguish in flight. They are most distinct in adult males, with less apparent differences in adult females and immatures.

"Atlantic" Eider is the largest-billed subspecies. Adult males have a dull olive green to yellow-green bill with a broad, rounded frontal lobe. The black line underneath the frontal lobe is quite narrow. The pale green wash on the nape extends farther forward than on other subspecies; it is generally only in a thin line directly underneath the black cap, but a pale green flush covers much of the cheek in some individuals. Immature males have rounded frontal lobes like adult males, though these lobes may not be as broad. Adult females tend to be bright rusty brown overall, but there is much variation.

"Northern" Eider is the smallest-billed subspecies. Adult males have a fairly bright yellow to bright orange-yellow bill with a fairly narrow, pointed frontal lobe. The black line that borders the frontal lobe is broader than in "Atlantic" Eider. The pale green wash on the nape does not extend forward onto the cheek. Immature males have a frontal lobe shape similar to that of adult males but have duller yellow bills lacking orange tones. Adult females tend to be dark to medium brown with faint rusty tones. Although "Northern" Eider do winter south to New England, they are rare, numbering only a handful in Maine and Massachusetts annually (Derek Lovitch, pers. comm.). Bright, small-billed male "Northern" Eider could likely be separated from "Atlantic" Eider in flight, though birds with intermediate characteristics between "Northern" and "Atlantic" Eiders exist.

"Hudson Bay" Eider is intermediate between "Northern" and "Atlantic" Eider in bill size and frontal lobe shape. It is rarely found outside the Hudson and James Bay regions, and vagrant "Hudson Bay" Eider are unlikely to be certainly identified in flight.

CORY'S SHEARWATER

Two subspecies exist, *Calonectris diomedia diomedia* and *C. d. borealis.* Although they are treated as subspecies by the American Ornithologists' Union, they are considered full species by the British Ornithologists' Union and other European authorities. The name "Scopoli's" Shearwater is used for *diomedia* and "Cory's" Shearwater for *borealis.* "Scopoli's" breeds in the Mediterranean. "Cory's" breeds on islands in the northeast Atlantic north to the Berlengas archipelago off Portugal.

"Scopoli's" averages smaller than "Cory's" with a thinner-based bill, smaller head, and thinner wings.

However, *Calonectris* shearwaters display distinct sexual dimorphism, and there is some overlap between large male "Scopoli's" and small female "Cory's." "Scopoli's" also tends to have a paler tan head and slightly duller yellow bill than "Cory's," but these traits are subtle. These taxa are best separated by the pattern of the underwing. "Scopoli's" has distinct pale vanes extending up the inner webs of the primaries, including P10, and a single dark spot on the primary underwing coverts. "Cory's" has no pale vanes on the primaries or indistinct vanes on some primaries but not on P10. It usually has two dark spots on the primary underwing coverts, but sometimes these spots overlap so they look like a single large spot. The overall difference in appearance of the underwing is similar to the difference in underwing pattern between Sooty and Bridled Terns; the division between the primaries and underwing coverts appears blended or uneven in "Scopoli's," whereas this division is sharply defined in "Cory's." It is often difficult to determine the precise pattern of the underwings while the bird is in flight, so it is helpful, whenever possible, to photograph every member of the Cory's Shearwater complex and make determinations from these photos.

There is still much to be learned about the distribution of "Scopoli's" Shearwater in North American waters. There are several records of "Scopoli's" off Massachusetts, but overall it seems rare in New England, though it is regular off North Carolina, making up 5–15 percent of birds in the Cory's Shearwater complex seen off North Carolina (Howell 2012). It seems "Scopoli's" makes up a greater percentage of the overall Cory's Shearwaters in the Atlantic waters off the southeast United States and in the Gulf of Mexico than it does in the Mid-Atlantic and New England. "Scopoli's" also seems to arrive in North American waters slightly later in the spring or summer than "Cory's" Shearwater.

BAND-RUMPED STORM-PETREL

In the northeast Atlantic four taxa of the Band-rumped Storm-Petrel complex breed on various island chains. These are all regarded as a single species by the American Ornithologists' Union. The British Ornithologists' Union, by contrast, has split the Atlantic breeders into three species and is still evaluating the status of a fourth taxa. Pacific populations of Band-rumped Storm-Petrel likely represent additional species and are not considered in this section.

"Madeiran" Storm-Petrel breeds on the Madeiran archipelago as well as on the Selvagens and Canary Islands during the hot season in that region (March–October). "Cape Verde" Storm-Petrel breeds only on the Cape Verde Islands, and during the cool season (October–June). "Monteiro's" Storm-Petrel is a hot-season (March–September) breeder on the Azores. "Grant's" Storm-Petrel has yet to be formally accepted as a distinct species by European authorities and is still considered part of "Madeiran" Storm-Petrel. It is a cool-season (August–March) breeder on the Madeiran archipelago, the Azores, Berlengas, Selvagans, and Canary Islands. "Grant's" Storm-Petrel represents the vast majority of the Band-rumped Storm-Petrels seen in North America, though at least one additional taxon has occurred.

"Grant's" Storm-Petrel and "Madeiran" Storm-Petrel overlap on some breeding islands, though they breed at different times of the year. There is some overlap in timing; "Grant's" Storm-Petrel may arrive back on the breeding ground, begin courtship, and even occupy nesting burrows that still contain "Madeiran" Storm-Petrel chicks!

These taxa differ in morphology, egg measurements, DNA, and vocalizations. Unsurprisingly, though, for a group only recently recognized to be different, the identifications traits used to identify birds are very subtle, and confident identification of birds in flight is probably impossible in most situations.

Characteristics that may have value for field identification include molt timing, the presence or absence of a forked tail and the depth of the fork if present, the width of the wings, the width of the white rump band, the extent that the rump band wraps around to the undertail, the presence or absence of dark flecking in the white rump band, and the degree to which the pale carpal contrasts with the rest of the wing.

"Grant's" Storm-Petrel molts from February to early August, though immature birds may molt on a slightly different schedule. Presumed "Grant's" Storm-Petrels seen off North Carolina in late May to early June have replaced primaries up through the middle to outer primaries and typically still retain at least two worn outer primaries. They have little or no tail fork, a weak ulnar bar, and typically show no dark flecking in the white rump band.

GLOSSARY

adult. A bird that is fully mature or a bird in the definitive plumage cycle. We use the term "adult plumage" in this guide, as it is more widely understood than the Humphrey-Parkes term "definitive plumage."

alternate plumage. A second plumage inserted into the annual cycle that alternates with basic plumage. Often occurs in the spring and is called "breeding" plumage by some authors.

arboreal. A species that inhabits trees.

arm. The inner portion of the wing from the wing bend to the body. Comprises the secondaries and secondary coverts. See **hand.**

auriculars. Feathers covering the region around the ear, on the sides of the face. Also called ear coverts.

axillaries (or axillars). Long, stiff feathers on the underside of the wing where it joins the body. The "wingpit."

basic plumage. The plumage attained by a prebasic molt (usually a complete or nearly complete molt). A base plumage worn by all birds for at least part of the year and comparable across all birds.

clinal. Showing changes along a gradient.

culmen. A ridge on the top of the upper mandible.

cycle. Abbreviation for "molt cycle." A regularly repeated molt or series of molts. A basic cycle extends from the start of one prebasic molt to the start of the next prebasic molt. Roughly 1 year in length in most species.

diurnal. Active in the daytime.

dynamic soar. A flight style used by most tubenoses; also by some gulls, jaegers, and sulids in strong wind. Birds arc up and down with little or no flapping, using their wings to catch the wind to carry them to the top of their arc, then adjust the wings to glide back down near the water.

eye crescents. Pale crescents above and below the eye broken by narrow dark areas at the corners of the eye.

flight feathers. The primaries, secondaries, and tail feathers. The tertials and alula are sometimes considered flight feathers as well.

flight line. A specific path taken by a particular species on a regular basis at a given location. Varies daily for some species, whereas other species use the same flight lines year after year.

formative plumage. A unique plumage worn by some birds only in the first cycle. It is brought about by a preformative molt.

gonydeal spot. A reddish spot near the bottom of the tip of the bill on adult and some subadult large gulls.

grinning patch. An opening along the sides of the bill of Snow Geese and some Ross's Geese where the upper and lower mandibles do not meet.

hand. The entire outer portion of the wing from the wing bend to the tip of the wing; comprises the primaries and primary coverts. See **arm.**

Holarctic. A region that includes North America, Europe, North Africa, and most of Asia.

immature/immature plumage. Any bird not in adult plumage or any plumage that precedes the adult plumage cycle.

Intracoastal Waterway. A 3,000-mile waterway along the Atlantic and Gulf Coasts that can be navigated by boats. Follows bays, inlets, sounds, and man-made canals for much of its length, to be sheltered from the open ocean.

juvenile. A bird holding its first set of vaned feathers, which are acquired by a complete prebasic molt. In Howell's modification of the Humphrey-Parkes system followed in this guide, juvenile plumage is considered equivalent to first-basic plumage.

kettle. A tight flock of birds using the same rising pocket of warm air to gain lift. Most closely associated with several species of raptors, though some gulls and other waterbirds also use this method.

kleptoparasitism. Parasitism by theft. Stealing an item such as food or nest material from another individual.

mantle. The back and upperwings on a gull or tern. Technically, it refers only to the back and scapular feathers, but as the color of the back and upperwings is the same across the entire back and upperwings in adult gulls and terns, it is convenient to refer to this area as the "mantle" and the color of this region as the "mantle color."

Mid-Atlantic. A region that includes the states of New

York, New Jersey, Delaware, Maryland, Virginia, North Carolina, and the District of Columbia.

mirror. Oval-shaped white spots near the tips of the outermost or outer two primaries of adult or subadult large gulls.

molt. Regular feather growth.

molt cycle. See **cycle.**

molt migration. A migration undertaken by male ducks to find a suitable location to molt.

morph. Different forms of a single species. Usually refers to different color morphs.

nocturnal. Active primarily at night.

Old World. Europe, Asia, and Africa.

P(1–10). See **primaries.**

pelagic. Referring to the water beyond the continental shelf. A pelagic bird is a bird found primarily at sea. Also an abbreviation for a boat trip that explores offshore waters looking for birds.

piscivorous. Fish-eating.

plumage. Used here in the standard, non–Humphrey-Parkes sense: all of a bird's feathers or its overall appearance.

plunge-dive. A headfirst dive made into water while flying. Many terns, sulids, and some small gulls use this method of feeding.

polymorphic. Having more than one morph.

preformative. The molt—occurring only in the first cycle—that produces formative plumage.

primaries. The main group of feathers that enable a bird to fly, attached to the hand bone (manus). All species covered in this guide have 10 primaries, numbered from the innermost (P1) to the outermost (P10).

primary shaft. The stiff shaft running along the center of a feather, to which the softer vanes attach.

scapulars. The feathers that protect the base of the wing when not in flight. They appear to grow in rows but actually all originate from the same point near the shoulder. In flight they lie flat on either side of the back.

secondaries. The secondary flight feathers attached to the forearm bone (ulna).

subadult. A bird that is not yet an adult but that is beyond the first cycle.

subflock. A flock within a flock. A tightly packed group of birds that maintain slight spacing from the rest of the flock while still being part of the greater flock.

subspecies. A taxonomic designation below a species. Populations that can be distinguished by differences in plumage, vocalizations, DNA, or other traits but are not considered sufficiently distinct to be considered a species.

taxon (plural: taxa). A general term for a discrete taxonomical unit. Subspecies, species, and families are all taxa. This term is often used when the taxonomic status of a population is unresolved.

terrestrial. Of or pertaining to the ground.

tertials. The inner secondaries that protect the wing when it is closed.

tomial stripe. A stripe that runs along the cutting edge of the lower mandible and that contrasts with the rest of the bill.

tongue-tip. A white area between dark primary tips or subterminal bands and the paler basal portion of the middle or outer primary. Usually found only on adult or subadult gulls; see particularly adult Mew ("Short-billed") Gull.

ulnar bar. A diagonal band across the secondary coverts from the wing bend to the base of the secondaries, roughly tracing the path of the underlying ulnar bone.

underparts. The entire lower half of a bird, from the underside of the bill to the underside of the tail.

upperparts. The entire upper half of a bird, from the bill to the tail.

waterbird. A nontechnical term that can refer to any fully or partially aquatic bird. This guide covers a subset of what could most broadly be considered "waterbirds."

waterfowl. Swans, geese, and ducks.

white flash. A crescent-shaped white patch at the bases of the primaries of skuas and jaegers. Usually larger and present on both the underwing and upperwing on skuas; smaller and only on the underwing on jaegers.

wing bend. The bend at the front of the wing; the place at the front of the wing where the arm meets the hand. Sometimes called the carpal, carpal joint, or elbow, though it is more analogous to the wrist.

wingtip. The tip of the wing, comprising the primaries. Usually refers to shape (a blunt wingtip or a pointed wingtip).

BIBLIOGRAPHY

Alderfer, J., ed. 2006. *National Geographic Complete Birds of North America*. Washington, D.C.: National Geographic.

American Birding Association. 2008. *ABA Checklist: Birds of the Continental United States and Canada*. 7th ed. Colorado Springs, CO: American Birding Association.

American Ornithologists' Union. 1998. *Check-list of North American Birds*. 7th ed. Washington, D.C.: American Ornithologists' Union.

Barnard, C. J., and D. B. A. Thompson. 1985. *Gulls and Plovers: The Ecology and Behaviour of Mixed-Species Feeding Groups*. London: Croom Helm.

Beaman, M., and S. Madge. 1998. *The Handbook of Bird Identification for Europe and the Western Palearctic*. London: Christopher Helm.

Beaton, G., P. W. Sykes, and J. Parrish. 2003. *Annotated Checklist of Georgia Birds*. 5th ed. Atlanta, GA: Georgia Ornithological Society.

Bellrose, F. C.. 1976. *Ducks, Geese & Swans of North America: A Completely New and Expanded Version of the Classic Work by F. H. Kortright*. 2d ed. Harrisburg, PA: Stackpole Books.

Blomdahl, A., B. Breife, and N. Holmström. 2007. *Flight Identification of European Seabirds*. London: Christopher Helm.

Cayuga Bird Club. 2007. The Loon Watch at Taughannock State Park. Downloaded at www.birds.cornell.edu/cayugabirdclub/loonwatch.htm.

Clements, J. F., T. S. Schulenberg, M. J. Iliff, B. L. Sullivan, C. L. Wood, and D. Roberson. 2012. The eBird/Clements Checklist of Birds of the World. Ver. 6.7. Downloaded from www.birds.cornell.edu/clementschecklist/downloadable-clements-checklist.

Cox, C., and J. Barry. 2005. The identification, molts, and aging of American and Eurasian Wigeons in female-type plumages. *Birding* 37(2): 156–164.

Cramp, S., ed. 1980. *Handbook of the Birds of Europe, the Middle East, and North Africa*. Vols. 1 & 3. Oxford: Oxford University Press.

Crossley, R. 2011. *The Crossley ID Guide: Eastern Birds*. Princeton, NJ: Princeton University Press.

Del Hoyo, J., A. Elliott, and J. Sargatal, eds. 1992. *Handbook of the Birds of the World*. Vol 1. Barcelona: Lynx Edicions.

Del Hoyo, J., A. Elliott, and J. Sargatal, eds. 1996. *Handbook of the Birds of the World*. Vol 3. Barcelona: Lynx Edicions.

Dunn, J. L., and J. Alderfer. 2011. *National Geographic Field Guide to the Birds of North America*. 6th ed. Washington, D.C.: National Geographic Society.

Dunne, P. 2006. *Pete Dunne's Essential Field Guide Companion*. Boston: Houghton Mifflin.

Dunne, P., D. Sibley, and C. Sutton. 1988. *Hawks in Flight*. Boston: Houghton Mifflin.

Dwight, J. 1925. The gulls (Laridae) of the world: their plumages, moults, variations, relationships, and distribution. *Bulletin of the American Museum of Natural History* 52: 63–401.

eBird. 2012. eBird: An online database of bird distribution and abundance [web application]. Ithaca, NY: eBird. Available at www.ebird.org.

Ewald, B. M., and D. F. Sherony. 2001. *A Summary of Hamlin Beach Lakewatch Fall and Winter Waterbird Migration Data 1993–1999*. New York: Federation of New York State Bird Clubs.

Flock, G., and A. P. Hecker, eds. 1994. *Birding Cape Cod*. Wellfleet: Massachusetts Audubon Society.

Gooley, M. 2002. The continental shelf-edge: an oceanographic primer for pelagic birders. Downloaded at www.neseabirds.com/wheretoshelfedge.htm.

Grant, P. J. 1982. *Gulls: A Guide to Identification*. Vermillion, SD: Buteo Books.

Harrison, P. 1985. *Seabirds: An Identification Guide*. Rev. ed. Boston: Houghton Mifflin.

Heil, R. S. 2001. Seabirds of Andrew's Point, Rockport, Massachusetts. *Bird Observer* 29(5).

Hess, G. K., R. L. West, M. V. Barnhill III, and L. M. Flemming. 2000. *Birds of Delaware*. Pittsburgh, PA: University of Pittsburgh Press.

Howell, S. N. G. 2010. *Molt in North American Birds*. Peterson Reference Guide Series. Boston: Houghton Mifflin Harcourt.

Howell, S. N. G. 2012. *Petrels, Albatrosses, and Storm-Petrels of North America: A Photographic Guide*. Princeton NJ: Princeton University Press.

Howell, S. N. G., C. Corben, P. Pyle, and D. I. Rogers. 2003. The first basic problem: a review of molt and plumage homologies. *Condor* 105(4): 635–653.

Howell, S. N. G., C. Corben, P. Pyle, and D. I. Rogers. 2004. The first basic problem revisited: reply to commentaries on Howell et al. (2003). *Condor* 106(1): 206–210.

Howell, S. N. G., and J. Dunn. 2007. *A Reference Guide to Gulls of the Americas.* Peterson Reference Guide Series. Boston: Houghton Mifflin.

Howell, S. N. G., and J. B. Patteson. 2008a. Variation in Cory's and Scopoli's Shearwaters. *Alula* 14: 12–21.

Howell, S. N. G., and J. B. Patteson. 2008b. Variation in the Black-capped Petrel: one species or more? *Alula* 14: 70–83.

Howell, S. N. G., J. B. Patteson, K. Sutherland, and D. T. Shoch. 2010. Occurrence and identification of the Band-rumped Storm Petrel (*Oceanodroma castro*) complex off North Carolina. *North American Birds* 64: 196–207.

Howell, S. N. G., M. O'Brian, B. L. Sullivan, C. L. Wood, I. Lewington, and R. Crossley. 2009. The purpose of field guides: taxonomy vs. utility? *Birding* 41(6): 44–49.

Humphrey, P. S., and K. C. Parkes. 1959. An approach to the study of molts and plumages. *Auk* 76: 1–31.

Imhof, T. A. 1976. *Alabama Birds.* Tuscaloosa: University of Alabama Press.

Jonsson, L. 1992. *Birds of Europe: with North Africa and the Middle East.* London: Christopher Helm.

Kaufman, K. 2011. *Kaufman Field Guide to Advanced Birding.* New York, Houghton Mifflin Harcourt.

Kortright, F. H. 1942. *The Ducks, Geese and Swans of North America.* Washington, D.C.: American Wildlife Institute.

Larivée, J., ed. 2011. Étude des populations d'oiseaux du Québec (Ver. 2011-03-12) [database]. Rimouski, Québec: Regroupement Québec Oiseaux.

Levine, E., ed. 1998. *Bull's Birds of New York State.* Ithaca, NY: Comstock Publishing.

Lewington, I., P. Alström, and P. Colston. 1991. *A Field Guide to the Rare Birds of Britain and Europe.* London: Collins.

Lovitch, D. 2012. *How to Be a Better Birder.* Princeton, NJ: Princeton University Press.

Madge, S., and H. Burn. 1988. *Waterfowl: An Identification Guide to the Ducks, Geese, and Swans of the World.* Boston: Houghton Mifflin.

Malosh, G. R. 2006. Bonaparte's Gull migration in southwestern Pennsylvania: understanding "The April 10 Effect." *Pennsylvania Birds* 20(2): 67–70.

McCarthy, E. M. 2006. *Handbook of Avian Hybrids of the World.* New York: Oxford University Press.

Mumford, R. E., and C. E. Keller. 1984. *The Birds of Indiana.* Bloomington: Indiana University Press.

O'Brien, M., R. Crossley, and K. Karlson. 2006. *The Shorebird Guide.* Boston: Houghton Mifflin.

Olsen, K. M., and H. Larsson. 1995. *Terns of Europe and North America.* London: Christopher Helm.

Olsen, K. M., and H. Larsson. 1997. *Skuas and Jaegers: A Guide to the Skuas and Jaegers of the World.* New Haven, CT: Yale University Press.

Olsen, K. M., and H. Larsson. 2003. *Gulls of Europe, Asia and North America.* London: Christopher Helm.

Onley, D., and P. Scofield. 2007. *Albatrosses, Petrels, and Shearwaters of the World.* London: Christopher Helm.

Patteson, J. B., and E. S. Brinkley. 2004. A petrel primer: the gadflies of North Carolina. *Birding* 36(6): 586–596.

Peterjohn, B. G. 2001. *The Birds of Ohio.* Wooster, OH: Wooster Book Co.

Petersen, W. R., and R. R. Veit. 1993. *Birds of Massachusetts.* Lincoln, MA: Massachusetts Audubon Society.

Poole, A., ed. 2012. The Birds of North America Online: http://bna.birds.cornell.edu/BNA/.Ithaca, NY: Cornell Lab of Ornithology.

Post, W., and S. A. Gauthreaux, Jr. 1989. *Status and Distribution of South Carolina Birds.* Charleston, SC: Charleston Museum.

Pulcinella, N. 1998. *Birds of Delaware County.* Delaware: Bird Club of Delaware County.

Pulich, W., Jr. 1982. Documentation and status of Cory's Shearwater in the western Gulf of Mexico. *Wilson Bulletin* 94(3): 381–385.

Pyle, P. 1997. *Identification Guide to North American Birds.* Part I. Bolinas, CA: Slate Creek Press.

Pyle, P. 2005. Molts and plumages of ducks (Anatinae). *Waterbirds* 28: 208–219.

Pyle, P. 2008. *Identification Guide to North American Birds.* Part II: Anatidae to Alcidae. Bolinas, CA: Slate Creek Press.

Reed, A., ed. 1986. Eider ducks in Canada. Canadian Wildlife Service Report Series no. 47. Ottawa: Canadian Wildlife Service.

Ripma, E. and R. Ripma. Where to Bird: Miller Beach, Gary, IN. Downloaded at nuttybirder.com/Wheretobird/Indiana/northwestin/millerbeachin.html.

Rottenborn, S. C., and E. S. Brinkley. 2007. *Virginia's Birdlife: An Annotated Checklist.* 4th ed. Virginia: Virginia Society of Ornithology.

Sherony, D. F. 2008. Greenland geese in North America. *Birding* 40(3): 46–56.

Sibley, C. G., and B. L. Monroe, Jr. 1990. *Distribution and Taxonomy of Birds of the World.* New Haven, CT: Yale University Press.

Sibley, C. G., and B. L. Monroe, Jr. 1993. *A Supplement to Distribution and Taxonomy of Birds of the World.* New Haven, CT: Yale University Press.

Sibley, D. 1997. *The Birds of Cape May.* Rev. ed. Cape May Point, NJ: New Jersey Audubon Society's Cape May Bird Observatory.

Sibley, D. A. 2002. *Sibley's Birding Basics.* New York: Alfred A. Knopf.

Sibley, D. A. 2000. *The Sibley Guide to Birds.* New York: Alfred A. Knopf.

Sibley, D. A. 2001. *The Sibley Guide to Bird Life and Behavior.* New York: Alfred A. Knopf.

Spear, L. B., and D. G. Ainley. 1997. Flight behaviour of seabirds in relation to wind direction and wing morphology. *Ibis* 139(2): 221–233.

Stevenson, H. M., and B. H. Anderson. 1994. *The Birdlife of Florida.* Gainesville: University Press of Florida.

Sutton, C., M. O'Brien, and D. Ward. 2004. Identifying and enjoying Atlantic coast seabirds from shore. Part I. *Birding* 36(3): 254–263.

Svensson, L., and P. J. Grant. 1999. *Birds of Europe.* Princeton, NJ: Princeton University Press.

Walsh, J., V. Elia, R. Kane, and T. Halliwell. 1999. *Birds of New Jersey.* New Jersey: New Jersey Audubon Society.

Walton, R. K. 1988. *Bird Finding in New England.* Boston: David R. Godine.

Ward, D., M. O'Brian, and C. Sutton. 2004. Identifying and enjoying Atlantic coast seabirds from shore. Part II. *Birding* 36(3): 264–276.

Wood, C. L. 2004. Photo salon: identification of birds in flight. *Birding* 36(3): 246–252.

INDEX

Index pages in **bold** refer to photographs.

PETERSON FIELD GUIDES®

Roger Tory Peterson's innovative format uses accurate, detailed drawings to pinpoint key field marks for quick recognition of species and easy comparison of confusing look-alikes.

BIRDS

Birds of North America

Birds of Eastern and Central North America
SIXTH EDITION

Western Birds
FOURTH EDITION

Birds of Britain and Europe
FIFTH EDITION

Birds of Texas

Eastern Birds
LARGE FORMAT EDITION

Feeder Birds of Eastern North America
LARGE FORMAT EDITION

Hawks of North America
SECOND EDITION

Hummingbirds of North America

Warblers

Western Birds' Nests

Eastern Birds' Nests

PLANTS AND ECOLOGY

Eastern and Central Edible Wild Plants

Eastern and Central Medicinal Plants and Herbs

Western Medicinal Plants and Herbs

Eastern Forests

Rocky Mountain and Southwest Forests

Eastern Trees

Western Trees

Eastern Trees and Shrubs

Ferns of Northeastern and Central North America
SECOND EDITION

Mushrooms

North American Prairie

Venomous Animals and Poisonous Plants

Southwest and Texas Wildflowers

Wildflowers of Northeastern and North-Central North America

MAMMALS

Animal Tracks
THIRD EDITION

Mammals
FOURTH EDITION

INSECTS

Insects

Eastern Butterflies

Moths of Northeastern North America

REPTILES AND AMPHIBIANS

Eastern Reptiles and Amphibians
THIRD EDITION

Western Reptiles and Amphibians
THIRD EDITION

FISHES

SPACE

GEOLOGY

SEASHORE

PETERSON FLASHGUIDES®

Portable and waterproof, FlashGuides are perfect for those who want to travel light. Covering 50–100 species, with brief surveys of habit and habitat, each opens to two rows with twelve full-color, laminated panels on each side.

PETERSON FIRST GUIDES®

The first books the beginning naturalist needs, whether young or old. Simplified versions of the full-size guides, they make it easy to get started in the field, and feature the most commonly seen natural life.

PETERSON FIELD GUIDES
FOR YOUNG NATURALISTS

This series is designed with young readers ages eight to twelve in mind, featuring the original artwork of the celebrated naturalist Roger Tory Peterson.

Backyard Birds

Birds of Prey

Songbirds

Butterflies

Caterpillars

PETERSON FIELD GUIDES® COLORING BOOKS®

Fun for kids ages eight to twelve, these color-your-own field guides include color stickers and are suitable for use with pencils or paint.

Birds

Butterflies

Dinosaurs

Reptiles and Amphibians

Wildflowers

Seashores

Shells

Mammals

PETERSON REFERENCE GUIDES®

Reference Guides provide in-depth information on groups of birds and topics beyond identification.

Seawatching: Eastern Waterbirds in Flight

Gulls of the Americas

Molt in North American Birds

Behavior of North American Mammals

PETERSON AUDIO GUIDES

Birding by Ear: Western

Birding by Ear: Eastern/Central

More Birding by Ear: Eastern/Central

Bird Songs: Eastern/Central
THIRD EDITION

PETERSON FIELD GUIDE / *BIRD WATCHER'S DIGEST* BACKYARD BIRD GUIDES

Identifying and Feeding Birds

Hummingbirds and Butterflies

Bird Homes and Habitats

Finding Your Wings: A Workbook for Beginning Bird Watchers

The Young Birder's Guide to Birds of North America

DIGITAL

Apps available on the App Store for iPad, iPhone, and iPod Touch.

Peterson Birds of North America

Peterson Birds Pocket Edition

Peterson Feeder Birds of North America

E-books

Birds of Arizona

Birds of California

Birds of Florida

Birds of Massachusetts

Birds of Minnesota

Birds of New Jersey

Birds of New York

Birds of Ohio

Birds of Pennsylvania

Birds of Texas